This book was donated
to honor
the birthday of

Jessica Bankston

by

Kathy and David Bankston

1994

HOCKEY

PROFESSIONAL

SPORTS TEAM

HISTORIES

HOCKEY

PROFESSIONAL SPORTS TEAM HISTORIES

MICHAEL L. LaBLANC, Editor

MARY K. RUBY, Associate Editor

  **Gale Research Inc.** DETROIT • WASHINGTON, D.C. • LONDON

This book is printed on acid-free paper that meets the minimum requirements of American National Standard for Information Sciences— Permanence Paper for Printed Library Materials, ANSI Z39.48-1984.

STAFF

Michael L. LaBlanc, *Editor*
Mary K. Ruby, *Associate Editor*
George W. Schmidt, *Indexer*
Marilyn Allen, *Editorial Associate*
Michael J. Tyrkus, *Assistant Editor*

Barbara Carlisle Bigelow, Suzanne M. Bourgoin, Dean David Dauphinais,
Kathleen Dauphinais, Kathy Edgar, Nicolet V. Elert, Marie Ellavich, Kevin
Hillstrom, Laurie Collier Hillstrom, Anne Janette Johnson, Janice Jorgensen,
Denise Kasinec, Paula Kepos, Jane Kosek, Mark Kram, Mary P. LaBlanc,
L. Mpho Mabunda, Roger Matuz, Tom McMahon, Louise Mooney, Les
Ochram, Jack Pearson, Terrie Rooney, Mary Ruby, Julia Rubiner, Aarti
Stephens, Debbie Stanley, Les Stone, Gerald Tomlinson, Roger Valade,
Kathleen Wilson,
Contributing Editors

Kevin Hillstrom, Keith Reed, Mary K. Ruby, *Photo Editors*
Willie Mathis, *Camera Operator*

B. Hal May, *Director, Biography Division*
Peter M. Gareffa, *Senior Editor, Contemporary Biographies*
David E. Salamie, *Senior Editor, New Product Development*

Jeanne Gough, *Permissions Manager*
Margaret A. Chamberlain, *Permissions Supervisor (Pictures)*
Pamela A. Hayes, Keith Reed, *Permissions Associates*
Susan Brohman, Arlene Johnson, Barbara A. Wallace, *Permissions Assistants*

Mary Beth Trimper, *Production Director*
Mary Kelley, *Production Assistant*
Cynthia Baldwin, *Art Director*
Mark C. Howell, *Cover Designer*
Kathleen Hourdakis, *Page Designer*

Cover photo by arrangement with AP/Wide World Photos

Contents

Introductory Essay

Atlantic Division

Central Division

Northeast Division

Pacific Division

Essay

INTRODUCTION

Professional Sports Team Histories is a multivolume reference series that chronicles the evolution of four major U.S. spectator sports: basketball, baseball, football, and hockey.

Hockey boasts the unique status of being a true partnership between Canada and the United States. Built on this foundation, it is not surprising that the sport has an international flavor. In its early years most players hailed from Canada, but recently more and more participants call the United States, the Commonwealth of Independent States, Sweden, Finland, or Czechoslovakia home. As the game has crossed borders, it has also won new fans with its combination of speed, finesse, and occasional battles on the ice.

Professional Sports Team Histories: Hockey traces the development of hockey from an ancient British field sport to an organized game played in eastern Canada in the 1870s. Challenges for Lord Stanley's prestigious Cup began in 1892, and organized hockey leagues sprang up thereafter. From Canada, hockey's influence seeped southward to major industrial centers of the northeast United States in the early twentieth century. The game's strong following in both countries has prompted several league expansions since 1967.

With an extensive prose entry on each National Hockey League (NHL) team, *Hockey* focuses on the formation and growth of each franchise and highlights the accomplishments of significant players and members of management. The volume also charts the creation of the NHL in the fall of 1917, the history of the league's precursors, the pioneering teams that engaged in post-World War I play, and the refinement of the game into the sport of the 1990s.

A Source of Convenient Reference *and* Interesting Reading

· **Informative historical essays,** many written by specialists in the field, offer an overview of each team's development from its inception through the 1992-93 season, with coverage of franchise moves, name changes, key personnel, and team performance.

· **A special entry on the history of the sport** follows the development of the game over the years and presents a thorough analysis of the factors that have led to changes in the way it is played.

· **Designed with a broad audience in mind,** the information in *Professional Sports Team Histories* is accessible enough to captivate the interest of the sports novice, yet comprehensive enough to enlighten even the most avid fan.

· **Numerous photos**—including shots of Hall-of-Famers—further enhance the reader's appreciation of each team's history.

· **Easy to locate "Team Information at a Glance"** sections list founding dates for each team; names, addresses, and phone numbers of home stadiums; team color/logo information; and franchise records.

· **Additional eye-catching sidebars** present other noteworthy statistics, interesting team-related trivia, close-up profiles of important players and management figures, and capsulized accounts of events that have become a permanent part of sports folklore.

Helpful Indexes Make It Easy to Find the Information You Need

Each volume of *Professional Sports Team Histories* includes a detailed, user-friendly index, making it easy to find information on key players and executives.

Available in Electronic Formats

Diskette/Magnetic Tape—*Professional Sports Team Histories* is available for licensing on magnetic tape or diskette in a fielded format. Either the complete, four-sport database or a custom selection of entries may be ordered. The database is available for internal data processing and nonpublishing purposes only. For more information, call (800) 877-GALE.

We Welcome Your Comments

The editors welcome your comments and suggestions for enhancing and improving any future editions of the *Professional Sports Team Histories* series. Mail correspondence to:

The Editor
Professional Sports Team Histories
Gale Research, Inc.
835 Penobscot Bldg.
Detroit, MI 48226-4094
Phone: (800) 347-GALE
FAX: (313) 961-6599

ACKNOWLEDGEMENTS

Professional Sports Team Histories represents the culmination of nearly three years' effort by a large and diverse group of people. The editors wish to acknowledge the significant contribution of the following individuals and organizations:

• The fine pool of sportswriters and historians who wrote the individual entries, especially Bruce C. Cooper, for sharing their considerable knowledge of the subject matter. In cases where the writers have drawn on reference materials in addition to their own archival resources, we have included a Sources section at the end of the entry. These sources contain a wealth of additional information, and we urge the interested reader to consult them for a more detailed understanding of the subject.

• Mr. Craig Campbell of the Hockey Hall of Fame and Museum, for assistance in securing photos of and information on its members. The Hockey Hall of Fame and Museum is a registered charity dedicated to the collection and preservation of information, records, and artifacts relating to the people who have performed outstanding services to the sport. The Museum is open to the public and features numerous displays, an extensive library, and a gift shop. For more information about the Hall, its Museum, and its publications, contact:

The Hockey Hall of Fame and Museum
BCE Place, 30 Yonge Street
Toronto, Ontario M5E 1X8
Phone: (416) 360-7735

• The media relations departments of the various teams, for their valuable cooperation and assistance in providing photographs, historical materials, information on current players, and for directing us to local sports historians and sportswriters.

• Lauren Fedorko and Diane Schadoff of Book Builders Incorporated, and to Jim Evans of Deadline Inc., for their help in securing knowledgeable and entertaining contributors of team essays.

• The talented and dedicated in-house Gale staff—especially Mary K. Ruby and the Contemporary Biographies and the Biographical References Group staffs; Keith Reed of Picture Permissions; Marilyn Allen, Mike Tyrkus, and Laura Standley Berger of the *Contemporary Authors Autobiographical Series;* Mark Howell and Cindy Baldwin of the Art Department; Patrick Hughes of PC Systems; MaryBeth Trimper, Dorothy Maki, Mary Kelley, and Eveline Abou-El-Seoud of Production; Don Wellman and Maggie Patton of Creative Services; and the entire Marketing and Sales departments—for their invaluable contributions to this series.

Editor's Note

The publication of *Professional Sports Team Histories: Hockey* seems fitting at a time when National Hockey League officials are seeking to bolster the game's following in the United States. This book provides the background and folklore of historic battles on ice that have promoted kinship between Canada and the United States. Gathered in the prose entries of *Hockey* are the legends, personal profiles, anecdotes, and statistics that make up a game that its fans smugly consider the best spectator sport in the world.

—Mary K. Ruby

THE HISTORY OF
PROFESSIONAL HOCKEY

On November 22, 1917, the often-squabbling owners of four of the five teams that made up the eight-year-old National Hockey Association (NHA), one of two "major" professional hockey leagues operating in North America, met at the Windsor Hotel in Montreal to decide how to save their troubled circuit. While pro hockey was growing as a spectator sport, many factors seemed to be conspiring against it in 1917—particularly the great war raging in Europe that had forced many of the game's best players into Canadian military service.

As a temporary solution to that problem, the NHA admitted an Army team to the league in 1917. The 228th Battalion of the Northern Fusiliers boasted many of Canada's best players who had been "recruited" in hopes of avoiding front-line duty. The following February, however, the 228th was ordered overseas, thereby removing many of the game's rising young stars from the ice. The NHA dropped down to five, and then just

four, member clubs at mid-season.

The most pressing problem for the NHA as the 1916-17 campaign approached was how to deal with Toronto Blueshirts' owner Eddie Livingstone. Livingstone was unhappy with his fellow owners for forcing him to fold his other NHA team, the Toronto Shamrocks, a year earlier because the league did not want one man owning two clubs and had bitterly objected to the revised NHA schedule when the Northern Fusiliers were forced to suspend operations.

The dispute between Livingstone and the owners of other clubs—the Ottawa Senators, Quebec Bulldogs, Montreal Canadiens, and Montreal Wanderers—became so intransigent that the league finally canceled all of Toronto's remaining games, assigning the Blueshirts' players to the surviving teams.

The NHA's 1917 playoff champion Montreal Canadiens were then defeated by the rival Pacific Coast Hockey Association's (PCHA) titlists, the

Seattle Metropolitans, in four games by an aggregate score of 23 to 11. This brought the 24-year-old Stanley Cup to a U.S.-based team for the first time and greatly embarrassed the Canadian clubs. In the fall of 1917, the future of pro hockey in eastern Canada looked bleak.

By the time the troubled NHA's November session—to which Livingstone had not been invited—got under way, Canadiens' owner George Kennedy, a particularly bitter Livingstone foe, proposed a way to get rid of the recalcitrant Toronto owner. Kennedy suggested that the team owners simply fold the NHA and establish a new league without Livingstone.

Thus on November 22, 1917, the NHA disbanded and the National Hockey League (NHL) was officially organized. Four days later the NHL chartered five member clubs—the old NHA Montreal Canadiens, Montreal Wanderers, Ottawa Senators, and Quebec Bulldogs, and a new Toronto franchise called the Arenas. Although Livingstone legally challenged the new circuit, claiming that the NHA's dissolution was the result of an illegal vote, the court sided with the NHL. Thus the problematical Eddie Livingstone was out, and the National Hockey league was on its way.

Hockey Before The NHL

Ice hockey, a game that had evolved from the ancient British field sports of Scotch "shinty," Irish "hurley" and English "shinney," appeared in North America in the early 1870s, although primitive forms of the game had been played in Kingston, Ontario, as early as the 1830s. While both Kingston and Halifax, Nova Scotia, claim to be the birthplace of hockey, the first game with rules is generally considered to have been organized by J.G.A. Creighton in Montreal between two teams of McGill University students in December of 1879.

The young sport's first formal governing organization, the Amateur Hockey Association of Canada (the predecessor to today's Canadian Amateur Hockey Association), was formed in Montreal in 1885 to develop rules and promote the sport. That same year, the first hockey league was also established in Kingston with four member clubs—Queen's University, the Royal Military College, Kingston Hockey Club, and the Kingston Athletics. At season's end, Queen's University defeated the Athletics 3-1 in the title game to become the world's first championship ice hockey team.

Hockey at that time, however, was a very different game from than today's elegant high-speed contact sport. Artificial ice was rare in Canada until the first two indoor rinks were built in Vancouver and Victoria, British Columbia, in 1911, and it did not become common in many cities until the 1920s. While today's game is played with five skaters and a goalkeeper per team on a 200' x 85' enclosed surface, early ice hockey was played on much smaller open outdoor rinks surrounded by boards no more than a foot high. Goals were two sticks or poles stuck in the ice without netting (which often led to disputes as to whether or not the puck had actually passed between the posts).

Teams consisted of nine players per side, and no substitutes were allowed. Equipment provided little protection, and skates consisted of crude blades clamped or strapped to street shoes. Sticks and pucks were often homemade, although by the 1880s sticks were being produced commercially in Montreal.

By the 1890s Canadian hockey was dominated by the five-team league established in 1886 by the Amateur Hockey Association (AHA). This circuit included the Montreal Victorias, Montreal Amateur Athletic Association (AAA), Ottawa Generals, Quebec Bulldogs, and Toronto Shamrocks.

As the 1893 champions of that league, Montreal AAA also became the first club to win the Stanley Cup. This trophy had been donated in 1892 by Canadian Governor General Frederick Arthur, Lord Stanley of Preston. Originally known as the "Dominion Hockey Challenge Cup," it was to be awarded annually to the top amateur hockey team in Canada. Despite Lord Stanley's original sentiment, however, by 1910 his cup was being competed for exclusively by professionals.

With "amateur" hockey—at least as far as the above-board payment of players was concerned—still the rule in Canada, acknowledged professional hockey was first introduced in the United States. In 1903 an enterprising Houghton, Michigan, dentist, Dr. J. L. Gibson, recruited some of the best amateur players from Canada to play exhibition games for his Upper Peninsula mining town team, The Portage Takes. They challenged the rough-and-tumble clubs of other such communities for the entertainment—but mostly the wagering—pleasure of spectators.

In 1904 these U.S.-based clubs were formally organized into the game's first professional circuit, the International Pro Hockey League—which was soon joined by the first Canadian-based pro team, the Sault Ste. Marie Soos. Among the players who performed in "Doc" Gibson's pro league for as much as $500 a game were many eventual Hall of Famers, including Fred "Cyclone" Taylor, Hod Stuart, Sprague Cleghorn, Edouard "Newsy" Lalonde, and Art Ross. Despite considerable early success, the league lasted just three seasons before folding in 1907 because of runaway expenses.

Play-for-pay hockey formally came to Canada in January of 1908 with the formation of the four-team Ontario Professional Hockey League (OPHL) with clubs in Toronto, Kitchener (then called Berlin), Brantford, and Guelph. That circuit was soon joined by the National Hockey Association (NHA) which began play in 1909-10 with the Colbalt Silver Kings, Haileybury, the Renfrew Creamery Kings, Montreal Canadiens, and Montreal Wanderers.

Two weeks into the NHA's inaugural season, the Canadian Hockey Association disbanded. Two of its three clubs, the Ottawa Senators and Montreal Shamrocks, joined the new NHA to bring that circuit up to seven teams. With an 11-1 record, the Wanderers captured their eighth and last Stanley Cup in March of 1910, as the NHA's first regular season champion and then defeated Berlin of the OPHL 7-3 in a single-game challenge to retain it.

In 1911 major league hockey spread west when brothers Lester and Frank Patrick, who had been star players with both the Wanderers and Renfrew, founded another circuit called the Pacific Coast Hockey Association (PCHA) thereby establishing pro hockey in Western Canada with teams in Victoria, Vancouver, and New Westminster, British Columbia. Bankrolling the new venture with their family's lumber fortune, the Patrick brothers proved to be great innovators and developed many of the game's lasting rules.

The Patricks also brought pro hockey indoors by building the first two artificial ice rinks in Canada—a massive 10,000-seat arena in Vancouver and a 3,500-seat building in Victoria. To provide their fans with the best hockey possible, the Patricks attracted many the game's top players, such as "Cyclone" Taylor and "Newsy" Lalonde, away from eastern Canada by offering to pay them far more than the NHA clubs.

The PCHA made its debut in Victoria on January 2, 1912, as a crowd of 3,500 saw the New Westminster Royals beat the Victoria Senators 8-3. Three nights later New Westminster opened Vancouver's new arena with a 8-3 victory over the Millionaires before 10,000 fans.

In addition, the PCHA brought the United States its first major league pro hockey team in 1914-15 when the Royals moved from New Westminster to Portland, Oregon (where they became the Rosebuds). The following season a second U.S.-based club, the Seattle Metropolitans, joined the circuit.

With a fourth PCHA team to stock, a second round of player raiding ensued with the NHA clubs as the primary targets. In 1916-17 Victoria also moved across the border to become the Spokane, Washington, Canaries, thereby leaving only the Vancouver Millionaires still in Canada among the PCHA's four clubs. In the meantime the NHA saw its members come and go. Colbalt, Haileybury, and the Montreal Shamrocks dropped out in 1910-11 while the Quebec Bulldogs were reactivated and joined the circuit. Renfrew dropped out in 1911-12.

On the ice, the seventh man "rover" position was eliminated from the NHA rules, dropping eastern hockey to a six-man game (the PCHA still retained seven-man hockey) and saving the cost of a player's salary. Two Toronto teams, the Blueshirts and the Tecumsehs, were added in 1912-13, bringing the NHA up to six clubs.

In 1913, for the first time, NHA and PCHA teams faced each other as their respective champions Quebec and Victoria played a three-game set. The PCHA club won two out of three games, but since it was considered an exhibition series, the NHA club retained possession of the Stanley Cup.

Eddie Livingstone's Toronto Blueshirts won the NHA title in 1913-14 and swept Victoria in an official challenge for the Cup. The 1914-15 NHA playoff champion Ottawa became the first club from the east's top pro league to lose the Stanley Cup to a PCHA challenger as the Vancouver Millionaires overwhelmed the Senators in three straight games. In this first Cup series played on the Pacific Coast, Vancouver outscored the Ottawas 26-8. (Despite losing the title, the stunned Senators nonetheless refused to surrender the Cup to the victorious PCHA team.)

The Montreal Canadiens, or Habs, won their first of many Stanley Cup titles in 1915-16, edging the Portland Rosebuds. The Habs lost the 1917 final (this time turning over the Cup) to the Metropolitans in Seattle, dropping the championship game 9-1.

The NHL's Formative Years

The NHA not only lost possession of the Stanley Cup in 1917, but, to the utter distress of all Canadians, they had done so to a team from the United States. The NHA's troubled 1916-17 season also brought the league other scandals to overcome. In addition to its problems with Toronto owner Eddie Livingstone, other problems included the shady recruitment of players Eddie Oatman and Gordon Meeking by the 228th, a center-ice fight between the 228th's Howard McNamara and referee Cooper Smeaton, the attempted union activities and messy defection of

Toronto star Cy Denneny to Ottawa, a violent brawl late in a game between Toronto and Quebec (which eventually involved officials and fans and required massive police intervention to quell), and the general level of greed and avarice displayed by the owners in their dealings with both the players and each other.

The best course of action in the fall of 1917, therefore, appeared to be to just dissolve the troubled circuit and start over under a new name—the National Hockey League. Thus the new NHL was chartered on November 22, 1917, although it elected to maintain essentially the same constitution and playing rules as the defunct NHA. The league began its life with new leadership at the top, however, as NHA president Frank Robinson declined to retain his post. NHA secretary Frank Calder was thus elected as the NHL's first president and secretary at an annual salary of $800.

Born in Scotland in 1877, Calder had emigrated to Canada at the turn of the century to begin a career as a schoolteacher. In 1909, however, the 32-year-old Calder gave up teaching to become a sportswriter. He gained the attention of Canadiens' owner George Kennedy, who was impressed with Calder's forthright writing style and no-nonsense approach to the business of hockey. Although he had never played the game, Calder became the NHA's secretary with Kennedy's support and then president of the new NHL, a post the taciturn Scotsman held for 25 years.

Calder guided the NHL from a fledgling three-team circuit to a major North American sports power. One of the Hockey Hall of Fame's first inductees, Calder has also been permanently honored by two major namesake hockey awards—the Calder Memorial Trophy (presented annually to the NHL's top rookie), and the Calder Cup (given to the winner of the American Hockey League playoffs).

While NHL franchises were awarded on November 26 to the Canadiens, Wanderers, Senators, Bulldogs, and Arenas, the Bulldogs had already announced that they would suspend operations—for at least the 1917-18 season—because

Hockey Hall of Fame and Museum

The 1915-16 Montreal Canadiens

of financial problems. Their players were immediately distributed among the new NHL's other four teams. Scoring great "Phantom" Joe Malone was snapped up by the Canadiens, and he collected 44 goals (assists were not yet kept) in just 20 games in 1917-18 for a still-standing NHL record average of 2.20 goals per game. When the Bulldogs returned to action two years later, they got all of their players back, including Malone, who scored an NHL record seven goals in one game for the Bulldogs on January 31, 1920.

NHL's first games were played on December 19, 1917. Joe Malone scored five goals for the Canadiens in a 7-4 home victory over Ottawa, while just 700 spectators showed up to see the

Montreal Wanderers upset the Toronto Arenas 10-9. That surprising Wanderers' victory would prove to be the club's only career NHL triumph as the team lost its next five games before folding when the Montreal Arena (which they shared with the Canadiens) burned to the ground on January 2, 1918. Wanderer owner Sam Lichtenhein used the fire as an excuse to get out of hockey, and the Habs moved to the 3,250-seat Jubilee Rink.

With the Canadiens winning the NHL season's first half and the Toronto Arenas the second half, those two clubs met in a two-game total goals series to crown the NHL's first playoff champion. Behind a surprising three-goal hat trick by Toronto winger Hairy Meeking, the Arenas won the NHL's

Frank Calder (wearing hat) in 1942

first ever playoff game 7-3, in a fight-filled affair before a crowd of 4,000 in Toronto. Although the Canadiens took the second game at Montreal in another evening filled with fisticuffs, the Arenas captured the NHL's 1917-18 playoff title on total goals, 10-7, to win the O'Brien Trophy and earn the right to face the PCHA champion Vancouver Millionaires for the Stanley Cup.

The Arenas hosted the Millionaires at Toronto for a best-of-five series which alternated between using the NHL's rules, which permitted six players on the ice, and PCHA's, which allowed seven. While the Millionaires dominated the two games played under "western" rules the Arenas

won all three games played under the NHL's six-man system to capture the championship. Five members of Toronto Coach Dick Carroll's club would eventually be enshrined in the Hall of Fame—wingers Reg Noble and Rusty Crawford, rover Jack Adams, blueliner Harry Cameron, and goalie Harry "Hap" Holmes.

The NHL's second season saw each of its three teams play an 18-game schedule as opposed to the 22-game slate of the previous year. First-half champion Montreal defeated the second-half winners, Ottawa, four games to one for the league playoff title. The Canadiens then departed for Seattle to take on the Metropolitans for the Stanley

Cup, but the series was suspended after five games because several players became seriously ill during the flu epidemic which was sweeping the United States and Canada. When Montreal defenseman Joe Hall died of the disease on April 5, the series was canceled without a winner.

The Quebec Bulldogs resumed play under new ownership in 1919-20 with all its players returned from the teams to which they had been distributed two years earlier.

Meanwhile, the Canadiens finally got out of the tiny Jubilee Rink and moved to the much larger Mount Royal Arena. The Toronto Arenas changed their name that year to the St. Patricks, and the league schedule was increased from 18 to 24 games. Despite having the league's top scorer in Joe Malone (who collected 48 points in 39 goals and 9 assists), the Bulldogs won only four games, while powerhouse Ottawa with Cy Denneny and Frank Neighbor won both halves of the league schedule with a combined record of 19-5-0 and then beat Seattle for the Stanley Cup.

The first franchise shift in NHL history came in 1920-21 when the Quebec Bulldogs were purchased by H. Percy Thompson of Hamilton, Ontario, for $5,000. He moved the club to Toronto's industrial sister city, where it would play until 1925 as the Hamilton Tigers. League officials worried, however, that the Tigers would be a poor draw in Hamilton if forced to play with the same weak lineup it had in Quebec, and thus permitted the club to draft players from the other three teams.

Among the players made available to the Tigers was a 22-year-old Toronto winger named Cecil "Babe" Dye, who had scored 12 goals for the St. Pats the previous year. After collecting a pair of goals in Hamilton's surprise 5-0 shutout of the Canadiens, Dye was reclaimed by the St. Pats. Without Dye, the Tigers won just 6 games. After defeating the St. Pats for the NHL playoff title, the Ottawa Senators captured their second consecutive Cup by defeating the Vancouver Millionaires.

While retaining the 24-game season in 1921-22, the NHL dropped its "split schedule" format, instead opting for a playoff between the first- and second-place finishers to determine the winner of

the championship O'Brien Cup. For the fourth year in a row, the powerhouse Senators were in the championship series after edging Toronto for the regular season title by three points, but they fell to the St. Pats in the playoffs.

Competition for players grew as a third pro circuit, the Western Canadian Hockey League (WCHL), sprang up with teams in Edmonton, Regina, Calgary, and Saskatoon. While the new league would soon swallow up the PCHA and then fold itself in 1926, it brought major pro hockey to the Canadian prairies for the first time.

This league introduced some of the game's greatest stars, including Dick Irvin (who later became a Hall of Fame coach), brothers Bill and Bun Cook (who both went on to star with the New York Rangers), Mervyn "Red" Dutton (the NHL's second president), and perhaps the greatest of them all, immortal Hall-of-Fame defenseman Eddie Shore.

In March of 1923, hockey took another important step forward with the first live broadcast of a game, which was called by Foster Hewitt from Toronto's Mutual Street Arena. Previously, the only way to follow the exploits of pro hockey across Canada was by newspaper or telegraph.

Speaking into an upright telephone, the 30-year-old Hewitt began a tradition that evolved into "Hockey Night in Canada" and earned him a berth in the Hockey Hall of Fame in 1965. Over his long career, Foster Hewitt's trademark call of "He shoots ... he scores!" brought the thrill of the NHL to millions of fans in every corner of Canada.

NHL Hockey Heads South

The 1923-24 season was the NHL's seventh, but also the fourth year in which the circuit operated with the same four franchises—Ottawa, Toronto, Hamilton, and the Montreal Canadiens. At the time, this constituted a remarkable record of stability for an organized hockey league. While Hamilton continued to be the NHL's weak sister, the other three clubs were all fairly strong. Club owners decided to expand into the rich, yet untapped markets in the northeastern quarter of the United States. Pro hockey had already proved its appeal and fan support in the United States by the success experienced by the Patricks' PCHA franchises in Seattle and Portland. And in the Roaring Twenties the United States was also where the money was.

The league received applications from New York, Philadelphia, Pittsburgh, and Boston, but the NHL owners decided to grant a franchise to a city with a strong amateur hockey tradition. Thus in October of 1924, the NHL formally awarded its first U.S. franchise to Boston sportsman Charles F. Adams. A Vermont native who had made his fortune in the grocery business, Adams knew that he would need an experienced hockey man to ensure the success of his new team, the Boston Bruins.

He chose NHL referee and former Hamilton Tigers' manager Art Ross. Ross, a former star defenseman, would be affiliated with the Bruins for three decades, winning Stanley Cup titles in 1929, 1939, and 1941.

To balance the league—up to an even six teams—the NHL also granted a second franchise to Montreal. Owned by Donat Raymond and Thomas Strachan of the Canadian Arena Company, the Maroons were meant to appeal to Montreal's large English-speaking population the same way that the Canadiens had won the hearts of the city's French-Canadians. While the new Montreal Forum was to be home ice for the Maroons, the first NHL game played in the world-famous hockey arena featured the Canadiens, who defeated the Toronto St. Pats there on November 29, 1924, when no ice was available that night at the Habs' then-home Mount Royal Arena.

With the addition of the Maroons and Bruins, the NHL schedule was extended to 30 games. As expected, the two new expansion clubs finished a distant fifth and sixth, while powerhouse Ottawa unexpectedly missed the playoffs by one point. The Tigers, who had finished last in each of their first four seasons in Hamilton, surprisingly beat out the St. Pats and Canadiens for first place. The Tigers' players were not happy, however, and contended that their salaries had not been increased to reflect the additional six games. They refused to play the winner of the St. Pats–Canadiens semifinal series for the league title unless each man were paid an additional $200. NHL president Frank Calder suspended the entire team, fined each man $200, and declared that the winner of the semifinal series, the Canadiens, were the league champs!

Over the summer the Tigers were sold for $75,000 and moved to the new Madison Square Garden in New York City, re-emerging as the New York Americans. Although the club did well at the gate, as the Americans it would never again come close to winning another divisional or playoff title during the 16 seasons it played in the Big Apple.

A third U.S.-based team also joined the expanding NHL in 1925-26, the Pittsburgh Pirates. This brought the league up to seven clubs. Under colorful player/manager Odie Cleghorn, the longtime Canadiens' star, the Pirates did surprisingly well in their first season. With a lineup made up largely of players from the Pittsburgh Yellow Jackets, the Steel City's highly successful amateur team, the Pirates finished third behind Ottawa and the Maroons.

Under Cleghorn, the Pirates introduced the practices of changing players on the fly and using set three-man forward lines. By 1929-30, however, the Pirates had plummeted in the standings to a dreadful 5-36-3 mark. The club moved to Philadelphia, adopting the name the Quakers, but had an even worse year at 4-36-4. The team folded at the end of the 1930-31 season and neither Pittsburgh nor Philadelphia would return to the NHL again until 1967.

In 1926-27 the NHL expanded for the third consecutive season, adding three more U.S. cities with the establishment of the New York Rangers, Chicago Black Hawks and Detroit Cougars. This also then placed a majority of the league's clubs (six of ten) outside of Canada just two years after the first American team was admitted.

With ten teams, the league split into two divisions for the first time with Boston, Pittsburgh, Detroit, Chicago, and the New York Rangers playing in the American Division, and the two Montreal clubs, Toronto, Ottawa, and the New York Americans competing in the Canadian Division.

Had it not been for the collapse of the six-team Western Hockey League (WHL) after the 1925-26 season, the NHL would have been hard pressed to stock all these clubs with quality players. However, Lester Patrick sold the rights to the WHL's players to Boston's Charles Adams for $300,000 who in turn sold them to off to his fellow NHL owners.

Patrick also came east, and stayed with the Rangers, serving variously as coach or manager for the next two decades. With the NHL as the sole surviving major professional hockey league after the 1925-26 season, the Stanley Cup also came under the circuit's exclusive control.

"Golden" Years

Although North America was in deep economic depression during part of the NHL's first 25 years, the period from the late 1920s to the beginning of World War II was in many ways a Golden Age for the league. As the Depression deepened in the 1930s, sports heroes and the teams they played provided spectators with something to cheer about. Many of the NHL's great arenas arose in the 1920s and 1930s, including the Montreal Forum, Madison Square Garden, Boston Garden, Chicago Stadium, Maple Leaf Gardens and Detroit's Olympia Stadium.

Competition among the league's clubs was also outstanding with eight different teams—Ottawa, New York, Boston, the Canadiens, Toronto, Chicago, the Maroons, and Detroit—all winning the Stanley Cup at least once between 1927 and 1936. Many of the NHL's greatest names, both on and off the ice, also were at their peak in these years. Among managers, Hall of Famers Lester Patrick of the Rangers, Art Ross of the Bruins, Jack Adams of Detroit, and Conn Smythe of the Leafs were at the helms of their clubs. On the ice, the likes of Bill and Bun Cook, Howie Morenz, Frank Boucher, Dit Clapper, Eddie Shore, Joe Primeau,

Hockey Hall of Fame and Museum

Jack Adams

Busher Jackson, Syl Apps, Aurel Joliat, Charlie Conacher, Toe Blake, Babe Siebert, Ching Johnson, Hap Day, King Clancy, Red Dutton, Lorne Chabot, Clint Benedict, Alex Connell, and Dave Kerr all starred during this period.

By 1929, the NHL had a corps of stable clubs—the Rangers, Canadiens, Black Hawks, Bruins, Maple Leafs, and Detroit Falcons. After years of success in three different leagues, however, the Ottawa Senators fell on hard times. After winning the Cup four times between 1920 and 1927, Ottawa was forced to suspend operations for the 1931-32 season and lend its players to the league's other teams while attempting to put its finances in order. With the Philadelphia Quakers also folding permanently after the 1930-31 campaign, the NHL suddenly dropped from ten to eight teams.

The Senators resumed operation in 1932, but after two more years of last-place finishes, the franchise was transferred to Missouri in 1934 where it operated as the St. Louis Eagles. The club

Hockey Hall of Fame and Museum

Conn Smythe

folded for good after winning just 11 games in 1934-35, thereby dropping the NHL down to eight teams. The Montreal Maroons folded after the 1937-38 season.

Although the Maroons had been successful for most of their 11 seasons in the league, the club seemed unable to win the hearts of Montreal's hockey fans away from the Canadiens. With the demise of the Maroons, the seven-team NHL dropped its American and Canadian Divisions in 1938-39 to function as a unified league.

The Toll of War

World War II severely impacted the NHL, almost causing the league to suspend operations when a majority of its prewar players were sent overseas. While all the league's cities were impacted, no venue was hurt more than the tenants of Madison Square Garden in New York—the Americans and the Rangers.

The cash- and talent-strapped Americans club operated under the Brooklyn Americans name in 1941-42. After finishing the year in last place,

however, "Red" Dutton's troubled club folded after 16 seasons. The NHL was reduced to six clubs, and would remain that way for the next quarter of a century.

The Rangers, who won their third Stanley Cup in 1940, finished the 1941-42 campaign in first place. They would not be able to repeat that feat, and in 1942-43 dropped to last place as the club's roster was decimated by the draft board. By the end of that season, 80 of the league's estimated 125 players had either enlisted or called to the Canadian or U.S. armed forces.

With so many of hockey's top players missing, NHL president Frank Calder suggested before the 1942-43 season that the league suspend operations for the war's duration. Government and Allied war leaders considered the continuation of pro sports good for morale, and prevailed on the NHL to keep going the best it could.

The league suffered a permanent loss during the 1942-43 season when Frank Calder died suddenly of a heart attack on February 4 at the age of 66. He was replaced by 45-year-old "Red" Dutton, who agreed to run the league on an interim basis until the end of the war. Unlike Calder, Dutton had played the game—having spent 14 years as a top defenseman in the WHL and NHL before his retirement in 1936.

Despite being seriously wounded in World War I, the Manitoba-born Dutton was known as one of the most aggressive and rugged blueliners in the game during his playing days and proved to be the perfect man to guide the NHL through the remaining war years.

Another curious effect of the war on the NHL was the reappearance on the ice of some of the most-penalized players the game had ever seen—as officials! With many of the circuit's referees and linesmen also called up to military service, retired stars, such as former Leaf captain—and notorious badman—George "Red" Horner were given whistles and put in charge of controlling the games they used to disrupt. Other ex-NHL stars that saw service as officials during the war years included Frank "King" Clancy, Charlie "Rabbit" McVeigh, and Aurel Joliat.

Campbell Began Reign

After World War II, NHL president "Red" Dutton retired and recommended Clarence S. Campbell as his successor. Campbell was a 41-year-old Oxford educated lawyer, ex-Rhodes Scholar, former NHL referee, Canadian Army Lieutenant Colonel, and a war crimes prosecutor at Nuremberg.

Elected president of the NHL before the 1946-47 season, Campbell would remain at the helm for 31 years. A consummate administrator, Campbell was famous for keeping on top of every aspect of the business and hockey operations of the league—doing so with a staff so small that he regularly answered his own telephone.

Despite being based in Montreal, Campbell showed no favoritism to that city's passionately supported hometown team, the Canadiens. Campbell had several famous confrontations with Montreal's hockey legend of the 1940s and 1950s, Maurice "Rocket" Richard. One such incident came after Campbell had suspended Richard's teammate Bernie "Boom Boom" Geoffrion for the seven remaining Canadiens-Rangers games left of the 1953-54 season after Geoffrion broke Ranger Ron Murphy's jaw with his stick.

In a ghostwritten column in Montreal's *Samedi Dimarche* newspaper, Richard called Campbell a dictator and threatened to retire if Geoffrion's suspension was not lifted. The unamused Campbell demanded that Richard give up

Hockey Hall of Fame and Museum

NHL President Clarence S. Campbell (center) with Red Wings great Gordie Howe (9)

his column, apologize publicly to Campbell and the league, and to post a $1,000 bond against any such recurrence.

Richard and Campbell came head to head again 15 months later. In a game in Boston on March 13, 1955, Richard punched linesman Cliff Thompson, who was breaking up a confrontation between Richard and the Bruins' Hal Laycoe. Campbell quickly suspended Richard for the final three games of the season and the playoffs. This suspension ended Richard's chance to claim the league's scoring title and dimmed his team's playoff hopes.

All of Montreal was furious, but Campbell refused to be intimidated, appearing in his regular seat at the Forum when the Canadiens met the Detroit Red Wings on March 17 as the two clubs battled for first place. With the Wings leading 4-1, a tear gas canister was thrown at Campbell from the stands. The crowd rushed for the exits, and fire officials closed the building, deeming it unsafe to continue the game.

Angry Canadiens' fans went on a rampage outside of the Forum in what became known as the "Richard Riot" but Campbell was unmoved. He forfeited the called-off game to the Red Wings, who beat the Canadiens again on the final night of the season to edge Montreal in the standings by two points. Although the Canadiens defeated the Boston Bruins to reach the finals, the Red Wings beat Montreal in seven games to win their fourth Stanley Cup in six years.

League Expansion

The NHL flourished under Campbell's steady leadership, but as the circuit approached its Golden Anniversary season in 1967 it remained accessible to just six cities in small geographic areas of the massive North American continent. The game was popular in Montreal, Toronto, Boston, New York, Detroit, and Chicago, but except for minor league development clubs outside those areas, live professional hockey was virtually unknown. In 1967, however, that changed.

The NHL owners were a highly conservative group who kept a tight rein on operations and had long resisted letting any outsiders share in their small but quite profitable business. In the early 1960s, however, the highly successful pro-development Western Hockey League (WHL) began to make serious noises about competing with the NHL. In 1963 that league—which already had flourishing franchises in Los Angeles, San Francisco, Seattle, Portland and Vancouver—notified the NHL that it would not renew its agreement to act as part of the NHL's farm system.

In September of 1963, New York Rangers' President William Jennings responded by sending a memo to his fellow members of the NHL Board of Governors that suggested expanding in 1964-65 by adding two West Coast franchises. The proposal was not adopted in 1963, but in early 1965 the NHL Board announced that at a meeting to be held the following February, it would consider applications for six new franchises for teams which would begin play in October, 1967.

In the NHL's 51st season, 1967-68, the league would double in size from six to twelve teams. No other professional sports league had ever made such a major change.

A dozen groups from eight different cities made presentations to the NHL Board in New York City on February 8, 1966, and the following day the six franchise winners were announced. A trio of cities which had brief flings with the NHL in the late 1920s and early 1930s—Pittsburgh, Philadelphia and St. Louis—all got a second chance to make a go of major league hockey.

No group had applied to put a franchise in St. Louis, but the city's ancient and massive St. Louis Arena was owned by the influential Wirtz (Chicago Black Hawks) and Norris (Detroit Red Wings) families who wanted a tenant. The awarding of a franchise to St. Louis was made conditional, however, on the receipt of an acceptable application by April 5, 1966. Otherwise, its franchise was to be awarded to Baltimore, Maryland.

Minnesota's twin cities of Minneapolis-St. Paul, a long-time hotbed of amateur, high school, college, and minor pro hockey, gave the league a second Mississippi River venue. The other two new franchises were awarded to established WHL markets in California—Los Angeles and Oakland.

Each new franchisee was required to either build or obtain a lease for an arena with a minimum of 12,500 seats and to pay $2 million to the NHL's "original six" owners for the right to join their number. While Pittsburgh, Oakland, and St. Louis all had access to existing buildings or ones under construction, over the next 18 months Los Angeles, Minnesota, and Philadelphia all built new privately financed structures.

Besides precluding unwanted competition from a new rival "major" league—at least for a while—the NHL had two other stated objectives it hoped to achieve with expansion. The first was to become "the only major professional league operating coast-to-coast in the United States and Canada."

The second was to do so "while not affecting the quality of NHL hockey in any material way during the establishment of (its) new Division," a tall order which the NHL Board nonetheless considered to be a realistic goal. "There are numerous players today in the minor professional leagues who could play effectively in the NHL," the league stated. (Previously, the NHL had purposely buried many such players in the minors for years as a means of keeping the supply of available players much greater than the demand and holding NHL salaries at artificially low levels.)

The NHL also stated, "With the acquisition by the new franchises of top caliber players through the New Division Player Purchase Plan, these other players will help provide the additional talent for competitive teams. Further with twice the number of NHL jobs available, many more of the fine Canadian junior players will continue their hockey careers than now is the case. An additional factor will be the potential introduction to NHL rosters of a substantial number of young United States players."

Four months before the new teams were to play their first NHL games, the league held an Expansion Draft in Montreal. The six new clubs were allowed to claim two goalies and 18 skaters from the rosters of the original six. The vast majority of players that were made available to the new clubs, though, were journeyman minor leaguers, a few aging stars at the end of their careers, and a number of untested rookies.

While several of the 120 players taken in the draft proved to be valuable performers, the only one who had a Hall-of-Fame career was goalie Bernie Parent, whom the Philadelphia Flyers claimed from the Boston Bruins. Parent shut out his old team 1-0 on May 19, 1974, to help the Flyers become the first expansion team to win the Stanley Cup.

To provide the new clubs with competitive opposition as they established themselves, all six were assigned to the newly created West Division, while the "original six" were assigned to the East Division. With each team playing the other five clubs in its own division ten times, each expansion club would play just 24 games against the six established teams.

Additionally, the first two rounds of the playoffs would be played within the divisions so that a representative of each would reach the Stanley Cup finals. Not surprisingly, no West Division team ever won a game in the Cup finals during the three seasons that system was used.

The NHL expanded for a second time in 1970 with the addition of the Vancouver Canucks and Buffalo Sabres, both of which teams replaced successful minor league franchises in the same cities. A third expansion took place in 1972 with the addition of the New York Islanders and Atlanta Flames, bringing the NHL up to 16 teams.

Yet the appetite for major league hockey in North America was growing, and the rival league that the NHL had so long feared came into being in 1970 with the birth of the 12-team World Hockey Association (WHA).

After 25 years with the same six teams owning the major league hockey market, the roster of big league clubs had increased to 28 in just five seasons. This greatly increased the demand for talented hockey players, and with competing leagues now vying for their services, salaries and expenses both exploded. This distressed the conservative fraternity of NHL owners. Nonetheless, the NHL continued to expand, adding the Washington Capitals and Kansas City Scouts in 1976 to bring the league up to 18 clubs. At this time the NHL realigned into two Conferences—the Campbell and the Prince of Wales—and four Divisions—the Smythe, Norris, Adams, and Patrick.

Offering huge salaries, the WHA attracted some of the NHL's best players to its ranks, including Bobby Hull, Gerry Cheevers, Bernie Parent and the already retired Gordie Howe. The WHA also began the careers of future stars, such as Mark Howe, Rod Langway, Real Cloutier, Mike Gartner, and Wayne Gretzky.

The WHA's seven-year life was volatile and often financially troubled, however. After dozens of franchise shifts and player defections, the league collapsed after the 1978-79 season when four of the WHA's six surviving franchises—Edmonton, Winnipeg, Quebec, and New England—joined the NHL in during the senior circuit's fifth expansion in 12 seasons.

The NHL's exponential growth did not come without some failures. Two franchises moved in 1976-77. The California (nee Oakland) Seals, a member of the first expansion class, became the Cleveland Barons, while the two-year-old Kansas City Scouts transferred to Denver as the Colorado Rockies. Neither venue would help the respective clubs, and two years later the bankrupt Barons merged with the Minnesota North Stars, and the Rockies moved east after the 1981-82 season to become the New Jersey Devils. The Atlanta Flames moved to Calgary in 1980 while the North Stars shifted after 26 seasons in Minnesota to Dallas, Texas, after the 1992-93 season.

The NHL's most controversial franchise move, however, is one that never happened—the transfer of the St. Louis Blues to Saskatoon, Saskatchewan. In 1983 the Blues' owners, the Ralston-Purina Co., announced that it would sell the club to a group headed by Saskatchewan businessman Bill Hunter, who intended to move the club to the relatively small city located in the heart of Western Canada's frigid prairie country. The NHL Board bitterly opposed the move

and was subsequently sued by Ralston-Purina. The league countersued. While a new local owner was eventually found to keep the Blues in St. Louis, one side effect of the dispute was that because its ownership was in limbo, the club was not represented at the NHL's 1983 June draft and made no picks that year.

After absorbing the WHA, there were a dozen seasons of quietude in the expansion department. The NHL began another growth spurt in the early 1990s, however, adding five teams between 1991 and 1993. In 1991-92 the San Jose Sharks brought the NHL back to the Bay Area for the first time since the departure of the Seals 15 years earlier. In 1992-93 the league brought back an "original" member city after a hiatus of almost six decades with the admission of the "new" Ottawa Senators.

The NHL placed a team in the "Sun Belt" for the first time with Florida's Tampa Bay Lightning. In 1993-94 two more clubs began play in resort areas, with the debut of the Miami-based Florida Panthers, and the Disney-owned Mighty Ducks of Anaheim located in Southern California's affluent Orange County.

The Post-Campbell NHL

With the retirement of Clarence Campbell in 1977, the league was run for the first time by an American, as 43-year-old Detroit lawyer and Red Wing executive John A. Ziegler, Jr. became just the fourth president of the NHL in 60 years.

The chairman of the NHL Board of Governors at the time of his election, Ziegler first became involved with the NHL in 1957 shortly after he graduated from law school at the University of Michigan as an attorney for the Detroit Red Wings, Olympia Stadium, and the Norris family. In 1966 he began to represent the Wings on the NHL Board as an alternate governor of the team.

The first major issue that Ziegler handled after taking over the NHL was negotiating the complicated merger with the World Hockey Association. The NHL's post-Campbell era proved to be a litigious one for the league. This occupied considerable amounts of Ziegler's time as did his negotiations with the NHL Players' Association and various overseas hockey organizations (especially the Soviet Hockey Federation) as the league increased its participation in the international exhibitions.

Unlike his predecessors, Ziegler rarely involved himself in player disciplinary matters, turning over this duty to league vice-president Brian O'Neill. Over the years this arrangement led to considerable friction between the players and the league because of what many considered inconsistent punishment for similar offenses. Ziegler was also criticized for avoiding NHL games (especially during the playoffs) and for being unavailable when he was needed to settle crisis issues.

The most notable example of that occurred during the 1988 Wales Conference Finals between the New Jersey Devils and Boston Bruins, when Devils' coach Jim Schoenfeld was suspended for a game by O'Neill because of a postgame confrontation with referee Don Koharski after a 6-1 loss to Boston.

Two days later, the Devils unexpectedly sued the NHL and obtained a restraining order from a New Jersey judge against the league which stayed the suspension because it had been imposed by O'Neill without a hearing and the league president could not be found to resolve the dispute. With Ziegler still unavailable, the on-ice officials who were scheduled to work the game refused to take the ice with Schoenfeld behind the bench, thereby delaying the game for several hours until local amateur officials could be found to referee the playoff game. Ziegler finally appeared in Boston (where the series had moved for the fifth game) two days later to deal with the matter, but the incident resulted in considerable criticism and embarrassment for the league.

The NHL's 75th Anniversary

The final major controversy of the Ziegler era came at the end of the 1991-92 campaign, when the league suffered its first league-wide players strike with just over a week left in the NHL's highly promoted 75th Anniversary Season.

The work stoppage, which threatened to cancel the Stanley Cup playoffs for the first time since 1919, came about because NHL leadership had failed to resolve the negotiation of a new collective bargaining agreement with the players' association (NHLPA) even though the old one had expired almost a year earlier.

While a one-year extension to the existing contract was finally worked out—following ten days of negotiations with the NHLPA to save the season and the playoffs just hours before both were to be canceled—the damage to Ziegler had been done.

Within a few weeks it was announced that after 15 years as president of the NHL, John Ziegler would retire to return to practice law. Long-time NHL Board Chairman William Wirtz also stepped down and was replaced by one of the league's progressive and relatively new owners, Bruce McNall of the Los Angles Kings.

Gil Stein, the league's vice-president and general counsel, was named interim president and chief executive officer while the league's Board debated as to whether the circuit's next chief executive should be another "president" or if the NHL should be governed by a "commissioner" patterned after the leaders of the other three major professional team sports in North America. It was eventually decided to appoint a commissioner, and the man selected for the job after an exhaustive search was a young New York lawyer named Gary Bettman.

Bettman had already earned high marks in sports administration as the number two man to National Basketball Association (NBA) commissioner David Stern. Bettman officially took office mid-way through the 1992-93 season with a full plate of issues facing him. Among those were the negotiations of new collective bargaining agreements with both the players and officials associations, the realignment of the 26-team league, and a controversy involving outgoing president Gil Stein's alleged orchestration of his own election to the Hockey Hall of Fame.

Although Bettman came to the NHL with considerable experience in sports administration, none of that was in hockey. Therefore, the new commissioner hired the general manager of the Hartford Whalers, Brian Burke, to be the league's number-two man as NHL director of hockey operations. Burke officially joined the NHL front office October 1, 1993.

Bettman started his tenure by reprimanding Stein for manoeuvering his ill-deserved Hall-of-Fame berth. The new commissioner also changed the historic division names—Norris, Smythe, Patrick, and Adams—to the generic terms, Atlantic, Northeast, Central, and Pacific. Indeed, one of Bettman's main challenges was promoting the Canadian-born game in the United States—beyond the traditional hockey hotbeds of Detroit, Chicago, Boston, and New York—and helping the game successfully compete against the three major U.S. spectator sports.

—Bruce C. Cooper

ATLANTIC DIVISION

FLORIDA PANTHERS

The player roster for the Florida Panthers' initial season, 1993-94, may be sprinkled with a few leftovers, has-beens, and no-names, but the franchise is led by an impressive management group that bodes well for the team's future. President Bill Torrey has been called "the premier expansion team builder" for his success with the California Golden Seals in the NHL's original expansion in 1967 and, most notably, for leading the New York Islanders from an expansion team in 1972 to a hockey dynasty within a decade.

The Panther's General Manager is Bobby Clarke. He captained two Stanley Cup Champion Philadelphia Flyers teams—the first franchise other than the NHL's original six to win the championship—and reached the finals twice as a general manager, once with Philadelphia, and once with the Minnesota North Stars.

The Panthers are coached by Roger Nielson. He hasn't won a Cup yet, but has earned great respect for emphasizing fundamentals and for his

talents as a teacher—skills much needed if the Panthers are to succeed.

At the top of the Panthers' management is owner Wayne Huizenga, who built a fortune through Blockbuster Video. Huizenga brought baseball to Miami with the expansion Florida Marlins in 1993. His commitment both to the Miami area and to his expansion franchises are personal as well as financial investments.

Huizenga's multimillion-dollar entertainment empire will back local and national marketing of the Panthers. While the team plans to sell hockey to the Miami area and its many northern transplants, they also hope to draw from the nearly half-million Canadian citizens who winter in Miami.

The excellent management group showed a touch of class by naming the team after the endangered Florida Panther that roams the Everglades. Naturalists estimate that only 30-50 of the sleek beasts remain. Adding to the $36,000 they donated to a wildlife fund, the team will make a donation to a Panther preservation fund for each save made by a Panther goalie during home games.

Fortunately for all Florida Panthers, the team has depth in goal. John Vanbiesbrouck, a former Vezina Trophy winner, was the team's first selection and the first player taken overall in the 1993 expansion draft to stock Florida and the Anaheim Might Ducks. Vanbiesbrouck posted a very respectable 20-18-7 record and 3.31 goals-against-average for the 1992-93 season for the New York Rangers, a team that failed to make the playoffs. He has over 200 career victories, and he was the fifth-best goalie in save percentage (.900) in the NHL the previous season.

Backing Vanbiesbrouck will be Mark Fitzpatrick, a strong prospect selected from the Islanders organization.

Unfortunately, the depth ends there. The Panthers will have to hope that the defensemen they drafted from the lower depth charts of other teams can improve with increased playing time. Brian Benning (27, signed as a free agent from Edmonton), Joe Cirella (30, drafted from the New York Rangers), Alexander Godynyuk (23, Calgary), and Gord Murphy (26, Boston), will be joined by promising but inexperienced Paul Laus (23, Pittsburgh) and Milan Tichy (24, Chicago).

With Laus, who racked up over 400 penalty minutes in the minor leagues during the 1992-93 season, and several scrappy veteran forwards, the Panthers should prove to be an aggressive team.

Observed General Manager Clarke, who bullied with hockey's ultimate tough-guy team—the Flyers of the 1970s: "Fighting may be down in the league, but intimidation is still a part of the sport, and I think a good part of it. I've never been comfortable with a team that got pushed around on the ice."

Brian Skrudland (30, selected from Calgary), Dave Lowry (28, St. Louis), and Scott Mellanby (27, Edmonton) are hustlers who should provide the team with veteran leadership as young forwards Jesse Belanger (24, Montreal), Tom Fitzgerald (25, New York Islanders), and the team's top 1993 Amateur Draft selection, Rob Niedermayer, take time to mature. Niedermayer, 18, is big (6-foot-2; 200 lbs.), fast, and a terrific scorer, tallying 43 goals and 34 assists in 52 games for Medicine Hat during 1992-93, his final year in junior hockey. Niedermayer is considered a leading candidate for the Calder Trophy, which is given to the NHL's Rookie of the Year.

The potential of solid netminding and aggressive veteran skaters should keep the Panthers in most games as their solid management group builds for the future. Perhaps the animal for which the franchise was named will also benefit as short-sighted goals are forsaken for the long-term good.

SOURCES

Inside Hockey: Yearbook '94, September, 1993.

TEAM INFORMATION AT A GLANCE

Founding date: December 9, 1992

Home ice: Miami Arena
701 Arena Blvd.
Miami, FL 33136
Phone: (305) 530-4400
Seating capacity: 14,500

Team colors: Red, white, black, gold.
Team Nickname: Panthers
Logo: Snarling panther, teeth and claws bared, above the franchise name.

NEW JERSEY DEVILS

The road to the "Meadowlands"—once a tract of cattail-filled New Jersey marshlands situated on the banks of Bergen County's Hackensack River just across the Hudson from upper Manhattan—was indeed a long and convoluted one for the New Jersey Devils. When the well-traveled but relatively young NHL club finally arrived in the Garden State in 1982, it was in fact undergoing its third incarnation in just eight years.

And when the red, black, and green-clad Devils played their first game in the cavernous 19,040-seat Byrne Meadowlands Arena on October 5, 1982, they were sporting their third combination of hues, competing under their third name and logo, playing in their third home time zone, and operating under the management of their fifth group of owners.

The National Hockey League (NHL) franchise that finally became the New Jersey Devils in June of 1982 had originally come into existence as the Kansas City Scouts in the NHL's two-team

expansion of 1974. However, like the club's fellow inductee into the league that year, the Washington Capitals, the Scouts were far from an instant success either on the ice or at the box office.

Part of the reason for that, no doubt, was that both the Scouts and the Capitals came into the National Hockey League just two years after the 1972 formation of the World Hockey Association, which was in direct competition with the older, established circuit. That and the NHL's own three recent expansions in 1967, 1970, and 1972 had sextupled the demand for major league caliber hockey players—from 125 to 750—over a period of just seven years.

The addition of the Scouts and Caps to the NHL boosted the league in 1974 from a two-division, 16-team circuit to a four-division, two-conference, 18-team confederation. That same season the WHA also expanded by a pair of franchises (Indianapolis and Phoenix), increasing its size to an all-time high of 14 clubs.

Thus, with 32 NHL and WHA teams all combing the limited universe of North America's top hockey talent for players (Europeans were still a novelty then), the starting-from-scratch Kansas City and Washington franchises were all but guaranteed to begin their careers as virtually talentless teams—and they certainly did.

Although Washington was able—barely—to survive its dreadful early years in its original market, after just two disastrous seasons in Kansas City the Scouts failed and began to seek both new ownership and a more receptive market. Both existed in Denver, Colorado, the bustling winter sports city located at the crossroads of the Rocky Mountains just 600 miles to the west of—and one mile higher than—Kansas City.

With a long history of participatory and fan support for amateur, college, and minor league hockey, Denver welcomed the transplanted franchise to town in the summer of 1976 as the Colorado Rockies. Unfortunately, however, the carpetbagging Rockies proved to be just as inept on the ice—and in the front office—in Denver as the Scouts had been in Kansas City. They lasted just half a dozen less-than-successful seasons there before having to pull up stakes again.

This time the eight-year-old orphan franchise moved two time zones east from the high mountainlands of Colorado to the low meadowlands of East Rutherford, New Jersey, where it finally lighted for good in June of 1982 as the New Jersey Devils.

In the eight years before their incarnation as the Devils, the lowly Scouts-cum-Rockies won 20 or more games in a season only twice (20 in 1976-77; 22 in 1980-81) and made just one brief appearance in the Stanley Cup playoffs in 1978. Away from their two homes during those eight years the clubs were especially inept, with a combined overall road-winning percentage of just .203 on a record of 42-232-46.

Their arrival in New Jersey did not immediately cure the vagabond franchise's propensity to consistently miss the play-offs by a mile, but the Devils finally did ice a team. Squeaking in on an overtime goal in the final game of the 1987-88 season, the club carried out a gritty postseason run which, incredibly, took it within one game of making the Stanley Cup finals. With the play-off ice thus finally broken, the Devils went on to qualify for Stanley Cup play in all but one of the next five years.

The Kansas City Scouts

After doubling in size in 1967-68 from a unified six-team league to a two-division circuit with a dozen member clubs, the National Hockey League continued to expand through the 1970s with boosts in membership in 1970, 1972, 1974, and 1979 to bring the loop up to 22 clubs by the end of that decade. Vancouver and Buffalo, two cities with long histories of hockey success in the minor leagues, joined in 1970-71 while two relatively virgin territories—Atlanta, Georgia, and the Long Island community of Uniondale, New York—were added in 1972-73.

In 1974-75 the NHL's fourth expansion in seven years brought in the Washington, D.C. suburb of Landover, Maryland, along with the established Central Hockey League market of Kansas City, Missouri, then home to the CHL Kansas City Blues.

The Kansas City franchise, awarded to local real estate developer Edwin G. Thompson, spurred the final development and construction of a new multipurpose indoor sports and entertainment facility, the $22 million Crosby Kemper Arena. Seating 16,500 for hockey, the new arena—which later hosted the 1976 Republican National Convention—was officially opened on October 18, 1974, and hosted its first hockey game on November 2nd when the Scouts were edged by the visiting Chicago Black Hawks, 4-3.

After opening their debut season with a winless (0-7-0) seven-game road trip and an eighth consecutive loss in their home debut, the first victory in franchise history finally came in the Scouts' ninth game with a 5-3 triumph at Washington on November 4, 1974. The Scouts' first home-ice win came nine days later on November 13th at the

TEAM INFORMATION AT A GLANCE

Founded in 1974 as the Kansas City Scouts;
moved and became the Colorado Rockies, 1976;
moved again and became the New Jersey Devils, 1982

Home ice: Meadowlands Arena
P.O. Box 504
East Rutherford, NJ 07073
Phone: (201) 935-6050
FAX: 935-2127

Seating capacity: 19,040

Team colors: Red, green, and white
Team nickname: Devils, 1982--
Logo: Letters "N" and "J" in red and fused together;
letter "J" has horns on top and tail at the bottom.

Franchise record	Won	Lost	Tie
(1974-93)	465	851	208

expense of the cross-state rival the St. Louis Blues, also by a 5-3 margin.

Detroit Red Wing Hall of Famer Sid Abel, who centered Gordie Howe and Ted Lindsay on Detroit's famous "Production Line" during much of his 13-year NHL playing career, became the franchise's first hockey employee when he was named the Scouts' general manager on April 17, 1973.

Already a 20-year NHL front office veteran, Abel had begun his management career in 1952-53 as player/coach with the Chicago Black Hawks, but returned to Detroit in 1957 to coach and later manage his old club until 1971. Immediately prior to joining the Scouts, Abel had been serving as general manager of the St. Louis Blues.

Abel hired 48-year-old Armand "Bep" Guidolin in June, 1974, as the club's first coach just after Guidolin had guided the Boston Bruins to the 1974 Stanley Cup finals against the Philadelphia Flyers. Guidolin, a former left winger who had played briefly with Abel in Detroit in the late 1940s, spent nine workmanlike seasons as an NHL player with Boston, Detroit, and Chicago before turning to coaching with the OHA Oshawa Generals and London Knights in the early 1960s. His main claim to hockey fame, however, came as a member of the war-depleted Bruins in 1942 when, at age 16, he became the youngest man to ever play in the NHL.

Although he survived his first season (15-54-11) as the Scouts' coach, Guidolin was let go 45 games into the 1975-76 campaign with a record of 11-30-4. After three games behind the bench (0-3-0) on an interim basis, Abel turned the hapless Scouts over to veteran minor league coach Eddie Bush for the remainder of the season, but he managed to guide them to just one more win (5-1 over Washington on February 13th) in the season's remaining 32 games (1-23-8).

Like almost all expansion teams, the Scouts' first year roster was pretty much a ragtag assortment of third string NHLers, older ex-minor league veterans, and inexperienced amateur draft picks. However, the club was not completely without talent, such as the Scouts' first captain and leading scorer (26-32-58), right wing Simon Nolet.

Nolet came to Kansas City in the expansion draft after having helped the Philadelphia Flyers to the 1974 Stanley Cup. Seven years earlier, in 1967 as a minor leaguer, Nolet had received his first chance to play in the NHL with the league's initial six-team expansion that had brought in Philadelphia. Rookie Wilf Paiement, another right winger, became the franchise's first amateur draft pick (second overall in 1974) and tied Nolet with a team-leading 26 goals.

The Scouts' debut season goaltending chores were handled by the trio of young NHL veterans—Peter McDuffe, Michel Plasse, and Denis Herron. Although the Scouts finished last in the new Smythe Division with just 41 points on a record of 15-54-11, they nonetheless did almost twice as well as their expansion co-inductees, the Washington Capitals, who only managed eight wins and a mere 21 points in 1974-75.

While the 1974-75 season was the NHL's first in Kansas City, its second in 1975-76 would also unexpectedly prove to be its last there. The Scouts' continued poor attendance and terrible on-ice performance (12-56-12; 32 points) proved to be too much to overcome, and at season's end the troubled franchise was sold to Denver oil man Jack Vickers and his partner, ex-NBA New York Knicks captain and network TV sportscaster Bud Palmer.

The new owners moved the club to the Colorado capital for the 1976-77 season. The franchise's cumulative record in its two seasons in Kansas City was 27-110-23 for a total of just 77 out of a possible 320 points. Twenty of their wins came at Kemper Arena, while the club won a total of just seven times in eighty tries on the road.

The Colorado Rockies

On October 5th, 1976, the franchise made its debut as the Colorado Rockies with a 4-2 victory over the Toronto Maple Leafs. The game was held in the year-old 16,400-seat William H. McNichols Sports Arena, located adjacent to Denver's Mile High Stadium, home of the NFL Denver Broncos.

Although the NHL Rockies would play in Denver for just six seasons, during that stretch the franchise went through players, coaches, and owners with startling alacrity. Between 1976 and 1982 well over 100 skaters appeared in one or more games for the Rockies, seven different men stood behind the club's bench, and the club was bought and sold three times.

Vickers and Palmer, who owned the Rockies for its first two seasons in Denver, brought in a completely new management team when they moved the franchise west. Former California Golden Seals' boss Munson Campbell became the Rockies' president and governor while veteran minor league executive Ray Miron left the presidency of the Central Hockey League—a job he had held for just three weeks—when he was named the franchise's new general manager in late August. As the first of seven head coaches in just six years, Miron named former Los Angeles Kings' and Detroit Red Wings' mentor Johnny Wilson to take over behind the Denver club's bench.

Veteran winger Simon Nolet became the Rockies' first captain despite the fact that midway through the previous season he had been traded by Kansas City to the Pittsburgh Penguins. However Nolet and goalie Michel Plasse, another original Scout, were reacquired by the transplanted team just prior to the start of the season in compensation for the Pens' signing of free–agent goalie Denis Herron.

Also joining the Rockies for their debut season in Denver was veteran goalie Doug Favell who came over in a trade with the Toronto Maple Leafs. Like Nolet, Favell had been an original Flyer in the NHL's first expansion in 1967.

Although the franchise won 20 games (20-46-14) in its debut season in Denver and improved from 36 to 54 points over its final year in Kansas City, the team nonetheless finished with the second worst record in the league in 1976-77, bettering only Detroit's dismal total of 41. With that, coach Johnny Wilson found himself out of a job and was replaced by 42-year-old Pat Kelly, a veteran minor league bench boss and the recent ex-coach of the WHA Birmingham Bulls, who had a long history of success as a player and coach in the game's "bus" circuits.

Even though the club improved by only five points in his first year to 59 on a record of 19-40-21, that was good enough to move the Rockies from last place to second in the weak Smythe Division and earn a play-off berth for the first time.

With the experienced Favell in goal, Colorado almost pulled off a monumental upset when Favell turned aside 40 shots at Philadelphia on April 11, 1978, to hold the powerhouse Flyers to a 2-2 tie through 60 minutes in the first Stanley Cup game in the franchise's history.

A goal by center Mel Bridgman just 23 seconds into overtime quickly ended their fantasy, however, and the Rockies then fell in the best-of-three preliminary round series in two straight games. It would be another decade before the franchise—as the New Jersey Devils—would ever again appear in a postseason contest.

In August, 1978, northern New Jersey trucking magnate Arthur E. Imperatore became the third owner of the franchise when he bought the financially floundering club from the Vickers group with the apparent hope of eventually moving it to the growing sports complex in the Meadowlands.

Imperatore's stepson, Armand Pohan, a former Hudson County, New Jersey, prosecutor and an officer of Imperatore's huge trucking business, replaced Munson Campbell as team president while Miron remained as general manager and Kelly stayed on—albeit briefly—as coach.

Just 21 games into his second season behind the Rockies' bench in 1978-79, Kelly was fired after a dismal 3-14-4 start and was replaced for rest of the season by Rockies' player/personnel director Aldo Guidolin, a cousin of the franchise's original coach, Bep Guidolin. In the season's remaining 59 games under Guidolin, however, the Rockies scored a poor 12-39-8 and finished the year with the league's worst record at 15-53-12 for 42 points—just one more point than in their first year in Kansas City.

The time had clearly come to make a bold move if the Rockies were to ever make a mark in Denver and, a few weeks later, they did just that by hiring the most colorful coach in the game. The Rockies' fourth coach, 45-year-old Don "Grapes" Cherry was outspoken, flamboyant, and controversial.

In five years of strutting behind the bench of the Boston Bruins, the NHL's most famous practitioner of sartorial splendor had guided the B's to four consecutive first-place divisional finishes—and two appearances in the Stanley Cup finals—while also being named NHL Coach of the Year in 1975-76.

Although Cherry's clubs were highly successful in Boston, his often outlandish personal style was a constant thorn in the side of management. He finally left the Bruins following the 1978–79 season as the result of a contract dispute and various other ongoing and much publicized flaps with conservative Boston General Manager Harry Sinden. Not unexpectedly, Cherry also soon proved to be a handful in Denver for both team management and more than a few of his players.

Since Cherry was a great advocate of old-time hard-nosed "lunch pail" school of hockey, players whose style differed from tradition (such as the talented but flaky defenseman Mike McEwen and the diminutive Swedish goalie Hardy Åstrom), often felt the coach's well-placed barbs with particular frequency.

While the Rockies were certainly more entertaining under Cherry, the club's real weakness was purely and simply a lack of talent. By season's end they had only improved by a modest nine points over the previous year to 51 on a record of 19-48-13 and again finished in the Smythe Division's cellar. Not surprisingly that was not enough to offset the aggravation of Cherry's loose canon style—of which management had already had their fill. They dismissed him after just one season.

Although he never coached again, Cherry nonetheless got the last laugh as two years later the Rockies were no more while "Grapes" went on to stardom on Canadian TV as host of *Don Cherry's Grapevine* and *The Coach's Corner* and became one of the most recognizable public figures in Canada.

Although highlights during Cherry's year with the Rockies were few and far between, one certainly came for him on December 2, 1974, when he returned to Boston Garden for the first time to coach a game against his old club. Behind the strong goaltending of journeyman Bill McKenzie, the Rockies upset the powerhouse Bruins, 5-3, to the great delight of Cherry's large legion of still loyal fans in Beantown.

In the 1980-81 season, the Rockies' fifth in Denver, the club skated for its fifth coach, 37-year-old former New York Islander assistant Billy MacMillan. MacMillan's relatively understated style proved to be a refreshing change to many after the turmoil of the previous season.

In addition to his term as an assistant to Islander coach Al Arbour in New York, during which he had earned a Stanley Cup ring in 1979-80, MacMillan had also played for the Isles, Atlanta Flames, and Toronto Maple Leafs from 1970 to his retirement in 1978. As a head coach in the Islander organization, he had guided the CHL Fort Worth Texans to the Central Hockey League playoff title in 1978.

Although again failing to make the play-offs, MacMillan's Rockies won a team-record 22 games in 1980-81. Future Hall-of-Fame winger Lanny McDonald and Joel Quenneville had been acquired from the Toronto Maple Leafs the previous season in exchange for for Wilf Paiement and Pat Hickey. When McDonald collected 81 points on 35 goals and 46 assists, the Rockies iced the first "point-per-game" scorer in franchise history.

The franchise also got a legitimate star goalie for the first time in its history on March 10, 1981, when it traded talented but eccentric defenseman Mike McEwen to the Islanders for veteran netminder Glenn "Chico" Resch and center Steve Tambellini.

The 1980-81 season also saw the third change of ownership for the franchise in Denver (and fourth overall) when Buffalo cable TV magnate Peter Gilbert bought the club in February, 1981. A native of Austria, the colorful Gilbert had, at age 19, become the youngest major in the British Army by the end of World War II .

Later, prior to emigrating to the United States, he flew bombers in the Israeli Air Force in that country's 1946 war of liberation. After building up several high tech manufacturing companies, Gilbert got into the cable TV business in 1970 and by 1981 was president and chairman of Comax Telcom Corporation (which did business as International Cable) when he bought the Rockies. Former Colorado Lieutenant Governor Mark Hogan became the club's chairman of the board.

Following the 1980-81 season Billy MacMillan was appointed to replace Ray Miron as general manager, and Bert Marshall, a former Islander teammate of MacMillan's, became the sixth head coach of the Rockies in six years. In the two seasons prior to joining the Rockies, Marshall had coached the Islanders top farm team, the CHL Indianapolis Checkers.

Unfortunately for Marshall, however, the talent-thin Rockies again faltered badly at the start of the 1981-82 campaign and the rookie NHL coach was replaced behind the bench after just 24 games (3-17-4). Assistant GM Marshall Johnston, a former coach of the University of Denver Pioneers, replaced Marshall, and finished out the year with a 15-32-9 mark in his 56 games as the Rockies' seventh coach.

Three days prior to Marshall's departure, Lanny McDonald also left Denver, having been traded by Billy MacMillan to the Calgary Flames for 29-year-old right wing Bob MacMillan (the general manager's younger brother) and veteran former Vancouver Canuck left wing Don Lever.

Although the club played somewhat better after these changes, at 18-49-13 in 1981-82 the Rockies were again dead last in the league at season's end in both ice proficiency and fan interest. Despite protestations during the season's closing weeks that NHL hockey was safe in Denver, it was, in fact, doomed, as by that time the club was playing to home crowds of as few as 4,775 people.

On April 1, 1982, when the Rockies traveled to Calgary for their final road game of 1981-82, the Flames defeated the franchise 11-0—the greatest margin in their history either before or since. The Rockies beat the same Flames two nights later at McNichols Arena, 3-1, in front of a crowd of 9,824.

The game, which marked the team's 113th victory in the six seasons since they had arrived in Denver, would also prove to be their last as the Colorado Rockies. Three months later on June 30, 1982, the franchise was sold for the fifth time in eight years to a group headed by New Jersey businessman John J. McMullen, and was officially transferred to East Rutherford, New Jersey.

NHL Hockey Comes To New Jersey

The National Hockey League first emerged in the New York City metropolitan area with two teams, the New York Americans in 1925 and the New York Rangers in 1926. Both of these teams played at Madison Square Garden on Eighth Avenue at 50th Street—just a stone's throw from Manhattan's glitzy Broadway theater district.

In those days New York's NHL fans were mostly city dwellers, but by 1968 when the Rangers moved to the new MSG built above Pennsylvania Station at 33rd Street and Eighth Avenue,

their fans were a much more diverse lot who came not only from Manhattan, but more and more from the city's outlying boroughs and its many fast-growing Long Island and New Jersey suburban communities.

In 1972 Long Island-based hockey fans got an NHL club to call their own when the New York Islanders were established at the Nassau County Coliseum in Uniondale. Not unexpectedly, that club—and its fans—quickly built up an intense rivalry with the long-established Rangers. At the same time, northern New Jersey's exploding population was actively seeking to attract major league sports franchises to the Garden State with the privately financed development of a major sports complex at the Meadowlands, a site adjacent to Exit 18W of the heavily traveled New Jersey Turnpike, halfway between the Lincoln Tunnel and George Washington Bridge.

With the construction of 77,000-seat Giants Stadium next to Meadowlands Race Track, the Garden State eventually attracted both of New York City's National Football League teams; the New York Giants relocated first from Yankee Stadium in the Bronx, and the New York Jets moved from Shea Stadium in Flushing. With the subsequent addition to the complex of the Byrne Meadowlands Arena, the NBA New Jersey Nets moved to East Rutherford from Rutgers, and the NHL Devils completed the Meadowlands' major league quartet with their arrival from Denver in 1982.

Bringing a third NHL franchise to the New York metropolitan area, however, would prove to be both a particularly expensive and a complicated proposition for new majority owner John J. McMullen and his two partners, Brendan T. Byrne, Jr., and John C. Whitehead.

Not only was there considerable expense in the purchase and physical uprooting of the existing Rockies' franchise, but winning the league's approval of the transfer to New Jersey required the payment of millions in territorial indemnification fees to the Flyers, Rangers, and Islanders. If any group of men had the wherewithal to pull it off, however, it was McMullen and his two partners, all of whom were already proven movers and shakers in their native New Jersey.

A graduate of the U.S. Naval Academy and MIT, McMullen also earned a doctorate in mechanical engineering in Zurich, Switzerland, before leaving the Navy in 1954 to become the chief of the U.S. Maritime Administration Office of Ship Construction and Repair. In addition to operating his own naval architecture and marine engineering firm since 1957, McMullen also ran several major shipping companies, including the United States Lines and Burmah Oil Tankers, Ltd. A onetime partner in the New York Yankees, McMullen was also the majority owner of the Houston Astros.

A former New Jersey prosecutor, Superior Court judge, and two-term governor of the state (1974-82), team co-owner Brendan Byrne's name was not only listed among the club's shareholders, but also appeared in large letters on the club's new home—"The Brendan T. Byrne, Jr., Meadowlands Arena." John Whitehead came to the group as a senior partner and co-chairman of the Wall Street investment banking house of Goldman, Sachs & Co. and later served as the nation's number two diplomat as Deputy Secretary of State (1985-1988) under George Schultz in the second Reagan administration.

The Rockies' principal hockey staff moved east with the franchise. Billy MacMillan remained as general manager while also returning to the bench after a year's hiatus to again coach the club. Former Washington Capitals general manager Max McNab also joined the Devils front office as vice president for hockey operations and eventually took over as GM as well when MacMillan was dismissed on November 22, 1983.

McNab had once been a linemate of Gordie Howe's in Detroit, as had been the franchise's first general manager in Kansas City, Sid Abel. He had also once been president of the Central Hockey League, as had former Rockies' general manager Ray Miron. The two men who had coached the Rockies in their last season in Denver, Marshall Johnston and Bert Marshall, also remained with the Devils as assistant coach and director of player

personnel respectively.

A "Mickey Mouse" Start

With Chico Resch in goal, the nomadic franchise made its third NHL debut in eight years by tying the Pittsburgh Penguins, 3-3, before a crowd of 13,663 at the Meadowlands on October 5, 1982. New captain Don Lever scored the Devils' first goal. Three nights later the club earned its first career victory before a home crowd of 19,023 by beating their new cross-river rivals, the New York Rangers, 3-2.

While the standing-room-only crowd for that game was by far the biggest to ever see the Scouts-Rockies-Devils play in their eight years as a team, such sellout throngs tended to reappear at the Meadowlands only on the three or four nights each season that the Rangers visited. In the years to come the Devils were largely unsuccessful in converting the many longtime Ranger loyalists who lived in New Jersey. Attendance figures on nights when the Rangers were not the opposition usually fell many thousands below capacity.

The first year Devils had a surprisingly strong if illusory start, losing just one of their first seven games (3-1-3). By the end of November, however, the Devils again looked very much like the dismal clubs that had characterized the franchise's Kansas City and Colorado eras.

After beating the Philadelphia Flyers, 3-1, at the Meadowlands on October 18th, the Devils did not experience victory again for another six weeks, when they won at Calgary, 4-3, on November 27th, breaking an 18-game winless streak (0-14-4). While that still represents the longest such stretch for the Devils, it is nonetheless far short of the overall franchise record of 27 (0-21-6) that was set by the Scouts from February 15th to April 4th, 1976.

By the end of their first season in New Jersey the club had a winning record against exactly one team—the Pittsburgh Penguins—with a 3-1-3 mark over their new Patrick Division rivals. The Penguins and Hartford Whalers were also the only two clubs to finish the 1982-83 season with worse records than the Devils' mark of 17-49-14 for 48 points (which was actually one point below what the club compiled in its last season in Denver the year before).

On April 15, 1983, the Devils brought in former Flyers president Bob Butera, a 48-year-old Philadelphia attorney and onetime Pennsylvania state legislator, to become the team's first president. GM/coach Billy MacMillan was also given a managerial vote of confidence with a three-year contract just prior to the start of the 1983-84 campaign, but the support was not strong enough to save either of MacMillan's jobs when the club virtually broke down in the first quarter of their second season in New Jersey.

In mid-November the team experienced perhaps the most embarrassing loss in franchise history: the so-called "Mickey Mouse game." On November 19, 1983, the Devils visited Northlands Coliseum in Edmonton for their twentieth game of the season in which they were beaten by the Oilers, 13-4, with Wayne Gretzky collecting eight points (3-5) and his linemate, Jari Kurri, scoring five times. This heartless thrashing—Edmonton scored five of its goals in the game's final ten minutes long after the outcome was certain—dropped the Devils record to 2-18-0, the second worst start in NHL history behind the 1930-31 Philadelphia Quakers' 1-19-1 opening.

After the game Gretzky compared the Devils to a Mickey Mouse operation that was "ruining hockey," an injudicious remark for which he later apologized. The damage, however, had already been done and three days later Billy MacMillan was dismissed as both general manager and coach, with Max McNab becoming GM and former Washington Capital and Winnipeg Jet coach Tom McVie being promoted from New Jersey's AHL Maine Mariners farm club to take over behind the Devils' bench.

Under McVie the Devils went 15-38-7 over the remaining 60 games of the season to give them an overall record of 17-56-7, matching the franchise's all-time low of 41 points from their first season in Kansas City. That lowly score did not prove to be the league's worst record in 1983-84, however, despite the Devils' finishing the season with a 1-10-1 run over their final dozen games.

A three-game winning streak at the start of March, which ended with a 6-5 victory over Pittsburgh on March 6th gave the Devils a three-point bulge over the Pens at season's end. With 38 points to the Devils' 41, the Penguins thus earned the first overall pick in the Entry Draft in June, 1984, while the Devils picked second. New Jersey got a very fine player with their pick in future captain Kirk Muller; Pittsburgh used its first overall pick to select a future captain of its own—Mario Lemieux.

The Carpenter Years

Tom McVie returned to the AHL's Mariners following the 1983-84 season and was replaced by 42-year-old Doug Carpenter, a longtime minor league defenseman who had spent the four previous seasons coaching the top farm clubs of the Toronto Maple Leafs in Moncton, New Brunswick, Cincinnati, Ohio, and St. Catharines, Ontario. As a junior coach Carpenter led the Cornwall Royals to the Memorial Cup title in 1980 as champions of Canadian junior hockey, and in the mid-1970s he had also guided the IHL Flint Generals.

The dozenth coach overall in the history of franchise and the third in New Jersey, Carpenter would remain with the Devils for three and a half seasons—by far the longest period any one man would ever coach the Scouts, Rockies, or Devils.

The Devils opened their third season in New Jersey on October 12, 1984, with what seemed to be a good omen—a 7-5 win over the New York Islanders, a team they had failed to earn a single point from in 14 previous meetings (0-14-0) over the two seasons since they had become Patrick Division rivals in 1982.

Over the next two months Carpenter also helped the Devils exorcise a pair of decade-long all-time franchise ciphers with first-ever road wins over the Flyers and Islanders, ending a 0-24-1 run in Philadelphia with a 2-1 win at the Spectrum on November 29th and an 0-24-2 stretch at Nassau

Coliseum with a 7-5 victory over the Isles on December 11th. For the first time since arriving in New Jersey the Devils beat another Patrick Division opponent, the Washington Capitals, with a 5-3 victory at the Meadowlands on January 12th.

Under Carpenter the Devils continuously improved each year to 54 points (22-48-10) in 1984-85, 59 points (28-49-3) in 1985-85, and 64 points (29-45-6) in 1985-86, but still continued to miss the play-offs in the strong Patrick Division. Nevertheless, after more than a decade of being little more than cannon fodder for the rest of the league, the franchise was finally icing competitive teams and making regular season games memorable enough to build fan interest.

On November 2, 1985, for instance, the Devils staged the most dramatic comeback in their history when Mel Bridgman scored 50 seconds into overtime to defeat the hated New York Rangers 6-5, after a five-goal Devils third period outburst erased a 4-0 Ranger lead. On March 27, 1986, 27-year-old veteran minor league goalie Sam St. Laurent unexpectedly got his first NHL start while on an emergency recall and shut out St. Louis, 1-0, to give the Devils their first victory over the Blues in a dozen tries since moving to New Jersey.

While the Devils' newfound success started to bring more people out to the Meadowlands, one of their most remarkable games of this era was actually played in front of almost nobody. On Thursday, January 22, 1987, the Devils were scheduled to host the powerful Calgary Flames, but on the day of the game the New York area was hit with an intense snowstorm that dumped more than 15 inches of wind-driven snow by game time. However, with the Flames already at the rink and the game scheduled to be televised both locally and in Canada, a decision was made to attempt to play if enough Devils players could make it in from their homes.

Only 13 New Jersey skaters were on hand by the scheduled 7:35 pm start time, but over the next hour and forty-five minutes the rest finally slogged their way in. The game got underway at 9:20 pm. To the utter delight of a hearty "crowd" of 334 who

had fought their way to the Arena, the Devils defeated the Flames, 7-5, behind a hat trick by Doug Sulliman. Not only was that victory the Devils' first ever over Calgary at the Meadowlands, but a very exclusive still-active fan club called the 334 Club was formed by the die-hard fans who had witnessed it.

1987: A New Boss

With the resignation of team president Bob Butera, who returned to practicing law just after the end of the 1986-87 season, the Devils appointed 44-year-old Lou Lamoriello as the team's second chief executive on April 30, 1987.

A native of Providence, Rhode Island, Lamoriello came to New Jersey after almost a quarter of a century with his hometown Providence College, where he had played both varsity hockey and baseball as an undergraduate and remained for another 20-plus years after graduation as a hockey coach and sports administrator.

Over his 15 seasons as head coach of the NCAA Division's Providence College Friars (1967-83), Lamoriello compiled a career record of 248-179-13 before becoming athletic director at Providence with responsibility for all 22 of the school's varsity programs as well as its extensive athletic facilities. Lamoriello had also helped establish "Hockey East" and then served as Commissioner of the seven-team Division league of New England-based colleges.

Five months after joining the Devils, Lamoriello added the duties of general manager to his portfolio just before the start of the 1987-88 season when former GM Max McNab became the Devils' executive vice president.

On the ice the Devils got off to their best start in franchise history in 1987-88, compiling a record of 12-6-2 over the first quarter of the season and carrying either first or second place in the Patrick Division through the end of December. With a 4-3 home loss to Washington on December 30th, however, the club began a January slide which saw them drop nine of their next 13 games (3-9-1), culminating with a 5-2 home loss to Buffalo on January 25th.

While such mid-season slumps are not at all uncommon even for the best of teams, the loss to the Sabres was the Devils' fifth in a row and the club dropped into fifth place for the first time. With that, Lamoriello dismissed Carpenter after three and a half seasons (100-166-24) and replaced him with his own choice for head coach, 35-year-old Jim Schoenfeld.

A top defenseman in the NHL for 13 seasons (1972-85), of which all but two and a half were spent with Buffalo, Schoenfeld's only coaching experiences prior to joining the Devils on January 26, 1988, were brief stints behind the benches of the AHL Rochester Americans (17-6-2 in 1984-85) and the Sabres (19-19-5 in 1985-86).

The coaching change did not have a stunning immediate impact, however, as the club went a modest 7-10-0 over Schoenfeld's first 17 games behind the bench. On March 1st, however, a second new arrival in New Jersey did have a salubrious effect.

Goalie Sean Burke, a surprise second-round draft pick of the Devils three years earlier, joined the club after finishing his stint with the Canadian Olympic team and competing in the XV Winter Olympic Games in Calgary. Burke got his first NHL start five days later and although he gave up six goals, he collected his first career pro victory with a 7-6 overtime win at Boston to begin a remarkable 10-2-1 play-off "march" by the Devils over the season's final full month.

In his first four weeks as a pro, Burke lost only once and helped to bring about two victories each over the Flyers and Penguins, also beating the Capitals, Blues, Rangers, and Islanders to return the franchise to its first play-off berth in a decade. By the time Burke led the Devils onto the ice at Chicago Stadium on April 3rd for their final game of the season, the club was tied in points (80) with the New York Rangers for the fourth and final Patrick Division berth.

With two more victories than New York, however, the Devils would earn the postseason nod if the two clubs remained tied in points after

their respective final games that night. As the Rangers' season closer against the Quebec Nordiques would start in New York an hour earlier than the Devils' final game in Chicago, however, by the time Schoenfeld's charges took to the ice for the third period they would already know how many points—if any—they would need to make the play-offs.

All the Devils would need to make the play-offs was to match the Rangers' result that night, but the Broadway Blues were not about to make it easy for them as they shut out the Nordiques, 3-0, which meant the Devils would have to beat Chicago to earn the final Patrick Division berth.

Despite being outshot by New Jersey by a considerable margin, the Blackhawks were holding a 3-2 lead as the game headed to its final eight minutes, when Devils' winger John MacLean finally beat diminutive 'Hawk goalie Darren Pang at 11:57 to deadlock the contest, 3-3. With the Rangers already having won, a tie would not be good enough to get the Devils in the play-offs, but that's how the game stood after 60 minutes.

In 31 previous career overtime road games, the Devils had only won five times while losing eight and tying 18, so the odds were definitely not in their favor as they began the five-minute sudden death extra period. Miraculously at the 2:21 mark, however, MacLean beat Pang again to give the Devils a storybook come-from-behind 4-3 victory—and to propel the franchise into the most memorable and dramatic six weeks in its history.

With 38 wins (38-36-6) and 82 points, the 1987-88 season had been by far the most successful in the 14-year history of the Scouts-Rockies-Devils franchise. Never before had the club won more than 29 games in a season, and only twice had it exceeded 22 wins. In its previous 13 years, the franchise had averaged just 50 points per season, which it had now bettered by an incredible 32. With 37 goals and 94 points, Devils' captain Kirk Muller had clearly emerged as one of the league's top centers, while Muller's left wing, Aaron Broten—the only former Rockie still with the club—had collected a career high 83 points and tied Muller with 57 assists.

Feisty Pat Verbeek (77 points), Muller's right wing, led the team in both goals, with 46, and penalty minutes, with 227. At 10-1-0, however, it was rookie goalie Sean Burke who, with just one month of NHL experience, had provided the Devils with the ingredient they had needed not only to finally make the play-offs, but to be successful in them as well.

The Patrick Division race was a most unusual one in 1987-88 in that its six clubs all finished the regular season within seven points of each other (88 to 81). [The distance separating the four teams from second-place Pittsburgh (85) to the fifth-place New York Rangers (82) at season's end was an even more minuscule three points.] As the Division's fourth-place finisher, the Devils drew their longtime nemesis, the Division champion New York Islanders in the first round.

Although they beat the Isles in all three regular season meetings at the Meadowlands in 1987-88, in 14 seasons as a franchise the club had only managed one win in 38 tries at Nassau Coliseum (1-34-3), where they would now have to win at least once to advance in the play-offs.

Incredibly, the Devils almost got that elusive road win in the opening game of the best-of-seven set on April 6th with late third period goals by David Maley at 12:05 and John MacLean at 13:04 to overcome a 3-1 Islander lead and force the game into overtime. However, at 6:11 of the first extra frame, Islander center Pat LaFontaine corralled the rebound of a shot by Derek King and beat Burke from the slot for a 4-3 Isles' victory, Burke's first loss since his only other NHL career setback at Quebec on March 17th.

While Burke had played well, Schoenfeld decided to go with a hunch the next night and started Burke's far more experienced backup, 12-year NHL veteran Bob Sauve, in game two. A former Vezina Trophy winner and onetime teammate of Schoenfeld's in Buffalo, Sauve's steady experience came through as he held the Islanders to just two goals while another experienced vet, 31-year-old 1980 U.S. Gold Medal-winning Olympian Mark Johnson, beat Kelly Hrudey for the game winner in the Devils' clutch 3-2 road vic-

tory, its first triumph in postseason play.

Burke returned to the Devils' net for game three on April 9th in spectacular fashion as he earned his first career play-off shutout, 3-0. The highly experienced Islanders proved they were not going to be easy to upset, however, as they evened the series and regained home ice advantage with another overtime victory in game four (and this despite giving up a tying goal to John MacLean with but a dozen seconds left in regulation to knot the contest at 4-4).

However, with five minutes left in the first overtime, and the Devils on a power play, veteran Isles' center Brent Sutter stole errant Tom Kurvers' pass to Craig Wolanin near the Devils' blueline and fired the puck at Burke from close in. Although the young Devil goalie managed to stop the original shot, Kurvers inadvertently knocked the rebound into his own net at 15:07 of overtime. With that Sutter became the second player in Stanley Cup history to be credited with scoring a shorthanded goal in overtime. With the 5-4 win, the Islanders also extended their club's incredible career play-off overtime record to 24-7.

With the Isles' victory in game four, the Devils were in the difficult position of having to win another game in Uniondale. After a fight-filled first period in game five that ended tied at 1-1, the Devils outscored the Isles, 3-1, in the middle stanza. Then, with the team's fate in his hands, Burke turned aside all 18 New York shots in the third period to give the Devils their second consecutive road win of the series, 4-2.

Two nights later the Devils again beat the Islanders at the Meadowlands, 6-5, to earn their first play-off series victory. At this point they found themselves faced by the team that had given them more trouble than the Isles since coming to New Jersey—the Washington Capitals.

The Caps had been every bit as dismal as the Scouts/Rockies when they and the Devils' ancestors had entered the NHL together in 1974, but during the 1980s the Caps, under Bryan Murray, had become one of the league's strongest clubs, despite often disappointing their fans in the play-offs. Like Nassau Coliseum, the Cap Centre had been a traditional house of horrors for the Devils, who, since joining the Patrick Division, had managed only one victory (1-19-1) at Landover, during which they were also 6-32-4 overall in 42 games against Washington. New Jersey's one career victory in Landover had come in their most recent visit when Sean Burke led the Devils to a 4-2 triumph there less than a month earlier on March 20th.

The Devils' one-game winning streak at Landover came to an abrupt end on April 18th, however, as the Caps outhustled the visitors in the first game of the Patrick Division finals and won with relative ease, 3-1. The victory proved to be a Pyrrhic one for the Caps, however, as they suffered a key personnel loss when their captain, Rod Langway, was cut on his left leg late in the third period by the skate of Pat Verbeek and sidelined for the rest of the series.

Two nights later the Devils came back in a rough-and-tumble (162 penalty minutes) game two to beat the Caps decisively, 5-2, for their second win in Landover in a month and to capture home ice advantage for the second series in a row.

It could be legitimately observed that the loss of Langway, one of the league's best defensemen, had contributed to the Caps loss in game two. A whole squad of Norris Trophy winners, however, probably would not have stopped the Devils in game three at the Meadowlands on April 24th. By the end of that remarkable night Devils winger Patrik Sundstrom had collected a single-game NHL play-off record of eight points on three goals and five assists, while linemate Mark Johnson added four goals on the way to a stunning 10-4 New Jersey rout.

Things began to look even bleaker for the Caps in game four when they lost two more key defensive players. Both goalie Pete Peeters and blueliner Gary Galley had to be carried off the ice on stretchers when injured in separate incidents by errant shots. Ironically, it was the Caps who came out on top in the game, 4-1, to even the series.

With Bob Sauve back in goal for the second time in the play-offs, the Devils won their second consecutive game at the Cap Centre, 3-1, but then lost game six at home behind Burke in a blow-out, 7-2, to set up the first seventh game in franchise history on April 30th. If the Devils were to survive, they would have to win for a third consecutive time in eight days at the Cap Centre. Incredibly, they did just that as John MacLean, the club's regular hero by then, beat Pete Peeters at 13:49 of the third period to give the Devils a 3-2 win.

League officials were no doubt happy to see this bloody series finally end as the two clubs had not only combined for 48 goals but also set new records for total penalties—219—and penalty minutes—656—in a Stanley Cup series.

Little did anyone know, however, that the confrontations of that series were nothing compared to what would soon happen between the Devils' head coach and key front office honchos and the NHL's game officials and most of the league's top mandarins.

Lawsuits and "Missing" NHL President

For the third series in a row, the Devils lost the opening game, 5-3, to the much stronger Bruins at Boston Garden on May 2nd, despite coming back from a 3-0 deficit to tie the game before Bruin co-captain Ray Bourque beat Bob Sauve early in the third period for the eventual game winner. As they had in each of the two previous series, however, the visiting Devils came back to win the second game.

Rookie right wing Doug Brown, a former Boston College star and Massachusetts native, beat veteran Bruin netminder Reggie Lemelin at 17:46 of overtime to give the franchise its first overtime play-off victory against three earlier losses. Burke had also returned to the Devils' goal that night and keyed the crucial road win by stopping 39 of 41 Bruin shots.

The two teams then returned to the Meadowlands for game three on Friday, May 6th, which the Bruins won easily, 6-1. As it turned out, however, the evening's on-ice activity proved to be a mere side show to the real action that took place in the runway between the team benches and in an adjacent corridor leading to the officials' dressing room.

"Have Another Doughnut"

Devils coach Jim Schoenfeld was so displeased with the work of referee Don Koharski that instead of going with his team to their dressing room after the game he waited for Koharski. During the ensuing confrontation between the two, the referee stumbled as he made his way past Schoenfeld to his locker room.

Regaining his balance, the hefty Koharski accused the Devils' coach of pushing him and advised Schoenfeld that he would never coach again. To that challenge the overwrought Devils mentor replied with the often-repeated comeback: "You fell down, you fat pig. Have another doughnut."

Had the incident—which lasted but a few seconds—not been caught on videotape by a local TV news crew the almost unbelievable sequence of events that unfolded over the next 48 hours may never have happened.

However, by the time that the crucial game four of the series got under way just over an hour late on Sunday evening, May 8th, the following unprecedented events had occurred: a lawsuit had been filed against the NHL by the Devils, resulting in a restraining order being issued against the league; NHL president John Ziegler was discovered to be "AWOL" and his office was unable to locate him to represent the league during this crisis; Jim Schoenfeld stood behind the Devils' bench during game four in defiance of a league-imposed suspension, and; the game itself was officiated not by the assigned NHL referee and linesmen but instead by a Yonkers, New York, ice rink manager, a Clifton, New Jersey, salesman, and a retired Long Island policeman. This game would forever be known as the "Mother's Day Amateur Referees Game."

After Koharski had filed his game report on Friday night, NHL executive vice president Brian O'Neill indefinitely suspended Schoenfeld without the right of appeal, for acting "in a manner that was dishonorable and prejudicial to the League and the game of hockey," even though O'Neill had not conducted a hearing, viewed the videotapes, or considered any evidence other than briefly talking to Koharski and Schoenfeld on the telephone.

When Lamoriello was unable to get O'Neill to rescind the suspension pending a hearing or to find the missing Ziegler to make a ruling, the Devils then sought relief in the only way left to the club—by filing a lawsuit against the NHL.

On Sunday morning the club was granted an emergency court hearing before New Jersey Superior Court Judge J. F. Madden who, shortly before game time, issued a temporary restraining order against the league, abating Schoenfeld's suspension because it had been imposed without granting him due process or providing for an appeal.

The NHL had no option but to obey Judge Madden's order and permit Schoenfeld to coach even though it did not officially lift the suspension, but when the three on-ice officials scheduled to work the game (referee Dave Newell and linesmen Ray Scapinello and Gord Broseker) were informed shortly before game time that Schoenfeld would be behind the Devils' bench they refused to work in protest.

With Ziegler's whereabouts still unknown it then fell to NHL Board of Governors Chairman William Wirtz, the owner of the Chicago Blackhawks, to order the game to be played with substitute officials and at 7:45—the game's scheduled starting time. An announcement was made to the fans that there would be an "indefinite delay," but that the game would be played that night.

Fortunately, three of the off-ice officials scheduled to work the game had amateur officiating experience—goal judge Paul MacInnis, game timekeeper Vin Godleski, and statistician Jim Sullivan.

MacInnis, the Yonkers rink manager and an experienced ECAC college hockey official, was appointed referee for the game while God-leski, the salesman and referee in chief of the Atlantic

Division of the Amateur Hockey Association of the United States, and Sullivan, the retired policeman, served as the linesmen.

After a delay of just over an hour the fourth game finally got under way at 8:51 p.m. with the amateur officials in charge. The first penalty MacInnis called was an easy one—an automatic delay of game on goalie Sean Burke who flipped the puck over the glass just 55 seconds into the first period.

As the game progressed, however, the two clubs forgot about cutting the amateur officials a break and a total of 88 minutes in penalties were eventually assessed with several fights having to be broken up. However, despite being outshot by Boston, 34-18, with Schoenfeld behind the bench and Burke in net the Devils again upset the Bruins, 3-1, to send the series back to Boston tied at two games apiece. Schoenfeld's suspension was officially rescinded the next day (Monday) pending a hearing to be held in Boston on Tuesday afternoon, May 10th, prior to the start of game five that evening. At 6:25 p.m. John Ziegler (who had finally been located) announced that Schoenfeld would be suspended for one game.

With Schoenfeld therefore unavailable, Devils president Lou Lamoriello coached that night for the first time since retiring as coach at Providence College in 1983. It did not take the Bruins long to take advantage of the unsettled situation: they defeated the disorganized Devils easily, 7-1. While the Devils came back in game six with a 6-3 win at the Meadowlands, forcing a seventh game for the second consecutive series, their magic carpet to fantasyland finally crashed in that game seven in Boston on May 14th when the Bruins cruised to a 6-2 series-clinching victory.

The 1987-88 season had been by far the most memorable and eventful campaign ever for the Devils and their fans. When it started in October the franchise had never even won a single play-off game. The addition of two fiery redheads—Jim Schoenfeld and Sean Burke—changed the Devils from a perennial never-ran to a team that came within one game of making the Stanley Cup finals that season.

"Easy Come, Easy Go"

When compared to their magical play-off run the previous spring, "easy come, easy go" seemed to pretty much describe the success—or lack thereof—experienced by the New Jersey Devils in 1988-89. After fluctuating between third, fourth, and fifth place in the Patrick Division through the season's first six weeks, the Devils dropped to fifth on November 29th and never left that spot for the rest of the year.

By season's end the club had dropped from 82 points to a disappointing 66 and missed the play-offs by 14 points with a 27-41-12 record. However, the salutary effect of the previous spring's play-off run continued to be felt at the box office as the Devils drew a dozen sell-out crowds at home and seldom played to an arena audience of less than 14,000.

On January 2, 1989, the team also brought international hockey competition to New Jersey for the first time when the powerful Central Soviet Red Army club visited as part of "Super Series 1988-89." Although New Jersey lost the game, 5-0, three future Devils made their long-anticipated Meadowlands' debuts that night skating for the Red Army—Viacheslav Fetisov, Alexei Kasatonov, and Sergi Starikov. Fetisov and Starikov signed with the club six months later on June 26, 1989, followed by Kasatonov on December 11th.

After the first 14 games of the 1989-90 season the Devils were in second place in the Patrick Division with a 6-6-2 record, but general manager Lou Lamoriello had again become dissatisfied with the direction in which his team was going.

On November 6th, therefore, he dismissed head coach Jim Schoenfeld after a 7-3 loss in Calgary two nights earlier and replaced him with assistant coach John Cunniff, a onetime All-American at Boston College and a member of the 1968 U.S. Olympic Hockey Team.

Prior to joining the Devils the previous May, the 45-year-old Boston-born Cunniff had spent virtually all of his playing, scouting, and coaching career in his native New England with the Hartford Whalers (both WHA and NHL) and the

NEW JERSEY DEVILS

Boston Bruins and had briefly served as head coach of the Whalers late in the 1981-82 season.

Over the remainder of the season Cunniff guided the Devils to a 31-28-7 record, which gave the team an overall mark of 37-34-9 for 83 points and a second-place finish in the Patrick Division, just two points behind the first place New York Rangers. Thus for the first time in 16 NHL seasons the franchise had not only made the play-offs with relative ease but, with a strong 5-0-1 run over the season's final six games, did so with 11 points to spare.

Two years earlier, when they needed sudden death overtime of the last game of the season to qualify for their first Stanley Cup trip in a decade, the Devils had entered the postseason without the external pressure of expectations for their success and responded with a spectacular nothing-to-lose run that brought them within a game of the finals.

In 1990, however, the expectations—and pressure—for postseason success would be different.

Unfortunately for the Devils, the team they drew for the first round of the 1990 play-offs was their longtime Patrick Division nemesis, the Washington Capitals. They had beaten the Caps two years earlier, four games to three in the 1988 Division finals, in the two clubs' only previous play-off confrontation. But in 56 regular season career meetings to date the Devils' record against Washington was still a quite poor 13-39-4.

Nonetheless, for the first time in franchise history, in 1990 the Devils opened a series with the luxury of home ice advantage to work with—if they could keep it. The two clubs opened their best-of-seven set at New Jersey on April 5th but by game's end the Devils' home ice edge had indeed vanished with a 5-4 Caps' victory over Sean Burke. Although the Devils won the next two

AP/Wide World Photos

Brendan Shanahan (11)

games, 6-5 and 2-1, with 1988 U.S. Olympian Chris Terreri in goal to regain home ice, the Caps then swept games four, five, and six to end the Devils' eighth season in New Jersey in a taxing fashion on April 15th.

Musical Coaches—Again

With 79 points on a record of 32-33-15 and a fourth-place finish in the Patrick Division in 1990-91, the Devils made the play-offs for the second year in a row for the first time in franchise history, but for the third time in four years the coach behind their bench at the end of the season was not the same man who stood there at the start. With just 13 games left in the campaign general manager Lou Lamoriello pulled the trigger on yet another Devils coach.

With the Devils in fourth place at 28-28-1, Lamoriello removed John Cunniff and replaced him with 55-year old Tom McVie, the same man who had replaced Billy MacMillan as Devils' coach some seven-and-a-half years earlier. In the almost seven seasons since ending his first stint in New Jersey, McVie had been the coach of the Devils' AHL farm clubs in Portland, Maine (1984-87) and Utica, New York (1987-91).

For the first time the Devils were also to meet a Patrick Division play-off opponent other than the Islanders or Capitals in their best-of-seven opening round as they came up against the Pittsburgh Penguins. Even though the Penguins would eventually beat the Devils in the series and go on to win their first Stanley Cup title the following month, McVie's pesky troops would prove to be no pushover.

For the first time (in six tries) the Devils actually won the opening game of a play-off series by beating the Penguins at the Igloo in the Steel City, 3-1, on April 3rd and then taking them to overtime two nights later before Penguin rookie Jaromir Jagr finally scored at 8:52 of the first extra period to even the set. After splitting the next two games in New Jersey, the Devils upset the Penguins again in game five in Pittsburgh, 4-2, to force Lemieux's club to the brink of elimination.

With All-Star Pittsburgh goalie Tom Barrasso having already given up 17 goals to the Devils and losing three times in five games, Penguin coach Bob Johnson decided to make a change in game six and switched to backup goalie Frank Pietrangelo, despite the fact that the 25-year-old netminder had never before played a single minute of Stanley Cup action. Johnson's hunch paid off: Pietrangelo not only beat the Devils at the Meadowlands, 4-3, to even the series, but then shut them out, 4-0, in game seven in Pittsburgh to send the Pens on to their eventual Cup title—and to end the Devils' season on Income Tax Day, April 15th, for the second year in a row!

A Lucky "Loss"

The Scouts-Rockies-Devils have not always been the luckiest franchise in NHL history—often far from it—but the prize the franchise won on September 3, 1991, was worth a bushel of four-leaf clovers. It all began six weeks earlier on July 25th when fourth-year right wing Brendan Shanahan, a "Type I" free agent acquired by New Jersey with the second overall pick in the 1987 draft, was signed away by the St. Louis Blues.

While New Jersey could not get Shanahan back, under league rules the Blues would have to compensate the Devils for their loss with one or more players (or draft picks) from their roster of "equal or greater value." Because the two teams could not agree on the compensation, each was required to submit its proposal to an independent arbitrator who would then pick the one which he felt most closely matched the value of the lost free agent.

As the arbitrator, Judge Edward Houston of Toronto could only pick one proposal or the other but not change either one. If St. Louis offered a package of considerably less value than Shanahan, Houston was obliged under the rules of free agency to award the Devils whatever they had asked for even if it was of greater value than the lost player—and that's exactly what happened.

Blues general manager Ron Caron offered a

NEW JERSEY DEVILS

package of players that Houston considered to be far short of Shanahan's value and therefore he awarded the Devils the one player they asked for—Blues captain and All-Star defenseman Scott Stevens. The 27-year-old Stevens, who had spent his first eight NHL seasons with the Washington Capitals, had been signed away from the Caps by St. Louis at tremendous expense just the year before in a similar free agent transaction.

With the dominating Stevens on defense and the wily McVie behind the bench in 1991-92, the Devils' tenth season in New Jersey, the club set new franchise records for home wins (24), overall wins (38), fewest losses (31) and total points (87). That only proved to be good enough for fourth place in the again highly competitive Patrick Division. The Patrick's top two teams— the New York Rangers (105 points) and the Washington Capitals (98)—were also the first and sec-

ond overall finishers in the league while the Devils tied the defending Stanley Cup champion Penguins with 87 points but finished behind them because Pittsburgh had managed one more win.

Although the Devils would have to face the team with the best regular season record in the league in the opening round of the 1992 Stanley Cup play-offs, that opponent would be the one with whom the Devils and their fans had been envisioning a series since the club moved to New Jersey a decade earlier—the New York Rangers.

No two NHL teams play their home games closer to each other than the Devils and Rangers, with the Meadowlands Arena and Madison Square Garden located less than seven miles apart. As far as many of the partisans of the two clubs are concerned, there may as well not be any other teams in the league. To fans, a best-of-seven play-off confrontation between these two by now bitter

Scott Stevens (4)

rivals was manna from hockey heaven, especially if the series was to eventually come down to a seventh and deciding game. And in April, 1992, the hockey fans of New York and New Jersey got their wish.

The high-profile Rangers had spent millions in the 1990s on the likes of Mark Messier, Brian Leetch, John Vanbiesbrouck, and Mike Richter to finally bring a winner to the Big Apple. With their first number one overall finish in the NHL since the wartime season of 1941-42, the pressure on the Broadway Blueshirts to not only beat the Devils in the opening round but also to finally end their increasingly gnawing 52-year championship drought since last winning the Cup in 1940 was intense.

The Devils-Rangers series opened at Madison Square Garden on April 19th. As usual, the Devils dropped their opening road contest, 2-1, but dominated play much of the night and by no means made victory easy for the Rangers. Only the strong netminding of New York's Vanbiesbrouck kept them from victory. With the loss, however, the Devils had the Rangers right where they wanted them. As they had against the Islanders, Capitals, and Bruins in 1988 and the Penguins in 1991, the Devils came back to win the second game of an opening road play-off pair as they routed the Rangers at the Garden, 7-3, on April 21st to even their series at a game apiece.

Although Mark Messier had opened the scoring in the game with an early shorthanded goal for New York, the Devils rallied with top performances from players such as goalie Chris Terreri, defenseman Scott Stevens, and forwards Peter Stastny and Claude Lemieux, managing to crush the Rangers on their own ice.

Things then went from bad to worse for the "All-Name" Rangers when the series resumed across the Hudson as the "No-Name" Devils took a two-games-to-one lead with a 3-1 victory in game three behind a sparkling 34-save performance by Terreri.

The Rangers seemed to regain their equilibrium with a 3-0 Mike Richter shut out in game four and then took a 5-0 lead in game five at Madison

Square Garden, only to have the Devils erase it with five unanswered goals of their own to tie the contest before finally bowing to New York, 8-5.

However the Devils would not die easily. They again outplayed the Rangers to win game six at the Meadowlands, 5-3, ending the evening with the added attraction of a ten-minute bench clearing brawl resulting in the imposition of an additional 13 penalties and $50,000 in fines after the game was over. Thus for the fourth time in their last five play-off series the Devils had forced a much stronger opponent to face them in a seventh and final winner-take-all game—and for hockey fans it doesn't get any better than that.

The rivalry among the two teams' partisans was at fever pitch before the game as a number of them clashed in the Madison Square Garden lobby prior to the game, resulting in injury to a security guard and six arrests. Outside, the Eighth Avenue scalpers had a field day as thousands more than the 18,200 who could fit in the Garden sought a coveted ducat. Five stories above street level the two clubs took to the ice for their high stakes May Day confrontation, the seventh time in a dozen days they would do deadly battle.

The script could not have been better or more unpredictable. Both teams had already won close games as well as blowouts in the series. Each had tasted victory in the other's building, and each had been blessed with great goaltending and cursed by bad. There had also been a shutout, a game-ending brawl, and a big comeback in the first six games, but none of that mattered as the opening round had been reduced to the basics—an all-or-nothing, best-of-one series.

Despite having been in the NHL since 1926, the Rangers had only played in a "seventh" game four times in 73 previous career play-off series over 66 years—and they had lost them all. As President's Trophy winner and a Stanley Cup favorite in 1992, however, a fifth such loss in this opening round would be a disaster for the Rangers of unmentionable proportion. A victory for the Devils, on the other hand, would be akin to David slaying Goliath. The stakes were high, the emotions intense.

By evening's end the faithful of both teams were drained of emotion, although the Rangers had come out on top by a wide margin with an 8-4 win. The Devils allowed the Rangers' special teams to score an incredible five goals—two while shorthanded and three on the powerplay.

By the midway mark of the game the Devils had fallen behind by a death knell five goals at 6-1, but as they had in game five they then began another incredible charge with three unanswered goals to pull within two at 6-4 and counting before the Rangers finally put away the comeback kids. But as coach Tom McVie observed later the Devils had spent too much of the game "smoking in the dynamite shed" and thus their season ended with their third seventh-game loss in four years.

Brooks Comes and Goes

Despite the Devils' strong season under Tom McVie, incredibly just a month later on June 5th, 1992, GM Lamoriello changed coaches again as he removed the popular McVie in favor of 55-year-old Herb Brooks, the hero of the 1980 U.S. Olympic hockey team's upset Gold Medal-winning performance in the XIII Winter Games at Lake Placid, New York.

With the promotion of Brooks from the AHL Utica Devils, with whom the former Ranger and North Star mentor had spent the 1991-92 season after a number of years out of coaching, the Dev-ils' GM had changed his bench boss for the fourth time since taking over from Max McNab in September, 1987.

By the end of Brooks's first season as coach of the Devils, 1992-93, the club had set yet another new team mark for most wins in a season with 40 (40-37-7) and tied the previous year's club high point total with 87. Also, as in the previous year, the Devils finished tied in points for third place in the Patrick Division—this time with the Islanders—only to be dropped to fourth on a tie breaker. As such, they were again matched in the opening round of the play-offs against the first place overall team in the regular season only this time it was to be the two-time defending Stanley Cup champion Penguins instead of the Rangers.

The Devils went on to lose in the opening round for the fourth year in a row as the Penguins defeated them, four games to one. The season had been a strong one overall for Brooks and his charges, but on May 31st, within weeks of its conclusion, Herb Brooks announced his departure due to a disagreement with management over the direction the team should take in the future.

Brooks had wanted to shape a club with greater emphasis on speed and youth than he apparently believed Lamoriello was willing to allow him. He was replaced by former Canadien center Jacques Lemaire, who had also coached the Habs from 1983 to 1985.

—*Bruce C. Cooper*

NEW YORK ISLANDERS

In the 75-year history of the National Hockey League (NHL), no club ever went from being as bad a first-year expansion team to becoming as truly great a dynastic force in the game as fast as the New York Islanders did. When the club entered the NHL with the league's third expansion in 1972, it managed just a dozen wins in its inaugural season and collected only 30 points (of a possible 156) for a paltry winning percentage of .192.

Within another two year's time, however, the Islanders had almost tripled their output to 33 wins and 88 points. That year the team made the playoffs for the first time, won their first two career postseason series, and reached the semifinals. Here the Islanders forced the defending Stanley Cup champion Philadelphia Flyers to a seventh game before finally bowing.

By 1975-76, their fourth season, the Islanders, or Isles, achieved the lofty heights of the "century plateau" with 101 points and repeated that feat

six more times over the next eight seasons. Then, in just their eighth season, the Islanders achieved every NHL team's ultimate goal by capturing the Stanley Cup for the first time. They held onto it for four years.

In a sport known for its frequent coaching changes, the Isles reaped this success with just one man continuously behind their bench for 13 years from 1973 to 1986—and again beginning in 1989—Al Arbour. And in a league where teams often trade high draft picks for instant short-term boosts, the Isles assiduously kept their draft choices and carefully turned them in to All-Stars, NHL individual trophy winners, and Hall of Famers.

The history of the Islanders is characterized by remarkable stability on the ice and a torrent of financial instability off of it. While General Manager Bill Torrey was building the Islanders into champions through the 1970s, the club's original general partner and largest shareholder, Roy L. M.

Boe, was mismanaging it into bankruptcy. By the time Boe was finally forced out by the courts in 1978, the Isles were running an annual operating deficit of $1 million, were $22 million in debt, had a $4 million judgement already entered against them in one suit, were the defendants in 13 additional pending lawsuits, and had less than $10,000 in the bank.

Nonetheless the club survived when Torrey helped convince John O. Pickett, Jr., a small minority investor who once held just one percent of the club, that this bleak situation was salvageable and to take on the unenviable challenge of saving the club financially.

In just three years Pickett, an entrepreneur and investment counselor, was able to restructure and greatly diminish the club's debt to put it back on sound financial footing. In November of 1981 Pickett bought out the remaining 45 percent of the stock from some 35 investors to become the team's sole owner. He remained the owner for the next dozen years.

The Isles earned their last Stanley Cup in 1983, and by 1991-92 the team had missed the playoffs in three of the previous four seasons. Yet the club began a turnaround in 1992-93 which took it to its best finish since 1988 and brought playoff triumphs over the Washington Capitals and the defending Stanley Cup champion Pittsburgh Penguins. The Islanders were eventually eliminated in the Wales Conference finals by the Cup-winning Montreal Canadiens.

While Torrey was no longer the club's general manager in 1992-93, the Islanders' 21st season, his hand was still clearly in evidence in the young, rebuilt roster.

Long Island Got NHL Franchise

The 1970s were a decade of unprecedented growth for pro hockey in North America. After doubling in size from six to 12 teams in 1967, the NHL conducted four more expansions in the 1970s. Two teams were added in 1970, 1972, and 1974, and the league absorbed the four surviving World Hockey Association (WHA) clubs in 1979 to boost the NHL from 12 to 21 teams. The new Long Island franchise was granted by the NHL's Board of Governors on November 8, 1971, to R.L.M. Sports, Inc., a large group of investors of whom the managing partner was Roy Boe, a 40-year old sports entrepreneur who had originally made his money in the garment industry. The Islanders began play in the NHL in the 1972-73 season as part of the "third" expansion.

The Islanders set up shop within 30 miles of one of the NHL's "original six" pre-1967 clubs, the New York Rangers. With the large migration of traditional Ranger fans to the suburbs following World War II, the new club in the Nassau County community of Uniondale was expected to attract many of those NHL patrons away from the Rangers, nicknamed the Broadway Blues.

The Rangers agreed to the new club's infringement into their territory, but the Islanders were charged nearly twice the franchise fee—almost $11 million— that other expansion clubs paid. Half of this amount went to the Rangers as an indemnity fee. In ensuing years, paying off this huge fee—and the interest that accrued during the high inflation of the 1970s—would nearly ruin the young Islanders.

The Man Who Built the Islanders

The two central figures in the history of the Islanders were William A. Torrey and Alger J. Arbour. Bill Torrey, the Islanders' first hockey employee, was named general manager on February 15, 1972. He held this position for the next two decades.

The Montreal-born son of American parents who grew up two blocks from the fabled Forum, the 38-year-old Torrey had a degree in psychology and business from St. Lawrence University in Canton, New York. He had also been a member of that college hockey power's varsity hockey team in the mid-1950s.

A self-described "slow-footed" defenseman, Torrey nonetheless once considered a professional

TEAM INFORMATION AT A GLANCE

Founding date: 1972

Home ice:
Nassau Veterans Memorial Coliseum
Uniondale, NY 11553
Phone: (516) 794-4100
FAX: (516) 542-9348

Seating capacity: 16,297

Team colors: Blue, orange, and white
Team nickname: Islanders or Isles
Logo: Blue circle with white intials "NY" (with "Y" forming a hockey stick), above
an orange represenatation of New York state with "Islanders" written underneath

Franchise record	Won	Lost	Tie
(1972-1993)	796	643	241

Stanley Cup Wins (4): 1979-80, 1980-81, 1981-82, 1982-83
League First-place Finishes (3): 1978-79, 1980-81, 1981-82

playing career in England where, he later recalled, they were "in desperate need of bad hockey players." Upon further reflection, however, he wisely decided it would be better for him to opt for a career in management after graduating.

The first players he was involved with were not hockey skaters but figure skaters and basketball players as he went into business in Pittsburgh as a promoter of the touring Ice Capades and Harlem Globetrotters. By 1960, however, Torrey returned to his first love as business manager of the American Hockey League's (AHL) Pittsburgh Hornets. In 1968 he finally reached the NHL when he was hired by Oakland Seals' General Manager Frank Selke, Jr., to be vice-president for hockey operations of the year-old expansion club.

Torrey remained with the Seals for three financially chaotic seasons, eventually working for one of the most colorful, and difficult, bosses in sports, Oakland A's owner Charles O. Finley, who acquired control of the Seals in 1970. While trying to help run a struggling team for the always involved and often meddlesome "Charlie O." was often trying and frustrating, the experience would serve Torrey well in the future. The lessons that he learned over those three seasons helped him as he skillfully negotiated his way through the financial pitfalls that were omnipresent during the Islanders' early years.

"Once you've worked for Charlie Finley," Torrey once observed, "you can face anything." Finally tired of Finley's managerial "assistance," Torrey left the team, now called the California Golden Seals after the 1970-71 season, having helped move them from last place to a pair of consecutive playoff appearances.

Although Torrey returned to his arena and event promotion business in Pittsburgh, it did not take him long to begin looking for another position in hockey. He sought the advice of old friend and Pittsburgh Steelers' respected owner, Art Rooney, who suggested Torrey apply to run the new hockey team on Long Island. There was another expansion club in Atlanta, but Rooney told his young friend, "Atlanta is a great city and a fun place to go, but you would have to spend most of your time there selling the game. In New York you can concentrate on building the team because the people already know and love hockey and will come willingly."

Torrey knew that Rooney was right, because before the Long Island franchise had even been awarded, more than 8,000 fans had requested season tickets. That cushion of fan interest would be important to Torrey as he planned to build his team through the draft; he would be judicious when it came to trading valuable high draft picks for immediate—although usually just temporary—respectability.

Torrey believed that the only way to achieve long-term success was to build from within and develop his own stars, as opposed to struggling from year to year with other teams' "castoffs, hand-me-downs and tradeoffs." The result of this approach was a first-year team of appalling ineptitude, derisively dubbed "Torrey's Turkeys." By the third year, however, Torrey's strategy began to pay off as the Isles emerged as an up-and-coming power.

Torrey's Turkeys

Torrey had been hired only four months before hockey's draft, and thus had little time to assemble a scouting staff to assess the "talent" available in the June 7, 1972, expansion draft or in the following day's amateur draft. In the long run, however, the lack of preparation did not appear to matter as the astute Torrey and his new scouts, especially Jimmy Devellano, had a long-term plan and knew how to achieve it.

While many of the players Torrey took in the expansion draft would, as expected, soon fall by the wayside as his young amateur draft picks started to develop, several others would play key roles in the club's rise to the top. Gerry Hart, a tough-as-nails defenseman claimed from Detroit, gave the club steady character over its first seven years.

"Steady Eddie" Westfall, a 32-year-old veteran right winger from Boston, served as the Isles' captain for their first four seasons and stayed on with the club as a broadcaster after his retirement in 1979. Most important of all, however, was the drafting of 21-year-old goalie Bill Smith from the Los Angeles Kings.

By the time "Battling Billy" retired in 1989, he had appeared in 675 regular season and 132 playoff games for the club. He also had won more playoff games than any other goalie in NHL history with 88 and helped the Isles to four consecutive Stanley Cups. (Smith was inducted into the Hockey Hall of Fame in 1993.)

Also in 1972, Torrey acquired a second key goalie in Glenn "Chico" Resch from the Montreal Canadiens—although he did not play for the team regularly until 1974-75 when Gerry Desjardins, the Isles' first overall expansion draft pick, jumped to the WHA Michigan Stags. Desjardins would not be the only defection to the WHA that Torrey would ever have to worry about, however; before the club opened its first training camp, seven of the original 19 players claimed in the June expansion draft had signed with the WHA, leaving Torrey with just 11 veterans to work with.

Torrey's plan was based on team development through the amateur draft. He immediately began to lay the foundation for the future Stanley Cup champs on June 8, 1972, when he took right wing Billy Harris from the Toronto Marlboros with the draft's first overall pick.

Torrey subsequently selected three more keys to the club's future success—Lorne Henning (17th overall), Bob Nystrom (33rd), and Garry Howatt (144th). Evidence of how well Torrey and his staff built through the draft in ensuing years is found in the team's record books; all but two of the top-

Hockey Hall of Fame and Museum

Denis Potvin

20 Islanders' all-time scoring leaders were amateur draft picks of Torrey's.

In July of 1972 Torrey selected his first coach, recently retired veteran center Phil Goyette. A 38-year-old native of Lachine, Quebec, Goyette had spent 16 years in the NHL with the Canadiens, Rangers, Blues, and Sabres, winning the Lady Byng Trophy for sportsmanship with St. Louis in 1969-70. Three months later, on October 7, 1972, the Isles took to the ice for the first time as they made their NHL debut against another expansion club, the Atlanta Flames, before an enthusiastic crowd of 12,221 at the Nassau Coliseum. Unfortunately for the home club, the visiting Flames prevailed 3-2, handing the Islanders the first of 60 losses in 78 games that year. Five nights later, however, the Isles picked up their first win—one of just a dozen that year—when Germain Gagnon scored with 1:09 left in the game to defeat the Los Angeles Kings 3-2.

There were precious few "highlights" for

Torrey's Turkeys in that inaugural season. On January 18, 1973, the Islanders visited the Boston Garden in the midst of a 12-game losing streak to take on Bobby Orr, Phil Esposito, and the defending Stanley Cup champion Bruins.

By mid-game, however, it was the Islanders who looked like champs as they had jumped to a 5-0 lead. By evening's end, the Isles were still on top as they held on for 9-7 victory. Five nights later the Islanders staged another offensive outburst as they crushed the California Golden Seals 8-1 at Nassau Coliseum behind a hat trick by generally low-scoring journeyman winger Craig Cameron.

But these two offensive displays were not enough to change the plummeting course being charted by the team, and Goyette was relieved as coach on January 29, 1973, with a record of 6-40-4. Earl Ingerfield, a retired veteran center who had finished his 13-year NHL career with the Seals while Torrey was working in that club's front office, was named interim coach. In 28 games under Ingerfield, the Isles compiled a 6-20-2 record. The Islanders' opening season came to an end on April Fools' Day with a 4-4 tie with the Atlanta Flames.

Building a Contender

The Islanders had ended their inaugural season with 30 points, an incredible 90 points behind first-place Montreal and 35 points behind fellow expansion club Atlanta. Torrey remained optimistic, focusing on ways to achieve future excellence. He had spent most of the season touring Canada scouting hundreds of junior players to find the right few with which to build his team. With the first overall selection in 1973, Torrey also had the pick of any draft-age player in North America; that choice was his easiest one—sensational Ottawa 67's defenseman Denis Potvin.

The only problem in drafting Potvin was the peskily competitive WHA, which had already spent millions to attract NHL stars. Torrey had already hedged against that possibility by trading veteran checking center Terry Crisp to the Philadelphia Flyers for a journeyman 24-year-old defenseman named Jean Potvin, Denis' older brother. On May 15th Torrey then selected the younger Potvin with the first pick in the 1973 amateur draft and signed Denis without difficulty.

Torrey then added another solid defenseman with his second pick (33rd overall) in Dave Lewis and later got two more eventual contributors in forwards Andre St. Laurent (49th) and Bob Lorimer (129th). Torrey's most important acquisition that summer, however, was 40-year-old coach Al Arbour, who signed a three-year contract on June 10, 1973.

Respected as a rock-solid defenseman during his 14-year NHL playing career, Arbour had won three Stanley Cup titles as a player with Detroit (1954), Chicago (1961), and Toronto (1964). He had also appeared in the Stanely Cup finals three more times with the St. Louis Blues, a team that he coached for parts of three seasons between 1970 and 1973.

As a player, Arbour was remembered for wearing glasses on the ice, which earned him the nickname "Radar." While Arbour scored only a dozen goals in his 626-game NHL career, he stopped hundreds from being scored by blocking shots and was known as one of the premier "defenseman's defenseman" of his era.

The Islanders surrendered a staggering 347 goals in their first season while scoring just 170. Torrey knew that the most important thing he had to do to build a winner was to improve the defense, and Arbour was the man to fill that bill. A devoted student of the game, Arbour had kept notebooks on opposing forwards while he was a player.

As a coach, however, his greatest strength was his forceful personality. Fair and forthright, he was also an outstanding teacher who rewarded those who gave their best effort—and sat those who didn't—whether they be rookie or veteran, journeyman or star.

With Potvin, Lewis, and Bert Marshall (another solid rear guard acquired from the Rangers in the 1973 intra-league draft) added to the blueline and the whole team playing Arbour's defense-oriented style, the Isles dropped their goals against

by 100 over the previous season to just 247 while also upping their goals scored to 187.

Although the Isles again finished in last place in the NHL's East Division, they nonetheless showed remarkable improvement with nine more and 19 fewer losses while almost doubling their point total in one year from 30 to 56 on a record of 19-41-18. With 17 goals and 37 assists, rookie defenseman Denis Potvin won the Calder Trophy as rookie of the year between.

The summer of 1974 saw Torrey continue to build the nucleus of his future champions through the draft. He took 20-year-old strapping left wing Clark Gilles from the WHL Regina Pats with the fourth overall pick, followed in the second round by 18-year-old center Bryan Trottier, who played with the WHL Lethbridge Broncos.

While the obviously talented Trottier could have helped the Islanders right away, Torrey insisted that he play another year of junior before joining the Isles. Although Trottier was disappointed by Torrey's decision, the extra season of junior competition helped him polish his game. In 1975-76, his rookie NHL season, Trottier scored 95 points and brought the Calder Trophy to New York for the second time in three years.

Respectability and a Playoff Appearance

By 1974-75 the increasingly talented Islanders made another jump in the standings in the newly realigned 18-team, four-division league, finishing in third place in the Patrick Division to qualify for the playoffs for the first time. Boasting a 32-point increase from the previous year's record, the team was tied at 88 points with the second-place Rangers. In just two seasons the Isles had made a staggering 58-point improvement from its first season's mark of just 30 points.

The goals allowed by Smith, Resch, and the Islanders' defense dropped by another 26 over the previous year's total while their own goals exploded by 82 to 264. With a 33-25-22 record, the Islanders had also broken the .500 plateau in just their third season and had become especially tough at Nassau Coliseum, losing just six games on home ice.

The Islanders' first ever playoff confrontation would come against its nearest and already bitter rival, the New York Rangers. The animus that had developed between these two neighbors and their fans was apparent even during the Isles' first two seasons when they were a far inferior team to their cousins from Manhattan. The events of their first ever playoff meeting would do nothing to cool that "friendly" rivalry.

On April 8, 1975, the Isles visited Madison Square Garden to open their best-of-three prelimi-

nary round set with the hated Broadway Blueshirts. Although the heavily favored Rangers held a comfortable 2-0 lead after 40 minutes, the complexion of the game changed drastically in the third period to the great distress of the Garden faithful. Unanswered goals by Billy Harris and Jean Potvin tied the game at 2-2, and then rookie winger Clark Gilles beat veteran Ranger goalie Eddie Giacomin with 6:30 left in regulation with what proved to be the game winner in the Isles first playoff victory.

The Rangers exacted revenge in a penalty-filled game two at Uniondale two nights later with an 8-3 drubbing of the Isles. In the deciding third

AP/Wide World Photos

Bryan Trottier (19) closes in on an opponent's goal

As a rookie, Mike Bossy scored 53 goals and averaged 59 a year between 1977 and 1986 while never potting fewer than 51 in any one season except his last, 1986- 87, when his chronically bad back limited him to "just" 38.

When Bossy retired after a ten-year career, he had collected 573 goals and 553 assists for 1,126 points in just 752 regular season games and added another 160 points (85-75) in 129 Stanley Cup contests to help earn the Islanders four Stanley Cups—and himself a berth in the Hockey Hall of Fame (he was inducted in 1991).

Among Bossy's individual awards were the Calder Trophy (1978), the Conn Smythe Trophy (Playoff MVP, 1982), three Lady Byng Trophies (1983, 1984, and 1986), and eight berths on the All-Star Team between 1978 and 1986.

Hockey Hall of Fame and Museum

game, the visiting Isles took a 3-0 lead into the third period only to lose it when the Rangers scored three unanswered goals to tie the match at 3-3, forcing the Isles to overtime for the first time. It took the Isles 11 seconds of overtime to win the game and eliminate the Rangers as left winger J.P. Parise deflected a centering pass by Jude Drouin past Giacomin for a 4-3 series victory.

Next up for the Islanders were the Pittsburgh Penguins, whose snipers scored 14 times in the first three contests to give the Pens a commanding three-games-to-none lead. Arbour replaced goal-tender Smith with Resch, and the Pens' seemingly insurmountable lead disappeared, leaving the series tied at three games apiece. Resch shut out Pittsburgh 1-0 in the series' final game.

With the Penguins behind them, the "Comeback Kids" from Uniondale next faced the defend-

ing Stanley Cup champion Philadelphia Flyers in the semifinals. The Flyers entered postseason play in 1975 with 113 points—25 more a than the Islanders' total of 88. In addition, Arbour's club had only beaten the Flyers twice in 16 career meetings.

The Islanders dropped the first three games to the Flyers, losing 4-0 in the series opener, 5-4 in game two (on an overtime goal by Bob Clarke), and being outshot 32-14 in a 1-0 loss in game three. The Islanders again faced elimination, but after 60 minutes it was tied at 3-3; Jude Drouin ended the Flyers' perfect run for the Cup by beating Bernie Parent at 1:53 of overtime to hand the Flyers their first loss in 21 starts.

The series returned to the Spectrum for game five, and the Isles won easily, 5-1. Then they edged the Flyers 2-1 in game six on Gerry Hart's third period goal to send the series back to Philadelphia for a seventh and deciding game. In game seven Flyer winger Gary Dornhoefer scored 19 seconds into the game, and Rick MacLeish netted what proved to be the series-winning goal just over two minutes later on a power play at 2:27. Drouin scored the Isles' only goal at 5:02 of the first period, but MacLeish added two more later on for a hat trick and a 4-1 Flyer victory. "This isn't the end for us," insisted a disappointed but proud Arbour outside the quiet Islander dressing room after the game, "it's only the beginning."

Building a Champion

The 1975 Stanley Cup playoffs were a turning point for the three-year-old Islanders. Prior to their remarkable postseason run, the club was considered a young, unaccomplished team (even though Torrey and Arbour were given high marks

for the club's progress). After defeating the Rangers and Penguins to take on the Stanley Cup champion Flyers, the hockey world quickly began to take notice. A month later Denis Potvin became the first Islander to make the NHL All-Star Team, an honor he would earn six more times.

The Islanders opened their fourth NHL season with a 1-1 tie in Kansas City. Two days later, rookie Bryan Trottier put in an amazing five-point performance in his first game at the Coliseum. With a 10-2 win over the Rangers in the season's final game, the Islanders became the youngest team in NHL history to break the 100-point barrier (with 101 points on a record of 42-21-17), but came in second place in the Patrick Division behind the Flyers.

In the playoffs the Isles again reached the semifinals, defeating the Vancouver Canucks (2-0) and Buffalo Sabres (4-2). The team lost to the eventual 1976 Stanley Cup champion Montreal

AP/Wide World Photos

Al Arbour

Canadiens in five games, although they were the only club to win a playoff game from the Habs that year.

Although the team had not reached the finals, a number of Islander players garnered individual honors. Potvin broke Bobby Orr's eight-year stranglehold on the Norris Trophy as the NHL's top defenseman and was also named a first team All-Star for the second year in a row. Trottier earned the Calder Trophy as the NHL's 1975-76 Rookie of the Year. Second-year goalie Chico Resch was also honored by being named a second team All-Star.

With 106 points (47-21-12) in 1976-77, the Islanders tied Boston for the third best record in the NHL but again finished in second place in the Patrick Division behind Philadelphia. In the playoffs they swept past Chicago and Buffalo with Clark Gilles setting an NHL playoff record with game-winning goals in four consecutive contests. After losing the first two games of the semifinals to the defending champion Canadiens in Montreal, the Isles won two of the next three before bowing to the Habs in game six.

On June 14 Torrey stole 20-year-old future Hall-of-Fame winger Mike Bossy with the 15th overall pick in the 1977 draft. Incredibly the dozen clubs selecting before the Islanders (the Rangers and Maple Leafs had already both picked twice) all passed on Bossy, despite his obvious goal scoring talent, because he was skinny and was not known as a checker.

But Torrey, who often placed as much importance on a player's character as he did on his talent, liked what he saw in Bossy. The scouting report on Bossy noted that he was raised in a poor family in suburban Montreal, and was intelligent, hard-working, eager to learn, and had wrists that were a "gift from God." Torrey rationalized that he had enough physical players to compensate for drafting a finesse-type winger.

In 1977-78 the Islanders finally supplanted the Flyers atop the Patrick Division with their third consecutive 100-plus point season. They notched 111 on a record of 48-17-15 and were virtually invincible at Nassau Coliseum, were they posted

a phenomenal 29-3-8 mark. Rookie Mike Bossy had greatly helped the cause by scoring 53 goals. While things were going well on the ice, the club was nonetheless in great peril as Roy Boe's mismanagement of team funds had brought it to the brink of bankruptcy.

The extent of the problem finally became apparent after Boe wrote millions of dollars worth of promissory notes against the Islanders' assets to prop up his failing New York Nets basketball team. Boe had also made the hockey club co-guarantors of various bank loans to the Nets. By 1977 the club's credit was so bad that hotels demanded to be paid up front and in cash when the team was on the road. In January of 1978, the NHL warned the Islanders to settle payments due on its franchise fee by June or risk losing the club.

In May of 1978, one of the Islanders partners who had no interest in the Nets found out about Boe's commingling of the two teams' funds and filed suit against Boe to recover his investment. With the club on the brink of both on-ice success and off-ice bankruptcy, Torrey went to investment counselor and minority investor John O. Pickett, Jr., to convince him to step in and help save the Islanders. Pickett officially replaced Boe as president of the club in July 6, 1978, and restructured the club's debt in three years. At the same time, Torrey and Arbour were brought the Islanders to the verge of winning their first Stanley Cup.

Although the Isles had become one of the league's premier teams, they were upset in the quarterfinals by the Toronto Maple Leafs in 1978. After winning the first two games at Uniondale, the Islanders dropped the next two contests in Toronto. Bob Nystrom brought New York within one game of advancing to the semifinals, however, with another overtime game winner to edge the Leafs in game five, but Toronto again prevailed on Garden ice, 5-2, to set up a seventh game at Nassau Coliseum. After a fearsome struggle, the game was tied at 1-1 at the end of 60 minutes, thereby putting the fate of the two teams in the hands of their netminders. The Leafs' Lanny McDonald scored at 4:13 of overtime to eliminate the Islanders.

Despite the disappointing loss to the Leafs, Torrey nonetheless added another important piece to the Stanley Cup puzzle on July 26, 1978, when he signed 21-year-old winger John Tonelli, the club's second round draft pick a year earlier, who had been playing with Gordie Howe and the Houston Aeros in the rival WHA since he was 18. Over the next eight seasons, the hard-nosed Tonelli would come to personify the grit and tenacity of the Islanders' championship teams.

The Islanders continued to edge closer to the Stanley Cup in 1978-79 with another record season. With a first-place finish and 116 points on a record of 51-15-14, the Isles had climbed from having the worst regular season record in the league to having the best in just seven years. In his third NHL season, Bossy had become the league's leading goal scorer with 69.

Trottier claimed the Art Ross Trophy as the NHL's scoring champion with 134 points on 47 goals and 87 assists and also won the Hart Trophy as the league's most valuable player. Potvin collected his third Norris Trophy in four years, and Coach Arbour was recognized with the Jack Adams Trophy as the NHL's coach of the year. Five Islanders also won berths on the league's two All-Star teams with Potvin, Trottier, and Gilles on the first team, while Resch and Bossy were named to the second team.

Over the 80-game season in 1978-79, the Islanders had clearly been the best team in the NHL and it looked as if by May the Stanley Cup would finally be back in New York State for the first time since the Rangers last won it in 1940.

First up for the Islanders were the Chicago Blackhawks who, although they had finished first in the Smythe Division, had finished with just 73 points—43 fewer than the Islanders. As expected, the Isles dispatched the Blackhawks quickly, in four straight games, while giving up only three goals in the series.

The Isles' next opponent was a surprise, however, as the New York Rangers had upset the favored Flyers in their quarterfinal round, four games to one, with former Flyer coach Fred Shero behind the New York bench. The tabloids were

delighted to have another "Battle of New York" to cover, and this time it would be a best-of-seven series between two excellent teams.

The series opened at the Coliseum with a surprisingly easy triumph by the underdog Rangers. By the start of the third period of game two it looked as if the favored Islanders might head to Manhattan down two games. The Isles eventually tied the game at 2-2 on a goal by Bob Lorimer, and then went ahead by one on Bob Nystrom's first goal of the playoffs only to have Phil Esposito tie the game at 3-3 late in regulation to force overtime. After eight minutes of furious end-to-end action, Potvin finally tied the series when Ranger defenseman Carol Vadnais inadvertently deflected the Islander blueliner's slapshot past John Davidson for a 4-3 Islander victory.

The Islanders split the two games at Madison Square Garden. Games five and six were decided by one goal, but the Islanders lost both contests and were eliminated in the semifinals for the fourth time in five years.

The Stanley Cup Arrives

After seven consecutive seasons of steady improvement, the Islanders suffered a drop in performance in the 1979-80 season. The club recorded 25 fewer points and 13 more losses than the previous year's totals. As the club staggered toward the playoffs they were clearly suffering through some sort of malaise and badly needed a change in their chemistry.

Torrey had already demonstrated his mastery of the amateur draft, but he also proved to be adept at claiming veteran players through trades. Torrey surprisingly made a deal at the trading deadline on March 9, 1980, for long-time Los Angeles Kings' star center Butch Goring. To pry the popular Goring from the Kings, Torrey had to give up two key players who had helped build the Islanders—Billy Harris and Dave Lewis.

Trading Harris was an especially difficult decision for Torrey; Harris was the club's first amateur draft pick and had played in every one of the club's 623 regular season and 59 playoff games. The 31-year-old Goring helped the Islanders needed go undefeated through their remaining 12 games of the season, contributing 11 points. The Islanders' first opponent in the 1980 playoffs was the Los Angeles Kings. The Isles won easily, three games to one.

In the quarterfinals the Islanders upset Boston in five games to move on to the semifinals against the Buffalo Sabres. With three straight victories, it looked as if the New Yorkers were finally going to make it to the championship round. The Sabres subsequently handed the Isles two consecutive losses, but the Isles rebounded in game six to earn the honor of meeting the Philadelphia Flyers in the finals.

Over the 80-game regular season in 1979-80, the Flyers had been by far the best among the 21 NHL teams, with a 48-12-20 record—and a record

35-game unbeaten streak. That roll continued in the first three rounds for the Flyers, as they defeated the Edmonton Oilers, New York Rangers, and Minnesota North Stars.

The Islanders won game one on a power play in overtime. Although the Flyers came back strong in game two to even the series with an easy 8-3 win led by Paul Holmgren's hat trick, the Islanders had taken away Philadelphia's all-important home-ice advantage.

In game three Flyer coach Pat Quinn unexpectedly switched from sensational rookie goalie Pete Peeters to the veteran Phil Myre. Although Myre played well, the Islanders power play decided the game, and they won easily, 6-2. The Isles took game four 5-2, and the series returned to Philadelphia with the Islanders holding a three-game- to-one edge. Peeters returned to the Flyer net for game five and, after trailing 1-0, Philadel-

AP/Wide World Photos

The Islanders celebrate victory

phia scored five of the game's next six goals to beat the Isles 6-3. Peeters was brilliant as he turned back 35 New York shots to deny the Isles in their first of three chances to clinch the title.

Game six was aired nationally in the United States on CBS on May 24, a sweltering Sunday afternoon. The game had intensity, drama, and action of a potential Cup-clinching match, but unfortunately it would also become mired in controversy as the outcome was ultimately decided by a pair of clearly illegal goals.

Flyer sniper Reggie Leach gave the visitors a 1-0 lead at 7:21 of the first period on a five-on-three power play with both Bob Nystrom and Denis Potvin in the box for the Islanders. (Referee Bob Myers would then give the Flyers just one more power play in the game while the Isles would enjoy eight.) Potvin scored on the power play at 11:56, although the Flyers argued—to no avail—that it had been scored with a high stick.

Just over two minutes later, Clark Gilles led a rush up ice and carried the puck over the blueline. A second later he dropped it back to a trailing Butch Goring who was at least five feet outside the zone. Goring in turn fed it back in to rookie winger Duane Sutter who lifted it over Peeters' shoulder and into the net for a 2-1 New York lead.

Incredibly, veteran linesman Leon Stickle failed to call the play offside and referee Myers let the goal stand. The Islanders had a 4-2 lead after 40 minutes, but the Flyers fought back on goals by Bob Dailey and John Paddock in the third to send the game into overtime tied 4-4. The Islanders got the game-winner at 7:11 of overtime, when Bob Nystrom scored his second goal of the game to give the Islanders the Cup-winning victory. With 29 points on a dozen goals and 17 assists Bryan Trottier won the Conn Smythe Trophy as the playoffs' most valuable player.

Torrey collected two more "prizes" a few weeks later. In the 1980 draft Torrey selected Brent Sutter with the 17th overall pick (who would eventually go on to succeed Denis Potvin as the Islanders' captain) and claimed future star goalie Kelly Hrudey with the 38th overall selection.

Islander Dynasty

The Islanders jumped back into first place overall in the NHL in 1980-81 with 110 points, and Potvin and Bossy regained their berths as first team All-Stars. Torrey realized, however, that if the Islanders were to remain champions, he could not afford to let them get complacent. As players aged or lost effectiveness, or the style of the NHL game changed, Torrey quietly but steadily made personnel changes to ensure the team's productivity.

Before the 1981 playoffs, Torrey dealt goalie Chico Resch, arguably the team's most popular player, and former top draft pick Steve Tambellini to the Colorado Rockies for offensive defenseman Mike McEwen. With 21-year-old goalie Rollie Melanson ready to move up as Billy Smith's backup, Resch was expendable, as was center Tambellini (who got little ice time behind Trottier, Goring and Wayne Merrick). McEwen proved to be a key performer in the 1981 playoffs, especially when fellow blueliner Stefan Persson was unexpectedly lost to the team when he suffered a broken jaw from an errant shot in the fourth game of the quarterfinals at Edmonton.

Behind the brilliant goaltending of Smith, the record scoring prowess of Bossy, and the inspired leadership of Conn Smythe Trophy winner Butch Goring, it took the Islanders just 18 games to collect the 14 wins they needed to win their second Stanley Cup. First they defeated the Toronto Maple Leafs in three straight games, and then downed Wayne Gretzky and the up-and-coming Edmonton Oilers four games to two. The Isles then drew the Rangers in the semifinals and swept them aside in four straight games.

In the finals the Islanders met the upstart Minnesota North Stars, a team that had only made the playoffs twice in the previous seven seasons. This matchup also pitted two of the closest friends in the game against each other—Islanders General Manager Bill Torrey and his North Star counterpart, Lou Nanne.

In many ways, Torrey had served as a valuable mentor and counselor to the younger Nanne

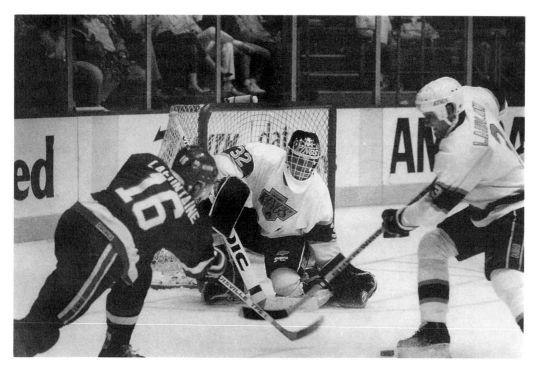

AP/Wide World Photos

Pat LaFontaine (16) takes a shot on goal but is turned away by the Kings' Kelly Hrudey

when he retired as a player and assumed the GM's chair in Minnesota in 1977. The North Stars had upset three strong clubs—Boston, Buffalo and Calgary—to earn their championship meeting with the Isles in 1981. The Islanders proved to be much too strong for the valiant Stars, however, as they swept past them in five relatively high-scoring games. The host Islanders took both the first and second games at the Coliseum by identical 6-3 scores and then captured the third contest in Minnesota in a 7-5 shoot out.

Nanne's Stars did get one taste of victory in the finals, however, with two late goals in game four to break a 2-2 tie and hand the Islanders their lone loss in the championship round, 4-2. It was all Islanders in game five, however, as Goring sandwiched a pair of goals around one by Wayne Merrick in the first ten minutes of the contest to lead the Isles to a 5-1 Cup-clinching victory.

With their second Cup freshly won the Islanders put together the best season in their history in 1981-82 as they dominated the league with 118 points on an outstanding record of 54-16-10, the best in their history before or since, and for the third time in five years they lost just three games at home (33-3-4). Although Mike Bossy (64-83-147) and Bryan Trottier (50-79-129) were the only two Isles among the league's top ten scorers, the club also collected a team high 385 goals, which was second that year only to run-and-gun Edmonton's stratospheric 417.

Although the Islanders were clearly the class of the NHL in 1981-82, they were almost upset by a team that had nothing to lose. After opening their best-of-five Patrick Division semifinal series against fourth place Pittsburgh with an 8-1 drubbing of the Pens, they notched another home blowout victory in the second game.

When the series moved to Pittsburgh, the Islanders seemed to forget their dominating style of hockey, while the Pens—who had finished the regular season campaign with 43 fewer points—rediscovered their strong checking game. Penguin netminder Michel Dion held the Islanders to one goal in game three, and Pittsburgh won 2-1 in overtime. The Penguins then tied the series by winning game four with surprising ease to force the series back to New York for a fifth and deciding game.

The underdog Penguins played with unusual calm and determination, while the Islanders seemed nervous and dispirited. By late in the third period, the Isles trailed 3-2. However, gritty New York winger John Tonelli picked off an errant clearing pass by Penguin defenseman Randy Carlyle and beat Dion with 2:21 left in regulation to send the game—and the series—into overtime. Shortly into "sudden death," Pittsburgh rookie Mike Bullard almost ended it all for the Isles with a fabulous scoring chance, only to be thwarted by an even more spectacular save by Billy Smith. At 6:10 Tonelli again beat Dion, and the Isles won the game 4-3. The relieved Islanders went on to face their hated neighbors from Manhattan, the Rangers.

After dropping the first game of the division finals 5-4 to the Rangers, Arbour's club finally recovered and dropped only one more playoff contest over the next month. The team swept both the Quebec Nordiques and Vancouver Canucks in the Conference and Stanley Cup Finals to become only the second team since the 1967 expansion to win hockey's "Grail" for more than two consecutive seasons. (The Montreal Canadiens held the Cup for four years, from 1976 to 1979.)

With seven goals in the finals and 17 overall in the playoffs, Mike Bossy took home the Conn Smythe Trophy. Bryan Trottier led the league in postseason scoring with 29 points on six goals and 23 assists. In goal, Vezina Trophy winner Billy Smith appeared in all but one game, compiling a 15-3 postseason record and a 2.52 goals-against average.

Crafty General Manager Bill Torrey topped off the year by making a steal in the 1982 draft a few weeks later. He was able to get talented University of Wisconsin winger Pat Flatley with the club's first pick—even though the Isles had only the 21st overall selection. Flatley made the team two years later without ever playing in the minor leagues by jumping directly from the 1984 Canadian Olympic team. In 1991 the steady winger also became just the fifth player to ever be named captain of the Islanders.

The Islanders dropped 22 points in 1982-83 to 96 and finished in second place in the Patrick Division, but when the playoffs ended, the Stanley Cup was again in Long Island—for the fourth consecutive time. Offensively the club's goal production dropped off dramatically during the regular season despite Mike Bossy's league-record, third consecutive 60-goal season. Defensively, however, no other NHL club allowed fewer goals, and the netminding tandem of Billy Smith and Rollie Melanson brought the William Jennings Trophy (fewest goals allowed) to Long Island for the first time.

While the Islanders did not sweep a playoff round that spring until the finals, they were never in any serious trouble during the 1983 Stanley Cup chase. The Washington Capitals went down easily in four games in the best-of-five Wales Conference semifinals while the Rangers extended the Isles to six games in the division final series. The Islanders most challenging series in 1983 came in the Wales Conference Finals against the league's best regular season club, the Boston Bruins and their Vezina Trophy-winning goalie Pete Peeters.

Like Billy Smith, Peeters was famous for being a highly territorial netminder who often reacted with a shove or sharp swing of the stick whenever opposing players wandered into the goal crease. Although Peeters had held the Islanders to just three goals total in a trio of regular season meetings, the Islanders managed to score 30 goals in their six playoff games against Boston.

The man most responsible for the talented Boston netminder's sudden loss of effectiveness was feisty utility winger Duane Sutter, who drove Peeters to distraction by constantly skating through his crease or bumping him whenever he roamed away from his net.

While Peeters twice held New York to a single tally in Boston's two series wins, in the other four games the Islanders scored more than 5 goals as Sutter's ploys successfully diverted Peeters' concentration from stopping the Islanders' snipers.

With their fourth consecutive trip to the Stanley Cup finals the Islanders had truly become a dynasty. The team they beat so easily that May, however, would be the NHL's next dynasty, the Edmonton Oilers (who would win the Cup five times over the next seven years). Conn Smythe Trophy winner Billy Smith did not allow four-time league MVP and Art Ross Trophy-winner Wayne Gretzky a single goal in the finals and held the high scoring Oilers—who had averaged 5.30 goals per game during the season—to just six goals in the series.

After a Presidential reception at the White House in honor of their fourth consecutive Cup, the Isles claimed one more prize in the spring of 1983 when Bill Torrey used the third overall pick in the draft (which he had acquired from the New Jersey Devils in 1981) to select St. Louis-born, Detroit-raised center Pat LaFontaine.

In just one season of junior hockey the 18-year-old had compiled 234 points on 104 goals and 134 assists. After playing with the 1984 U.S. Olympic team, LaFontaine turned pro and played 15 games with the Isles in the 1983-84 season. The nifty center collected 287 goals and 566 total points in just 530 games with the Isles, but a bitter contract dispute ended LaFontaine's Islander days in 1991.

He was traded at his request to the Buffalo Sabres in October of 1991 as the key figure in a seven-player deal that brought high-scoring winger Pierre Turgeon, the first overall player taken in the 1987 draft, to the Isles.

Every Dynasty's Destiny

The Islanders entered the 1983-84 season—just its 12th since joining the NHL in 1972—as the four-time defending Stanley Cup champions and the winningest team in pro sports for its age. However, the stars that had built the team's fortunes got older, and it became more difficult to maintain a championship level of performance without consistent access to high draft picks.

Nonetheless, the Isles won 50 games in 1983-84 to recapture the Patrick Division with 104 points and reached the Stanley Cup Finals for the fifth consecutive year. Edmonton, however, proved too powerful for the Isles. The Islanders had been able to hold Gretzky & Co. to only six goals in the 1983 finals, but just a year later, Smith and Melanson were scored upon 19 times in the final three games. Thus, the Isles fell to the Oilers four games to one, and the Cup left the United States for Canada.

With the official departure of the Stanley Cup from Uniondale in the spring of 1984, the Islanders soon fell from hockey's pinnacle. In 1984-85 the club dropped to 86 points and a third-place finish in the Patrick Division, their poorest season in 11 years. The Isles won the division semifinal against the Washington Capitals, but lost in the next round. The first-place Flyers downed them in five games, with Philadelphia's Vezina Trophy-winning Swedish goalie Pelle Lindbergh shutting the Isles out twice on his way to leading the Flyers to a finals appearance.

In 1985-86 the Islanders finished fifth overall in the league with 90 points, but only managed a third-place finish in the strong Patrick Division. The Isles met the Washington Capitals in the opening round of the playoffs, but were swept aside in three games. In March General Manager Torrey traded the club's popular right winger John Tonelli to the Calgary Flames. Shortly after, 53-year-old Al Arbour, the club's coach for 13 of its 14 seasons, announced that after 1,209 regular season and playoff games, he was taking a front-office job with the team as vice-president for player development.

The man Torrey eventually chose to take Arbour's place behind the Islanders' bench was 43-year-old junior hockey coach Terry Simpson.

Despite his lack of professional experience, Simpson's successful record in 13 years with the Prince Albert (Saskatchewan) Raiders earned him his ticket to guide one of the NHL's top teams.

Unfortunately for the rookie coach, however, the club he would take over in the fall of 1986 was fast losing all semblance to the championship teams that had dominated the NHL in the early 1980s. In August, veteran winger Bob Nystrom retired but remained with the club as an assistant coach. In October two more key veterans of the Stanley Cup years, Clark Gilles and Bob Bourne, were lost in the waiver draft.

During Simpson's first two seasons behind the bench, the Isles earned 82 and 88 points. In 1987-88 they finished in first place in the suddenly weakening Patrick Division, but Islander fans had been spoiled by the club's past success and expressed dissatisfaction. Simpson's Islanders did provide hockey fans with one unforgettable—if prolonged—thrill, however, when they visited the Washington Capitals for the seventh game of the Patrick Division semifinals. After falling behind three games to one in the series, the Islanders fought back to force a seventh game.

With former U.S. Olympian Bob Mason in goal for the Caps and Kelly Hrudey guarding the Isles' twine, the two clubs played a cautious, low-scoring contest. The Caps were leading 2-1 when Bryan Trottier tied it with 5:23 left in regulation.

With the score still knotted at the end of 60 minutes of play, the series went into overtime. Pat LaFontaine eventually scored at the 8:15 mark of the fourth overtime—six hours and 15 minutes after the game had started. In the next round, the Isles made a similar gritty comeback from a three-games-to-one deficit against the Flyers, but then lost the seventh game 5-1 to end their season.

Hitting Bottom

With the retirements of Mike Bossy and Denis Potvin after the 1987-88 season and the suddenly diminishing effectiveness of 32-year-old Bryan Trottier, the Islanders finally crashed in

AP/Wide World Photos

Pierre Turgeon (77)

1988-89. Twenty-seven games into the season, the club was a dismal 7-18-2. General Manager Bill Torrey decided to shake up his team, and he dismissed Coach Terry Simpson and brought back Al Arbour.

The club improved somewhat after Arbour's return, but they missed the playoffs for the first time since 1973-74 and tied with the Quebec Nordiques for the fewest points in the league with just 61. At season's end, the last remaining original Islander, goalie Billy Smith, hung up his skates. Smith had appeared in just 17 contests that year with a 4.44 goals-against average.

Arbour's team improved somewhat in 1989-90, notching 73 points and a fourth-place finish in the rapidly weakening Patrick Division. After being swept in the first round of the playoffs by the Ranger, Torrey announced that the last major star of the Stanley Cup years would not return, and he bought out the remainder of Bryan Trottier's contract.

Although Trottier ranked as the all-time leader in points (1,353) and games played (1,123), he had scored just 39 goals in his final three years. While no longer a scoring threat, Trottier's experience and leadership were just what the Pittsburgh Penguins were looking for, and they signed the Islander great as a free agent in 1990. (Over the next two years, the Pens won two Stanley Cup titles to give Bryan Trottier the fifth and sixth championship rings of his distinguished playing career.)

Meanwhile, the 1990-91 season saw the Islanders in last place with 16-year lows in points (60) and wins (25). The team struggled both on the ice and at the turnstile as season-ticket and box-office sales continued to fall off dramatically—on some nights the team played in front of more empty seats at the Nassau Coliseum than occupied ones.

The Islanders showed improvement in 1991-92, although they would again miss the playoffs.

Absentee owner John O. Pickett, a Florida resident, was looking to sell the club that he had helped save from bankruptcy in 1978. In December of 1991, it was announced that four local Long Island investors—Robert D. Rosenthal, Stephen Walsh, Jerome H. Grossman and Ralph Palleschi—had agreed to purchase 50 percent of the team from Pickett and completely take over its business management.

"The New Ice Age"

In June of 1992, as he had 20 times before, General Manager Bill Torrey presided over the Islanders' table at the NHL's entry draft. He used his club's first pick to select talented 20-year-old Lithuanian-born defenseman Darius Kasparaitis who had starred for the gold medal-winning CIS

AP/Wide World Photos

Vladimir Malakhov

team in the 1992 Olympics. That draft, however, was Torrey's last official public appearance as the Islanders' general manager.

In August, the team was officially sold to Cablevision Systems, and as part of the club's reorganization under the new ownership, Torrey agreed to step down as president and general manager. He was replaced by Jerome Grossman as president and former New York Ranger winger Don Maloney—who had finished his playing career with the Islanders in 1991 and had spent 1991-92 as Torrey's assistant general manager—as general manager. Although Torrey remained briefly as a consultant to the new group, he severed all ties with the Islanders midway through the 1992-93 season when he was name president of the NHL expansion Florida Panthers in Miami.

The new management team quickly settled in

by declaring the start of "The New Ice Age" on Long Island, and on the ice Al Arbour and his young team began to make that promise a reality.

With 58 goals and 132 points in his first full season with the team, 24-year-old Pierre Turgeon emerged as a new star for the Islanders. With 166 penalty minutes, the feisty Kasparaitis quickly became a fan favorite. He and fellow Soviet blueliner Vladimir Malakhov also compiled the two best plus/minus ratings among the team's defensemen. In goal, Glenn Healy and Mark Fitzpatrick were often stellar, and they helped the club back into the playoffs with a third-place Patrick Division finish on a record of 40-37-7, the team's best mark since 1987-88.

Although the Islanders' 87-point 1992-93 regular season was an impressive improvement, what they accomplished in the first two rounds of

AP/Wide World Photos

Glenn Healy

the playoffs brought back fond memories of the grit and determination characteristic of their championship teams a decade earlier. After losing the opening game of their best-of-seven division semifinal series to the second-place Capitals, the Islanders won games two, three, and four in overtime.

After losing the fifth game of the set, the Islanders captured the series with a 5-3 win in game six. That victory earned the Isles the dubious honor of facing the two-time defending Cup champion Pittsburgh Penguins whose league-best 119 regular season points were 32 more than the Islanders had earned.

That task was made even tougher after the Caps' Dale Hunter blindsided Pierre Turgeon into the boards while the Islanders' leading scorer celebrated his goal at 11:29 of the clinching game's third period. Although Hunter's vicious cross-check earned the aggressive Cap veteran a long suspension to start the 1993-94 season, it also separated Turgeon's shoulder making him unavailable for at least the first five games of the Penguin series.

With the Islanders' best player sidelined, it appeared as if they would be lucky to win even one game from the league's top team. Surpris-ingly, they won the opening contest as Islander goalie Glenn Healy turned aside 28 shots in a 3-2 New York road win. New York picked up a second series victory on game four, and, after losing game five at Pittsburgh, again stunned the champion Penguins with a 7-5 victory to tie the series and force a seventh game. With another incredible goaltending performance from Glenn Healy, the Islanders carried a 3-2 lead into the final minute of regulation time before Rick Tocchet scored to send the game into overtime.

Rarely used Czech-born forward David Volek stunned the Penguin faithful after just 5:16 with a blast from the top of the right circle that beat Tom Barrasso and completed the Isles' storybook upset series victory. The eventual 1993 Cup champion Montreal Canadiens would end the Islanders' magical run just ten days later in the Wales Conference Finals. The Habs, however, would need two overtime goals to earn that series victory over the now clearly up-and-coming New York Islanders, hockey's once—and perhaps soon again future—champions.

—Bruce C. Cooper

NEW YORK RANGERS

Despite more than 50 years since their last championship (1940)—the longest such championship drought experienced by any of the six surviving pre-War NHL clubs still competing in the league—the New York Rangers nevertheless hold a special place in the hearts of New York sports fans and have ever since their founding in 1926 by colorful boxing and arena promoter George Lewis "Tex" Rickard.

In the years since, the Rangers have been both a stylish heartthrob of America's biggest city and the purveyor of many of the town's most heartbreaking sports disappointments. But whether playing like champs or chumps, the New York Rangers have always been a reflection of both the city in which they played and of the fans who, for almost 70 years, have faithfully streamed through the turnstiles to see them perform.

From its founding in 1917 until 1924, the National Hockey League (NHL) was a cozy confederation made up of several teams in Quebec and Ontario, Canada. With the 1924-25 season, however, the league expanded to six clubs and ventured south of the border for the first time, adding the Boston Bruins. Two more U.S. cities, Pittsburgh and New York, joined the growing NHL fraternity in 1925-26. The Hamilton (Ontario) Tigers were sold for $75,000 to millionaire New York bootlegger William "Wild Bill" Dwyer. He moved the club to Gotham where, as the New York Americans, they became the first tenant of the newly erected Madison Square Garden.

Built on the site of a former trolley car barn just one block off Broadway on Eighth Avenue between 49th and 50th streets, the new Madison Square Garden was actually the third such New York sports and entertainment facility to bear the name. The first was P.T. Barnum's old Great Roman Hippodrome, a converted onetime passenger station, horse stable and freight shed for Commodore Cornelius Vanderbilt's New York & Harlem Railroad. In 1890 a second far more lavish Madison Square Garden rose on the same site.

By 1920, however, the second Garden had fallen into physical disrepair and was mired in bankruptcy when Rickard, a flamboyant boxing promoter, noted gambler, former South American cattle baron, and onetime operator of saloons from Alaska to Nevada, came to the rescue. Rickard, who had just made a financial killing as promoter of the July 4, 1919, Jack Dempsey-Jess Willard heavyweight boxing title fight, signed a ten-year, $200,000-a-year lease to operate New York high society's onetime favorite nightspot.

Rickard soon returned Madison Square Garden to profitability by emphasizing boxing and bringing in such high profile events as the 1924 Democratic National Convention. Shortly after the Convention ended, however, the New York Life Insurance Company, the Garden's mortgage holder, announced plans to demolish the arena and build its 40-story headquarters building on the site. Undaunted, Rickard assembled a syndicate of rich New York businessmen (whom he dubbed "my 600 millionaires") and organized a new Madison Square Garden Corporation. To assure his investors that the new enterprise would be well managed, Rickard gave himself a 20-year contract as president of the Garden.

While the old Madison Square Garden would not host its last event until May 5, 1925, construction on the new Garden began on January 9, 1925, and was completed in a mere 249 days. With anywhere from 14,290 to 18,500 seats to fill depending on configuration, Rickard was constantly on the lookout for new attractions for the Garden.

Garden executive John S. Hammond believed that ice hockey would be just such an attraction and attempted to persuade Rickard to purchase a franchise. Although Rickard doubted that a "Canadian game" would go over in sophisticated New York, he was more than willing to let "Wild Bill" Dwyer take the risk of finding out as a rent-paying tenant. A shrewd businessman, Rickard exacted a steep rent in exchange for giving Dwyer an unwritten "guarantee" that the Garden would not bring in another hockey team to compete with the Americans.

Hockey Hall of Fame amd Museum

Rival New York Americans' star Billy Burch

Madison Square Garden formally opened on December 15, 1925, as Dwyer's New York Americans, or Amerks, hosted the Montreal Canadians before a sell-out crowd of 17,442. Although the Americans lost to the Canadiens 3-1, the evening proved to be a sensational financial and critical success. Unfortunately for Dwyer, however, Rickard also began having second thoughts about hockey and the non-competition guarantee he had given the Amerks' owner.

"Tex's Rangers"

After just one night of hockey at the Garden, Rickard apparently overcame his earlier resistance to the game—as the great financial potential for hockey in New York became clear to him. While Madison Square Garden was already making a

TEAM INFORMATION AT A GLANCE

Founding date: May 15, 1926

Home ice: Madison Square Garden
4 Pennsylvania Plaza
New York, NY 10001
Phone: (212) 465-6486
FAX: (212) 465-6494

Seating capacity: 17,520
Team colors: Blue, red, and white
Team nickname: Rangers

Logo: A shield with "New York" across top and "Rangers" written diagonally

Franchise record:	Won	Lost	Tie
(1926-93)	1,863	1,881	706

Stanley Cup Wins: 1927-28, 1932-33, 1939-40

tidy sum from the Americans' hefty rental fees, it was obvious that much greater profits could be made from a team owned and operated by the Garden. Acquiring a new NHL franchise would be no problem, Rickard soon learned, as the league was anxious to add three more U.S.-based clubs to increase the circuit to a two-division, ten-team league.

Madison Square Garden made formal application to the NHL for a new franchise even before the 1925-26 season came to a close, and it was granted on May 15, 1926. The NHL's U.S. expansion was completed a short time later with the addition of the Chicago Black Hawks and Detroit Cougars. Naturally, Dwyer was furious that Rickard had reneged on his promise to not compete with the Americans. The bad blood that the situation engendered resulted in a fierce on-ice battle between the two teams. (This was fine with New York fans, who always liked a good fight.)

The new club was soon dubbed "Tex's Rangers" in honor of the Garden president, a one-time Texas sheriff, and the moniker stuck. For team colors the Rangers shamelessly mimicked their Garden co-tenants by adopting the same red, white, and blue hues sported by the Americans. As neither Rickard nor Hammond, who became the team's first president, knew anything about the technical part of the game, however, they immediately brought in a qualified hockey man to form a team. They settled on a fiery 31-year-old Canadian war hero named Constantine F. K. "Conn" Smythe.

A highly successful amateur hockey manager and coach in Toronto, Smythe had impressed Rickard and Hammond when he visited the Garden a few months earlier as coach of the University of Toronto Varsity Grads. In two sterling exhibition games, Smythe's club had easily defeated Yale and Princeton despite having only nine players. A few months later, Smythe guided his club to the 1926 Allen Cup title as the senior amateur hockey champions of Canada.

An experienced amateur hockey player, coach, and manager, Smythe liked to build teams with amateur athletes who loved the game more than money. Hammond, however, had a building to fill and wanted Smythe to bring in established pros and marquee players who would sell tickets.

The player Hammond especially wanted was Toronto winger Cecil "Babe" Dye, a three-time NHL scoring champion whom the St. Pat's were willing to trade. The headstrong Smythe refused to acquire him, however, on the grounds that Dye was only interested in money. With that, Smythe's and Hammond's philosophical differences reached an apex. Smythe considered hockey a pure sport while Hammond viewed it as entertainment that needed high ticket sales to survive financially.

Unable to reach agreement, Smythe and the Rangers parted company even before the start of the new club's first training camp. Yet Smythe found legendary success in the NHL. On February 14, 1927, Smythe and a group of fellow World War I veterans purchased the Toronto St. Patricks and renamed the club the Maple Leafs. Except for military service during World War II, Smythe remained with the Leafs continuously as a coach, manager, president and/or owner-governor for the rest of his long and distinguished hockey career.

With Smythe's sudden and unexpected departure, Rickard and Hammond needed to quickly find a new manager and coach. Fortunately for them, however, the greatest innovator in pro hockey, Lester Patrick, had become available following the demise of the Western Canada Hockey League and consequent folding of the club he owned and operated in that league, the Victoria Cougars. Patrick was promptly hired and, over the next 20 years, brought the Rangers more credibility, success, and glory than anyone else who would ever be associated with the club.

Hockey Hall of Fame amd Museum

Lester Patrick

"The Silver Fox"

The Patrick family could be considered pro hockey's royal family. Ever since family patriarch Lester helped lead the ECAHA Montreal Wanderers as a rover to successful Stanley Cup challenges in 1906 and 1907, three generations of Patricks have won Stanley Cup titles as players, coaches, and managers. In 1911 Lester and his younger brother Frank cofounded the Pacific Coast Hockey Association (PCHA) with the proceeds from the sale of their family's business, the Patrick Lumber Company of British Columbia.

By the time Lester—whom the press had dubbed "The Silver Fox" for his shrewdness as a manager, coach and promoter of his sport—came to New York 15 years later, he and Frank had all but invented and developed much of what today constitutes modern hockey.

During their long careers, the Patricks were by far the greatest innovators and promoters in pro hockey. In 1911 they introduced Canada's first indoor artificial ice plants to house Lester's club in Victoria and Frank's in Vancouver. Later they conceived of and developed the lucrative playoff system now used by all sports to determine championships, were the first to put numbers on their player's sweaters, and instituted many of the playing rules still in use in the 1990s, such as the penalty shot, the blueline, offsides, awarding of assists, and allowing the goaltender to leave his feet to make a save.

The PCHA folded in 1924 with Lester's Victoria Cougars and Frank's Vancouver Millionaires joining the four-team Western Canada Hockey League. (In 1925 the Cougars became the last non-NHL club to win the Stanley Cup.)

With the addition of the Montreal Maroons and Boston Bruins to the NHL in that same 1924-25 season, the Pittsburgh Pirates and New York Americans in 1925-26, and three more clubs including the Rangers in 1926-27, the western teams soon discovered that they could no longer com-

pete financially with the richer eastern cities for players. Therefore just as "Tex" Rickard was purchasing his NHL franchise, the Patricks came east to sell all of the WCHL's players to the NHL for $300,000—with the exception of Saskatoons, who had already been purchased by the Maroons for $60,000.

The only club that initially balked at Patrick's offer was the Rangers. Then manager Smythe was still looking for his preferred amateur sportsmen as opposed to high-priced professionals. With the other teams quickly loading up with WCHL talent, however, Smythe was soon forced to relent.

Among his signings were three memorable defensemen, "Iron Man" Murray Murdoch (who never missed a game in 11 seasons as a Ranger), bald tough guy Ivan "Ching" Johnson, and steady Clarence "Taffy" Abel, who became Johnson's longtime defensive partner.

Smythe also acquired three key forwards who would quickly become one of the league's top lines and remain so for a decade—center Frank Boucher and his wingers, Bill and Fred "Bunny" Cook.

"The Broadway Blueshirts ... Classiest Team in Hockey"

Under the expert tutelage of Lester Patrick, the Rangers quickly established themselves as a power in the NHL. After completing their first training camp at Ravina Gardens in Toronto, the team made their NHL debut at Madison Square Garden on November 16, 1926. Their opposition that night was the defending Stanley Cup champion Montreal Maroons.

New York's second hockey team came out a winner as Bill Cook scored the game's only goal at 10:37 of the second period while goalie Lorne Chabot earned the first of his 21 shutouts in just two years in New York.

Rickard and Hammond pulled out all the stops for the debut of their new attraction with marching bands, flags hanging from the rafters, a between periods "fancy skating" exhibition by

Hockey Hall of Fame amd Museum

Frank Boucher

Hockey Hall of Fame amd Museum

Bill Cook

figure skater Katy Schmidt, and a personal appearance by movie star Lois Moran, who dropped the ceremonial first puck.

Although there was only one goal scored that evening, referee Lou Marsh was busy calling penalties by ringing a dinner bell. The game was so rough that Frank Boucher—who went on to win the Lady Byng Trophy for sportsmanship seven times before the league finally gave it to him permanently—had the only fight of his career as he tussled with diminutive Montreal forward Merlyn "Bad Bill" Phillips.

"In a fast and savagely played hockey game the New York Rangers took up their stand last night and defeated the fast traveling Montreal Maroons by the airtight score of 1-0 on the ice at Madison Square Garden before a crowd of over 13,000 spectators," wrote Seabury Lawrence in the *New York Times.*

If Rickard had any doubts about bringing a second hockey team to the Garden, he was more

than assuaged after opening night—the Rangers were a hit. Four nights later the club notched its first road win at Toronto. By season's end, the nascent Rangers had won the five-team American Division handily with a record of 25-13-6 for 56 points, 11 ahead of second-place Boston.

Winger Bill Cook collected a league leading 33 goals to edge Chicago Black Hawk captain Dick Irvin by one point and win the Art Ross Trophy as the NHL's top scorer. Although the Bruins eliminated New York in the opening round of the playoffs, the Rangers were the toast of the town after just one season.

Attending a New York Rangers game in the club's early years was a formal social affair. Many of the gentlemen in the celebrity-filled Garden crowd would arrive in dinner jackets accompanied by gowned and bejeweled lady friends. The puck was not dropped until 8:45 pm to coincide with the traditional curtain time of the nearby Broadway theaters.

Among the faces frequently spotted in the crowd in these years were two of New York's biggest sports stars, Babe Ruth and Lou Gehrig. Also frequently on hand were many of America's best-known show people, including such luminaries as Humphrey Bogart, George Raft, Edward G. Robinson, Paul Muni, Lucille Ball, Dezi Arnez, and Frederick March.

With the proximity of New York's Broadway theater district and the team's high society and show business following, it didn't take Rickard's club long to earn a new popular moniker: "The Broadway Blueshirts ... The Classiest Team in Hockey."

The First Stanley Cup

In 1927-28, the Rangers finished in second place in the American Division on a record of 19-16-9. The young club, however, blossomed fully in the playoffs; they won their first Stanley Cup with one of the most dramatic and storied postseason performances in NHL history. After dispatching the Pittsburgh Pirates in the first round and downing the first place Bruins in the two-game division finals, Patrick's charges had to face the powerful Montreal Maroons in the Stanley Cup finals—without a single game contested on their home ice.

The Garden's longtime biggest moneymaker, the Ringling Brothers & Barnum and Bailey Circus, played Madison Square Garden every April. For that reason, prior to 1968 the Rangers were often forced to play many of their postseason "home" games on the road. Therefore all of the games in the 1928 championship series were scheduled for the Maroons' home ice at the Montreal Forum. The Rangers were shut out 2-0 in the series opener by Maroons' Hall-of-Fame goalie Clint Benedict.

In game two, which lasted approximately three hours, the Rangers had written one of the greatest and most dramatic chapters in the history of sports as 44-year-old General Manager and Coach Lester Patrick took to the ice for injured goalie Lorne Chabot and helped defeat the Maroons 2-1 in overtime.

After a scoreless first period in which Chabot was spectacular while turning aside 15 Montreal shots, Maroons' winger Nels Stewart's shot hit Chabot in the left eye. Bleeding heavily, the Ranger netminder was carried from the ice and taken to Royal Victoria Hospital. (Although it was feared that Chabot might lose his eye, he recovered and played nine more years In the NHL.)

With no backup goalie, Patrick appealed to the Maroons' manager Eddie Gerard to allow the Rangers to dress Ottawa netminder Alex Connell who was in the stands watching the game. The Maroons' players violently protested, however, because Connell had set an NHL record during the season with six consecutive shutouts.

Patrick then asked if he could use minor league goalie Hughie McCormick who was also in the stands, but Gerard again refused. Patrick returned to the Rangers' dressing room to ask for suggestions from his team, and Frank Boucher half-kiddingly suggested that Patrick himself play. Patrick, a one-time defenseman, had once played goal in an emergency for his PCHA Victoria Cou-

Hockey Hall of Fame and Museum

Alex Connell

gars. Patrick reluctantly stepped in as his team's goaltender.

"Lester went in, and stayed in until the bitter end, performing prodigies of net minding, backed up by as capable defensive play as (Ching) Johnson and (Taffey) Abel could muster, and while he had all the airy grace of a flounder in a dry bath tub, he played like a bull whale, and turned the laugh on the overconfident Maroons who only scored one goal on him. The refusal of the Maroons to allow another alien goal tend to replace the stricken Chabot filled Rangers with a frenzy and zeal that might have been lacking had the red team acceded to the request."

Patrick stopped all five shots he faced in the second period, but Benedict turned in his fifth consecutive shutout period of the finals to keep the game at 0-0 after 40 minutes. Just 30 seconds into the third, however, Bill Cook gave the Rangers their first lead of the series. At 14:20 Nels Stewart scored for Montreal to send the game into overtime. A reporter noted that after Stewart's goal, "the Silver Fox stuck his pads and chest in front of everything fired his way and, after making a few stops, became lucky as goaltenders will and turned loose some circus saves that even Benedict could not have beaten." In overtime Benedict and Patrick each made three stops, but Boucher scored and the Rangers won the game and the Stanley Cup.

Just 18 months after making their debut, Rickard's Rangers had brought him a world title. Unfortunately, however, Rickard died on January 6, 1929, from an acute attack of appendicitis. In a rite that the New York press likened to that for "an archbishop in the cathedral he had built," some 15,000 mourners filed past Rickard's massive $15,000, 2,200-pound bronze casket as his body lay in state in the Garden for two days.

Another Stanley Cup

The Rangers' third season saw them reach the Stanley Cup finals for the second consecutive year. This time, though, they were swept by the Boston Bruins. In 1931-32 the team clinched their second American Division title and made the finals for the third time in just six NHL seasons, but were swept in the championship series by Conn Smythe's high scoring Toronto Maple Leafs. Although Patrick's club fell to third place in the division in 1932-33 behind Boston and Detroit, they reached the Cup finals for the fourth time in their short history.

With 28-year-old rookie netminder Andy Aitkenhead between the pipes, the high-scoring Rangers swept past both the Montreal Canadiens and Detroit Red Wings to earn a second straight finals meeting with the Toronto Maple Leafs and their famous "Kid Line" of Joe Primeau, Busher Jackson, and Charlie Conacher. The circus, however, again intruded, and the Rangers only played one game on home ice, a 5-1 New York win, before being forced out of town to the year-old Maple Leaf Gardens for the rest of the best-of-five championship series.

Aitkenhead stymied the Leafs in game two, a 3-1 Rangers' win, but the Leafs got back into the

series in game three with a 3-2 victory. Game four was a classic playoff contest as neither team scored in regulation. In overtime referee Odie Cleghorn penalized Leaf defenseman Alexander "Mine Boy" Levinsky and rookie Toronto center Bill Thomas within a few seconds of each other to give the Rangers a two-man advantage. Ranger captain Bill Cook capitalized on this situation and scored to bring New York its second Cup in five years.

"With a rising drive into the corner of the net over the shoulder of Lorne Chabot, his one-time teammate, Bill Cook, scoring king of the National Hockey League, broke up the fourth game of the Stanley Cup series with the Toronto Maple Leafs, firing the shot that shocked 14,000 pop-eyed Canadian rooters and sent the New York Rangers to the apex of their rocket-like drive to the world's hockey championship," noted hockey writer Kerr N. Petrie.

While Cook and Aitkenhead got most of the publicity, the star of the playoffs for the Rangers that year clearly was 25-year-old Cecil Dillon, who scored eight goals in the postseason. Then in his third year with the Rangers, the 5'10" 175-pound Dillon played with distinction for the club until 1939.

The Depression Years

The Garden and Rangers got a new president in 1933 in John Reed Kilpatrick, a distinguished military man and All-American football player at Yale, who would remain at the club's helm for more than 25 years. Although hockey and the nation were mired in the depths of the Depression in the 1930s, the duo of Patrick and Kilpatrick kept the Rangers an NHL power.

Patrick continuously proved his mettle as both a judge of talent and an astute businessman. To maintain his club's strength, Patrick developed a four-tiered system, called the "Four-R" chain, to develop and oversee hockey talent. The Rangers were fed by the International-American League Philadelphia Ramblers, the Eastern Amateur League New York Rovers, and the Canadian junior Alberta Roamers. Over the years these clubs graduated a steady stream of new young stars such as Bryan Hextall, Sr., Alex Shibicky, Phil Watson, Neil and Mac Coville, and Lester Patrick's own two sons, Lynn and Muzz.

Although by finishing fourth in the American Division in 1935-36 the Rangers missed the playoffs for the first time in their history, their low standing was deceptive; they tied two other teams with 50 points and finished only six points behind the first-place Detroit Red Wings, who went on to win the Stanley Cup.

By 1936-37 the team found itself back in the finals—although they lost to Detroit—as Patrick's youth movement paid off with the blossoming of son Lynn and his linemates Watson and Hextall, and the addition of Neil and Mac Coville, who played on a line with Alex Shibicky. Key figures on the Ranger blueline were Muzz Patrick, Ott Heller, and the irrepressibly fun-loving "Babe" Pratt.

This home-grown talent program was so successful that when the Rangers won their third Stanley Cup in 1940, only two players on the team had not come up through Patrick's development system—goalie Dave Kerr and defenseman Art Coulter. Kerr came to the club from the Montreal Maroons in 1934 and backstopped the Rangers until 1941. Forty of Kerr's 157 wins as a Ranger were by shutout, and his goals-against average with the club was 2.07 in 324 games. Coulter came to the Rangers during the 1935-36 season from the Chicago Black Hawks and replaced Bill Cook as captain of the club the next year.

While the Rangers prospered during the 1930s, the Americans struggled to match the success of their Garden rivals. Unlike the Rangers, the Amerks seldom reached the Stanley Cup playoffs, appearing in postseason action only five times between 1926 and 1942 and winning just two series overall.

While the Americans shared the Garden with the Rangers for 15 seasons, the two clubs met only once in Stanley Cup play. It was the underdog Amerks who came out on top—although it took triple overtime in the deciding game to do it. With

Hockey Hall of Fame and Museum

Clint Smith

60 points on a record of 27-15-6, the Rangers finished second in the American Division in 1937-38 while the Amerks were second in the generally weaker Canadian Division with 49 points.

The Americans won the first game of the best-of-three set, however, but the Rangers took game two. In the third game, Rangers led 2-0 after two periods. However, the Amerks scored twice in the third to force overtime, and it was well past midnight when former Ranger Lorne Carr beat Dave Kerr to give the Amerks the biggest win in their history.

The Rangers show-business image also once brought Hollywood to Broadway in the late 1930s when MGM decided to make a feature film about the club called "The Great Canadian" starring matinee idol Clark Gable and silver screen siren Myrna Loy. Although the picture was never completed, the hockey scenes were filmed on location at the Garden with Phil Watson doubling for Gable and "Babe" Pratt skating as the movie's villain.

By the end of the 1938-39 season the Rangers had existed for 13 years with Lester Patrick as coach. With the conclusion of that campaign, however, the 55-year-old hockey legend handed the club's reins over to former star winger Frank Boucher, who had spent 1938-39 coaching the New York Rovers to the EAHL title.

Patrick compiled a record of 281-216-107 in 604 regular season games as Ranger coach as well as a superb 31-23-8 mark in postseason play with five trips to the finals and a pair of Stanley Cup titles. While the Silver Fox no longer patrolled the Ranger bench after 1939, he remained the club's manager through 1945-46.

In his last season behind the Rangers' bench, Lester Patrick led the club to a second-place fin-ish in the seven-team, one division NHL with a 26-16-6 record. Although Patrick's team did not reach the finals, his club stretched the eventual Stanley Cup champion Boston Bruins to seven games in the 1939 semifinals.

"1-9-4-0"

When Frank Boucher took over the Rangers in the fall of 1939, he inherited a well-balanced team. Although Cecil Dillon had moved on to Detroit, his place on the roster was taken by 22-year-old rookie center Alf Pike, who would go on to play six strong seasons in New York and later coach the team. Left wing Kirby MacDonald,

Hockey Hall of Fame amd Museum

Bryan Hextall, Sr.

another first-year player, won the Calder Trophy as NHL rookie of the year in 1939-40.

The Coville and Patrick brothers were solid veterans, as were teammates such as Phil Watson, Alex Shibicky, Clint "Snuffy" Smith, Wilfred "Dutch" Hiller, Bryan Hextall, Sr., "Babe" Pratt, and Ehrhardt Henry "Ott" Heller. With Vezina Trophy-winner Dave Kerr in goal and captain Art Coulter leading the blueline corps, the Rangers were a formidable aggregate.

Nonetheless, the Rangers started poorly in the 1939-40 season, winning just one of their first six games. With a 1-1 tie at Montreal on November 23, however, the club began a run of 19 consecutive games without a loss (14-0-5) which included a stretch of ten straight wins. Although the club again finished second behind the Boston Bruins, they had cut the margin back from 16 points in 1938-39 to just three and had won most of their regular season meetings with Boston.

As the NHL's top two finishers, the Bruins and Rangers met in a best-of-seven semifinal series. Kerr continued his brilliance of the regular season by shutting out the Bruins—the league's highest scoring team—in the opening game in New York.

The Bruins won the next two contests on their home ice, but Kerr posted consecutive 1-0 shutouts in games four and five before finishing off the Bruins in New York, 4-1. While Kerr gave up eight goals in the Rangers' two losses, in their four victories he held the Bruins—a team which scored an average of 3.54 goals per game in the regular season—to just one goal total for an average of 0.25.

With the Bruins out of the way, the Rangers were back in the finals for the sixth time in 13 years. For the third time their opponents were the Maple Leafs, this time coached by Hall-of-Famer Dick Irvin, Sr. The Rangers won the first two games, but the Leafs took advantage of their home ice to even the set with wins in games three and four.

Game five went into overtime tied at 1-1 with Kerr and Hall-of-Fame Leaf netminder Walter "Turk" (for "Turkey Eyes") Broda playing stone-

wall goal, but the Rangers finally prevailed when light-scoring defenseman Muzz Patrick—who had only three career goals—beat Broda at 11:43 of the extra frame.

In game six of the finals, the Leafs held a comfortable 2-0 lead at the second intermission. However as Kerr kept the Leafs at bay over the final 20 minutes of regulation time, Alf Pike and Neil Colville each scored on Broda to send a game into overtime for the third time in the championship series.

Barely two minutes into overtime, left wing Wilbert "Dutch" Hiller won the puck behind the Leaf goal and passed it to Phil Watson, stationed at the blueline. Watson soon found Bryan Hextall, the Rangers' leading scorer that year, cutting toward the net and fed the puck to the winger, who backhanded into the Leaf net at 2:07 for the Cup-winning goal. After a jubilant locker room celebration, the team met at the Royal York Hotel where General Kilpatrick hosted a victory party.

With three titles in 14 seasons, arguably hockey's best manager in Lester Patrick, and a talented young lineup, the Rangers appeared to be on the verge of becoming a dynasty. No one could foresee how war, bad luck, fate, and numerous other factors would combine over the next 50 years to keep the Stanley Cup away from New York.

The War Years

World War II was a disaster for hockey, and no NHL town felt its sting more than New York. The Americans dropped to last in the league in 1940-41 winning just eight games and, after struggling through one more last place season under the name "Brooklyn Americans," folded altogether in the spring of 1942.

The Rangers avoided immediate collapse and even finished first in 1941-42 with 21-year-old "Sugar Jim" Henry in goal in place of the departed Dave Kerr. As the war progressed, though, more and more of the club's top players were called away to the service, and the team suffered accordingly.

Hockey Hall of Fame amd Museum

Chuck Rayner

By 1942-43 Henry had also gone to war, and the Rangers fell from first place to last while using four different goalies that season. They remained in last place for the next four years while putting together extended losing streaks. In 1943-44 the club won only six of 50 games and scored just 162 goals while netminder Ken "Tubby" McCauley gave up an average of 6.20 goals per game.

Starting in January of 1944, the Rangers posted a team record 25-game winless streak (0-21-4) which stretched over two seasons. Things were so bad that when coach Frank Boucher—who had already been retired for six years—briefly strapped on the skates again during the 1943-44 season, the 43-year-old proved better than most of his regular players, collecting four goals and ten assists in just 15 games.

Near Return to Glory

With the end of World War II, the Rangers slowly began to rebuild. In 1947-48 the club finished fourth to make the playoffs for the first time in six years, but lost in the opening round to the Detroit Red Wings. After missing the playoffs after another last-place finish in 1948-49, the club rebounded the next year to fourth and then almost stole the 1950 Cup with a remarkable playoff that carried them to overtime of the seventh game of the finals.

Although losing their 14-game regular-season series to the Canadiens, the Rangers, coached by Lynn Patrick and managed by Frank Boucher, upset the Maurice Richard-led Habs four games to one in the playoffs. Then it was on to the finals to meet the first-place Red Wings, who not only boasted veteran All-Star goalie Harry Lumley, but also had the league's three top scorers—the "Production Line"—Ted Lindsay, Sid Abel, and Gordie Howe (although Howe missed the finals due to a serious head injury he had suffered in the previous round).

After losing the first game in Detroit and splitting the next two on neutral ice in Toronto (the Rangers, as usual, had been expelled from the Garden by the circus), the Rangers traveled to Olympia Stadium for the last five contests, trailing two games to one. Although the Wings built up a 3-1 lead by the third period of game four, they were forced into overtime after Edgar Laprade, the Rangers' leading scorer in 1949-50, and defenseman Gus Kyle scored unanswered goals.

After Chuck Rayner made three big saves on Ted Lindsay early in the extra period, New York winger Ed Slowinski found center Don "Bones" Raleigh with a pass from behind the Detroit net, and at 8:34 the diminutive Ranger pivot put it past Lumley with a desperate backhand swipe as Detroit defender "Black Jack" Stewart knocked him viciously to the ice.

Two nights later the Rangers appeared to be on the verge of taking game five in regulation with Rayner shutting out Detroit 1-0 when Lindsay tied the match with just two minutes remaining. For

Hockey Hall of Fame amd Museum

Andy Bathgate

Ted Lindsay tied the game with his second goal of the night and Sid Abel completed the Detroit comeback with the game-winner at 10:34 to send the finals to a seventh and deciding game. Although the Rangers again took a 2-0 first period lead, the contest went into overtime as the Red Wings came from behind to tie it at 3-3 after 60 minutes.

The Rangers almost won it in the first overtime period, but winger Nick Mickowski's shot hit the post and bounced harmlessly away. As the second overtime progressed the Red Wings kept getting good chances as the tiring Rangers faded with exhaustion. Then, as the two clubs moved into their 88th minute of play, Detroit center George Gee broke in on Rayner, but the Ranger goalie smothered the puck to force a face-off. Detroit won the draw and left wing Pete Babando fired blindly toward Rayner and beat him with a shot two feet off the ice. Thus ended the Broadway Blues' dream of a fourth Stanley Cup.

Two Decades of Comings and Goings

The Rangers trip to the 1950 Stanley Cup finals brought hockey back to the front pages in New York, but the team's hopes of returning to the glory days of the 1920s and 1930s were dashed. After their heartbreaking loss to Detroit, the Rangers missed the playoffs for five straight seasons—and 12 of the next 16—while failing to win another playoff series until 1971.

Although the team had just three coaches in its first 24 seasons, there was soon a revolving door of former Ranger players for the bench job. Neil Colville replaced Lynn Patrick in 1950 but lasted just 93 games.

Bill Cook took over midway through the 1951-52 campaign only to be replaced by General Manager Frank Boucher, who returned for his second tour of bench duty at the start of the 1953-54 season. After 39 games, however, Boucher installed Muzz Patrick behind the bench. Patrick replaced Boucher as general manager following

the second consecutive game, however, Slowinski fed Raleigh from behind the net who then beat Lumley between the pads from ten feet out just 1:38 into overtime to give the underdog Rangers a three-games-to-two lead in the finals.

In game six the Rangers built a 4-3 third-period lead on goals by Allan Stanley, Dunc Fisher, Pentti Lund, and Tony Leswick. However at 4:13

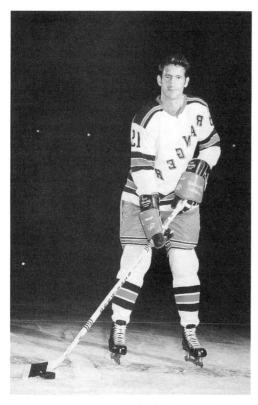

Hockey Hall of Fame amd Museum

Jean Ratelle

playoffs for three consecutive seasons (1955-56, 1956-57, and 1957-58) due in no small part to the influx of young talent developed by the Guelph Baltimores, the Junior "A" club the Rangers sponsored in the Ontario Hockey Association.

Among those who came up from Guelph and played with distinction in New York were Lou Fontinato, Dean Prentice, Ron Murphy, Aldo Guidolin, Harry Howell, and the Rangers' top three all-time leading scorers—Rod Gilbert, Jean Ratelle, and Andy Bathgate. These eight players appeared in a total of 5,279 regular season Ranger games and accounted for 3,538 points.

Madison Square Garden "IV"

By 1960 the "new" Garden on 50th St. was 35 years old and fast becoming obsolete. At the same time Jim Norris was forced by a federal court to sell his interest in the Garden Corporation to Irving Mitchell Felt, head of the Graham-Paige Investment Company, who acquired 80 percent of the Garden's stock.

With the arrival of Felt, John J. Bergen replaced Kilpatrick as president of the Rangers from 1960 to 1962. William M. Jennings then ran the club from 1962 until his death in 1981. On November 3, 1960, Felt announced his plans to build a fourth Madison Square Garden complex.

Two days after Felt made his announcement he was contacted by J. W. Ewalt, vice-president for real estate of the Pennsylvania Railroad, who suggested that the proposed new Garden be built above Pennsylvania Station at 33rd St. and Eighth Avenue. Not only would the railroad be willing to make the "air rights" of the 455' x 800' two block area available, Ewalt noted, but the site already had an existing basement-level transportation hub in the form of one of the world's most famous and busiest train stations.

Within eight months Madison Square Garden and the Pennsylvania Railroad reached agreement. Plans were drawn up for the new complex, which included a sports arena, an office tower, and complete entertainment and convention center. Con-

the 1954-55 campaign and remained in that office, once occupied by his father, until 1964.

Phil Watson took over the Rangers' bench next and lasted until a month into the 1959-60 season when ex-teammate Alf Pike became the eighth ex-Ranger to coach his old team. Over the remainder of the 1960s the club changed coaches six more times as Doug Harvey (as player/coach), Muzz Patrick (again), George "Red" Sullivan, Emile Francis, Bernie Geoffrion and Emile Francis (also for a second time) guided the team.

All of these men had stints with the Rangers as players. In 1964 the team also got its fourth general manager as Emile Francis, a seldom used back up goalie to Chuck Rayner in the early 1950s, took over the reins from Muzz Patrick.

The most successful stretch in the 1950s came when Phil Watson was able to get the club to the struction of the Garden officially commenced on May 1, 1964.

By the time the new Garden formally opened for business in February of 1968, the hat box-shaped main building had risen 13 stories over Eighth Avenue with the Rangers' ice surface located some 60 feet above street level on the fifth floor.

The Rangers played their last game at the old Garden on 50th St. on February 11, 1968, while the "new" Garden was celebrating its gala opening. Bob Hope and Bing Crosby headlined Madison Square Garden IV's opening night festivities before a black tie crowd of 19,832 who were also treated to Jack Dempsey and Gene Tunney shadow-boxing. Meanwhile 15,925 Ranger faithful watched their club close out its 42-year run in its original home as Jean Ratelle scored the last goal in the "house that Tex built" to earn a 3-3 tie with the Red Wings.

A week later, the Rangers made their debut in Madison Square Garden IV as they hosted the Philadelphia Flyers, one of the six new expansion teams that had joined the NHL in 1967-68. Within a few years of Madison Square Garden IV's opening, Gulf & Western (later called Paramount Communications) became the majority shareholder of Madison Square Garden Corporation.

This gave the international entertainment conglomerate effective control of the Garden complex including the Rangers, the NBA's Knicks, and the Madison Square Garden television network among other entities. (G&W/Paramount eventually became the Garden's sole owner by the late 1970s.)

The Emile Francis Years

Although the Rangers failed to win a Stanley Cup during the dozen-year reign of Emile "The Cat" Francis as general manager—and often coach—of the club from 1964 to 1976, they regained respectability for the first time since before the war and became an NHL power over the first half of the 1970s, finishing either second or third

overall for three consecutive seasons from 1970-71 to 1972-73.

The Rangers won only 20 games in Francis' first year as general manager (20-38-18) and 18 in his second (18-41-11). He took over behind the bench for the first time by replacing "Red" Sullivan on December 5, 1965. Over the next five years, however, the Rangers' points climbed steadily from a low of 47 in 1965-66 to 92 by the 1969-70 season.

In 1970-71 Francis guided the Rangers to the club's first 100-point season with 109 points on a record of 49-18-11, second only to the then defending Stanley Cup champion Boston Bruins. New York was especially tough at Madison Square Garden that year where the club tasted defeat just twice (30-2-7).

More important, however, for the first time since their trip to the finals in 1950 they also won

Hockey Hall of Fame amd Museum

Eddie Giacomin

a playoff series by downing the Toronto Maple Leafs in the quarterfinals, four games to two, to end their embarrassing 21-year drought. New York's visions of another trip to the finals were dashed in the semifinals by high flying Chicago, although it took the Black Hawks seven games to finish them off.

The 1971-72 season brought New York two more firsts—a 50-goal scorer and the club's first 100-plus point-getters. Vic Hadfield, a 31-year-old journeyman winger who, in a decade with the Rangers, had averaged just 16 goals a year, exploded for 50 goals and 106 points when Francis put him on a line with center Jean Ratelle and right wing Rod Gilbert.

Ratelle, meanwhile, collected 109 points—a club record—on 46 goals and 63 assists despite missing 15 games, and Gilbert completed the Rangers' "G-A-G (Goal-a-Game) Line's" production with 97 points on 43 goals and 54 assists. Besides pacing the Rangers, the trio also finished third, fourth, and fifth in overall league scoring. Also blossoming that year was 24-year-old defenseman Brad Park, whose 24 goals and 73 points placed him second only to Bobby Orr among the league's blueliners.

The 1972 Stanley Cup playoffs saw the Rangers reach the finals for the eighth time in their history—but only the second time in 32 years. Pitted against the Montreal Canadiens in the first round, they defeated the defending Cup champions four games to two in what many observers considered a Ranger upset. The semifinals saw New York avenge the previous year's loss to Chicago with a four game sweep to earn a finals meeting with the powerhouse Bruins.

The 1972 Bruin-Ranger final represented the first time in a dozen years that the NHL's top two regular season finishers had made it to the championship series. The finals opened on April 30 in ancient Boston Garden and the game was tied 5-5 in the third period. Bruin winger Garnet "Ace" Bailey scored with just over two minutes left in regulation to give Boston a 6-5 victory. Both coaches switched netminders for game two with Gilles Villemure going in for New York and Eddie

Hockey Hall of Fame amd Museum

Brad Park

Johnston taking over for Boston. The Bruins again came out on top, 2-1, on a third period goal by Ken Hodge.

New York took early charge of game three, solving Cheevers three times on the power play by the 13 minute mark of the opening period. The Rangers went on to win their first finals contest in 22 years, 5-2, behind Giacomin's excellent goaltending. After losing game four, 3-2, New York staved off ultimate defeat in game five with a come-from-behind 3-2 road victory.

In game six, with New York's Walt Tkaczuk off for hooking midway through the opening period, Bobby Orr collected his fifth goal and 23rd point of the playoffs—his second Cup-winner in three years. Wayne Cashman officially iced the season for the Rangers with a pair of third period insurance goals while WHA-bound Gerry Cheevers earned a 3-0 shutout.

In 1972-73 the Rangers finished third behind Montreal (120) and Boston (107) in the powerful

East Division with 47 wins and 102 points. Francis turned the coaching reins over to yet another former Ranger, Larry Popein, for the 1973-74 season, but the general manager returned himself to the bench—for a third time—on January 11, 1974. After upsetting the Canadiens in the opening round of the 1974 playoffs, Francis' Rangers almost got to the finals again in a hard fought semi-final series with the eventual champion Philadelphia Flyers, but lost the seventh game at the Spectrum 4-3.

After losing in the preliminary round of the 1975 playoffs to the third year New York Islanders, Francis permanently stepped down as Ranger coach and replaced himself with Ron Stewart, a recently retired 21-year NHL veteran winger who had played almost four seasons with the Rangers in the late 1960s and early 1970s.

By mid-season, however, Stewart was gone, but this time so too was Francis, with both men being replaced on January 6, 1976, by former Montreal Canadien "badman" John Ferguson. Just two months before Francis left, though, he pulled off one of the biggest trades in NHL history.

On November 7, 1975, Francis dealt Rangers' second all-time leading scorer Jean Ratelle, 26-year-old All-Star defenseman Brad Park, and recently acquired former WHA blueliner Joe Zanussi to Boston for the Bruins' second all-time point leader, Phil Esposito, and key veteran defenseman Carol Vadnais. (Winger Ken Hodge, Esposito's high-scoring linemate, would also come over from the Bruins after the season for Rick Middleton.)

Turbulent Transition Years

The John Ferguson era in New York lasted just two-and-a-half turbulent seasons and is probably best remembered for two fashion statements. Ferguson imposed "New Look" uniforms on the club for two years—starting with the 1976-77 season—and coach Jean-Guy Talbot wore jogging suits behind the bench.

On the ice, however, the Rangers were all but invisible, making the playoffs just once in three tries under Ferguson. In their lone postseason appearance, they fell quietly in a best-of-three preliminary round to the Buffalo Sabres.

The 1978-79 season saw the return of the team's management to a "member of the family" as onetime Ranger defenseman and minor league development coach Fred "The Fog" Shero was hired away from the Philadelphia Flyers—where he won a pair of Stanley Cup titles in seven years. (New York was eventually required to surrender its first round draft pick in 1978 to the Flyers in exchange for Philadelphia's releasing Shero from the last year of his contract.)

Hockey Hall of Fame and Museum

Rod Gilbert

Hockey Hall of Fame and Museum

Harry Howell

Shero officially took over the Rangers hockey operations on June 2, 1978, and among the first accomplishments of his stewardship—after announcing that the club would return to wearing its traditional uniforms—was the signing of a pair of high-priced, free-agent Swedish scoring stars, Anders Hedberg and Ulf Nilsson.

From 1974 to 1977, center Hedberg and right wing Nilsson had skated on a line with Bobby Hull for the WHA Winnipeg Jets, where each had four consecutive 100-plus point seasons. While neither ever broke the century mark in the tighter checking NHL, in their first season in New York they helped carry the Rangers into the 1979 playoffs and into the finals for the first time since 1972.

The Rangers improved by ten wins and 18 points in Shero's first year at the helm. The team then defeated Los Angeles, Philadelphia, and the New York Islanders with a cumulative 10-3 playoff record to reach the 1979 finals. There they met the three-time defending champion Canadiens.

By the time the championship series opened at the Montreal Forum, Shero was being billed as a miracle worker; his reputation grew even more after the Broadway Blues took the opening game 4-1, driving Ken Dryden from the nets in the process. Undaunted, the Canadiens took the next four games to win their fourth consecutive Cup and send the Rangers home empty-handed.

Shero began his second year in New York with another big trade as he acquired hulking defenseman Barry Beck from the Colorado Rockies. This deal cost him Pat Hickey, Lucien De Blois, Mike McEwen, Dean Turner, and Bobby Crawford. While Beck became a major force on the Ranger blueline and eventually the team's captain for five seasons, the trade deprived the Rangers of much-needed depth. The club dropped five points over the previous year's total and was then eliminated in the quarterfinals by the Flyers.

In the spring of 1979 Fred Shero was the toast of Broadway, but when the Rangers faltered unexpectedly at the start of the 1980-81 season by winning just four of their first 20 games, Shero got all of the blame. On November 19, 1980, Shero was dismissed and replaced in both of his jobs by 34-year-old Craig Patrick.

A former journeyman NHL winger and 1980 U.S. Olympic Hockey Team assistant manager-coach, Patrick had joined the Rangers the previous July as director of operations. Although he had never played for the Rangers, Patrick's roots with the team were deep. He was the son of former star Ranger winger and onetime coach Lynn Patrick; the nephew of ex-Ranger defenseman, coach, and general manager Muzz Patrick; and the grandson of the Rangers' patriarch and original manager and coach, Hall of Famer Lester Patrick. On November 21, 1980, Craig Patrick officially became the third generation of his distinguished hockey family to run the New York Rangers.

The Third Patrick Era

The new Ranger boss went behind his club's bench for the rest of the 1980-81 campaign to evaluate its talent firsthand. During his 60-game stint, Patrick compiled a creditable 26-23-11 record—good enough to earn the club a 1981 play-off berth. His new charges played well enough, defeating the Los Angeles Kings and St. Louis Blues, to reach the Stanley Cup semifinals to face the defending champion Islanders. The Islanders swept the Rangers in four games en route to their second consecutive Cup. With a relatively satisfying season and playoffs over, Patrick set about finding a new coach for the Rangers.

Patrick hired his top assistant from the 1980 Gold Medal-winning U. S. Olympic Hockey Team, 44-year-old Herb Brooks, on June 4, 1981. By leading that club of underdog collegians to their "Miracle on Ice" at Lake Placid, the Minnesota-born Brooks had become probably the best known and most highly praised coach in any sport in the United States.

Brooks at first eschewed the NHL limelight and instead headed off to Switzerland, where he spent the 1980-81 season coaching Davos in the Swiss Elite League. When Brooks agreed to coach in New York, the world's biggest and richest professional sports market, it caused a sensation and quickly returned the Rangers to being one of the highest profile clubs in pro sports. Unfortunately for both the new coach and his team, three of the Rangers' Patrick Division rivals—the Islanders, Flyers, and Washington Capitals—were also at their peak at the time.

In the Patrick Division of the early 1980s, the competition was stiff and the pace unrelenting. In Brooks' first season, the Rangers improved by 16 points to 92 and earned second place in the division, but the team failed to finish any higher than fourth during the remainder of his tenure and never advanced out of the Patrick Division in the playoffs. The Rangers had their best year under Brooks in 1983-84 when they amassed 93 points on a record of 42-29-9; they still finished in fourth place behind the Islanders (104), Caps (101), and Fly-

AP/Wide World Photos

John Vanbiesbrouck

ers (98). The next season, however, Brooks' Rangers went into an unexpected tailspin despite the addition of rookie goalie John Vanbiesbrouck.

While the team's goal production dropped slightly, their goals allowed jumped markedly and by mid-January the Rangers were mired in fifth place with a record of 15-22-8. On January 21, 1985, Ranger General Manager Craig Patrick removed Brooks and returned to the club's bench. Although eventually making the playoffs with just 62 points—31 fewer than the previous season—on a disappointing 26-44-10 record, the Rangers were quickly swept away by the Flyers in three straight first-round games.

Patrick's next choice to coach the Rangers was another American, 35-year-old Utica, New York, native Ted Sator, a onetime draft pick of the WHA New York Raiders who had spent several years as an assistant coach under Bob McCammon and Mike Keenan with the Philadelphia Flyers. As with Brooks, Sator was a product of U.S. college hockey, having played and coached at Bowling Green University. Prior to joining the Flyers, Sator had spent five highly successful years coaching in Sweden.

Under the highly regimented Sator, the Rangers became a far better defensive team, cutting down their goals against in one season by nearly one per game and improving their point total from 62 to 78. A key factor in this improvement was goaltender John Vanbiesbrouck, who blossomed in his sophomore season to bring the Vezina Trophy to New York. He was also named a first team All Star.

Although again finishing fourth, the club had a strong playoff in 1986 advancing to the final four by pulling off major upsets of both the first-place Flyers and second-place Caps before finally falling to the eventual Cup champion Canadiens in the Wales Conference Finals.

Despite the Rangers' marked improvement and strong playoff performance, by mid-summer the third Patrick era came to an end after just six years.

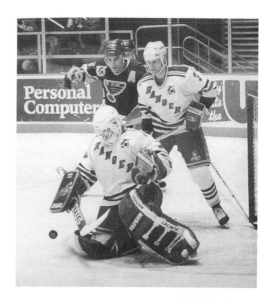

Mike Richter (foreground)

Trader Phil

On July 14, 1986, Phil Esposito, one of the greatest players in NHL history, became just the eighth man in six decades to assume the top hockey job with the New York Rangers. Traded to the Rangers in November of 1975, Esposito spent the last six seasons of his 18-year, Hall-of-Fame career skating in New York before retiring in 1981 to join the Rangers' broadcast team as a television color commentator.

Although lacking managerial and coaching experience when hired to be the Rangers' vice-president and general manager, the outgoing Esposito was a natural born salesman. Throughout his tenure, he pulled off so many trades and made so many other roster moves that he soon became known in the hockey world as "Trader Phil."

During his several weeks on the job, for instance, Esposito traded goalie Glen Hanlon and two draft picks to Detroit for Kelly Kisio, Lane Lambert, and Jim Levins. He then acquired Walt Poddubny from Toronto for Mike Allison, signed free agents Lucien DeBlois and Doug Soetaert—both former Rangers—from the Montreal Canadiens, and signed college free agents Mike Donnelly and Norm Maciver. Esposito's dealings even included a trade for a coach—a 1988 first round draft pick to Quebec for Michel Bergeron. Although Esposito would be general manager of the Rangers for just three years, during that relatively short span his club dressed 67 different players.

On the coaching front, Esposito initially retained Ted Sator even though he had been selected by his predecessor. However the stark difference in the two men's personalities and approach to the game—"Espo" being an emotional, extroverted former NHL star player and Sator a no-nonsense technocrat—made it clear to most observers that this setup would not last long. Sator's inevitable departure came just six weeks into the season, when Esposito removed him 19 games into the 1986-87 campaign with his revamped Rangers sitting in last place in the Patrick Division.

Esposito's choice to replace Sator was 38-year-old Tom Webster, a former star winger with the WHA New England Whalers who had gone on to become a highly successful junior and minor league coach. Unfortunately for Webster, however, shortly after joining the Rangers he developed a chronic inner ear problem that affected his balance and prevented him from traveling by air.

Mark Messier

Webster's medical condition forced him to withdraw as the Rangers' coach after only 16 games. With Webster sidelined, Esposito and assistants Wayne Cashman and Ed Giacomin coached the club through the remaining 45 games of 1986-87. The Rangers finished in fourth place, for the fifth consecutive season, with a 34-38-8 record, and were eliminated in the first round of the playoffs by the Flyers in six games.

"Espo" and "Le Petit Tigre"

With a few notable exceptions, the general demeanor of the 24 Ranger coaches between 1926 and 1987 was conservative, staid, and relatively colorless. Michel Bergeron, the 25th man to coach the club, exhibited none of these traits. Known by the nickname "Le Petit Tigre"—the "Little Ti-ger"—the 41-year-old Bergeron was snatched by Esposito in June of 1987 from the Quebec Nordiques, which the highly emotional and outspoken diminutive French-Canadian had coached with considerable success—and often controversy—for the previous seven years.

(As was the case with Fred Shero nine years earlier, the Rangers surrendered a first-round draft pick to the Nordiques in exchange for their releasing Bergeron from the rest of his coaching contract with Quebec.)

Esposito and Bergeron were alike in personality and approach. Temperamental, sometimes intemperate, demonstrative, passionate, impetuous, ardent, ambitious, egocentric, self-indulgent, affable, and sentimental—each of these adjectives could be applied equally to Esposito and Bergeron at one time or another. Not surprisingly, neither man was good at taking a back seat to the other,

James Patrick (left) outhustles Montreal's Guy Carbonneau to the puck

and over the next two years that would lead to plenty of fireworks. The New York media loved it, because if something controversial wasn't happening on the ice, they could be sure that Esposito and/or Bergeron would soon do something to help them sell papers.

Even though there were almost constant roster comings and goings in 1987-88 (20 of the 39 men who played for the Rangers that year had not appeared with the team the previous season), the club improved its record by six points to finish with 82. That year, however, the Patrick Division's six teams ended the season in a virtual dead heat with only seven points separating the first-place Capitals (88) from the last-place Islanders (81). Unfortunately for the Rangers, they ended up fifth and missed the playoffs for the first time since 1977.

During the 1988-89 season, Esposito made 55 separate transactions—trades, waiver claims, free agent signings, recalls, and reassignments. His most controversial move came on April 1, 1989, when he fired coach Michel Bergeron on the grounds, among other things, of insubordination. Esposito took over the bench that night but his charges lost the final two games of the regular season.

Despite the frequent player moves during the season, Bergeron kept the Rangers at or near first place for most of the 1988-89 campaign, only to falter in March when the club went 4-10-0. Although the club won only four of its final 16 games, it still finished in third place with 80 points and qualified for the playoffs. In their series against the Penguins, Esposito's Rangers continued their lassitude of the season's final month and were thoroughly outplayed by Pittsburgh, who beat them in four straight.

In the three years since Esposito had replaced Patrick, the club had gone through six coaches, compiled an overall regular season record of 106-108-22, and won just two playoff games. The club missed the playoffs, in 1988, for the first time in a decade. In six seasons under Craig Patrick, on the other hand, the Rangers had three coaches, were 183-174-58, won six of twelve playoff series, and

AP/Wide World Photos

Brian Leetch

reached the Wales Conference finals twice. While Espo's years in New York were doubtless more colorful—and almost certainly more expensive—than Patrick's, the bottom line comparison was far less favorable. Thus, on May 24, 1989, the Madison Square Garden bosses fired Esposito.

Mr. Smith Goes To New York

On July 17, 1989, the Rangers installed their ninth general manager in 63 years, 35-year-old Neil Smith. Although he was the first Ranger general manager who had never been an NHL player or coach, Smith had experience in the front offices of the New York Islanders and Detroit Red Wings.

A native of Toronto, Smith was an All-American defenseman at Western Michigan University and had been drafted by the Islanders in 1974. After two seasons playing in the Isles' minor league system, however, Smith retired in 1980 to become a scout and learn about hockey management.

A protege of former Islander head scout Jimmy Devellano, Smith followed his mentor to the Red Wings in 1982 and remained in the Detroit organization for seven years. Among Smith's major accomplishments with Detroit was winning two AHL Calder Cup titles as general manager of the Adirondack Red Wings, Detroit's top farm club, in 1986 and 1989. In addition to his duties with Adirondack, Smith also served Detroit as director of scouting and player procurement.

Within a month after coming to New York, Smith had revamped the Rangers' hockey department and brought in 55-year-old veteran NHL coach Roger Neilson. Known as "Captain Video" for his heavy use of videotape to scout, teach, and coach, Neilson arrived in New York with a reputation as a superb technical coach whose teams always played strong defense and were well disciplined on offense.

Although the Rangers finished the 1989-90 season with just 85 points on a record of 36-31-13, for the first time since the 1941-42 season they also won their Division. After beating the hated Islanders easily in five games in the first round of the 1990 playoffs, however, the Rangers fell unexpectedly to the Capitals in the Patrick Division finals, winning just one game. Despite their disappointing exit, however, the season was by no

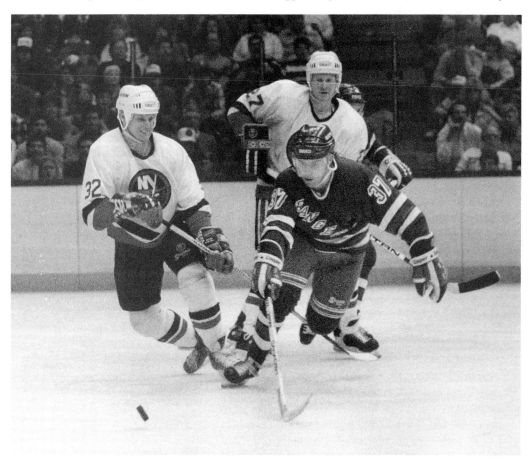

Norm Maciver

means a loss, as Smith had made two key late-season trades to bring the Broadway Blues a pair of proven scorers who would either directly or indirectly go on to pay big dividends in the seasons to come.

On January 20, 1990, Smith sent popular forwards Tony Granato and Tomas Sandstrom to Los Angeles for veteran center Bernie Nicholls, who had notched 150 points the previous season while playing on a line with Wayne Gretzky. Smith's second major deal took place on March 6 when he acquired veteran right wing Mike Gartner, one of the game's most consistently prolific all-time leading goal scorers, from the Minnesota North Stars for Ulf Dahlen and a fourth-round draft pick. Gartner produced 11 goals in the final 12 games of 1989-90 season and contributed 40 or more in each of his next three seasons in New York.

Although Smith made no major trades in 1990-91, two U.S. Olympians who had joined the Rangers after the 1988 Winter Games in Calgary emerged that season to become legitimate NHL stars—goalie Mike Richter and defenseman Brian Leetch. Richter, a 24-year-old native of the Philadelphia suburb of Flourtown, paced the Rangers between the pipes with a 21-13-7 record and was named a finalists for the NHL's Vezina Trophy.

With 88 points, 23-year-old Leetch earned an All-Star team berth and became just the third blueliner to lead the Rangers in scoring. Despite the excellent performances by these two players, the Rangers finished 36-31-13 and were upset in the playoffs by the Washington Capitals.

A "Messianic" Season

Between 1984 and 1990, the Edmonton Oilers won five Stanley Cups under the leadership of just two captains—centers Wayne Gretzky and Mark Messier. Gretzky, who wore the "C" on four of those five Cup-winning Oiler teams, was traded to the Los Angeles Kings in August of 1988, immediately gave that long suffering club credibility. Messier, who captained the 1989-90 Oilers to the Cup, left Edmonton on October 4, 1991, in a blockbuster trade that sent him to New York. He was dealt to the Rangers in exchange for Bernie Nicholls and two promising prospects, Steven Rice and Louis DeBrusk.

Messier made his Ranger debut at Montreal on October 5 by helping lead the Broadway Blues to a 2-1 victory over the Canadiens. Two nights later he made his debut in New York in a 2-1 win over the Boston Bruins while also wearing the "C" for the Rangers for the first time. Over the next few months, Messier's dynamic leadership combined with a Norris Trophy-winning season by Leetch had its intended effect on the Rangers. On January 23, the club pulled ahead of Washington into first place in the Patrick Division with a 3-1 victory in Edmonton.

The Rangers remained atop their Division for the rest of the season and improved by 20 points over the previous campaign to 105. With 107 points, Messier led the club in scoring, followed closely by Leetch with 102. For the first time in team history, the Rangers had five players with 30 or more goals. The team scored a record 321 while Richter and Vanbiesbrouck allowed just 245, the fewest to be surrendered by a Ranger team since 1972-73. Despite winning the President's Trophy for having the league's best record, this strong regular season did not guarantee postseason success. Although New York defeated the New Jersey Devils in the first round, they were stretched to seven games.

In their second-round series against the defending Stanley Cup champion Penguins, the Pens—who had finished 18 points behind the Rangers—defeated them in six games. In the final game, Penguins' fans taunted the crestfallen Rangers with the same chant that so many enemy crowds—and sometimes even the Rangers' own crowds—had inflicted on them for many years: "1-9-4-0."

Although the Rangers failed to bring the Stanley Cup to New York in 1992, many other honors did come their way. Messier captured the Hart Trophy as the NHL's most valuable player and also received the Lester B. Pearson Award. Brian Leetch brought the James Norris Trophy to

Joe Cirella (left) checks an unidentified Washington Capitals player in 1993

New York as the NHL's defenseman of the year. The *Sporting News* named Tony Amonte its top rookie and selected Neil Smith as the NHL executive of the year. On June 19, Smith became the first general manager in Rangers' history to also be named president of the club.

Back to the Future

Prior to the 1992-93 season, Smith gave coach Roger Neilson a new three-year contract in recognition of the club's excellent performance the previous year. However, less than three months later the Rangers were again underachieving, and on January 4, 1993, Roger Neilson was gone. (Longtime Neilson assistant Ron Smith, coach of New York's AHL Binghamton Rangers farm team, was brought in as interim coach for the remainder of the season.)

It certainly did not help Neilson or the Rangers that All-Star defenseman Brian Leetch was injured for much of the year, or that just a few games after he finally returned in March, he broke his ankle after slipping on a patch of ice. Richter and Vanbiesbrouck also had bad stretches in goal. Although Messier again led the team in scoring with 91 points, he too had his problems, including a painful late-season rib injury that hampered his effectiveness.

By the latter part of the 1992-93, the Ranger had lost their way. By season's end the team had dropped from first overall in 1991-92 to 19th in the 24-team league, and were last in the Patrick Division with 79 points. Within days of the season's conclusion, the rebuilding process began anew with the hiring of Mike Keenan, the former iron-handed coach of the Philadelphia Flyers and Chicago Blackhawks, to be the 28th man to guide the New York Rangers.

As with the others who held that position before him, beginning with the legendary Lester Patrick in 1926, Keenan's marching orders were simple: bring the Stanley Cup to long-suffering hockey fans in New York, where they have waited for more than half a century.

—Bruce C. Cooper

PHILADELPHIA FLYERS

Philadelphia, one of America's oldest and most important cities, is widely regarded as the historical "birthplace" of the United States. But, in spite of its political and cultural status, most of the major league professional sports teams that called Governor William Penn's "greene countrie towne" home over the first seven decades of the twentieth century usually found themselves close to the bottom of their leagues' standings at the end of each of their respective seasons.

There were some notable exceptions, such as Connie Mack's Philadelphia Athletics, an American League baseball team that racked up victories from 1910 to 1915 and again from 1929 to 1931; the National League Phillies' "Whiz Kids" of 1950; the postwar Philadelphia Eagles, who won NFL titles in 1948, 1949, and 1960; the NBA Warriors who became play-off champs in 1947 and 1956; and the Wilt Chamberlain-era NBA 76'ers of the late 1960s. But prior to 1970, the City of Brotherly Love was far more often a city of losers, not winners, when it came to major league sports.

As bad as its baseball, football, and basketball teams generally were, however, Philadelphia's first—and fortunately short-lived—major league hockey club proved to be even worse. At the close of the 1929-30 season, the woeful Pittsburgh Pirates of the National Hockey League (NHL) pulled up stakes after five seasons in the Steel City and moved 300 miles east to become the Philadelphia Quakers. Pennsylvania's largest city thereby became home to "major league" hockey for one depressing "Depression Era" season (1930-31) by icing a club that even more than 60 years later still held the NHL single season record for futility.

It should be noted that establishing such a standard was no mean feat for the 1930-31 Quakers, considering that the year before in Pittsburgh the club had "crashed" right along with the New York Stock Exchange to a dismal 5-36-3. In their lone season in Philadelphia, however, the Quakers managed to best that by winning just four (4-36-4) of its 44 games. The club folded altogether at season's end, and for another 36 years neither Pennsylvania city saw NHL hockey played within their confines again.

Curiously the Quakers were managed and coached by a veteran hockey man who had never worked at either job before, J. Cooper Smeaton. Smeaton was one of the league's original referees, and his one-year experiment behind the bench ended with the Quakers' demise; he returned to officiating the next year as the NHL's referee-in-chief. Among Smeaton's players in Philadelphia was a 19-year-old center named Syd Howe, who had been loaned to the Quakers by the Ottawa Senators. Many years later both Smeaton and Howe went on to be elected to the Hockey Hall of Fame after distinguished careers in the game—despite their season in Philadelphia.

In the years before and after the Quakers, a number of minor league professional teams (the Arrows, Rockets, and Ramblers) took to the ice of the city's only indoor hockey rink—"The Arena," located at 46th and Market Streets in West Philadelphia—but the NHL was not to be seen again in the city until 1967. It came back when the league doubled in size in 1967-68 from six to twelve teams. Within just a few years, both on the ice and at the box office, big league hockey proved to be a smashing success in the Delaware Valley.

After seven decades of big league sports mediocrity in Philadelphia, it took less than seven years for the new NHL Philadelphia Flyers to completely reverse the city's lackluster professional sports image. Hockey's success also proved to be contagious, with the Flyers serving as the catalyst that finally inspired each of the city's three other long suffering major league franchises to finally achieve excellence as well.

On the muggy Sunday afternoon of May 19, 1974, just six years and eight months after playing their first game in October of 1967, the "Broad Street Bullies" completed Philadelphia's sports metamorphosis with a home ice 1-0 shut-out of Bobby Orr, Phil Esposito, Ken Hodge and the rest of the powerhouse Boston Bruins. That stunning victory completed their play-off upset of the Bruins, four games to two, to make the Flyers the first "expansion" team to capture the Stanley Cup.

The "Orange and Black" continued its reign as one of the world's top performing sports franchises for almost a decade and a half. They repeated as Stanley Cup champions in 1975 and reached the finals four more times in 1976, 1980, 1985, and 1987, during the 13-year stretch from 1974 to 1987. In regular season play over that same period, the club finished in first place in its division nine times, in second place three times, and as low as third only twice.

The Flyers' most remarkable feat of all, however, was "the Streak" of 1979-80. After splitting the first two games of that campaign, the club went on to establish an unprecedented all-time major league professional sports standard by not losing again for almost three months as they fashioned their historic unbeaten "Streak" of 35 games (25-0-10).

The Flyers' years of success clearly seemed to inspire the three other major league tenants of Philadelphia's massive sports complex at the south end of Broad Street. In the ten years after 1974, when the Flyers brought the Stanley Cup to town for the first time, each of their neighbors awoke from their prolonged doldrums to also win a title. After literally decades of dead last place finishes, the almost century old Phillies captured their first World Series in 1980—and reached the fall classic again in 1983. The NFL Eagles dovetailed with the Phillies in 1980 by defeating their archenemies, the Dallas Cowboys, in the NFC Championship Game to win a trip to Super Bowl XV. In 1983, the NBA 76'ers—another record-setting loser just a few years before—dethroned the defending champion Los Angeles Lakers to win their first crown since 1967.

In addition to the great success the Flyers had as a team in those glory years, many individual honors were also bestowed upon its members both on and off the ice. In 1984, two-time Vezina (best goalie) and Conn Smythe (play-off MVP) trophy-winning netminder Bernie Parent became the first player ever elected to the Hockey Hall of Fame

TEAM INFORMATION AT A GLANCE

Founding date: June 5, 1967

Home ice: The Spectrum
Philadelphia, PA 19148
Phone: (215) 465-4500
FAX: (215) 389-9403

Seating capacity: 17,147

Team colors: Orange, black, and white
Team nickname: Flyers; "Broad Street Bullies"
Logo: The letter "P" drawn as if it is flying.

Franchise record	Won	Lost	Tie
(1967-93)	1,021	715	322

Stanley Cups (2): 1973-74, 1974-75

based on a career spent almost entirely with an expansion club. Parent was followed into the Hall in 1987 by three-time league MVP and all-time Flyer scoring champion (with 1,210 points) Bob Clarke. The club's all-time leading goal-scorer, Bill Barber (420), joined his two Stanley Cup teammates in the players' section of the Hall in 1990.

In addition to Parent, goalies Pelle Lindbergh (1984-85) and Ron Hextall (1986-87) also captured the Vezina Trophy as the league's top goalie. In 1976 high scoring winger Reggie Leach won the Conn Smythe Trophy as the Stanley Cup MVP despite his club's loss in the finals to the Montreal Canadiens, and Hextall did the same as a rookie goalie in 1987 when the Flyers lost to the Edmonton Oilers in seven games. Only two other NHL players—both goalies—have been honored as play-off MVP while playing for the losing Cup

finalist since the Smythe Trophy was first presented in 1965.

The Flyers' front office is also represented in the Hall by the club's majority owner, Ed Snider, who was elected as a "Builder" in 1988. He was followed four years later by the man who literally "built" the Flyers' greatest teams on the ice, Keith Allen. Allen, the Flyers' senior employee who was hired to be the club's first coach a year before the team played its first game, was the Flyers' general manager (GM) for 13 of its most successful seasons.

Three of the Flyers' first six head coaches—Fred Shero in 1973-74, Pat Quinn in 1979-80, and Mike Keenan in 1984-85—won the Jack Adams Award as NHL Coach of the Year. Shero, Allen, Snider, and Clarke (who retired as a player in 1984 to become just the fourth GM in Flyer history) have each also won the league's prestigious Lester

Hockey Hall of Fame and Museum

Bobby Clarke

Patrick Trophy for "outstanding service to hockey in the United States."

Through hard work on the ice—and astute management off of it—after winning the Stanley Cup for the first time in 1974, the Flyers were able to maintain their status as one of the premier teams in sports for almost 15 years. By the late 1980s, however, the club finally slipped off that pedestal as too many of its key players grew older and less effective all at once without being adequately replaced.

The bottom fell out quickly. In 1990—just three years after the Flyers had played the Edmonton Oilers even until the final 20 minutes of the seventh game in the 1987 Stanley Cup finals—the team failed to qualify for the post-season chase for the first time in 17 years. They missed again after each of the next two seasons as well. However, the Flyers' lowest point—at least emotionally—in

their first quarter-century of existence came on April 16, 1990. On that day the sports world witnessed something never thought possible in Philadelphia as GM Bob Clarke—the Flyers' heart and soul both on and off the ice for the previous 21 years—was fired.

Despite their late downturn, however, as the club completed its silver anniversary season in 1991-92 it could still boast the NHL's third best overall career winning percentage (.580), trailing only the Montreal Canadiens and Edmonton Oilers by a narrow margin. The weeks that followed the end of that 25th campaign also saw the club "serve notice" of its determination to return to its far more accustomed level of excellence as it began its second quarter-century.

In May of 1992, that process began as the Flyers' first superstar—Bob Clarke—was brought back into the fold as senior vice president and a part owner. It continued a month later as the Flyers added the game's next superstar—Eric Lindros—to lead the club on the ice well into the next century.

1965-67: NHL Hockey Comes To Philadelphia

When the NHL announced in 1965 that it was going to double in size from six teams to twelve beginning with the 1967-68 season, the city of Philadelphia looked like quite a long shot to get one of those half dozen new franchises. For one thing, no adequate playing arena was either in place or on the drawing board. At a minimum, the NHL had announced that it would require a 12,500-seat indoor facility be already available (or undergoing construction) for a franchise bid to even be accepted for consideration.

In 1965 the only existing building that had ever hosted pro hockey in Philadelphia was the old and by then considerably rundown "Arena" in West Philadelphia—a structure with barely 6,000 seats and virtually no parking. Although the NBA Philadelphia 76'ers played only a few blocks away from the Arena in the city's 1930s-vintage Civic

Center Convention Hall, that building had no permanent ice plant and could seat no more than 8,500. (Later the World Hockey Association [WHA] Philadelphia Blazers [1972-73] and the NAHL [1974-77] / AHL [1977-79] Philadelphia Firebirds used Convention Hall for hockey playing on a portable rink.)

However the lack of existing facilities did not discourage 35-year-old William R. Putnam, a former New York banker, ex-Navy demolition expert, and onetime University of Texas quarterback who had been raised in Shanghai, China. Putnam's introduction to the Philadelphia sports scene had come in 1964, when he handled the intricate financial arrangements for the $5.5 million purchase of the NFL Eagles by two Washington, D.C. businessmen—Jerry Wolman and Earl Foreman. Although Putnam had since moved to Los Angeles to work for sports and media mogul Jack Kent Cooke, he had studied the Philadelphia sports market closely and believed that hockey could be successful there.

Putnam returned to Philadelphia to discuss his idea with Wolman, Eagles vice president Edward M. Snider, and Jerry Schiff, a Washington, D.C. building contractor. They soon formed a group to explore making a bid for an NHL expansion franchise for the city. When Wolman agreed to build the necessary new arena with seating for approximately 15,000, the group began planning in earnest.

After a year of almost secret preparation, Putnam's group made a formal presentation before a meeting of the NHL Board of Governors in New York City on February 8, 1966, along with a dozen other expansion franchise applicants from a total of eight cities.

Although many hockey people and Philadelphia city officials had long known about the group's interest, the formal submission of the proposal came as an almost complete surprise to the city's sports fans. "We tried to keep it quiet," Putnam told the Philadelphia *Bulletin* later that day as he and his partners nervously awaited the NHL's decision. "We were just afraid we might foul it up otherwise."

The next day, Wednesday, February 9, the NHL announced that Philadelphia was one of the six winners in the expansion derby. Along with the other new entries to be located in Minneapolis-St. Paul, Pittsburgh, Oakland, St. Louis, and Los Angeles, Philadelphia would join the league's new "West" division and begin play in just 20 months. In the meantime, each new club would have to pay the league an entry fee of $2,000,000—a pittance by today's standards—and find a place to play that met NHL requirements.

From the Ground Up: Building the Spectrum

While three of the new cities had suitable existing buildings already available, the franchises in Philadelphia, Los Angeles, and Minnesota would have to build new arenas from scratch. A site in Philadelphia was quickly made available by the city—a municipally-owned, five-acre tract adjacent to the 100,000-seat JFK (formerly called Municipal) Stadium, then the longtime home of the Army-Navy Game, at the south end of Broad Street and just north of the sprawling U.S. Navy Yard.

On May 19, 1966—eight years to the day before the Flyers brought the Stanley Cup to Philadelphia—the city granted a 50-year lease for the land to Wolman. Just 12 days later on June 1— less than four months after the NHL awarded Philadelphia its franchise—ground was broken for the new arena to be called the Spectrum. While the new NHL team was to be the building's principal tenant, the NBA 76'ers quickly agreed to move to the new facility, and together these two clubs immediately guaranteed the new arena up to 100 dates a year. Ice shows, other indoor sporting events, circuses, concerts and other shows soon added another 150 or more dates annually to the building's calendar, eventually making it one of the busiest arenas in the country.

Three-and-a-half years after the Spectrum hosted its first event (an ice show) in September of 1967, construction of the city's long awaited

"He was the best in the world at what he did," Flyer coach Fred Shero once said of his Hall of Fame goalie Bernie Parent. For 13 seasons, Bernard Marcel Parent plied his goaltending art in the NHL with grace, skill, and beauty. During two of those seasons, 1973-74 and 1974-75, it could well be argued that Parent did so better than any player before or since, as he not only earned consecutive "Triple Crowns"—the Vezina Trophy, Smythe Trophy, and the Stanley Cup—but even appeared on the cover of *Time* magazine.

Parent's "numbers" for those two seasons still seem unbelievable. In regular season action he played 141 games, compiling a record of 91 wins, 27 losses, and 22 ties—a winning percentage of .729. He posted an even dozen shutouts in each of those two campaigns, in which he compiled goals-against averages of 1.89 and 2.03 respectively.

As spectacular as those numbers were, Parent was even better in play-off competition. In 32 Stanley Cup games, he recorded 22 wins—including six by shutout—against just ten losses with miserly goals-against averages of 2.02 in 1974 and 1.89 in 1975. To top it off, Parent did not allow a goal in either of his Cup-winning games, whitewashing the Boston Bruins 1-0 in 1974, and the Buffalo Sabres 2-0 in 1975.

For those two consecutive years, there was truly no better goaltender in the world than Bernie Parent, and he proved it with his pair of "Triple Crowns": the Vezina Trophy as the league's top regular season goalie, the Conn Smythe Trophy as the Most Valuable Player in the play-offs, and of course the most important of all, the Stanley Cup for himself and his teammates. "We all knew that any one of us could have been replaced except Bernie and the team could have still won," said Bob Clarke, who was then the team captain and in the midst of three Hart Trophy-winning seasons in four years. "Parent was absolutely indispensable to the team. Without him there would have been no Stanley Cups in Philadelphia."

Parent's first real taste of success as a goalie came a decade before his Stanley Cup seasons, when he and his original Philadelphia goaltending mate Doug Favell led another "Flyer" team to a national championship. That came in 1964-65 with the OHA Niagara Falls Flyers, who won the Memorial Cup as the champions of Canadian junior hockey. He went to the NHL the following year with the Boston Bruins, where in two seasons his record was 14-31-5 for the club that was about to get, but still didn't have, Bobby Orr, Phil Esposito, and Gerry Cheevers. In Parent's days in Boston, the Bruins were still a last place team.

Both Parent and Favell (then in the Boston system in Oklahoma City) were selected by the Flyers in the 1967 expansion draft. They teamed together in Philadelphia until Parent was traded to Toronto in a three-way deal with Boston on January 31, 1971. The trade brought the Flyers Rick MacLeish, who would score the Flyers' first Cup-winning goal against the Bruins three years later.

After a year and a half with Toronto and another season with the WHA Philadelphia Blazers (to whom he jumped in 1972-73), Parent came back to the Flyers in 1973. Ironically, the Flyers had to give up Favell to Toronto to regain Parent's NHL rights, and the two faced each other at the Spectrum on opening night of

new 65,000-seat multipurpose outdoor sports facility, Veterans Stadium, was completed. Located directly across Pattison Avenue from the Spectrum, the "Vet" opened its gates in April of 1971, as the Phillies hosted the Montreal Expos, the same club that had helped them close their old park, Connie Mack Stadium, in North Philadelphia the previous September.

The Phillies were soon followed by the NFL Eagles, who had played for many years at the University of Pennsylvania's ivy-covered, brick-walled Franklin Field in West Philadelphia. With that final move completed, the three-year transfer of all four of the city's major league franchises to the massive new South Philadelphia sports complex.

the 1973-74 season. Parent prevented the Leafs from scoring, and the Flyers won the game 2-0. This was only the first of 30 shutouts he would post over the next two seasons and play-off years.

After leading the Flyers to a third trip to the Stanley Cup finals in 1976 before falling to the Montreal Canadiens, Parent was sidelined for most of the 1976-77 season because of a serious neck problem that had required off-season surgery. He came back strong, however, in 1977-78 with a 35-13-12 (2.71 GAA) record in 61 games and a 29-6-3 (2.22 GAA) mark in 49 starts in 1977-78. As he entered the 1978-79 season, Parent was 33 years old and looked as if he could play effectively into his 40s. But tragically that would soon all come to an end.

Parent and the Flyers were leading the New York Rangers 1-0 early in the first period of a Saturday afternoon contest at the Spectrum on February 17, 1979, when New York's Don Maloney and Flyer defenseman Jimmy Watson fell in front of the Flyer net. The tip of Watson's stick hit Parent in the right eye, and the goaltender skated quickly to the bench in pain just 6:11 into the game. As it turned out, Parent's playing career had just ended.

Bernie Parent, who played a total of 486 regular season games for the Flyers between 1967-71 and 1973-79, not surprisingly still holds all the team's goaltending records. He had an even 50 shutouts and a goals-against average of 2.42 while winning 232 games, losing 141, and tying 103. His record in Stanley Cup action was 35-28 in 63 games with six shutouts and a 2.20 GAA.

While Parent could no longer play goal for the Flyers, he could help to teach his successors in the Flyer nets as the club's goaltending instructor. It should come as no surprise that three of his students—Pete Peeters, Pelle Lindbergh, and Ron Hextall—went on to win Vezina Trophies on their own.

In 1984, Parent's accomplishments were formally recognized by the hockey world when he became the first expansion team player elected to the Hockey Hall of Fame. The reason was simple. "He was the best in the world at what he did."

Photo: *Hockey Hall of Fame and Museum*

From the Ice Up: Building a New Franchise

As the Spectrum began to rise at the corner of Broad Street and Pattison Avenue, Philadelphia's new hockey club was being built from the ice up at the as yet unnamed team's temporary city offices at 15th and Locust Streets. Soon, a public contest was held to pick the team's moniker, and "the Flyers" emerged as the people's choice.

The club also needed an experienced hockey staff and started building that with veteran hockey executive Norman "Bud" Poile, who had been GM/coach of the Edmonton Flyers of the minor pro Western Hockey League. Poile was recruited as the new NHL club's first GM, and he quickly hired his old friend and WHL rival, longtime Seattle Totems GM/Coach Keith Allen, to be the Flyers' first coach.

The league's six new franchises acquired the bulk of their first skaters from the rosters of the "original six" NHL clubs in an expansion draft held at the Queen Elizabeth Hotel in Montreal on June 6, 1967. However, to develop its future players and provide the roster with some needed depth, the Flyers also bought an established American Hockey League franchise, the Quebec Aces. A number of the AHL players whose rights were acquired with the Aces, such as Andre Lacroix and Simon Nolet, became some of the Flyers' first stars.

Poile and Allen spent much of the 1966-67 season scouting the NHL, AHL, CHL, WHL, and IHL evaluating the players expected to be made available in the draft or who could be signed as free agents. As there was very little player turnover in the NHL in pre-expansion days, many of the "minor leaguers" who would be available were actually very skilled veterans with many years of pro experience.

At the expansion draft, each club first selected two goalies followed by 18 defensemen and forwards. While most clubs went for at least one veteran NHL netminder by taking the likes of Terry Sawchuk (Los Angeles), Glenn Hall (St. Louis), Charlie Hodge (Oakland) and Cesare Maniago (Minnesota), the Flyers decided on another approach by selecting a pair of young, inexperienced goalies whom they expected to be stars in the future—Bernie Parent and Doug Favell. It proved to be a very smart move.

Both Parent and Favell were claimed from the Boston Bruins organization, although it would not be the first time the pair had been "Flyer" teammates. (Three years earlier, they had back-stopped the Niagara Falls Flyers of the Ontario Hockey Association to a Memorial Cup title as the playoff champions of Canadian major junior hockey.)

The Philadelphia Flyers also took five skaters from the Bruins, including defenseman Joe Watson and right wing Gary Dornhoefer, who

were also both just starting their careers. Seven years later, Parent, Watson, and Dornhoefer were all key members of the Flyer club that defeated Boston in the 1974 Stanley Cup finals.

1967-68: An Eventful First Year

The Flyers' first season proved to be an eventful one on and off the ice. After opening on the road with losses in Oakland and Los Angeles before winning for the first time in St. Louis, the Flyers returned to Philadelphia for their home ice debut on October 19, 1967. At the very moment that the new team was shutting out the Pittsburgh Penguins 1-0 on the Spectrum ice that night, the original management team that had brought the franchise to Philadelphia was breaking up.

Two months earlier, Ed Snider and local businessman Joe Scott had bought out the interests of Wolman, Schiff, and several other small stockholders in the team, making Snider the majority owner. On May 1, 1968, the financially troubled Wolman's final ties with the team were severed when he lost control of the Spectrum, which was taken over by court-appointed trustees under Federal Bankruptcy Law. (In January of 1972, the Court approved a plan to transfer ownership of the building to Snider and his brother-in-law, Earl Foreman, when they arranged to satisfy all major claims against the building.)

The Flyers' most unusual challenge of their inaugural season, however, came not from anything that happened on the ice, but from far above it. On March 1, 1968, the Flyers were literally "blown away" from Philadelphia for the final month of the season by a violent wind storm that ripped away several sections up to 20 x 30 feet each from the northwest corner of the Spectrum roof, forcing the city to close the building for a month while the roof structure was redesigned and permanent repairs were made.

With the Spectrum indefinitely unavailable, the Flyers played their final seven regular-season home games on the "borrowed" ice at Madison Square Garden in New York, at locations in Boston, and at Maple Leaf Gardens in Toronto before setting up shop at Le Colisee in Quebec City, then home of their AHL Quebec Aces farm club and now home ice to the NHL Quebec Nordiques.

Quebec City remained the Flyers' "home away from home" for five more games, which saw them earn three shutouts—2-0 over the Minnesota North Stars, 2-0 over the St. Louis Blues, and a classic exhibition of goaltending in which Hall of Famers Bernie Parent and the late Terry Sawchuk of the Los Angeles Kings each whitewashed the other team for the Flyers' first career 0-0 tie.

Despite the difficulties of playing away from Philadelphia for a month, the Flyers fashioned a 3-2-2 record in their seven "road" home games and that was good enough to make them the first regular season champion of the NHL's new West division. Philadelphia's first NHL hockey season since 1930-31 officially came to an end in mid-April when the St. Louis Blues knocked Philadelphia out of the Stanley Cup play-offs in a thrilling first-round series that ran the full seven games—two of which were decided in double overtime.

1969-70: The Philadelphia "Tiers" and Front Office Shakeups

The 1969-70 season, the Flyers' third, was one of the most unusual—and heartbreaking—in the team's history. Over the summer, coach Keith Allen had moved up to the front office as assistant GM and was replaced behind the bench by Quebec Aces' mentor Vic Stasiuk, a hard-nosed former winger who had played 14 years in the NHL with Chicago, Detroit, and Boston from 1949 to 1963.

The next big change came just a few months later when GM Bud Poile was relieved of his duties midway through the season in a dispute with ownership over his authority to run the club. Poile was replaced by Allen, who during his 13-plus year tenure in the GM's chair would deservedly earn the reputation as one of the best hockey executives in the business, especially when it came

Hockey Hall of Fame and Museum

Bill Barber

to making trades. Allen's unmatched skill in that important area of the game earned him the grudging but admiring nickname among his peers of "Keith the Thief"—as well as his eventual election to the Hockey Hall of Fame in 1992.

On March 22, 1970, the Flyers beat the Oakland Seals at the Spectrum 3-2 for just their 17th victory of the season in 70 starts, with six games remaining in their then 76-game regular season schedule. While the Flyers had also lost 29 games to that point, remarkably they had tied two dozen more earning themselves the nickname of the Philadelphia "Tiers." (Those 24 ties are still a single-season NHL record.)

To clinch their third play-off berth in three years in the league, the Flyers would need but one

In the century-plus history of professional sports in Philadelphia, few coaches or managers (with the possible exception of Connie Mack) had a greater influence on the success of their team than did Fred Shero during his seven seasons behind the Flyers' bench from 1971 to 1978.

Only a handful of coaches in the history of any professional sport won as many overall play-off championships in their careers as "The Fog"—seven in the 23 years he coached professional hockey teams. Even more amazing, however, was that he won those seven play-off titles in no fewer than five different leagues: the Quebec Professional League (Shawinigan, Quebec); the International Hockey League (St. Paul, MN); the Central Hockey League (Omaha, NE); the American Hockey League (Buffalo, NY); and of course the National Hockey League with the Flyers in 1974 and 1975.

In the four seasons the Flyers existed before Shero became their third head coach in 1971, the club had compiled a modest record of 96-135-73 for a winning percentage of .436, and in the play-offs had won just three of 15 games (.200). Over the next seven seasons, however, Shero's Flyers were 308-151-95 (.642), while in Stanley Cup play over the same period they were 48-35 with three trips to the finals and a pair of titles. The often enigmatic Shero was behind the Flyers' bench for 637 regular season and play-off games in his seven years as their coach, more than any of the other seven men who held that position through the club's first 25 seasons.

Shero came to the Flyers after a long minor league coaching career spent mostly in the New York Rangers' organization, where he had also seen his only NHL playing time as a defenseman (1947-50). Soon after he arrived, Shero was given the nickname "Freddie the Fog" by original Flyer winger Gary Dornhoefer because he so often seemed completely oblivious to what was going on around him. "Sometimes I see him and think he doesn't know what day it is," Scotty Bowman, then coach of the Montreal Canadiens, concurred. "Other times I'm sure he is a genius who has us all fooled."

Bowman was right on both counts. During his career, Shero was probably the most advanced thinker in the game, often leaving people baffled by his theories and methods because he was so far ahead of his time. Shero also proved to be a master motivator—even though he almost never talked to his players one-on-one but instead left little notes in their lockers or wrote his aphorisms—such as "Win together now and we walk together forever"—on the locker room blackboard.

There is no doubt that Shero's players had great love and respect for their coach, but he never wanted them to really get to know him. After playing on the team for a couple of years, defenseman Larry Goodenough was asked what he was like. "I couldn't really tell you," he replied matter-of-factly. "I've never actually met the man."

Shero left Philadelphia following the 1977-78 season to become GM/coach of the only other organization he had served for a longer period in his career than the Flyers: the New York Rangers, with whom he had spent so many years both as a player and a minor league coach. Not surprisingly, in his first season back in New York (1978-79), Shero led New York to the Stanley Cup finals. Less than two years later, however, Shero was fired just 21 games into his third season with the team—ironically after a home-ice loss to the Flyers—and would never coach another game in the NHL.

In the spring of 1990, Fred Shero was elected to the Flyers' Hall of Fame and also officially rejoined the organization as a special consultant. Unfortunately, Shero's return ended much too soon: on November 24, 1990, he lost a long battle with cancer and passed away at the age of 65.

more point out of a possible 12—just one more of those all-too-frequent ties—in the six games remaining. However over the next five the Flyers lost four times by one goal and dropped the other by a 4-1 score, which meant that making the play-offs came down to the 76th and final game of the season, a Spectrum matinee with the Minnesota North Stars, on Saturday, April 4, 1970.

With the Flyers, North Stars, and Seals all tied for the final two play-off spots with 58 points, a win would give the Flyers third place and a tie fourth. A loss, however, would drop them to fifth and out of the play-off picture because Oakland had more wins.

Future Hall of Famers Bernie Parent and Gump Worsley were the goaltenders that afternoon, and the sell-out crowd of 14,606 saw these two great netminders stop everything that came their way through the first two periods. A little over a third of the way into the Flyers' final period of the season, however, Stars defenseman Barry Gibbs lofted what appeared to be a harmless wrist shot into the Flyers' end from the center ice red line. However Parent lost sight of the puck in a shaft of sunlight shining through a portal from a window in the concourse, and incredibly the puck sailed into the net for a Minnesota goal.

It was just the third goal of the season for Gibbs, but it proved to be enough to end the season for the Flyers as Worsley did not allow a Flyer goal and the North Stars won the game 1-0. That goal still stands as the cruelest ever scored against the Flyers on home ice, as it ended their 1969-70 season without a visit to the play-offs. The team that had set the NHL record for ties in a season couldn't get just one more to beat out Oakland for the final play-off berth.

At the season's end, another of the Flyers' original founding group left the organization: team president Bill Putnam sold his 25 percent interest in June, 1970, to local sportsman F. Eugene Dixon, Jr. (Putnam reappeared in the NHL two years later as a member of the founding group of the Atlanta Flames when that team joined the league with the expansion of 1972.) Also departing over the summer was coach Vic Stasiuk, whom Allen replaced with a longtime minor league coach from the New York Rangers' organization, Fred Shero.

Like Allen and Stasiuk before him, Shero arrived in Philadelphia without ever having coached a game in the NHL. By the time he left town seven years later to return to the Rangers as their GM/Coach, however, the enigmatic Shero had led the Flyers to glory unsurpassed in Philadelphia by any other pro sports team in the city's history.

Keith Allen Builds a Champion

By the midway point of the 1970-71 season, it was clear that the Flyers would have to make some major personnel moves if they were ever to become a true Stanley Cup contender. While drafting Bob Clarke in 1969 had brought them the one young player whose leadership both on and off the ice would prove to be one of the essential ingredients in the team becoming a champion, the supporting cast was not yet in place.

In 1972, three of the key players of the Flyers' championship clubs were added in just a single draft: Bill Barber, Tom Bladon, and Jim Watson. But the Flyers would almost certainly have not won their two Stanley Cups in 1974 and 1975 without three blockbuster trades Allen pulled off in a period of just two-and-a-half seasons.

The first of these came on January 31, 1971, when Parent was moved to the Toronto Maple Leafs in a complicated three-way deal with the Leafs and Boston Bruins that also sent Toronto's Mike Walton to the Bruins and brought the Flyers veteran Leaf goalie Bruce Gamble, Boston minor league forward Danny Schock, and 21-year-old Boston center Rick MacLeish.

"It took a lot of soul searching throughout our entire organization to make this trade," Allen said at the time. "But in order for us to make a marked advance we had to deal a goaltender. MacLeish was the key for us and has the ability to be an outstanding hockey player. He is the kind of young player we must have to build a Stanley Cup contender, and the only way we could get him was to move one of our goalies."

"I feel both teams profited," said a shaken Parent as he left for Toronto, where he would play with his boyhood idol, Jacques Plante. "I don't blame the Flyers for making the trade, however. I know that the Flyers had to make the deal to improve themselves for the future. I just wish I could have been a part of it."

Of course, as it turned out, Parent would be part of it. After a year and a half in Toronto and another stint in the WHA with the Philadelphia Blazers, Parent came back to the Flyers in the summer of 1973 in the third of Allen's key deals. The following May, Parent shut-out the Bruins at the Spectrum, 1-0, as MacLeish—the key player Boston had sent the Flyers in January, 1971—scored the lone goal in the victory which brought the Stanley Cup to Philadelphia for the first time.

Allen made his biggest trade of all on January 28, 1972—just three days short of a year after the Parent-MacLeish deal—when he sent almost a quarter of his team's NHL roster to the Los Angeles Kings in a monumental eight-player swap. The Kings got veteran forwards Bill Lesuk and Jimmy Johnson, the highly touted but disappointing Serge Bernier (who had been the Flyers' first ever amateur draft pick in 1967), and veteran defenseman Larry Brown.

In return Allen acquired four players, two of which—wingers Ross Lonsberry and Bill Flett—would be key members of the 1974 Stanley Cup team. Forward Ed Joyal and defenseman Jean Potvin (traded a year later to the New York Islanders for center Terry Crisp) completed the deal.

"Flett gave us some big scoring when we needed it and Lonsberry was a regular with us for six years," Allen said many years later. "Although Joyal left for the WHA the next year and was not a factor, Potvin brought us Crisp in a trade late in the 1972-73 season and he proved to be the checking center we needed to be a winner. Without this, the 1971 Parent-MacLeish, and 1973 Favell-Parent deals, we probably would have never won the Cup."

On May 15, 1973, Allen made his most important trade of all as he dealt the Flyers' first round pick in the 1973 Amateur Draft—and a

"player to be named later"—to the Toronto Maple Leafs for that club's second round pick in the same draft and the NHL rights to Parent, whom he had traded away to them two-and-a-half years earlier. In 1972, Parent had jumped from the Leafs to the new WHA and had played the 1972-73 season just a few blocks away from the Spectrum at the Civic Center with the rival league's Blazers.

However, Parent left the WHA club during the play-offs in a contract dispute and shortly thereafter the team was sold and moved to Vancouver. The new owner made it clear, however, that Parent was not part of the deal and was free to return to the NHL.

And Parent wanted to return to the NHL—but not with Toronto. That being the case, the Leafs traded Parent's NHL rights back to the Flyers, and five weeks later, on June 21, the then-27-year-old netminder signed with the team. The final step in the deal was for the Flyers and Leafs to agree on the identity of the "player to be named later." It turned out to be the Flyers' other original goalie and Parent's longtime junior and NHL teammate, Doug Favell.

Two Milestone Goals

While the Flyers' transition to a contender was in effect made by those three trades, it was embodied in two goals scored exactly one year and eight days apart. The first was the cruelest ever scored against the Flyers—home or away. The second was such a milestone in the team's history that it is memorialized today in a larger-than-life bronze statue outside the Spectrum.

As had been the case two years earlier when the Flyers missed the play-offs by losing to Minnesota, 1-0, on the final day of the season, the team entered the final game of the 1971-72 season needing a victory for third place or a tie for fourth. A loss, however, would again drop them out of the final play-off berth, but this time that pivotal final game was to be played on the road at the "Aud" in Buffalo on April 2, 1972.

With the game tied 2-2 as the final seconds

ticked off the clock, goalie Doug Favell kept the Flyers alive by making two sparkling saves in the final two minutes. With the clock down to single digits, however, Sabres left wing Gerry Meehan—a former Flyer who later became the Sabres' GM—beat Favell on a desperation shot from the top of the left circle.

As the goal light went on, the clock read "00:04". Just four seconds from the making the play-offs, the Flyers' season was suddenly over. "I felt the same way about that goal and this loss as I did when my mother and father died," said Shero, who just two years earlier had led the AHL Buffalo Bisons to a Calder Cup championship in the same building.

Another goal scored 373 days later, however, proved to be as sweet to Shero and his team as the one in Buffalo was bitter. It came at the Spectrum on April 10, 1973, in game five of the Flyers' opening round play-off series against the Minnesota North Stars, who were then tied at two games apiece.

Although the 1972-73 season was the Flyers' sixth in the NHL, up until that point the club had never even held a lead in a play-off series—let alone won one. In their first two seasons, they lost to St. Louis in seven games in 1968 and in four straight in 1969. In their only other trip to the play-offs prior to 1973, the Flyers were swept in four straight games in 1971 by the Chicago Blackhawks, leaving them with a career play-off mark of 3-12.

After 60 minutes of play in game five at Philadelphia, the '73 series was still tied at a pair—and so was the game, 3-3—sending the Flyers into overtime for the first time since their monumental 2-1 win in St. Louis in double-overtime five years earlier, a game which still ranks as the longest in Flyer history.

The fifth game against Minnesota was the first ever overtime match played at the Spectrum, but this time it took just 8:35 for Gary Dornhoefer to win it with his first goal in 14 career play-off games with the team. As Dornhoefer sailed down the left boards on his off wing, it didn't look as if he had an authentic scoring chance, but he eluded

Stars defenseman Barry Gibbs at the blueline, cut for the net, and got off a backhand shot to beat a sprawling Cesare Maniago just as Stars defenseman Tom Reid knocked him to the ice.

The Flyers won the next game at Minnesota 4-1 to capture their first ever play-off series victory. Although they lost in the semifinal round to eventual Cup champion Montreal in five games, the Flyers gave notice that they would soon be making a serious run for the Cup by winning the opening game of the series at the Forum in overtime and going into overtime again in the second.

"I've been through it all with [this] club so far," Dornhoefer said after scoring his overtime goal against the Stars. "We've lost in seven games, lost in four straight, and missed the play-offs with four seconds to go in the season. But I think we've turned the corner and I want to be here when this team wins the Stanley Cup." One year later they did—and he was.

1974: "The Flyers Win the Stanley Cup!"

Two years after missing the play-offs in 1972 with 66 points and a fifth place divisional finish, the Flyers exploded in 1973-74 to a record of 50-16-12 for 112 points—exactly double their point total of just two seasons earlier. After sweeping aside the Atlanta Flames in four straight games in the opening round, the Flyers then met the New York Rangers in the semifinals.

Although New York had finished third in the Eastern division with 94 points (19 fewer than the first place Bruins' 113) and had not won a Cup since 1940, Fred Shero nonetheless believed going in that the Ranger series would be the toughest test his team would have to pass on its way to a Cup championship. He was right. After six bitterly fought, grinding games of the best-of-seven series, each team had won all three of its home games to set up a seventh and deciding meeting in Philadelphia.

"The Spectrum Ice is two hundred by eighty-five feet," said Ranger GM/Coach Emil Francis.

"It has boards and glass. There's no reason why we can't win there." But some of Francis' troops were not so sure. "There seems to be more contact and less room for skating there," said Ranger star Rod Gilbert. "We are going to have to be physical to win."

It was the Flyers, however, who won the final game, 4-3, in a close and fiercely contested Sunday afternoon of hockey in which the newly dubbed "Broad Street Bullies" beat the New Yorkers along the boards, in the clinches, and most importantly of all, on the scoreboard. "You feel like the world has ended," said Francis, Shero's longtime friend and mentor, whose Rangers were now 0-4 in Stanley Cup seventh games. "It's the toughest feeling in the world."

While the Flyers had won the series and earned a trip to the finals, they also had suffered a terrible loss as one of their stalwarts on defense over the previous four seasons, 34-year-old veteran blueliner Barry Ashbee, had been struck down in overtime of the fourth game when a rising shot by the Rangers' Dale Rolfe caught him in the eye. Although Ashbee regained most of his sight, the injury ended his playing career.

Ashbee remained with the team as an assistant coach, joining Shero's other assistant, Mike Nykoluk. Less than three years later, however, tragedy struck Ashbee again when he discovered unexplained bruises on his arms just before the start of the 1977 play-offs. Ashbee was hospitalized and within a few days was diagnosed with a virulent form of leukemia. Less than one month later, on May 12, 1977, he died at just 37 years of age. The following season Ashbee's jersey number—"4"—became the first ever to be retired by the club. It was later joined in the Spectrum rafters by Bernie Parent's "1" in 1979, Bob Clarke's "16" in 1984, and Bill Barber's "7" in 1990.

With the Rangers behind them, the Flyers were in the Stanley Cup finals for the first time in their seven NHL seasons. Their opponents, however, were Bobby Orr and the Boston Bruins—winners of the Cup in 1970 and 1972 and the only team to finish with more points than the Flyers in 1973-74. With 113 points—one more than the Fly-

ers' 112—the Bruins had home ice in the finals which presented Philadelphia with a major psychological obstacle.

To win the Cup, the Flyers had to win at least one game at Boston Garden—a building where they had not won since their first ever visit some six and a half years earlier. Philadelphia's record in Boston since then was 0-17-2, and their overall career mark versus the Bruins as they entered the finals was an unimpressive 4-30-4.

The Flyers almost got the win they needed in game one in Boston when Bill Flett hit the post in the final minutes of the third period with the score tied 2-2, but a minute later Orr won it for the Bruins with just 22 seconds left before sudden death. The second game two nights later was equally tense with the Bruins holding a 2-1 lead as the final minute ticked off the Garden clock, but this time low-scoring Flyer defenseman Andre Dupont tied it with just 52 seconds left.

After 12 minutes of sudden death overtime play, the Flyers beat the Bruins, winning against them on the road for just the second time in 21 tries. The Flyers still had only three career victories against the Bruins at the Spectrum; to win the Cup they would have to beat the them in Philadelphia as many times in two weeks as they had in the previous seven seasons.

The spectacular goaltending of Parent, however, gave the Flyers two of those three victories in the next two games as they won with relative ease, 4-1 and 4-2. The Bruins then took a fight-filled game five 5-1 in Boston to send the series back to Philadelphia for the potential clincher to be played at the Spectrum on Sunday afternoon, May 19.

As usual, the Bruins came out flying, outshooting the Flyers 14-3 in the game's first 14 minutes. But Parent let nothing past him. Then with a little over five minutes left in the first period and the Flyers on a four-on-three power play advantage with Philadelphia's Bob Clarke and Boston's Terry O'Reilly and Bobby Orr all in the penalty box, Rick MacLeish won a face-off from Greg Sheppard to Gilbert's left and fed the puck to Dupont stationed at the blueline.

As MacLeish cut for the net, Dupont lofted a shot toward Gilbert, which deflected off the toe of Boston defenseman Carol Vadnais's skate, caught the heel of MacLeish's stick, and flew into the Bruin net for a goal. At that moment few expected that this would also be the only goal scored that day.

Parent earned both a 1-0 Cup-clinching shutout and the Conn Smythe Trophy as the 1974 playoff MVP. The next day the millions of fans who could not get into the Spectrum for the game were in the streets of Philadelphia as the Flyers carried the Stanley Cup down Broad Street for what has been known ever since as "The Parade."

"The Parade" exceeded every other celebration in the city's history. It started at the Spectrum at midmorning and took almost three hours to move the three-and-a-half miles up Broad Street and out Market Street to Independence Mall. Kate Smith, the Flyers' special good luck charm, started the ceremonies off as she had the game 24 hours earlier by singing "God Bless America"—six times. There were speeches by the mayor, the coach, the players, and others but nobody heard the words. It didn't matter. It was a "happening" experienced by an estimated two million people.

1975: Stanley Cup II

The Flyers' first defense of their Stanley Cup title in the spring of 1975 almost ended before it started at the hands of a team that two years earlier had lost 60 games in a 78-game season—the New York Islanders. But by their third season, the Isles improved their record dramatically to 33-25-22 and made the play-offs for the first time with 88 points to the Flyers' 113.

While the Flyers had sailed past Toronto in four straight games in the quarterfinals, the Islanders took the hardest possible route to advancement by downing the Pittsburgh Penguins in seven games—after losing the first three games of the series—to set up what should have been a routine semifinal between the Flyers and the upstart Islanders.

As they had in the previous series, New York lost the first three games but then won the next three to send the series back to Philadelphia for a seventh—and suddenly frightening—final game. If the Flyers lost again, the Isles would be in the Stanley Cup finals in just their third season—and would have gotten there at the expense of the defending Cup champions. But the Flyers won convincingly 4-1 on a hat trick by Rick MacLeish.

For the first time in NHL history, two post-1967 teams met in the finals as the Flyers were opposed by the Buffalo Sabres. Parent and the Flyers won the first two games easily 4-1 and 2-1 but game three in Buffalo was one of the most memorable—and obscure—play-off contests in NHL history. While the Flyers lost the game 5-4 on Rene Robert's goal 18:29 into the first overtime period, the biggest obstacle both teams—and especially the goalies—had to overcome was a thick fog that hung over the ice for much of the game. The ancient "Aud" is not air conditioned and the sell-out crowd of 15,863 plus a 90-degree spring heat wave combined to turn the ice surface into a fog generator.

Ironically, seven of the game's nine goals were scored during the first two periods when goalies Bernie Parent, Gerry Desjardins, and Roger Crozier (who had replaced Desjardins after the first period) could actually see the shots coming at them, and the Flyers held a 4-3 lead after 40 minutes. The game was halted 11 times during its final half because of the fog, and it took over four hours from the opening face-off to Robert's overtime winner to complete the contest.

The Flyers entered game six holding a three-games-to-two lead. While neither team scored in the first two periods, just 11 seconds into the third, "bull-in-a-china shop" Flyer winger Bob "The Hound" Kelly sneaked out from behind the Buffalo net to beat Crozier for what would prove to be the Cup-winning goal. Checking center Bill Clement added a late insurance goal set up by Orest Kindrachuk to give each player his first and only point of the play-offs.

At the other end of the ice, Parent turned aside all six Buffalo third period shots to win his second championship game in two years by a shut-out, which gave him a brilliant 1.88 average in 15 post-season games in 1975 and earned him his second consecutive Conn Smythe Trophy.

The "Post-Cup" Years

While the Flyers did not win a third consecutive Stanley Cup in 1976, they did do something that in many ways was far more significant and memorable. On January 11, 1976, the Flyers took on what many thought was the best hockey team in the world—the Central Soviet Red Army (CSKA) club from Moscow—and beat them at the Spectrum 4-1 in the eighth and final game of a highly charged exhibition swing by the two top Soviet teams (CSKA and Soviet Wings) against the eight best clubs in the NHL.

The Flyers not only soundly defeated the Soviet Union's best before a worldwide television audience of millions, they also forced the Red Army to "retreat" from the battlefield. After a hard but clean check by Ed Van Impe on Valarie Kharlamov midway through the first period, CSKA coach Konstantin Loktev sent his club to the dressing room complaining that the Flyers were "too rough." When they refused to continue the game, Loktev was told pointedly: "No play, no pay." *That* the Red Army understood, and the team returned after a 16-minute delay. "When we won the Stanley Cup in 1974 I told the team we would walk together forever," Fred Shero said afterwards. "Today I told them that we won and are now standing at the top of the mountain."

The Flyers finished the 1975-76 season with 118 points, the most in their history, on a record of 51-13-16. They entered the play-offs as the two time defending Stanley Cup champions looking to bring the Cup back to Philadelphia for a third straight season. But to do so they would have to defeat three of the NHL's original six: Toronto, Boston, and Montreal.

The feisty Leafs gave the defending champion Flyers a scare as they took them to seven games in a high scoring, fight-filled series before

falling. The Flyers then lost the opening game of the Boston series but won the next four to earn their third consecutive trip to the finals.

While the clinching game with Boston to give the Flyers their ninth consecutive play-off series was an easy 6-3 win, the victory proved to be secondary in importance as right wing Reggie Leach accomplished something that no other Flyer has ever done before or since: score five goals in one game.

The goals were Leach's 72nd through 76th of the season and 11th through 15th of the play-offs, which he finished with another still-standing NHL record of 19 goals in a play-off year. When added to his 61 regular season tallies it gave Leach a total of 80 goals in 1976-77. Leach's five goals in a single play-off game matched NHL play-off performances that had been accomplished by only two other men in modern Stanley Cup history.

Montreal's Maurice Richard did it first 32 years earlier in a 5-1 Canadien victory over Toronto on March 23, 1944; exactly two weeks earlier, Toronto's Darryl Sittler netted five goals in an 8-5 Maple Leaf victory over the Flyers in game six of the quarterfinals. (Mario Lemieux later matched the feat with five goals against the Flyers on April 29, 1989, in a 10-7 Penguin victory at Pittsburgh.)

While the Flyers eventually lost the Cup to the Montreal Canadiens in the finals, Leach's record 19 play-off goals kept the Conn Smythe Trophy in Philadelphia for the third consecutive season after Bernie Parent had won it the two previous years.

1978-79: Turmoil Behind the Bench

After seven exceptionally successful years behind the bench of the Flyers, Fred Shero suddenly got "wanderlust" in the spring of 1978, following the club's second consecutive elimination by the Boston Bruins in the Stanley Cup semifinals. Despite having a year left on his contract, the always unpredictable and enigmatic Shero announced in May that he was returning to the organization with which he had spent so many years prior to coming to the Flyers—the New York Rangers—as that club's GM and coach. "I've done all I can do here," Shero said, "and I wanted to get a situation in which I would have complete control of who played for me as well as what they did on the ice."

Shero's unexpected departure was especially painful because it was to one of Philadelphia's most heated rival sports towns. The fact that Shero was still under contract to the Flyers made the deed all the more dastardly in the eyes of the Philadelphia faithful. Shero, however, was determined to leave, so the Flyers did the only thing they could do to resolve the situation—effected a post facto "trade" of their coach to the Rangers in exchange for New York's first pick in the upcoming draft, which they then used to select highly touted center Ken Linseman, a player in the rival WHA. (The night prior to the draft, the Flyers also acquired Pittsburgh's first-round pick for veterans Tom Bladon, Ross Lonsberry, and Orest Kindrachuk, which they used to select defenseman Behn Wilson.)

With Shero's departure problem settled, Flyer GM Keith Allen then had the unenviable task of selecting his replacement. His choice was finally narrowed to three men, all of whom were already in the organization—Maine Mariners coach Bob McCammon, who had just led the first year AHL Flyer farm club to a Calder Cup title; longtime Flyer center Terry Crisp, who had been a de facto assistant coach the previous season; and first year Shero assistant and recently retired veteran NHL blueliner Pat Quinn.

Shortly after the June NHL meetings, Allen announced his choice. To the surprise of many, it was McCammon, a veteran of many years as a player and coach in the minor league—but without a single day of NHL experience. (It should be noted that none of the Flyers' three previous coaches had any NHL bench experience when they took over the club either, although all had played in the league.) Quinn, whose only coaching experience was his one year as Shero's assistant, was tapped to replace McCammon in Maine,

while Crisp (who would later coach the Calgary Flames to a Stanley Cup title) took over Quinn's spot in Philadelphia as McCammon's assistant.

Not unexpectedly, the job of filling Shero's shoes was not an easy one, and by the time the team reached the 50-game mark of the 1978-79 season they were, by Flyer standards, in disarray. As they skated out on the Spectrum Ice to meet the Montreal Canadiens on January 29, the club sported an un-Flyer like 22-16-11 record and were in the midst of an unacceptable 0-2-5 winless streak, which by game's end had reached eight as they lost 7-3 in a lackluster performance.

By the next morning McCammon's Flyer coaching career was over—at least for the time being. Allen promoted Pat Quinn from Maine while McCammon returned to the Mariners. The shock of that wake-up call appeared to bring the Flyers out of their lethargy as they finished out the final 30 games of the season under Quinn with an 18-8-4 mark.

After almost being upset in the best-of-three preliminary round of the play-offs by the hapless Vancouver Canucks, the Flyers fell unexpectedly in the quarterfinals to none other than Fred Shero's Rangers, four-games-to-one, as the Broadway Blues marched on to the Stanley Cup finals. Meanwhile in Maine, McCammon led the Mariners to a second consecutive Calder Cup title. Ironically, the turbulent events of that season would prove to not be the last time that Shero's, McCammon's and Quinn's fates would intersect on the way to the coach's employment—and unemployment—line.

1979-80: "The Streak"

Pat Quinn's first full season as coach of the Flyers proved to be one of the most remarkable in the history of professional sports. After two games of the 1979-80 season, the Flyers were a modest 1-1-0 with an opening night 5-2 win over the Islanders at home on October 11th—and a dreadful 9-2 loss two nights later in Atlanta in game two. The single digit in the loss column would remain unchanged for almost three full months, however, as the Flyers then embarked on the most amazing unbeaten streak in professional sports history—35 games without a loss. "It's impossible," said Scotty Bowman, then coach of the Buffalo Sabres. "But it's not impossible because they've done it."

Quinn's Flyers were really a transition team between the veteran Fred Shero clubs that had averaged 112 points per year over his last five seasons (1973-78) and the Flyer teams of the 1980s. The 1979-80 club was built around a core of original Flyers and drafted players that had come to the team between 1969 and 1972, and the second generation Flyer teams whose first member, Brian Propp, arrived in 1979.

The 1979-80 season was one in which virtually all the vets—Bob Clarke, Bill Barber, Reggie Leach, Rick MacLeish, Bob Kelly, Jimmy Watson, Bob Dailey, Mel Bridgman, Andre Dupont—had outstanding seasons while the "role" players promoted from Maine, such as Al Hill, Tom Gorence, Norm Barnes, Frank Bathe, and John Paddock, among others, made great contributions to the team. There were also several transition players, including Propp, Ken Linseman, Behn Wilson and a new pair of goalies—rookie Pete Peeters and veteran Phil Myre, who had been acquired from the St. Louis Blues in an off-season trade.

"The Streak" started on Sunday, October 14, with a 4-3 Spectrum win over Toronto which featured a penalty shot goal by the Leafs' Lanny McDonald with ten seconds to go in the game. The Flyers won ten of their next 11 to give them an overall record of 13-1-1 by mid-November.

Starting with a 3-3 tie in St. Louis on November the 17th, the Flyers' winning percentage "plunged" to .750 for the next 14 games, which saw them win seven and tie seven—but lose none. That extended their "Streak" to 27 games without a loss (19-0-8) and put the Flyers in a position to tie the Montreal Canadiens' then-league record of 28 when they met the Pittsburgh Penguins at the Spectrum on December 20th. It wasn't easy, however.

As the center ice clock ticked down to the game's final five minutes, the much weaker Pens were holding onto a slim 1-0 lead while Pittsburgh's rookie goalie Greg Millen had already turned away over 30 Flyer shots. It looked as if the magic were about to run out. With 4:39 to go, however, referee Dave Newell called a controversial hooking penalty on Pittsburgh's Bob Stewart. Behn Wilson converted it into a power play goal 31 seconds later—and "the Streak" remained alive with a "skin-of-their-teeth" 1-1 tie.

Two days later, on December 22, 1979, the Flyers were in Boston Garden for a Saturday afternoon game with a chance to make the record their own. The Garden had been notoriously unkind to the Flyers over the years as being a building in which they almost never won or tied. But the team wanted to bring this record to Philadelphia for Christmas and won easily 5-2 in a masterful game against the Bruins.

"The Streak" continued for another six games with a 4-2 victory in Buffalo on January 6, making it 35 games since the loss on October 12th at Atlanta. They finally lost their second game of the year in Minnesota, 7-1, on January 7th. But after splitting their next two games, the Flyers fashioned another streak of 16 games (13-0-3) without a loss for a record of 39-3-13 after 55 games—a phenomenal winning percentage of .827.

The Flyers finished the 80-game regular season schedule with a 48-12-20 record good for 116 points and went on to defeat Edmonton (three-games-to-none), the Rangers (4-1) and upstart Minnesota (4-1) on their way to the Stanley Cup finals for the first time since 1976.

The 1980s: The Transition Years

In the 1980 Finals, the Flyers met the New York Islanders, who were there for the first time since joining the NHL in 1972. After losing the first game—and their "home ice" advantage—on an overtime power-play goal, the Flyers came back in game two to even the series. The Islanders then took a three-games-to-one lead in the series with a pair of wins on Long Island and needed just one more victory in the next three games to upset the Flyers and take the Cup.

Philadelphia won game five easily 6-3 to return the series to Uniondale for game six, which was played on the sweltering Sunday afternoon of May 24th and seen nationwide on network (CBS-TV) television. While the Flyers scored twice in the opening period, so did the Islanders—with a pair of highly controversial goals that virtually all observers but the three on-ice officials agreed should have been disallowed. The first was scored by Denis Potvin who put the puck past Pete Peeters with a high stick. The second, by Duane Sutter, came on a play that was at least five feet offside.

New York's Mike Bossy and Bob Nystrom both scored unanswered goals in the second period to give the Islanders a 4-2 lead going into the third, but the Flyers fought back again on goals by

Bob Dailey and John Paddock to send the game into overtime. At 7:11 of overtime, however, the Flyers' luck finally ran out when Nystrom scored his second goal of the game to give the Islanders a 5-4 Cup-winning victory.

The Flyers' record-breaking "Streak" season ended one game short of a seventh-and-final "championship" at the Spectrum, which would have almost certainly brought Philadelphia a third Stanley Cup had it been played. Instead the Isles had the Cup—and would keep it for four years.

The Flyers dropped 19 points in 1980-81 (116 to 97) and lost to the Calgary Flames in the quarterfinals in seven games. Despite trading for Toronto captain Darryl Sittler in January, 1982, they continued to slide in 1981-82, leading to the second in-season coaching change in Flyer history when Pat Quinn was dismissed on March 19, 1982, with just eight games remaining in the sea-

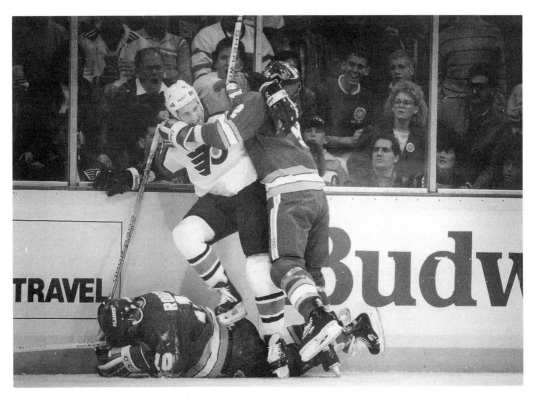

AP/Wide World Photos

Former Flyers' captain Ron Sutter (in white) tangles with two Calgary Flames

son. He was succeeded by the same Bob Mc-Cammon whom Quinn had himself replaced three and a half years earlier.

Over the summer, the Flyers added two key figures to their blueline as Brad McCrimmon was acquired from Boston for Pete Peeters, and Mark Howe came from Hartford for Ken Linseman, Greg Adams and several draft picks. Peeters had become expendable with the rapid development in Maine of Swedish Olympic goalie Pelle Lindbergh. Also beginning to show promise was rookie right wing Tim Kerr, who had been signed as a free agent in 1979 while still a junior and who would go on to have four consecutive 50+ goal seasons from 1983 to 1987.

McCammon added the GM's portfolio to his coaching duties following the 1982-83 season as Keith Allen moved up to become executive vice president. Just a year later, however, McCammon was out of both jobs after going 1-9 in the play-offs over three years. He was replaced as GM by Bob Clarke on May 15, 1984, who ended his 15-year playing career to take on the new assignment. Nine days later Clarke named 34-year-old University of Toronto coach Mike Keenan to replace McCammon behind the Flyers' bench.

Clarke and Keenan—Two More Trips to the Finals

The 1984-85 season brought two new men to the helm of the Flyers—Bob Clarke as GM and Mike Keenan as coach. While both were "rookies" in their jobs at the NHL level, neither was lacking in experience at leading hockey teams to championships from either on the ice or behind the bench.

Clarke, the Flyers' all-time leading scorer and a three-time NHL Most Valuable Player, had helped lead the Flyers to six divisional championships, four trips to the play-off finals, and a pair of Stanley Cup crowns in his 15 years as a player. As a coach, Keenan had already had won titles in Jr. B, OHL, AHL, and Canadian College ranks, while as a player he had skated on championship

teams with the University of Toronto and the SHL Roanoke Valley Rebels.

When the 1984-85 season opened, however, neither had ever managed or coached a game in the NHL. By the time the Flyers played their last game of that campaign on May 30th, however, their club had finished the 80-game regular season schedule with the best record of the 21 teams in the NHL (53-20-7) and had come within three games of a Stanley Cup championship.

After sweeping the Rangers in three games, the Flyers met the New York Islanders—the club that held the Cup for four years after winning their first championship in 1980 over the Flyers—and eliminated them in five games to meet the Quebec Nordiques for the Prince of Wales Trophy and a trip to the Stanley Cup finals.

Although the Flyers won the Quebec series in six games, injuries to three key players suffered against the Nordiques would prove to doom them in the finals against Edmonton. Tim Kerr—then in the midst of scoring 216 goals in just four seasons—went down to a knee injury, team captain Dave Poulin suffered cracked ribs but continued to play, and Pelle Lindbergh—who had three shut-outs against New York and Quebec—was hit on the knee by a shot that eventually sidelined him by late in the finals.

Although the Flyers defeated the defending Stanley Cup champion Edmonton Oilers in the first game of the finals, the Wayne Gretzky-Mark Messier-Grant Fuhr led Oilers swept the next four from the battered Flyers.

While the Cup had eluded the Flyers in the finals for the third straight time, the team that lost it in 1985 was a young one on its way up as opposed to the aging club of 1980 that was not going to get better with the players it had. It was clear that Clarke's and Keenan's young Flyers would challenge for the Cup again.

Although the Flyers failed to bring back the Stanley Cup in '85, Pelle Lindbergh won the Vezina Trophy as the top goalie in the NHL for 1984-85—and at just 26, it appeared as if he would carry the Flyers' goaltending load well into the 1990s. However, early in the morning of November 10, 1985, that all ended as Lindbergh lost control of his sports car, struck a retaining wall, and died three days later without regaining consciousness.

Despite their great loss, the Flyers pulled together and ended the season with 110 points for the second best record in the league. But the fourth place Rangers—who had finished 32 points behind Philadelphia—dashed the Flyers' Stanley Cup hopes early as they upset Philadelphia in the best-of-five opening round of the play-offs, picking up two of their three wins on the Flyers' own ice.

While veteran goalie Bob Froese and rookie Darren Jensen were excellent replacements for Lindbergh in 1985-86 and won the Bill Jennings Trophy for the fewest goals allowed, the Flyers surprisingly opened the 1986-87 season with a new rookie in goal—Ron Hextall. Despite having a new "number one" goalie in their nets for the third year in a row, the Flyers again won the Patrick Division easily with 100 points to finish 14 points ahead of second place Washington. Not unexpectedly, by May they had also reached the finals for the sixth time in 14 years.

Once again Philadelphia would face Edmonton for the Stanley Cup. Unlike two years earlier, the Oilers had the home ice advantage, having finished the regular season with 106 points. As it turned out, they would need every bit of that "advantage," as, for the first time since 1971, the championship series went a full seven games be-

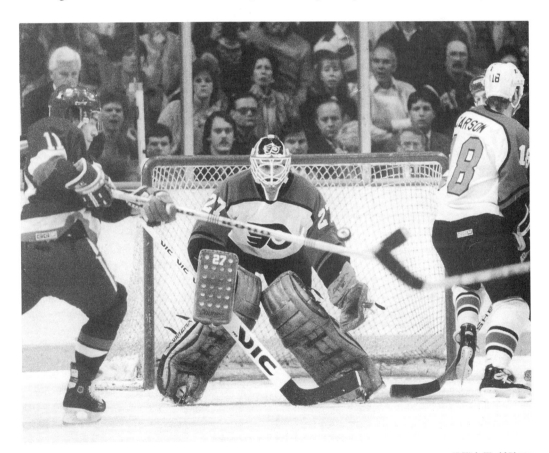

AP/Wide World Photos

Ron Hextall

fore a winner was crowned. (When added to the 19 games the Flyers needed to eliminate the Rangers, Islanders, and Canadiens in the first three rounds, the Flyers would play in an NHL record 26 Stanley Cup games in 1987.)

While the first two games in Edmonton were close, the Flyers lost them both—4-3 and 3-2 in overtime. However Philadelphia then went on to win three of the next four behind Hextall's brilliant play in goal to force a seventh and deciding game.

The high-powered Oilers poured shot after shot on Hextall (outshooting the Flyers 43-20 in the final game) but the rookie netminder turned all but one of them aside until late in the second period when Jari Kurri scored to finally give Edmonton their first lead of the game at 2-1.

While the Flyers continued to press for the tying goal through the third period, with just 2:24 left in regulation time Glenn Anderson beat Hextall to make it 3-1 for the Oilers. That proved to be the last goal scored in the NHL in 1986-87 and gave Edmonton their third Cup title in four years. However, the Conn Smythe Trophy went to the rookie Flyer netminder as the play-off MVP (15-11, 2.77, 2 shut-outs) just as it had to Bernie Parent twice before in 1974 and 1975.

A few weeks later Hextall's rookie regular season record (37-21-6, 3.00, one shut-out) earned him a berth on the NHL's First All Star Team as well as the Vezina Trophy—the same two honors the late Pelle Lindbergh had captured as a Flyer just two years earlier.

1987-1992: Causes and Effects

After almost a decade and a half of unbroken success as one of the NHL's premier teams, the Flyers' run seemed to come to an end with their heartbreaking seventh game loss in the 1987 Stanley Cup finals. Not surprisingly, this downfall had many causes—and many effects.

Among those causes were a series of long-term injuries to key players, aging talent not adequately replaced, a string of unproductive drafts, and some ill-advised, ineffective trades. Among the effects were a number of expected, and some unexpected changes on the ice, behind the bench, and in the front office.

Among the injuries, the most serious damage to the club's on-ice fortunes resulted from a series of shoulder problems suffered by winger Tim Kerr, who had averaged 56 goals a year for the Flyers from 1983 to 1987. In 1987-88, however, he would score just three times in eight games while being sidelined most of the year by the first of a long series of shoulder surgeries.

Although Kerr returned to productivity in 1988-89 with 48 goals, he would score just 34 more times in his final two years as a Flyer before leaving the team in the 1991 expansion draft. Kerr's shoulder (and later knee) problems kept him out of a total of 176 games in his last four seasons with the team.

Mark Howe, the Flyers' all-time leader on defense, suffered chronic back problems in his final years with the team, eventually leading to surgery and a long lay-off. While the Flyers generally did quite well when he could play, when he couldn't the club's winning percentage invariably faltered. Howe eventually left the team in 1992 to sign with his hometown Detroit Red Wings as a free agent.

The third significant loss to the roster was goalie Ron Hextall, which came at the start of the 1989-90 season—and did so in a most unexpected way. As the result of an unprovoked attack on Montreal defenseman Chris Chelios in the closing seconds of the Flyers' final play-off game the previous spring, Hextall was scheduled to miss the first month of the season under a league-imposed suspension. That, however, was only one of three reasons why he would eventually play in just eight games for the Flyers that year.

The second manifested itself just prior to the opening of training camp when Hextall called a tearful press conference to announce that he wanted his contract renegotiated and would refuse to report to the team in any capacity until it had been. Although the Flyers eventually gave him a new deal a few weeks after his suspension expired, Hextall suffered a bad groin pull soon after rejoining the club and was sidelined for many weeks.

Ap/Wide World Photos

**Flyers goalie Ken Wregget fights off a Bob Gainey shot during
1989 play-off action against the Montreal Canadiens**

When finally cleared to play again, Hextall was assigned to the AHL Hershey Bears for a one-game-conditioning-stint to test his readiness prior to rejoining the Flyers. Before Hextall could finish that game, however, he pulled the muscle again much more severely than the first time and missed most of the rest of the season. After averaging 64 games and 33 wins in each of his first three seasons as a Flyer, Hextall's eight appearances in 1989-90 yielded just four wins.

Of far greater significance, however, was that when the season ended, the Flyers had failed to qualify for the Stanley Cup play-offs for the first time in 17 consecutive campaigns.

Injuries were not considered to be the only reason for the Flyers' problems, however. For the second time in his first three seasons as the Flyers' coach—one year after taking the team to the

Stanley Cup finals in 1987—Mike Keenan was dismissed by GM Bob Clarke in May of 1988, despite his outstanding four-year winning percentage of .638 and record of 190-102-28.

Over each of Keenan's four seasons, however, the Flyers' point total had consistently dropped from 113 to 110 to 100 to 88—and in 1987-88 the team had come within three points of missing the play-offs. Then, after taking a three-games-to-one lead over the Washington Capitals in the 1988 Patrick Division semifinals, the Flyers dropped the next three and were eliminated by losing the seventh game in overtime.

The main reason given for Keenan's dismissal was that the club no longer responded positively to his authoritarian coaching style and a new approach was needed. On June 1, Clarke named the team's assistant coach and one-time Flyer teammate Paul Holmgren to take over the reins, making the Minnesota-born former right winger the first ex-Flyer player to coach the club.

Although the Flyers finished fourth in Holmgren's first season with just 80 points—the team's lowest total since last missing the play-offs in 1971-72 with 66—the club made a remarkable play-off run knocking off Washington and Pittsburgh before finally falling to the Montreal Canadiens in six games in the Wales Conference finals. However that would be the last time the Flyers would see post-season action for quite awhile: the next April they would begin the longest play-off drought in their history.

In 1989-90, the Flyers' regular season production dropped nine more points to 71—and for the first time in their history the club finished in last place in their division. Not surprisingly, heads rolled again, but this time it was Clarke who was dismissed on April 16th by Flyer president Jay Snider when the two couldn't agree on how to restructure the team for the future. The search for Clarke's replacement lasted almost two months, but on June 6th, 1990, the Flyers finally named a new GM, 34-year junior hockey executive Russ Farwell.

Farwell became the first GM to jump directly to the NHL from junior hockey since Wren Blair had been named GM of the expansion Minnesota North Stars in 1967. A native of Calgary, Farwell had experience only as a coach or GM with clubs in the Western Hockey League. He was serving as GM of a team in Seattle, Washington, when the call came from Philadelphia, but his greatest successes had come during his six seasons as GM of the WHL Medicine Hat Tigers, which had won consecutive Memorial Cup titles under his stewardship in 1987 and 1988.

Meanwhile, for the first time since being drafted in 1969, Bob Clarke was not a Flyer. Clarke was not out of hockey for long, however, as he was hired to be GM of the Minnesota North Stars even before Farwell had replaced him in Philadelphia. After a mediocre regular season in 1990-91, Clarke's new club surprisingly caught fire in the play-offs and knocked off the top two teams in the league—Chicago and St. Louis—on its way to the Stanley Cup finals. The Flyers, in the meantime, missed the play-offs for a second year in a row.

While Farwell made virtually no personnel moves in his first NHL season, 1991-92 was a far different story as he pulled off no fewer than eight major deals to bring in such new key new players as Rod Brind'Amour from St Louis for former Flyer captain Ron Sutter, Kevin Dineen from Hartford for Murray Craven, and 113-point scorer Mark Recchi from the Stanley Cup champion Pittsburgh Penguins for team captain Rick Tocchet and defenseman Kjell Samuelsson.

Twenty-four games into his second season, Farwell also made his first coaching change as he relieved Paul Holmgren and replaced him with Flyer scout Bill Dineen. A veteran of almost four decades in pro hockey as a player, coach, scout, and manager, the 59-year old Dineen had an excellent reputation coaching young players while also having proven himself to be a winner with four play-off titles to his credit in a dozen years behind the bench in the WHA and AHL.

Despite eventually missing the play-offs for the third year in a row in 1991-92, under Dineen's experienced hand the many new players who had joined the Flyers played well down the stretch, compiling an 18-13-2 record over the final 33 games of the season.

1992-93: A New Franchise

Everybody who gathered in Montreal for the NHL Annual Congress and Entry Draft in June of 1992, knew for sure that one thing would happen before the week was out—the NHL rights to Eric Lindros, the highly touted first overall pick in the 1991 draft, would be traded by the Quebec Nordiques, with whom Lindros had steadfastly refused to sign for a full year. The only questions were where he would go—and what he would cost.

Marcel Aubut, the Nordiques' president, entertained many impressive offers from other clubs

Eric Lindros

On Tuesday, June 30, arbitrator Larry Bertuzzi finally announced that Lindros would play for the Philadelphia Flyers. The terms of the trade, as expected, were unprecedented. In exchange for Lindros's NHL rights, the Flyers would send the Nordiques five top quality players—goalie Ron Hextall, defensemen Steve Duchesne and Kerry Huffman, and centers Mike Ricci and Peter Forsberg, who had been the Flyers' first round draft picks in 1990 and 1991 respectively. In addition Quebec also would get left wing Chris Simon, the Flyers' first round picks in both the 1993 and 1994 Entry Drafts—and $15 million in cash.

Of course all that only brought the Flyers Lindros's rights—not a signed contract for the 19-year-old center. It would take the club another two weeks to get his signature on the dotted line for the next six seasons—at roughly $3.5 million a year. (It should be remembered that 25 years earlier, the Flyers' NHL franchise had cost just $2 million.) On July 15, 1992, however, the Flyers were finally able to call a press conference to introduce what, in a very real sense, could be considered a new hockey "franchise" to the sports fans of Philadelphia: Eric Lindros.

1992-93: The "Lindros Era" Begins

Although the Flyers would miss the play-offs for an unprecedented fourth consecutive year in 1992-93 with a 36-37-11 record and a fifth place finish in the soon-to-be-disbanded Patrick Division, the first season of the club's "Eric Lindros Era" nonetheless gave every indication that he would prove to be well worth the high price in current and future talent—and money—that they had paid to get him.

Despite missing 23 games with knee problems, the 19-year old center collected 41 goals and 75 points while also leading the team in the official category of +/- at +28—and the *unofficial* one of "opposing players left in a heap" after absorbing one of his thundering checks. Lindros didn't have to wait long for his first NHL goal, which came in his debut game against the Stanley Cup

but was determined to get the very most he possibly could for Lindros, whom everybody agreed was a sure fire "franchise" player. The rumor mill worked overtime all week, but when the draft began at noon on Saturday, June 20, surprisingly there had still been no announcement made by the Nordiques as to where Lindros was going.

By late that afternoon, however, the secret was out. Aubut had apparently made deals to trade Lindros to two different teams—the Flyers and the New York Rangers—which, of course, was impossible. In order to resolve this embarrassing situation quickly, all parties immediately agreed to place the matter under binding arbitration. Over the next ten days countless hours of testimony were taken and considered in order to finally determine to which team Eric Lindros's rights would go.

champion Pittsburgh Penguins in a 3-3 tie in the Steel City on the season's opening night, October 6th. His first Spectrum marker came three nights later in the team's home opener, when he scored the game winner in an emotional 6-4 comeback victory over the New Jersey Devils with a spectacular individual rush after stealing the puck at center ice.

Over his first 20 games, Lindros collected an impressive 15 goals and a total of 28 points to put him well on the road to a 100+ point rookie season, but in his 21st game—a 4-4 Spectrum tie with the Buffalo Sabres on November 22nd—that all changed when he suffered a severe knee strain after falling against the boards while throwing a bodycheck on Sabre defenseman Petr Svoboda.

The injury not only sidelined Lindros for the next month, but it also severely impacted his team's position in the standings: the Flyers faltered badly without him, winning just two (2-7-0) of the nine games he missed. Although Lindros returned on December 19th, he aggravated his injury twice more in December and January, eventually keeping him out of another 14 of the next 22 games.

The starkest indication of Lindros's importance to the Flyers' level of performance in his rookie year is a comparison of the team's record with him in and out of the lineup in 1992-93. In the 61 games in which Lindros played, the Flyers had a record of 29-23-9 for a .549 winning percentage, which—if carried over the whole season—would have placed the team in the upper half of the league and easily earned a berth in the playoffs.

In the 21 games for which Lindros was not available, however, the club was a dismal 7-14-2. By late January, the Flyers were in a hole from which they could not escape, despite finishing the season with an impressive eight-game winning streak.

"The Philadelphia Flyer center is the anti-Wayne Gretzky," opined *The Hockey News* in its 1993-94 season preview, as it named Lindros its pick for the second best player in the NHL behind only Mario Lemieux. "A cocky, arrogant player, he will be hated everywhere but the Spectrum where he will be worshipped because he plays the game which such skill and snarl."

As impressive as Lindros's rookie season was, however, it was not the Flyers only bright spot in 1992-93. With 53 goals and 70 assists for 123 points, right wing Mark Recchi not only became the first Flyer to exceed the 100-point plateau since 1975-76, he also broke Hall-of-Famer Bobby Clarke's 15-year-old single season team record of 119 points.

The loss of the combative Hextall was also soon forgotten with the emergence of Swedish Olympic netminder Tommy Soderstrom who, after missing the first two months of the season with a heart problem, earned five shut-outs on his way to compiling a record of 20-17-6 and a 3.42 GAA as a rookie pro. The combination of Soderstrom and 23-year-old NHL sophomore Dominic Roussel gave the Flyers one of the youngest—and potentially one of the best—goalkeeping tandems in their history by the end of the 1992-93 campaign.

While the Flyers were rebuilding with youth on the ice, two veteran Stanley Cup winners who started the 1992-93 season in Philadelphia were no longer affiliated with the team when the 1993-94 campaign opened a year later. A little over six months after his emotional return, Bob Clarke resigned his front office advisory job to accept the position of general manager of the Florida Panthers, an expansion team that began play in the NHL in 1993-94.

Departing shortly after the season was 61-year-old head coach Bill Dineen, a two-time Cup winner as a player with the Detroit Red Wings in the 1950s who returned to his duties as a scout after a season and a half behind the Flyers' bench. Dineen was replaced in June by 50-year-old Terry Simpson, a one-time coach of the New York Islanders and a legendary junior hockey mentor who had spent the previous three seasons as an assistant coach with the Winnipeg Jets.

Despite their problems in the early 1990s, in the first two-and-a-half decades since the NHL's 1967 expansion the Philadelphia Flyers were a premier team. With a pair of Stanley Cups, a half dozen appearances in the finals, ten divisional titles, five Hall of Famers, four Vezina Trophies, four Conn Smythe Trophies, three Hart Trophies, and a raft of All Stars and other honors, the Philadelphia Flyers had long since turned William Penn's "greene countrie towne" into an "orange and black" town too. With Eric Lindros and company, they expect to keep it that way for a long time to come.

—*Bruce C. Cooper*

Tampa Bay Lightning

Hockey in Florida would seem to have a snowball's chance in a tropical climate, but the Tampa Bay Lightning enjoyed a strong first season on the ice and in the stands. The team is primed to move from modest Expo Hall (capacity 10,400) to St. Petersburg's Thunder Dome, a 28,000-seat stadium that will be the largest venue in the NHL.

Much of the Lightning's success can be attributed to discretion. General Manager Phil Esposito kept in check his love for wheeling and dealing that earned him the nickname "Trader Phil" when he was general manager of the New York Rangers. His trades have been modest, generally involving a swap of an older player for a younger one or for draft choices. He bolstered the team's lineup with older players acquired without great risk.

Terry Crisp controlled his fiery style that helped win a Stanley Cup championship and, soon after, led to his dismissal as coach of the Calgary Flames. Crisp is concentrating instead on encour-

agement and teaching as coach of the Lightning.

Like the team's media darling, minor league goalie Manon Rheaume, 20, the first female to play in an NHL preseason game, the Lightning franchise is making the most of its opportunity: "Trader Phil" is being selective, Terry Crisp preaches and practices patience, and Manon Rheaume works hard, maintains her perspective and values, and resists overexposure.

Rheaume supplements her $35,000 contract with the minor league Atlanta Knights (International Hockey League) through commercial endorsements. A book and a made-for-TV movie are in the offing. Kevin Allen, in *Inside Hockey*, reports that Rheaume has turned down several good offers to maintain her practice schedule and her personal values. "I was a simple person before all this happened," stated Rheaume. "I want to be a simple person when it's over." She stands a good chance of being the first female to play in a regular season NHL game.

Tampa Bay's inaugural season included 23 victories, 11 on the road—third most in NHL history by an expansion team. Yes, they lost 54 games, but 16 of those were by one goal, and 7 others were by two goals with the second goal scored after the Lightning's goalie was removed for an extra attacker late in a game.

The team lit off with a 9-8-1 start, surprising then division rivals Chicago and Detroit along the way. With realignment for the 1993-94 season, the team moves into the Atlantic (formerly Patrick) Division, where, according to some analysts, speed and scoring are more prevalent than they were in the Central (formerly Norris) Division.

The Lightning needed better offensive production anyway, having finished 21st in goals scored and last in power-play proficiency among 24 teams. In the off-season, Esposito acquired Petr Klima, a six-time 30-goal scorer, Denis Savard, whose waning offensive wizardry at age 32 is compensated by increased leadership skills, and Gerard Gallant, who had several high-scoring seasons as Steve Yzerman's linemate in Detroit. Chris Gratton (19 years-old, 6'2"; 200 pounds), the Lightning's first selection and third overall in the 1993 amateur draft, is a skilled center who should contribute offensive firepower as well.

These newcomers join Brian Bradley, an All-Star who led the Lightning with 42 goals and 44 assists. Chris Kontos ignited the Lightning's early season surge by scoring 19 goals in the team's first 21 games, but scored only 8 more in his next 45 games. Other returning forwards include Adam Creighton (19 goals, after 4 straight 20-goal sea-

AP/Wide World Photos

Brian Bradley (19)

TEAM INFORMATION AT A GLANCE

Founding date: 1992

Home ice: Thunder Dome
1 Stadium Dr.
St. Petersburg, FL 33705
Phone: (813) 825-3120

Capacity: 28,000

Team colors: Black, white, purple, and gray
Team Nickname: Lightning
Logo: Bolt of white lightning with black borders in a gray circle outlined in purple, with the city name on top and the nickname running out of the lower right side

Franchise Record	Won	Lost	Tie
(1992-1993)	23	54	7

sons elsewhere), John Tucker (17 goals), Rob Zamuner (15 goals), and Danton Cole (12 goals).

The Lightning's veteran defensive corps was somewhat respectable, yielding 332 goals--19th most in the league--but finishing better than such established teams as the Hartford Whalers, the Edmonton Oilers, and the Los Angeles Kings, Stanley Cup runners-up. The unit consisted of Marc Bergevin, Joe Reekie, Shawn Chambers, and 19-year-old rookie Roman Hamrlik. Hamrlik was the first player taken in the 1992 amateur draft. For the 1993-94 season, the Lightning added Donald Dufresne, who played 32 regular-season games and two playoff games for the Montreal Canadiens, 1993's Stanley Cup champions.

During their first season, Tampa Bay went with three goalies—J.C. Bergeron, Pat Jablonski, and Wendell Young. In the off-season they acquired Daren Puppa, who sported an impressive 17-7-4 record and a 3.32 goals-against average with Buffalo and Toronto in 1992-93 and was expected to become the team's top netminder.

While Tampa Bay should rise from the cellar in their second season, by virtue of the fact that a newer expansion team, the Florida Panthers, is joining their division, they will be hard pressed to improve or even match the 53 points they accumulated in their first year.

They have added highly paid veterans in Klima and Savard to an expansion franchise that already has a fairly high payroll. And the 28,000-seat Thunder Dome, originally built to lure a major league baseball team, has the potential for looking mighty empty, especially since it has almost three times the capacity of Expo Hall. But, with selective transactions, patience, and the ability to keep values in perspective, Tampa Bay can build on its strong beginning.

WASHINGTON CAPITALS

The task of making the National Hockey League work in the capital of the United States has been anything but easy. Despite calling on a couple of the sport's fabled names, Red Sullivan and Milt Schmidt, the first Washington entry in the NHL won just eight games in an 80-game season. Then, when winning teams finally arrived after eight years of struggle, the Capitals were beset with a Stanley Cup playoff jinx that taxed the imagination, and drove reporters to seek new ways to explain the unbelievable.

A $6 Million Odyssey

Abe Pollin picked the legendary Milt Schmidt as general manager of the first Capitals, plunked down $6 million for the privilege of accompanying the Kansas City Scouts into the NHL in 1974-75, then named Jim Anderson, a Pembroke, Ontario, native who never before—or since—had

handled an NHL team as his head coach. When the year was history, one wondered who had the biggest headache.

Thanks to the rapid expansion of the NHL and the existence of a rival World Hockey Association, there weren't many top calibre players available when the Washington and Kansas City teams started. Anderson lasted 54 games, only four of which were victories. Sullivan, a great star in his playing days with the New York Rangers, took over for 19 contests, and pulled out six wins. Schmidt finished the season, coaching the final seven games and overseeing the last two triumphs of an opening season that is best forgotten.

Though the future of the first Washington team looked rather grim, other teams that season had records equally as bad: Kansas City won just 15 games, California, 19 and even the "original six" Detroit Red Wings finished 23-45-12. Sure, the Caps were bad, but there were plenty of bad hockey teams to keep them company.

It Takes a Long Time to Win

The trials of building a winner at this stage in hockey history are no better illustrated than in Washington. This was a franchise with experienced hockey leadership, but its failure to connect with successful draft choices meant that the club was dependent upon fringe players in its early seasons.

Nelson Pyatt, for example, was the team's top scorer in 1975-76, a season when Schmidt and Tom McVie shared the coaching agonies. Pyatt played seven years in the NHL for Detroit, Washington and Colorado without topping his 26-23-49 numbers in that Capitals' season. Second on the club was Hartland Monahan, whose 23-27-50 campaign one year later was his best in a similar seven-year NHL career.

The Caps didn't strike it rich with a draft choice until 1977-78 when they acquired Ryan Walter with the second overall selection and started a reasonable run of success. Mike Gartner was the number four overall selection in 1978-79 and Darren Veitch arrived as the No. 5 pick in 1979-80. But early picks and prospects who required too much time to develop weren't the immediate answer, as Washington tried to grab a foothold in a sports town that was used to success.

Guy Charron, signed as a free agent from Colorado (nee Kansas City) in September, 1976, was the first skater to give the Caps a goal-scoring threat. He logged 36-46-82 numbers in the 1976-77 season when Washington more than doubled its victories.

The Capitals' second season had produced just three more wins than their dismal opening year, so 24 victories represented major improvement and a fourth-place finish in the Norris Division. That, incidentally, was 21 points ahead of the Red Wings, proof that the new kids on the block were struggling right along with the veterans. McVie finished as runner-up in coach-of-the-year voting.

Charron added 38 goals the next season, but the Caps' wins dipped to 17, and they finished last in the Norris. Part of the reward was the selection of Walter, who would become the team's first major contender and, ultimately, the bait in a major trade which many credit with turning the Caps from NHL cannon fodder into a team to be reckoned with. It was Montreal's desire to grab Walter which led them to part with defenseman Rod Langway in September, 1982.

The First Big Catch

Ryan William Walter had won just about everything available in 1977-78, his last season of Canadian Junior Hockey. The 6-foot, 200-lb. left wing from New Westminster, B.C. had played three seasons with Kamloops in the Western Hockey League where he'd scored 54 goals, added 71 assists and tallied 125 points and won the WHL Most Valuable Player award, the WHL Player of the Year Trophy and first team WHL All-Star status.

He also collected 148 minutes in penalties, proof that he was not just a silky scorer, but a player able to take care of himself in the inevitable scrapes which characterize professional hockey.

Walter was chosen first by the Caps, second overall, in a 1978 draft that contained several future stars. Minnesota had taken Bobby Smith first that year, while players of the calibre of Wayne Babych, Behn Wilson, Ken Linseman, Brad Marsh, Larry Playfair and Al Secord all went in the first round. Indeed, Minnesota was able to select Steve Payne on the second round that year and Buffalo found Tony McKegney with the 32nd overall pick, testimony to depth in Walter's year.

If Walter didn't immediately take the NHL by storm, his selection served as the first building block in what would ultimately be a competitive Washington team.

He began his NHL career with 28-28-56 figures in 69 games, but was never a player who could be judged strictly by his numbers. He had presence, a confidence on the ice which attracted observers from the start; he communicated the ability to win, something any struggling franchise must acquire.

TEAM INFORMATION AT A GLANCE

Joined the NHL in 1974

Home ice: Capital Centre
Landover, MD 20785
Phone: (301) 386-7000

Seating capacity: 18,130

Team nickname: Capitals
Team colors: Red, white, and blue

Franchise record	Won	Lost	Tie
(1974-93)	624	704	196

Maruk Hits 90

While Walter made a stunning debut in 1978-79 it was another acquisition, 5-foot, 8-inch, 165-lb. Dennis Maruk, who actually made the bigger noise. Acquired just after the start of the season in trade with Minnesota for an early round draft choice the following season, Maruk came to Washington and made an immediate impact. He scored 31 goals and added 59 assists in his first season with the club, registering a team-leading 90 points. Soon he was a 50-goal scorer (1980-81), then a 60-goal sniper (1981-82)——the exchange looked very good, indeed.

That Capitals' team matched the club high 24 wins, then in 1979-80, when Garry Green arrived as coach 16 games into the season, broke through to the 27-win level with the help of a youngster who had been selected in the 1979 draft lottery. He was Mike Gartner, whose record was two points better than Walter that season. Bengt-Ake Gustafsson, an import from Sweden, also arrived to contribute.

Goaltender Wayne Stephenson played well that season, winning 18 games and posting a 3.57 goals-against average as the Capitals began to show signs of real development.

Already a Pro

The selection of Gartner in 1979 proved an inspired move by the Capitols. A native of Ottawa, the 6-foot, 190-lb. right wing was already a professional, with Cincinnati of the WHA, when the Caps chose him in the draft. He had scored 27 goals in 78 games and his 123 minutes in penalties indicated that he, like Walter, was not a player who would back away from the hard work needed to get both goals and respect.

Gartner turned out to be even better than expected. He played the major part of 10 seasons in Washington before he was dealt to Minnesota in a major deal for Dino Ciccarelli, during which time he could be counted on for 30-plus goals. His best year was 1984-85, a 50-goal, 52-assist campaign, but it was his consistency, rather than the occasional spectacular season, which served to make him a very special player.

Gartner played in five NHL mid-season All-Star games for the Caps and held several career club records when he was traded. He collected 397 goals in 758 games and added 392 assists to top the career point getters with 789. His 102-points in 1984-85 also stood as the top production by a right wing after the 1992-93 campaign.

When the Caps named Veitch in 1979-80 and then tabbed Bobby Carpenter in the 1980-81 draft, their days as consistent losers were nearing an end. The 1980-81 season was frustrating both for the clear achievement and the fact that coach Green's second season wound up a last place finish. Maruk scored 50 goals that year, Gartner contributed 94 points and goalie Mike Palmateer turned in a 3.87 gaa in 46 decisions, but the Caps wound up four points behind the New York Rangers in the Patrick Division and missed the playoffs. Their finish netted them Carpenter, however.

One year later, when Green's team started 1-12, general manager Roger Crozier turned to a McGill University graduate to chart the course for the Capitals future. It was the start of a long relationship between Washington and the Murray family.

The Future Arrives

Bryan Clarence Murray was no stranger to reclamation projects when he responded to Crozier's call after 14 games of the 1981-82 season. After completing his degree work at McGill, he had gone to Regina, in the Western Hockey League, where he transformed the last-place Pats into a WHL championship club. That earned him a boost to Hershey of the American Hockey League, where he won the *Hockey News*' award as minor league coach of the year after guiding the Bears to their best season in 40 years. He started 1981-82 in Hershey, but moved to Washington to post a 25-28-13 record over the remainder of the season. He never again coached a Capitals' team to an under-.500 season.

A native of Shawville, Quebec, Murray was known as something of a taskmaster. He worked hard and expected the same from his players. He instilled a sense of purpose into the club, a work ethic which helped to transform the Capitals from a team on the verge of being good to a club that could win anywhere. A competitive, aggressive bench coach, Murray quickly won the respect of players and fans alike.

His first season saw Maruk score 60 goals and add 76 assists, and Walter (38-49-87), Gartner (35-45-80) and the rookie Carpenter (32-35-67) were all showing signs of being ready to excel. Murray had the makings of a good team. With the fifth pick of the 1982 draft, the Capitols selected Scott Stevens, a big, mobile defenseman, and one more piece was added to the puzzle.

A Rookie All-Star, a New GM

Had he been judged soley on statistics, Scott Stevens might not have caught the eye in that 1982 draft. He could not be accused of setting the Ontario Hockey League ablaze in his final season as junior where he scored six goals and added 36 assists in 68 games. But his 158 minutes in penalties and 11-points in 15 playoff games suggested that there was a toughness and an ability to play under pressure. It didn't take long for everyone in the NHL to appreciate Stevens' competitive virtues.

He broke into the Washington lineup and immediately won NHL all-rookie team honors. Five years later he was an NHL first team all star.

That summer of 1982 also saw an addition to the Washington franchise that would prove most important: David Poile, a 33-year-old graduate with a degree in business administration, moved from a management position with the Atlanta Flames to the general manager's job in the nation's capital. As a collegiate player he'd won the MVP award in his senior season; during his first two seasons in Washington he was twice named Executive of the Year as the Caps became winners and began their Stanley Cup saga.

More than a decade later, when the NHL was undergoing major change with the naming of a new commissioner, Poile's name was the one prominently mentioned as a possible right-hand man for new boss Gary Bettman. His hockey knowledge and ability to work with all parties in the league had gained him respect and admiration that argued for his inclusion in the NHL administrative hierarchy.

One Final Piece

Rod Langway came to Washington on September 9, 1982. Poile's first major deal as Capitals' general manager was something of a gamble. He packaged Walter and Rick Green together to entice Montreal to part with Langway, Doug Jarvis, Craig Laughlin and Brian Engblom.

The Canadiens coveted Walter, and Poile knew that the key to turning Washington into a winner was to secure defensive stalwarts like Langway and Jarvis. Both teams, it can be argued, got exactly what they sought, because Walter served admirably in Montreal just as Langway proved to be the keystone of the winning Washington team.

Langway had played college hockey for a year at New Hampshire before turning pro in 1977-78. He skated with Birmingham in the last year of the WHA, before coming to Montreal. After an initial season that included some time at Nova Scotia in the American Hockey League, he took his regular place on the Canadiens' backline.

A thoughtful, careful defenseman, Langway was not a goal-scorer in the modern, attack-oriented backliner. Instead, he was a throwback to the days when defenders thought first of protecting their goaltender, then of making sure that the clearing pass got the puck out of the zone. He was never going to threaten goal-scoring records, but the Caps had traded for leadership and stability. Langway delivered both.

A big man at 6-foot, 3-inches, 218-lbs., Langway skated with his head up and a sense of purpose. He won the Norris Trophy as the top NHL defenseman in both 1983 and 1984 and might have gone on to win again, but the high-scoring feats of modern stars like Edmonton's Paul Coffey helped to change the definition of the award-winner.

He was twice a first team NHL All Star and was a regular participant in the mid-season all-star game for six seasons. That kind of excellence was new in Washington, and it helped to make the Capitals a very different kind of team.

Rod Langway

Jarvis was another player whose skills might not have been noticed by fans who only watched the high-scorers. He had broken into the NHL in 1975-76 with the Canadiens at the age of 20, and established himself as a hard-working center who would contribute some points each season, but, more important, could play the defensive game—watch the opposition's big gun, forecheck effectively and do it without collecting penalty minutes.

Veterans of the NHL, who remembered the days when every team had defensive stars as well as the goal-scorers, appreciated the skills that Jarvis brought to a team. So did the voters from the Professional Hockey Writers Association; they made Jarvis the Frank Selke Trophy winner in 1984, complementing Langway's recognition as the best defender in the circuit.

Winning Season No.1

Bryan Murray and Poile oversaw the first winning year in 1982-83 when the Caps went 39-25-16 and wound up third in the Patrick. Maruk led the attack with 81 points, but the strength of the team was on defense.

The Caps had allowed 338 goals in 1981-82; in 1982-83 the reinforced team surrendered just 283. A year later, the goals-against figure would be 226, best in the NHL. Murray's system was working just fine; he was voted NHL coach of the year in 1984.

The new coach and general manager not only had a stronger team, they had a couple of goaltenders about to emerge as steady workers. Al Jensen had come from Detroit, Pat Riggin, from Calgary. Together they would lead the NHL in 1983-84 as the Capitals took strength from solid netminding behind the sturdy backline. The pair won the Jennings Trophy that season; Riggin was 2.66 in 41 games while Jensen finished 2.93 in 43 decisions.

The defense would become even better in a couple of seasons because the Caps drafted Kevin Hatcher with the 17th pick in the 1984 draft, a year when they also gambled the 59th selection on an 18-year old from Kladno, Czechoslovakia. Michal Pivonka was not a household name on that day, but he would lead the 1991-92 Capitals in scoring, proof that the making of a championship team often has as much to do with prescience on draft day as anything else.

What didn't happen at the end of the first two triumphant seasons was a Stanley Cup run. In 1982-83 the Caps fell to the four-time Cup winning New York Islanders, 3-1. The next season produced a 3-0 first round win over Philadelphia in the Patrick Division semi-finals, but it was the Islanders, 4-1 in the Patrick finals. But the real frustrations lay ahead.

Gartner broke through the 100-point level in 1984-85, scoring 50 goals for the first time in his career. Carpenter had his biggest season as a Capital (53-42-95) while Stevens also chose that year to make his first major statement as a point-get-

Dale Hunter

ter. The big backliner scored 21 goals and added 44 assists and rang 221 minutes in penalties. Riggin was top-class again, finishing 28-20-7 with a 2.98 gaa, Jensen played only 14 times that season. It all added up to a 45-25-9, 101-point season and second place in the Patrick Division.

What happened next was heartbreaking, or proof of the playoff jinx. When the first round series against the Islanders began in Washington, the Caps immediately jumped into the lead. Alan Haworth scored at 2:28 of overtime to win game one, 4-3, then Gartner got the game-winner 21:23 into sudden death to give Washington a 2-1 victory in game two.

That was as far as the Caps went in 1985: amazingly the Islanders came back to win the next three games and scuttle the Washington hopes.

A year later, after a 50-23-7 season that netted another second place Patrick Division finish, the Caps exacted some Stanley Cup revenge. This time they kayoed the Islanders in three straight, only to run into the other New York entry. Though the Rangers had finished fourth in the division, a distant 29 points adrift of Washington in the regular season, it was the Broadway Blueshirts who prevailed in May. The Rangers won the series, 4-2.

The 1985-86 season had included a major trade as Poile sent Riggin to Boston on November 14, 1985 in a straight exchange for Pete Peeters. Peeters had been the 1983 Vezina Trophy winner after an outstanding year in Boston, while Riggin's record in Washington was top flight. Capitals' fans may have had initial misgivings, but Peeters proved Poile's judgment sound; he performed well in his first season, then excelled in 1987-88 and 1988-89 when he posted sub-3.00 goals-against-averages in better than 30 decisions each season.

The Longest Night

While there could be no doubt that the Capitals were one of the stronger Patrick Division teams, those playoff woes continued to plague the club. In 1986-87, the misery increased. This time, after a 38-32-10 season and another second place Patrick finish, the Caps again faced the New York Islanders in the first round of the playoffs. The series' were all best-of-seven, but there was a virtual repeat of the 1984-85 scenario. Washington won twice on Islander ice to lead the playoff, 3-1 and had two remaining home chances to get the series clincher. They never did.

The seventh game was historic—the fifth-longest Stanley Cup overtime struggle. Pat Lafontaine settled it in the wee hours of Sunday morning with a goal 8:52 into the fourth overtime to give the Islanders a 3-2 victory. That was a total of 68 minutes, 52 seconds of sudden-death play. The teams played more than two full contests in a single night.

Bryan Murray was at the helm two more seasons, winning a Patrick Division regular season title in 1988-89. There were some key additions to the roster: Geoff Courtnall was obtained from Edmonton in the summer of 1988 and contributed

42 goals in the Patrick Division championship year; Dino Ciccarelli was a late addition in 1988-89, obtained from Minnesota in a trade of big name players. Gartner moved to the Twin Cities; Dale Hunter came along with goalie Clint Malarchuk in a June, 1987 deal; while Malarchuk was traded to Buffalo in March, 1989, for Calle Johansson and a second round draft pick.

Amidst the changes, one thing remained constant: the Stanley Cup playoffs ended too soon. There was a first round victory over Philadelphia, a seven-game dogfight in 1987-88, but the Caps then fell to New Jersey 4-3 in the Patrick Division final. In Murray's final full season, the Flyers administered a first round kayo, 4-2.

Another Murray Takes Over

The 1989-90 season saw the end of one Murray administration in Washington and the start of another. Bryan's eight-plus years ended after 46 games when the Caps had an 18-24-4 record; replaced by his younger brother, Terry, eight years his junior, Bryan then moved on to oppose his sibling the next season when he became coach and general manager of the Detroit Red Wings.

Terry Murray was no stranger to Washington when he took control. He had been an assistant coach for six seasons with the Capitals following the conclusion of his playing career, one spent largely in the American Hockey League. In 1988-89 he took over as head coach of the Baltimore Skipjacks in the AHL, where he served for 124 games before being called back to the Cap Center.

Although Terry Murray's coaching record was four-games over .500 that first year, Washington suffered its first losing season since 1981-82, finishing 36-38-76. Naturally, given the luck the Caps had experienced in post-season play, that proved to be the year they finally escaped from the Patrick Division playoffs.

Ciccarelli, Courtnall, and Mike Ridley had finished as the club's top scorers with Pivonka, who had spent 31 games in Baltimore with Terry

Murray the season before, emerging as a scoring threat. Don Beaupre, whose career in the NHL had appeared shaky when he spent 1988-89 with four different teams, including two minor league stints, came back to form with a 23-18-5 performance and a 3.22 goals-against average that sent him into the playoffs with momentum.

Beaupre and the veteran Mike Liut, picked up from Hartford in March, 1990, were in the nets for the Capitals' longest-ever Stanley Cup run. The Caps eliminated New Jersey, 4-2 in the opening round, then got game-winning overtime goals from Rod Langway and John Druce to upset the regular season Patrick champion New York Rangers in five games. The Cinderella story didn't have a happily ever after. Boston swept the Prince of Wales Conference final in four straight.

Back on the Winning Side

The next two seasons saw Washington return to winning records but also to the Patrick playoff woes. Now it was the Pittsburgh Penguins who stood in the way as the Patrick boasted the strongest division in the league. The 1991-92 Caps were 45-27-8 in the regular campaign and still finished seven points behind the New York Rangers in the race. They were kayoed in the first round by the Penguins, en route to their second straight Stanley Cup despite finishing only third in the regular season Patrick race.

They had added another potential star, Dmitri Khristich, whose 14 powerplay goals and seven game-winners highlighted a 73-point second season in the NHL. Only 21, he had joined the Capitals from Sokol Kiev in the midst of the 1990-91 season, a delayed payoff on a sixth round draft selection in 1988. The 120th overall choice, the native of the Ukraine had needed only 120 games to reach 100 NHL points.

By then, the Capitals had achieved a remarkable turnaround in the franchise history. A team which suffered eight years before finding the winning formula had now evened off its ledger. In 18 seasons, nine were winners. The overall Washing-

ton record had been improved to 581-670-189 despite the team's daunting start.

A 43–34–7 record in 1992-93 earned the Caps a second-place finish in the Atlantic Division (tenth overall), but they suffered a first-round play-off elimination at the hands of the New York Islanders. The most noteworthy event of the Caps' performance was offensive threat Dale Hunter's cheap shot on Pierre Turgeon, who suffered a shoulder injury. A stiff fine and a 20-game suspension were slapped on Hunter, resulting in his absence from the team for the first quarter of the 1993-94 season.

Following their frustrating play-off loss, the Caps entered a rebuilding period, with plans to have goalie Rick Tabaracci, an acqusition from the Winnipeg Jets, replace Don Beaupre as the team's number-one netminder. A pair of free-agent centers—11-year veteran Dave Poulin and standout Keith Acton—were signed to strengthen the team's offenseive production, and muscle was added in the person of enforcer Craig Berube, picked up from the Flames.

All that remains to complete the story is an appearance in the Stanley Cup finals, the goal which has proved so elusive over the past decade.

SOURCES

BOOKS

Calabria, Pat, (1984-85 Season Review) *The Sporting News Hockey Guide and Register.*

Diamond, Dan, *The Official National Hockey League 75th Anniversary Commemorative Book,* NHL Publications, 1991.

Eskenazi, Gerald, *A Thinking Man's Guide to Pro Hockey,* E.P. Dutton, 1972.

Fischler, Stan and Shirley Fischler, *The Hockey Encyclopedia*, MacMillan. 1983.

Greenberg, Jay; Orr, Frank; and Ronberg, Gary, *NHL: The World of Professional Hockey*, Rutledge Press, 1981.

Matheson, Jim. Season Reviews, *The Sporting News Hockey Guide & Register,* editions for 1986-87 and 1989-90 seasons.

Romain, Joseph and Diamond, Dan, *The Pictorial History of Hockey*, Gallery Books, 1987.

Trecker, Jerry, (Season Review) *ESPN Sports Almanac '83*, Total Sports Publications, 1983.

OTHER

Various *NHL Official Guide & Record Book*, Sporting News *Guide and Register* for basic statistical data.

Various media guides & yearbook information.

—*Jerry Trecker* for Book Builders, Inc.

WASHINGTON CAPITALS

CENTRAL DIVISION

CHICAGO BLACKHAWKS

The Chicago Blackhawks are one of the most fabled franchises of American sport. Their fiery red sweaters with the big, black hawk in full head-dress are a symbol of competitive energy; their home ice, Chicago Stadium, has passed into legend among sporting arenas; and their great stars, from Charlie Gardner and Max Bentley through Glenn Hall, Bobby Hull and Stan Mikita, are among the best known in hockey.

For all that, the last of the National Hockey League's "original six" to join the league in 1926-27 has tasted the ultimate Stanley Cup success just three times in its history, testimony to the power of the opposition in so many seasons when Chicago seemed to have all of its aces lined up exactly right. Montreal, in particular, proved a bedeviling foe, five times defeating the Hawks in the finals, while there were also memorable title battles against the great Detroit Red Wings and Toronto Maple Leafs teams of the NHL's pre-expansion era.

The Blackhawks have contributed much to the sport, both on and off the ice. In addition to fabled players, eight Chicago representatives will be found in the Builders Wing of the Hockey Hall of Fame. James D. Norris, Arthur M. Wirtz, and William Wirtz have also contributed much to the administration and growth of the sport during more than 40 years of association with hockey and the NHL.

There have also been famous coaches behind the bench at Chicago Stadium, among them Sid Abel, Dick Irvin, Tommy Ivan, Rudy Pilous, and Billy Reay, the latter serving nearly 14 years in charge of some of the NHL's finest teams.

And don't forget the organ, that famous blaster which is supposed to equal the sound of 25 brass bands at full volume and is said to be capable of breaking all the glass in the Chicago Stadium if fully cranked up. Then there's the tradition of out-yelling the national anthem and a fog horn which makes visiting goaltenders positively determined to keep the Blackhawks at bay, just so that they don't have to stand there while the crowd roars and the horn blasts behind them. These things are all part of a story that began in 1926-27 when the Chicago franchise joined a then 10-team National Hockey League.

Opening day for the NHL's Chicago franchise was November 17, 1926, but the Chicago Stadium was just a dream for the future on that night. The first game was played in the Chicago Coliseum, a 4-1 Blackhawk victory over the Toronto St. Pat's, who were coached by one of hockey's great founders, Conn Smythe.

The Hawks were led in that initial season by Peter Muldoon, who coached the 15-man roster to a 19-22-3 finish, good enough for third place in the American Division behind the champion New York Rangers and the second place Boston Bruins. Ottawa won the Canadian Division and the Stanley Cup in that debut Chicago season, but the Blackhawks served immediate notice that they would make their contribution to hockey history.

Cecil "Babe" Dye finished second in goal-scoring with 25, and Dick Irvin topped the league in assists with 15, finishing a point behind Bun Cook of the New York Rangers in overall scoring. Cook collected 37 points, Irvin had 36, and Dye was in fifth position with 30, in an era when scoring was much lower and the teams played a 44-game regular season.

The Hawks' first goaltender was Hugh Lehman, whose 2.64 goals-against average looks terrific by modern standards but was actually the highest in the NHL among regular netminders. In that season, five of the ten regulars allowed fewer than 2.00 goals per game.

That first season proved something of a mirage, however, because reality hit the Hawks in a big way in the next two campaigns, as they totalled only 14 wins and finished last on each occasion. There was something to look forward to, however, when the Chicago stadium was completed and opened to a boxing show on March 28, 1929. The Blackhawks would call the Stadium home at the start of the 1929-30 season.

Chicago produced no NHL leaders in its sec-

Hockey Hall of Fame and Museum

Chuck Gardiner

ond two seasons but did introduce the first major star of the franchise, goaltender Chuck Gardiner, who would go on to lead the Hawks to Stanley Cup glory in a career that spanned 1927-1934. He won the Vezina Trophy—given to the league's best goaltender—twice during that period and was a fan favorite. He died tragically of a brain tumor at the age of 30, just after he had led the club to its first championship. In his second NHL season, although the Hawks were a miserable 7-29-8, Gardiner's 1.93 goals-against average marked the first time that the team had a netminder of outstanding calibre.

The Turnaround Begins

That first season in their new Stadium saw Chicago return to winning ways and lay the foundation for the first Blackhawk team to reach the Stanley Cup finals. The 1929-30 crew posted a 21-

TEAM INFORMATION AT A GLANCE

Founding date: September 25, 1926

Home ice: Chicago Stadium
1800 West Madison St.
Chicago, IL 60612
Phone: (312) 733-5300
FAX: (312) 733-5356

Seating capacity: 17,317

Team colors: Red, black, and white
Team nickname: Black Hawks, 1926-77; Blackhawks, 1977—
Logo: Profile of Native American head with feathers in hair

Franchise record	Won	Lost	Tie
(1926-93)	1,828	1,930	692

Stanley Cup Championships (3): 1933-34, 1937-38, 1960-61

18-5 mark, good enough for second place, but the Hawks were well behind the 77-point Boston Bruins, who dominated the regular season only to lose the Stanley Cup. Irvin, who would coach the 1930-31 Stanley Cup finalists, and Dye were gone from the lineup by now so there were new heroes in front of Gardiner.

Tom Cook (14 goals, 16 assists, 30 points) and John Gottselig (21-4-25) were the top point-getters, with Gottselig the leading goal-scorer. Captain Duke Dutkowski, a defenseman, took over Irvin's leadership mantle and collected seven goals along with 10 assists from the back line. In an era of great defensemen, headed by Ottawa's King Clancy and Boston's Eddie Shore, Dutkowski wasn't among the league leaders, but his tally topped the Chicago defense conclusively.

And Gardiner continued to excel. Even though goals were coming more frequently throughout the league, his 2.52 goals-against average and three shutouts placed him third in each category in the NHL.

The next season, with Irvin behind the bench, saw Gardiner post a 1.77 goals-against average and 12 shutouts, as the Hawks went 24-17-3 in the regular season then enjoyed their first run to the Stanley Cup finals. Chicago had previously appeared in the playoffs but was eliminated in the first round in both 1927 and 1930, so the 1930-31 season marked the coming of age of the Hawks as a competitive force in the league.

Gottselig led the Hawk scorers in the regular season with 20 goals and 12 assists, and Cook was right behind him with 15-14-29 figures. The team was captained by Ty Arbour, a forward who played 38 games and registered six points, and featured a defense that was so stingy that only the New York Americans allowed fewer than the 78

---

goals the Hawks conceded in 44 games.

In the playoffs, that defense came to the forefront again. In the quarterfinals Chicago upset Toronto 4-3 in the two-game, total-goal series; then Gardiner produced back-to-back shutouts as the Hawks swept past the New York Rangers, 3-0, in another total-goal playoff. That sent Chicago against the Montreal Canadiens for the first time in a Stanley Cup final. No one knew then that it would be the start of a jinx pairing which has never seen the Blackhawks top their Quebec rivals in the championship series.

This was a classic series, with four games decided by a single goal. Montreal finally won the decisive fifth game, 2-0, as the clinching goal came off the stick of Howie Morenz in the final five minutes of the third period. Two of the games went into lengthy overtime, each to be won by the Hawks.

Montreal took the opener, 2-1, before Gottselig's goal after 24:50 of overtime gave the Hawks a 2-1 decision in the second match. The April 9, 1931, game was a classic. The Hawks rallied with two goals in the space of 18 seconds in the third period to tie the contest, then won it 53:50 into overtime. Harold "Mush" March, who would turn out to be the hero three years later when Chicago finally lifted Lord Stanley's cup, got the first goal of the great comeback at 16:20 of the third period on a feed from Gottselig, then Cook set up

Dick Irvin in his last season as Chicago's coach (1955-56)

Stewart Adams at 16:38 to make it 2-2. Marvin Wentworth, who had scored only four goals in the regular season, got the game-winner at 13:50 of the third overtime on a feed from Adams.

Montreal, however, returned the favor in game four, rebounding from an early 2-0 deficit to reply with three unanswered tallies. Chicago's Stanley Cup hopes faded away when they played the last five periods of the five-game series without scoring a goal against Montreal's future Hall-of-Fame goaltender George Hainsworth. The fact that Gardiner actually finished with the second-best goals-against average in the playoffs, ahead of Hainsworth, was all the consolation available to the Hawks.

The Blackhawks' goaltender, who had been born in 1904 in Edinburgh, Scotland, put together three great seasons from 1931-34, winning two Vezina Trophies and a Stanley Cup to cap his career. Gardiner died at the age of 30, however, still at the very top of his game. Oddly, two of his best seasons were losing ones for the Chicago team, which actually fell all the way to last place before coming back to capture the sport's top prize.

In 1931-32, a season that saw Gardiner post a 1.92 goals-against average, the Hawks failed to take advantage of their goalie's brilliance, limping into an 18-19-11 finish that was good for second place in the American Division, but a shadow of the season before. First round elimination by Toronto—who eventually won the Cup—quickly followed.

The 1932-33 year was no better, since the Hawks had the misfortune to be playing in a stronger division. Their 16-20-12 record (44 points) would have gotten them a third-place finish—ahead of even the Montreal Canadiens—in the Canadian Division, but it was only good for propping up the bottom in the American Division. Boston was on top, with both Detroit and the Rangers ahead of the Hawks by 10 points or more.

The year also contained an unwanted piece of Chicago history, when the Hawks were forced to forfeit a game. On March 14, 1933, coach Tom Gorman was ejected by famed referee Bill Stewart, and when the Hawks' players refused to

return to the ice after the ejection, Stewart awarded Boston a 1-0 victory. Gardiner, however, had put together another good year, yielding goals at only a 2.10 rate, while Paul Thompson led the offensive attack with 33 goals. Thompson would later become coach of the club he was about to lead to its first Stanley Cup.

An All-Star Game and a Cup

The 1933-34 Blackhawks weren't the best regular season team in the National Hockey League, but they put everything together at playoff time to cap Gardiner's career and bring Chicago its first championship. The team finished second in the American Division with a 20-17-11 record that was seven points behind Detroit and only a point better than the third-place New York Rangers. Over in the Canadian Division the Toronto Maple Leafs, despite losing star forward Ace Bailey to a controversial career-ending injury, had an 11-point cushion over the Canadiens and were favorites heading into the post-season action.

Chicago had actually been the center of NHL attention before their playoff run. The league used Chicago Stadium to stage a February 14, 1934, All-Star benefit for Bailey, who had undergone surgery for a fractured skull after being checked from behind by Eddie Shore in an infamous game in Boston in December of 1933. Shore was suspended for 16 games as a result of the check, a blow that *The NHL's Official 75th Anniversary Commemorative Book* claims was actually intended for King Clancy, who had tripped Shore on a breakaway immediately before the incident.

The NHL doesn't include this benefit contest among its All Star Game results. That official series did not start until 1947, when the tradition of a season-opening game between the defending Stanley Cup champion and a team of All Stars was begun. In 1970 the format was changed again to the inter-divisional contest which prevails today.

Thompson was a 20-goal scorer during the regular season for a Chicago team which had important contributions from Gottselig (16-14-30),

Elwyn "Doc" Romnes (8-21-29), and Lionel Conacher, the team's fourth player to get 10 or more goals. But, as in 1931, this was a team that owed much to their defense. Built around Conacher, Art Coulter, and Roger Jenkins—in front of the redoubtable Gardiner—the Chicago defense led the league in goals-against, conceding only 83, 15 fewer than number two Detroit. Gardiner's goals-against average was 1.73, and he added 10 shutouts in a Vezina Trophy-winning season. Romnes was fourth in the NHL in assists and Conacher second in penalty minutes.

The playoffs began in dramatic fashion, with the Hawks traveling to Montreal to win the first game of a total goals series against the Canadiens, 3-2. Then the Hawks needed overtime in their own building to get a 1-1 tie and capture the aggregate victory, 4-3. The semifinal was easier, a clear-cut 6-2 aggregate win over the Montreal Maroons, as Gardiner posted another shutout in the 3-0 opener in Montreal. This time there was no extra period needed as the Hawks won the return match in Chicago, 3-2. They advanced to the final against Detroit, which had won the series of first-place finishers, beating Toronto three games to two.

The Hawks never trailed in the finals, but two overtime victories were required—including the decisive fourth game—before the celebrations could begin. A feature of the series was the match-up of two of the game's top lines: Chicago's March, Romnes, and Thompson paired against the Red Wings' Larry Aurie, Cooney Weiland, and Herbie Lewis.

Conacher gave the Hawks a 1-0 first period lead in game one, but Detroit's Lewis forced overtime with a goal 4:45 into the third period. It took 21:10 before Thompson won it for Chicago. Game two was 1-1 after two periods before Romnes, Rosie Couture, and Gottselig scored for Chicago, allowing the Hawks to take a two-game advantage to Detroit for game three. Once again, the Hawks, with goals from Thompson and Gottselig, were tied going into the final session, but it was Detroit's turn to score three times—twice in the final two minutes—for a 5-2 win.

There was plenty of drama in what turned out to be the final game of the best-of-five series. Gardiner and Detroit's Wilf Cude allowed no goals over the first 90 minutes of action. March, on a feed from Romnes, eventually got the game-winner at 10:05 of the second overtime to settle the titanic battle between the Scotsman in the Chicago goal and his rival from Barrie, England. Chicago had its first Stanley Cup.

An Encore Four Years Later

Although the Hawks were able to replace Gardiner in goal with another Vezina Trophy-winner, Lorne Chabot—who backstopped another set of league-leading defensemen while recording a 1.83 goals-against average—Chicago had to wait four years before it could claim another Stanley Cup. The 1934-35 Hawks again finished second in the American Division, just a point behind Boston. However, in the playoffs they were shut-out twice in successive games, eventually losing the total-goal Stanley Cup quarterfinal series to the Montreal Maroons in overtime of the second game, 1-0.

A year later the team finished in a three-way dead heat with Boston and the Rangers for second place in the American Division, but once more playoff action ended in the first round. This time it was a 7-5 total-goals loss to the New York Americans. Romnes won the Lady Byng Trophy, the first Blackhawk to be honored for his combination of skills and gentlemanly play. The 1936-37 Hawks dropped off sharply, finishing at the bottom of the American Division with just 14 wins.

It was obviously time for a change of direction. Bill Stewart replaced Clem Loughlin behind the bench, becoming the 13th head coach in the team's 11th season, indication enough that the Hawks' owner, Manor House Coffee heir Fred McLaughlin, was not long on patience. In this case the change paid off against the odds.

Stewart's single year as coach of the club was hardly a rousing success in the regular season, as the Blackhawks just barely got into the playoffs

CHICAGO BLACKHAWK FIRST TEAM ALL-STARS

Goaltenders

Chuck Gardiner 1931, 1932, 1934
Lorne Chabot 1935
Glenn Hall 1958, 1960, 1963
Tony Esposito 1970, 1972, 1980
Ed Belfour 1991

Defensemen

Lionel Conacher 1934
Earl Seibert 1942, 1943, 1944
Pierre Pilote 1960, 1961, 1962, 1963, 1964, 1965
Elmer Vasko 1963, 1964
Bill White 1972, 1973, 1974
Chris Chelios 1991

Centers

Max Bentley 1946

Stan Mikita 1962, 1963, 1964
Ed Litzenberger 1957
Denis Savard 1983

Left Wing

Paul Thompson 1938
Doug Bentley 1943, 1944, 1947
Roy Conacher 1949
Bobby Hull 1960, 1962, 1964
Dennis Hull 1968, 1969, 1970, 1972, 1973

Right Wing

Ken Wharram 1964, 1967
Bud Poile 1948

Coach

Paul Thompson 1940, 1942

with a 14-25-9 record that was only two points better than last-place Detroit. They could hardly see American Division champ Boston, 30 points ahead of them, and were 23 points adrift of the second-place Rangers. But that didn't mean a thing when the playoffs began.

Thompson had enjoyed a strong 22-22-44 regular season, finishing third among both NHL goal-scorers and point-getters, while Carl Dahlstrom's 10-9-19 rookie year was good enough to earn him the Calder Trophy as the NHL's top first-year player. In goal, Mike Karakas had a 2.90 goals-against average, which didn't rate among the NHL's leaders but indicated that he was better than the relatively ineffective team in front of him. Romnes was still effective, too, scoring 10 goals and collecting 22 assists.

And as things turned out, the Blackhawks had a "secret weapon." The playoffs would include the only appearance of goalie Alfie Moore, whose entire NHL career spanned just 21 regular season games and three Stanley Cup playoffs, one each with the New York Americans, Detroit, and Chicago. He won only one post-season game, that important one with the Hawks.

Post-season play began with a 2-1 series victory over the Canadiens, the deciding game won in the Forum in overtime by the Black Hawks. That meant a test against the New York Americans, who also found the Hawks tough to handle in extra sessions. Although New York won the opener, 3-1, they fell 1-0 in overtime in Chicago, then lost in New York. Against all the odds it was the Hawks and the Maple Leafs in the final.

The series began in Toronto with Moore in goal because Karakas had suffered a broken toe in the last game against the Americans. Two goals by Gottselig and one by Thompson were enough, combined with Moore's netminding, to produce a 3-1 Chicago win.

Moore didn't get the call in game two, however; Paul Goodman was beaten by a 5-1 Maple Leafs onslaught before Karakas returned wearing a steel-tipped boot. Goals by Carl Voss—who had scored just three in the regular season—and Romnes carried the Hawks to a 2-1 victory at home. Two nights later Dahlstrom, Voss, Jack Shill, and March scored in the Cup-clinching 4-1 triumph. Chicago had its second Stanley Cup in 11 seasons.

Thompson Changes Roles

Stewart didn't last through the next season, as Chicago reverted to the form it had displayed in the regular campaign of 1937-38. The slide, in fact, was complete, with the Hawks finishing last in a seven-team league and winning only 12 games. That was Thompson's last season as a player, his 13-year career having included five seasons as a New York Ranger before he pulled on the Black-hawk jersey in 1931-32.

The man who would coach Chicago through the World War II years wound up with 153 goals in 586 NHL games. His best season was 1937-38, when he tallied 44 points in 48 games. Thompson had played a major role in two Stanley Cup triumphs, collecting seven points and four goals in both the 1934 and 1938 victories. A native of Calgary, Alberta, he turned to coaching at age 34.

There was not quite the same success for Thompson behind the bench, although his Hawks were by no means without achievement during the war years. The best finish was fourth (twice), but there was an appearance in the 1940-41 Stanley Cup semifinals and a 1943-44 run to the finals where the Hawks again ran into Canadiens. As history would repeat over and over again, they lost.

Despite the inevitable roster changes caused by wartime hockey, the Hawks had some stars to keep the Chicago faithful entertained while the troops were engaged in Asia and Europe. Chief among them were the Bentley brothers, Doug and

Max, while "Mush" March, the hero of 1934, skated on right wing to the end of the hostilities. He was 37 when he called it quits, having appeared in 758 NHL games, all of them in a Chicago uniform. As a 36-year-old in 1943-44, he managed 37 points in a 48-game season. By then, Doug Bentley was taking center stage.

Bentley led the NHL in goal scoring in both 1942-43 (33 goals) and 1943-44 (38 goals) en route to his place in the Hall of Fame. His career began in 1939-40 and included NHL assist-leading years in 1947-48 and 1948-49; but it also contained some controversy when his brother Max was traded to Toronto in 1947, one of the most-discussed moves in Chicago history.

Max Bentley joined Chicago for the 1940-41 season. Two years later he finished second in the NHL in assists, before being called for Canadian service. His return in 1946-47 presaged two Art Ross trophies as the top scorer in the NHL before the trade.

The team had its share of drama during the war years. On March 18, 1940, the Hawks became the first team to fly to an engagement when they chartered a plane and flew to Toronto for a Stanley Cup game. A year later, in a game against Boston, goaltender Sam LoPresti faced 83 shots. He saved 80 of them but the Hawks lost 3-2 to the Bruins. On March 16, 1941, in the final game of the season, Thompson pulled goaltender LoPresti for an extra attacker. No one had ever done that before in the NHL.

In 1943 Max Bentley picked up the Lady Byng Trophy to start a Chicago streak that would include Clint Smith in 1944 and Bill Mosienko in 1945. On January 28th of that year Max Bentley collected seven points in a single game, getting four goals, three assists against the New York Rangers. Doug Bentley won the Art Ross trophy as NHL scoring leader in 1942-43 with a 33-40-73 season. On February 20, 1944, the Hawks played a "perfect game" against Toronto. There were no goals and no penalties at Chicago Stadium that night.

The highlight of the Thompson era behind the bench came in 1943-44 when Chicago reached the

Hockey Hall of Fame and Museum

Earl Siebert

Stanley Cup finals. They had Doug Bentley (38-39-77) in top form along with Clint Smith (23-49-72) and Bill Mosienko (32-38-70) to lead the offensive attack, while Karakas, sharing duty with Hec Highton, was still in goal. For Bentley, the 38 goals and 77 points were both career highs, but the star was far from the only Chicago regular reaching unusual heights in 1943-44.

Smith, a 31-year-old center from Assinobia, Saskatchewan, had been obtained from the New York Rangers that season. His 72-point performance was the best of his 11-year NHL career and helped him to win the Lady Byng Trophy. Mosienko, who would later team with the Bentley brothers to form the "Pony Line," was just 22 and playing his first full season in the league. Like Smith, he would never top the 70-point figures he achieved that year, although his 14-year NHL career was marked by consistent offensive output.

Carl Dahlstrom, a 32-year-old center from Minneapolis, was another Hawk for whom 1943-44 would mark the high point of his NHL career.

His 20 goals, 22 assists, and 42 points were all career highs. George Allen, a defenseman from Bayfield, New Brunswick, made it four of five top Chicago scorers who were having a career year. Like Dahlstrom, his goals (17), assists (24), and points (41) that season were the best numbers he ever posted.

Karakas, whose heroics had keynoted the 1938 Cup triumph, also made 1943-44 his last outstanding season. His 3.04 goals-against average in 26 regular season games was topped by his 2.62 performance in nine Stanley Cup starts. They were numbers he never approached again as his career drew to a close after the 1945-46 season.

For all of those personal achievements, the Hawks didn't have a magic march to the Cup. They easily eliminated Detroit, 4-1, in the semifinal round, but had no answers against the Canadiens in the final. Montreal swept the series, 4-0, with a team that included Stanley Cup goal-scoring leader Maurice Richard, Toe Blake, and another Hall of Famer, Bill Durnan, in goal. Richard's 12 goals were four more than Bentley picked up in the playoffs, while Blake and Elmer Lach each had three more assists than Smith's eight.

A Long, Long Wait

It would be 17 seasons before the Black Hawks again played in a Stanley Cup final—they won it all in 1961 to launch a great era for the club. The post-World War II era belonged instead to Detroit, Montreal, and Toronto, with Chicago struggling through a long dry spell. In the 15-year period after the 1944 Stanley Cup finals appearance, there was just one winning season (1945-46) and far too many last place finishes (nine) for a proud franchise.

There were numerous coaching changes along the way, with Gottselig, Charlie Conacher, Ebbie Goodfellow, Sid Abel, and Frank Eddols all taking a turn. Even Dick Irvin returned, 25 years after he had led the Hawks to the 1930-31 Cup finals. Irvin had gone on to win three Cups in a long tenure at Montreal, after winning one with Toronto, but he had no magic left when he got back to the Windy City. His 1955-56 Hawks finished 19-39-12, last in the six-team league.

Tommy Ivan—listed in Stan Fischler's *Hockey 100* as one of the ten best coaches and ten best general managers in the history of the game—even took a shot at turning things around. He had presided over the great Detroit teams from 1947-54, winning three Stanley Cups with the Red Wings, but his 1956-57 Blackhawks were no better than Irvin's of the year before. In fact they won three fewer games, tied three more, and lost exactly the same number, 39. They were the fourth consecutive Chicago team to finish last in the NHL and the seventh in eight years.

The long drought was not without some individual highlights, however. Mosienko won the Lady Byng trophy in 1945 after a 54-point season that included 28 goals. He was third overall in goals scored that season, just one behind Montreal's Blake and Toronto's Ted Kennedy, who tied for second. Hockey's great star, Maurice Richard, led the league with 50 goals that season. The "Rocket" was clearly in a class by himself. Max Bentley led the NHL in total points in both 1946 and 1947, barely edging Richard 72-71 in the second of his Art Ross Trophy seasons.

Max Bentley was also at the center of one Chicago's most controversial moves on November 4, 1947. Coming off those two scoring championships, Bentley was traded to the Toronto Maple Leafs for five players, but the massive infusion of new talent into the Chicago lineup couldn't lift the Hawks out of last place in the 1947-48 season.

Toronto, meanwhile, won both the regular season title and the Stanley Cup. However, it was during this season that Bill Gadsby, who would enter the Hall of Fame in 1970, began his illustrious career in Chicago. Roy Conacher (26-42-68) won the Art Ross trophy in 1948-49, with teammate Doug Bentley (23-43-66) right behind him, although Chicago missed the playoffs with a fifth-place finish.

The first afternoon game in NHL history was played at the Stadium on January 20, 1952. True to their performance in that era, the Hawks lost to Toronto, 3-1. On March 23rd, in that same season—which they finished with a dismal 17-44-9 record—Mosienko scored the three fastest goals in NHL history. He needed just 21 seconds to accomplish the feat on the last day of the season as the Hawks beat the New York Rangers, 7-6. Mosienko, assisted by Gus Bodnar on all of the goals, hit the goal post seconds after completing the pure hat trick. Ranger goalie Lorne Anderson never played another NHL game.

In 1953-54, when the Hawks won only 12 games and were outscored 242-133, the NHL voters paid the ultimate tribute to a beleaguered goaltender. Chicago's Al Rollins, who played all but four of the games in that long season, was awarded the Hart Trophy as the league's most valuable player. Rollins, who won a Vezina Trophy with Toronto in 1950-51, had been traded to the Hawks along with three other players for Harry Lumley in 1952.

Rollins played five seasons in Chicago, starting every one of the 70 games during two of those. He never played on a winning team, but posted creditable goals-against averages in every season, so his Hart Trophy win was some reward for performance against the odds. Another player was commended for his performance despite the losing fortunes of the team as a whole. Eddie Litzenberger came into the league in 1954-55 with a 26-24-40 season that earned him the Calder Trophy as rookie of the year.

The Blackhawks were in deep trouble in the 1950s and it took a revitalized ownership, a new direction in the front office, and some excellent scouting to save the franchise. Joseph Romaine and Dan Diamond, in *The Pictorial History of Hockey*, explained what took place: "The Chicago Black Hawks were a have-not team saved from the brink of dissolution in the mid-1950s by new ownership and a commitment to rebuild in the old style.... Crowds in the old Chicago Stadium had dropped below the 5000 level as prospects for improvement were bleak. Jim Norris, Jr. bought the Chicago club in 1954 and hired Tommy Ivan, the successful coach in Detroit as his general manager and Dick Irvin, the coach of the Canadiens, as his coach. Ivan set out to build a solid farm system of sponsored junior and minor-pro clubs. The system began to bear fruit before the end of the 1950s as first Bobby Hull and then Stan Mikita graduated from the St. Catherines, Ont. juniors to the Hawks."

The long tunnel finally ended with a convergence of forces in Chicago that began during the 1956-57 season. That was the first full year for defenseman Pierre Pilote, who would evolve into one of the great NHL backliners and win numerous awards. Elmer "Moose" Vasko also made his full-time debut in that season under Ivan. They would team up at the heart of the defense on a team building from mediocrity to Stanley Cup glory.

In 1957-58 Rudy Pilous took over behind the bench from Ivan, and a newcomer on the forward line, Bobby Hull, made his debut with 13 goals and 34 assists in 70 games. This was a mere hint of what the future would hold. That same year saw the Blackhawks introduce a new goaltender. Glenn Hall, eventually to earn the nickname "Mr. Goalie," didn't miss a game until November 8, 1962, after 552 consecutive starts. By then the Hawks had won a Stanley Cup.

In 1958-59 another piece of the puzzle was fitted neatly into the pattern. Stan Mikita made his first appearances in Chicago, playing three games that season before breaking in as a regular the following campaign. In that 1959-60 season another rookie, Bill Hay, won the Calder Trophy in Chicago colors.

The rest of the 1960-61 Cup-winning cast was being slowly assembled during this era, as Hull and Mikita, along with the remarkable Hall, attained superstar status.

Pilous, a Winnipeg native, had never coached in the NHL when he was tapped to succeed Ivan. In the next six years he created history in Chicago. It took three years to gain a winning season, although the Hawks twice fell only one victory short of the break-even level. But once they were at the top of their game, Chicago was a match for anybody in the NHL.

Hockey Hall of Fame and Museum

Pierre Pilote

A Steady Climb to the Top

In Pilous's first season, 1957-58, Chicago finished 24-39-7, 14 points behind fourth-place Boston. The improvement was marked, however; Chicago had not won as many as 20 games since 1952-53, the only time the Hawks had qualified for Stanley Cup action since the war. Hall's first season saw him post a 2.89 goals-against average and seven shutouts, ranking him fourth behind Montreal's Jacques Plante in average and second behind the great Canadien in shutouts. Eddie Litzenberger was third behind Dickie Moore of the Canadiens in goal-scoring, as he led the Hawks with 62 points.

They called him "Mr. Goalie." Born in Humboldt, Saskatchewan, on October 3, 1931, Glenn Hall played 18 years in the National Hockey League, won or shared the Vezina Trophy three times, won the Conn Smythe Trophy for playoff excellence, and entered the Hockey Hall of Fame in 1975. He was the man behind some of Chicago's finest teams.

Hall came to Chicago in a blockbuster trade in July of 1957, but he wasn't the centerpiece of the deal. The Hawks obtained him and Detroit's folk hero, Ted Lindsay, for four players. The Red Wings had been careful to reacquire Terry Sawchuk before letting Hall go. The Detroit club had "lost faith in Hall after his mouth was shattered by a puck in the 1957 playoffs. Although he returned and played admirably, he was blamed for Detroit's elimination," reports Dan Diamond in *The Official NHL 75th Anniversary Commemorative Book.*

Detroit's decision gave Chicago a goaltender who would play 10 remarkable seasons in Chicago Stadium during which he never had a goals-against-average above 2.97. From the day Hall first skated in a Blackhawk uniform, he played 552 consecutive NHL league and playoff matches before a pinched nerve forced him to the sidelines. So much for being affected by that playoff injury.

Diamond profiles Hall as "a man who loved poetry and the wide open Alberta spaces . . . [he] often needed coaxing to show up for Chicago training camps. The rumor always had him painting his barn outside of Edmonton. He would show up, it was said, as soon as the paint dried. In fact, Hall always dreaded the prospect of another year of hell. A substantial raise usually helped the paint dry faster."

Hall was one of a bevy of memorable netminders in one of the NHL's golden eras. He will be remembered as much for his style of play as his proficiency at the game. "Hall's `spread-eagle' style (today called the 'butterfly') in which he'd fan his knees out in an inverted V formation nearly covered the area post to post to protect against deflections while keeping his swift glove hand free for the high shots. By digging his toes into the ice he could quickly regain his feet, ready for the rebound," Diamond reports in the *Official NHL 75th Anniversary Commemorative Book.*

Gerald Eskenazi, in *A Thinking Man's Guide to Pro Hockey,* offers a view of the era's great trio, Jacques Plante, Hall, and Sawchuk: "Big leads never prevented Plante from trying his best when he was with the Canadiens. Always in the back of his mind was the Vezina Trophy. But the other great goalies of his era, Hall and Sawchuk, had a different mental approach. They wouldn't consider it a tragedy to yield a goal when they had a big lead. Hall and Sawchuk had high-scoring teams, too, but their defenses were not nearly so expert as the Canadiens'." That fact, alone, makes Hall's career all the more special. He didn't play on teams that emphasized defense; in fact he, himself, criticized that attitude. As quoted by Eskenazi, Hall said, "I was once fighting for the Vezina in the final week of the season and the players didn't even know it. They were just intent on getting their own goals."

There was playoff hockey for Chicago in 1958-59 as the club just missed a winning season. The Hawks finished 28-29-13, four points behind second-place Boston but well adrift of the league and Cup winners from Montreal. Hall was third in goals-against average, and Litzenberger was fourth in goals scored and fifth in total points. Hull did not improve upon his first year figures, finishing 18-32-50, but he was just a year away from becoming the "Golden Jet."

Chicago made Montreal work for a 4-2 semi-final Stanley Cup victory in their first taste of post-season action since 1953. After dropping the first two games in the Forum, the Hawks returned to the Stadium to even the series, but there was to be no repeat of that in the next two contests. The Canadiens won 5-2 in the Forum, then closed out the series with a 5-4 victory April 4 in Chicago.

Hockey Hall of Fame and Museum

Glenn Hall (in goal)

The 1959-60 season was uncannily like the one before. The Hawks again finished just under .500 (28-29-13) and were third in the NHL. They again faced Montreal in the Stanley Cup semifinals, and once again they were beaten—this time in four straight games—as the Canadiens were in the midst of one of their greatest eras. They would win their fifth straight Stanley Cup that spring, but Chicago would need to wait only one more year

to take revenge in the sweetest possible manner.

That 1959-60 season saw Hull come into his own. He won the Art Ross Trophy with a 39-goal, 42-assist season that enabled him to edge Boston's Bronco Horvath by a single point for the NHL scoring crown. His 39 goals equalled Horvath in that department. Hay, the Calder winner, was second in scoring with 55 points while Mikita contributed 26 in his first full season. Hall, meanwhile, stepped up to second place in the goals-against averages, his 2.57 just narrowly behind the 2.54 figure of Montreal's Plante, while he led the league in shutouts with six.

The season was notable for more than just the battle between Plante and Hall for goaltending leadership. On November 7, 1959, the Montreal netminder had made history when he became the first goalie ever to play an NHL game while wearing a facemask. Fittingly, Hall was Plante's opponent that night in the Montreal Forum as the teams finished tied at 2-2.

It All Comes Together

What had taken years to build bore fruit for Pilous and the Hawks in 1960-61. They finished the regular season in third place, but achieved that elusive winning season with a 29-24-17 mark. Hall again led the league in shutouts with six and was his usual stingy self (2.57 GAA) between the pipes. Pierre Pilote and Reg Fleming were first and second in penalty minutes, with Eric Nesterenko fifth. The Hawks were taking nothing lying down.

Surprisingly, perhaps, the season wasn't a big

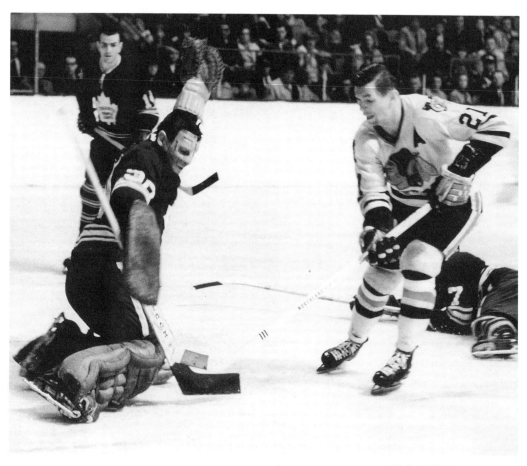

Stan Mikita (21) scores on Toronto's Terry Sawchuk

one for Hull. He was fifth in goals with 31, though this was well behind Montreal's 50-goal marksman Bernie Geoffrion. The key was offensive balance rather than one superstar's output. Hay made a mockery of the sophomore jinx, following his Calder Trophy year with an 11-48-59 season that led the Hawks. Hull was next with 56 points and there were important contributions from many others. Mikita had 53, Murray Balfour, Ken Wharram, and Ron Murphy all hit for 40 or more, and Pilote, one of the acknowledged best at his profession in an age when there many standout defensemen, weighed in with 35 points including 29 assists.

Nevertheless, when the playoffs started with the Hawks matched with Montreal yet again, not many people would have wagered on a different outcome from the past. The Canadiens still had Plante in goal and Doug Harvey and Tom Johnson on defense. "Rocket" Richard had retired, but Geoffrion, Jean Beliveau, Dickie Moore, Henri Richard, Ralph Backstrom and Bill Hicke led a still-potent attack. They had won the regular season title with 92 points, just two ahead of a strong Toronto team, but 17 points better than Chicago.

The playoffs, however, proved dramatically different, turning in the third game of the series when Balfour's goal 12:12 into the third overtime gave Chicago a pulsating 2-1 victory and the lead in the series. Even though Montreal rebounded to win game four in Chicago Stadium, there was to be no sixth straight Cup for the Canadiens. Glenn Hall personally saw to that. He shut out Montreal in successive 3-0 games on April 1 and April 4.

For Hall, goaltending was never easy, but a way to earn a living. His heroics in the 1961 finals were just normal for the 11-time All Star, but he never mastered the art of taking each game in a calm, relaxed manner. "I hate every minute I play," he admitted in *The NHL's 75th Anniversary Commemorative Book*. "I'm sick to my stomach before the game, between periods, and from the start of the season to the end. I sometimes ask myself, 'What the hell am I doing out here?' But it's the only way I can support my family. If I could do it some other way, I wouldn't be playing goal."

The finals pitted Chicago against Detroit—which had also sprung a semifinal upset, beating Toronto—and the Stanley Cup final was an all-American affair for the first time in more than a decade. The Hawks prevailed, 4-2, in the final series, with the final 5-1 triumph an indication of how the entire team produced under the pressure of the championship series.

Mikita and Balfour finished the playoffs atop the goal-scoring list, while Pilote (15 points) and Hull (14) were right there with Detroit's great Gordie Howe (15) in the Stanley Cup point-scoring race. But the goals in the finale came from the "supporting cast" which had done so much to define the Chicago work ethic: Fleming, Ab McDonald, Eric Nesterenko, Jack "Tex" Evans and Wharram were the marksmen who put the champagne in the big Cup for the Blackhawks on April 16, 1961. Only Nesterenko and Wharram had been double-figure goal scorers in the regular season; Evans had not scored at all, but his unassisted effort 6:27 into the final period was the backbreaker for the Red Wings.

The next season saw the Hawks produce another 75 point campaign (31-26-13) and another third place-finish. They again beat the Canadiens in the Cup semifinals, but there was to be no second straight Stanley Cup. Toronto saw to that by winning the final series four games to two with aid from an unexpected source. The finals had begun as a duel between legendary goalies, Chicago's Hall and Toronto's Johnny Bower, but the Leafs' coach, Punch Imlach, produced a master stroke in game four. He lifted Bower in favor of Don Simmons, a left-hander who had languished on the bench during most of his days in Toronto, after having been obtained from the Boston Bruins. Simmons had played in just nine regular season games, but he was ready when called upon and wound up winning the final two playoff games, including the decisive sixth contest in Chicago Stadium, 2-1.

Hall had seen his record string of consecutive games come to an end at 552 in that season, after he suffered a pinched nerve in the November 8, 1962, game and had to leave the ice. However his performance was as consistent as ever—2.66 GAA and a league-leading nine shutouts. Hull won the Art Ross Trophy after matching Geoffrion and "Rocket" Richard with 50 goals in an NHL season. Four years later the "Golden Jet" became the first player to break through that barrier when he scored 54 goals in the 1965-66 season. Mikita was fast becoming one of the most feared and respected centermen in the game—renowned for his stick-handling and playmaking as well as his tenacious style of play. He finished behind the Rangers' Andy Bathgate in assists with 52, a number equalled by teammate Hay. A great Chicago era was in progress.

What Might Have Been

From the 1962-63 season, Pilous's last behind the bench, through the 13-year Billy Reay era, Chicago was consistently one of the finest teams in the National Hockey League. The Blackhawks never had a losing season in that stretch, claiming six divisional championships and one overall NHL title. They had individual award winners with Hall, Hull, Mikita, and Pilote, and the brilliant Tony Esposito was added to the cast as Hall's successor. Hull became the most feared goal scorer of his era and Mikita went on to establish himself as one of the greats.

Hockey Hall of Fame and Museum

Bobby Hull (9)

For all that, there will be some critics who will always suggest that the Blackhawks never quite realized their full potential during this remarkable era. They didn't win a Stanley Cup, despite three appearances in the final—on each occasion a Montreal team was in their way at the last hurdle. The loss in the classic 1971 seven-game series was a particularly hard one to swallow.

This was also the beginning of NHL expansion, a period when the game was undergoing major growth and change. For the Hawks, expansion meant a change in the tradition of Chicago hockey. New rivalries were created with nearby teams in St. Louis and Minnesota when Chicago moved to the Western Division in 1970-71. This also meant the end of a long-standing era—the rest of the "original six" teams stayed in the Eastern Division when the first realignment was made.

It is worth taking a quick look at three seasons during this era, because they show the depth of talent that Reay commanded during his tenure on the Stadium bench. In 1963-64, when the Hawks finished second to Montreal, Mikita won the Art Ross Trophy, edging Hull 89-87, while Hull topped the goal-scoring charts with 43. Hall finished with a 2.31 GAA and seven shutouts. In 1964-65, when Montreal beat the Hawks in the Cup finals, Mikita won his second straight scoring title with a 28-59-87 season. Pilote outdistanced all defensemen with a 14-45-59 year that was a harbinger of things to come as the game changed. The 1965-66 season was Hull's record-smashing season, the "Golden Jet" getting 54 goals and 97 points to run away from the competition. He was 22 goals better than runner-up Frank Mahovlich in that department and 19 points ahead of Mikita, who surrendered the Art Ross Trophy to his teammate.

An NHL Championship at Long Last

The 1966-67 campaign was extra special because the Blackhawks won the overall NHL title for the first time in their history. Their 41-17-12 performance saw them run away from the pack and finish 17 points ahead of second-place Montreal. There was disappointment in post-season, however, when Toronto upset the champions four games to two in the semifinals, but at least one fabled piece of Chicago lore had been laid to rest.

Dan Diamond tells the story in *The NHL 75th Anniversary Commemorative Book*: "The Black Hawks captured their first league championship in forty years, breaking what had become known as the 'Curse of Muldoon.' Pete Muldoon was the Hawks' first coach, who, upon being fired, vowed that the team would never finish in first place. Muldoon, in fact, said no such thing: the 'Curse' was invented by a sportswriter in 1941."

If there was anyone directly responsible for lifting the curse, imaginary or not, it was Mikita, the 5-foot, 9-inch, 169-pound Czech who had transformed himself from a one-time league leader in penalty minutes to a model forward. He finished the 1966-67 season with just 12 penalty minutes, an astonishing figure for a player who had logged more than 100 on four previous occasions and racked up 154 just two seasons before. Mikita became the first player to win three major trophies in that championship season, capturing the Art Ross, the Hart, and the Lady Byng. He never again had triple figures in penalty minutes and ultimately finished his 22-year NHL career with his feisty days a distant memory.

The Hawks couldn't maintain the pace, but their record stayed well above .500 as expansion hit with whirlwind force. In 1967-68 the NHL introduced six new teams, placing all of them in a new division. As a result, the entire Eastern Division (the original teams) finished above .500 while no one in the West managed to play winning hockey. Chicago sank to fourth in the East in a season that was notable in goal; for the first time since 1957-58 Glenn Hall didn't play a game for the Blackhawks. He had been made available in the expansion draft and was snapped up by St. Louis, where he had one more league-leading season (1968-69, 2.17 GAA) before retiring in 1971 and heading straight for the Hall of Fame.

Chicago actually finished last in the East in 1968-69, but that was no fault of Robert Marvin

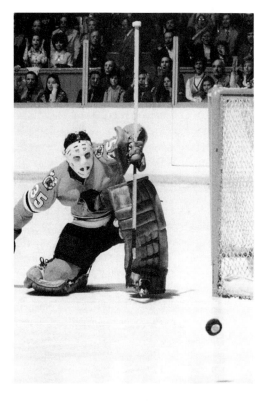

Tony Esposito

Hull. He scored 58 goals that season, the fourth of what would be five 50-goal seasons in a Chicago sweater. The Hawks still finished a game above .500 (34-33-9), but that was as much due to the expansion factor as to the team's strengths. They were 26 points behind Montreal, and even expansion St. Louis finished with 11 more points than the Blackhawks. It was definitely not the high point in Reay's tenure.

All changed immediately. In five of the next seven seasons Chicago finished at the head of its division, in part because of a little-noticed move made at the end of that disappointing 1968-69 year. On June 11, 1969, Chicago paid just $25,000 for a Montreal goaltender named Tony Esposito. Esposito had played just 13 games for the Canadiens, who had Rogie Vachon and veteran Gump Worsley ahead of him as well as youngster Phil

Myre and a talent named Ken Dryden in the system. They could afford to let Esposito go.

It is hard to understate just how much Esposito meant to Chicago in the next decade. He moved right into the lineup as the kind of workhorse netminder that Hall had been, starting off with a Rookie of the Year season in 1969-70 that included a 38-17-8 record and a 2.17 goals-against average. His goals against over the rest of the decade show how valuable he was to the team: 1971, 2.27; 1972, 1.77; 1973, 2.51; 1974, 2.04; 1975, 2.74; 1976, 2.97; 1977, 3.47; 1978, 2.63; 1979, 3.27.

The Eastern Division winning team of 1969-70, when Esposito led the league in wins, GAA, and shutouts (with a remarkable 15), may have been among the best of the Blackhawk teams. It had Mikita and Hull in their primes, Pat Stapleton, Doug Mohns, and Keith Magnuson on defense, and talented depth across the lines: Dennis Hull, Mikita, and Cliff Koroll; Bobby Hull, Pit Martin, and Jim Pappin; Lou Angotti, Eric Nesterenko, and Chico Maki were all names to be reckoned with.

The Hawks did not win a Stanley Cup, however. In fact they only finished first in the division by virtue of posting five more wins than the Boston Bruins, who also accumulated 99 points. The Bruins were led by two of the greatest players of their era, the now-mature Orr (33-87-120) and Esposito's brother Phil, who led the NHL in goals with 43 en route to a 99-point season.

In the playoffs, Chicago sailed past Detroit in a four-game sweep, while the Bruins were working hard to defeat the New York Rangers in six games. It didn't matter, however. In the showdown between the East's best, Boston prevailed decisively in a four-game sweep, then did the same to St. Louis in the inter-division Stanley Cup final. One of the best-ever Chicago teams came up empty-handed.

A Classic Final Battle

The next season may have been even more

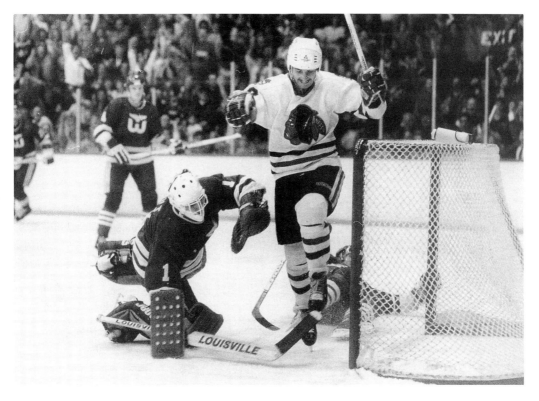

AP/Wide World Photos

Denis Savard scores against Hartford's Mike Liut

frustrating for Chicago fans. Now in the revamped Western Division, the Hawks cruised away from the pack to win the regular season crown by 20 points over St. Louis. Their 49-20-9 record was the best in the team's history. Hull had a 96-point season, 11 Blackhawks made the Western Division All-Star team, and all that seemed necessary to put the cap on the outstanding era was a fourth Stanley Cup triumph.

The Hawks swept past Philadelphia in four games to open their Cup bid, while Montreal was engaged in a seven-game struggle with the Bruins before getting safely into the semifinals. There it was the Blackhawks who labored, needing seven games to subdue the Rangers while the Canadiens dispatched Minnesota in six. The stage was set for still another Chicago-Montreal showdown. It turned out to be one of the very best in history.

Esposito was matched not against a veteran Montreal goaltender but the rookie Dryden, called into the front line after playing just six regular season games. In those, Dryden had a 1.65 GAA, presaging the kind of hot hand he would carry through the finals.

The Hawks actually won the first two games of this grinding final, with Pappin scoring after 21:11 of overtime on opening night for a 2-1 victory, and Angotti getting a pair of goals in the second game as Chicago took a 5-3 victory and a 2-0 series advantage. Undaunted, Montreal snapped back with two wins in the Forum, where the Mahovlich brothers, Frank and Peter, took turns bedeviling Chicago. It was now a best-of-three finale with the Hawks enjoying home-ice advantage.

Esposito, who finished the playoffs with a

Mike Keenan

the finals, losing four games to two to Dryden and his mates after a 42-27-9 regular season that notched another Western Division crown. This time, however, Chicago was no better than fourth overall, and it was a different team. Bobby Hull, for so long the signature around which the Hawks wrote their scripts, had jumped to the Winnipeg Jets of the rival World Hockey Association. The "Golden Jet" truly could not be replaced.

A Near 20-Year Wait

Remarkably, it would be the final decade of the 20th century before Chicago again reached a Stanley Cup final. There would be seven more divisional titles after Bill White replaced Reay in 1976-77 and a new generation of stars, but success at the very top level continued to elude the franchise.

Bob Pulford had two turns as coach, winning three divisional titles in five full seasons behind the bench. Orval Tessier came from the minor leagues and had a 47-win season in 1982-83, but couldn't repeat the act the next season. Mike Keenan, a success in Philadelphia and with Team Canada, brought his firm coaching style to the Windy City and won divisional honors, but when the one Stanley Cup chance appeared, Mario Lemieux and Pittsburgh stood in the way. Even in 1992 it seemed that Chicago always had the misfortune to face a French-Canadian in the showdown. Lemieux, after all, had gone from the Montreal suburb of Laval to stardom in Pittsburgh.

Along the way the Hawks had plenty of happy moments, perhaps none better than the day they plucked Darryl Sutter with the 179th pick of the NHL entry draft. Sutter's family produced six NHL players and three coaches, so it is odd that he was overlooked for so long that June afternoon.

There were also notable achievements. Mikita collected his 500th career goal on February 27, 1977, and had his jersey retired on October 19, 1980, capping a fabled career. The No. 21 sweater was the first ever hoisted to the rafters by Chicago. Denis Savard, plucked from under the nose of

2.19 GAA, blanked the Canadiens in game five, so goals by Dennis Hull and Koroll were more than enough for the Hawks. But the Mahovlich brothers played executioners again in game six with third-period goals—Frank tying the game, Peter winning it—as Montreal prevailed, 4-3, to force the seventh game in the Stadium.

This game may be remembered as the worst cut of all for Chicago fans. Dennis Hull gave the Hawks a 1-0 first-period lead, then Dan O'Shea, scorer of just four regular season goals, made it 2-0 early in the second. Dryden allowed nothing more, however.

Montreal came back on a controversial long-range goal by Jacques Lemaire and a pair by Henri "Pocket Rocket" Richard. The Rocket's third-period goal was the game-winner that allowed Montreal to take the Cup. Chicago was left to reflect on another missed opportunity.

A year later the Hawks fell more meekly in

107 points. (That was just two years after he had been selected third in the draft.) In 1982-83 Al Secord became the second Blackhawk to score more than 50 goals in a season when he netted 54. Only Bobby Hull (five times) had done it before.

The club's two great modern netminders, Esposito and Hall, were jointly honored on November 20, 1988. Hall's No. 1 and Esposito's No. 35 were retired on the same evening. Happily for Chicago fans, an heir apparent, Ed Belfour had been signed the spring before.

Defenseman Doug Wilson earned all-star status and recognition as one of the most accomplished skaters and playmakers among backliners in the game. Wilson, who did it all without sacri-

ficing the defensive skills, was one of the last NHL regulars to play without a helmet. Steve Larmer earned recognition as one of the club's standout wingers with three 90-plus point seasons, five years with 40-plus goals, and a record-setting 59 assists in 1989-90—the best ever racked up by a Chicago right wing.

Jeremy Roenick came out of Boston, Massachusetts, and Thayer Academy to achieve NHL stardom. His 53 goals in the 1991-92 season broke Savard's club mark for a centerman and put him on the same plane with Hull and Secord. His future loomed brightly ahead of him.

In the meantime Belfour was coming into his own in goal. His 1990-91 season included a Calder

AP/Wide World Photos

Ed Belfour (30)

In the meantime Belfour was coming into his own in goal. His 1990-91 season included a Calder Trophy and 43 wins, despite playing for Keenan, the coach who had earned the nickname "Captain Hook" based on his reputation for pulling goalies quickly. Belfour had the temperament to ride the wave and was the mainstay of the Hawk team that reached the 1992 finals. In those playoffs he played 18 games and allowed just 2.47 goals per game, figures that belied the wide-open, free-scoring nature of modern hockey.

Pittsburgh had the last statement in 1991-92, sweeping four games from Chicago, but that 4-0 result is misleading. Three of the games were decided by a single goal. Prior to the final, the Hawks had swept past Edmonton and Detroit in the previous two rounds after needing six games to eliminate St. Louis. Overall, the Hawks finished with a 12-6 post-season record, second only to Lemieux and the fabulous Penguins.

By 1992, Keenan's fiery disposition had grown tiresome and he was dismissed. Darryl Sutter assumed the role of head coach, while Bob Pulford took over as general manager. In 1992-93, the Blackhawks finished first in the Norris Division and third overall in the league with a record of 47-25-12. Team defense was stellar, as Chicago allowed only 2.7 goals per game. With high hopes, the team entered the playoffs, but were knocked out in four games by the St. Louis Blues. The team's lack of offensive production (six goals in four games) killed them. Pulford realized that many of Chicago's core players were aging, and set a goal for the 1990s of infusing youth into his lineup.

SOURCES

BOOKS

Diamond, Dan, editor, *The Official NHL 75th Anniversary Commemorative Book,* Montreal: NHL Publications, 1991.

Eskenazi, Gerald, *A Thinking Man's Guide to Pro Hockey,* New York: E. P. Dutton, 1972.

Fischer, Stan and Shirley Fischer, *The Hockey Encyclopedia,* New York: MacMillan, 1983.

Greenberg, Jay, Frank Orr, and Gary Ronberg, *NHL: The World of Professional Hockey,* New York: The Rutledge Press, 1981.

Romain, Joseph and Dan Diamond, *The Pictorial History of Hockey,* New York: Gallery Books, 1987.

—*Jerry Trecker* for Book Builders, Inc.

DALLAS STARS

Beginning in the 1993-94 National Hockey League season, the Dallas Stars replaced the Minnesota North Stars in professional hockey's top circuit. Some deemed this replacement shocking; in 1967, when the NHL doubled its size, Minneapolis-St. Paul was named as one of the first expansion franchises. While hockey in Texas is not all that unnatural—the state supported the World Hockey Association during the days when there were a pair of leagues at war—the absence of an NHL hockey presence in Minnesota seems incongruous.

Minnesota is one of the greatest hockey-player producing states in America, rivalled only by Massachusetts for the excellence of its high school programs. In addition, it has some of the finest college hockey in the United States. The state would seem to be a perfect locale in which to place an NHL franchise, but the region never became attached to the professional team.

Through their 26-year history, the North Stars

too often struggled for an audience. When the move to Dallas was announced, there were the usual cries of protest, but it had long been obvious that fan support was not sufficient to satisfy ownership in the modern age.

The last great North Stars' success, the run to the 1991 Stanley Cup finals, illustrated the conundrum: early in the season there was no trouble getting a ticket for Minnesota games. Only as the playoff run gained momentum were the games sellouts. Since modern franchises no longer are satisfied with such erratic attendance, it was only a matter of time before the Stars would head elsewhere.

Those troubles were far in the future when the NHL decided to add Minnesota to the six Western Division teams who would begin play in the 1967-68 season. As Dan Diamond in *The NHL's Official 75th Anniversary Commemorative Book* relates, the potential of the new franchise was widely hailed. The new owners—Gordon Ritz,

Bob McNulty, and former college player Walter Bush, Jr.—had Central Hockey League experience. There was a new rink in Bloomington, and Wren Blair was coach and general manager. Noted Diamond, "Blair, a veteran junior and minor pro coach and manager, had considerable experience as a scout and director of minor-league personnel for the Boston Bruins. Blair also had a background in international hockey, having managed the Whitby (Ontario) Dunlops, IHHF world amateur champions in 1958."

There was good news, too, at the first expansion draft. The North Stars selected Cesare Maniago from the New York Rangers. He would prove to be a consistently fine goalie in the team's early years. They also tabbed Wayne Connelly and Bill Goldsworthy from Boston. Goldsworthy emerged as one of the team's major stars in its first decade of existence.

But the North Stars also exhibited one of the problems that often plague expansion teams in their early years. Anxious to make an immediate impact, the new clubs were wont to exchange draft choices for players. Because the established clubs had many players, stockpiling talent in the minor leagues and utilizing territorial choices, this was a guessing game that often worked against new teams.

Diamond related some of the machinations that characterized the immediate aftermath of expansion: "The ingenuity of owners and managers of both established and expansion teams was demonstrated in their efforts to outflank the Expansion Draft. Managers of established clubs were willing to part with cash, players and future draft choices to induce their expansion counterparts to pass over the best unprotected players on their lists.

The Canadians, for example, traded three players from their talent-rich farm system (Andre Boudrias [the Stars' second-leading scorer in their first year], Bob Charlebois and Bernard Cote) to Minnesota for the North Stars' first choice in the 1971 amateur draft. What didn't appear in the official trade record was the North Stars' agreement to select someone other than the Habs' Claude Larose with the first overall pick in round

three of the 1967 Expansion Draft. Minnesota used its pick to select Dave Balon from the Montreal roster, enabling the Habs to keep Larose."

Two Hats for Wren Blair

There was another challenge facing the new teams—the players were no longer the compliant chaps who had once simply been happy to have a job in the six-team NHL. Expansion, coupled with the advent of the new World Hockey Association a few seasons later, created a players' market and made new demands on coaches and officials.

Fred Shero, who was busy building the Philadelphia Flyers into a team that would be the first great expansion juggernaut, expressed the attitude of many old-timers: "It used to be that a player gave out 110 percent," he was quoted as saying in Gerald Eskenazi's *A Thinking Man's Guide to Pro Hockey.* "But there's less desire around today. If a guy can't make it with Montreal what's he got to worry about? He knows there are so many expansion teams around he can make it with one of them."

Minnesota had picked Blair, a hockey veteran, to serve as general manager, but he also wound up coaching the better part of three years because he, like Shero, had difficulty with the "new breed." "The problem today is finding a coach who can relate to the new breed of younger player," Blair said in Eskenazi's book. "I'm having a hell of a time finding a coach who's young enough to talk to them. The old ways are finished. You can't just tell a kid to play for you because you're the boss. You've got to find ways to motivate the new player. The old threats, the old ways, don't work anymore. This is going to be the biggest problem hockey is going to face over the next years."

The tension that is always present when major change ensues was obvious. It would be easier to grant franchises and draw up schedules than to put new, competitive teams on the ice.

That first Minnesota season was a reasonably successful one (27-32-15, fourth place in the

TEAM INFORMATION AT A GLANCE

Founding date: June 5, 1967, as the Minnesota North Stars;
moved to Dallas, became the Dallas Stars, 1993

Home ice: Reunion Arena
777 Sports Street
Dallas, TX 75207
Phone: (214) 748-1808

Seating capacity: 16,000 (app.)

Team colors: Black, gold, and green
Team nickname: North Stars, 1967-93; Stars, 1993--
Logo: Star

Franchise record	Won	Lost	Tie
(1967-93)	758	970	334

Western Division, and a series win over Los Angeles in the first round of the Stanley Cup playoffs), but it contained a tragedy that was to influence many players in the NHL. Joseph Romain and Dan Diamond, in *The Pictorial History of Hockey,* explained: "Near the season's halfway mark, journeyman player Bill Masterton was fatally injured after striking his head on the ice. Masterton was a longtime minor pro player who was enjoying his first NHL season with the Minnesota North Stars when the accident occurred. The freakish nature of the incident—no rough play was involved—accelerated the trend that today see almost universal use of helmets for skaters at the NHL level."

Masterton, a popular player, was honored by the NHL Writers' Association, which presents the Bill Masterton Memorial Award to a player each season. Each team nominates a player who shows the qualities of perseverance, sportsmanship, and dedication to hockey. Although there is only one overall winner, the nomination of a player in each

city is a way of extending the value of the trophy and keeping Masterton's memory alive. One future North Star, Al MacAdam in 1980, was to win the award. Claude Provost, of Montreal, was the initial honoree.

It Takes Time to Win

Although the North Stars had a Calder Trophy winner, Danny Grant, in their second season and a runner-up, Jude Drouin, for the same rookie of the year award in 1971, it was five years before they put their first winning team on the ice in Minnesota. That was no fault of Maniago, who immediately came to the new franchise and established himself as a fine, hard-working goalie. It seemed that the pool of players available for the original expansion draft simply wasn't that strong.

Eskenazi pointed out this situation, with particular reference to the Stars: "But the major statement about expansion, after the maneuvering, or the poor selections, is that the players generally are of lesser quality or over the hill. When the expansion of 1967 took place, 120 players were drafted. Each of the six new teams took 20 players apiece. Yet, in 1970, when the second expansion took place, only 28 of the original 120 draftees were still with their clubs. The North Stars, three years later, had only two players still around."

One of the players whom Minnesota let go in 1970 was Ray Cullen, a former Detroit Red Wing, who had been the third-leading scorer on the first-year North Stars. He was picked up by Vancouver when the next round of NHL expansion took place.

There were other paradoxes as well. Larose, the Montreal player whom Minnesota bypassed in the initial draft maneuvering, wound up as a North Star in the team's second season and finished as the third-leading scorer on a team that won just 18 games. He was picked up along with Danny Grant for the North Stars' first amateur draft choice in the 1971-72 season. It was apparent that, while the new clubs were still looking for immediate help, the older teams were stockpiling for the future by assembling draft picks.

Grant was the Calder Trophy winner that same 1968-69 season, leading the North Stars with 34 goals and 31 assists (Cullen was the second top marksman, a point behind), and Maniago had a solid 3.30 goals-against average. But there were precious few wins. The third season was not much different, although the Stars lost eight fewer games.

They still finished with only 60 points, and the year was most noteworthy for the arrival of two players who would prove to be long-serving assets: Jean-Paul Parise and Bill Goldsworthy. Forward Charlie Burns even took a stint at coaching that season, part of it in a player-coach role, as Blair finally left the bench altogether.

Long-Term Helpers

Parise was 26 years old and in just his third NHL season when he was sold to the North Stars by the Toronto Maple Leafs in December, 1967.

He had played just 22 NHL games and scored only twice when his chance came via an expansion club. The 5' 7", 168-pound left winger proved to be a good acquisition by Minnesota. In eight seasons he was a solid regular, three times scoring more than 20 goals and twice topping the 70-point mark. In 1969 and 1970. He led the North Stars in scoring as he skated on the top line with Tom Williams and Goldsworthy. He was the second leading scorer in the 1972-73 season with a 27-goal and 48-assist (75 points) season.

Goldsworthy had been picked up in the initial expansion draft as a 23-year-old. The Kitchener, Ontario, native, a 6-foot, 190-pound right wing, had played parts of three seasons in Boston but had been unable to win a regular place on the strong Bruins team. When he went to the North Stars he took full advantage of his chance, and his number ultimately was retired at the end of his Minnesota career. Only Masterton shares the same honor.

Goldsworthy, like Parise, was a consistent producer. He topped the 30-goal level five different times and could be counted upon for 60-plus point seasons. He was also one of those players who could be expected to dress for every game, able to shrug off the continual bumps and bruises that are an accepted part of the professional hockey player's life.

Two Great Goalies

Perhaps the most noteworthy aspect of the North Stars' early years was the presence of Maniago and, later, Lorne (Gump) Worsley, two of the game's better goaltenders in an age when there were a number of high quality netminders.

Cesare Maniago, born in Trail, British Columbia, on January 13, 1939, was 28 years old before he had a real chance to demonstrate his skills in the National Hockey League. At 6' 3" and 195 pounds, Maniago was a big man with quick reflexes and a flair for the dramatic. He had played seven games with Toronto in the 1960-61 season and drank the proverbial "cup of coffee" in Montreal in 1962-63 (14 games) before getting a shot in the New York Rangers' organization in the 1965-66 season. He shared the job with Ed Giacomin that first year, but Giacomin then turned workhorse, starting all but six Rangers' games over the next four seasons. That made Maniago expendable at the time of the first expansion. The big netminder was arguably Minnesota's best pick. It wasn't easy for him, though, especially in the early seasons.

Eskenazi quotes Maniago in *A Thinking Man's Guide to Pro Hockey* on the difficulties with an expansion club: "You finish a game in Minnesota," relates Maniago. "You need time to unwind from all those slap shots. But no. You've got to rush to catch a plane to New York. On the plane you're not relaxing. You're thinking of the goals you let in. You try to sleep, but you just can't. So after a while, you don't even try. Then you land in New York. Because of the time difference, it's an hour closer to morning. By the time you get into bed it's three o'clock. You're still tense. You try to sleep. You've got a game that night. Sometimes, I don't roll over till four or five."

Eskenazi points to such experiences as the rationale for the two-goalie system that became a pattern for modern hockey. But that change wasn't easy, either, especially for goalies like Maniago, who had been reared in the other tradition.

Again, the writer quoted the Minnesota netminder: "You're always hoping you're going to play," said Maniago. "When I used to back up Eddie Giacomin it was a big disappointment to find the coach chose him. I prepared myself mentally to play for a day and a half. It's like telling a quarterback or a pitcher that they won't start. You work like heck in practice and find out you're not going to be in the game."

Maniago played the lion's share of the games until Worsley arrived in Minnesota for the 1970-71 season. He played in 52 contests in the first season and turned in remarkable numbers. On a team that had a losing campaign, Maniago was a winner (21-17-9), and his 2.77 goals-against average was excellent. His six shutouts placed him second in the NHL behind only Giacomin.

Maniago was in the net for 64 games in the 1968-69 season, 50 in the 1969-70 season, and 40 in the 1970-71 season, when Worsley arrived to take some of the workload. Maniago's goals-against averages were 3.30 and 3.39 in the two years before Gump became his partner, then dipped to 2.70, 2.65, and 2.89 in the next three years respectively, affirmation that Maniago benefited from the alternating goalie system.

The Gump, One of the Best

Lorne Worsley, born May 14, 1929, had an extraordinary National Hockey League career. Elected to the Hall of Fame in 1980, Worsley broke into the league in the 1952-53 season as a Calder Trophy winner with the New York Rangers, a time when winning was not a habit on Broadway. Four times he led the NHL in losses as he played 60 or more games in seven seasons. His ten years with the Rangers made him a favorite with fans who noted his refusal to complain about the team's penchant for allowing too many shots on goal.

There was a certain satisfaction, then, for Worsley fans when he was traded to the powerful Montreal Canadians in 1963. He shared two Vezina Trophies while playing in The Forum and led the NHL in goals-against with a 1.98 average in the 1968-69 season. Minnesota purchased him on February 27, 1970, when he was 41 years old. Happily for the North Stars, this was one veteran who was far from washed up.

"Worsley was one of the best-liked men ever to play the game," wrote veteran Toronto hockey columnist Frank Orr in *NHL: The World of Professional Hockey*. "The Gumper had a consistent good nature, plenty of fast lines and [the] ability to stop the puck.... Chubby at five-foot-seven, 185 pounds, Worsley never ducked an issue, never hesitated to answer a question. His Ranger days were a succession of feuds with coach 'Fiery' Phil Watson, a large part of the war inspired by Watson's dislike for the size of Gump's girth." "Worsley is nothing but a beer-belly," Watson once roared. "As always, Watson doesn't have the faintest idea what he's talking about," Worsley shot back. "I never drink beer, only good Canadian whiskey."

The Gump also was one NHL goalie who never followed the lead of Jacques Plante, the first man to wear a face mask for NHL games. Orr reports that, typically, Worsley offered two explanations for his remaining maskless for so long. "Would it have been fair not to give the fans the chance to see my beautiful face?" Worsley asked rhetorically, then told Orr what actually lay behind his decision not to cover up. "Seriously, I had troubles adjusting to the mask because I had played so long without one. When I wore a mask I kept losing sight of the puck when it was at my feet. Eventually, I got accustomed to it enough to wear a mask. It sure saved a lot of stitches."

Worsley gave Minnesota four seasons before finally becoming a scout at the age of 45. His goals-against figures of 2.50, 2.12, 2.88, and 3.22 proved that he still had his extraordinary reflexes and competitive desire, even when he was one of the oldest players in his sport. He also helped the North Stars to enjoy a winning season.

The Jack Gordon Era

Jackie Gordon got his chance to coach at the NHL level in the 1970-71 season after a lengthy career in the minors. He needed a full season to get the club playing the kind of defense he wanted, but it paid off in the 1971-72 season when the North Stars finished 37-29-12, good for second place in the West.

That team had Doug Mohns, Barry Gibbs, Tom Reid, and Ted Harris in front of the redoubtable Maniago and Worsley, and posted the second-best defensive record in the regular season. Goldsworthy and Jude Drouin, who had been Calder Trophy runner-up the season before, were helped in the scoring department by Murray Oliver, while Lou Nanne, who had begun life in Minnesota as a defenseman, contributed 49 points on right wing. Maniago was fifth in the NHL that

Gump Worsley (shown during his playing days with Montreal)

year with his 2.65 goals against average; Worsley didn't appear in enough games for his 2.12 to rank among the leaders.

The major disappointment came in the Stanley Cup playoffs when Minnesota fell in a seven-game series to St. Louis in the first round. The final game was decided in overtime. But there was another winning year immediately afterward. Dennis Hextall, acquired from California in a May 1971 trade, had contributed just 16 points in 36 games in his first North Star year, but he burst out with 30 goals and 52 assists (82 total points) in the 1972-73 season. That enabled him to finish ahead of both Parise (75 points) and Drouin (73) in the team scoring battle, while Maniago posted five shutouts and another strong season in goal. Gilles Gilbert was now part of a three-man rotation in the Minnesota net, as Worsley played just 11 times that season.

The playoffs proved the end of the Minnesota run, a first-round loss to Philadelphia signalling not only a second straight Stanley Cup frustration but serving as a reminder that the North Stars were not as solid as the record appeared to indicate. They would go the next six seasons without a winning team, and the financial problems that beset both the Minnesota club and the struggling Cleveland franchise would ultimately drive the teams to discuss a merger.

Some Long, Long Years

Gordon's three-year reign at the helm ended in the 1973-74 season when the club plummeted precipitously to seventh place in the Western Division. He was gone after just 17 games, with Parker MacDonald finishing the year behind the bench. It was a strange season in that Hextall, with 62, wound up third in the NHL in assists, and Goldsworthy continued his fine offensive play. But the North Stars failed because the defense was no longer tight. Where the previous season's club had scored 254 goals and allowed just 230, this one registered 235 and gave up 275. That swing spelled the difference between success and failure.

Gordon returned as coach for 39 games in the 1974-75 season, with Burns handling the other 41 contests, but the defensive woes accelerated dramatically. The team scored only 221 times and surrendered 341 goals and again missed the playoffs. The offensive weakness was obvious: Hextall's 74 points and Goldsworthy's 72 led the scoring, but next in line was Murray Oliver, who tallied 19 goals and 15 assists in totalling only 34 points.

The 1975-76 North Stars team was no better, allowing 16 short-handed goals as they finished ahead of only the Kansas City Scouts in the Smythe Division. Tim Young broke in with an 18-goal, 33-assist season for 51 points in his rookie

year. He would improve greatly to garner 29 goals and 95 points the next year, a season when Swedish player Rolie Eriksson made his Minnesota debut with a 25-goal, 44-assist, 69-point season.

There still was not much to cheer, although a second-place finish in the weak Smythe Division did earn the North Stars a playoff spot despite a 23-39-18 record. It was no surprise when Minnesota was quickly bundled out of the Stanley Cup, losing two straight to Buffalo in the first round. Maniago was no longer in the Minnesota goal, having been dealt to Vancouver along with Jerry Korab for Gary Smith, a swap of leading netminders. Smith joined Pete LoPresti in Minnesota, where neither could point to a solid defense.

The downward trend that had begun in the 1973-74 season continued as well. The 1975-76 North Stars scored only 195 goals while yielding 303; the next season the attack was better, netting 240, but the defense continued to be porous, allowing 310 goals.

From the 1971-72 season, when Minnesota had allowed only 191 goals in 78 games, the goals-against figure had soared out of control. It would not crest until the next year, when Minnesota had three different coaches in an 18-53-9 nightmare season that saw them outscored 325 to 218. By the end, Lou Nanne, who had been a fixture with the club from the start, was given the job of coach and general manager to try to get things sorted out.

Merger with Cleveland

Against this background of losing seasons, there were also financial problems facing the franchise. This was the height of hockey warfare as the World Hockey Association's battle for players and territory was taking its toll on all sides. The WHA would eventually die, though four of its teams were absorbed into the older league, but the NHL continued to experience problems with its own expansion teams.

The 1976-77 season had seen two of the league's strugglers move to new sites: Kansas City went to Denver to become the Colorado Rockies and the California Golden Seals, who had experienced problems attracting support almost from the start of their franchise, were moved to Cleveland. In neither case did the new homes solve the problems. Colorado eventually was relocated to Byrne Arena as the New Jersey Devils. California-Cleveland survived until the 1978-79 season when they were merged with the North Stars. Minnesota had switched to the Adams Division in Cleveland's place, but the Twin Cities franchise was saved by the deal.

There was another piece of good fortune for the North Stars in that same year when they selected 20-year-old Bobby Smith as the number one pick in the 1978 entry draft. He turned out to be quite a catch, starring in two different stints with the Minnesota club.

A Calder Trophy Winner

Smith was a 6'4", 210-pound center with excellent instincts for the game, an accurate shot, and a nifty passing touch. Because of his size he suffered a bit from the critics who claimed he wasn't as physical as he should be, but the North Sydney, Nova Scotia, native always preferred to showcase his skills. His competitiveness was never questioned, and he time and again exhibited his ability to rise to the big occasion, as his career in both Minnesota and Montreal attests.

Smith had attracted attention in his final two seasons with Ottawa in the Ontario Hockey Association. In the 1976-77 season he earned OHA second team all-star recognition with a 65-goal, 70-assist season and a 32-point (16 goals, 16 assists) performance in the playoffs. His final junior season was even better—69 goals and 123 assists for 192 points in the regular campaign. He topped the OHA in both assists and points and won the Canadian Major Junior Player of the Year award as well as first team OHA all-star recognition. In the playoffs he matched his previous year's work with 15 goals and 15 assists in 16 games.

If Smith never quite matched those gaudy OHA numbers in the NHL, he was a consistent

point producer right from the start in Minnesota. He collected 30 goals and 44 assists and won the Calder Trophy during the year as the North Stars improved by 23 points under the tutelage of Glen Sonmor. Smith's best year in a Minnesota uniform came in the 1981-82 season when he garnered 114 points (43 goals and 71 assists), but he was arguably just as valuable in 1990-91, when he was a key force in leading Minnesota to a quite unexpected berth in the Stanley Cup finals. By then he was a 33-year-old veteran of the NHL.

The Drought Ends

Helped no little bit by the infusion of talent from the Cleveland dispersal draft, Minnesota finally ended the long walk in the wilderness in the 1979-80 season, Sonmor's first full season in charge. The club finished 36-28-16 with major contributions from Al MacAdam and Gary Edwards, a pair snatched from the Cleveland roster.

MacAdam had played with Philadelphia and the California-Cleveland combination before being protected by Minnesota on June 15, 1978, when players from the combined franchise were dispersed. He gathered 58 points in the 1978-79 season, a performance in keeping with his career numbers at previous stops. The 6-foot tall, 180-pound right winger with a left-handed shot chose the 1979-80 season to have his career year.

A total of 42 goals and 51 assists gave MacAdam a team-leading 93 points and helped him win the Masterton Trophy as the North Stars broke their long losing spell. It was the only time in 10 years that he would get more than 63 points in a season. The fact that he was the fourth-best sniper in the league that year, fashioning a 24.7 shooting percentage, explains part of the story.

Edwards, too, was on a roll during the 1979-80 season. A journeyman goaltender who had played in St. Louis, Los Angeles, and Cleveland—he would eventually see duty in Edmonton, Pittsburgh, and, again, in St. Louis—his 3.20 goals-against average in 26 games was the second-best he ever recorded in an NHL season. He teamed with Gilles Meloche in a season that finally stopped the bleeding on defense. For the first time since the 1972-73 season, the North Stars scored more goals (311) than they conceded (253).

A Rare Man in the NHL

Sonmor, who had been tapped to move behind the Minnesota bench during the 1978-79 season, was an unusual figure for his day in the National Hockey League. He came into the league with experience as an American collegiate coach, one of only two coaches in the league at the time with a United States background.

Frank Orr, writing in *NHL: The World of Professional Hockey,* takes up the unusual aspects of Sonmor's position: "Although coaching techniques in the NHL and, because of the major-league influence, in Canadian junior hockey as well, had remained stagnant for many years, large advances were made in coaching at other levels of the game, notably Canadian and U.S. college hockey."

"I feel that the coaching in U.S. college hockey always has been extremely competent," said Sonmor, who started his coaching career at the University of Minnesota after an eye injury ended his playing days. "For one thing, working in the university milieu is entirely difference than coaching a Canadian junior or a pro team. The athletes are in an educational setting, involved in the learning process all the time and therefore are very open to learning new things in hockey.'"

When Sonmor stepped up to the NHL he took new ideas with him, prepared to give the North Stars a different way to play. "Tempo! That's a big word in our plans for the North Stars," Sonmor related in *NHL: The World of Professional Hockey.* "We have a team that skates well and has excellent quickness. We want our team to keep the pace of the game, the tempo of the play, as high as possible. We want the puck on the move all the time when we have it and we want our team to 'counter-punch' well, to go from defense to offense very quickly when he get the puck. That has

always been a great asset of the Canadians, their ability to break up your attack and mount one of their own all in one motion. A club that can do that keeps opponents on edge all the time."

One reason there was all this talk about tactics and approach to the game was that new coaching blood, like Sonmor, was filtering into the sport. Another factor was the beatings the Soviet Union had been regularly administering to the best of the NHL. It was no longer possible for North American hockey people to shrug off the losses as the result of superior Soviet preparation for a short series. The visitors had a different, more puck-possession oriented approach to the game. North American coaches began to realize there was much to be assimilated.

Help from Cleveland

Sonmor had been picked by Nanne, whose 11-year NHL career was spent entirely with Minnesota. Although a Canadian by birth, the Sault Ste. Marie, Ontario, native became a well-known advocate of the Americanization of the NHL. He was one of the first to extensively scout the United States colleges for talent and to take an active role in support of player-development programs, including Olympic and international level play. For the next four seasons the Sonmor-Nanne team helped Minnesota to a place among the best in the NHL.

The 1979-80 team, led by MacAdam, Steve Payne (42 goals and 43 assists for 85 points) and Smith (27-56-83) went 36-28-16 and finished third in the Adams Division. Craig Hartsburg, who would spend his entire ten-year career with the North Stars, made his NHL debut on defense and produced a 44-point (14 goals, 30 assists) season that stamped him as a most important addition. Meloche and Edwards, of course, combined in goal.

The postseason yielded a pair of series wins, including a major upset in seven games against the Canadiens. Montreal was attempting its fifth straight Stanley Cup win that spring and led the second round confrontation 3-2 before the North Stars sprung the surprise. Ultimately, the Philadelphia Flyers eliminated the North Stars in five games, but the year marked a dramatic change of direction for the franchise.

The next year mirrored the previous season, as the North Stars compiled a 35-28-17 record. Smith had a big year with 93 points (29 goals, 64 assists), Payne was a 30-goal contributor, and Hartsburg escaped the sophomore jinx, tallying 43 points over the course of the season.

More Important Additions

This was also the season when Curt Giles made his first major contributions in what was to be a 12-year Minnesota career. He had come to the Stars from the University of Minnesota-Duluth in 1979-80, but was with Oklahoma City of the Central Hockey League for more than half of that year. In 1980-81 he was a regular, a steady defenseman who added skill and polish to the backline.

In goal, the North Stars unveiled another new talent. Don Beaupre made his NHL debut so effectively that Meloche was relegated to the number two role. Beaupre had been the club's second choice (32nd overall) in the 1980 entry draft, after earning a first team Ontario Hockey Association all-star berth in his final junior campaign. He didn't have great figures with the Sudbury Wolves, but obviously Nanne spotted something he liked about the 5'10", 172-pound netminder.

Although Beaupre would ultimately spend three different short stints in the minors before four seasons as Minnesota's number one goalie, he stepped directly into the line of fire in his rookie season. Just 20, he appeared in 44 games and posted an 18-14-11 record with a 3.20 goals-against average. In the playoffs he added a 6-4-2 ledger, though his goals-against average rose to 4.33.

Dino Ciccarelli also emerged as a star in these playoffs. Ciccarelli demonstrated during the postseason how much of an offensive force he

would be with the North Stars. He had split his first NHL year between Oklahoma City and Minnesota, getting 50 goals between the stops. In the playoffs, however, he turned into a postseason terror with 14 goals in 19 games. His 14 goals and 21 points were NHL playoff records for a rookie. Along with Payne and Smith he led the North Star attack.

Uncharted Territory

Those playoffs gave Minnesota fans their first taste of a Stanley Cup finals and, although the team eventually lost, the playoff run gave them plenty to cheer about in the spring of 1981. First Boston was eliminated in three straight games before Buffalo (4-1) and Calgary (4-2) fell. The last opponent for the North Stars was the New York Islanders, just starting to take firm command of all they surveyed in the league. This was the second of four straight Stanley Cup wins for the Isles, who dismantled the Stars in five games.

Ciccarelli blossomed fully the next year as the North Stars won the regular season Norris Division crown with a 37-23-20 campaign that matched the then-club record for wins in a season. In postseason play, however, the Chicago Blackhawks sprung a first round upset on the division champs, nailing Minnesota with an awkward chapter at the conclusion of an otherwise well-plotted season.

Broten Joins Ciccarelli

The 1981-82 season not only was the best regular campaign in many years for Minnesota, it also marked the first full seasons from two of the players who would dominate North Stars' scoring for much of the decade, as Ciccarelli was joined by Neal Broten.

Dino Ciccarelli didn't look like the archetypal scorer. At 5'10", 175 pounds, he gave the impression of power rather than agility, but that was deceptive. A quick skater with a very fast release on

Central Division

his shot, the Sarnia, Ontario, native was a scorer par excellence, gifted with a sixth sense for being in the right place. He was also a tough competitor who was particularly adept at fending off defensemen in front of the net, holding his position in front of the goaltender to get those vital deflected goals.

Ciccarelli had played his junior hockey with London in the OHA, where he won second team all-star honors in 1977-78 after a 142-point season at the age of 17. Injury curtailed his contributions the next year and he wasn't drafted. Minnesota subsequently picked him up as a free agent. He went back to London for the 1979-80 season, where he finished with 103 points, then spent that first pro season with Oklahoma City and Minnesota before the record playoff debut.

Ciccarelli scored 40 or more goals four times in the next eight years, topped by 55 in the 1981-82 season. Twice he went over the 100-point level, before he was eventually dealt to Washington for Mike Gartner in a major trade on March 7, 1989.

Broten hailed from Roseau, a small Minnesota town with a great high school hockey tradition. He starred at the University of Minnesota, then was part of the "Miracle of Lake Placid" in 1980, when the U.S. hockey team won the Olympic gold medal. He won the Hobey Baker Award as the top United States collegian in 1981 and was a first team Western Collegiate Hockey Association all-star the same season. He then moved right over to the Minnesota North Stars and became a local hero.

At 5'9"and only 170 pounds, Broten was no physical giant on the ice. Shrugging off the pressures of always playing in front of demanding home fans, he combined guile and skill into an NHL package that made him an 80-plus point producer four times in a decade with the North Stars. His best season statistically was 1985-86, when he collected 105 points on 29 goals and 76 assists. That was the fourth straight season that he appeared in the mid-season NHL All-Star Game.

In their first season together as full-timers, Ciccarelli and Broten finished 1-2 in the point parade as Minnesota put together that outstanding 1981-82 campaign. Broten and Smith tied for the scoring lead a year later when another touted prospect, Brian Bellows, was added to the cast.

The Perils of Top Choices

For Minnesota, both the 1982 and 1983 entry drafts offered great opportunities. As more than one hockey organization has learned in the era of an amateur selection process that culls unfinished 18-year-olds, along with opportunity comes the burden of missing on player evaluations of prospects so young.

The advent of the modern-day draft (featuring selections of 18-year-olds) had come as a direct result of the World Hockey Association and Ken Linseman's bid to be allowed to play in that circuit before the then-usual age of 20. Linseman's signing led the NHL to lower its draft-eligible age in the face of a possible court case that would have made them do so, anyway. But the change was not one welcomed by scouts and general managers, who often labeled the task of selecting youths "a crapshoot."

In 1982 the Stars struck a form of gold with their first pick, Bellows, the second overall selection in the draft. In 1983, conversely, when they had the first selection, they picked an American high schooler, Brian Lawton. Lawton never went on to NHL stardom, although he probably would have been the top choice of many teams in that draft.

What makes all of the draft talk so pressure-packed is the fact that draft selections are so open to second-guessing. In 1982, for instance, Boston had maneuvered to obtain the top pick so they could select defenseman Gord Kluzak in a season where most experts had Bellows rated No. 1. Kluzak, plagued by injury, never could deliver all his talent to Boston; the North Stars selected Bellows, who proved his worth.

The Lawton selection, however, has haunted the North Star brain trust. Other players available in that draft that the Stars bypassed included Pat LaFontaine, Steve Yzerman, and Tom Barrasso, all of whom would go on to enjoy fine careers in the NHL.

Some Winning Years

Bellows came into the NHL in 1982-83 with 65 points in 68 games. That helped the North Stars to a 40-24-16 season and second place in the Norris Division, as well as a first round playoff triumph over Toronto. The Chicago Blackhawks won the Norris Division title in the Stanley Cup action, however, sidelining Minnesota in five games. Meloche and Beaupre formed an almost identical tandem in goal, the former compiling a 20-13-11 record (3.57 goals against average) and Beaupre posting a 19-10-5 record (3.58 goals against average) in the regular campaign.

Bill Mahoney was behind the bench in 1983-84 when the North Stars posted a first-place finish in the Norris Division after a 39-31-10 regular season, the club's finest performance of the decade. Broten led the attack with 89 points while Bellows scored 42 goals and added 41 assists in his second season. Brad Maxwell (19 goals and 54 assists) and Ciccarelli (38 goals and 33 assists) also were major contributors in a strong season. Beaupre and Meloche were both over the 4.00 goals-against mark, though, a sign that the defensive tightness was slackening.

In the playoffs, Minnesota triumphed over Chicago in five games and St. Louis in seven before reality intruded. The North Stars faced the Edmonton Oilers in the Campbell Conference finals. Edmonton, which would win the first of four Stanley Cups in five years that season, swept the North Stars 4-0 in the series. There was no disgrace in losing at that stage, but that playoff failure, coupled with the regular season defensive woes, presaged a slide for Mahoney's club.

His next season was a 25-43-12, 62-point campaign softened somewhat by a first round upset victory over St. Louis in the playoffs. Chicago then put an end to Minnesota's season, posting two overtime victories to eliminate the North Stars in the Conference finals, 4-2.

Bellows led all scorers that year, but there were some who said that his 26 goal, 36-assist season wasn't all that was expected. Like all highly-touted players coming out of junior hockey in his era, Bellows suffered in comparison to Wayne Gretzky, who had redefined the standards in the NHL to such an extent that newcomers were hit with a tidal wave of expectations. Bellows wasn't a graceful, nifty player but rather a sturdy, hard-working citizen who could be counted upon for a steady performance night after night. Too many of the "new hockey" set wanted panache from everyone, a goal well beyond the level of most newcomers.

Three goaltenders played in that 1984-85 season for Minnesota. Beaupre and Meloche were joined by Rollie Melanson, who appeared 20 times between the pipes for the Stars. Beaupre enjoyed the best season statistically, tallying a 3.69 goals against average in 31 games, while Meloche finished with a 3.80 goals against average in 32 appearances and Melanson totaled a 4.10 goals against average in 20 appearances.

One More Winning Year

The 1985-86 season found Lorne Henning in the coaching hot seat; it proved to be the last winning campaign of the decade. Minnesota finished 38-33-9 that year, second in the Norris, as Broten had an excellent campaign. The local hero scored 29 goals and added 76 assists for a 105-point year that left him well ahead of Ciccarelli (44-45-89) and Bellows (31-48-79) at the conclusion of the regular season. Beaupre played 52 games in goal that season, while a newcomer, Jon Casey, made his first impact in the league with 26 appearances and a 3.89 goals-against average.

For Casey, arrival in the NHL proved to be a sometimes-difficult achievement. He was overlooked as a junior goaltender so he headed to the University of North Dakota, where he proved to be a reliable netminder for the better part of three years. After just five appearances for the traditionally strong Fighting Sioux in his freshman year,

Casey shared duties the next two, then was the workhorse in his senior season when he went 25-10-2 with a 3.13 goals against average in 1983-84. Signed as a free agent at the end of that collegiate season, he played twice for the North Stars in April 1984 but spent the next year in the American Hockey League.

At Baltimore in 1984-85 Casey won the Baz Bastien Trophy as the AHL's most valuable goaltender and was named to the AHL first team all-star squad. In 46 games he put together a 30-11-4 record, including four shutouts, and had a 2.63 goals against average. He added an 8-3 playoff record and a 3.31 Calder Cup goals against average to those statistics. Nevertheless, he didn't jump back to the NHL in one leap.

The 1985-86 season was split between Minnesota (26 appearances) and Springfield of the AHL. In 1986-87 Casey suffered through a 1-8-0

campaign in Springfield and a 14-15 season at Kalamazoo in the International Hockey League. At neither site did he keep his goals against average below the 4.36 per game level. When he played only 14 times in Minnesota the next year, compared with 52 games at Kalamazoo, it seemed unlikely that he would ultimately turn out to be the star of the 1991 Stanley Cup finals and a top-level NHL netminder.

The 1986-87 season was a disappointing one, as the North Stars suffered through a losing campaign. Nanne quit as general manager and the club resumed its downward slide. Ciccarelli scored 52 goals and added 51 assists for 103 points. His point total was more than 40 points ahead of that of his nearest teammate, Brian MacLellan.

Henning and Sonmor, back for a second turn at the helm, were the coaches that year as time ran out on Nanne. Kari Takko teamed with Beaupre

Goalie Jon Casey thwarts Ranger Mike Gartner (24)

in goal, but both Bellows and Broten were below form. Each finished with 53 points for the season, as an injury limited the latter to only 43 games.

Local Hero No. 2

The next season saw the North Stars played a wild card, hiring Herb Brooks as coach. Brooks, who had guided the United States to the Olympic Gold Medal in 1980, was a native of St. Paul and very much a hockey icon in the United States, but, unlike Broten, he was unable to add to his stature in Minnesota.

Brooks was 50 when he became the first Minnesota native to coach a team in the state. He had won 100 NHL games more quickly than any coach in the history of the New York Rangers during a 1981-85 stint on Broadway, but ultimately his attempt to graft a European-based style on NHL pros had failed. Before that he had won three NCAA titles at the University of Minnesota (1974, 1976, and 1979), where he compiled a .627 winning percentage. The Olympics success merely added to the American notion that he was some kind of hockey miracle man.

It didn't turn out that way. The season was not a productive one for the North Stars. The club produced a 19-48-13 ledger that relegated them to the cellar of the Norris Division. Brooks was replaced at the end of the campaign by Pierre Page. Page couldn't reverse the momentum in two years, either, although each of the next seasons was better.

Ciccarelli was traded to Washington for Mike Gartner in the 1988-89 year, as Dave Gagner emerged to lead the team in scoring. With Casey playing 55 games in goal there were signs of better things ahead.

In 1989-90 Bellows nearly hit the 100-point mark as he racked up 55 goals and 44 assists. Highly-regarded rookie Mike Modano tallied 75 points (29 goals and 46 assists) and placed second in the Calder Trophy voting that season as the North Stars went 36-40-4. Broten was back in top form with an 85-point year and Gagner again put up good numbers but, as had been the case in the past, issues off the ice were distracting from the action between the boards.

Relocation Rumors Return

Faced with continuing financial losses in the Twin Cities, the North Stars' owners, George and Gordon Gund, began exploring the possibility of moving the Minnesota franchise out west. Undeterred by the failure of a previous team in the Bay Area, the Gunds were looking at San Jose, which had an arena and an interest in an NHL franchise.

The NHL wasn't interested in promoting franchise relocation, however. As a result, an intriguing compromise emerged. When the league announced it would expand into the San Jose area it awarded the franchise to the Gunds and worked out a deal that allowed new investors to operate in Minnesota. There was even an agreement that allowed the San Jose franchise to draft some players from the North Stars' organization when expansion took place.

Dan Diamond, in *The Official NHL 75th Anniversary Commemorative Book*, adds that there was a longer term impact of the agreement: "The North Stars management team departed when the franchise was sold. General manager Jack Ferreira went to San Jose and coach Pierre Page and assistant Dave Chambers joined Quebec as general manager and coach respectively. The new North Stars' organization was headed by owners Howard Baldwin (a former managing partner with the Hartford Whalers) and Morris Belzberg. Shortly after the deal was completed with the Gunds, Norman Green, who had been a part-owner of the Calgary Flames, became a partner in the North Stars."

For Minnesota hockey fans that reorganization was to prove a turning point. It was Green who would eventually take control of the Stars and move the team to Dallas at the end of the 1992-93 season.

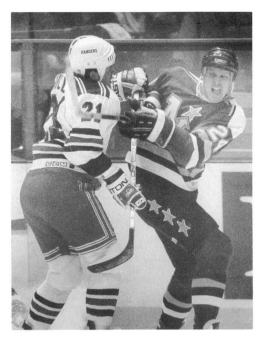

**Mark Tinordi (24) mixes it up with
Ranger Jody Hull (21)**

One Wonderful Memory

Before the team left Minnesota, however, the Stars left its fans in the North with a final burst of excitement. The 1990-91 season had Bob Gainey in charge and Bobby Smith back in the city where he had begun his NHL career. But even the convergence of two men who had spent enough time in Montreal to learn what it took to reach the top was not expected to produce an appearance in the Stanley Cup finals.

Perhaps it was the additional presence of Bobby Clarke, the inspiration of so many great Philadelphia Flyers' teams, in the general manager's role that tipped the balance. In any event, the North Stars enjoyed a tremendous run in the postseason that brought them to the very brink of an NHL championship.

Gainey had prepped for an NHL coaching job by going to Epinal in the French Hockey League at the conclusion of a brilliant 16-year career with the Canadians. While in Montreal Gainey played on five Stanley Cup winners, so he was certainly familiar with the requirements of postseason success. Minnesota's run was nonetheless a surprise given their unremarkable regular season: a record of 27-39-14, good only for fourth place in the Norris Division.

Gagner had 82 points, while Bellows added 75 and Broten posted 69; Casey was outstanding with a 2.98 goals-against-average. Still, few would have wagered the farm on a Minnesota appearance in the Stanley Cup Championship series.

The postseason began with a stunning upset as Casey became a playoff hero on the strength of his spectacular goaltending. Regular season Norris Division champ Chicago was kayoed in six games. St. Louis fell in the division finals by a similar 4-2 count and Edmonton was dispatched 4-1 in the conference championship. Suddenly, Minnesota was in the final, pitted against Pittsburgh, led by superstar Mario Lemieux.

The North Stars actually won two of the first three games in that final as it appeared that Gainey had some kind of magic touch. Broten scored twice in the first game as the Stars triumphed, 5-4 in Pittsburgh, then both Gagner and Smith found the net in game three when the Stars won 3-1 to take the lead in the series. It was all Pittsburgh thereafter but the Stars had reclaimed their fans, playing to sellout crowds, and offered a platform for the future.

Bellows was a big gun in the playoffs, getting 10 goals and 19 assists, just ahead of Gagner's 12 goals and 15 assists. Broten (22 points) and Modano (20 points) also came up big in the postseason. The leadership provided by Smith, however, may have been the key to the achievement.

He contributed eight goals and eight assists in the playoffs after a 46-point regular season, proving that he not lost the edge that had always made him special in the minds of North Stars' fans. After all, they appreciated the little skills of hockey—finishing the check, making the key pass or winning the vital face off. Those were skills Smith had always exhibited.

The euphoria of the 1991 playoffs didn't prove enough to save the Minnesota franchise, however. The following season was a losing year (32-42-6) made particularly disappointing in the playoffs when the Stars surrendered a 3-1 series edge to Detroit.

The Stars won 4-3 and 4-2 on the Red Wings' ice, then took an apparently winning edge by capturing game four at home, but Detroit threw a pair of shutouts (3-0, 1-0) at Minnesota and then won the pivotal seventh game at home, 5-2.

The next season, with relocation rumors rampant, Minnesota turned in a 36-38-10 record. The club struggled throughout the season to make the playoffs but were turned away. Soon after the end of the season it was confirmed that the club would relocate to Dallas, where the team would be known as the Dallas Stars.

SOURCES

BOOKS

Diamond, Dan, *The Official National Hockey League 75th Anniversary Commemorative Book,* NHL Publications, 1991.

Eskenazi, Gerald, *A Thinking Man's Guide to Pro Hockey,* E. P. Dutton, 1972.

Fischler, Stan, and Shirley Fischler, *The Hockey Encyclopedia,* MacMillan, 1983.

Greenberg, Jay, Frank Orr, and Gary Ronberg, *NHL: The World of Professional Hockey,* Rutledge Press, 1981.

Romain, Joseph, and Dan Diamon, *The Pictorial History of Hockey,* Gallery Books, 1987.

The Sporting News Hockey Guide & Register, Sporting News Publishing Co., 1984-85, 1986-87, 1989-90.

Trecker, Jerry, "Season Review," *ESPN Sports Almanac '83,* Total Sports Publications, 1983.

—Jerry Trecker for Book Builders, Inc.

DETROIT RED WINGS

Detroiters began a love affair with professional hockey when the city was granted a franchise for the sport in 1926, becoming the home of one of the original six teams in the National Hockey League (NHL). The team, initially named the Detroit Falcons, lost considerable money during its first two seasons. In 1932 American industrialist James Norris and a partner bought the floundering club, and the Norris family retained control of the franchise for 50 years.

At this time the Detroit team was christened the Red Wings and, over the next quarter century, achieved considerable success, winning seven Stanley Cups and finishing first in the league 12 times—including an unprecedented seven league championships in a row from 1948-49 to 1954-55. Based on these statistics, the Red Wings teams of the early 1950s are considered among the best ever in the NHL.

Beginning in the late 1950s, the Red Wings finished first in the NHL only once, and the club's season records generally placed them among the bottom half of the league. At the conclusion of the 1961-62 season, an era ended as Jack Adams was forced to resign after a 35-year association with Detroit as both coach and general manager.

The year the league expanded, 1967, signalled the beginning of a dismal era for the Red Wings, with a revolving door for both coaches and players. During this time—from the late 1960s to the mid-1980s—the team's atrocious play earned them the moniker "The Dead Wings"; while individual players racked up impressive statistics, the team remained in the cellar of league standings. The Norris-owned organization was in disarray and nearly bankrupt, and in 1982 Bruce Norris sold the franchise to another family-oriented business man, pizza mogul Mike Ilitch.

The Red Wings flirted with success in the 1980s, twice reaching the semifinal round of the playoffs, but Detroit eventually lost and returned home to observe the Stanley Cup championships on television. During the late 1980s and early 1990s, club management developed talent-laden teams through trades and drafts, but despite high expectations, the Red Wings continued to fall short in playoff competition.

In 1992 hockey aficionados witnessed the first players' strike, which threatened the year's playoff schedule, the next season, and the comparative innocence to other sports that hockey seemed to possess. Just as the hockey world survived its first strike, Detroit fans have weathered the team's woes and the disappointing decades since the Red Wings captured a championship, still faithfully filling the arena to capacity to support their team.

Joe Falls explained this phenomena in a 1987 column for the *Detroit News:* "Hockey has always had a strange kind of hold on the sports fans of this city. It is a Canadian game by nature but the people around here have always loved it. They have always understood it.... Detroit has always been a hockey town and probably always will be."

Detroit Joined NHL

On September 25, 1926, a group of Detroit business leaders secured a National Hockey League (NHL) franchise for the city. The price tag: $100,000. Named the Detroit Cougars, the team consisted of players from British Columbia's Victoria Cougars of the Western Hockey League. Notable among the club's original players were Frank Frederickson, Frank Foyston, and Jack Walker, all of whom were later inducted into the Hockey Hall of Fame.

No home stadium existed in Detroit during the team's first season, so the Cougars played at Windsor, Ontario's Border Cities Arena. The Cougar's debut was less than promissory, as they lost—by a score of 2-0—to the Boston Bruins. The season too was forgettable; the team finished last in the American Division, winning only 12 of 44 games.

In the team's first year of existence, club president Charles Hughes reported that the Detroit

Hockey Hall of Fame and Museum

Ebbie Goodfellow

organization lost $84,000. Sensing an impending front-office change in the Motor City, NHL president Frank Calder urged Jack Adams—who had previously helped lead the Ottawa Senators to

TEAM INFORMATION AT A GLANCE

Founding date: September 25, 1926

Home ice: Joe Louis Arena
600 Civic Center Dr.
Detroit, MI 48226
Phone: (313) 567-7333
FAX: (313) 567-0296

Seating capacity: 19,275 (in addition, the fire marshall
allows 600 standing-room tickets to be sold)

Team colors: Red and white
Team nickname: Detroit Cougars, 1926-30; Detroit Falcons, 1930-32;
Detroit Red Wings, 1932—
Logo: Winged wheel

Franchise record	Won	Lost	Tie
(1926-1993)	1,849	1,895	706

Stanley Cup Wins (7): 1935-36, 1936-37, 1942-43, 1949-50, 1951-52, 1953-54, 1954-55
League First-Place Finishes (13): 1933-34, 1935-36, 1936-37, 1942-43, 1948-49, 1949-50,
1950-51, 1951-52, 1952-53, 1953-54, 1954-55, 1956-57, 1964-65
League Last Place Finishes (3): 1958-59, 1976-77, 1985-86

hockey's championship, the Stanley Cup—to apply for the Detroit coaching job, stating, "I think Detroit might be looking for a firebrand like you," according to *Hockey: The Story of the World's Fastest Sport.*

Calder was right, and the 1927 season marked the beginning of Adams's 35-year tenure with the Detroit hockey club, which culminated with his selection to the Hockey Hall of Fame. With Adams at the helm on November 22, 1927, the Cougars opened up their second season at Detroit's new Olympia Stadium, losing to Ottawa 2-1.

In the club's early days, attendance hovered around 80,000 for an entire season. However, with the stock market crash of 1929 and the ensuing Great Depression, penniless hockey fans came up with inventive ways to watch their team.

In *Hockey: The Story of the World's Fastest Sport,* Adams recounted a story about a 1930 charity game for which fans were instructed to pay what they could. One man had no money but did have several bags of potatoes. Sympathetic Olympia officials subsequently granted him standing room admission.

Because team owners could not depend on gate receipts to foot the bills for the team, the Red Wings were not faring much better than the general population. Adams once joked that if Howie

Right wing Larry Aurie was a standout for the Red Wings during the club's early years. Aurie played with the Red Wings from 1927-28 to 1938-39, although he missed most of the 1928-29 season due to sickness.

In a 1935 series on the Red Wings, *Detroit News* reporter Lloyd Northard summarized Aurie's capabilities: "Larry Aurie has been one of the best right wings in the National [Hockey] League since he joined the Wings.... Not only is he a good scoring wing but he is rated among the best back checkers and puck raggers."

In a *Detroit News* article, Olympia usher Charlie Clyde recalled Aurie's strong points as a player: "You should see him kill penalties. He was better than anyone else at it. In a tribute to his contributions, the team retired Aurie's jersey, number six.

AP/Wide World Photos

Morenz, a league superstar, would have been available for approximately two dollars, it still would have been out of Detroit's price range.

New Start With Norris Family

In 1930 the team's name was changed to the Detroit Falcons at the urging of local media members who thought the new sobriquet might bring good fortune to the club that had not qualified for the playoffs the previous year. Although this new name did not immediately alter Detroit's fortunes, significant changes loomed for the Detroit club.

In 1932 American industrialist James Norris and investor Arthur M. Wirtz bought the team and Olympia Stadium from the bankrupt Detroit Falcons organization. Because the country was still in the throes of the Great Depression, the two men got a bargain price: they paid $500,000 for both

the team and arena, whereas five years earlier Olympia Stadium had cost $2.2 million to build.

In the summer of 1932, Norris renamed his team the Detroit Red Wings. Norris had once played hockey for the Winged Wheelers of the Montreal Athletic Association and considered that squad's emblem particularly appropriate for Detroit, the hub of the nation's automobile manufacturing aptly nicknamed the "Motor City." Hence, Detroit's jersey logo became a winged automobile tire.

A demanding boss, Norris gave Adams a one-year probation as coach and general manager. The arrangement worked out well, and Adams never signed a contract while James Norris was alive. Norris oversaw other innovations for the club; in 1933, the Red Wings offered their fans the option of purchasing season tickets, becoming the first major sports team with such a program. Fans flocked to Olympia Stadium because the team was also improving under the direction of Adams, who had a knack for finding talented players.

By 1933-34 Detroit was earning respectability in the league. They finished on top in the league standings and beat the Toronto Maple Leafs to make their first bid for the coveted Stanley Cup. The 1933-34 championship series featured a matchup of two of the top forward lines in the league: the Chicago Blackhawks's Harold Marsh, Elwyn Romnes, and Paul Thompson versus the Red Wings's Larry Aurie, Cooney Weiland, and Herbie Lewis. Chicago, however, claimed the Stanley Cup, three games to one.

Adams Built Championship Teams

The 1934-35 season was not successful for the Red Wings as they finished last in the six-team league. To reverse the fortunes of his club, Adams began dealing, acquiring Syd Howe and Scotty Bowman at a cost of more than $50,000, and adding Hec Kilrea to the roster for another $7,500. The coach's zeal to win the Stanley Cup was evident in these moves, because this amount of money was enormous considering the country was still suffering the effects of Depression.

Adams also acquired center Marty Barry and, with wingmen Larry Aurie and Herbie Lewis, this forward line became one of the best in the league. In 1935-36 Adams's transactions paid off as the team rebounded from its dismal showing the previous year to place first in the American Division.

Detroit's 1935-36 playoff run was distinguished by a marathon game with Montreal in the first round. The Red Wings beat the Maroons on a goal by rookie Mud Bruneteau that was scored after 116 minutes and 30 seconds of overtime.

Detroit goaltender Normie Smith contributed to the victory by stopping 92 shots. With the winning goal not tallied until the sixth overtime period, *Detroit News* reporter Sam Greene remarked, "The goal judge was so surprised, or so sleepy, that it seemed half a minute before he flashed the red light behind [Maroon goaltender Lorne] Chabot. The game was over."

Detroit won that series and moved on to the finals against the Toronto Maple Leafs, winning their first Stanley Cup by a three-game-to-one margin. Two-way player Ebbie Goodfellow, whom *Detroit Free Press* reporter George Puscas later called the Wings' "first great star," led the team to their premiere championship.

During the 1936-37 season, the Red Wings again finished first in the American Division. They faced a physical first-round playoff series against the Montreal Canadians, but a goal by Hec Kilrea in the third overtime period of game five clinched a finals appearance. The tough series against Montreal, however, had reduced Detroit's roster to nine healthy players, requiring the team to play minor-league goalie Earl Robertson as starter Normie Smith was also injured.

In the five-game finals series against the New York Rangers, Robertson earned two shutouts and center Marty Barry led all playoff scorers with four goals and seven assists as the Red Wings won their second Stanley Cup, becoming the first team to repeat as champions.

After two consecutive championship seasons, many hockey insiders predicted the Red Wings would become the league's new dynasty. Adams also believed this and, surprisingly, the man known as "Trader Jack" made no roster changes. The Red Wings won only 12 games and finished in fourth place during the 1937-38 season. Adams later admitted that he should have pursued trade possibilities and vowed that he would never again hesitate to break up a championship team.

World War II Affected NHL

For the next three seasons the Red Wings languished in the bottom half of the standings, but the NHL itself underwent changes. During the 1938-39 season, the league changed its structure by merging the previously separate Canadian and American divisions. At the same time the teams' rosters increased from 14 to 15 players.

The following year, despite the outbreak of World War II, NHL officials decided to pursue a regular schedule. While war still raged in Europe and the Pacific, Detroit qualified for the Stanley Cup finals in 1940-41, but the team was swept by the Boston Bruins.

In 1941-42 the Red Wings finished fifth in the division, but still qualified for the playoffs. In an impressive playoff run, they reached the finals against the Toronto Maple Leafs and appeared in control of the series after winning the first three games.

In the fourth game Detroit was leading 3-2 with 15 minutes remaining in the third period, but Red Wings Eddie Wares and Don Grosso were both penalized, and the Maple Leafs scored two goals to win the game. An irate Adams confronted referee Mel Harwood after the game and allegedly hit him. Adams was suspended for the remainder of the series and was forced to watch his club lose the series after holding a seemingly insurmountable advantage.

Detroit Secured Third Championship

Detroit fought back from this disappointment to take honors as regular season and Stanley Cup champions in 1942-43. In the playoffs, left wing Carl Liscombe tied a club record with 14 points (six goals, eight assists), but it was goaltender Johnny Mowers, however, who emerged as the hero of the championship series, earning two shutouts in four straight victories.

In the third period of game four, Mowers was hit with a puck in the face. Although bleeding from this gash, he refused to delay the game to get stitches. Mowers played the last five minutes of the contest with blood streaming down his face.

Later, on the victorious train ride home, a *Detroit News* reporter recounted the Wings's celebration with their proud possession, the Stanley Cup: "Water was poured in for teetotaler Adams to take the first drink from the historic cup.... After Adams' drink the cup was filled with beer. Liscombe was the first player to get a drink. He also nearly got a beer bath as the train lurched."

The Red Wings were out of playoff contention for the next two years, but some players achieved personal records. Carl Liscombe and Syd Howe each reached career highs in scoring with 36 and 32 goals respectively during the 1943-44 season. And, on February 3, 1944, Howe became the first Red Wing to score six goals in one game.

The ongoing war offered young players a shot at the big leagues, as the continuing need for soldiers whittled away at previously static NHL rosters. During the 1944-45 season two rookies—goalie Harry Lumley and forward Ted Lindsay—made their mark on the Detroit club. The Red Wings reached the Stanley Cup finals but lost to the Toronto Maple Leafs in seven games.

Howe Ushered in Era

October 8, 1946, marked the beginning of a new and prosperous era for the Red Wings. On that day, 18-year-old right wing Gordie Howe signed with the Red Wings and, eight days later—in the opening game of the season—scored his first NHL goal. Howe was noted for being down-to-earth; his unflinching demand before signing a contract with the Red Wings was that he receive a Detroit jacket as a bonus.

Describing his rookie season and how he viewed his teammates in Jim Vipond's book *Gordie Howe Number Nine,* Howe remarked, "I guess I held everybody in awe. All I wanted desperately to do was hang on for a full season so I could go back to Saskatoon and brag about it."

In October of 1947, Howe switched jersey numbers from 17 to 9. Roy Conacher, who had previously worn number nine, was traded to Chicago. During this era when the Wings traveled by train, lower sleeping bunks were prized. These berths, however, were given to players with seniority and low uniform numbers. When Conacher left, trainer Carl Mattson urged Howe to grab the lower number merely to secure a good position on the train. This seemingly innocent move became part of hockey folklore; 24 years later, when Howe retired as the league's all-time leading scorer, he

| PROFILE | Gordie Howe |

The most illustrious career in Red Wings's history belongs to Gordie Howe. Howe's name became synonymous with longevity as he played in the NHL for 25 years and missed only 57 regular season games due to injuries. Howe played the most games (1,687) and scored the most points (1,809) of any player in Red Wing history. The right wing was named to the All-Star team a league record 21 times. Howe won both the Hart Trophy as the NHL's most valuable player and the Art Ross Trophy as the leading point scorer six times. In 1963 Howe was voted Canada's outstanding male athlete, and in 1967 he won the Lester Patrick Trophy for contributing to hockey in the United States. In a tribute to the contributions of number nine, Howe's jersey was retired by the Detroit Red Wings's organization in 1972.

During his career, Howe's average playing time was 40 minutes out of 60. He took a regular shift, served on the power-play unit, and killed penalties. In the days before curved sticks—which limited players to either right or left-handed shooting— Howe was distinguished by his ambidexterity. Howe was strong enough to score with defenders draped on him and tough enough to fight with other players and for the puck in the corners. Number nine also had the ability to remain calm in tense situations. Sid Abel recalled that in overtime playoff game, Howe was relaxed on the bench, telling a story about his youth.

In *Hockey: The Story of the World's Fastest Sport*, Howe was judged: "There has never been a better player than Gordie Howe.... Nobody ... combined the arts of shooting, scoring, stickhandling and *all* other hockey skills to the degree Howe did." Jean Beliveau, the captain of the Montreal Canadians during the heated Montreal-Detroit rivalry of the 1950s, simply stated, "He's the best hockey player I've ever seen." In Jim Vipond's *Gordie Howe Number Nine*, Red Wing general manager Jack Adams was quoted as saying, "... nobody compares to Howe. There is Gordie Howe and there are other hockey players who are merely great."

was one of the most famous number nines in NHL history.

At the end of the 1946-47 season, Tommy Ivan took over coaching duties from Adams, who retired as skipper, but stayed on as general manager. In his second season, Ivan made two significant moves; he added rookie defenseman Leonard "Red" Kelly to the Detroit roster and composed a forward line featuring Gordie Howe, Sid Abel, and Ted Lindsay. These three served as a unit from November 1, 1947, through the 1951-52 season and were soon dubbed the "Production Line" for their prolific scoring.

Although Howe and Lindsay—the two wingers—were touted as superstars, Abel also had impressive credentials; he had picked up the Hart Trophy as the league's most valuable player in 1942 and 1949. In a 1991 *Detroit Free Press* article, Lindsay explained the reason for the line's success: "We had talent, and by talent I mean the ability to anticipate plays.... We knew what was going to happen" on the ice.

In the 1948-49 season the Production Line led their team to first overall in the standings, despite Howe's 20-game absence with torn cartilage in his right knee. Bill Quackenbush garnered praise as one of the league's best rushing defensemen and, due to his penalty-free season, picked up the Lady Byng trophy, annually awarded to the most gentlemanly player. The same year Quackenbush added the Hart Trophy to his collection.

Although the Red Wings lost the Stanley Cup finals to the Maple Leafs, a new era—dominated by Detroit—was beginning. In his essay "Power and Production: Jack Adams's Red Wings" in *The Official National Hockey League 75th Anniversary Commemorative Book,* Trent Frayne remarked that during this "swashbuckling period the Red Wings were dominating, pugnacious, and arrogant.... They carried their sticks like lances and plastered visiting players against the boards as though they were advertisements."

Hockey Hall of Fame and Museum

Sid Abel

"Trader Jack" Earned Nickname

Having learned his lesson in the late 1930s about the perils of complacency, general manager Adams continued to tinker with his lineup. In the spring of 1949, Adams traded Quackenbush and Pete Horeck to Boston for Pete Babando, Jimmy Peters, Clare Martin, and Lloyd Durham. Under Ivan's tutelage in 1949-50, the Red Wings were led by forwards Howe, Abel, and Lindsay, defensemen Red Kelly and Leo Reise, and goaltender Harry Lumley.

Detroit also had talent waiting at its minor-league club, the Indianapolis Capitals. When Lumley was injured, Detroit called up Terry Sawchuk, and he soon earned his first shutout in

the NHL. The Production Line solidified its reputation as the league's top forward line by finishing first, second, and third in overall scoring in the 1949-50 season (Howe 68 points, Lindsay 78, and Abel 69).

The Production Line was temporarily dismantled during the 1949-50 playoff series against Toronto, after Howe collided with Maple Leaf Ted Kennedy, crashing head-first into the boards and suffering a concussion, broken nose and cheekbone. Because no penalty was called on the play, the Detroit team was eager to retaliate against the Maple Leafs. Although the remainder of the series was marred with penalties, Detroit emerged victorious.

The championship series against the New York Rangers was evenly matched, with three contests decided in overtime. Left wing Pete Babando scored a goal in the second overtime period of the seventh game to help the Red Wings clinch the Stanley Cup.

Living up to his nickname "Trader Jack," Adams masterminded another player swap before the 1950-51 season. Playoff hero Babando along with Harry Lumley, "Black Jack" Stewart, Al Dewsbury, and Jim Morrison were exchanged for Chicago players Jim Henry, Bob Goldham, Gaye Stewart, and Metro Prystai. The trade of goalie Lumley was possible because of talented newcomer Terry Sawchuk. In 1950-51 Sawchuk played all 70 games and recorded 11 shutouts, winning the Calder Trophy as rookie of the year. Forward Alex Delvecchio also joined the team, earning the epithet "a smooth young newcomer," according to *The Official National Hockey League 75th Anniversary Commemorative Book*.

This same year Red Kelly received the Lady Byng Trophy and Howe picked up his first Art Ross Trophy for most points. With his 43 goals and 43 assists for 86 points, Howe set a single-season NHL scoring record. Despite the accolades showered on its players, Detroit did not fare well in the playoffs, losing the semifinal playoff series to the Montreal Canadians.

Detroit Captured Fifth Cup

In 1951-52 the Detroit Red Wings returned to their winning ways by again capturing the Stanley Cup. Detroit, bolstered by a fan's good luck charm **[see sidebar]**, did not lose a game during the semifinal and championship series. Sawchuk—supported by the play of defensemen Red Kelly, Leo Reise, and Bob Goldham—gave up only five goals in eight games, an NHL record.

This fifth Stanley Cup victory fell on the Red Wings's 25th anniversary. After the game Adams sought Sawchuk out to thank him for the "anniversary present." Area media members also credited coach Tommy Ivan's contributions. A *Detroit News* writer remarked that Ivan "ran virtually the perfect bench through the whole year."

The next season featured a change in Detroit's front office. On December 4, 1952, owner James Norris died; his daughter, Marguerite, assumed the role of club president. With this appointment,

Octopus on Ice

In 1952 a playoff tradition began for the fans in Detroit. During a game, seafood merchant Peter Cusimano and his brother heaved a partially cooked octopus on the ice. Each of the creature's eight tentacles stood for the needed victories to win the Stanley Cup. The Wings won the game. Since then, brave fans have sneaked the creatures into the Wings's home arena—usually during the playoffs—to show support for their team.

Purists, like Cusimano, disdain the practice of throwing uncooked, slippery beasts, pointing to the animated bounce—and colorful appearance—a cooked octopus will create. The *Wall Street Journal* recorded one 1987 hurler's reaction to his feat: "It was slimy and smelly, but throwing it out there was exhilarating."

During the 1986-87 playoffs after such an incident, center John Chabot scooped up the uncooked octopus with his stick, holding it up as a salute to Detroit's frenzied fans after a victory.

Marguerite Norris became the first female executive in league history and the youngest person—at age 26—to head an NHL team.

On the ice during the 1952-53 season, goaltender Glenn Hall appeared in six games for Detroit as the backup for Sawchuk. The Production Line's reign was over, because with the emergence of Alex Delvecchio at center, Detroit felt comfortable sending veteran Sid Abel to Chicago. The Red Wings produced impressive statistic, leading the league in goals scored with 222 and fewest goals allowed with 133, but the team was upset by the Boston Bruins in the Stanley Cup semifinals.

Wings Captured Consecutive Cups

In 1953-54 the Wings again doubled as season and Stanley Cup champs. Detroit led Montreal

Ted Lindsay

three games to one in the best-of-seven series, but the Canadians fought back, setting the stage for a seventh game at Detroit's Olympia Stadium. At the end of regulation the game was tied 1-1. Detroit won its sixth championship in stunning fashion when Tony Leswick dumped the puck into the Montreal end and it caromed off Doug Harvey's glove and past goalie Gerry McNeil to end the series. An instant hero, Leswick later told reporters that he had never before scored an overtime goal. During the dressing room celebration, the contributions of other key players were noted. Defenseman Bob Goldham had blocked numerous shots in the series, and a *Detroit News* writer reported that captain Ted Lindsay proposed a toast, calling Goldham "the greatest competitor in hockey."

To complement their 1953-54 championship, several Red Wing players picked up postseason honors. Howe received his fourth consecutive Art Ross Trophy, and Red Kelly became the first re-cipient of the Norris Trophy for the league's best defenseman and was also awarded the Lady Byng Trophy. After leading the team to three Stanley Cup championships, Detroit coach Tommy Ivan moved to Chicago as general manager of the Blackhawks, and Jimmy Skinner took over the helm for the Red Wings.

Although Skinner never played professional hockey, he had coaching experience in the minor leagues. In a 1955 *Detroit News* article, Adams described his new coach: "He's sincere and very human, but he's tough enough to fight [boxing heavyweight champion Rocky] Marciano in a pinch."

Near the end of the 1954-55 season, the Red Wings were involved in an incident that would come to be known as the Richard Riot. Before a Montreal-Detroit contest on March 17, 1955, Montreal fans learned that Canadians scoring sensation Maurice "Rocket" Richard had been suspended by league president Clarence Campbell—for the remaining regular-season and playoff games—for his part in an altercation with a referee.

With only three games left, Richard was leading the league in scoring and his team—tied with Detroit for best record—was fighting for a first-place finish in the league. With the Wings leading 4-1, a spectator heaved a tear gas bomb onto the Forum ice. Detroit won by forfeit and Montreal fans, angered by the suspension and the team's second-place finish, instigated a riot that spilled into downtown Montreal.

At the conclusion of the regular season, Detroit swept Toronto in four games in the playoff semifinals. The Red Wings then met Montreal—albeit without "Rocket" Richard—in the finals and the series stretched to a full seven games. Gordie Howe, Tony Leswick, Metro Prystai, Pete Babando, Joe Carveth, Marty Barry, and Pete Kelly each contributed to the championship by scoring important goals.

Detroit News reporter Harry Stapler recounted the reactions of several Detroit players and executives after this seventh championship. General manager Adams called the Red Wing squad

FRONT OFFICE | Jack Adams

Serving the Detroit Red Wings's team from 1927 to 1963, Jack Adams had the longest reign as both coach and general manager. Adams was recognized as a founding father of the National Hockey League. In *Hockey: The Story of the World's Fastest Sport,* Adams was designated as "among the advance men who blazed the NHL to a big-league level—combative, bold, frank, cussed, big-headed and amiable."

Adams earned the nickname "Trader Jack" for engineering numerous player swaps. In *The Official National Hockey League 75th Anniversary Commemorative Book,* a writer stated, "Jack Adams had an eye for talent; it seemed everyone he brought up from the minors turned into a star. And those the Red Wings' farm system didn't develop were acquired through trades."

Detroit News columnist Joe Fall described Adams: "He was loud, he was colorful, he was bombastic." While addressing his players in the dressing room between periods of games, Adams was know to throw pieces of oranges at athletes whose performances he was displeased with.

Hockey Hall of Fame and Museum

Another one of his ploys was to walk around the locker room with one-way train tickets to Indianapolis—where the Red Wings minor-league club was located—sticking out of his pockets. Adams was equally rough on hockey writers, screaming at them when they wrote something he did not like.

Adams's dedication to the sport were noted in 1966 when he became the first recipient of the Lester Patrick Award honoring the person contributing most to hockey in the United States.

"the greatest clutch team I've ever had." In the postgame celebration Lindsay shouted, "Earlier in the season they called us bums, and I guess it took bums to win it." Coach Skinner earned acclaim for leading his team to a regular and postseason championship in his first year on the job.

Postseason Woes Began

In a front-office change in 1955, Bruce Norris replaced sister Marguerite as club president.

Adams continued to make player transactions. Confident that Glenn Hall could assume goaltending duties, the general manager traded playoff-proven Terry Sawchuk to the Boston Bruins. Sawchuk was devastated, but Hall responded by leading the league in 1955-56 with 12 shutouts and earning the Calder Trophy as top rookie in the NHL.

That year, in game two of the first-round playoffs against Toronto, Maple Leaf Tod Sloan had run-ins with both Lindsay and Howe. Later that game, Sloan and Howe crashed into the boards

Goaltender Terry Sawchuk played with the Red Wings for 14 years and, during this time, won the Vezina Trophy as the league's top goaltender three times and posted 85 shutouts, the most of any goaltender in Red Wing history. Sawchuk was an old-time goalie, and before making a mask a part of his outfit in 1962, he required nearly 400 stitches in his head and face.

Trent Frayne, writing in *The Official National Hockey League 75th Anniversary Commemorative Book,* called Sawchuk "the most acrobatic goaltender of his time. He didn't move so much as he exploded into a desperate release of energy ... he sometimes seemed a human pinwheel. He played the whole game in pent-up tension, shouting at his teammates, crouching, straightening, diving, scrambling, his pale face drawn and tense."

Terry Sawchuk (bottom)

Hockey Hall of Fame and Museum

together and Sloan emerged with a fractured shoulder. Angry Toronto fans believed Sloan was intentionally injured, and the *Toronto Star* received several anonymous calls from a man threatening to shoot Howe and Lindsay if they played at Maple Leaf Garden that night. Both played, however, as the Wings won 5-4 in overtime. Revelling in the victory, Lindsay played upon his tough-guy reputation and mocked Toronto fans by holding his stick like a gun and shooting at the crowd. Detroit won that series 4-1, but lost by the same margin to Montreal in the finals.

Detroit finished first in the 1956-57 season, but made an early exit in the playoffs, losing to the Boston Bruins. In 1957 Adams angered Detroit fans by trading forward Ted Lindsay and goaltender Glenn Hall to Chicago for Hank Bassen, Forbes Kennedy, Bill Preston, and Johnny Wilson.

The team then went on a downward trend.

In 1957-58, under the leadership of former player Sid Abel, they finished third in the league and were swept by Montreal in the first round of the playoffs, and in 1958-59 the Red Wings came in last in the league and missed the playoffs for the first time since 1938.

The Red Wings continued their slide during the next two years. Although the team did not match their previous regular-season success, they managed to grab the last playoff spot both years. In 1959-60 the team lost to Toronto in the opening round. Adams again turned heads by trading star defenseman Red Kelly to Toronto for the less talented Marc Reaume. In 1960-61 the Red Wings again reached the Stanley Cup finals, but eventually lost to the Chicago Blackhawks, four games to two.

Adams Ended Detroit Association

The next season produced one bright spot, as Gordie Howe scored his 500th career goal in the 1961-62 season, stretching his string of 20-goal seasons to 13. Detroit, however, finished fifth in the league and did not qualify for the playoffs. Based on his team's uncharacteristic woes, owner Bruce Norris decided to shake up the organization. After more than 30 years with the Red Wings, Jack Adams was asked to resign and Sid Abel added general manager duties to his coaching role.

The Red Wings bounced back under Abel and reached the Stanley Cup finals in both the 1962-63 and 1963-64 seasons. Each time, though, the team lost to the Toronto Maple Leafs. In 1964-65 the Red Wings lured Ted Lindsay out of a four-year retirement, and his experience—along with the saves of Calder Trophy-winning goaltender Roger Crozier—helped lead the team to a first-place finish. The Red Wings narrowly lost to the Chicago Blackhawks in the playoffs.

In 1965-66 the team again made it to the finals, but was defeated in six games by Montreal. Crozier made history when he earned the Conn Smythe Trophy as the most valuable player in the playoffs; he was the first goaltender and first member of a losing team to capture the award.

The Red Wings missed the playoffs each of the next three years, heralding the beginning of a low point in Detroit hockey history. The league gained six teams in the 1967-68 season, but the Red Wings were ill prepared to handle the change. Detroit's farm system degenerated and, when the amateur draft was introduced, the organization had no good scouting system in place.

Instead of addressing the root of the problem, Detroit management sought quick fixes, and this era was marked by high turnover of coaches and a series of bad trades. In the 1969-70 season, second-year coach Bill Gadsby was fired after two games—which were both victories. Although protocol dictated that general manager Abel was responsible for the change, *Detroit News* columnist Pete Waldmeir remarked, "It is pretty generally acknowledged that [executive director of the club, Jim] Bishop was behind the firing of Bill Gadsby."

Despite high-level disorganization, the Red Wings appeared to be primed for playoff contention, led by defenseman Carl Brewer and left wing Frank Mahovlich. Nonetheless, they lost in four straight games to Chicago.

Harkness Began Stormy Reign

During the 1970-71 season, in which they would finish in seventh place, a reorganization was engineered for the Red Wing franchise. Due to Bishop's lobbying, Ned Harkness was hired as coach. Although successful in the college ranks at Cornell University, Harkness had no NHL experience. Defenseman Carl Brewer left the team after the appointment was announced, and, in a *Detroit News* article, Vartan Kupelian noted that most of the other players "revolted at the coach's rah-rah approach and discipline geared for college athletes, not professionals."

This disapproval showed in the team's record; after playing 37 games, the Red Wings had only 12 victories. According to *Detroit News* columnist Pete Waldmeir, general manager Sid Abel wanted Harkness fired in an attempt to halt the team's lopsided losses. Waldmeir speculated that owner Norris rejected this plan because he did not want to admit he made a mistake in hiring Harkness. Dismayed, Abel resigned, telling *Detroit News* writer Bill Brennan, "I can't accept this guy [Harkness] coaching the team."

Harkness promptly took over as general manager and executed a series of trades that altered the Detroit line-up and brought in younger players less likely to question team management. Notable among these transactions was the departure of Frank Mahovlich to Montreal for Mickey Redmond, Bill Collins, and Guy Charron.

One significant change did not involve a player swap, however; after the 1970-71 season the seemingly immortal Gordie Howe retired after 25 years with the Detroit club. Soon, Howe too became disillusioned with the Red Wings's organization. Although promised a front-office position with the club, he was not allowed to make any significant contributions and disassociated himself from the Red Wings.

During the next two seasons, the Red Wings finished fifth in their division. One bright spot for Detroit was the acquisition in the 1971 amateur draft of Marcel Dionne. Although playing only four years with the team, Dionne would dart up to 13th overall in Red Wings's career scoring. Coaching changes continued, and 11 games into the 1973-74 season, former player Alex Delvecchio was installed as coach. His leadership qualities were already proven; Delvecchio had served as Red Wing captain for 12 years. He lasted as head coach for 156 games and as general manager for three seasons.

In February of 1974, general manager Harkness resigned and was replaced by Delvecchio. Harkness's four-year reign had been stormy; three coaches were fired, players revolted at his coaching methods, and fans lambasted him for his bad trades. Harkness, while not overtly bad-mouthing his bosses, remarked to Jerry Green of the *Detroit News* that Detroit "was a seedy organization when I came here." Another writer for the *Detroit News,* Bill Brennan, surveyed players and found that most had anticipated the change, but none expressed regret about Harkness's departure.

In both 1974-75 and 1975-76, Detroit finished fourth in its division. Billy Dea and Larry Wilson split coaching duties in 1976-77, but the Red Wing team earned only 41 points and finished last in the Norris Division. The following year the club moved up to second place in the division, but lost to Montreal in the first round of the playoffs. For the next two seasons, the Red Wings settled for fifth-place finishes.

Team Moved to Joe Louis Arena

The Detroit organization ended an era by moving to a new arena in 1979. Old Olympia Stadium, while steeped in tradition as the home ice of star players such as Aurie, Howe, Lindsay, and Abel, was getting old and was too small to accommodate Detroit's many fans. Before the move, former Red Wings players told *Detroit News* writer Vartan Kupelian of their memories of Olympia. Hall-of-Fame defenseman "Black Jack" Stewart recalled, "It was a thrill the first time I ever saw the building.... I'll be sorry to see it go. It was a landmark." And Metro Prystai remarked, "The thing I'll always remember ... was the ice at Olympia. It was the best ice in the league and the boards were very lively."

Joe Louis Arena, located on Detroit's riverfront, opened December 27, 1979, and the Red Wings—upholding a team precedent—lost their inaugural game in a new arena, this time by a score of 3-2. For the next several years Detroit remained near the bottom of league standings, and most headlines about the team involved coaching or managerial changes.

Ilitch Bought Club

A significant change for the Red Wing club occurred on June 22, 1982, when Bruce Norris sold the team to pizza magnate Mike Ilitch, ending the Norris family's 50-year ownership of the team. Local media members welcomed Ilitch's arrival; *Detroit News* columnist Jerry Green stated, "Ilitch's purchase of the Red Wings is the best damn thing that has happened to hockey in Detroit over the last 25 years."

The new owner told *Detroit News* reporter Jack Berry, "I've sponsored amateur hockey since 1964 and I love the game.... I think this is the best franchise in the world. It's a sleeping giant, waiting for someone to do something with it." Ilitch retained part of the Red Wing tradition by making ownership a family affair. Wife Marian serves as secretary and treasurer; daughter Denise Ilitch-Lites held the post of general counsel for the organization; and son-in-law Jim Lites served as executive vice-president.

[Jim Lites and Denise Ilitch-Lites ended their association with the Red Wings in 1993, when Lites was named president of the Dallas Stars hockey club.]

Fighting has always been a part of hockey. There are those who believe that the ability to intimidate other teams directly correlates with wins. A fight can also signify a shift in momentum during a game. According to Doug Beardsley in his book *Country on Ice,* league patriarch Conn Symthe once said (although he later denied it): "If you can't beat 'em in the alley, you can't beat 'em on the ice." Through the years, Red Wings players have adhered to this maxim.

"Black Jack" Stewart (1938-39 to 1942-43; 1945-46 to 1949-50): Stewart played for the Red Wings for nine seasons beginning in 1938-39 and coach Jack Adams regarded him as one of the strongest players he'd ever seen. Trent Fayne, in *The Official National Hockey League 75th Anniversary Commemorative Book,* remarked that Stewart "could hit with terrific force, [he was] a rib-rattler of grim application." Stewart sported scars over both eyes and one down his cheek and received more than two hundred stitches during his career.

Ted Lindsay (1944-45 to 1956-57; 1964-65): Lindsay's scarred face was a testament to his willingness to battle; he led the team in penalty minutes for nine years. Despite his small stature (Lindsay was only 5'8" and 165 pounds), teammate Sid Abel recalled in the *Detroit Free Press* that "Ted was always very fiery. He wouldn't back down from anybody." One night Lindsay and frequent opponent Bill Ezinicki of the Toronto Maple Leafs pounded away at each other for three straight minutes. Lindsay severely bruised his right hand, but required only one stitch to Ezinicki's 15. Beardsley restated the rumor that Lindsay was the first to say, "The hockey stick is the great equalizer."

Gordie Howe (1946-47 to 1970-71): Howe solidified his tough-guy reputation in a game against the New York Rangers in February of 1959. Howe had roughed up Eddie Shack, and Lou Fontinato, the reigning NHL heavyweight, came to his teammate's defense, pummeling Howe. Beardsley, in his book *Country on Ice,* explained that Howe took this barrage "without flinching. Then, he turned on Fontinato and delivered a series of blows that broke Fontinato's nose and reduced his face to pulp." With this exhibition, Howe earned respect in the NHL and more leeway on the ice because players were afraid to check him. Howe was also known for his effective—and sneaky—paybacks with his stick. In his book *The Thinking Man's Guide to Pro Hockey,* Gerald Eskenazi recounted an incident in which referee Vern Buffey was quoted as saying, "You're working a game ... and you see a player is down. You know that Howe did it. But how can you prove it?"

Howie Young (1960-61 to 1962-63; 1966-67 to 1967-68): On February 17, 1963, Young was charged with 27 penalty minutes in a 6-1 loss to Montreal. For the season Young recorded 273 penalty minutes—then an NHL record.

Joe Kocur (1984-85 to 1990-91): Berger remarked that "Kocur is one of the NHL's most feared players and that fear is generated because of his fighting ability. He is an exceptional fighter, a true NHL heavyweight who can literally knockout opponents with one punch."

Bob Probert (1985-86—): Probert led the NHL with 398 penalty minutes in the 1987-88 season. One of the most feared men in the NHL, Probert was described by *Chicago Tribune*'s Mike Kiley as "the league's most famous agitator, ... he'll hit anything." In the *Hockey Scouting Report, 1990-1991,* Michael A. Berger assessed that power is Probert's "greatest component in his game. He hits people hard and he hurts them."

AP/Wide World Photos

Jacques Demers

maining 45 contests. After the last game of the 1985-86 season, Vartan Kupelian of the *Detroit News* received feedback from players about the team's disappointing year. "It's a relief that the season is over," remarked Steve Yzerman. Captain Danny Gare called it a "frustrating year" that was "dismal for everybody."

Demers Ignited Hope in Detroit

In an attempt to turn around the club, owner Mike Ilitch hired Jacques Demers as coach beginning in the 1986-87 season. In a *Sports Illustrated* article, Ilitch—who ranked the former St. Louis Blues skipper as the best coach in the NHL—remarked, "I can't believe we got him." Demers endeared himself to Detroit fans and media members with his blue-collar work ethic and engaging personality.

Demers turned heads by appointing Steve Yzerman the youngest captain in team history at the age of 21, leading *Washington Post* staff writer Robert Fachet to comment, "to call Yzerman precocious would be a classic understatement." In a *Sporting News* article, coach Jacques Demers explained to Keith Gave, "My No. 1 priority was to pick a good captain, I wanted to build from youth.... I can tell you it was one of the best decisions I've ever made. Let me put it this way: Steve Yzerman is a winner."

In Demers's first year on the job, the Red Wings became the most improved club in the NHL by making a 38-point turnaround from the previous year and qualifying for the playoffs. Detroit swept Chicago in the first round of the 1986-87 playoffs and fought back from a 3-1 deficit against Toronto in round two to win that series and reach the Campbell Conference finals against Edmonton in 1987. Detroit players, coaches, and fans were ecstatic and celebrated the team's unexpected accomplishments.

Realizing that hockey aficionados might point to weak opponents as reason for the Red Wings' success while laughing at Detroiters' premature celebrations, *Detroit Free Press* columnist

Ilitch brought in Jimmy Devellano as his general manager, and he immediately made a smart decision. Detroit chose fourth overall in the 1983 entry draft. The Red Wings's first pick was a center named Steve Yzerman. Yzerman joined the team as an 18-year-old and wowed fans by scoring 87 points and making his first all-star game appearance. In Yzerman's first two seasons, the Red Wings under coach Nick Polano finished third in their division, but made early exits in the playoffs.

Although there were high expectations at the start of the 1985-86 season, the team set a record for most losses with 57 and finished last in the NHL. Skipper Harry Neale lasted only 35 games of the season, with former Red Wing defenseman Brad Park assuming coaching duties for the re-

Mitch Albom nonetheless defended the city's elation: "Remember the failure that has been hockey around here in recent years, the red faces, the 'Dead Wings' jokes, the revolving door of coaches and players. It was as if a filmy residue had dried on this franchise.... Forget that now.... These players have brought a cleansing rinse that leaves them fresh and new and ready to establish their own tradition in this town."

Detroit eventually lost to Edmonton, four games to one. Such improvement in their overall performance, however, elicited support from Edmonton player Marty McSorley, who explained in a *Sporting News* article, "Everyone in the [Edmonton locker] room is surprised by the heart of their hockey club. You've got to respect what they're doing and how they're going about it."

Based on their positive showing in the 1986-87 playoffs, the 1987-88 season held promise for fans and team members alike. The Red Wings finished with 93 points and placed first in the Norris Division. This marked the first season in which centerman Steve Yzerman scored 50 goals. He also added 50 assists to reach one hundred points.

On March 1, 1988—a day of infamy for some Red Wing supporters—captain Yzerman, shortly after scoring his 50th goal of the season, cut toward the net, but lost his balance and crashed into the goal posts, suffering a potentially career-ending knee injury.

Foregoing surgery, Yzerman returned for game four of the division semifinals to a rousing ovation from an appreciative Joe Louis crowd. The Red Wings repeated their Campbell Conference final appearance, losing once again to the Edmonton Oilers.

Yzerman's heroic comeback was marred, however, by several of his teammates' off-ice shenanigans. On the eve of the fifth game in the best-of-seven series against the Edmonton Oilers for the Campbell Conference championship, eight Red Wing players—including two suspected alcoholics, Bob Probert and Petr Klima—were sighted drinking at Edmonton's Goose Loonies bar at two a.m., three hours past team curfew.

While Probert—Detroit's leading scorer in

AP/Wide World Photos

Bob Probert

the playoffs—and John Chabot, were allowed to play the game, the rest of the group was benched. Not surprisingly, Detroit lost the game 8-4. Albom, in *Live Albom II,* stated that the rest of the team "deserve[d] better than a betrayal from their own ranks." Those offenders, Albom judged, "lost trust. They lost spirit. They broke their coach's heart."

Demers Lost Magic Touch

In each of his first two seasons with the Detroit club, Demers received the Jack Adams Award as coach of the year and achieved near cult status with Detroit-area fans. Such adoration—from fans, players, and management—did not last. In 1988-89 the Red Wings, although finishing first in the Norris Division, lost in the first round of the playoffs, and the following year the team finished fifth and did not earn a chance for postseason play.

On July 13, 1990, Demers was fired amidst rumors that players—notably Yzerman—had expressed discontent with his coaching methods. In the shake-up, Jimmy Devellano moved from general manager to senior vice-president. Some media members cited Demers's pandering to Bob Probert as a reason for the coach's firing.

During the 1987-88 season, Probert had set a club record with 398 penalty minutes and also made major offensive contributions with 62 points. Probert's personal life, however, was tumultuous: he was an alcoholic, and in March of 1989 was arrested and charged with bringing 14.3 grams cocaine across the U.S.-Canadian border.

Detroit Free Press columnist Mitch Albom restated coach Jacques Demers's reaction to this incident: "He has given this team some black eyes in the past ... but this time, he split the eye right open." Demers gave Probert repeated chances to reform though, and after a one-year suspension the NHL did too. Probert was reinstated by the NHL on March 9, 1990, but remained unable to travel to Canada until the 1992-93 season because of a restriction from the U.S. Immigration and Naturalization Department.

In July of 1990, Bryan Murray joined the Red Wings' organization, gaining the posts of general manager and coach. Formerly the coach of the Washington Capitals, Murray was known for his disciplined approach, which resulted in top regular-season finishes for his team. In *The Wings,* Murray recalled how he looked forward to the appointment, commenting that the hockey tradition in Detroit "is tremendous. The enthusiasm and interest in the community is an everyday thing.... The people care very much about their hockey team." In Murray's first year on the job, the Red Wings finished third in the Norris Division.

New-Look Wings in 1990s

Although the Detroit organization had previously featured foreign players on their roster, most were proven NHLers. The Red Wings expanded their scope in scouting by making international deals. In 1990 the Red Wings acquired centerman Sergei Fedorov from the Soviet Red Army team. Joe Lapointe, in the *New York Times* remarked that Fedorov "has a dazzling, up-tempo style" and added that "unlike some players from Europe, he is willing to carry the puck and battle for it in the corners and along the boards."

Joining his fellow countryman on Detroit ice for the 1991-92 season was defenseman Vladimir Konstantinov, distinguished by his pesky play. Praising his debut, a writer for *Hockey Digest* added, "Expect even better things from this former Red Army captain, especially since he likes to hit and plays obnoxious." Another young Soviet prospect, Vyacheslav Kozlov, joined the team at the end of the 1991-92 season despite court battles with his former Soviet team. Two Swedish players, Johan Garpenlov and Niklas Lidstrom, also joined the team, making the Detroit dressing room multilingual.

During the 1991-92 season, as a commemoration of the 75th year of the NHL's existence, the original six teams planned to wear replicas of old-fashioned jerseys. The Red Wings wore the design of their sweaters of the 1927-28 season—a white jersey with Detroit written across the front, surrounded by several red bands.

After superstitious Red Wings players suffered through an 0-3-1 record in historic garb, they instructed the equipment man to "forget" the uniforms; the team did not wear them for the remainder of the season. Despite superstitions, the 1991-92 season held overdue promise for Detroit fans. Five players—Steve Yzerman (45), Ray Sheppard (36), Paul Ysebaert (35), Jimmy Carson (34), and Sergei Fedorov (32)—scored 30 or more goals, tying a team record set during the 1969-70 season.

Detroit also set a new attendance record as 788,920 (an average of 19,723) fans watched the team during the 40 home games at Joe Louis Arena. These supporters were excited about the Wing's playoff chances.

Accumulating 98 points and finishing first in the Norris Division, the Red Wings had their most

Although a member of the Red Wings for only a decade, center Steve Yzerman ranks third on the team's list of scoring leaders. During the 1988-89 season, Yzerman won the Lester B. Pearson Award as the league's best player as voted by his peers in the NHL. With his 155 point total for that season, Yzerman joined an elite group of hockey players: only four players in NHL history have scored more than 150 points in a season. In 1992-93, Yzerman scored 137 points, stretching his string of 100-point seasons to six. During the 1992-93 season, Yzerman became only the 37th player in NHL history to reach 1000 points in scoring.

For many hockey fans, however, what makes Yzerman's accomplishments even more impressive is his character. *Detroit Free Press* reporter George Puscas judged, "If not the smartest young guy on hockey skates, the Red Wings' Steve Yzerman must be the most patient and thoughtful." In a *Detroit News* column, Joe Falls remarked that Yzerman "is one of the finest hockey players I have ever known.... He fascinates me every moment he is on the ice, not only because of his brilliance as a player, but also because of his amazing work effort. I've never seen him give less that his best, even when he was worn out from overuse."

Michael A. Berger, writing in *Hockey Scouting Report 1990-1991,* was equally enthusiastic, stating, "Yzerman is a superior hockey player in every phase of the game.... Yzerman is an exemplary leader. His character, work ethic, and dedication are second to none, and the Red Wings are lucky to have him."

AP/Wide World Photos

Steve Yzerman

successful season since 1969-70 and were considered a top contender for postseason play. Third-year goaltender Tim Cheveldae was primed to lead his team in the playoffs.

First Strike Jarred Wings

The postseason was jeopardized, however, as bargaining talks between the NHL Players' Association and the league's Board of Governors stalled. By a vote of 560-4, the first players' strike in league history began on April 1, 1992, when most teams had two regular season games remaining.

Players sought free agency, improved pension benefits, and a greater percentage of both playoff money and revenue from trading cards. A *Sports Illustrated* reporter noted that Red Wings management would be hard hit by a strike. As owners of the arena and concessions, their losses would be in the millions of dollars.

Detroit News hockey writer Cynthia Lambert recounted how the realization of the impending strike hit second-year player Keith Primeau the night before the walkout. Primeau recalled, "I was afraid to get off the ice because I don't know when we'll get back on it." Steve Yzerman was asked to be one of nine players on the union negotiating committee, but admitted to *Detroit Free Press* reporter Keith Gave, "I never thought it would come to this." Mike Ilitch was a member of the owners' committee, but he stepped down in frustration about the lack of progress. In an 11th-hour session, an agreement was hammered out and hockey continued in the Motor City.

The layoff from the strike seemed to adversely affect Red Wings players. In the first round of the 1991-92 playoffs, Detroit was tested by the Minnesota North Stars, a team the Wings had finished 28 points ahead of in the divisional standings. Detroit fought back from a 3-1 deficit to win that series.

The Red Wings then faced the rival Chicago Blackhawks—who had beaten them only once during the regular season—in the second round,

AP/Wide World Photos

Paul Coffey

but to the surprise of many hockey fans, Detroit was knocked out of the playoffs after losing four straight games.

Ray Sheppard confessed to *Detroit News* writer Cynthia Lambert, "It's going to bother me for a long time because we have a lot of potential." Captain Steve Yzerman was similarly upset, telling Bob Wojnowski of the *Detroit News,* "I've never worked so hard and accomplished so little."

The 1992-93 season began with high hopes. Murray had traded for veteran winger Dino Ciccarelli and defenseman Mark Howe, Gordie's son, was signed as a free agent, with fans finding it fitting that the 37-year-old should close out his career in Detroit. His legal troubles resolved, Probert was allowed to travel across the U.S.-Canada border again.

In mid-season, Murray traded center Jimmy Carson to Los Angeles for Paul Coffey, one of the best offensive defensemen in NHL history. This move seemed to spark the Red Wings; Coffey made contributions as a leader in the locker room as well as on the ice. Yzerman earned another laurel in February by becoming only the 37th player in league history to score 1,000 points.

The team finished with 103 points, leading the NHL in both scoring (369 goals) and power-play efficiency. Yzerman had his second-best season by chalking up 137 points. Yet for fans hoping for a Stanley Cup appearance for their team, the postseason was again a time of disappointment. Detroit put in only a lackluster performance, and critics charged that the Wings played scared in their series with the Maple Leafs. The team twice lost in overtime—including the deciding seventh game—to Toronto.

Disappointed with his team's subpar performance, owner Ilitch pressured Murray to resign as coach, but retained him as general manager. Some in the media cited Murray's history of coaching teams to high-place finishes in the regular season and coming up short in the playoffs as the reason for his dismissal. Yet the players supported Murray's coaching abilities and accepted much of the blame. A *Hockey Digest* contributor noted that "as a general manager, Bryan Murray has been brilliant" and has not made a bad trade.

Hoping to finally propel his team to a championship, Ilitch hired the winningest active coach in the NHL, Scotty Bowman. Bowman, who found fame in Montreal by leading his team to five Stanley Cup victories and by gaining another championship in Pittsburgh, was known as a disciplinarian who remained somewhat aloof from both his players and the media.

Detroit Free Press staffer Charlie Vincent observed, "Undeniably, [Bowman] marches to his own drummer, an idiosyncrasy you can afford when you've won more games than any other man

in the history of your sport." In a *Sports Illustrated* article, Cliff Fletcher, a former associate of Bowman's, stated, "When the puck is dropped, there has never been anyone who could run a bench better than Scotty."

Detroit entered the 1993-94 season saddled again with the expectations of postseason success. A reporter for *Hockey Digest* noted that "with five solid forward lines and a half-dozen mobile defensemen at their disposal, the Wings are arguably the NHL's most talented team." Bowman believed that Detroit's previous disappointments could serve as valuable lessons to the club, telling a *Detroit Free Press* reporter that his new team "know[s] the adversity of the playoffs, and you really don't get anywhere in this league unless you've had a little adversity."

There were several changes awaiting the team, including a restructured league. Hoping to have hockey catch on in areas of the United States not familiar with the sport, the league expanded in the 1990s, with two teams apiece to California and Florida, and one in Ottawa. Another change was the league's decision to replace the historic names of the divisions, including the Norris and Adams, with generic terms such as Central and Northeast.

Despite the modernizing of the NHL, Detroit fans remained proud of their team's status as an "original six" team and, persisting in their high hopes for the club, looked to Bowman to bring the cherished Stanley Cup back to the Motor City.

SOURCES

BOOKS

Albom, Mitch, *Live Albom II, Detroit Free Press,* 1990.

Albom, Mitch, *The Live Albom, Detroit Free Press,* 1988.

Beardsley, Doug, *Country on Ice,* Paperjacks, 1988.

Beddows, Richard, Stan Fischler, and Ira Gitler, *Hockey: The Story of the World's Fastest*

Sport, Macmillan, 1969.

Berger, Michael A., *Hockey Scouting Report, 1990-1991,* Summerhill Press, 1990.

Diamond, Dan, and Lew Stubbs, *Hockey: Twenty Years,* Doubleday, 1987.

Diamond, Dan, editor, *The Official National Hockey League 75th Anniversary Commemorative Book,* McClelland & Stewart, 1991.

Eskenazi, Gerald, *The Thinking Man's Guide to Pro Hockey,* Dutton, 1972.

Fishchler, Stan, *Heroes of Pro Hockey,* Random House, 1971.

Rennie, Ross, *Detroit Red Wings,* Creative Education, 1990.

Vipond, Jim, *Gordie Howe Number Nine,* Ryerson Press, 1968.

PERIODICALS

Chicago Tribune, May 13, 1988; November 29, 1990.

Detroit News, February 3, 1935; March 25, 1936; April 9, 1943; April 16, 1952; April 17, 1954; March 25, 1955; April 15, 1955; January 6, 1971; January 31, 1971; February 7, 1974; February 6, 1977; August 4, 1977; December 16, 1979; June 4, 1982; April 7, 1986; February 12, 1987; October 1, 1991; April 14, 1992; May 4, 1992; May 10, 1992.

Detroit Free Press, October 3, 1991; April 2, 1992; September 10, 1993; September 16, 1993.

Goal, April, 1992.

Hockey Digest: Hockey 1993-94 Yearbook, September, 1993.

Inside Hockey, February/March, 1993.

Maclean's, October 14, 1991.

New York Times, November 7, 1990.

Sporting News, March 23, 1987; May 18, 1987.

Sports Illustrated, March 16, 1987; April 13, 1992; May 10, 1993.

Wall Street Journal, April 9, 1987.

Washington Post, January 22, 1989; July 14, 1990.

The Wings, Professional Sports Publications, 1991.

—Mary K. Ruby

ST. LOUIS BLUES

Although they have existed for only a quarter century, the St. Louis Blues have created their own niche in National Hockey League (NHL) history. Some of the game's greatest players have skated in the old Arena, legendary general managers Lynn Patrick and Emile Francis have been a part of the club's management, and there have been enough memorable games to keep the hot stove leagues sizzling.

There has also been something of a roller-coaster ride associated with St. Louis, a city which has experienced the vagaries of hosting professional teams. The Blues became an instant hit when they were founded in 1967-68, survived a lean patch in the early 1980s when the rumor mill had them headed to Saskatoon, and have now entered the final decade of the 20th Century with every reason to believe that the worst is past.

Along the way the Blues' fans have thrilled to goaltending by two of the game's greatest figures, Glenn Hall and Jacques Plante, and were

cheering a standout rookie, Curtis Joseph, as the 1990s arrived. They have seen three Plager brothers, the best of Brian Sutter as player and coach, Red Berenson, Bernie Federko, and Joey Mullen. There was the wonderful 1990-91 season when youngsters Brett Hull and Adam Oates led their NHL rivals a merry dance, and three Stanley Cup final appearances in the first three years of the franchise.

Not to be overlooked, either, is the competition that quickly developed between the Blues and one of the original six, the Chicago Blackhawks. The two cities had been opponents in baseball for so long that the extension of the rivalry to include a new sport seemed quite natural. What no one could have anticipated was how soon the new Blues would prove a real test for the older Chicago franchise. Their precocious development helped to insure that the rivalry would be realistic from the start.

St. Louis was one of six expansion teams created in the 1967-68 season when the National Hockey League, acknowledging the threat of rivals and the need to broaden its exposure, doubled in size by admitting an entirely new division. The Blues were joined by two California franchises, a Minnesota entry, and teams in Philadelphia and Pittsburgh, competing in the new-born Western Division of hockey's toughest circuit.

It was not the first time that the Missouri city had been in the NHL, but only sports trivia buffs recall the St. Louis Eagles of the depression era. They lasted one season, 1934-35, but were too far away from the rest of the league in the era of train travel.

The new team was the property of Sid Salomon, Jr. and his son Sid Salomon, III, who paid $6 million for the privilege of joining the NHL. Gerald Eskenazi, in *A Thinking Man's Guide to Pro Hockey*, explained that there was some behind-the-scenes drama involved in locating a team along the Mississippi River: "Pretty soon it [the NHL expansion plans] boiled down to the following: the Minneapolis-St. Paul area, Los Angeles, the San Francisco Bay area, Philadelphia, Pittsburgh, Vancouver."

Interestingly, no one from St. Louis was making a bid. One day, the league announced it was holding St. Louis open—even though no one had applied for a franchise. The reason? The [Chicago] Blackhawks owned the St. Louis arena, an old, dingy cavern that couldn't pay for itself. It was, however, the only rink of major-league size in the city. If a hockey club played there, it would have to use the arena. So the league waited for someone to make a bid for St. Louis and the Hawks contemplated, happily, the prospect of unloading their white elephant."

The fight over expansion sites was by no means without rancor. Buffalo wanted to be part of the new division but ran into opposition from Toronto, which had a huge television audience in the city just across Lake Ontario. Vancouver also faced opposition, because its admission would have meant Montreal and Toronto would have to share Canadian television rights and attention with the club in British Columbia.

When the Salomons came forward, not surprisingly, their offer of $3 million for the old arena and a concomitant bid for a franchise was welcomed by the old hands in the NHL. Whatever the backroom motivations may have been, the decision to put a team in the city proved to be a fortuitous one.

Famous Names, Fast Start

Most expansion teams in any sport start slowly. St. Louis began with a bang and the momentum has carried the franchise along ever since. The Salomons' first decision, to hire Lynn Patrick as their first general manager, proved a superior judgment. The Patrick name was already special in hockey, Lynn's father and his uncles having helped to lay the foundation for the National Hockey League. Lynn would play a role in St. Louis for a decade, helping to guide the franchise through early growing pains.

One of the smartest early moves was Patrick's decision to hire a 34-year-old player development specialist out of the Montreal system as his coach. Twenty-five years later Scott Bowman is headed for the Hall of Fame, one of the great coaches the sport has ever seen; perhaps Patrick saw that potential when he hired the young Bowman in that 1967-68 season.

That first St. Louis club, a team that finished 27-31-16 and reached the Stanley Cup finals, had an unusual depth of character. The array of special talent that was gathered together in that opening season included Gordon (Red) Berenson, the first big scoring star in St. Louis, who would go on to coach the Blues, then turn his attention to building one of the top college hockey programs in the United States at his alma mater, the University of Michigan; Don McKenney, a silky smooth forward who later would also coach at one of the United States' top college programs, Northeastern University.

There was also Terry Crisp, a tough forward known for his nonstop work ethic, who later made his name as a coach in Canadian junior hockey,

TEAM INFORMATION AT A GLANCE

Founding date: June 5, 1967

Home ice: St. Louis Arena
5700 Oakland Ave.
St. Louis, MO 63110
Phone: (314) 781-5300

Capacity: 17,188

Team colors: Blue, white, gold, and red.
Team nickname: Blues
Logo: Blue musical note

Franchise record	Won	Lost	Tie
(1967-93)	853	894	315

then led the Calgary Flames to a Stanley Cup when he moved up to the NHL; Al Arbour, the Blues' first captain, who had emerged as key defenseman with the Chicago Blackhawks' Stanley Cup champions at the start of the decade; and the Plager brothers, Barclay and Bob, both of whom would endear themselves to St. Louis fans by their courageous style of play, then go on to coach the Blues.

Bowman played a key role in coaxing the very best out of some of those aging stars. His second season was notable for the remarkable goaltending of two sports veterans, Glenn Hall and Jacques Plante. His ability to instill a strong defensive style, based on a sense of positional play, was to become his trademark.

Twenty-five years later, when Bowman had one of the sport's most explosive offensive aggregations—the Stanley Cup champion Pittsburgh Penguins with Mario Lemieux and a redoubtable supporting cast—he still emphasized the need to have defenders covering the passing lanes and protecting their goalkeeper.

The Grey-Haired Heroes

If some could criticize the Blues for relying too much on aging stars, three consecutive Stanley Cup finals appearances were a sensible reply. What doesn't make sense in the long view is the fact that St. Louis suffered three consecutive four-game sweeps in those finals. Fans who watched those 12 games know how unkind that statistic is to the NHL's expansion club.

True, lack of a truly strong offense was the Achilles heel in Stanley Cup finals, but the Blues' defensive strengths deserved far more than three straight whitewashes. In their first appearance in the finals, 1968, they lost a pair of overtime games to the Montreal Canadiens. The next season they managed just three goals in four games against the same opponents and so never allowed their own defensive strength to come into play.

The third finals, against the Boston Bruins, left North American sports fans with one of those indelible memories: Bobby Orr flying through the air after scoring the deciding goal in the fourth

Hockey Hall of Fame and Museum

Glenn Hall (in goal) during his playing days with Detroit

game. No one doubted that the Bruins were deserving Stanley Cup winners; that clinching goal served to encapsulate all that Orr meant to a sport just starting to create new heroes in the modern age.

The first St. Louis season finished 27-31-16, the 70 points good enough for third place in the new Western Division. Berenson, with 22 goals, 29 assists, led the team with 51 points, while Gerry Melnyk went 15-35-50 to finish second. Hall, who had been made available in the initial expansion draft by the Chicago Blackhawks, quickly demonstrated that he was nowhere near reaching his prime. He played 49 games, compiled a 2.48

goals-against average, and recorded five shutouts in his first year with the Blues.

In an ordinary year, Hall would have been among those honored, but the first expansion season in the NHL was anything but ordinary. There were four goalies ahead of him, including Lorne (Gump) Worsley, the best of the bunch with a 1.98 average in Montreal. There was no complaint about finishing behind the likes of Johnny Bower, Bruce Gamble, or Ed Giacomin, either. Giacomin, the star of the New York Rangers, had eight shutouts that year.

One Blue did lead the NHL in 1967-68. That was Barclay Plager, the oldest of the trio from

Kirkland Lake, Ontario, who would all eventually wear St. Louis sweaters. He chalked up 153 minutes in penalties, the first of six consecutive seasons when he would spend more than 100 minutes in the sin bin. His combative style won the applause of Blues' fans and the respect of opponents.

Plager's younger brother Bob was also a member of that first team, playing 53 games, while the youngest of the three, Bill, was added in an off-season deal that also brought Camille Henry and Robbie Irons from the New York Rangers for a pair of players. Henry was actually the prize catch in the trade, an exquisite little forward whose ability to avoid checks and worry defenses had earned him the nickname "The Eel" during his days on Broadway. Henry was among the NHL's best in shooting percentage the next season when the Blues topped the West.

That second year brought a 37-25-14 record, 88 points, and a stellar year from Berenson. He wound up with 82 points to outdistance the rest of the cast in scoring, but much of the attention was focused on the Hall of Famers in goal. Hall figured in 39 decisions, had eight shutouts and finished with a 2.17 goals-against average; Plante had 36 decisions, five shutouts, and a 1.96 gaa in his first season in St. Louis colors. They shared the Vezina Trophy and may well have been the finest duo ever to play together on the same team.

One of the Game's Greats

Jacques Plante was born on January 17, 1929, in Mont Carmel, Quebec. He played 19 professional seasons with the Montreal Canadiens, New York Rangers, St. Louis Blues, Toronto Maple Leafs, Boston Bruins, and Edmonton Oilers (WHA). Plante was 46 when he finally hung up his equipment, including his now-famous goaltender's mask.

Plante won a Hart Trophy with Montreal, won or shared the Vezina Trophy seven times, and entered the Hall of Fame in 1978. All of the awards give testimony to his greatness at the toughest

position in the game. For all of that, he probably performed his greatest service to the sport in November of 1959, when he came back onto the Madison Square Garden ice to play against the New York Rangers after having been struck in the face by a shot. That night he became the first goaltender ever to wear a face mask in the NHL.

The mask stayed on when he started the next game in Montreal against the Chicago Blackhawks. He faced the ridicule of veterans who said he lacked courage, and the complaints of traditionalists who said he should not have been allowed to tamper with the macho image of his sport, but he paid no attention. His conviction changed both the position and the game.

Plante had already set about changing the position long before he wore a mask or arrived in St. Louis. He was the first goalie to skate behind his net to stop the careering puck, the first to venture forward with the puck in his possession and set up an attack, the first to turn the goal position into a comprehensive hockey post. He claimed that he had started to wander for the simple reason that he was a better skater than his defensemen as a youth, and he simply carried the pattern into his professional career.

His daring, inventiveness, and panache in goal were all accepted, because he was also the consummate performer: in big games it was almost impossible to get the puck past him.

Eskenazi recalled that neither Hall nor Plante was immune to the pressures of the sport. In *A Thinking Man's Guide to Pro Hockey*, he wrote that Hall never was able to attain calm before a game, often retching before the first face off and being sick between periods. Although one of the greatest ever to play between the pipes, Hall said that he hated the pressure of the position.

Plante was different. Those who knew him said that he knitted his own socks and studied philosophy; his coaches sometimes wondered how they would ever be able to deal with his hypochondria. "Was it goaltending that made Plante a hypochondriac?," Eskenazi asked in his book. "Nobody knows. But he did have asthma as a child and a host of allergies. Goaltending didn't help. There was a time when Plante couldn't play in Toronto. He claimed he was allergic to the city. He had a bright idea: He'd sleep in a motel on the outskirts of Toronto and go into town just to play. That worked fine for a time. But one night, Plante dreamed he was in Toronto—he woke up wheezing." That only served to certify Plante's reputation as an eccentric goalie. In fact, when he wound up in Toronto in the 1970-71 season, he played better at Maple Leaf Gardens than anywhere else.

St. Louis Arena—Home of the Blues

It is one of the ironies of sport that the Blues, not expected to be able to give the veteran NHL clubs a moment's worry, should have been so close to Stanley Cup glory those first two years. Their final games were nationally televised across the United States, and anybody who worried about the finals turning into a rout needed have no fears in those days. The Blues didn't win a game, but they made the Canadiens and Bruins fight for their Cups.

One reason for that was their home, the old, decrepit St. Louis Arena that the Blackhawks had been so happy to unload. Thanks to renovations carried out by the first owners, the Blues' home turned out to be a remarkable place. Later, when Ralston Purina took over the team, they called it the Checkerdome, but the reputation had been established in those earliest days.

"It was louder in that building than it had ever been in Montreal," Plante told Jay Greenberg in *NHL: The World of Professional Hockey*. "Just unbelievable, a standing ovation every time we took the ice. It just caught on like crazy. Every time . . . they got a big crowd they'd have a spectacular game. Overtime or beating one of the six original teams. More and more people kept coming and soon it was full every night. Noise like that I couldn't believe. They were two of the happiest years I had in hockey."

The Salomon brothers had done a major renovation job on the building when they took over. Greenberg tells us that they cut the seating capac-

ity back to 14,500 by installing theater style seats, tiled the lobby and added a private dining club. The also remodeled the bathrooms and hired an attendant for each one. Eventually, buoyed by the team's early success, capacity was increased to 17,967. That proved overly ambitious when the team later slumped in the mid-1980s, but the plain fact was that the building's ambiance and the team's early success had worked together to weld hockey onto the Missouri mind.

The Blues finished first in the Western Division in 1969-70 with Phil Goyette, formerly a Montreal Canadien star, having one more fine NHL season. He led the team with 78 points, finished fifth in the NHL in assists, fourth in points, and first in shooting percentage. Berenson was right there with a 72-point season, while Plante, Ernie Wakely, and Hall combined for another historic season in goal. Plante, in 32 decisions, had a 2.19 gaa; Wakely, in 25, was 2.11; while Hall, in 18, finished 2.91. This was the team that lost to Boston and Orr's dramatic shot in the final.

The season had been marred, however, by an event that happened back in an exhibition game. Wayne Maki, who played only 16 games in a St. Louis sweater, swung his stick at one of the NHL's renowned tough guys, Ted Green, and the consequences rebounded across a sport still trying to get a handle on violence.

Gerald Eskenazi described the event: "The most controversial defenseman . . . was the Bruins' Ted Green. Nicknamed Terrible Teddy, Green built his reputation as a vicious fighter.... During an exhibition game in St. Louis in 1969 Green and Wayne Maki waggled their sticks at each other. Green brought his up and then turned away, figuring it was over. But Maki came down with the stick hard and smashed Green in the head. Green suffered a fractured skull. Although there was a cry, temporarily, for helmets and stiffer fines for stick-fighters, there was not that much sympathy for Green."

Happily, Green recovered and returned to top class hockey, eventually becoming a valued coach in the NHL. Helmets, too, would make their appearance, although that took the impetus of expo-

| PROFILE | Colorful Blues |

In their relatively short history, the Blues have had an ample share of hockey characters. Easily the most eccentric was Gilles Gratton, whose peculiarities were far more memorable than his achievements in the nets. According to Frank Orr's *NHL: The World of Professional Ice Hockey*, Gratton's interests encompassed "reincarnation, meditation, playing the piano, [and] streaking."

Reincarnation, at least, Gratton took seriously. He attributed one leg injury not to his exertions on the ice but to an old war wound--from the Franco-Prussian War. He also believed that he'd been a tiger in a previous life, thus his face mask was decorated with tiger stripes. His identification with his feline past went a little too far one night while Gratton was still with the Rangers. His teammates became alarmed when they noticed him growling behind the mask during the warm-up. As he related to Orr, Coach John Ferguson was untroubled until a fight broke out during the game and Gratton began skating around "hunched up like an angry cat, snarling and holding his hands in the claw position. He jumped on someone like a cat pouncing on a mouse."

Of more lasting impact on the Blues were the battling Plager brothers--Barclay, Bob, and Billy--genial, fun-loving fellows known equally for their love of hockey and personal combat. The two older siblings, Barclay and Bob, were key defensemen for the Blues in the early years. Billy was picked up for parts of three seasons. The Plagers' hockey fights, some with each other, were legendary, their enthusiasm summed up by Barclay's credo, "it's not how many fights you win that's important, it's how many you show up for." Even before they made their junior hockey debut, Bob claimed the boys had won their father, a hockey referee, the nickname "Squirrel" because "he raised three nuts".

Fittingly, their swan song occurred in St. Louis, where the Plagers were hugely popular. Bob and Barclay had been dispatched on a public relations visit to a local women's club. The meeting was a great success, the members impressed with the Plager Brothers' prefect manners. Unfortunately, the brothers stopped at a local restaurant on the way home. As Bob recalled in *NHL: The World of Professional Hockey*, "We ordered alphabet soup and the waiter spilled it on my good suit. I didn't like the words the noodles spelled, we got into a little beef, a couple of punches were tossed, and somebody called the cops."

sure to the international game and stiffer rules for youth hockey that brought a generation of players used to headgear into the NHL.

It was unrealistic to think that a team could reach the Stanley Cup finals every season. Nevertheless, when the Blues finally faced that reality, they did it without Bowman at the helm. He had been replaced by Arbour during the 1970-71 year, exiting with a parting shot at the Blues' management.

Eskenazi quoted Bowman as saying, "A few years ago there wasn't even an NHL team in St. Louis. The owners didn't know a thing about hockey. Now the team gets successful—and sud-denly the owners are smarter than you are. I had to get out of that situation. If I'm not in control, I don't want to be part of the club." Bowman would prove to be just as tough-minded in later coaching stints even as he won numerous Stanley Cups and carved out a Hall-of-Fame career.

The Bowman-Arbour team of 1970-71 finished well, 34-25-19, the 87 points good for second place behind Chicago in the Western Division. Wakely, who had replaced Plante in the goaltending tandem, had another fine year (45 decisions, 2.79 gaa) and Hall played 32 games with 2.42 figures. Barclay Plager had become captain of the team by now, but one of the early fixtures, Red Berenson, was shipped to Detroit in mid-season. Some blamed Berenson's active players' union work for his transfer. Without the redhead, Christian Bordeleau won the team scoring title with 53 points.

Three Years in the Wilderness

The next three seasons were unsteady, a succession of coaches, losing records, and only one Stanley Cup series victory to cushion to shock. They were notable, however, for the presence of Garry Unger, the player acquired along with Wayne Connelly for Berenson and Tim Ecclestone in February of 1971.

Unger had broken into the NHL as a 20-year-old with the Toronto Maple Leafs in the 1967-68 season before being part of a blockbuster trade with Detroit that include the Leafs' star, Frank Mahovlich. His arrival in St. Louis in the Berenson deal began a career that would see him become the perennial top scorer for the Blues as well as set a standard for reliability and longevity in a tough game. From 1971-72 through 1978-79 he never missed a game in St. Louis.

In Unger's first year, the Blues had three coaches, Sid Abel, Bill McCreary, and Arbour, back for a second stint, but none could find the winning formula. The team finished 28-39-11, third in the West. They beat Minnesota in six games in the opening round of the playoffs, but fell in four straight to the Bruins in the next scene. Hall was gone by this time, and Wakely, Jacques Caron, and Jim McLeod shared the goaltending. Bowman, in the meantime, had moved into the head coaching job in Montreal, where he would reestablish the Canadiens as the top team in the league.

Arbour and Jean-Guy Talbot were behind the bench in 1972-73, a second straight losing year. The Blues finished 32-34-12 with Unger leading the attack, and Wayne Stephenson and Caron combining for a good season in the nets. Stephenson finished with a 3.03 gaa, while Caron, who later would be a goaltending coach in the league,

had a 3.53 average.

The Blues were also noted for Steve Durbano's 231 penalty minutes, third in the league, and might have had more if Moose Dupont had not been moved on to Philadelphia during the season. Dupont finished fourth in sin-bin time in an era when the league was noted for the physical nature of its play.

Talbot began the 1973-74 season but didn't finish it as head coach. Lou Angotti handled the last 23 contests in a 26-40-12 season notable mainly for the arrival of 20-year-old rookie goalie John Davidson, who would go on to a successful career with the New York Rangers, then become one of the game's most eloquent spokesmen as a television analyst.

Davidson played 39 games and had a 3.08 goals-against average in his first full season, sharing the responsibility with Stephenson, whose 3.13 gaa was more than respectable on a team that could finish only sixth in the West. Unger was again the top scorer with 68 points, but there was no postseason play for St. Louis.

The 1974-75 NHL season marked the advent of the four-division system. St. Louis was placed in the original Smythe Division alignment and immediately regained winning ways. Angotti, Lynn Patrick, and Garry Young, who was to coach only 98 NHL games, were in charge that season.

Young had coached just 12 games in California before being tapped to take over the club. He would be in charge for the final 69 games of this season then start the next in a cameo NHL career.

Davidson shared the goaltending work (39 decisions, 3.66 GAA) with a veteran, Ed Johnston (30 games, 3.10), and Unger (80 points) was once more the top marksman on a team that still struggled to get goals.

Bob Gassoff, a 5-foot, 10-inch, 195-pound defenseman picked up 222 penalty minutes in that season, the fifth most in the league. When he wrapped up his career two years later, his would be among the four St. Louis numbers to be retired. That spoke volumes for his popularity and the willingness to do the little things that hockey clubs need.

There was no perfect ending to Young's brief NHL year in the sun. Pittsburgh defeated the Blues in the first round of the Stanley Cup playoffs in two straight games. Young was gone after 29 games the next year, Patrick going back behind the bench for the last time, serving eight games before ex-Boston Bruin star Leo Boivin was tapped to handle the remaining 43 contests of a disappointing year. St.Louis wound up 29-37-14, third place in the Smythe Division, then fell 2-1 to Buffalo in the first round of the playoffs.

There was a big season from an unexpected source—Chuck Lefley edged Unger for the club scoring lead after having been acquired the season before in a deal with Montreal that sent Don Awrey to the Canadiens. Lefley had notched 49 points in 57 games with the Blues in his first year, but his 43-42-85 the next season represented a career year for the 26-year-old Winnipeg native. Unger came in with 39-44-83.

Johnston was now the number one goaltender, playing 37 games and putting up 3.62 figures. He was partnered by Yves Belanger, whose only full season in the NHL amounted to 31 decisions and a 3.85 gaa. Gassoff again finished among the leaders in penalty minutes, but it was clear that the Blues needed a change of direction.

Enter Emile "The Cat" Francis

The bantam-sized Emile Francis had always been a battler. A native of North Battleford, Saskatchewan, Francis worked his way into the National Hockey League at the age of 20, playing in goal for the Chicago Blackhawks and the New York Rangers. It wasn't a distinguished career, only 95 NHL games in five different seasons, most of them in Chicago.

Francis, however, was canny, a player who was alert to everything going on around him. Even as he was playing, he was "in training" for his true NHL career, that of coach and general manager with three different teams, all of whom he lifted to success after they were down. He first earned the nickname "The Cat" because of his quickness between the pipes; by the time Francis had suffered

the slings-and-arrows of team rebuilding in New York, St. Louis, and Hartford, the appellation was appropriate for his ability to move from one hockey life to the next without missing a step.

Francis had spent ten years on Broadway in the high-pressure New York Rangers' job before answering the call to head west in 1976-77. He was not expected to coach as much as to manage the Blues, but he wound up in two different stints behind the bench and presided over a team that struggled, particularly in the early 1980s, when Ralston Purina, their parent company, was looking to get out of hockey. That was when Francis may have done his best work, keeping the team focused as much as possible on playing the game, while the off-ice talk was all about proposed moves, rumored amalgamations, and suggested trades.

Francis's first season in St. Louis produced a Smythe Division championship, but it was hardly the kind of title that initiated celebrations. The team finished 32-39-9 in a division where no one had a winning record. Rewarding the Blues with a first round Stanley Cup bye simply delayed their elimination; Montreal, now coached by Bowman, took care of that business in four straight games.

In a bit of poetic justice, Francis was reunited with Bob MacMillan, a winger he had traded from the Rangers to the Blues the season before. MacMillan led St. Louis in scoring with 58 points, one more than Unger, while Johnston and Ed Staniowski shared the goaltending duties.

Francis had already insured the success of that first season before a game was played. Although The Cat has sometimes been accused of being too quick to trade young talent for proven veterans, no one could question his acumen when it came to drafting for St. Louis' future. In the spring of 1976, the Blues picked Bernie Federko with the seventh selection and used the 20th pick to tab Brian Sutter. Two years later Francis took Wayne Babych with the third overall pick. All three played an important part in turning the Blues back into a winning aggregation.

Federko, from Foam Lake, Saskatchewan, came into the pros off an impressive Western

Hockey League career. The center with the strong left-handed shot had gone 39-68-107 in his second season with Saskatoon, then won the WHL's most valuable player award in his last junior campaign, one that saw him score 72 goals and add 115 assists, numbers that were astonishingly high in the pre-Gretzky era.

Federko needed just half a minor league season, with Kansas City in the Central Hockey League, before he was ready to make an impact in St. Louis. He played 31 games in his rookie year of 1976-77 and was a full-time regular from then on. Included in his sparkling Blues' career would be four 100-point plus seasons, two NHL All Star game appearances, and a level of consistency that saw him produce 30 or more goals seven times. When he was eventually traded to Detroit along with Tony McKegney in June of 1989, the package value was still so high that St. Louis got one of the league's bright young stars, Adam Oates, along with Paul MacLean in return.

A Sutter for St. Louis

Brian Sutter, one of six brothers from Viking, Alberta, played 12 seasons with the Blues, then moved behind the bench as coach of the only NHL club he ever played for. His 779 NHL games produced 303 goals, 333 assists, and 1786 minutes in penalties. He ranks second in club history in games, goals, assists and points, but the numbers don't tell of the leadership, will to win, and sheer competitiveness of the man.

He had played his junior hockey in Lethbridge of the Western Hockey League and, like Federko, joined Kansas City after he was drafted by the Blues. He, too, spent only a minimal apprenticeship in the minors, playing 38 games in the CHL before making the jump to the Blues. In just two years, at the age of 23, he was named captain of the club, a position he retained until his retirement in 1987-88. He was 33 when he went behind the bench for his first season, the youngest head coach in the NHL.

Sutter's mother was the subject of a likely apocryphal story that made the rounds in later years after the rest of the clan had followed Brian into the NHL. Francis, known for his quick wit, is supposed to have told his scouts that he would have done even better for the Blues "if I had drafted Mrs. Sutter."

The building process took time, naturally. Francis went upstairs to concentrate on the administrative side of things in 1977-78, Leo Boivin taking over as coach. Bovin was replaced after 54 games by Barclay Plager, who had wrapped up a notable 10-year career with St. Louis the season before. Overall, St. Louis finished 20-47-13 and missed the playoffs after a fourth place finish in the Smythe Division.

The next year was also a losing campaign (18-50-12), but it was notable for the emergence of Sutter and Federko as stars of the future. Sutter, who had gotten just 22 points the preceding season, leaped to 41-39-80, while Federko offered the evidence that his junior scoring feats were to be repeated at the top level, when he collected 31 goals and added 64 assists to finish with 95 points.

The Blues still didn't have the kind of airtight defense and goaltending that would produce a winning team, but that was about to change.

Mike Liut Arrives

Emile Francis, a raconteur whose collection of lore entertains audiences of all types, will spend hours talking hockey. Listen carefully, however; the same message comes through time and again: winning teams start with excellent goaltending, pay attention to defensive checking, and make the best use of their opportunities. The Cat likes players who do the little things like completing their checks or winning pressure face offs, which explains why he always found room on his teams for such specialists. The goaltender, though, was always a key.

In 1979-80, when Red Berenson took over for Plager after 28 games, St. Louis not only put together a .500 season, they also found the goalie Francis had been looking for. He was Mike Liut, a strapping netminder who wore leadership on his

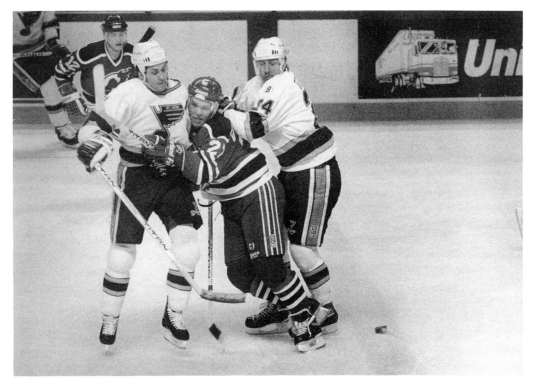

**Doug Gilmour (left) and Bernie Federko (right) make a New Jersey
Devils sandwich with the assistance of Randy Velischek**

shoulder and could make the big saves with the best of them.

Liut had actually been chosen by the Blues back in the 1976 amateur draft, when he was a fifth round selection after completing his college career at Bowling Green. There he had played his junior and senior years with goals-against averages of 2.56 and 2.72, not easy in the sometimes wide-open collegiate game, but he elected to join Cincinnati in the rival World Hockey Association rather than move to the Blues.

In 1979, when the NHL-WHA accommodation was completed, one of the first things St. Louis did was reclaim their prize in the expansion draft that preceded the merger. Liut became a workhorse for the next six seasons with the Blues, starting 60 or more games four straight seasons, win-

ning first team NHL All Star recognition in 1981, and a berth on Team Canada for international play against the Soviet Union.

He also endeared himself to Francis, so much so that when The Cat eventually moved to Hartford, Liut was a major acquisition in a February 1985 trade that involved two of the fan favorites in Connecticut, goalie Greg Millen and 1980 U.S. Olympic hero Mark Johnson. Francis braved the storm of criticism and Liut responded with an All Star season in his new city in 1987.

The first Liut campaign in St. Louis was marked by 64 appearances, a 3.18 goals-against average, and the .500 record that was the first time in five years that the Blues had avoided a losing campaign. Federko followed up his big season with a 94-point year, Babych came aboard to contribute 61 points, and there was also a worthy contribution from Mike Zuke, one of those specialist players Francis always seemed able to spot.

A face-off expert and defensive star, Zuke was a master at outsmarting the opposition; his 64 points that season and 68 the next represented nearly half of his career total of 282, picked up in eight seasons in St. Louis and Hartford. Like Liut, Zuke was one of those players Francis liked for his for special contributions.

Berenson's 1980-81 team improved radically; they finished 45-18-17, the 107 points representing a gain of 27 over the previous season. Liut was outstanding, his 3.34 goals-against average in 60 games and consistently high calibre play earning him the Lester B. Pearson Award, the player-of-the-year accolade. He finished second in voting for the Hart Trophy in the same season.

There was plenty of firepower, too. Federko went 31-73-104 to achieve his first 100-point season in St. Louis, while Babych scored 54 goals and finished with 96 points. Blake Dunlop, acquired from the Philadelphia Flyers in midseason when it was obvious that back-up netminder Phil Myre could be traded, finished 20-67-87 and Sutter added 35 goals on the line with Federko and Babych.

Although taken to the full five games by Pittsburgh in the first round of the playoffs, the Blues survived that test, then were favored to get by the Rangers in the quarterfinals. In one of sport's ironies, St. Louis fell in six games to New York, now being guided by Craig Patrick, son of Lynn Patrick, the original mastermind in St. Louis.

Having touched the heights in 1980-81, there was a fall-off the next season. Berenson was replaced with 11 games to go, Francis moving behind the bench for his second tenure as St. Louis coach as the team slumped to 32-40-8. Liut was again in goal most of the time, playing 63 games, but his 4.06 gaa reflected the amount of work he had to do. Federko got 92 points, Dunlop, 78, and Sutter, 75, and there was even a first round playoff win over Winnipeg, but a generally disappointing year was again ended in the Cup quarterfinals by Chicago.

That St. Louis survived the 1982-83 campaign intact turned out to be something of a miracle. This was a dismal, 25-40-15 campaign, Francis and Barclay Plager sharing the work behind the bench, but to say there were extenuating circumstances is putting it mildly. Ralston Purina, the Blues corporate owner since 1977, spent much of the year attempting to organize a move to Saskatoon, Saskatchewan, with rumors blowing hot and cold throughout the season.

Francis, himself, became the center of rumors in March of the same season, when he was reported in Hartford when the Whalers, struggling through a dreadful season, began thinking of new leadership at the top. Eventually Francis took over in Connecticut after the end of the campaign; he admitted that the uncertainty in St. Louis had made the final year difficult.

There were success stories, however, that should not go unnoticed. Liut bounced back to 3.72 numbers behind a weaker team. Federko continued his production, and an import from Sweden, Jorgen Pettersson, came up with 35 goals and 38 assists for 73 points. That was also the season that Joe Mullen, the New York native, made his first impression, collecting 47 points in 49 St. Louis games.

The chaos in the organization continued at the end of the year when the NHL denied Ralston Purina's planned move to Saskatchewan. Dan Diamond, in *The NHL's Official 75th Anniversary Commemorative Book* elaborated: "When the NHL prevented the move, Ralston Purina closed the Blues' front office and announced it would no longer operate in the city. Despite the league's urging it to participate in the entry draft, the company refused to do so. Beverly Hills businessman Harry Ornest bought the Blues at the end of July, hiring Ron Caron as his general manager. Caron had been the director of scouting and player personnel in Montreal and would need all his talents as a dealmaker to make up for St. Louis' lost draft choices."

To Caron's credit, and with more than a little help from Jacques Demers, a coach who turned out to be an extraordinary motivator of players, the

Blues overcame the missed chances more quickly than might have been expected.

Some Overtime Heroics

Demers's first season produced a 32-41-7 record, good for second place in the Norris Division. Federko had his second 100-point campaign, going 41-66-107, while Mullen demonstrated his full potential, finishing 41-44-85, and Sutter was right behind at 32-51-83. There was also a debut season for Doug Gilmour, who would give five years of solid service in St. Louis, and another good year from Liut. He played 58 games (3.45) while Rick Heinz worked the other 22 (4.29) regu-

lar season games in goal.

The playoffs produced so̶ Blues skated by Detroit 3-1 Game three went into double̶ *en the* Mark Reeds won it at 37:07, w̶ *und.* fourth game was also an overtime̶*pre* netting the winner after just 2:42 ̶*de* play. Minnesota ended any dream̶ bigger, however, winning the Norr̶ nal in a seven-game grinder.

St. Louis won the Norris Divisi̶ 1984-85, finishing 37-31-12, as Fed̶ topped the 100-point level, Mullen we̶ and Rick Wamsley provided strong s̶ Liut in goal. In fact, this was the year tha̶ swung the deal to get his old favorite in ̶

AP/Wide World Photos

Coach Jacques Demers celebrates the Blues' 1986 Norris Division finals victory over Toronto

...iging Greg Millen and Whalers' cold Pettersson in a contro- Mark Johnson...had played 32 games that versial sprin...while Wamsley finished season wit... 3.26 mark. The season with 40 ...t, when Minnesota swept ended i...first round of the playoffs. the Bl...ore full season in charge ...got the underdogs all the in S... p finals. The regular season wa... from the one before (37-34- ...vision was stronger, so the w... espite the narrow three-point ... tion. ...ll the most reliable marksman ... Mark Hunter emerged that

year to provide assistance, and Rob Ramage, in the midst of a six-year career as the big man on the Blues' backline, was his usual steady self. There was another dramatic deal in mid-season, when Mullen was dealt over to Calgary in a six-player swap.

Millen, who had been a consistent, if sometimes poorly-supported, goaltender in Hartford, proved a solid addition, teaming with Wamsley in the nets. In his first full season in St. Louis, Millen finished 3.57 in 36 decisions, comparing very favorably with Wamsley's 3.43 average in 42 appearances.

The playoffs were dramatic right from the start. The Blues first edged Minnesota, 3-2, then won a seven-game thriller from the Toronto

AP/Wide World Photos

Curtis Joseph

Maples Leafs. Mark Reeds again proved an over-time hero, scoring 7:11 into sudden death to win game five. The deciding game was a 2-1 nailbiter in favor of the Blues.

That sent St. Louis into their first Campbell Conference final, where the opponent turned out to be Calgary and their old star, Mullen. The series went all the way to seven games, Doug Wickenheiser keeping the Blues alive with an overtime game-winner in the sixth contest, but this time history repeated in the wrong manner for Demers's club. The seventh game again finished 2-1 but the Blues were on the wrong side of the result. Shortly thereafter Detroit lured Demers away as they sought to rebuild their fortunes.

St. Louis turned to Jacques Martin, a 34-year-old native of Rockland, Ontario, who had built a solid reputation in Canadian junior hockey. Martin's coaching career began in 1979-80 with the Rockland Nationals, a Junior B team, then took over the Peterborough Petes of the Ontario Hockey League in 1983-84. His final Petes' season was a glorious one, Peterborough winning the divisional title, but even better finishes lay in the immediate future. Martin moved to the Guelph Platers, another OHL club, and achieved all that a coach can win in the junior ranks. Guelph won the 1985-86 OHL title and then captured the Memorial Cup, the annual tournament which decides the Canadian national junior champion. He was named OHL coach of the year, finishing with a 126-76-10 record in three league seasons.

Martin carried that winning habit into St. Louis, although it took some Norris Division weakness to do it. His initial Blues' team wound up below .500 (32-33-15) but still finished first in a year when no Norris team had a winning record. Gilmour was the top gun (42-63-105), but although both Millen and Wamsley were again sharp, but the momentum didn't carry into the playoffs. Toronto got immediate revenge for the previous season, ousting the Blues in six games to open the Stanley Cup competition.

Tony McKegney bagged 40 goals for the Blues in 1987-88 while Federko and Gilmour topped the 80-point level. But the biggest news in a season when St. Louis came second in the Norris Division happened off the ice. On March 7, 1988, the Blues traded Ramage and Wamsley to the Calgary Flames for Brett Hull and Steve Bozek. Bozek, ironically, would be dealt right back to Calgary the following September in another major trade, but this particular swap was all about the potential of young Hull.

Living Up to a Great Name

Brett Hull was 21 years old when he left the University of Minnesota-Duluth to skate with the Flames knowing that he would face the inevitable comparisons with his famous father, Bobby Hull, the fabled Golden Jet. Hull had done nothing to discourage such talk in his one Junior season or during two standout years at UMD. With Penticton, B.C., in 1983-84, the future superstar "announced" his arrival with 105 goals and 83 assists in a 56-game performance. He went on to the Western Collegiate Hockey Association Bulldogs the next year and immediately made an impact. He scored 32 goals in his first season, then got 52 in 42 games the next year when he won WCHA all-star status and then turned pro. He made a pair of Stanley Cup playoff appearances in 1985-86 without collecting a point.

His real NHL debut was delayed another year because he spent 1986-87 at Moncton in the American Hockey League. There he scored 50 goals en route to a first-team AHL All-Star berth and the Red Garrett Award as the AHL's top rookie before joining the Flames for 1987-88.

Hull had scored 26 goals in 52 games in Calgary before finishing that season in St. Louis, where he collected 14 points in 13 games, then added nine more in ten playoff games. It was just a hint of what the future held.

After an 84-point season in his first full year as a Blue, Hull blossomed into a consistent NHL All Star. He posted gaudy figures in each of the next three years: 72 goals, an All Star berth, and the Lady Byng Trophy came in 1989-90; 86 goals, 131 points, All Star status, the Hart Trophy, and the Pearson Trophy were his in 1990-91; and 70 more goals in 1991-92 by way of establishing his own high standards and making modern hockey fans think "Brett" as often as "Bobby" when they heard the famous last name

Hull's first full season in St. Louis was also the debut season for Brian Sutter behind the Blues' bench. With Brett leading the team in scoring with 84 points, a mid-season addition from Philadelphia, Peter Zezel, adding points and precision checking up front, and Federko still a contributor on the attack, the Blues finished 33-35-12 and took second in the Norris. Millen had a standout season in goal, leading the NHL with six shutouts and finishing with a 3.38 gaa in 52 decisions. He was now partnered with Vincent Riendeau, a goalie of promise.

The playoffs were dramatic in round one—Hull's overtime goal won the opener, and another by Rick Meagher accomplished the same in game two—as the Blues bounced Minnesota aside, 4-1. Chicago was too strong at the next stage, winning in five games, but Tony Hrkac did give Blues fans a memory when he scored 33:49 into overtime to give St. Louis a win in the second game.

After the playoffs were over, the Blues swung a deal that was to help transform the team. On June 15, 1989, the veteran Federko was sent to Detroit

Brett Hull

along with McKegney for Adam Oates and Paul MacLean. Oates, who had slipped through the draft net as a youngster, emerged at RPI as a collegiate star before signing as a free agent with Detroit. In fact, his bargaining power led the NHL to create a supplemental draft to select just such collegians whose rights had not been assigned at the amateur draft of 18-year-olds.

Certainly Oates's arrival in St. Louis marked a new era. With his deft passing and Hull's deadly sniping, the statistics grew quickly. In 1989-90, when Hall first topped the 70-goal level, Oates picked up 79 assists. Zezel contributed 72 points in his first full St. Louis season, while another rookie, Rod Brind'Amour, made a 61-point debut.

That all added up to a 37-34-9 season, second place in the Norris Division and a mini-playoff run. Toronto was handled 4-1 in the first round, while Chicago was taken to the seven-game limit in the Norris finals before the Blackhawks finally prevailed.

The year was also notable for the arrival of rookie goalie Curtis Joseph, who came from the University of Wisconsin and appeared in 15 games. His presence enabled the Blues to send Millen to Quebec in a December deal that brought Jeff Brown, a defenseman, back to Missouri.

In 1990-91, Oates tied a club record held jointly by his coach, Sutter, and Federko when he picked up five assists in a game on the way to a 90-assist haul for the season. Hull had his Hart Trophy season, and the club collected 105 points with a club record 47 wins and 11 ties in the 80-game season.

There was a club record seven-game win streak to go along with a nine-game home victory skein, as well as a dramatic playoff comeback in the first round when the Blues came from a 3-1 deficit to knock off Detroit in the Norris semifinals. Minnesota, though, sprung a 4-2 upset at the next stage to end the season earlier than most observers expected.

The 1991-92 season, a third place finish in the Norris, included a first round playoff loss to Chicago and the controversial trade of Oates to Boston for Craig Janney. Joseph played 60 games and had a 3.01 goals-against average, but questions remained about the club's ability to translate the regular season excellence into postseason triumph.

Before the 1992-93 season, Brian Sutter was fired as coach and was replaced by the more mild-mannered Bob Plager. Plager's tenure, however, lasted less than a month; he resigned after 11 games, leaving the team in chaos. Assistant general manager Bob Berry took over the helm.

After a dismal start of 13-20-6, the club picked up its intensity and made the playoffs by finishing fourth in the Norris Division. Joseph proved able to lead the team, and a writer for *Inside Hockey* noted that the team "walked a tightrope ... and only the unflappable Joseph kept them from going splat down the the stretch." Hull notched a 54-goal year (his lowest total in four seasons), Janney led the team in points with 106, and Brendan Shanahan scored a career-high 51 goals.

In the playoffs, the inspired Blues swept Chicago—a team that had finished 21 points ahead of them in the divisional standings. The Blues then took Toronto to a seventh game before succumbing to the Leafs.

SOURCES

BOOKS

Diamond, Dan, *The Official National Hockey League 75th Anniversary Commemorative Book,* NHL Publications, 1991.

Eskenazi, Gerald, *A Thinking Man's Guide to Pro Hockey,* E.P. Dutton, 1972.

Fischler, Stan and Shirley Fischler, *The Hockey Encyclopedia,* MacMillan, 1983.

Greenberg, Jay, Frank Orr, and Gary Ronberg, *NHL: The World of Professional Hockey,* Rutledge Press, 1981.

Romain, Joseph and Dan Diamond, *The Pictorial History of Hockey,* Gallery Books, 1987.

Trecker, Jerry, "Season Review," *ESPN Sports Almanac '83,* Total Sports Publications, 1983.

PERIODICALS

Calabria, Pat, "1984-85 Season Review," *The Sporting News Hockey Guide and Register.*
Matheson, Jim, "Season Reviews," *The Sporting News Hockey Guide & Register,* 1986-87, 1989-90.

—*Jerry Trecker* for Book Builders, Inc.

TORONTO MAPLE LEAFS

The Maple Leafs' record of 13 Stanley Cups is an achievement second in the NHL only to that of the Montreal Canadiens, as is their record of 54 playoff appearances. During the decades when the National Hockey League (NHL) was a six-team league, the Leafs were virtually the national team of English-speaking Canada, inspiring fanatical loyalty from the Maritime Provinces to British Columbia. Their history includes periods of dynastic glory—and yet the glory, from the standpoint of the 1990s, seems very much a thing of the past.

Not since 1967 have the Leafs played in the Stanley Cup finals. Not since 1963 have they finished higher than third in their division. With the far-flung expansion of the NHL, which eventually brought citizens of Winnipeg, Edmonton, Calgary, Vancouver, and Ottawa major-league teams of their own to root for, the Maple Leafs have had to settle for being the home team of a single city. More damaging has been the sheer mediocrity, at best, of recent Maple Leaf teams' play and management. Yet the arrival of coach Pat Burns for the 1992-93 season, brought new hope for fans and an appearance in the Campbell Conference finals.

At their height, the Leafs' franchise was based on team play and guts rather than on stellar individual talents. Often members of the Leafs' management were better known than players. In the past generation, the Leafs have had neither a superstar nor the spirit to win without one. Nor have they recently had a leader like Conn Smythe, Hap Day, or Punch Imlach to guide their fortunes and inspire their players. And throughout their history, the Leafs have repeatedly stumbled through mismanagement or sheer bad luck.

Auspicious Beginnings

The team's beginnings were as auspicious as possible. It all began with the Toronto Arenas of the original 1917 NHL, winning the Stanley Cup in the league's first year of existence. They were the fifth team to enter the league and the only one at that time to play on artificial ice. After finishing second to the Canadiens in the first half of the split season, the Arenas finished first in the second half behind left wing Reg Noble's 28 goals in 22 games and defenseman Harry Cameron's 17. In the NHL finals—a two-game, total-goals series—the Arenas beat the Canadiens 10 goals to 7. They then went on to overcome the Vancouver Millionaires in a five-game Stanley Cup series, with left wing Corbett Denneny scoring the winning goal.

Typical of the team's fortunes, however, they finished third—in a league reduced to three teams—and out of the playoffs the following season. Noble's production was down to 14 points and Cameron had been sent to the Ottawa Senators. Despite being favored for a repeat, the Arenas lost six of their first seven games and never recovered.

The team's name was changed to the St. Patricks, or St. Pats, for 1919-20 as part of a rebuilding effort. Right winger Carol "Cully" Wilson, who had been banned from the Pacific Coast Hockey Association (PCHA) for his rough play, joined Toronto and proceeded to lead the NHL in penalty minutes with 79. He also contributed 26 points, eighth in the league. Denneny scored 23 goals and 12 assists, fourth in the league in points, as Toronto again finished third, but this time in a four-team league.

During the 1920-21 season, the St. Pats rose to second place in the first half and first place in the second half. Right winger Cecil "Babe" Dye, who had been drafted by Hamilton and then reclaimed by Toronto in mid-season after he scored two goals in a December 22 game against them, led the league in goals with 35 (and was third in points with 37). Unfortunately, the St. Pats were shut out by the Ottawa Senators 5-0 and 2-0 in the two NHL playoff games.

Babe Dye's acquisition continued to pay off for Toronto, however, as he scored 30 goals and 7 assists in 1921-22. The team finished eight points

behind Ottawa for second place, and then defeated Ottawa for a shot at the Stanley Cup finals with 5-4 and 0-0 playoff performances. The first four finals games against Vancouver were evenly split. In game five, Dye scored four of his team's five goals for a 5-1 victory and a second Stanley Cup for Toronto.

Dye led the league in points in 1922-23, with 26 goals and 11 assists, and teammate Jack Adams, a center, scored 19 and 9 for third in the league. The team itself was only third in the league, however—another disappointment. They missed the playoffs in 1922-23 and the next season.

Dye blazed back in 1924-25 to lead the league in scoring with 38 goals and 6 assists in 30 games. Reg Noble had been picked up by the Montreal Maroons, but rookie left wing Clarence "Hap" or "Happy" Day scored 22 points to fill the gap. (Hap would go one to become team captain in 1927, head coach in 1940, and general manager in 1957.) The St. Pats finished second to Hamilton in the regular season, and faced the Canadiens in the playoffs because of the Hamilton players' strike. The Canadiens beat them 3-2 and 2-0.

Enter Smythe

The league expanded to seven teams in 1925-26; the St. Pats had the misfortune to be sixth place, out of the playoffs again. For the next season, the NHL split into Canadian and American divisions. The St. Pats finished last in their five-team division with a 15-24 record. Owner Charlie Querrie put his team up for sale and Conn Smythe, disgusted by his recent experiences building the New York Rangers, made the $165,000 purchase with the help of backers. Smythe patriotically changed the team's name to the Maple Leafs and launched an era of improved fortunes.

After another poor year in 1927-28, the Leafs climbed to third place in 1928-29 as Ace Bailey led the league in scoring with 22 goals and 10 assists. Ace was part of a crew of young players Smythe was acquiring with the sage advice of Frank Selke. Others who arrived in this era in-

TEAM INFORMATION AT A GLANCE

Founding date: 1917

Home ice: Maple Leaf Gardens
60 Carlton Street
Toronto, Ontario M5B 1L1
Phone: (416)977-1641
FAX: (416) 977-5364

Seating capacity: 15,642

Team colors: Blue and white
Logo: Maple leaf with "Toronto Maple Leafs" written inside

Franchise Record	Won	Lost	Tie
(1917-93)	2,001	1,993	682

Stanley Cup Wins (13): 1917-18; 1921-22; 1931-32; 1941-42; 1944-45; 1946-47;
1947-48; 1948-49; 1950-51; 1961-62; 1962-63; 1963-64; 1966-67
League/Division First Place Finishes: 1917-1918*; 1920-21*; 1932-33; 1933-34;
1934-35; 1937-38; 1947-48; 1962-63
(* second half of split season)

League/Division Last Place Finishes: 1918-19**; 1926-27; 1957-58;
1969-70; 1980-81; 1988-89; 1990-91; 1991-92
(**both halves of split season)

cluded Alex Levinsky, Harold "Baldy" Cotton, and goalie Lorne Chabot. The tough, experienced Smythe did far more than assemble players, however. He pioneered modern training methods, making his players work out before the season began rather than using the early regular-season games as toners. Smythe's teams were also scrappy, reflecting his often-quoted motto, "If you can't beat 'em in the alley, you can't beat 'em on the ice." And despite the stock market crash of 1929 and the skepticism of investors, his vision extended to the possibility of a new arena, Maple

Leaf Gardens, on which work was begun in June of 1931.

The climb was bumpy at first: after beating the Red Wings in the 1928-29 playoffs, the Leafs fell to the Rangers. In 1929-30, they finished fourth. Big right wing Charlie Conacher had joined the club as a rookie, scoring 20 goals and 9 assists for the start of a Hall-of-Fame career.

Things really began to turn around in 1930-31, the Leafs' last season in the old arena. Maple Leaf Gardens was being successfully built, to the surprise of many, by union workers who accepted shares of stock as partial payment in lieu of wages. Smythe's next step was to acquire a star.

The one he had in mind was Francis Michael "King" Clancy, a stocky, 5'9" rushing defenseman who had weathered nine seasons in Ottawa. The price was two players plus a stratospheric $35,000. Smythe had the players, in Art Smith and Eric Pettinger, but how to find the $35,000? In typically Smytheian fashion, he scrounged some cash from friends and bet it on a horse named Rare Jewel that he owned. Rare Jewel won the race, allowing Smythe to buy King Clancy.

Clancy gave the Leafs 14 assists in his 1930-31 season and became the off-rink nucleus for a solid lineup of rough-hewn practical jokers that has often been compared to baseball's "Gas House Gang," the St. Louis Cardinals of the same era. The team's scoring nucleus was the famed "Kid Line" of Conacher, Harvey "Busher" Jackson at left wing, and little Joe Primeau, a future Leafs head

Hockey Hall of Fame and Museum

King Clancy

coach, at center. The trio, known for speed and for the trick plays they invented during practices, inspired passionate devotion among fans. Conacher's 43 points were third in the NHL in 1930-31, while Ace Bailey's 42 and Primeau's 41 were fifth and sixth. This flashy roster produced a second-place divisional finish, but the Leafs were defeated in the playoffs by the Chicago Black Hawks.

Maple Leaf Gardens

Spiffy, well-kept Maple Leaf Gardens made its debut on November 12, 1931, before a crowd of 13,542 largely middle-class Torontonians. Unfortunately, the Leafs lost their inaugural game to the Black Hawks, 3-1, and after one month were in last place in their division. Smythe kicked out his recently hired head coach, Art Duncan, and put in the classy Dick Irvin, who had been fired by Chicago.

The Maple Leafs were soon moving upward. By season's end they were in second place, as Busher Jackson led the league in scoring (28 goals, 25 assists), with setup man Primeau second (13 and 37), and Conacher tied for fourth (34 and 14). Primeau won the Lady Byng trophy and Jackson was named All-Star left wing.

The playoff series against Chicago was an occasion of personal vindication for Dick Irvin. The Leafs were shut out in game one, but their 6-1 victory in game two gave them the edge in the total-goals series. The semifinals against the Montreal Maroons (who featured Charlie Conacher's brother, Lionel "Big Train") were tied at three goals apiece at the end of regulation in the second game. Which Leafs would show up—the solid scorers or the shaky defenders? It was the former, as rookie wing Rob Gracie scored the winning goal after predicting to the coach he would do so if put into the game.

The finals were against the Rangers. Game one was a 6-4 war of attrition against both teams' goalies, with Jackson scoring a second-period hat trick. Game two was played in Boston Garden, of

Hockey Hall of Fame and Museum

Charlie Conacher

all places, as Madison Square Garden had been rented to the circus.

The Rangers took a 2-0 lead, but the Maple Leafs' three Cs—Conacher, Clancy, and Cotton—scored six goals against Ranger goalie Johnny Roach, who had broken training the previous night. (It must have been the New York atmosphere, for when Roach was traded to Detroit the following season, he became an All-Star.)

"It was like tossing a puck into an open net," Clancy said. In game three of the sweep, a third straight six-goal score prompted the press to call it "the tennis series." Later, Smythe praised his players' uprightness in not dragging out the series for monetary reasons.

Flash and Frustration in the 1930s

It looked like dynasty time for the Leafs, but as things turned out, the 1930s were a decade of

frustration as they lost the Stanley Cup finals again and again—six times between 1932-33 and 1939-40. They finished first in the regular season in 1932-33, with Jackson's 44 points coming in second in the league, and faced the Boston Bruins for the first-place playoff series. It was grueling. Four of the five games went into overtime, including six overtimes in the decisive game.

In that epic game five, played before 14,000 incredulous Toronto fans, the score was 0-0 after four overtimes when league president Frank Calder suggested a coin toss to decide the outcome. The Bruins agreed, as did Conn Smythe. But in the Maple Leafs' dressing room, Baldy Cotton led the players in protest. The fans, too, having come so far, raised a ruckus against the coin-flip idea, and it was nixed.

Early in the fifth period, Cotton slapped a shot which he claimed went into the net, but after much arguing the goal judge refused to allow the score. It was almost two in the morning when 5'7", 133-pound forward Ken Doraty skated around an exhausted defenseman and took a point-blank shot at goal to win it.

The finals, in New York, were only 18 hours away. The exhausted Leafs could muster only one goal, by Levinsky, in game one and another goal, by Doraty, in game two. Doraty continued his heroics with two goals in game three, which the Leafs won 3-2 on a goal by their aggressive defenseman Reginald "Red" Horner. Game four was another scoreless overtimer, but at 7:34, with Toronto shorthanded by two men to New York's one, Ranger Bill Cook's goal gave the Leafs a summer-long rest.

The Maple Leafs of 1933-34 came out ahead of the pack in the Canadian Division, with Conacher (52 points) and Primeau (46) first and second in the league in scoring and Jackson (38) seventh. Conacher, Primeau, and King Clancy were named All-Stars. The team finished 11 points ahead of the second-place Canadiens, but lost their playoff series to the Red Wings.

The most memorable event of the season, however, was a tragic one: the game in which Ace Bailey's career was ended by the Bruins' Eddie

Hockey Hall of Fame and Museum

Ace Bailey

Shore. It happened in Toronto in December. Toronto was two men short, and Bailey, an expert stickhandler, was killing the penalty successfully. After Bailey sent the puck into the Boston end, Shore came back with it and was clobbered by Clancy.

Getting up, Shore skated for the tired Bailey and gratuitously flipped him from behind with a shoulder. Bailey hit the ice and lost consciousness. Red Horner took revenge by flooring Shore with a punch. It might have been just another hockey brawl except that Bailey was seriously injured and taken to a hospital, where he lay near death for days. He recovered but was never able to play hockey again. In February, the Leafs held a benefit day for Bailey at which he and Shore were reconciled at center ice in front of a hushed then approvingly roaring crowd.

Conacher won a second straight scoring title

in 1934-35, and the Kid Line again led the team to a first-place finish. Goalie Lorne Chabot had gone to Chicago—where he would win the Vezina Trophy—but Toronto replaced him with the legendary George Hainsworth, longtime goalie of the rival Canadiens.

The team led the Canadian Division by 11 points over the Montreal Maroons, who would defeat them in the Stanley Cup finals. In the playoffs against the Bruins, the Leafs lost the first game but went on win to three straight by scores of 2-0, 3-0, and 2-1. The Leafs went on to the first all-Canada finals since 1926, and were favored over the Maroons. But veteran goalie Alex Connell held off the Toronto scorers, gaining upsets of 3-2 and 3-1 in the first two games. Game three was tied 1-1 at the halfway point when Montreal scored two goals in 12 seconds and coasted to a 4-1 victory for the last Stanley Cup in their team's history.

The following year was a turnabout, as the Maroons topped the Maple Leafs for first place in the regular season but the Maple Leafs went to the Stanley Cup finals. Conacher was down to fourth in league scoring, tied with teammate Bill Thoms, a center, at 23 goals and 15 assists apiece. The Leafs beat the Bruins in the opening round of the playoffs.

In the semifinals against the lowly New York Americans, the Leafs won game one, but the Amerks threatened an upset, winning game two, 1-0, and tying game three at 1-1 in the third period; but Thoms and Clancy came through with goals for Toronto in the clutch, and the Leafs faced the Red Wings for the championship.

These Leafs were in the autumn of their careers, and members of the Kid Line were fully blossomed veterans. Game one was a 3-1 Red Wing victory, as Clancy and Day looked tired. Game two saw the Red Wings overwhelm the Toronto defense, 9-4, for a Cup one-game total goals record that was to stand until 1973. The Leafs seemed about to be swept as the Red Wings took a 3-0 lead in game three, but in the latter half of the third period they rallied for a goal by Primeau and two by 5'6" forward Regis "Pep" Kelly. Frank "Buzz" Boll scored the winning

The Maple Leafs of the 1930s, though short on Stanley Cups, were long on skill, style, and entertainment value. Key members were:

• **Francis "King" Clancy:** Born February 25, 1903 in Ottawa, Clancy was a 5'9" defenseman who played for the Ottawa Senators during the 1920s before being purchased by Conn Smythe. He was the court jester of the Gas House Gang, sometimes called "150 pounds of muscle and conversation," and was known for his rushing ability and likeable personality. Clancy was often the butt of practical jokes by Charlie Conacher and Hap Day, who once locked him out seminude on a freezing hotel balcony after Clancy boasted about having a "wonderful" physique. When Eddie Shore dropped his gloves to punch Clancy during a game, the smaller but quick-thinking Clancy grabbed Shore's hand and shook it, saying, "Why, hello, Eddie. How are you tonight?" Clancy retired as a player in 1937, but continued his antics as a referee; once, after challenged a heckling fan to a fight, he learned the heckler was heavyweight champ Jack Sharkey. Clancy coached the Maple Leafs from 1950-53, and then became vice-president and a chief Harold Ballard crony. He was elected to the Hall of Fame in 1958.

• **Clarence "Hap" Day:** Born June 14, 1901 in Owen Sound, Ontario, Day studied pharmacy at the University of Ontario, and then joined the St. Pats in 1924. A 5'11", 175-pound left wing, Day played for Toronto until 1937, then for the New York Americans for one year. A nondrinker, nonsmoker, and fierce competitor, Day was adept at holding without getting caught. He captained the Leafs from 1927 to 1937. Day served two seasons as referee, and then coached the Leafs throughout the 1940s, winning five Stanley Cups (including three consecutively). He was highly respected by his players, who went through grueling practices for him. Day honed and toughened the Leafs' defense, particularly their penalty-killing. He became general manager in 1950, retiring in 1957, and was elected to Hall of Fame in 1961.

• **Charlie Conacher:** Born December 10, 1909, in Toronto, Conacher was the younger brother of Ottawa Senators star Lionel Conacher. A 6'1", 195-pound right wing on the Kid Line, he played nine years for the Leafs, one for the Red Wings, two for the New York Americans, and retired in 1941 with a total 225 goals and 173 assists. A premier practical joker on the Leafs, Conacher was known for his friendly antagonism of Baldy Cotton (whom he once hung feet-first from a New York hotel window). He served as the Leafs' captain in 1937-38 and coached the Black Hawks from 1947-50. He then retired into business before succumbing to cancer in 1967. Conacher was elected to Hall of Fame in 1961.

• **Ralph Harvey "Busher" Jackson:** Born in Toronto on January 19, 1911, Jackson was a 5'11" left wing on the Kid Line who won the scoring title in 1932-33 and was a four-time first-team All-Star. He spent ten years with the Leafs, two with the Americans, and three with the Bruins, retiring in 1944 with 241 goals and 234 assists. Jackson was elected to the Hall of Fame in 1961.

• **A. Joseph "Joe" Primeau:** Born January 29, 1906, in Lindsay, Ontario, the 5'11", 155-pound Primeau did not learn to skate until he was 12. He was an expert stickhandler, playmaker, and penalty-killer, playing nine NHL seasons with the Leafs and centering the famous Kid Line. Primeau coached Leafs from 1950-53, won the Stanley Cup in 1951, and was elected to Hall of Fame in 1963.

• **George Reginald "Red" Horner:** Born May 29, 1909, in Lynden, Ontario, six-foot, 190-pound defenseman Horner was known for rough play. He amassed 1,264 penalty minutes in 12 seasons as a Leaf and led the league in penalties for eight consecutive seasons, 1933-40. He held the record for penalty minutes in a season with 167 PIM in 1935-36 (a 48-game season). Horner retired in 1940, enjoying business and farm interests and a home in Portugal. He was elected to Hall of Fame in 1965.

• **Irvine Wallace "Ace" Bailey:** Born July 3, 1903 in Bracebridge, Ontario, the 5'10", 160-pound right wing joined the Leafs in 1926. Bailey retired prematurely after skull was fractured by Eddie Shore in a famous near-fatal incident. He led the league in goals in 1928-29 and was known for effective penalty-killing. His jersey, number 6, is one of the only two retired by the Leafs. Bailey worked in the insurance business after retirement and was elected to Hall of Fame in 1975.

TORONTO MAPLE LEAFS

Joe Primeau

Toronto goal at :31 of overtime. Game four seemed destined to be a comeback for the Kid Line, as Primeau scored in the first period.

It proved to be the last goal of his career, however, and the next three goals were by the Red Wings. The only other Maple Leaf score was a meaningless tally by Bill Thoms late in the game. The Cup had again gone south of the border.

And the Leafs were changing. The Kid Line had broken up. Bush Jackson was the offensive leader in 1936-37, scoring 40 points and becoming an All-Star. A more future-oriented bright spot was rookie Sylvanus "Syl" Apps. Conn Smythe first became aware of Apps's athletic talent when watching him play halfback for the McMaster University football team. Apps also competed in the Olympics as a pole vaulter and was initially hesitant to turn professional as a hockey player.

Nonetheless Apps scored 16 goals and 29 assists in his rookie year—second best in the NHL—winning the first Calder Trophy (for rookie of the year) ever given. He would go on to become captain of the team during the Golden Forties. An equally good omen for the future was the arrival of rookie goalie Walter "Turk" Broda, a native of Brandon, Manitoba.

Smythe discovered Broda during a minor-league game between the Detroit Bulldogs and the Detroit Olympics; Smythe was scouting the Bulldogs' goalie, but was more impressed with Broda, in the net for the Olympics. Broda started the season so well for the Leafs that Smythe dealt Hainsworth to the Canadiens. Rookie unevenness plagued the team throughout 1936-37, though, as the Maple Leafs came in third in the four-team division and were beaten in the playoffs by the Rangers.

Out Go the Old Kids, In Come the New

The 1937-38 Leafs were nothing if not young. Conacher retired because of nagging injuries, Cotton retired as well, and Hap Day was sold to the Americans. The oldest veteran on the team was now 28-year-old Red Horner. The average age was 23. Youthful enthusiasm did the trick, as the Leafs finished first in their division, with All-Star Gordie Drillon leading the league in scoring (52 points) Apps second (50), and Thoms sixth (38).

Drillon also won the Lady Byng Trophy. In the semifinals, Toronto swept the American Division-leading Bruins on the strength of Broda's goalkeeping, as the Bruins scored a total of three goals in three games. The finals were against the Black Hawks, who had barely made it into the playoffs and, to top it off, were using a minor-league goalie because of a toe injury to their starter. The inspired Hawks won the first game 3-1. For the second game, the substitute goalie was ruled ineligible and the Hawks used another minor leaguer, bringing him out of a movie theater two hours before game time. This time the glamour

Hockey Hall of Fame and Museum

Gordie Drillon

17 players were fined $25 apiece for prolonging the fracas. In the finals against the New York Rangers, Broda's goalkeeping kept the Leafs close (except for game two, in which he was shelled 6-2). Three of the games went into overtime—but New York won all three, and took the Stanley Cup.

The NHL was decimated by World War II military service the following season, and many of the Maple Leafs joined the Toronto Scottish Reserve on the advice of Conn Smythe. When on the ice, however, the Leafs were in fine form, with Stanowski, Schriner, and Broda on the first All-Star team and Apps on the second. New coach Hap Day guided the club to a second-place finish and Broda became the first Vezina Trophy winner in Leafs history. In the playoffs against first-place Boston, the Leafs took a 2-1 lead after three games, but Boston won the next game and the series eventually went to the full seven, with Boston prevailing by a single goal.

The Great Comeback

1941-42 was a great comeback season. The Leafs had acquired right winger Lorne Carr, who joined Taylor and Schriner to form a solid scoring line. Injuries hampered the team throughout the season, but they finished second to the Rangers. Fortunately, the Leafs had regained their health for the semifinals against the New Yorkers. The Leafs came from behind in each of the first two games in Madison Square Garden, then lost game three at home. Before game four, Conn Smythe gave the Leafs an inspiring pep talk, and they went out to a 2-1 defensive triumph in which defenseman Wilfred "Bucko" McDonald blocked so many shots he functioned virtually as a second goalie. The semifinals extended to six games, with Toronto winning at 19:54 of the final period on a surprising goal by low-scoring Nick Metz, who was usually a setup man.

That year's finals against the Red Wings provided perhaps the most memorable comeback in hockey history. The fast-skating, hard-checking, underdog Wings won the first three games, and no

faded, as the Leafs triumphed, 5-1. In game three, Chicago's regular goalie was back, and the Black Hawks won 3-1. Game four completed a devastating upset as the Black Hawks clinched the Cup in front of 17,000 cheering Chicago fans. Unsettled, Smythe continued to trade for young players in the coming years, adding such names as Wally Stanowski, Pete Langelle, Sweeney Schriner, and Billy Taylor to the roster.

The Leafs finished third in 1938-39, with Apps and Drillon named All-Stars. They coasted past the fourth-place Americans in the playoff opener, then won the three-game semifinals against the Red Wings. But then came the mighty Bruins, who, after splitting the first two games, won the next three straight for the Stanley Cup.

The 1939-40 season was another frustrating one. The Leafs finished third and knocked off the fourth-place Black Hawks in the playoff opener. The semifinal round against Detroit was marred by a fight in the final game that lasted 12 minutes;

team in Stanley Cup history had ever returned from a three-game deficit. Before game four, Broda told the press, "Detroit is unbeatable." But teammate Billy Taylor joked, "Don't worry about us, we'll beat them four straight"—and that's exactly what the Leafs did. Hap Day pulled every trick in the coaching book: he benched regulars McDonald and Drillon, played subs Gaye Stewart, Don Metz and Ernie Dickens, and tacked to the locker-room wall a letter from a 14-year-old girl who wrote that she was praying for a Leafs victory. (Benching Drillon was a crushing blow to that star's Toronto career. He was traded to Montreal the following season.)

The crowd at Olympia Stadium expected a Red Wings sweep to emerge from game four, and well into the third period they seemed to be getting their wish. But Apps scored at 6:15, and at 12:45 Don Metz passed to his brother, Nick, for the winning goal. Detroit fans could not have been very worried at that point, but slight frustration turned to disbelief as the Leafs took game five, 9-3, in Toronto, and game six was a triumphant 3-0 shutout for Broda. The 16,200-odd fans in Maple Leaf Gardens for game seven formed the largest crowd in Canada's hockey history to that point. The first period was scoreless, but Syd Howe gave the Red Wings a lead early in the second. The Wings protected the puck until 7:46 of the third period, when Schriner fired in a shot from in front of the goal to tie it. Langelle scored two minutes later, and Schriner capped it with the third Toronto

Hockey Hall of Fame and Museum

Turk Broda

PROFILE	The Founder: Conn Smythe

It is hard to believe that the Maple Leafs existed—although under another name—before Conn Smythe took over. His purchase of the team in 1927 marked a new era that began with revamping the roster and constructing Maple Leaf Gardens. For decades, Smythe was the unofficial leader among NHL owners, continually pressing for innovations that would make the game more popular, and he was a familiar, authoritative voice to millions of radio listeners and television viewers in Canada.

Constantine Falkland Cary Smythe was born February 1, 1895, in a working-class Toronto neighborhood, the son of a journalist of Irish heritage and Theosophical religious views. Smythe's mother died when the boy was seven years old, and at the boarding schools in which his father enrolled him, he was the butt of bullies, a mediocre scholar—and a sports fanatic. Young Conn learned to love sports by accompanying his reporter father to the racetrack. Growing to only 5'7" and 120 pounds, he nevertheless played center for the University of Toronto. In 1914 he joined the Canadian artillery, winning the Military Cross, and later became a reconnaissance pilot. Shot down behind enemy lines, he was a prisoner of war for 14 months, and twice attempted to escape, but was recaptured both times. Back home after the war, he tried civil engineering, and though he failed at that profession, he learned enough of its background to establish a lucrative sand and gravel business.

Simultaneously, he was staying in touch with hockey, coaching the University of Toronto team that won a 1928 Olympic gold medal. His growing reputation among sportsmen caused his selection by John Hammond, the New York Rangers' owner, to put that team together—which he did, only to be fired ungratefully. Smythe took his severance pay and parlayed it, with gambling winnings, to buy the Toronto St. Pats. Smythe's history and the team's were synonymous during the late 1920s and 1930s. Building the team around "strength down the center," and carefully balancing enthusiastic young players with wily veterans, he was invaluable in making the Leafs a major power. By enlisting retired players into front-office jobs, he created a pool of gifted coaches, managers, and scouts, and by tending his minor-league teams like a well-stocked nursery, he ensured a continuing supply of playing talent.

For a second time, however, a world war intruded into more enjoyable pursuits, and for the second time the Little Major answered the call. In 1942, at the age of 47, he formed the 30th Light Anti-Aircraft Battery, nicknamed the Sportsmen's Battery because its members came largely from the athletic world. Known for its high morale, the battery spent more than a year and a half in England waiting for orders to attack. When the D-Day order finally came in June, 1944, Smythe was suffering from four broken ribs incurred the previous day in a softball game. He had his ribs taped, and telling his men, "Anyone who mentions this can expect a court martial," took part in the Normandy landing. A month later, near Caen, he was seriously injured by a shell fragment to the spine, requiring long hospitalization. From his hospital bed he initiated a media attack on Canada's military, which eventually led to the resignation of the Defence Minister.

A nondrinker, nonsmoker, and arch-conservative, Smythe sent out feelers for a political career after the war but did not succeed in persuading the Conservative Party to let him run. Returning to hockey, he guided the Maple Leafs to their great 1940s and 1950s successes despite being somewhat slowed down by his war wound. As age set in, he began taking six-week vacations in Florida every year and giving first priority to his racing stable. His power over the team ended in 1961 when he sold majority control to the Stafford Smythe-Harold Ballard-John Basset consortium, though Conn Smythe remained chairman of the board. In March 1966, he resigned that position over a matter of political principle, objecting to the fact that heavyweight champion Muhammad Ali, then a Vietnam War protester, had been allowed to fight at Maple Leaf Gardens. Smyth was elected to the Hall of Fame in 1958. A Trophy was named after him in 1964, and an entire division of the NHL in 1974. He died November 18, 1980, on his Ontario farm.

goal of the period. Toronto's first Stanley Cup since 1932 had been won miraculously.

Military duty sapped the team during the 1942-43 season, and the Leafs sank to third place. Gaye Stewart won the Calder Trophy, however, and Lorne Carr gained an All-Star berth. The Leafs lost the semifinals to the Red Wings. Carr repeated on the All-Star team in 1943-44, joined by team-mate Babe Pratt, a 6'3" defenseman who had recently arrived from the Rangers and who won the Hart Trophy, with 17 goals and 40 assists.

Rookie center Ausut "Gus" Bodnar won the Calder Trophy, scoring 22 goals and 40 assists, and set a record for fastest goal by a rookie, 15 seconds into his first NHL game. The Leafs finished third in the regular season and were polished off by the first-place Canadiens in the opening round of the playoffs.

The 1944-45 season seemed destined to belong to the Montreal Canadiens, who finished in first place by 13 points over Detroit and 28 points over third-place Toronto. But surprises were in store. Toronto had 26-year-old rookie goalie Frank McCool—a pale, thin man who had been discharged from the army with ulcers and was considered too nervous to succeed in the NHL. McCool overcame such predictions to win the Calder Trophy.

The Leafs also had Ted "Teeder" Kennedy, a center from Humberstone, Ontario, who at the age of 19 became the team's emotional leader. His 29 goals led the Leafs, and he added 25 assists. The team finished third for the third consecutive season. The semifinals against Montreal were as tense and exciting as a finals series.

Game one was a goalies' duel between Mc-Cool and Bill Durnan, as Kennedy scored the game's only goal in its final minute. Kennedy scored again in game two, a 3-2 Toronto win in which Montreal suffered key injuries to Elmer Lach and Buddy O'Connor. Game three seemed to turn things around for the Canadiens, as they coasted to a 4-1 win and the Leafs lost Nick Metz to an injury.

Game four began well for the Canadiens—a 2-0 lead after two minutes—but Toronto tied the score at 2-2, and later at 3-3. McCool's saves in the third period led to an overtime, with Toronto prevailing 4-3 on an incredibly swift faceoff goal by Bodnar. Game five was a 10-3 Montreal rout, but game six was a hard-fought 3-2 Leafs win, in which the Canadiens missed an easy chance to tie in the last half-minute, as Toe Blake's shot at an open goal went over the net.

That put the Leafs in the finals against the Red Wings, who looked vastly superior on paper. But McCool, consuming a quart of milk before each contest, shut out the Wings 1-0, 2-0, and 1-0 in the first three games, tying Clint Benedict's Stanley Cup record for consecutive shutouts.

Then the Red Wings won the next three games—games five and six on shutouts—and it looked like a reversal of the 1942 comeback. But Mel "Sudden Death" Hill scored early in game seven on a pass from Kennedy, and there was no scoring in the second period. After the Red Wings had tied the score midway through the third period, Babe Pratt slipped the puck past the Detroit goalie, getting the rebound from a saved Nick Metz shot. The Leafs retained their lead for the next eight minutes and took the Stanley Cup.

Postwar Glory

The Leafs finished fifth, out of the playoffs, in 1945-46, despite All-Star play by Stewart. They bounced back with a vengeance in 1946-47, though, as Smythe's personnel changes assembled a new dynasty. The 19-man squad now had six rookies, along with veterans Broda, Stewart, and Bodnar, captain Apps, and young veteran Kennedy.

Young defensemen Jimmy Thomson and Gus Mortson, the "Gold Dust Twins," served effectively, as did Garth Boesch. Apps's line, with Harry Watson on left wing and hard-checking "Wild Bill" Ezinicki on the right, and Kennedy's line, with former defenseman Vic Lynn at left wing and heroic grenade-blast survivor Howie Meeker at right, helped make Toronto a power again.

The team brawled its way into contention: "They are the worst team in the league for holding, tripping, and interfering," said Rangers' manager Frank Boucher. The Leafs finished second to the Canadiens in the regular season. They defeated the Red Wings in a five-game semifinals, then faced the Canadiens in the finals for the first time ever. Game one, a 6-0 Montreal shutout, was not geared to improve Leaf fans' morale or Turk Broda's self-esteem. But in game two, Ezinicki shadowed and pester "Rocket" Richard, who was ejected for slashing open Wild Bill's head with his stick. The Leafs won 4-0.

Game three was a 4-2 Leafs win, and in game four Syl Apps broke a 1-1 tie at 16:36 of the third period by going behind the Montreal net, chang-

ing direction, and scoring. The Habs won game five, but the Leafs came back in game six, outshooting their rivals for a 2-1 victory. The Canadian press acclaimed them as the youngest Stanley Cup team in history. Montreal coach Dick Irvin refused to offer the traditional handshake after it was over.

The Maple Leafs repeated as Stanley Cup champions in 1947-48. Between seasons, Conn Smythe traded away five good players—an entire forward line and two defensemen—for one star, the Black Hawks' Max Bentley, a strong-wristed former Saskatchewan farm boy. It was a gamble. Many predicted that Bentley would not function well outside his beloved Chicago, away from his linemate and brother, Doug. Max Bentley was a

Hockey Hall of Fame and Museum

Ted Kennedy (in white)

hypochondriac to boot, but a month into the season, when his wife and children arrived in Toronto, his anxieties diminished and he immediately scored a hat trick.

A rookie teammate, Bill Barilko, also contributed mightily as the Leafs finished in first place after a tight race with Detroit. Broda won his second Vezina Trophy after a nip-and-tuck battle with Detroit's Harry Lumley. The Leafs beat the third-place Bruins in a five-game playoff, then swept the Red Wings for the championship.

The odds for a third consecutive Cup didn't look good, as the Leafs fell to fourth place in 1948-49. Detroit's Production Line of Sid Abel, Gordie Howe, and Ted Lindsay was dominating the league.

No Maple Leafs were named All-Stars or won important trophies. But the playoffs made the Leafs hungry for a three-peat. In the semifinals against second-place Boston, they went ahead by two games, then lost game three in overtime.

In game four, Hap Day called on Sid Smith, a bald minor-league forward who would eventually become the team comedian and captain. Smith proceeded to score two goals in a 3-1 victory. A Max Bentley goal in game five for a 3-2 victory put the club into the finals again.

The Maple Leafs were 3-7-2 for the year against the Red Wings, their opponents in the Stanley Cup championship series. The Maple Leafs won game one 3-2 on an overtime back-hander by Joe Klukay. Game two was Sid Smith

Max Bentley (center)

3, Red Wings 1, prompting Gordie Howe to ask afterwards, "Who's Sid Smith?" Game three had the same final score, on three Toronto goals in the second period, and game four completed the surprise sweep, 3-1. The 1949 Maple Leafs were the lowest-placed team in history to win the Stanley Cup.

Syl Apps retired after that season. The Leafs faltered to third place in the 1949-50 regular season, and in the playoffs they faced Detroit. The Leafs had defeated the Red Wings in 11 straight playoff games. In the opening game of the series, Gordie Howe suffered a nearly fatal injury when he fell face-first into the boards after Ted Kennedy sidestepped his check.

The Maple Leafs beat the stunned Red Wings 5-0 in that game. In game two, the Red Wings attacked Kennedy, whom they mistakenly believed to have caused Howe's injuries, and weakened him for the rest of the series. The Wings won the series in seven games, the decisive game going into overtime.

Hap Day was promoted to assistant general manager for 1950-51, and new coach Joe Primeau produced a 95-point team, taking second place to the awesome Red Wings.

The deep Leafs now had Al Rollins alternating with Broda in the net, with young center Tod Sloan increasing his offensive contribution and Fern Flaman hitting hard on defense. Bentley, Kennedy, Sloan, Smith, and Cal "Finger" Gardner were all among the league's scoring leaders, and Rollins won the Vezina with a 1.75 goals-against average in 40 games.

Gus Mortson led the league in penalty minutes and was a second-team All-Star, while Barilko kept improving his game. In the semifinals, the Leafs beat Boston in six games.

The finals against Montreal are still remembered as the series in which all five games went into overtime. They are also remembered as Bill Barilko's Stanley Cup, although Barilko only scored one goal, and no assists, in the series. Two and a half minutes into the overtime of game five, with the score 2-2, Barilko took a pass from Howie Meeker, who was behind the Montreal net, and

Hockey Hall of Fame and Museum

Hap Day

made a slapshot over the shoulder of Montreal netminder Gerry McNeil, falling on the follow-through so that he almost missed seeing his own winning goal.

Slapshots were new and controversial at the time and this goal helped put them into the standard NHL repertoire. But it was the last goal of Bill Barilko's career. In the summer of 1951, Barilko was flying over northern Ontario on a hunting trip when his small plane crashed. Bizarrely, his body was not found until May 1962—a month after the Maple Leafs won their next Stanley Cup.

After the Crash

Barilko's death traumatized the team and contributed to its decline. For seven years—until 1958, when Punch Imlach became general manager—the Leafs never finished above third place.

Busher Jackson

During those seven years, they either finished out of the playoffs or were quickly eliminated.

Why the decline? Sports historian Jack Batten offers the following reasons: pitiful offense; the failure of the Maple Leafs' farm system to continue supplying first-rate young talent; ill-advised personnel moves, caused by Smythe's anger against the fledgling Players Association and resulting in players panicking over their jobs; and rapid-fire changes in the head coach position.

Joe Primeau lasted through 1952-53, then retired to his concrete block business. King Clancy, after a stint as a referee, spent three years as Leafs head coach and was then kicked upstairs. Howie Meeker was in for a year, then out, and Billy Reay, in his one full year as Leafs' head coach, steered them into last place.

During those years, Smith's and Sloan's names occasionally appeared among the league's top ten scorers, and Lumley was All-Star goalie in 1953-54 and 1954-55—scant glory compared

to the team's past record. Teeder Kennedy continued to play solidly and won the Hart Trophy in 1954-55. And in 1956-57 a rookie named Frank Mahovlich joined the team, winning the Calder Trophy in 1957-58.

Something more was needed, however, and that was leadership. Conn Smythe had been paying more attention to his race horses than to his hockey team of late.

Toward the end of the 1956-57 hockey season, Smythe traveled from Florida to New York to call a press conference in which he declared that the Leafs' operation was out of date and obliquely asked for Hap Day's resignation. Day, who had not been privately informed before this, said, "My legs have been cut out from under me." A few months later, after Day had sold his interest in Smythe's gravel company and bought a factory that made tool handles, Smythe phoned Day and asked him to return. "There's no chance of that happening," Day said.

The Imlach Era

Day's successor was Stafford Smythe, Conn Smythe's son, an abrasive, cocky young man who had grown up in his father's shadow but had capably led the Leafs' minor-league system. Officially, Stafford was part of a committee, nicknamed the Silver Seven, that led hockey operations, but in fact he was the team's ruler. His first major decision was a brilliant one: he hired an obscure 40-year-old minor-league coach named George "Punch" Imlach.

Physically unprepossessing but mentally tough—too harsh, in fact, for some of his players—Imlach revived the team over several months during 1958-59 and became one of the most colorful, controversial figures in Toronto sports history. First as assistant general manager, then general manager and coach, he made crucial moves that included the acquisition of defenseman Allan Stanley from New York and goalie Johnny Bower from the Cleveland minor-league team.

Bower, a mild-mannered, hard-working 33-

year-old who had spent 15 years in the minors, was such an unlikely choice as an NHL goalie and had suffered so much frustration during his bumpy career, that he himself resisted the promotion at first; but he changed his mind and became one of the great major-league goalies of the era, with a 2.74 goals-against average in his first season in Toronto and a 2.52 lifetime average. He retired in 1970 at the age of 45.

The 1958-59 season was an uphill climb for fourth place, and the Leafs magically clinched that last playoff spot on the last day of the season, when the rival Rangers lost and the Leafs overcame a 2-0 deficit against the Red Wings to win 6-2. The Leafs made it all the way to the finals, beating the Bruins in a seven-game semifinals.

Against the Canadiens in the finals, the Leafs had the advantage of not having to face Jean Beliveau and Rocket Richard, who were injured. The Canadiens won the first two games anyway, and after the Leafs took game three on an overtime goal by clutch left winger Dick Duff, went on to win a 3-2 squeaker and a 5-3 coaster. But the Leafs had surprised the hockey world by getting that far.

The 1959-60 season, the last of Montreal's five-Stanley-Cup dynasty, marked a further ascent for the Leafs. Imlach had acquired 11-year veteran Red Kelly from the Red Wings to center his first line. With the Wings, Kelly had played defense, winning the Norris Trophy once, the Lady Byng three times, and showing scoring prowess as well.

Though he seemed past his prime to some, he easily made the conversion to center and stayed on the Toronto team for eight years. Explaining his reasoning in his book *Hockey is a Battle*, Imlach wrote, "My big aim at the time was to build a team for one function: to beat the Canadiens. To do that we had to be more powerful at center.... I knew how well [Red] skated, checked, made plays, and so on.... He was one guy I could put out against Jean Beliveau and make Beliveau work for any goals he got." The reasoning worked well enough to propel Toronto to second place and, once again, the finals against Montreal. Montreal swept the series, 4-2, 2-1, 5-2, 4-0.

Hockey Hall of Fame and Museum

Dave Keon

The 1960-61 team was of championship caliber according to Imlach and other observers, but it did not reach the finals. Bower won the Vezina Trophy and an All-Star spot, and the hugely talented Mahovlich had a great year with 48 goals and 36 assists, overcoming his usual inconsistency. Little center Dave Keon won the Calder Trophy as top rookie, and rookie right wing Bob Nevin had the first of four fine years for Toronto.

Rushing defenseman Carl Brewer continued his career as one of the Leafs' most solid assets. As late in the season as February 12, 1961, the Leafs were six points ahead of Montreal for first place. But that night, in a close, rough game against Detroit, rogue defenseman Howie Young slammed into Johnny Bower when Bower was out of the crease, putting him out of action for five weeks. That, and injuries to Eddie Shack and Bert Olmstead, crippled the team. They were nudged out of first place by Montreal by one point, and lost their semifinals to the Red Wings in an upset.

Dominating a Decade

The 1960s saw the Maple Leafs becoming a dominant hockey team. The franchise was restructured, as the 66-year-old Conn Smythe sold his shares to Stafford, Harold Ballard, and Toronto *Telegram* publisher John Bassett—a combination that would spell future trouble. On the ice, however, the 1961-62 team was in top form. With basically the same squad as the previous year, they aimed at the Stanley Cup rather than at beating Montreal for first place.

After a second-place finish, 13 points behind the Habs, the Leafs played a tight playoff series against the Rangers. The series was tied going into the fifth game, and that game went into overtime, with the Leafs winning on a freak goal by Red Kelly. It happened this way: Ranger goalie Gump Worsley had made a save by landing on the puck, flat on his back; not knowing exactly where the puck was, he leaned forward, expecting a whistle. The puck was under his neck and Kelly, spotting it, pushed it in. The sixth game was a 7-1 rout for the Leafs.

In the finals, the Leafs faced the fearsome Black Hawks of Bobby Hull and Stan Mikita. Bowers's goaltending helped the Leafs win the first two, 4-1 and 3-2, in front of home crowds. Back in Chicago, the Black Hawks took two games by scores of 3-0 and 4-1, with Don Simmons replacing the injured Bower in game four. The Leafs were down 3-2 in game five when they got five straight goals, winning the game 8-4.

Game six in Chicago was scoreless going into the third period, a goalies' classic between Simmons and Glenn Hall. When Bobby Hull scored

Hockey Hall of Fame and Museum

Frank Mahovlich (27)

at 8:58, the Chicago fans went wild, throwing so much garbage onto the ice that the game was delayed for ten minutes. It cooled the Black Hawks off and gave the Leafs incentive.

A minute and a half later, Bob Nevin scored the tying goal. Dick Duff scored the winner at 14:14. The victorious Leafs, after finishing the game before a silent Chicago crowd, returned to a welcome by 50,000 Torontonians in front of City Hall, as Eddie Shack stood on the seat of an open automobile and did the Twist.

The following season saw a fine addition to the roster in Kent Douglas, who became the first defenseman ever to win the Calder Trophy. Mahovlich and Brewer had All-Star seasons, with defenseman Tim Horton on the second team. Keon won his second straight Lady Byng, and the cast of veterans, sprinkled with some new players, caught fire toward season's end. The Leafs finished 1962-63 in first place, after a tight race in which the top four teams were bunched within five points of each other. The team was now viewed as a bunch of senior citizens, but they played hard and Punch Imlach got the most out of his aging goalies by platooning.

They took care of the Canadiens in a five-game semifinals, then confronted the Red Wings. In game one, Duff scored two goals in the first 68 seconds, and Nevin later scored two for a 4-2 victory. The leafs won game two by the same margin, a goal and two assists by slow-skating Black Hawk castoff Ed Litzenberger. The series shifted to Detroit, where the Wings took game three, but game four was another 4-2 Toronto triumph, after which the Detroit cognoscenti threw eggs at the departing victors.

Game five was tied 1-1 at 13:28 of the third period when the puck, ricocheting off a Detroit defender's skate, bounced against Shack's stick and went into the net without any conscious effort on his part. "I was just trying to get the hell out of the way," Shack said of his Stanley-Cup-winning fluke.

The same two teams met again in the 1963-64 Cup finals. Toronto had only finished in third place with a revamped—in mid-season—squad that included former Rangers Andy Bathgate and Don McKenney. (Duff, Nevin, Rod Seiling, and two minor leaguers went to New York in the deal.)

Adding to the strain, Red Kelly was now a member of Parliament—quite a double burden! Toronto's top two lines were now Bathgate-Kelly-Mahovlich and McKenney-Keon-George Armstrong. The two new Maple Leafs starred in the

---

PROFILE   ## The Voice from the Gondola

Foster Hewitt conducted the first radio broadcast of a hockey game, which took place in March of 1923 from the Mutual Street Arena. Hewitt announced Maple Leafs games for fifty years, becoming the most famous radio voice in Canada and adding his own personal expressions to the lexicon of the nation.

Growing up as the son of the sports editor of the Toronto *Star*, Hewitt got off to an early start in both hockey and journalism. A cub reporter for the *Star*, he switched to broadcasting when the newspaper started a radio station. Encouraged by Conn Symthe—who saw that broadcasting had a future—Hewitt broadcast Saturday games from Mutual Streets, and when Maple Leaf Gardens opened, his broadcasts became national.

The gondola is central to Hewitt's legend. It was a broadcast booth hanging 56 feet above the rink, reachable only by a catwalk that had no guard rail. Brave men such as Conn Smythe and Frank Selke, Sr., refused to cross that catwalk. Hewitt himself, on his first visit, crawled to his booth instead of walking. Once, according to biographer Scott Young, actor George Raft visited Hewitt. Warned that the trip across the catwalk might be a problem, the Hollywood tough guy laughed. Halfway across, however, Raft froze in fear. This happened after side cables had been added to make the pathway safer.

The term "gondola" entered the Canadian lexicon as a synonym for "broadcast booth." And Hewitt's trademarked shout, "He shoots! He scores!" was echoed by hockey-loving youngsters through the years, as the imitated their heroes on neighborhood rinks, frozen ponds, and playgrounds. The gondola was demolished in 1979, for Hal Ballard needed more private boxes for the arena. When Hewitt heard the news, he wept. Ballard, laughing, told Hewitt he could build a new gondola, adding, "I'll pay for the nails."

Hewitt prospered through his ownership of Toronto radio station CKFH (now CJCL) and other investments. His son Bill continued his broadcasting tradition for the Leafs. Foster Hewitt was elected to the Hall of Fame in 1965. The Foster Hewitt Memorial Award for oustanding broadcasters is named in honor of his contribution to hockey.

---

seven-game playoff victory against Montreal and then in the rematch against Detroit, combining for 9 postseason goals and 12 assists.

Game one of the finals was a 3-2 Toronto home victory on a shorthanded goal by Bob Pulford in the last two seconds. Game two, also in Toronto, went to the Red Wings in overtime. In game three, the Leafs surged back from a 3-0 road deficit to tie the game in the final two minutes, but the Wings came back on a goal by Alex Delvecchio. Game four went to the Leafs and game five to the Wings, both teams winning on the road.

Game six, in Detroit, was tied 3-3 late in the third period when a puck broke the ankle of Toronto defenseman Bob Baun. Baun was removed from the ice on a stretcher, but with true, old-time hockey spirit, he ordered the doctor to freeze the ankle, and returned to score the winning goal in overtime, his shot caroming off the stick of a Red Wing. Baun played game seven with a hairline fracture, and it was a 4-0 Maple Leafs shutout for a third straight Stanley Cup. It was a glorious moment, but cracks had already begun to

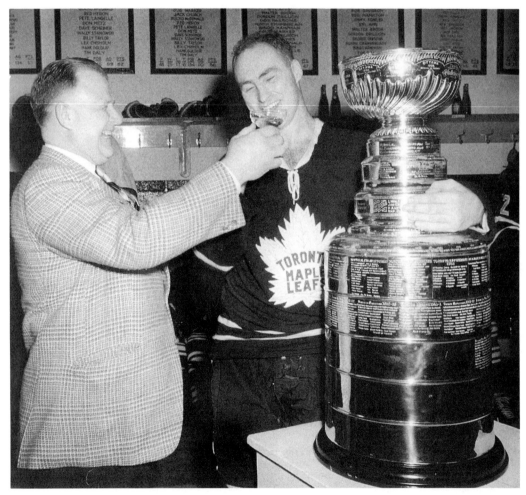

Hockey Hall of Fame and Museum

Leafs' owner Harold Ballard (left) with Red Kelly

Central Division

appear in the Maple Leaf dynasty. Imlach's excessively grueling practices had led to vocal protests by some players, especially Bathgate, who was soon traded to Detroit.

Imlach's intimidation techniques visibly hurt the play of Mahovlich, who began to be booed by fans, was put into the hospital twice for exhaustion, and was eventually traded. Contractual disagreements embittered Carl Brewer. The Leafs had none of the league's top scorers. They had, however, acquired great Red Wing goalie Terry Sawchuk, who split the season and the Vezina Trophy with Bower. After finishing fourth, they slugged it out with the Canadiens in the playoffs, and lost.

The following year was a reprise: a third-place finish and a penalty-filled playoff series against Montreal, who won in a sweep. Left wing Brit Selby won the Calder Trophy.

The team was steadily aging. Seven Maple Leafs were 36 years old or more in 1966-67. The hard-playing but sensitive Brewer had retired at the age of 27 after a patented Imlach curse out; and Eddie Shack had been sent to the minors. After a ten-game losing streak, Imlach was admitted to a hospital with ulcers and exhaustion, and his absence picked the team up, for replacement coach King Clancy eased up during practice.

Imlach returned for the postseason and led the team through a triumphant playoff series against Chicago in which an injured Sawchuk put on a marvelous goaltending exhibition in game five. The Leafs were underdogs to the Canadiens in the finals, and after Sawchuk gave up six goals in game one, he told the press, "I got one thing to say, gentlemen. I didn't have a good night."

Game two was a 3-0 Johnny Bower shutout despite Bower's nose having been broken by a Canadien's stick. In game three, Bower made 60 saves, 20 of them in the two overtime periods, and Toronto prevailed, 3-2. But the forty-something Bower pulled a muscle before game four, and Sawchuk had another not-good night, 6-2.

Wondrously, however, Sawchuk caught fire in game five, a 4-1 Leafs win. "Some nights you stop them, and some nights you don't," Sawchuk

Hockey Hall of Fame and Museum

Darryl Sittler

said philosophically. Game six was a goalies' duel between Sawchuk (46 saves) and Gump Worsley (36), and a 3-1 Maple Leafs win. It was the team's 13th Stanley Cup, and its last to date. Imlach, foreseeing the team's decline through expansion and other factors, said in the dressing room, "they're going out as champs."

The Skids

The Leafs finished out of the playoffs in 1967-68. From that year through 1991-92 their record was abysmal, never rising above third place in their division. Between 1969-70 and 1991-92, only one Maple Leaf was named a first-team All-Star: Swedish defenseman Borje Salming in 1975-76. After Salming in 1979-80, no Maple Leaf was even named a second-team All-Star.

During the 1980s the team's won-lost percentage was the poorest in hockey for a non-expansion team, and among the poorest in all major-league sports. In May of 1989, in a *Financial Post* analysis of 106 professional North American sports teams in the 1980s, the Leafs ranked 101st.

The Leafs' on-ice problems were clearly

linked to off-ice ones. Under the control of Harold Ballard, a hugely controversial figure whose public image was comparable to that of New York Yankees' owner George Steinbrenner, only Ballard was more uncouth and less successful (though he did share Steinbrenner's penchant for often berating and changing players and management.)

The Leafs organization became frazzled and the public's attention became focused on a long series of soap operas involving, among other things, Ballard's and Stafford Smythe's arrest for defrauding the Gardens, the swift deterioration and death of Stafford Smythe from the stress of an alcohol-related ulcer, Ballard's conviction and incarceration on 47 counts, and an accusation of assault against Ballard's son by Ballard's lover.

Even without these extracurricular activities, Ballard's interference in the running of the team often destroyed morale. He hired inept front-office personnel, publicly and privately berated players, antagonized some sportswriters while befriending others, once barred all reporters from the dressing room in an attempt to exclude women, and habitually issued racist, sexist, and homophobic quotes. He also showed a remarkable indifference to such emblems of Leafs tradition, including the gondola from which legendary and beloved announcer Foster Gewitt broadcast games; Ballard ordered it destroyed.

While quite adept at turning a profit by renting Maple Leaf Gardens to non-hockey attractions, Ballard was less skillful at the sport itself. He was deeply suspicious of modern coaching techniques, scoffing at the use of videos and refusing to spend significant amounts of money on hiring auxiliary staff such as strength coaches and physical therapists.

The Leafs' management consistently failed to draft good players and allowed good ones to escape to other teams, sometimes even forcing them away. Although the Leafs pioneered the NHL in scouting and drafting European players in the early 1970s, a drastic policy turnaround occurred, and the team drafted no Europeans between 1974 and 1988, although the quality of available European talent had increased.

A key mistake, characteristically made for short-term financial gain, was the Leafs' sale of two fine minor-league teams, the Victoria Cougars in 1967 and the Rochester Americans in 1968. It was sometimes said that the Rochester team of the 1960s could have competed in the NHL. The Leafs received virtually nothing for the Cougars and Americans, except a total $900,000. This, plus roster depletions in the 1967 expansion draft, meant that the Leafs had very little in the way of developing talent.

When the Leafs did acquire star-quality players, they tended to depart soon after. Goalie Bernie Parent fled to the WHA. Future Hall-of-Fame defenseman Lanny McDonald was drafted by the Leafs in 1973 but spent some of his finest years helping the Calgary Flames. The banishing of McDonald on December 28, 1979, is perhaps the most bizarre of the team's many bad trades: on the one hand it involved a long feud between Ballard and General Manager Imlach (rehired in a desperate attempt to revive the franchise) and, on the other, McDonald and his best friend, team captain Darryl Sittler.

A series of petty disputes led to animosity between Sittler and Imlach, then to public remarks on both sides. Since Sittler had a no-trade clause in his contract, Imlach did what he considered the next-best thing—he traded Sittler's best friend. The reaction from Leafs players was indicative of their dissatisfaction.

According to Toronto *Star* reporter Jim Kernaghan, they gathered in a bar and threw darts at a picture of Imlach. After the McDonald trade, Sittler resigned the captaincy. (He resumed the post the following season, only to demand a trade in December of 1981.)

Coaching and management were also major problems in the 1980s. Popular, innovative Roger Neilson was fired after one year. His successor, Floyd Smith, was involved in an auto accident in which two people were killed, and had to step down; he was acquitted of charges of impaired driving and criminal negligence. His replacements, Dick Duff and Joe Crozier, were unpopular with players and were quickly fired.

Mike Nykoluk, an easygoing, indecisive Ballard crony with only minor-league playing experience and a dubious record as an assistant coach, led the team into the cellar. General Manager Imlach was then dismissed and replaced by Gerry McNamara, a Leafs scout who proceeded to amass a remarkable record of bad moves. Hardworking assistant coach Dan Maloney stepped in for the fired Nykuluk in 1984-85, but was gone the next season after refusing a one-year contract, and went on to coach the Winnipeg Jets.

His replacement, John Brophy, was a 21-year veteran of the Eastern Hockey League, where he was feared as one of the meanest stick-fighters in hockey history. As coach he relied on screaming and insults to motivate players. Brophy's firing in 1988-89 led to the hiring of George Armstrong, the former Leaf star of the 1960s glory years—a nice guy and reluctant coach who was himself fired between seasons. Doug Carpenter, Tom Watt, and former Canadiens coach Pat Burns followed in quick succession in the late 1980s and early 1990s.

Nor has the team had a stable captaincy: after Sittler's departure, Rick Vaive was captain, but was demoted for missing a practice, and the spot remained open from 1986-87 through 1988-89. Vaive was eventually traded to Chicago. Rob Ramage and Wendel Clark have been Leafs captains since.

There were some high points after 1967. Under General Manager Jim Gregory, the team tried to rebuild in the mid-1970s. It drafted Borje Salming, a fast-skating star of the Swedish national team who was to spearhead the defense until 1988-89. Future Hall-of-Famer Sittler, at center, spent 11 of his 15 NHL seasons in Toronto, once scoring a record ten points (six goals, four assists) in a game in February of 1976. The top line of Sittler, McDonald, and Errol Thompson was one of the best in the NHL in the mid 1970s.

In 1975-76 the Leafs were 34-31-15, for third place in the Adams Division, but bowed to the eventual champion Philadelphia Flyers in a playoff series marred by violence. The Leafs again broke .500, by a slimmer margin, in 1976-77. In

Grant Fuhr

1978 their record was 41-29-10, a highly respectable third place behind Boston and Buffalo, and they upset the Islanders in a seven-game playoff series when Lanny McDonald scored the winning goal in overtime. The Leafs were swept by the champion Canadiens in the next round, however. The following season was another third-place, above-.500 finish, but a tailspin followed.

The Leafs got as far as the division finals in 1985-86, despite a 25-48-7 regular-season record. The following season was an improvement to 32-42-6 and another division final, taking the St. Louis Blues to seven hard-played games. At this point the Leafs seemed to be an improving young club.

Tough, skillful left winger Wendel Clark, a Saskatoon native who was the NHL's top draft pick in 1985, was becoming the team leader and the most popular player with fans, but was hampered by back problems. Right winger Gary Leeman had several good years for the Leafs during the 1980s. However, personnel mistakes outweighed these good signs.

Between December 26, 1987, and January 25, 1988, the team was winless for 15 games (11 defeats, 4 ties), the worst winless streak in its history; there had been an 18-game *road* winless streak from October 6, 1982, to January 5, 1983.

1989-90 was the only .500 year of the decade at 38-38-4, a third-place finish. The division semifinal was lost to the Blues, 4-1. The next two seasons, the Leafs were out of the playoffs, finishing last in the Norris Division both years.

In the summer of 1992, Fletcher lured an unhappy Pat Burns away from Montreal to coach for his team. With the emergence of Felix "The Cat" Potvin in goal, Fletcher traded Grant Fuhr to Buffalo in exchange for goalie Daren Pupa, a number-one draft pick, and Dave Andreychuk, a 50-goal scorer. Toronto finished the regular season with a club-record 99 points.

Leading the way was veteran center Doug Gilmour, acquired in a ten-player trade that sent Leeman and four others to Calgary. Despite finishing third in the Norris Division, the Maple Leafs charged through the postseason. The Leafs upset the Detroit Red Wings—who many hockey observers thought would make the Stanley Cup finals—in seven games, and then met, and fell to, the Los Angeles Kings in the Campbell Conference Finals.

Sources

BOOKS

Batten, Jack, *Hockey Dynasty*, Toronto: Pagurian Press Ltd., 1969.

Batten, Jack, *The Leafs in Autumn*, Toronto: Macmillan of Canada, 1975.

Beddoes, Dick, *Pal Hal: A Biography of Harold Ballard*, Toronto: Macmillan of Canada, 1989.

Beddoes, Dick, et. al., *Hockey!*, Toronto: The Macmillan Company, 1969.

Devaney, John, and Burt Golblatt, *The Stanley Cup: A Complete Pictorial History*, Rand McNally & Co., 1975.

Fischler, Stan, *Hockey's Greatest Teams*, Chicago: Henry Regnery Co., 1973.

Harris, Billy, *The Glory Years*, Scarborough, Ontario: Prentice-Hall Canada,Inc., 1989.

Hollander, Zander, *The Complete Encyclopedia of Hockey*, Detroit: Visible Ink Press, 1993.

Houston, William, *Ballard*, Toronto: Summerhill Press Ltd., 1984.

Houston, William, *Inside Maple Leaf Gardens*, Toronto: McGraw-Hill Ryerson, Ltd., 1989.

Imlach, George, *Hockey Is a Battle*, Toronto: Macmillan of Canada, 1969.

Kariher, Harry C., *Who's Who in Hockey*, New Rochelle, NY: Arlington House, 1973.

McDonald, Lanny, with Steve Simmons, *Lanny*, Toronto: McGraw-Hill Ryerson, Ltd., 1987.

McFarlane, Brian, *60 Years of Hockey*, Toronto: Pagurian Press, Ltd., 1976.

The National Hockey League Official Guide & Record Book 1992-93, Chicago: Triumph Books, 1992.

Pagnucco, Frank, *Heroes*, Scarborough, Ontario: Prentice-Hall Canada, 1985.

Ronberg, Gary, *The Ice Men*, Crown Publishers, Inc., 1973.

Ronberg, Gary, *The Illustrated Hockey Encyclopedia*, New York: Balsam Press, 1984.

Smythe, Conn, and Scott Young, *Conn Smythe: If You Can't Beat 'Em in the Alley*, Toronto: McClelland & Stewart, Ltd., 1981.

Young, Scott, *The Leafs I Knew*, Toronto: Ryerson Press, 1966.

—*Richard Cohen* for Book Builders, Inc.

WINNIPEG JETS

Although the Jets didn't join the NHL until the 1979-80 accommodation between that league and the rival World Hockey Association, the sport has a long history in Manitoba. In fact, the Winnipeg Victorias won a Stanley Cup as far back as 1895-96 and repeated the achievement in 1900-01. Winnipeg, too, was a junior hockey city before it achieved a WHA franchise when the new league was conceived in 1972.

Winnipeg has a reputation for harsh, cold winters where the snow flies and indoor entertainment is the obvious answer. Indeed, hockey was a major presence in western Canada long before the National Hockey League got around to recognizing that fact. Although Canadian Football League teams like the BC Lions, the Calgary Stampeders, Ed-monton Eskimos, Regina Roughriders, and Winnipeg Blue Bombers proved that pro sports would sell in the prairies, the NHL didn't have a team west of Chicago until its 1967 expansion. Then, western Canada was ignored in favor of franchises in California.

The failure of the NHL to expand into spots like Winnipeg was one reason Ben Hatskin, the original Jets owner, got into hockey. He got a club in the new Western Canada Junior Hockey League in 1967; he named it after the New York Jets, another sports franchise fighting against the odds, because he was a friend of Jets owner Sonny Werblin.

When talk of forming a new professional hockey league started in earnest in the spring of 1972, Hatskin was one of the original insiders who helped to shape the future of the organization. In fact, once Winnipeg was confirmed as a charter member of a the 12-team league, Hatskin made the move that "announced the arrival" of a true challenge to the NHL: he went after one of the league's biggest stars, Chicago's Bobby Hull.

Hull later recalled that he didn't think the WHA and the Jets would be able to produce the big money to sign him and admitted that his statement that it would take a $1 million contract to get him away from Chicago was only a bargaining ploy to get more cash from the Blackhawks. Hatskin and the WHA weren't bluffing, however, and Hull was signed on June 6, 1972. Winnipeg received help from other WHA members to raise the $2 million necessary to guarantee the blockbuster deal.

The WHA would be criticized in some circles for latching on to fading veterans, but there could be no doubt they meant business when they signed The Golden Jet. Hull was 32 at the time he jumped to the new league, still very much in his prime. He had just completed a 50-goal season in Chicago, playing every one of the 78-game schedule. He had been the NHL's top goal-scorer seven times in a 15-year career that began when he was just 18. He had won two NHL most valuable player awards, three scoring titles, and a Lady Byng Trophy. No one doubted that he was on his way to the Hockey Hall of Fame.

His signature gave the Jets immediate star quality and ignited the battle over players that would persist for almost a decade with potentially devastating effects for both circuits. The first major loser in the war was the NHL because it backed the Blackhawks, who contended that Hull's signing with a rival league violated his NHL contract's reserve clause. Although the legal wrangling meant that Hull missed the first 15 games of the initial WHA season, the outcome of the case eventually favored the WHA. A Philadelphia judge threw out the NHL's reserve clause; the player war was on in earnest.

Hull As Coach?

When the WHA opened for business in 1972, Bobby Hull was coach of the Jets. When the courts ruled in favor of his contract, he became player-coach and actually spent two seasons in that role. The first season—during which Hull teamed with Christian Bordeleau and Norm Beaudin to lead the Jets to a first-place finish in the WHA Western Division—was decidedly good. That season the

Jets also made a run to the WHA play-off finals, where they were beaten by the Boston-based New England Whalers. The second was a losing year that ended with the club facing its first financial crisis.

Hull's debut season in the WHA saw him finish third in goals, with 51, and fifth in scoring, with 103 points—not bad for a player who missed almost a quarter of the 78-game regular season. Beaudin was fourth in the league in assists, while Bordeleau completed a trio of 100-point scorers.

Hull went on to score 53 more goals in his second season and finished fourth in WHA scoring on 95 points, five fewer than evergreen Gordie Howe, who had also joined the new league and was playing with his sons in Houston. The Jets' ousting by Howe's Aeros in the first round of the play-offs was the prelude to an offstage drama that would last through a round of negotiations with city and provincial governments.

Although there had been success on the ice, the fans were not filling the 10,000-seat Winnipeg Arena. The WHA was always a hard sell in Canada, its sophisticated hockey fans having been educated on the Hockey Night in Canada telecasts that still brought the "competition," in the form of the NHL, into every home across the Dominion. The cost of starting and running a competing league was high, too, so Hatskin and his partners put the club on the market. There were the usual rumors that the franchise might even be relocated, a move Hatskin resisted.

Eventually, a scheme of public ownership was formulated. As it worked its way through the local government approvals and to the provincial level, where monetary support was not forthcoming, hockey fans in the city responded to a "Save the Jets" campaign with contributions of their own. Ultimately, a new ownership structure ensured that the team would remain in Winnipeg.

Robinson Gets His Men

While the behind-the-scenes negotiations to preserve the financial stability of the Jets were

TEAM INFORMATION AT A GLANCE

Founding date: 1972 (WHA); June 22, 1979 (NHL)

Home stadium: Winnipeg Arena
15-1430 Maroon Rd
Winnipeg, Manitoba, Canada R3G 0L5
Phone: (204) 783-5397
FAX: (204) 788-4668

Capacity: 15,393

Team colors: Blue, red, and white
Team nickname: Jets
Logo: Red circle with "Winnipeg Jets" written inside;
letter "J" of Jets is a hockey stick, and a red jet is protuding leftward from stick

Franchise record	Won	Lost	Tie
WHA (1972-79)	302	227	26
NHL (1979-93)	430	544	150

WHA Avco Cup Championships (3): 1975-76, 1977-78, 1978-79

grabbing headlines, personnel director Billy Robinson had been dispatched to Sweden to look for talent. Hatskin, ever the innovator, was willing to gamble Winnipeg's playing future on a complete change of style.

"I told him to go over and get me the two best Swedish forwards he could find," Hatskin said. "We'd known for years that the Swedes played the most exciting hockey in Europe. I wanted the Jets to be the most exciting team in hockey."

Hatskin may have been stretching the point, however, when he suggested that a lion's share of Canadian hockey fans were familiar with European, let alone Swedish, hockey. The 1972 Super Series between Team Canada and the Soviet Union had shocked North Americans, Canada struggling to win the eight-game set on the final

night in Moscow when it had been widely thought the best NHL pros would easily defeat the Russians. Nevertheless, conventional wisdom, especially at the pro level, suggested that European hockey, played on a bigger rink and not nearly as physical as the North American style, could not produce players capable of crossing the Atlantic and contributing to clubs.

Thus, when Robinson went on his talent search, there were few people in either the NHL or the WHA who appreciated the importance of that journey. By the end of the decade, once Anders Hedberg, Ulf Nilsson, and Lars Sjoberg had been seen from one side of the New World to the other, the only question about European-based players was "How many potential stars are there?," not "Can they play?"

The Swedish Superstars

Robinson obviously had an eye for talent, just as Hatskin had a flair for the dramatic gamble, but the Jets undoubtedly had luck in their corner as well; not only did they sign three talented players, but the Swedes also proved able to make the adjustment to life in North America with an ease that some later hockey immigrants could not muster. It didn't hurt, either, that Hedberg was both handsome and personable, a born public relations expert.

Anders Hedberg was a 23-year-old native of Ornskoldsvik when he decided to accept the offer from the WHA Jets. He was a blonde, swift right wing, not huge, but compact at 5'11" and 175 pounds.

He played four full seasons in the WHA with startling effect. In his first season, during which he played only 65 games, Hedberg scored 53 goals and added 47 assists for an even 100 points. That was his lowest total as a Jet. The next three seasons included a 70-goal campaign and a 29-point play-off spree during the year in which the Jets lost the final series to Quebec.

Ulf Nilsson, who came from Nynashamn, was 24 when Robinson signed him for the Jets. The same size as Hedberg, he was not a goal-scorer but the consummate playmaker, who filled the WHA record book with assists while setting up snipers like Hull and Hedberg. In his first season in Winnipeg he rolled up 94 assists, then followed that with 76, 85, and 89.

Lars-Erik Sjoberg did not grab as many headlines as Hull's high-scoring partners, but his presence demonstrated another facet of the European reservoir of talent. A veteran Swedish national team member, he was 30 when he joined the Jets, a 5'8", 179-pound defenseman whose leadership was key.

He was a "quarterback" in the European style of play, one that utilized a passing-oriented attack structure in marked contrast to the North American dump-and-chase approach. He brought that play-making skill with him to Winnipeg and consistently piled up impressive assist figures.

More Europeans Arrive

The immediate success of the Swedish imports led the Jets to look for even more help from the new breeding ground of talent. They added players like Veli-Pekka Ketola of Finland and another Swede, Willy Lindstrom, and, at one time, had as many as nine Swedes or Finns at their disposal. The Jets also adopted the high-speed European style of play, an approach that concentrated on play-making in the neutral zone—or even the defensive end—with the wingers circling back to accept the pass, then hitting the attacking blue line at full speed.

The WHA Jets, having got the jump on everyone else, were probably the best North American team utilizing the style, one that more coaches and teams gradually implemented. When Winnipeg sprang its European surprise, it was the defenses who were caught napping; adjustments to the quicker game came later, but it can be argued that the Jets' example inspired a generation of young Canadian and American players to try something different.

Through it all there was the continuing presence of Hull, who seemed to get better with age. There were the inevitable critics who said that he wouldn't have gotten the same numbers in the "tougher" NHL, but there was more than a bit of envy in such talk.

The Golden Jet was still a grand player no matter which rink he skated on. In 1974-75, the first year that Hull teamed with his Swedish linemates, the Jets finished 38-35-5 and missed the play-offs.

Hull, however, was dynamite: he scored 77 goals to lead the league, added 65 assists, and his 142 points were five behind the WHA scoring champ, Andre Lacroix of San Diego. Nilsson went 26-94-120, and Hedberg 53-47-100 in that season. Veteran coach Rudy Pilous had two different terms behind the bench that season, then was replaced for 1975-76 by Bobby Kromm.

Hull scored 53 goals and added 70 assists in 1975-76, Nilsson was 38-76-114, and Hedberg went 50-55-105. Ketola added 32 goals, Lindstrom scored 23, and the "Europeanized" Jets rolled away to the Canadian Division title with 52 wins and 106 points. They didn't slow down in the play-offs, either, performing almost perfectly to claim their first Avco Cup. Calgary was the only team to win a post-season game that spring; Edmonton and Houston, in the final series, were swept.

The First of Three

The Jets were finalists again in 1976-77, as Kromm completed a two-year stay in Winnipeg before moving to the NHL Detroit Red Wings at the end of the season. Hull played only 34 games that year because of injuries, so the burden now fell on Hedberg and Nilsson, who answered any remaining questions about their abilities.

Those who said their gaudy scoring figures owed much to Hull's presence now had to explain these statistics: Hedberg led the WHA with 70 goals and still picked up 61 assists, finishing second in scoring in the league; Nilsson got 39 goals and added a WHA-leading 85 assists. Lindstrom weighed in with 44 goals and 80 points, while Joe Daley, a regular in goal since the first WHA season, had another strong season.

Daley was 25 before he got a chance to play in the NHL and 29 when he opted to sign with the Jets after failing to earn a regular starting job with Pittsburgh, Buffalo, or Detroit. He slotted into the workhorse role in 1973-74, playing 41 games, and played 50 or more for the next three seasons. His goals-against figures ranged from 2.84 in 1975-76, when he posted five shutouts in the supposedly offense-only atmosphere of the WHA, to 3.99 during that period. He gave the Jets consistent minutes, eventually retiring at age 36 after an 11-year career.

The play-offs were tougher in 1976-77, San Diego extending the Jets to a full seven games before bowing and Houston losing in six games. The Winnipeg bid for a second straight title fell a game short when Quebec won the Avco Cup in seven games. As it turned out, that series prevented

Winnipeg from finishing its WHA history with four straight play-off championships.

Add Another Nilsson, Another Title

The 1977-78 season was memorable for several reasons, including a change in ownership as the Jets survived another threat of bankruptcy midway through the year. It also contained an Avco Cup and a memorable victory over the Soviet National team at a time when the Big Red Machine seemed unstoppable. There was also the addition of a second Nilsson, Kent, the younger brother of Ulf.

A 6'1" centerman, Kent Nilsson arrived at age 21 and immediately began to make his contribution with a 42-goal, 65-assist season. That meant that the Jets had four 100-point scorers in a 50-28-2 season. Hull went 46-71-117 in his last full season; Ulf Nilsson was second in assists and third in scoring after a 37-89-126 year; and Hedberg finished second in goals and fourth in the scoring race off a 63-59-122 season.

The December win over the Soviets included a three-goal performance by Hull, a 5-3 triumph that attracted a capacity crowd of 10,418, but the overall financial picture for the club was not so bright. Playing big-time hockey was expensive; the patched-together community ownership that had saved the team in its first crisis was under siege. To make matters worse, it was clear that both Hedberg and Ulf Nilsson were being wooed by the New York Rangers, who would ultimately sign them away from the WHA with a $2 million offer. Hull, too, was coming to the end of his career.

New Ownership Again

When the club declared bankruptcy in January of 1978, an eight-man group, including Hull, got together to see out the year. This arrangement turned into Jets Hockey Ventures, headed by Michael Gobuty. The new owners immediately said that the hockey future in Winnipeg lay in the NHL, but it would be another full season before that dream could be realized.

Having swept past Birmingham 4-1 and New England 4-0 to win the 1977-78 Avco Cup, the Jets went into what was to be the WHA's last season as defending champions but with a quite different-looking team. Kent Nilsson remained, but the rest of the stars who had formed the nucleus of the team were gone. In their places were some new heroes.

Morris Lukowich, who had been acquired from Houston when that team disappeared, contributed 65 goals—second best in the WHA—and Pete (Silky) Sullivan enjoyed his best year in the league with 46 goals and 40 assists. Terry Ruskowski, who had also been picked up from Houston, was third in the league with 66 assists, while Kent Nilsson matched his initial North American pro season with another 107-point campaign.

And, just to prove that the Jets hadn't forgotten about their European connection, the number-one goalie in the team's final WHA season was a Finn, Markus Mattsson. He went 25-21-3 with a 3.63 goals-against average.

The last Avco Cup was won at the expense of Quebec and Edmonton, but with an NHL-WHA accommodation an "open secret," it may have seemed an anti-climax.

A General Manager Arrives

Perhaps the most important change in that 1978-79 season came in November, long before it was certain that the Jets would be playing NHL hockey in 1979-80. John Ferguson, whose playing career had been notable for its pugnacity during an eight-year stay with the powerful Montreal Canadiens, was named general manager of the Winnipeg franchise.

There was more than a bit of irony in the appointment, because it had been Ferguson, in his role as coach and general manager of the New York Rangers, who had so actively pursued the Jets' Hedberg and Nilsson. Ferguson remained in the position until October 30, 1988, during which time the Jets made the transition from one league to another and produced their first NHL superstar.

Entry into the NHL proved extremely difficult for Winnipeg, in part due to the rules of accommodation between the two leagues. Part of the hefty price that the four WHA survivors (Edmonton, Hartford, and Quebec also came into the NHL in 1979-80 when the two leagues amalgamated) paid was that the National Hockey League teams could exercise their claims on players who had been drafted but elected to sign with WHA clubs. Winnipeg was especially hard hit.

Kent Nilsson, for example, was reclaimed by the Atlanta Flames. He went on to post 263 goals in an eight-year NHL career. Terry Ruskowski was reclaimed by the Chicago Blackhawks and went on to an effective 10-year NHL career. Defenseman Barry Long was snapped up by Detroit, and Chicago claimed another backliner, Rich Preston. Under the regulations in force, the Jets could "reclaim" only two skaters and two goalies after the NHL clubs were through pouring over the talent. They kept Lukowich and Mattsson at that point of the "expansion" process, but Ferguson admitted the club had been decimated.

Remarkably, Winnipeg managed to play .500 hockey just three years after losing the core of its team, but getting there was no fun.

Two Long Seasons

Tom McVie, who knew a bit about the rigors of putting together an expansion team, was the first coach of the NHL Jets. He had spent the 1975-76 season in Washington, relieving Milt Schmidt in the Capitals' second season. Washington had won only eight games in 1974-75 and was destined to win just 11 in that second year with McVie the coach during eight of those triumphs. He then stayed two more years in the nation's capital, steering the Caps to 24 wins in 1976-77 before his release after the 1977-78 season.

So McVie, at least, knew what to expect when he assumed the Winnipeg challenge. His first team won 20 games, better than had been expected, and finished with 51 points, but the next year marked the nadir of Winnipeg hockey history. McVie lasted only 28 games (winning one), and the Jets experienced a 30-game winless streak that attracted national media attention.

Ultimately they finished 9-57-14. The 32 points were 11 better than Washington had managed on its maiden voyage (and one more than the 1989-90 Quebec Nordiques accumulated), but it didn't take a hockey expert to figure out that the Jets needed help. Fortunately, they got it right away.

Working the Draft

While the team's performance on the ice was nothing to get wildly excited about, Ferguson and the management team got things right in June, when the future was determined for many teams; in 1980 Winnipeg had named the big defense-man Dave Babych as the second selection of the entry draft. They had the first pick in 1981 and took Dale Hawerchuk. Both proved to be inspired selections.

Babych was a 6'2", 215-pound backliner who had won Western Hockey League All Star selection and was recognized as the league's top defenseman in his final season of junior hockey. He could run the power play, as his 59- and 60-assist seasons in Portland (WHL) attested, and he didn't pick up needless penalty minutes. Although he didn't turn 20 until after completing his first NHL season, he was one of those rare youngsters who could make the difficult jump directly from junior hockey to the highest level of the game.

Babych took time, naturally, to recoup full value for the Jets, but he earned the reputation of a solid, talented defender within the first three years on the roster. By then, 1982-83, he was a 74-point scorer in the NHL, with 61 assists from a defensive position.

Hawerchuk was the acknowledged number-one player in the 1981 draft. He had led the Cornwall Royals of the Quebec Major Junior Hockey League to a Memorial Cup, emblematic of Canadian Junior Hockey supremacy, in his final season and won just about everything in sight. He was named to the QMJHL first All Star team, won the league's player of the year award, and added the Canadian Major Junior player of the year trophy for good measure. The numbers that season included 81 regular season goals and 102 assists. In the play-offs Hawerchuk scored 15 goals and assisted on 20 more to bring his two-year post-season total to 80 points, proof enough that he was a big-game player, too.

Ferguson labeled Hawerchuk "one of the best junior players I ever saw," and if that added any pressure to the 18-year-old's shoulders, it wasn't noticed; his first season in the NHL saw him register 103 points and win the Calder Trophy as Winnipeg broke through to the .500 level.

Watt Takes Over

Part of the change that took place in 1981-82 involved coaching. The Jets had turned to the University of Toronto Blues for their mentor, hiring Tom Watt. He was one of a growing number of coaches in the league who had come from a nontraditional background, and his immediate impact on a young, developing club was recognized when the awards were handed out at the end of the season.

After Winnipeg finished 33-33-14, second in the Norris Division, Watt was named winner of the Jack Adams Award, coach of the year in the NHL.

Hawerchuk clearly was a driving force behind the improvement, his 45 goals and 58 assists leading the team that season, but there were others who made important contributions. Lukowich was still a valuable scorer, getting 43 goals and 92 points; Dave Christian, one of the heroes of the 1980 Gold Medal U. S. Olympic team, was now an important cog, having scored 71 points in his first season and adding 76 this year; Paul Mac-Lean, Willy Lindstrom, and Babych all were vital as well. In goal, Ed Staniowski and Doug Soetaert shared the load.

Christian had been the fortieth draft choice in 1979, when the Jets first participated in the entry process. They had to wait for the Warroad, Minnesota, native, who had gone to the University of North Dakota and then dedicated the 1979-80 season to the Olympic team. He joined the Jets for 15 games after the Lake Placid victory, scoring 18 points. The 1981-82 season was his best in Manitoba, although he went on to a pair of 80-point seasons in Washington after the Jets traded him for a first-round draft pick in 1983.

There were no play-off heroics to complement the first successful season, however. The Jets fell to St. Louis in the opening round of post-season play.

The Seesaw Appears

Having gotten to the 50-50 level, the Jets couldn't stay there. Watt's second season produced a 33-39-8 ledger, fourth place in the Smythe Division, and a first-round play-off loss to the Edmonton Oilers, on their way to dominating the NHL for the better part of the decade. There was a bit of irony there, too, because the Oilers were led by the incomparable Wayne Gretzky, a player who might have wound up in Winnipeg in the hectic final year of the WHA, when teams and owners were fighting to stay alive.

According to current Winnipeg president Barry Shenkarow, a key figure in the 1978 rescue act, the Jets received a call from Indianapolis Racers owner Nelson Skalbania, who was looking to sell Gretzky before the Indianapolis team folded. Because of the uncertainty surrounding the possible merger with the NHL and the fact that Gretzky wouldn't come cheaply, the Jets declined to match Skalbania's demand of $500,000 for a player then just past 16 years old. Edmonton's Peter Pocklington eventually got The Great One.

Hawerchuk may not have equalled Gretzky in achievements, but he proved to be the real thing in Winnipeg. His second season produced 40 goals and 51 assists, while MacLean, a powerful right wing who had been acquired from the St. Louis

Blues along with Staniowski and Bryan Maxwell in July of 1981, continued to prove a good pick-up. After his 61-point 1981-82 season, MacLean raised his numbers to 32-44-76 in 1982-83 to edge out Babych for third in team scoring. That was the season Babych notched 61 assists on the way to a 74-point year.

There was also a growing contribution from Thomas Steen, another in the Winnipeg line of Swedish imports. Steen, a center from Tocksmark, had been signed as a 20-year-old free agent in March of 1980 after five seasons in the Swedish League. He broke into European hockey as a 16-year-old with Leksand, eventually gaining national team recognition in 1978-79 as an 18 year old. Steen's last season in Sweden was split between Farjestad and the national team, and saw him produce 46 points in 51 games.

It took Steen a while to realize his full potential. His first NHL season included 42 games and produced just 16 points, but after that he became a consistent scorer. It was 44 points in 1982, 59 in 1983, then 65 in 1984, as each season showed improvement. A tough forward with good skills, he developed into a player who could be counted on for 60-plus points and close to 20 goals per season (his high came in 1984-85, when he scored 30). In Winnipeg's continuing battle to rebuild a team that had been stripped of depth at the time of its NHL entry, players like Steen proved extremely important.

A "Long Season" Is Just Fine

Watt, Ferguson, and ex-Jets defenseman Barry Long took turns in 1983-84 as Winnipeg finished on 73 points, fourth in the Smythe, and again fell to the Oilers in the first play-off round, but Long was firmly in charge the next year when the Jets achieved their first winning season in the NHL.

That 43-27-10 campaign, which enabled them to finish second in the Smythe Division, earned Long the runner-up spot in the annual Adams Award voting for coach of the year. It also showcased Hawerchuk and MacLean in their best seasons in Winnipeg colors.

Hawerchuk broke through with 53 goals and 77 assists in a 130-point year, while MacLean put together 41 goals and 60 assists to also top the 100-point plateau. Steen would surpass his 30-54-84 statistics only once, in 1988-89, while Laurie Boschman, who had been acquired the season before, and Brian Mullen, one of those fortunate lower-round draft choices, were also over the 70-point level. In goal, the Jets relied on Brian Hayward, who responded with a 33-17-8 year and a 3.86 goals-against average.

In the play-offs, the Jets got past Calgary 3-1 in the best-of-five first round, but Edmonton was still the obstacle waiting in the Smythe Division final. The Oilers swept 4-0.

By then, the up-and-down Winnipeg story had become a pattern; after the fine 1984-85 season, Long found the magic missing in 1985-86. Fer-guson actually finished the year behind the bench before turning to Dan Maloney for coaching duties in 1986-87.

Hawerchuk again produced triple figures in 1985-86, finishing 46-59-105, but the rest of the cast that had struck gold the year before fell off. Hayward, for instance, saw his goals-against average soar to 4.79 in 52 starts and found himself on the way to Montreal the following summer. There, playing behind a different defense, Hayward teamed with Patrick Roy to win the Jennings Trophy three straight years, between 1987-1989.

At the end of the season the Jets tabbed Pat Elyniuk with the eighth pick of the entry draft and named Teppo Numminen with the 29th choice. Neither was ready for immediate delivery, but both would ultimately strengthen the franchise.

One Up, Two Down

Maloney enjoyed a winning season in 1986-87, leading the Jets to third place in the Smythe Division and a first-round play-off victory over Calgary, but the Oilers swept again in the Smythe finals, and the Winnipeg story of the seesaw continued with a pair of losing seasons finishing Maloney's stay in Manitoba. Rick Bowness finished the 1988-89 season in charge.

Hawerchuk was still putting up 100-point seasons, while MacLean was second in team scoring in both 1986-87 and 1987-88. But the Jets surrendered over 300 goals in both 1987-88 and 1988-89 as they tumbled all the way to the Smythe basement.

Fortunately, the spring again proved a time when patient Winnipeg fans could take heart. In 1988, Teemu Selanne was chosen tenth overall, but it would be the 1992-93 season before he came to Winnipeg. When he finally arrived, Jets fans immediately saw what he could deliver. His debut season produced 76 goals and 56 assists for a team that by then had six different top draft choices on board.

Selanne was also the last big pick of the John Ferguson era. The veteran general manager was sacked in October of 1988 and replaced by Mike Smith as the Jets moved to retool their front office. Ironically, Smith, a 43-year-old native of Potsdam, New York, had begun his NHL career as Ferguson's assistant coach with the New York Rangers in 1976-77. Now he was replacing his mentor, though he was no stranger to the Jets organization.

Smith had joined Winnipeg in the initial NHL season, taking charge of the Jets' Central Hockey League club in Tulsa. He actually had a brief spell as head coach in the 1981-82 season before settling into the role of director of recruiting. So, in tandem with Ferguson and the rest of the club's scouts, he had been party to the rebuilding job that would ultimately pay off with a strong start to the 1990s.

What is interesting about that rebuilding is that the Jets have turned back to their initial strategy: the 1992-93 club, which was the first to post back-to-back winning seasons since Winnipeg entered the National Hockey League, had nine Europeans in its lineup. The difference was that many of them came from Eastern Europe, territory that had been impossible to mine when the Jets were launching their life in the WHA.

Murdoch Wins, Then Loses

Smith's first coach was Bob Murdoch, who presided over a 37-32-11 season in 1989-90, but once again the Oilers got in the way come playoff time. Murdoch won the Adams Award as coach of the year in a season that saw Hawerchuk, Elyniuk, and Steen top the scorers, while a Swede, Frederik Olausson, confirmed his status as an important contributor.

A defenseman, Olausson is a 6'2", 200-pounder from Vaxsjo, who had been claimed with the 81st overall pick in the 1985 draft. At that time he was playing with Farjestad, where he would spend another full season before crossing the Atlantic. He broke into the NHL in 1986-87, but it was two years before he was able to put together a solid, 62-point season. That included 15 goals and indicated that he could be a major contributor. In the 1989-90 season he scored nine goals and added 46 assists from his backline position, proof that he was coming of age in the NHL.

In goal, that 1989-90 team featured Bob Essensa, a Toronto native who had been chosen 69th way back in 1983. Essensa elected to attend Michigan State University rather than head to the NHL, playing four seasons for the perennial Central Collegiate Hockey Association, where he teamed with Norm Foster as one of the finest goaltending tandems ever to play the collegiate game.

Essensa's best college season was 1984-85, when he posted a 1.64 goals-against average in 18 appearances. Overall, he finished with a 62-13-2 record and earned second-team All Star status in the CCHA in 1986. For all that, Essensa didn't have an easy transition to the NHL; he spent the 1987-88 season at Moncton of the American Hockey League but didn't have a successful campaign.

Despite finishing with a 4.66 goals-against average in 27 games, Essensa got a look in Winnipeg in 1988-89 for 20 games but played 22 with the Fort Wayne Komets of the International Hockey League. Thus it wasn't until 1989-90 that he really came of age at the top level; he won 18

of 36 starts and finished with a 3.15 goals-against average and a spot on the NHL all-rookie team.

In the spring, when it came to draft, the Jets continued a practice they had begun in 1989. In that draft they had used their last two selections on Evgeny Davydov, number 235 overall, and Sergei Kharin, number 240 on the list. In 1990 they gambled the 77th choice on Alexei Zhamnov. A year later they would opt for Igor Ulanov with the 203rd selection in the annual grab bag.

One Great Big Trade

If anyone thought Smith would play it safe when he moved into the general manager's chair, they were surprised on June 16, 1990. That's when Smith sent the Jets' "franchise player" to the Buffalo Sabres. He traded Dale Hawerchuk and a first-round draft choice to Buffalo for Phil Housley, Scott Arniel, Jeff Parker, and a Sabres draft choice.

It wasn't a case of trading a player who had begun to wane, either. Hawerchuk's career in Winnipeg was still going strong, but the Jets simply weren't a consistent team. Even the team's media guide allowed that "through the '80s the Jets were considered a one-man hockey team in a lot of ways. Dale Hawerchuk was the recognized leader and captain. His performances through nine prosperous years speak for themselves. However, in continuing to restructure the club Smith made [the] bold deal."

It was probably a case of two clubs figuring they needed to shake up the mix in order to take a real step forward. Like Hawerchuk, Housley had been a rookie star with Buffalo from the moment he was drafted sixth overall in 1982. An offensive backliner who could also play the wing, he had put up a 60-assist season in his final year in a Sabres uniform. Thus the swap was a risky gamble for Buffalo, too.

Smith's final move to turn things around at the start of the new decade was to name John Paddock head coach for the 1991-92 season. A right winger who had played just 87 NHL games, Paddock had spent most of his coaching career in the

American Hockey League before getting the summons to Manitoba, but he had put together some impressive figures in the minor leagues. His first team was the Maine Mariners, where, while still a player, he took over for Tom McVie when the latter was named head coach of the New Jersey Devils in 1983-84.

He wound up guiding the Mariners to the AHL play-off championship, winning the Calder Cup in his first season as a coach. After one more season with the Mariners, Paddock moved to the Hershey Bears for four seasons, winning another Calder Cup and collecting two coach of the year awards between 1985 and 1989. He spent the 1990-91 season with the Binghamton Rangers, making it six winning seasons in as many full years as a head coach, before taking over in Winnipeg.

In two seasons, the Brandon, Manitoba, native did something no one else in NHL-Winnipeg history could accomplish—he posted a pair of winning records, collecting the dividend for the earlier draft choices and capitalizing on the trade that brought Housley to Winnipeg Arena.

Two In a Row

The 1991-92 campaign finished 33-32-15, still just fourth place in the Smythe Division, but it was a breath of fresh air for the franchise. Housley led the scorers with 86 points in his first season in the Jets sweater, while Essensa improved to 2.88 goals-against in the nets and registered five shutouts. Even though there was a first round play-off loss to Vancouver, the Jets carried the Canucks to seven games. More importantly, they carried their momentum into the next campaign.

The 1992-93 team was markedly better. The Jets battled Calgary and Los Angeles for second place in the Smythe a good part of the year before finally settling for fourth with a 40-37-7 mark, just a point behind the eventual Stanley Cup finalist Kings. The big reason was Selanne, who burst into the NHL with a 132-point season. Selanne, at 6' and 181 pounds was still just a 22-year-old when he decided to leave home and cast his lot with the

National Hockey League. Born in Helsinki, he had broken into Finnish hockey with the Jokerit Juniors while just a 17-year-old, lighting up the league with 66 points in just 33 games. He scored 43 goals that season and even played five games in the senior league. Jokerit couldn't wait any longer for a talent of this type and jumped him to the major league the next season.

It seemed to make no difference that he was facing older players: Selanne scored 35 goals and got 68 points in 34 games. Just as he had when in juniors, he averaged two points per match. Injury cost him most of the 1989-90 season, but he was back with abandon the following two years; he scored 33 goals in 1990-91 and topped that with 39 in his final year in Finland. He bettered that before the NHL All-Star game in his first year in the NHL, netting 42 goals. Then a 20-goal outburst in March helped him to rewrite the Winnipeg record book.

Selanne set 16 individual club records in his rookie year and added two NHL standards for good measure. The NHL marks were his 76 goals and 132 points; among the pick of the new Winnipeg marks was his nine-game goal-scoring streak, which produced 14 goals between March 14 and April, 12 two-goal games, and five hat tricks by way of introducing the young man to the toughest hockey competition in the world.

More Than Selanne

In addition to Selanne, the Jets also began to reap the benefits of other draft picks that might once have seemed fanciful. Zhamnov, for example, made his debut in 1992-93 after three seasons with the Moscow Dynamo in the old Soviet Elite League. He was only 23 when he let the NHL see his left wing work; it was good enough for 25-47-72 and four game-winning goals.

Then there was Davydov, an older Russian who also picked the 1992-93 year to impress the NHL. A slender six-footer from Chelyabinsk, Davydov was good enough to have played with the famed Soviet Army team (CSKA Moscow) in its heyday and elected to remain at home through the 1992 Olympics, where he collected a gold medal with the hybrid Commonwealth of Independent States. That done, he went west, playing the final 12 games of the 1991-92 season as an appetizer for what lay ahead. In 1992-93 Davydov made 28 goals and 21 assists as he began to get his skates under him in the new environment.

Two other former Soviet players were also part of the best season in Winnipeg since 1986-87: Sergei Bautin had been the 17th pick in the 1992 draft; a big defenseman from Murmansk, he was 26 when he joined the Jets from Moscow Dynamo. Igor Ulanov, that 203rd pick back in 1990, brought his 6'2", 202 pounds of defense to the Jets from Khimik midway through the 1991-92 season and played 56 games in 1992-93.

The remaining European contribution came from Numminen, the 29th pick back in 1986, when he was an 18-year-old with Tappara in his native Finland. He made his NHL debut in 1988-89, so he was a veteran by 1992-93.

If the Jets had remade themselves in their old image, the transformation was far from complete. The 1992-93 organization, already with so many key contributions from players born outside North America, was tracking no fewer than 19 players still plying their trade in Czechoslovakia, Finland, the old Soviet Union, or Sweden.

Who could tell how many of them might arrive before the end of the century? Maybe they would have NHL fans thinking back to the earliest days when Winnipeg showed the way with some Swedes who disproved the notion that the only way to play winning hockey was with home-front personnel.

SOURCES

Diamond, Dan, *The Official National Hockey League 75th Anniversary Commemorative Book,* NHL Publications, 1991.

Fischler, Stan, and Shirley Fischler, *The Hockey Encyclopedia,* MacMillan, 1983.

Jets Media Guide, 1991-92.

Romain, Joseph, and Dan Diamond, *The Pictorial History of Hockey,* Gallery Books, 1987.

Taylor, Scott, *Winnipeg Jets History,* Winnipeg Jets Yearbook, 1991.

NORTHEAST DIVISION

BOSTON BRUINS

Since becoming the first U.S. entry in the National Hockey League, the Boston Bruins have embodied the tough-checking, violent style of professional hockey. Their roster has featured some of the most storied players in history, and some of the best teams. The "Big, Bad Bruins" of the late 1960s and early 1970s was the league's marquee team after the 1967 league expansion and during the subsequent "hockey boom" in the United States.

Its best player—flashy, high-scoring defenseman Bobby Orr—was the top superstar of the era. The photograph of Orr flying through the air after scoring the game-winning overtime goal to beat St. Louis for the 1970 Stanley Cup remains one of the most vivid images in sport.

While Orr's explosive skating and flashy offense changed the concept of offense and the defenseman's role, star blueliners have been a Boston mainstay dating back to the highly skilled and violently hard-nosed Eddie Shore, who played

from 1926-27 to 1939-40 and won the Hart Trophy as league most valuable player four times. Of the seven Bruins to have their numbers retired by the team, four were defensemen. Shore, Lionel Hitchman, Dit Clapper (who played forward as well) and Orr were joined by forwards Phil Esposito, John Bucyk, and Milt Schmidt. Bruins captain Ray Bourque will likely join his predecessors in the future.

Orr was not the only great Bruins player of the late 1960s-early 1970s era. Center iceman Phil Esposito became the first player to crack the 100-point mark in a season in 1968-69, and set a league record for goals with 76 and points with 152 in 1970-71. Three other players, including Orr, joined him with 100 points that season, an unprecedented feat.

But that high-flying team was upset by rookie goaltender Ken Dryden and the Montreal Canadiens in a 1971 Stanley Cup series, and the Canadiens went on to win the league champion-

Eddie Shore

ship. While the Bruins of the early 1970s won two Stanley Cups, Orr's ravaged knees and the defection of several stars to the new World Hockey Association—a rival league formed largely because of the popularity created by Boston and its stars—kept the team from putting together a prolonged string of championships. That, unfortunately, is illustrative of their history as a formidable but largely unsuccessful contender in Stanley Cup play—overachieving with teams of modest talent, but underachieving with great talent. The best Bruins teams have never produced dynasties, partly because of their own deficiencies, partly the victims of outside forces.

Just as Boston won the Cup in spring 1970 and then failed the next season, the Bruins of 1929-30 followed up a Stanley Cup-winning campaign with a dominant regular season, but were upset by

the Canadiens for the Stanley Cup. The Bruins put together perhaps their best club in the late 1930s and early 1940s, and won Cups in both 1938-39 and 1940-41. In between, however, was a semifinal loss to a very good New York Rangers team in 1939-40, and when World War II broke out in 1941, a number of the team's best athletes enlisted in the service. When stars such as Schmidt, Woody Dumart, and Frankie Brimsek returned after the war, the team remained competitive, but their moment had passed.

In other years, particularly the 1950s, the Bruins have performed better than expected in the play-offs, advancing to the finals despite average-to-mediocre regular seasons. Masterful trading and drafting have kept the team competitive since the Orr years, and the Bruins hold the record in all sports of qualifying for the play-offs in every year dating back to 1967-68. They've failed to win the Cup since Orr left the team, however, and overall have won it just five times, despite making it to the play-off finals 17 times.

The Adams Legacy

The early years were successful ones. Vermont's Charles Francis Adams started his working life sweeping a store and wound up as founder and president of the First National grocery store chain. The self-made millionaire was a fan of amateur hockey in the Boston area, and after attending a Stanley Cup playoff game in Montreal, determined that professional hockey could succeed in the United States. Negotiations with the NHL were concluded in mid-October, and on November 1, 1924, Adams was formally accepted as a league owner—for a reported $15,000.

Adams would later co-found the Suffolk Downs horse racing track and also owned baseball's Boston Braves for a time. The Adams family owned the Bruins for 49 years, and three members of the clan served as team president: Charles's son Weston held the post from 1936 to 1951, and then again from 1964 to 1969 (Boston Garden and Celtics president Walter Brown held the position

TEAM INFORMATION AT A GLANCE

Founding date: November 1, 1924

Home ice: Boston Garden
150 Causeway St.
Boston, MA 02114

Dimensions: 191 x 83 feet
Seating capacity: 14,448

Team colors: Black, gold, and white
Team nickname: Bruins, 1924-present
Logo: Black "B" outlined in gold, inside a black circle with white background and gold spokes

Franchise record:	Won	Lost	Tie
(1924-1993)	2,171	1,675	670

Stanley Cup championships (5): 1929, 1939, 1941, 1970, 1972
Divisional regular season titles (21): 1927-28, 1928-29, 1929-30, 1930-31,
1932-33, 1934-35, 1937-38, 1938-39, 1939-40, 1940-41,
1970-71, 1971-72, 1973-74, 1975-76, 1976-77, 1977-78,
1978-79, 1982-83, 1983-84, 1989-90, 1990-91

between his stints). His son Weston Jr. was president from 1969 to 1975. The club held a contest to pick a name for the team, which would wear the same colors Adams used at his stores, brown with yellow trim. Adams also stipulated that the name should "relate to an untamed animal embodied with size, strength, agility, ferocity, and cunning while also being the color brown." From that description it might seem Adams already had the name in mind, but it was his secretary who came up with the moniker "Bruins."

To stock his team, Adams hired former player Art Ross as manager and coach, and put him in charge of building the team. It proved a good choice. Ross ran the hockey side of the operation until 1953-54, and also had four different stints as

coach totalling 16 years, winning two Stanley Cups. Ross was also an innovator within the game, designing some early helmets, and a new style of goal and puck that were adopted by the league. In 1941 he donated a trophy to be awarded annually to the league's outstanding player. In 1947-48, the purpose of the trophy was amended, with it going to the player who led the league in scoring.

In 1924 Ross scoured up some players and coached them to a 6-24 record. The team's first game was played December 1, just a month after Adams had officially founded the club, and was undoubtedly the highlight of the season. At Boston Arena, the Bruins defeated the Montreal Maroons 2-1, with Fred "Smoky" Harris and Carson Cooper scoring second-period goals for the home

Hockey Hall of Fame and Museum

Art Ross

Shore was the Bruins' first superstar and, some say, the best of all time. He was not only the first defenseman to rush the puck up ice from behind his own net, he was also a rock on defense and tough as nails. As Gerald Eskenazi wrote in his book *Hockey,* Shore "was involved in more unusual happenings, more fights, more hockey lore, than any other single player."

More Shore Lore

The most famous Shore story—there are a number of different versions—describes the time another player's stick severed his ear. Legend varies as to how many doctors he visited with this injury, but all but the last one told him it was impossible to save it. Shore refused an anesthetic as the doctor sewed the ear back on.

The most infamous Shore incident came during a December 12, 1933 game, when Shore's blindside charge into Toronto's Irvine "Ace" Bailey caused a fractured skull that ended Bailey's career and nearly killed him. The Maple Leafs star underwent two operations in 10 days, and though he recovered, he never played again. Shore was suspended for 16 games, and Toronto defenseman Red Horner—who had decked Shore with a punch that left him knocked out on the ice—was suspended for nearly three weeks.

A Bruins game to benefit Bailey's family raised $6,642, and a second benefit game pitted the Leafs against an NHL all-star team. Shore skated for the all-stars.

Teamed with rangy Lionel Hitchman, Shore helped form an impenetrable defense. The Bruins improved to a second-place finish in the American Division in 1926-27 and went to the finals of the Stanley Cup play-offs, where they were defeated by the Ottawa Senators, who had two wins and two ties. At that time, the preliminary rounds would be two-game, total-goals series, and the final was a best-of-five series.

The final game was penalty-filled, and ended with Bruin Billy Couture knocking down the referee and jostling with his assistant. League Presi-

team. The lowlight was likely the 11-game home losing streak that remains a league record. Among the losses in that streak was a 10-2 defeat to the Ottawa Senators on December 15, and a 10-1 loss to the Toronto Maple Leafs seven days later.

The next season the Bruins went 17-15-4 and finished fourth in the league, which had expanded from six to seven teams. That was not good enough for a playoff berth, in days when only the first three teams made it to post-season play. Adams accelerated the building process before the 1926-27 season, when he bought a number of top stars from the defunct Western Hockey League, among them future Hall of Famers Harry Oliver and Eddie Shore.

The players he didn't keep Adams sold to two other U.S.-based NHL entries, the New York Americans and the Detroit Cougars. Shore, a big farm boy from Edmonton, Saskatchewan, made an immediate impact, and not just by leading the Bruins with 130 penalty minutes in 44 games.

dent Frank Calder fined Couture $100 and later suspended him for life. Although the suspension was eventually lifted, Couture never made it back to the NHL. The Bruins finished in first place in 1927-28, with Shore setting the NHL record with 165 penalty minutes in 44 games, and goaltender Hal Winkler recording 15 shutouts, which remains a team record. They were beaten in the first play-off round by the eventual Cup champion, the New York Rangers, who had entered the league just one season before.

In 1928-29 the team won both their division *and* the Stanley Cup, defeating the defending champion Rangers two games to zero in the NHL's first all-U.S. Stanley Cup final series. The final game was a 2-1 Bruins win in front of 14,000 fans at Madison Square Garden—"a rather slim crowd for a championship game," according to the *New York Times*'s Grover Theis. The game-winning goal was scored by Bill Carson with 1:58 remaining in the game.

A number of factors went into making 1928-29 a landmark one for the Bruins, starting with the November 20, 1928 opening of the Boston Garden, whose small ice surface was well-served by a hard-checking style of play, and which has remained the Bruins' home rink since, although construction has begun for a new arena.

The season marked the debut for goaltender Cecil "Tiny" Thompson, and the creation of one of the game's all-time great forward lines: Ralph "Cooney" Weiland centering right winger Aubrey "Dit" Clapper and left winger Norman "Dutch" Gainor.

In a scenario that would be repeated 39 years later, the defending Stanley Cup champs steam-

Hockey Hall of Fame and Museum

Cecil "Tiny" Thompson

BOSTON BRUINS

Hockey Hall of Fame and Museum

Dit Clapper

rolled the league the next season, but were upset by Montreal in the playoffs.

Led by the dominant defenseman Shore, the Bruins posted a 38-5-1 record during a season filled with individual milestones. Thompson won the first of four Vezina trophies as the league's best goaltender. The "Dynamite Line" scored 102 of the team's total 179 goals, with Weiland scoring a staggering 43 goals during the 44-game season, and also leading the league in points with 73.

There were a number of strong teams in the league then, however, and the Montreal Canadiens beat the Bruins in the final play-off series in two games, including a 4-3 win in the decisive contest.

In 1930-31 the Bruins' season ended with a goal by Montreal's Wilder Larochelle 19 minutes into overtime of the fifth game of their semifinal series. It would be the first of many early exits for Boston in the 1930s. The playoffs were not without dramatics—the 1933 semifinal series with Toronto ended with the longest game in hockey

history (2:44:46) up to that point—but the results were the same.

The Bruins finished in first place in their division in 1931-32, 1932-33, 1934-35, and for four seasons from 1937-38 through 1940-41. In two other years they finished second. The club advanced to the Stanley Cup finals only twice during that period, although on both those ocassions, the Bruins won.

The Kitchener Kids and Mr. Zero

The mid-1930s brought an influx of talent, with Ross earning an assist from some of his players, particularly young forwards Bobby Bauer and Woody Dumart. Growing up in Kitchener, Ontario, Bauer and Dumart had always played on the same line, centered by their younger friend Milt Schmidt.

Although Schmidt was considered a talented prospect, Ross thought the 17-year-old was too young for pro hockey. Bauer and Dumart pestered Ross to sign their friend as well. Ross did, and in 1936 Schmidt joined his two friends in the NHL, where they formed one of the best lines in the game's history. They were called the "Sauerkraut Line" (Kitchener had been called Berlin at one time), which was shortened to the "Kraut Line," and the "Kitchener Kids." They dazzled opponents with their passing and teamwork and stood up against attempts to intimidate. Although Bauer was a three-time Lady Byng Trophy winner, given to the player who combines excellence with sportsmanship, Dumart and Schmidt were not so honored.

A less-celebrated but also vital offensive cog was Bill Cowley, who came to the Bruins from the St. Louis Eagles (formerly the Ottawa Senators), a club that folded after one season, 1934-35. As Stan Fischler chronicled in *Golden Ice: The Greatest Teams in Hockey History,* teammate Albert "Babe" Siebert convinced Ross to move Cowley from winger to center ice, saying, "That kid can fly. Put him at center, and he'll rattle in the goals." The advice helped put Cowley in the Hall of Fame,

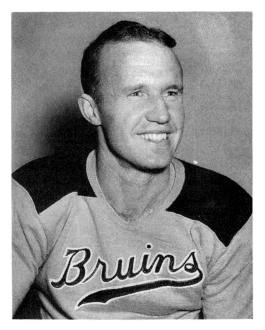

Hockey Hall of Fame and Museum

Bill Cowley

and he led the team in scoring six times and in three seasons set up linemate Roy Conacher for the team lead in goals. In the Cup-winning year of 1938-39, Conacher had a team-high 26 goals as Cowley led the team with 42 points, just three less than league leader Toe Blake of Montreal.

Along with veteran defensemen such as Shore and Clapper, the Bruins added Bill "Flash" Hollett, a defenseman with strong offensive abilities who would one day score 20 goals, splitting time between the blueline and up front, and solid Jack Crawford, one of the first NHL players to wear a helmet. Crawford's reasons had less to do with safety than with vanity; it's said he was sensitive about his bald pate.

The 1938-39 season also marked the debut of goaltender Frankie Brimsek. Thompson had won his fourth Vezina the season before but was sold to the Detroit Red Wings to make room for Brimsek, who was born in Eveleth, Minnesota. The rookie won over Boston fans by posting three consecutive shutouts beginning in his second

game, earning himself the nickname "Mr. Zero." He won both the Calder Trophy and Vezina that season, and backstopped the Bruins to the Stanley Cup.

The Bruins finished 16 points ahead of the second-place Rangers during the regular season to take first place in the NHL, which was now a seven-team league with all teams in one division. In the Stanley Cup final, they handled the Toronto Maple Leafs in five games of a best-of-seven final series, but the real test came in a seven-game semifinal series against the Rangers, a series that etched a place in hockey history for winger Mel "Sudden Death" Hill.

Skating on a line with Crowley and Conacher, Hill scored three overtime goals in the series. His first came in the third overtime of game one; the second, eight-and-a-half minutes into overtime in game two. The Bruins won the third game of the series as well, and took the lead in game four when Schmidt batted home a rebound just 49 seconds into the contest. But the Rangers put on an all-out offensive, scored twice, and held on to win the brawl-interrupted game (Shore finished with a broken nose), then won the next two games, setting up the final in Boston. Again, Hill was the star, in a game history recalls as one of hockey's best.

In front of nearly 17,000 fans, the teams played two overtimes with the score tied 1-1. The Bruins carried the play in those two stanzas, but the Rangers rallied early in the third overtime period and nearly won it when Brimsek turned aside a bid from Bill Carse, sent in alone. At the eight-minute mark Cowley (who set up all three Hill overtime scores) stole the puck and passed to Hill 10 feet in front of the net. Hill's wrist shot beat goaltender Bert Gardiner, ending the physically grueling series. The feat remains an NHL record. Shore, Clapper and captain Weiland all played on both the 1928-29 and 1938-39 Cup winners. Clapper would also play for the 1940-41 Cup winners, which would be coached by Weiland.

In 1939-40, the Bruins again led the league and became the first team to have linemates as the top three scorers in the league. Schmidt and Dumart led all scorers with 52 points, with Bauer

Frank Brimsek

The Bruins made history against Detroit, becoming the first NHL team to sweep a best-of-seven final series. They finished in Detroit, in front of a crowd of just 8,125, one of the smallest in playoff history. According to an Associated Press account, by winning in four games instead of seven, the Bruins "deprived hockey tills of an estimated $18,000 in revenue." After the game, Ross proclaimed his team the greatest ever assembled.

There was to be no dynasty, however, as outside forces came into play. Canada joined the fighting in World War II, and in February of 1942 Schmidt, Dumart, and Bauer enlisted in the Royal Canadian Air Force. Other teammates joined the service as well, including Brimsek, who enlisted in the Coast Guard. The Bruins dropped to third place in 1941-42 and were eliminated in the playoff semifinals.

The next season, Cowley won his second Hart next. The Rangers gained revenge, however, winning a six-game semifinal series over Boston, and going on to beat Toronto for the Stanley Cup. The season would mark the end of Shore's days in Boston. In January, he was dealt to the New York Americans after announcing that he'd purchased the minor league Springfield Indians and would only be available to the Bruins for home games.

World War II Thins Bruins' Ranks

The Bruins' young stars were just coming of age, however, and the team won its fourth straight division championship in 1940-41. Cowley led the league with 62 points and won the Hart Trophy, Conacher had 24 goals, and Boston had a 23-game unbeaten streak that remains a team record. Again, the Bruins' toughest series came in the semifinal round, where they edged Toronto in seven games.

Woody Dumart

Trophy as league MVP as Boston improved to finish in second place and advanced to the Cup finals, where Detroit—now calling themselves the Red Wings—beat the Bruins in four straight games, with goaltender Johnny Mower shutting them out in the final two.

Left winger Herb Cain led the team with 36 goals and broke a 14-year league record with 82 points in 1943-44, but the team did not qualify for the play-offs, and in the next season lost to Detroit in a seven-game semifinal series.

With the war over and the Kraut Line returning in 1945-46, hopes were high. Brimsek returned from service with the season in progress, but the Kraut Line was on hand for the start, as were returning servicemen Don Gallinger, Armand "Bep" Guidolin, Bill Shill, and Terry Reardon. Reardon, a winger before the war who converted to defense in the season of his return, suffered a shoulder wound during the war. On the eve of the team's opener in Boston, Reardon said, "This is the night I've been waiting for, and there were days and nights I feared I'd never see them again."

The October 24 opener—the earliest opener the Bruins had played, coming at the start of a 50-game season—was a charity game that raised $21,456.75 to benefit the Hearst Fund for Disabled Veterans, and was witnessed by league president Red Dutton along with a full house at Boston Garden. The crowd filled the arena and roared for its returning veterans during the introductions. Unfortunately, the Bruins lost the opener as Chicago Black Hawks captain Red Hamill, returning from the war as well, scored with 45 seconds left for a 5-4 win.

Player/coach Dit Clapper had "retired" at the end of the previous season, but came back "for one more year" in 1945-46—something he would do again in 1946-47. The season would be memorable as the team's war veterans rounded into shape and the team finished second, then defeated Detroit in five games to advance to the Stanley Cup finals.

With Clapper coaching from the bench, Montreal took the first game on a Maurice "Rocket" Richard overtime goal, 4-3, and went on

Hockey Hall of Fame and Museum

Milt Schmidt

to a five-game series win. Boston's lone victory came in game four, when Reardon scored the winning goal for a 3-2 victory. Schmidt and Dumart played productively into the early 1950s and wound up in the Hall of Fame, but Bauer retired after the 1946-47 season, discounting his one-game "comeback" in 1951-52, in which he scored a goal and Schmidt scored his 200th (he would finish with the team record for career goals and points, since broken). Management tried to talk Bauer into coming back, but he felt he needed to concentrate on his Kitchener-based skate business.

Hockey's First "Shadows"

Although the Bruins didn't finish in first place again until the 1970-71 season, they were a competitive team, with hard-hitting Fern Flaman, Hal Laycoe, and Bill Quackenbush anchoring the de-

Hockey Hall of Fame and Museum

Fern Flaman

son before. He'd played well that year, but midway into 1956-57 he left the club with mononucleosis, and the Boston newspapers asserted that he'd quit. Sawchuk threatened to sue them. The Bruins purchased goaltender Don Simmons from Shore's Springfield team, and he starred as Boston upset first-place Detroit in the play-off semifinals. Simmons also played well against Montreal, but the Canadiens were in the midst of a five-year run of Stanley Cups, and proved too strong.

Sawchuk was dealt back to Detroit before the next season, and the Bruins received a young left winger named John "Chief" Bucyk, who would go on to play 21 years and set most of the team's career scoring records.

Bucyk was placed with Vic Stasiuk (obtained in the original Sawchuk trade) and Bronco Horvath on the "Uke Line." Bucyk and Stasiuk were from the Ukraine, and Horvath said he didn't mind being identified as such for the sake of the nick-

fense, and in the 1950s the team played their best hockey in the play-offs. They advanced to the Cup finals three times despite finishing as high as second place just once during the decade. Lynn Patrick became coach in 1950-51, and his innovation helped boost Boston past a heavily favored Detroit team in the 1952-53 semifinal series.

Detroit was the defending Stanley Cup champ and had finished in first place for five straight seasons, but Patrick devised a system in which Dumart and Joe Klukay would concentrate solely on checking Detroit stars Gordie Howe and Ted Lindsay, respectively. They became hockey's first shadows, along with Schmidt, who would replace them when they took a breather. "If Howe goes to the men's room," Patrick told Dumart, "you go with him." After a shaky start, the strategy worked and Boston won the series.

Unfortunately, the Bruins were beaten by Montreal in five games in 1952-53, as they were again under coach Milt Schmidt in 1956-57. That season was notable for the saga of goaltender Terry Sawchuk, who was traded to the Bruins from the Detroit Red Wings in a nine-player deal the sea-

Hockey Hall of Fame and Museum

Bill Quackenbush

name. It became another of Boston's great forward lines. Gentlemanly Don McKenney, meanwhile, developed into a consistent 20-goal scorer for those teams.

They were never good enough, however, to displace the Canadiens as Stanley Cup champs. The Bruins-Canadiens final series went to six games in 1957-58. The 1956-57 series was a bloody, brawl-filled one, which carried over. The Canadiens wrapped it up in Boston when early goals by Bernie "Boom Boom" Geoffrion and Maurice "Rocket" Richard put the Bruins in a hole, and an empty net goal made it 5-3. In winning those games, the Canadiens were further extending their playoff mastery of the Bruins. From 1945-46 until the Bruins broke the streak in 1987-88, the Canadiens won every Stanley Cup series between the two clubs.

The Bruins broke the NHL color barrier when forward Willie O'Ree played two games in 1957-58. He returned for 43 games in 1960-61, scoring four goals, but didn't stick in the NHL.

Boston was also involved in a number of notorious brawls and peripheral controversy over the years. During an early-season Boston-Montreal game in 1929-30, according to Charles L. Coleman's *The Trail of the Stanley Cup*, "at one stage in the third period the game was stopped in order to scrape blood from the ice."

In 1948, New York Ranger (and former Bruin) Billy Taylor was banned for life for gambling on hockey, and Bruin Gallinger was suspended "indefinitely" for associating with a known gambler. He never played again in the NHL.

One of the most infamous incidents in NHL history was touched off by events in Boston. On March 17, 1955, Montreal's Richard, already the most heavily fined player in league history, was suspended for the three remaining games of the season and for the playoffs because of his actions at a Bruins game a few nights before.

After being high-sticked by Boston's Laycoe, Richard went after Laycoe with his stick and punched linesman Cliff Thompson. NHL President Clarence Campbell received some threatening phone calls, and his appearance at the Montreal

Hockey Hall of Fame and Museum

Johnny Bucyk

Forum that night touched off a riot.

Bobby Orr and the Big, Bad Bruins

Under a succession of different coaches in the 1960s, the team finished last in six seasons, and failed to make the playoffs for eight straight. Fans still turned out at Boston Garden to root for the Uke Line, and later the "BOW" line: Bucyk, Murray Oliver, and U.S.-born Tommy Williams (a Squaw Valley Olympic gold medalist in 1960). They also found a hero in bashing defenseman "Terrible" Teddy Green, but the club was no longer competitive.

Help was on the way in the form of a smallish kid from Parry Sound, Ontario. The Bruins had first spotted Bobby Orr as a five-foot-two, 110-pound 12-year-old playing in a Bantam tournament. Rarely were players scouted that young, but the parent club was in the first year of a precipitous decline in 1960, and an entire entourage of Bruins executives, including president Weston Adams, was scouting for talent. They had shown up to look at two other players, but were struck by Orr's tremendous skill, and wooed him for over a year, trying to sign him into Junior A hockey (at that time, junior teams served as NHL farm clubs).

The organization donated $1,000 a year to the Parry Sound youth hockey program, and Wren Blair, a coach in the Boston system, made regular visits to the Orr household. Montreal, Toronto, Detroit, and Chicago also vied for young Orr, but Boston prevailed when Orr signed with the Oshawa Generals of the Ontario Junior A Hockey Association.

Orr was a tremendously strong, agile skater who would dominate the game at both ends of the ice with his stick handling, shooting, and reckless aggressiveness. He entered the NHL as the most hyped player in history. The Bruins had become cellar dwellars, and hopes rested on Orr to bring the franchise back to prominence. On February 20, 1965, *Maclean's*—Canada's leading magazine—put Orr on its cover with the line, "How hockey's hottest sixteen-year-old is groomed for stardom—has Boston captured the NHL's next superstar?"

The next year Blair, now the GM for the Oshawa Generals, suggested that Orr would become a bigger star than the two greatest stars of the day—Chicago's Bobby Hull and Detroit's Gordie Howe. With Boston GM Leighton "Hap" Emms holding fast to a low figure during Orr's first pro negotiation, Orr hired attorney Alan Eagleson and wound up signing a two-year contract for between $50,000 and $70,000.

It made him the highest-paid NHL rookie ever, boosted the league's salary structure, and helped to establish a reputation for Eagleson, who would eventually head the NHL players' union and become one of the most powerful men in the game. A *Sports Illustrated* story was headlined "A high price for fresh northern ice." It would not be the last time Orr made an impact on the business of pro hockey.

Although the team finished last again in 1966-67, rookie Orr made a strong first impres-

Hockey Hall of Fame and Museum

Bobby Orr

sion, scoring 13 goals and 28 assists, winning the Calder Trophy as the league's top rookie, and being selected a second-team all-star. Upon receiving the Norris Trophy as the league's best defenseman, the New York Rangers Harry Howell said, "I might as well enjoy it now, because I suspect it's going to belong to Bobby for the next 10 years."

Howell was close; Orr won the Norris the next eight seasons, and also won the Hart Trophy as league MVP for 1969-70 and 1974-75, and the Conn Smythe Trophy as playoff MVP in 1970 and 1972—two years Boston won the Stanley Cup. In 1969-70 he also won the Art Ross Trophy, becoming the first defenseman to lead the league in scoring and the first player ever to win four major NHL awards in one season. He remains the only NHL player to accomplish the feat.

The comparisons with Shore began immediately, with Shore's former teammate Schmidt putting the two in the same category. "In the old days there was no forechecking," Schmidt said. "Shore could wind up without interference behind his net and start a big rush. Now there is excellent forechecking and the modern defenseman has to think faster. Bobby does just that."

In the same year, the Bruins welcomed a new coach, 34-year-old Harry Sinden, and at the end of the season replaced Emms with Schmidt as general manager. In one of his first acts as GM, Schmidt swung one of the best trades in hockey history: dealing Pit Martin, Gil Marotte, and Jack Norris to the Chicago Blackhawks in exchange for Phil Esposito, Ken Hodge, and Fred Stanfield. The players Boston traded away were talented, but those they received formed the core of a team that would become the best in the league, and two-thirds of the highest forward line ever assembled.

Esposito, a big man with soft hands whose job in Chicago had been to set up high-scoring winger Bobby Hull, would develop into the premier scorer of the day. Hodge would play the right wing for Esposito and become a prolific scorer as well, and Stanfield's two-way play would be a key to Boston's offensive depth.

In addition to Esposito and Stanfield at the center ice position, the Bruins promoted young Derek "Turk" Sanderson from the minor leagues in 1967-68. A "dead end" kid from Niagara Falls, Ontario, Sanderson was a superior face-off man and penalty killer, a defensive specialist and a consistent 20-goal scorer.

He was also flamboyant, charismatic, and made no secret of his love for the night life. He grew his hair long and wore a mustache. Pundits called him "the Joe Namath of Hockey." He bought a Rolls Royce, appeared in a movie, and wrote a book, *I've Got to be Me.*

Another thing happening at that time also played a key role in the legend of Bobby Orr and the Bruins: the National Hockey League expanded from six teams to 12. It was the largest expansion in modern professional sports, and roughly half the players who were in the NHL in 1967-68 would have been considered minor league material the year before.

For a team like the Bruins, suddenly stocked deep with young talent, the expansion clubs were destined to become cannon fodder for their high-

Hockey Hall of Fame and Museum

Phil Esposito

scoring arsenal. In the coming years, critics would point to expansion and the dilution of talent as a primary reason for Boston's record-breaking scoring, but while other teams' stars put up big scoring numbers, none did so like the wide-open Bruins. Then again, other teams didn't have Orr.

Boston improved from sixth in Orr's rookie year to third in the East Division, comprised of the NHL's six pre-expansion teams, in 1967-68. Esposito scored 35 goals and Bucyk 30—a sign of things to come. The team was swept by the Canadiens in the first round of the play-offs.

In the next season, Esposito exploded as a scorer with 49 goals and 77 assists to become the first player to top the 100-point mark. A rangy 6-foot-1, 220-pounder, Esposito would camp in front of the net and stave off enemy defensemen while linemates such as Hodge worked the corners and tried to set him up. He'd tip home Orr blasts from the point, or snap in rebounds. Although his reputation was that of a "garbage collector," he was also a gifted stickhandler and passer, as indicated by Hodge's 45-goal, 90-point season.

The Bruins finished second in the division and made it to a six-game semifinal series with eventual Cup champ Montreal.

Continuing the Tradition of Toughness

With Hodge, Esposito, and big Wayne Cashman on one line, and Stanfield centering between Bucyk and scrappy Johnny "Pie" McKenzie on the other, the Bruins had two high-scoring units. Sanderson was paired with defensive specialist Ed Westfall, a veteran and one of the top "shadows" in hockey on the third line, with a variety of left wingers.

That line, too, could score, particularly with Orr rushing the puck up ice and creating havoc in the enemy zone. Defensemen such as Dallas Smith, Green, and Don Awrey, and goaltenders Gerry Cheevers and Ed Johnston formed a solid supporting cast. Cheevers wound up in the Hall of Fame.

Boston scored, but also carried on the Bruins tradition of being physical and tough. Orr, challenged often, used his quick hands and superior skating to great advantage in fisticuffs. Sanderson once pulled a player's jersey off in a fight, then flipped it into the stands. On another occassion, Sanderson and teammate Garnett "Ace" Bailey went after a fan at Maple Leaf Gardens, and chased him out of the building, still wearing uniforms and skates. Southpaw Cashman, in addition to being a battler in the corner, was one of the game's best fighters. Sanderson once told the *Boston Globe,* "We've got 22 players who can fight and we're going to."

The toughest, meanest Bruin through the 1960s had been Green, who regularly led the team in penalty minutes but was also a talented defenseman, as his second all-star team selection in 1968-69 suggests. Like Shore, Green used intimidation as a weapon. "Lots of times, because of the reputation I've picked up in the past, I can go into the corner after the puck and come right out with it without ever getting bodychecked at all—lots of times," he told Stan Fischler in *Bobby Orr and the Big, Bad Bruins.* "Maybe a guy figures if he hits me I'm going to turn around and rap him with the stick. I probably won't, but . . . he doesn't know that."

In 1965 Green had stuck the Rangers diminutive Phil Goyette in a well-publicized spearing incident. When matched up against forward Wayne Maki in a pre-season 1969-70 stick fight, Green was nearly killed. In one of the most frightening incidents in hockey history, Maki shattered Green's skull, causing minor brain damage. A plate was inserted in the 29-year-old defenseman's head. Although he sat out the Bruins' 1969-70 Stanley Cup-winning season, he made a dramatic comeback in 1970-71.

Orr was unstoppable in 1969-70, becoming the first defenseman to top 100 points, with 120, including a league record 87 assists. Esposito was second with 99 points (43 goals), and those two, plus right winger McKenzie (29 goals, 70 points), were selected to the NHL's first all-star team. The Bruins finished second to Chicago in the East Division that season, and although both teams finished with 99 points, Chicago had won more games.

Because of the alignment of expansion teams in the West, in those days the Cup final series was a lopsided affair. The Bruins' lone test came in the first round, when the New York Rangers won the third and fourth games on their home ice, tying the series at two games apiece. Game three was significant for its then-record 174 minutes in penalties and brawling in the first period.

Sanderson claimed that goaltender Eddie Giacomin skated out to him before an early face-off and said, "We are getting paid to get you." Eleven seconds later, he went into the corner with two Rangers, and came out swinging. Rangers coach Emile Francis denied the allegations. New

Hockey Hall of Fame and Museum

Gerry Cheevers

York won 4-3. Esposito rallied the Bruins in game five, and backstopped by Cheevers, the Bruins dispatched the Rangers in six. They then ripped through Chicago in four straight to win the East, ditto for the St. Louis Blues in the finals. Although the St. Louis series was a quick one, the Blues made the decisive win tough for the Boston club.

With goaltender Glenn Hall playing spectacularly, the game was tied 3-3 going into overtime. Orr settled things with a give-and-go pass to Sanderson in the corner, who fed a cutting Orr in front of the net. Orr was tripped on the play, but not soon enough to prevent him from tucking the puck past Hall. Orr scored in all 14 play-off games, and Esposito led play-off scorers with 27 points.

Shortly after the play-offs ended, Sinden got

an offer from a private business and left the Bruins after the team refused to give him a raise that would bring his salary up to the level that other top coaches were making: $25,000 to $30,000. That would become a pattern for Boston in the 1970s, but when assistant general manager Tom Johnson moved in as coach in 1970-71, the team continued its ascent—until play-off time.

That was a record-setting, highlight-film season that ended abruptly and disappointingly for Boston when the Canadiens, backstopped by rookie Ken Dryden—an All-America fresh out of Cornell University with just six NHL games under his belt—stymied them in the first round, and went on to win the Cup.

During the season the Bruins had been virtually unstoppable, the first team in NHL hockey to boast four 100-point scorers: Esposito, Orr, Bucyk, and Hodge, who finished in that order in the scoring race. Esposito's feat of 76 goals and 76 assists in 78 games was astounding, as was the fact that 10 Bruins—every regular forward plus Orr—finished with 20 goals or better.

Stunned as the Bruins were, they came back in 1971-72 to win both the East Division title (in a realigned league) and the Stanley Cup. The Bruins scored far fewer goals during the season, but won a like number of games, and both Orr and Esposito—who was in the second year of a four-year run as scoring champ (he won five overall)—scored over 100 points.

The Bruins added all-star defenseman Carol Vadnais in a trade, and routed Toronto, St. Louis, and New York in the play-offs. The final series went the longest, six games, with Orr scoring twice despite being hobbled by an injured knee and Cheevers shutting the Rangers out in the deciding game, 3-0.

The team was less explosive than it had been the previous year, but also less inclined to mental letdowns and chippiness. "This is the best of the Bruins teams," Bucyk said. The Bruins were the most popular team in the NHL, which had again added teams (two) in 1970 and would do so again in 1972. Games were shown each weekend on national television, and the Bruins were featured most often. New rinks went up all over New England, and hockey was being imported into new areas.

That popularity was one of the reasons a group of investors founded the World Hockey Association. The Bruins were already losing young prospects drafted away to stock the new teams, and in the May, 1972 expansion draft Boston lost Westfall to the New York Islanders and promising goaltending prospect Dan Bouchard to the Atlanta Flames, both new teams. The Bruins wouldn't match the contracts offered some stars by WHA teams, and so lost Cheevers, Sanderson, McKenzie, and Green.

Worse, Orr underwent his third knee operation in the off-season, and missed almost all of the historic Team Canada-Soviet Union series and also some games in 1972-73, though he still scored 101 points. Montreal was on the ascent, and won the regular season title and the Stanley Cup. New York beat Boston in five games in the first play-off round. Orr underwent knee surgery again at the conclusion of the season.

Again, Boston retooled and in 1973-74 won the East Division with the top four scorers in the league: Esposito, Orr, Hodge, and Cashman. With a new goalie, Gilles Gilbert, obtained in a trade for Stanfield, Boston made it to the Cup finals, but was dispatched in six games by the Philadelphia Flyers, who'd incorporated Boston's style of brawling and intimidation along with tenaciousness and talent. They'd also taken something else from Boston: both Rick MacLeish, who scored the only goal in the 1-0 deciding game, and goaltender Bernie Parent, who had the shutout, were Boston property at one time.

Another significant event from 1973-74 is that it was the first year that the team was not owned by a member of the Adams clan. Both the team and its rink (purchased a couple of years before) were sold to Storer Broadcasting, which would turn them over a year later to the Delaware North Companies, Inc., owned by Jeremy Jacobs and his family. Delaware North has owned the Bruins since.

The team they purchased was in decline and slipped even further the next season, finishing second to the fifth-year Buffalo Sabres in a re-aligned NHL (which now had four divisions), and leaving the play-offs in one round. Orr and Esposito were still scoring 100 points per season, but the team had seen better days. Former player Bep Guidolin, who had been coaching a Boston farm club, replaced Johnson as coach midway through the 1973 season, and would be replaced himself by Don "Grapes" Cherry to start 1974-75.

That was a significant move, as had been the one in the fall of 1972, when Sinden was brought back to the Bruins fold as general manager. Sinden's job outside of hockey had soured when the company folded, but Sinden got a reprieve when Eagleson asked him to coach Team Canada in the dramatic 1972 series with the Soviet Union, an eight-game set that heavily-favored Canada won after spotting the Soviets a 1-3-1 lead. From there, he was hired back by Boston.

Don Cherry and the Lunch Pail A.C.

Sinden would be directly involved in the rebuilding of the Boston franchise, with moves that placed him directly in the middle of controversy, starting with the November 7, 1975 trade that sent Esposito and Vadnais to the New York Rangers for two future Hall of Famers, defenseman Brad Park and center iceman John Ratelle, along with journeyman Joe Zanussi.

The trade of all-stars was so unpopular in Boston, Sinden received death threats. "The deal was fraught with danger," Sinden told *Sports Illustrated* several years later. "The fans hated it, the team hated it, the press hated it. But I had a gut feeling it would work because of Park, who was a dominant defenseman, and because we knew that Orr's knee was in peril. Once you feel in your gut a deal will help your team and you don't act on it, then it's time to look for a new job." Later that season, Sinden swung another trade with New York, sending longtime Esposito sidekick Hodge for young Rick Middleton in an exchange of right wingers.

AP/Wide World Photos

Don Cherry

The trades proved to be excellent for Boston. Ratelle led the team in scoring and won the Lady Byng Trophy for excellence coupled with sportsmanship in his first Boston season, and lasted through 1980-81. Park, unpopular in Boston during his Ranger years, was twice a first-team all-star and anchored the defense until his retirement after 1982-83. Middleton blossomed into a star, leading the team in goals for six straight years and in overall scoring four times.

Sinden won the NHL's Executive of the Year Award for 1976-77, but first had one more controversy to withstand. At the end of the 1975-76 season, after dispatching Esposito, he bore the brunt of criticism when the Bruins let Orr become a free agent, following a contract impasse. Although the Chicago Black Hawks' contract was rumored to be in the vicinity of $3 million, a Bruins alternative offer would have given Orr 10 to 18.6 percent ownership in the team (reports vary). The Bruins have not been sold since, but given the escalation of the worth of franchises, Boston's proved the better offer. Orr played only a handful of games over three seasons for Chicago.

The Bruins, meanwhile, continued to win, albeit with a different style than the teams of a few years before. Cherry retained the traditional toughness—he was an open fan of rough-and-tough play—but played a tight-checking, grinding game. Goaltender Cheevers had returned from his WHA sojourn, and with Gilbert gave Boston a strong goaltending tandem. Nicknamed "The Lunch Pail A.C." (athletic club), the Bruins won four straight Adams Division championships during the last four seasons in Cherry's five-year tenure.

The team was typified by Terry O'Reilly, a rugged right winger who led the team in both scoring (90 points) and penalty minutes (211) in 1977-78. In 1976-77 and 1977-78, the team advanced to the Stanley Cup finals but was defeated by Montreal, which was in the process of winning four straight Stanley Cups. The first final series went four games, the second one six games, and in 1978-79 the teams met in a semifinal series that was the most competitive by far.

It was hard-fought and pugnacious, with the slower Bruins trying to overcome Montreal's speed and offensive depth. The series went to seven games, and Boston led 4-3 late in the deciding game when the Bruins were given a two-minute penalty for having too many men on the ice. Guy LaFleur's goal sent the game into overtime, and Yvan Lambert won it at 9:30, beating goaltender Gilbert. The Canadiens went on to win the Cup.

Although he only coached in Boston for five years, Cherry is one of the Bruins' best-known bench bosses. An engaging, entertaining personality who would go on to great success as a television personality in Canada, Cherry had the perspective of a minor league lifer, which he was—he played just one game in the NHL, for the Bruins in the 1955 play-offs.

He played three-and-a-half years for Shore's Springfield team, and told of being made to skate around the rink for four hours and 20 minutes, after Shore caught him peeking at the clock during a practice. In another story, he recalled, "One time, at Rochester, I'm playing for Joe Crozier and I say, 'Joe, I think ...' and Joe says, 'Grapes, don't think. You'll hurt the club.'"

By the end of the 1978-79 season, Cherry's relationship with Sinden had deteriorated, and he was replaced by Fred Creighton. There followed a succession of coaches, including Sinden to close out both the 1980 and 1985 campaigns.

Cherry was the only Bruins coach to win the Jack Adams Award as coach of the year, in 1975-76.

The Bourque Era

The Bruins ensured their continued success in 1979 when they selected Ray Bourque in the first round, eighth overall, of the amateur draft. Bourque proved to be the best player in the draft that year, becoming the first non-goaltender to win the Calder Trophy and to be named a first-team all-star in the same season. His 17 goals and 48 assists broke Orr's rookie records, and in his first few seasons he accepted the blueline mantle from Park. Middleton and linemate Barry Pederson were Boston's scoring stars when Bourque broke in, but in 1984-85 Bourque led the team in scoring for the first of five seasons.

But scoring is only part of Bourque's game: asked which player he'd rather have if he could choose between Orr and Bourque, Sinden once said that if he were behind he'd take Orr, and if he were ahead he'd take Bourque. That's testament to Bourque's worth, as was the $1.3 million contract he signed in 1990, making him the Bruins' first million-dollar-a-year player. The Bruins have finished in first place in the Adams Division five times during Bourque's tenure, and have twice gone to the Stanley Cup finals.

Although the NHL's playoff structure (which allows a vast majority of the league's teams to compete for the Stanley Cup) taints the accomplishment of making it to post-season play every season since 1967-68, the Bruins' streak of 26 years without a losing season is second only to

Montreal's run of 32 years between 1951-52 and 1982-83.

Another shrewd Sinden deal paid off for Boston in 1986, when he dealt Pederson, nearing the end of his career, to the Vancouver Canucks for little-used Cam Neely, a powerful young right winger who led the Bruins in scoring twice and in goals five times. Sinden also picked up a draft pick in that deal, which turned out to be talented defenseman Glen Wesley.

Sinden had signed goaltender Reggie Lemelin as a free agent before the 1987-88 season, which turned out to be fortuitous in that season's play-offs. With Lemelin stifling Montreal's offense, the Bruins snapped their string of 18 series losses to the Canadiens, beating them in five games in the Adams Division finals. Lemelin's play-off goals-against average was 2.63, best in the league.

Under coach Terry O'Reilly, the Bruins also defeated Buffalo and the New Jersey Devils as they advanced to the Stanley Cup final in the 1987-88 season, against an Edmonton Oilers team that was in the process of winning five Cups in seven years. The Oilers dispatched Boston in four games.

Two footnotes to those play-offs: 1) New Jersey coach (and former Bruin) Jim Schoenfeld pushed referee Don Koharski after a game, and non-NHL officials worked as referee and linesmen during a one-game protest when the NHL didn't discipline Schoenfeld; and 2) a final series game was cancelled after a blackout at the Boston Garden in mid-game.

Late in that season, the Bruins dealt young goaltender Bill Ranford to Edmonton for veteran Andy Moog, who shared the duties with Lemelin and eventually supplanted him as the team's top goalie.

In 1989-90, the Bruins got another shot at the Oilers in the finals. This time they were dispatched in five games. The Bruins had the NHL's best record that year, but couldn't match the Oilers' offensive firepower and swifter speed. They were also burned by their former goaltender, Ranford, who was named play-off MVP.

A hit to Neely's knee during the 1991 playoffs caused him to develop an unusual condition in which muscle calcified, and he missed much of the next two seasons, though he returned for the end of the season and the play-offs in 1992-93.

Sinden had traded disgruntled Craig Janney to St. Louis for holdout Adam Oates in a 1991-92 deal, with the idea of pairing Oates with Neely. Though the plan never worked out, Oates did lead the team in scoring with 45 goals and 96 assists in 1992-93, when the Bruins had the league's best record. That season ended abruptly, with a first-round sweep to the Buffalo Sabres. Three of the games were decided in overtime.

SOURCES

BOOKS

Beddoes, Richard, Stan Fischler, and Ira Gitler, *Hockey! The Story of the World's Fastest Sport,* Macmillan, 1969.

Cheevers, Gerry, with Trent Frayne, *Goaltender,* Dodd, Mead, 1971.

Coleman, Charles L., *The Trail of the Stanley Cup,* National Hockey League, volume 1, 1966; volume 2, 1969.

Devaney, John, *We Love You Bruins, Boston's Gashouse Gang From Eddie Shore to Bobby Orr,* Sport Magazine Press, 1972.

Eskenazi, Gerald, *Hockey,* Follett, 1969.

Fischler, Stan, *Bobby Orr and the Big, Bad Bruins,* Dodd, Mead, 1969.

Fischler, Stan, *Golden Ice: The Greatest Teams in Hockey History,* Wynwood Press, 1990.

Fischler, Stan, *Those Were The Days, The Lore of Hockey by The Legends of The Game,* Dodd, Mead, 1976.

Fischler, Stan and Shirley Fischler, *Great Book of*

AP/Wide World Photos

Cam Neely

Hockey: More Than 100 Years of Fire on Ice, Publications International, 1991.

Hollander, Zander and Bock, Hal, editors, *The Complete Encyclopedia of Ice Hockey,* revised edition, Prentice-Hall, 1974.

Jones, Thomas C., editor, with Buck Dawson, *The Halls of Fame,* J.G. Ferguson Publishing Co., 1977.

McFarlane, Brian, *50 Years of Hockey: A History of the National Hockey League,* Pagurian Press Limited (Toronto).

McFarlane, Brian, *The Stanley Cup,* Pagurian Press Limited.

National Hockey League Official Guide & Record Book 1992-93, National Hockey League, 1992.

New York Times Encyclopedia of Sports, New York Times Publishing Co., 1979.

Orr, Frank, *Hockey Stars of the 70s,* Putnam, 1973.

Romain, Joseph and Dan Diamond, *The Pictorial History of Hockey,* Gallery Books, 1987.

Ronberg, Gary, *The Ice Men: The Violent World of Professional Hockey,* Crown Publishers, 1973.

Sanderson, Derek with Stan Fischler, *I've Got To Be Me,* Dodd, Mead, 1970.

Sinden, Harry and Dick Grace, *The Picture History of the Boston Bruins, from Shore to Orr and the Years in Between,* Bobbs-Merrill, 1976.

PERIODICALS

Boston Globe, various dates in April and May of 1970; April 15, 1993.

Boston Magazine, March 1992.

Maclean's, November 6, 1989.

Sports Illustrated, April 25, 1988; May 16, 1988; April 1, 1991; May 18, 1992.

OTHER

Boston Bruins Guide and Record Book, 1973-74, 1991-92, 1992-93; *Bruins History I, II and III* (article on file with Boston Bruins for publication as needed) by Heidi Holland; and assorted newspaper and game program clips from the New England Sports Museum, dated 1944-46.

—*Steve Marantz*

BUFFALO SABRES

When the National Hockey League doubled its size in 1967-68, Buffalo was most unhappy to be left on the sidelines. A town on the edge of Canadian hockey territory, the western New York city had knowledgeable fans and a tradition of following the sport. Paradoxically, these very assets worked against them. The Toronto Maple Leafs were apparently afraid that their hold on the television audience on both sides of Lake Erie would be diminished, while Chicago Blackhawks' owner James Norris was even more direct in his put-down of the would-be NHL city.

"I don't want a town named Buffalo playing in my building," Norris is quoted as saying in Gerald Eskenazi's *A Thinking Man's Guide to Pro Hockey*. Twenty-five years later, more than one NHL owner or general manager might make the same assertion but for quite different reasons. Since the Buffalo Sabres joined the NHL for the 1970-71 season, they have almost always iced powerful teams.

They had the good fortune of picking Gilbert Perreault in the 1970 entry draft, and right from the start the Sabres have had the support of fanatic fans in a grand old building. Beyond that, the Sabres have made the most of their opportunities during more than two decades of NHL excellence. The only thing that hasn't come their way is a Stanley Cup, but you can make that statement about a fair number of hockey's top professional teams.

By choosing Perreault in 1970, Rick Martin and Craig Ramsay in 1971, and Jim Schoenfeld in 1972, the Sabres quickly established themselves as top-flight judges of talent. Guided by coaches who already were, or would ultimately prove to be legendary, the franchise got a kick start into the NHL wars and has rarely lost momentum.

George (Punch) Imlach, a coach who had restored the headiest of days to the Maple Leafs, was the initial leader of the 1970-71 expansion Sabres. He signed on as both coach and general manager but he knew full well that there is only one end to which an NHL leader comes.

"As a coach or general manager, for that matter, you must always remember that when you're on your way in, you're on your way out," Imlach says in Dan Diamond's *The Official NHL 75th Anniversary Commemorative Book*. "It all depends on how fast the old wheel is turning because your only end is the boot into the street."

For all that, Imlach had a method when he put together the first Buffalo team. Having won the lottery to get the first pick (Perreault) in the 1970 entry draft, the veteran mentor dealt with Detroit for a veteran goalie, Roger Crozier, and added some other experienced players to the first Buffalo team. That paid off when Phil Goyette produced a 15-46-61 point season, while Eddie Shack scored 25 goals for the initial Sabres.

Perreault, destined to become an all-time great, was better than any of the vets (38-34-72) but the presence of some old hands helped the Buffalo club earn a fifth place Eastern Division finish, better than expansion Vancouver and long-time NHL member Detroit.

Crozier's first season in Buffalo was better than the record indicated. He finished 9-20-7, but had a 3.69 goals-against average. Perreault won the Calder Trophy as rookie of the year.

Proof that the Buffalo front office knew what it was doing came in the entry draft of 1971. The Sabres tabbed Rick Martin with the fifth overall pick, then landed Craig Ramsay with the 19th choice. Both players were to prove cornerstones of the franchise. A year later the organization named Jim Schoenfeld with the fifth selection to complete a remarkable first three years of drafting. He, too, became a fixture on Buffalo ice.

Imlach didn't survive the club's second year, coaching for 41 games before Joe Crozier was called behind the bench to handle the last 36 games of a 16-43-19 season. As so often has happened, once the euphoria of the first expansion year wore off, the franchise found itself struggling in year two. The Sabres were sixth in the Eastern Division that season, still better than expansion partner Vancouver, but they were by no means a team in trouble.

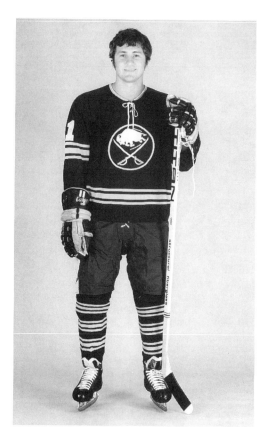

Hockey Hall of Fame

Gilbert Perreault

Martin, who broke in with a 44-30-74 year that was equal to Perreault's 26-48-74 point total, finished second in the Calder Trophy voting, while both Crozier and Dave Dryden performed well enough in the nets for the cognoscenti to recognize that the 51-point year was just a blip on the radar screen.

The Mixture Gets Richer

Led by Perreault's 88-point season and a 40-game outburst from Rene Robert, who had been obtained near the end of the previous season in a deal with Pittsburgh for Shack, the Sabres put up their first winning numbers in 1972-73. Crozier coached the club to a 37-27-14 mark, good for

TEAM INFORMATION AT A GLANCE

Founding date: 1970

On December 2, 1969, Buffalo was granted an expansion franchise for the 1970-71 season

Home ice: Memorial Auditorium
140 Main St.
Buffalo, NY 14202
Phone: (716) 856-7300

Dimensions: 196 X 85 feet
Seating capacity: 16,433

Team colors: Blue, white, and gold
Team nickname: Sabres
Logo: A charging buffalo poised between two crossed swords

Franchise record	Won	Lost	Tie
(1970-93)	866	674	296

Stanley Cup Wins: None
Division First-Place Finishes (3): 1974-75, 1979-80, 1980-81
Division Last-Place Finishes (2): 1985-86, 1986-87

fourth place in the East and a first crack at Stanley Cup action. That didn't last long, Montreal eliminating Buffalo in six games, but there was the satisfaction of having joined the better clubs in the NHL.

That same season saw Perreault finish fifth in the NHL in assists and win the Lady Byng Trophy, emblematic of excellence and gentlemanly play. Martin showed that his rookie year was no aberration, scoring 37 goals and adding 36 assists. Robert finished on 40-43-83 and Jim Lorentz, who would make annual contributions to the club, had 27 goals and 35 assists.

Roger Crozier finished fourth in the NHL in goals-against-average (2.76 after a 23-13-7 season) and Dave Dryden contributed a winning year,

as well. He was 14-13-7 with a 2.65 gaa, a preface to his fine 1973-74 campaign.

Despite an even better year from Martin in 1973-74 the Sabres couldn't overcome the loss of Perreault to a broken leg after 55 games. Without their big gun, the Sabres fell to 32-34-12, good just for fifth place in the East. That was hard luck for Martin, whose 52 goals placed him second behind NHL leader Phil Esposito's 68.

Robert, too, had a second strong season while Don Luce and Lorentz also finished well. Dryden went 23-20-8 (2.97) for the season. When it was all over, the Sabres proved once again that they knew how to take advantage of the NHL's entry draft. This time they picked Danny Gare with the 29th selection. He, too, would prove a gem.

With Floyd Smith replacing Crozier behind the bench and Perreault back at full speed, the 1974-75 season turned heavenly for Buffalo's fans. A popular movie of the era, *The French Connection,* gave its name to the Sabres' top line: Martin, Perreault, and Robert. The trio was almost unstoppable in a 49-16-15 season that gave Buffalo the first Adams Division title and carried the Sabres right to the Stanley Cup finals. Robert led the way with 40-60-100, while Perreault went 39-57-96 and Martin finished 52-43-95. He was third in goal-scoring that year.

Ramsay, too, was emerging as one of the top defensive forwards in the game, without sacrificing his value on attack. He went 26-38-64 while companion Don Luce, the Masterton Trophy winner that season, was 33-43-76 and a remarkable plus-61.

There were big contributions from Rick Dudley and Lorentz, and from the defensemen Jocelyn Guevremont and Jim Schoenfeld, too. Roger Crozier was spectacular in goal (17-2-1, 2.62) partnered by Gary Bromley, who finished 26-11-11 (3.10) in his only full season with the Sabres.

The playoffs turned out to be memorable, not only because Buffalo got all the way to the final round, but also because that dramatic series against the Philadelphia Flyers became known as "The Fog Bowl." Buffalo featured comedic scenes of players skating around the ice with large towels as they tried to disperse a rising fog which made play impossible. It apparently didn't occur to the folks who ran the NHL that their playoffs might be running too deep into the spring.

The Stanley Cup playoffs began with a 4-1 rout of Chicago, then continued with a 4-2 victory over Montreal. The last opponent was the Flyers, then in their Broad Street Bullies image, anchored by the remarkable Bernie Parent in goal. Games three and four were plagued by the warm weather in upstate New York, but nothing interrupted the Flyers' concentration. They won in six games.

One could argue that Buffalo still won the spring, however. As they had done in the past, the Sabres used the NHL entry draft to demonstrate their front office acumen, naming goaltender Bob Sauve with the 17th pick of the first round. He would one day lead the NHL in shutouts and put up goals-against numbers that ranked with the best in the game.

Gare Gets 50

Danny Gare came up in the 1975-76 season with a 50-goal effort that placed him sixth overall in NHL scoring and added to the idea that the Sabres drafted as well or better than anybody else in the business. Imlach, a wily veteran who had forgotten more hockey than most coaches and general managers knew, was still the general manager in this era.

That 1975-76 team, again coached by Smith, finished second in the Adams Division after a 46-21-13 season. Perreault finished third in the NHL with 69 assists and 113 points, while the other pieces of the French Connection line performed at their usual high standard. Martin collected 49 goals and Robert added 35. Ramsay (22-49-71) and Luce (21-49-70) gave strong assistance while defensemen Guevremont (12-40-52) and Jerry Korab (13-28-41) played their parts, too. Gerry Desjardins, who had played with three other clubs, came to Buffalo and went 29-15-11 (2.95) in goal.

The playoffs produced a first round win over St. Louis, but the Sabres fell to the emerging New York Islanders, 4-2, after winning the first two games of the second round series. In the 1976-77 post-season play the Islanders were again in the way, spoiling another excellent regular campaign. Smith guided the team to a 48-24-8 season, second again in the Adams. Perreault was now an acknowledged superstar, finishing fifth in the league with 95 points, while Martin (65) and Robert (73) continued to play the perfect supporting cast. Desjardins was fourth in the league with his 2.63 gaa after a 31-12-6 season, while Don Edwards, soon to become a major Buffalo star, made his first contributions. He was 16-7-2 (2.51) and clearly the goalie of the future along with the promising Sauve.

After defeating Minnesota in two games to open the playoffs, the Sabres fell in four straight to the Isles. Therefore it was once again the spring and the NHL entry draft that were the most memorable parts of the season. This time the pick was Ric Seiling, chosen 14th in the first round, adding another future regular to the Buffalo lineup.

While Buffalo success on the ice was gaining notice, the atmosphere inside the Memorial Auditorium—an imposing WPA project of the 1940s that was expanded to 16,000-plus capacity when the Sabres came into the NHL—was also part of the reason why Sabres' hockey made such an impact on the National Hockey League.

The rink's seats—for some reason painted a bright yellow—fall sharply from the roof in a cascade of fluorescence, giving spectators at the top level a sense that they are about to plunge straight down onto the center face-off circle. For those who don't have a fear of heights the view is breathtaking, affording a look at all of the patterns of the game.

The rink is also compact, shorter than regulation by ten feet and seemingly as constricted as the old Boston Garden. Games in the Aud are often noted for their banging in the corners; in recent seasons, Buffalo has made a greater effort, like the Bruins, to fit the team to its home surroundings. In the early days, quick skaters like Perreault and Martin may actually have been hindered by their own home ice.

Smith was gone for the 1977-78 season, succeeded by Marcel Pronovost. The Sabres hardly missed a beat, gaining another Adams Division second spot with 44 wins and 105 points. Perreault connected on 21.4 per cent of his shots that year to score 44 goals while Gare had 39. Craig Ramsay made his debut with 28-43-71 numbers and Edwards (38-16-17, 2.64, five shutouts) was fifth best among NHL goaltenders. The playoffs produced what was becoming a bad habit: a first round win (over the Rangers this time), then a second round elimination (to the Flyers).

Still, Buffalo fans could look at the spring with a smile. They had drafted Larry Playfair 13th and Tony McKegney with the 32nd choice. Arguably, no one else in hockey has come close to matching the Sabres when it comes to picking the youngsters. Every spring they seemed to pick players who would ultimately turn into effective NHL pros. Other teams were fortunate if they grabbed a winner every couple of seasons.

Pronovost was replaced by Bill Inglis after 24 games of the 1978-79 season, when the Sabres won 36 games and finished second again in the Adams. Inglis's presence couldn't alter the recent playoff hex, however; this time Pittsburgh sidelined the Sabres in the preliminary round. Ric Seiling made his first NHL impact that year with 20 goals and 22 assists, Edwards was outstanding in goal again (16-18-9, 3.02), and Sauve took his turn on a more regular basis, going 10-10-7, 3.73. The draft proved beneficial once again, Buffalo naming Mike Ramsey and Lindy Ruff. These were two more players who would provide depth and skill for the future.

The Bowman Era Begins

The Sabres made a pair of major changes in 1979-80, ushering in a new era of success in Buffalo. First, Scotty Bowman, who had won four Stanley Cups in Montreal, was hired away from the Canadiens to the dual role of General Manager-Coach in Buffalo. His top priority was to tighten the Sabres' defense, so he gambled by trading a part of The French Connection, Rene Robert, to Colorado for 27-year-old John van Boxmeer, a 6-foot, 190-pound backliner.

Both moves paid immediate dividends: Bowman's first Buffalo team won the Adams Division with a 47-17-6 record and reached the Prince of Wales Conference playoff finals before losing to the New York Islanders. The defense was so much better that the goal-tending tandem of Sauve and Edwards finished first and second, respectively in the NHL and collected the Vezina Trophy. Sauve had a 20-8-4 record, a 2.36 goals-against average and four shutouts, while Edwards was 27-9-12 and 2.57.

Gare was one of three players to score 56

goals that season, finishing level with Hartford's Blaine Stoughton and Los Angeles' Charlie Simmer in the goal-scoring race. Perreault (40-66-106) was fourth in both assists and points while Schoenfeld's 60-plus figure led the league in that important statistical category.

Bowman turned to Roger Neilson for the head-coaching role the next season, concentrating, himself, on the administrative side. Although it lasted just one year, Neilson's presence in Buffalo confirmed the notions that the Sabres had risen to a position of power in the league because of precision planning and hard work.

Bowman had hired Neilson as associate coach for the 1979-80 season and persuaded his former player in both St. Louis and Montreal, Jimmy Roberts, to come on as an assistant. When Bowman left coaching—temporarily as it turned out—Neilson and Roberts were already in place to maintain the organization's continuity.

In addition, Neilson was one of the "new breed" of NHL coaches, a mentor willing to take the game apart for his players through the use of technology. His passion for reviewing tapes earned him the nickname Captain Video, but it also helped him to produce winning teams in a long coaching career with several NHL clubs.

Frank Orr, the veteran Toronto hockey writer, got to know Neilson during his coaching stop with the Maple Leafs. Writing in *NHL: The World of Professional Hockey*, Orr described the attention to detail which made Neilson different: "Neilson does much more with video tapes of games than a simple overview. He breaks them down carefully into a statistical rating of the Sabre players' performances and retapes from them highlights in specific areas." Neilson, himself, liked to take collections of tape on special teams and splice them together so that players could study their strengths and weaknesses. He was also noted for preparing extensive pre-game reports on the opposition.

Bowman, too, was an innovator. He was the first NHL bench coach to use two-way radio to keep in touch with upstairs spotters, Roberts in the case of the Sabres. Schoenfeld, who had been reared in the more traditional manner of hockey coaches, told Orr he was skeptical at first about the new approaches, but quickly learned to value them. Schoenfeld admitted that after a while he relied on Roberts' observations from high above the ice, even asking questions if he needed specific information about the opposition's tactics.

Bowman's stay with the Sabres' front office lasted through the 1986-87 season, by which time much of what he had brought to Buffalo was being mimicked around the NHL. He later spent some time as a successful television analyst before returning to coaching duties with the Stanley Cup champion Pittsburgh Penguins of the early 1990's. His penchant for controlling the organization in which he worked never faltered, either; in 1993, Bowman left what many considered the best team in the league, the Penguins, for Detroit and another opportunity to try his ideas out in the competitive NHL world.

Over the five seasons between 1980-81 and 1984-85, the Sabres always produced a winning team but never went as far in the playoffs as they would have liked. Bowman had three different spells as coach, and Neilson and Roberts had one apiece. The organization continued to make excellent draft selections and had as much depth as any, but the club had the misfortune to be playing in what most observers thought was the NHL's toughest division, the Adams.

Starting in 1981-82, the league had realigned its schedule and playoff structure in an attempt to "create rivalries" and bring some order to the geographical structure after several years of expansion and the eventual absorption of four teams from the old World Hockey Association.

The Adams wound up with the Sabres, Boston Bruins, Hartford Whalers, Montreal Canadiens, and Quebec Nordiques. The Bruins and Canadiens had always been powerful NHL franchises, riding the wave of their glorious histories and adapting effectively to changes in the game. Quebec and Hartford were newcomers from the WHA who proved tougher than many expected; the Nordiques turned into a power when they lured the three Stastny brothers away from the Czech national team at a time when East European players were not free to leave their countries; the Whalers had an era of success when they hired the wily Emile Francis away from St. Louis to rebuild their struggling team.

As a result, just getting out of the Adams Division playoffs was a struggle that some observers felt left the winners exhausted before they reached the New York Islanders or Edmonton Oilers. For Buffalo, those Adams playoffs were particularly frustrating.

The Bruins were in the way in 1981-82, winning a first round series in four games; a year later the Sabres swept past Montreal in a first round upset but again were halted by the Bruins, losing the seventh game of the Adams final struggle in overtime in the Boston Garden; then Quebec administered the bad medicine in two consecutive seasons. The playoff miseries were that much more annoying because the Sabres continued to add star players through their successful drafts.

Housley, Barrasso Arrive

The 1982 draft saw Buffalo tap an American high school player, Phil Housley, from South Saint Paul, Minnesota. He was the number six selection in a first round when the Sabres had three picks. They went on to claim Paul Cyr and Dave Andreychuk to complete a good haul. Housley, a quick, shifty defenseman who could play equally well at the back or as a winger, immediately made an impact with 66 points in his first season in the league.

Buoyed by that success, the Sabres gambled on another American high school kid in 1983, striking gold again when they chose goalie Tom Barrasso with the fifth selection. This draft also included Adam Creighton, John Tucker, and way down, far from the super-hyped top five, Christian Ruuttu. A Finnish center, he was chosen on Buffalo's ninth pick, the 134th overall selection. Ruuttu would not arrive until 1986-87 but the wait

Tom Barrasso

proved worthwhile.

Barrasso's selection made him the third American-born player taken in the top five of the 1983 draft. Brian Lawton, a Rhode Island prep school player, had gone to Minnesota with the number one choice, while Pat Lafontaine, a Detroit area youngster who had gone to Verdun in the Quebec Major Junior Hockey League for his final honing, was the third pick in that remarkable amateur draft.

In his final season at Acton-Boxboro High School, Barrasso had yielded only 17 goals in 23 games (0.73 gaa) and recorded ten shutouts. At 6-feet, 3-inches and 210 pounds he was both big and quick, but there were not many people who believed an American kid could jump right out of a high school net into the Vezina Trophy. Barrasso did exactly that in a fine 1983-84 season.

Bowman was back behind the bench by now, en route to establishing his still-escalating NHL record of wins by a coach. He split the season between the rookie and Bob Sauve, Barrasso appearing in 42 games and compiling a 2.84 goals-against average while Sauve was 3.49 in 40 matches. Barrasso not only collected the Vezina off that performance, he also was named the league rookie of the year and added the Calder Trophy to his cabinet as well. Bowman finished runner-up in coach of the year voting.

The next season, when Bowman officially passed Dick Irvin's total of 690 victories, Barrasso and Sauve combined to lead the league in netminding when the Sabres went 38-28-14 and finished third behind Montreal and Quebec in a tough Adams race.

Craig Ramsay, who had been runner-up three

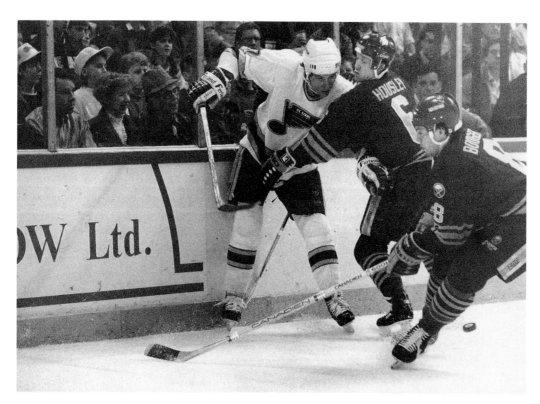

AP/Wide World Photos

Phil Housley (center) and Doug Bodger (8) double-team Blues' Gino Cavallini

times before, finally won the Frank Selke Trophy, given to the forward who "best excels in the defensive aspects of the game" while Barrasso and Sauve shared the Jennings Trophy, annually awarded to the club with the best goaltending record. That award, created for the 1982 season, recognized that goalies now worked in pairs; the Vezina Trophy, remained to honor the top individual as selected by the league's general managers.

Great Careers End

The Sabres fell off in 1985-86 and 1986-87, a pair of fifth place finishes marking the end of the Bowman era. Schoenfeld, Bowman, Ramsay, and Ted Sator all took a turn as coach before Sator was teamed with a new general manager, Gerry Meehan at the start of the 1987-88 campaign.

Before that, however, three of the Sabres' cornerstones wound up distinguished careers. In 1984-85, Ramsay retired after 14 seasons of excellence. He had pulled on a Buffalo sweater for 1,070 regular season games, scored 252 goals, and garnered 420 assists, but he would always be best known for his defensive skills and tenacity, which characterized much of the Buffalo spirit.

That same season, Schoenfeld, the big redheaded defenseman, called it quits after stops in Detroit and Boston followed his stay in Buffalo. He played a total of 719 NHL games, earning the reputation of a solid defenseman who could handle the high-pressure situations.

The 1986-87 year marked the conclusion of Gilbert Perreault's wonderful 17-year NHL career. The Sabres' first draft choice left an indelible print on the club where he had been the first superstar and lived up to all of the high expectations. Over those 17 seasons, Perreault played in 1,191 games, scored 512 goals and collected 814 assists for 1326 points. All stand today as Buffalo team records.

Perreault also rolled up 113 points in 1975-76 to set the club record for a center, had three five-assist games, a feat equalled only by Dale Hawerchuk, and enjoyed one seven-point outburst to

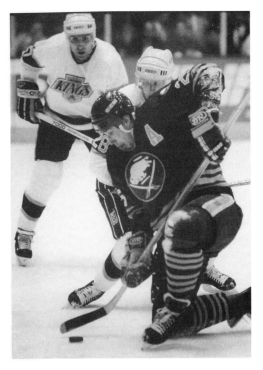

AP/Wide World Photos

Dave Andreychuk (in foreground)

establish a Buffalo record. He was elected to the Hockey Hall of Fame in 1990.

Of course, for much of Perreault's career in Buffalo he was accompanied by Martin and Robert, each of whom posted impressive career numbers. Martin's 11 seasons in Buffalo and Los Angeles produced 384 goals in 685 games, while Robert, who played with four teams in 12 NHL seasons, finished with 284 goals in 744 appearances. The big days of The French Connection, naturally, played a key part in those achievements.

Enter the New Stars

There may have been poetic justice when Perreault's retirement came at the end of the 1986-87 season. Buffalo had the first overall pick in the 1987 NHL entry draft and used it to select Pierre Turgeon, a 6-foot, 1-inch, 200-pound center who had racked up 154 points in his last season with Granby in the QMJHL. Within three years, Turgeon would be putting up 100-point NHL seasons.

In 1987-88, however, the impetus for recovery came from several new sources. They included Andreychuk, now a veteran of five NHL seasons after being picked in that strong 1982 draft; Christian Ruuttu, that remarkable ninth round choice in 1983; Housley; and another rookie, Ray Sheppard.

Sheppard had been picked 60th in the 1984 draft, another of those players the Sabres were so adept at finding in the later rounds. He stayed in junior hockey with Cornwall through 1985-86, winning OHL Player of the Year honors in 1986 when he led the league with 81 goals and 142 points. He then spent a season with Rochester in the American Hockey League before coming to

Buffalo to win a place on the NHL All-Rookie team and finish runner-up in the race for the Calder Trophy.

Turgeon made his NHL debut that season, getting 14 goals and 28 assists. It would be 1989-90 before he made his full impact on the league. The season also included another honor for Barrasso—he was runner-up in Vezina Trophy voting after a 54-game, 3.31 season. The return to playoff action brought an old story, however: the Sabres lost a first round Adams series to the Boston Bruins, 4-2.

Sator's in the Tradition

Ted Sator had taken control of the Sabres's coaching chores on December 22, 1986, succeed-

Alex Mogilny (center)

ing Craig Ramsay. Although just 37 at the time, he was already a coaching veteran. And, like Bowman and Neilson before him, he was a coach with a different background and approach to the game. In that sense he fit neatly into the already-established Buffalo pattern.

Sator, a native of Utica, New York, had cut his coaching teeth in Europe, building a successful program in the Swedish Elite League, where he won five consecutive titles. He moved to the Philadelphia Flyers in 1984-85 as an assistant to Mike Keenan, working with a club that reached the Stanley Cup finals. Then it was on to a stint with the New York Rangers before he moved to Buffalo.

The Sabres improved by 25 points in Sator's first full season, then came home with almost an identical record in 1988-89. That team won 38 games and finished third in the Adams. Turgeon broke through to the top level with a 34-54-88 campaign, Ruuttu contributed 60 points, and Housley was still on the mark with a 26-44-70 season.

There was one scary scene that year, however—Malarchuk suffered a partially severed jugular vein in a goalmouth collision. The goalie admitted in *The Sporting News Hockey Guide and Register, 1989-90* that he didn't realize the seriousness of the accident until he noticed that "as my heart would beat, it would squirt blood. I thought I was dying."

Change was in the air, however, as the Sabres moved to remake their club. In the off-season, Rick Dudley, who had played 279 games in Buffalo from 1972-1981, returned to the club as head coach after a seven-year minor-league apprenticeship. Dudley never had a losing season behind the bench during stops in the Atlantic Coast Hockey League's Carolina Thunderbirds, the International Hockey League's Flint Generals, and the American Hockey League's New Haven Nighthawks.

He took over a team that included one of the most sought-after and controversial players to come into the NHL in several seasons. Russian Alexander Mogilny, who had burst onto the international scene as a star player in World Junior

Tournaments. Mogilny didn't wait for the NHL and the old Soviet hockey federation authorities to smooth all the pathways for players to move across the Atlantic. Instead, he opted to leave on his own, signing with Buffalo while still claimed as property by the Russian Army club, CSKA.

The 20-year-old Mogilny took a while to adjust to the longer NHL schedule and the rigors of adapting to a new culture, but did contribute 15 goals in 65 games during his first season. By his third full campaign, which brought 39 goals and 45 assists, there were no longer any questions about the talent which was pointing him toward super-stardom.

Turgeon led that 45-27-8 club to a second place Adams Division finish with a 106-point season, while both Andreychuk and Housley collected 81. It was to be the final season in Buffalo for Housley, his eight years as a Sabre star ending when he was involved in a major trade with the Winnipeg Jets. The Sabres sent their star defenseman to the Jets in exchange for center Dale Hawerchuk, a player whose status in Manitoba was the equal of Housley's in Buffalo.

Hawerchuk immediately contributed an 89-point season in 1990-91, Turgeon chipped in with 79, and the Sabres made it two straight winning years to keep Dudley's coaching record perfect. But the Sabres still couldn't find playoff success, losing in the first round both seasons to their old nemesis, the Montreal Canadiens.

Dudley began the 1991-92 season but didn't finish it: John Muckler, the former coach at Edmonton, replaced him in a year that included another blockbuster trade. This time it was Turgeon on the move, sent to the New York Islanders in exchange for Pat Lafontaine, the superstar forward who had been involved in a lengthy contract dispute on Long Island. It turned out to be a trade that helped both teams, Lafontaine fitting neatly into a Buffalo team that now had Hawerchuk and Mogilny going full speed, while Turgeon helped the rebuilding Islanders to reach the Stanley Cup semifinals a year after the big deal.

In 1992-93, Buffalo finally shook off the playoff bug which had plagued them, sweeping regular season champion Boston in the first round of the Adams Division playoffs. They were then swept, themselves, by eventual champion Montreal in a remarkably close series. Every game was decided by a single goal, three of them going into overtime.

Thus, when the Sabres promoted Meehan to a front office administrative job and gave Muckler control of the club in the summer of 1993, there was a renewed sense of optimism on the shores of Lake Erie.

SOURCES

BOOKS

Diamond, Dan, *The Official National Hockey League 75th Anniversary Commemorative Book,* NHL Publications, 1991.

Eskenazi, Gerald, *A Thinking Man's Guide to Pro Hockey,* E.P. Dutton, 1972.

Fischler, Stan and Shirley Fischler, *The Hockey Encyclopedia,* MacMillan, 1983.

Greenberg, Jay, Frank Orr, and Gary Ronberg, *NHL: The World of Professional Hockey,* Rutledge Press, 1981.

Romain, Joseph and Dan Diamond, *The Pictorial History of Hockey,* Gallery Books, 1987.

PERIODICALS

Calabria, Pat, "1984-85 Season Review," *The Sporting News Hockey Guide and Register.*

Matheson, Jim, "Season Reviews," *The Sporting News Hockey Guide & Register,* 1986-87, 1989-90.

—*Jerry Trecker* for Book Builders, Inc.

HARTFORD WHALERS

Since the early 1900s, U.S. hockey teams across the country have faced off, competing against each other and against Canada's reputation for having the best teams in the world. In the history of hockey, the Hartford Whalers, formerly the New England Whalers, constitute a relatively new team. Although the Whalers have struggled through their seasons, they gained notoriety through such legendary greats as Gordie Howe and Emile "The Cat" Francis as well as through their successful transition from the World Hockey Association to the National Hockey League.

As one of four teams to survive the turbulent years of the WHA and to merge with the NHL in 1979-80, the Whalers owed much of their early existence to the persistence and vision of Howard Baldwin, who not only charted the team's early course but wound up guiding the WHA through its final days. Very much an example of hockey's "new breed" of leaders, Baldwin insisted that creative salesmanship and a solid effort could make

hockey successful in one of the league's smallest markets.

Along the way, the Whalers got the backing of one of Hartford's major insurers, Aetna, and financial support from a number of corporations. They were part of the revitalization of the downtown business area, the major tenants in the new Hartford Civic Center.

It was that same Civic Center roof which collapsed under the weight of heavy, rain-fed snow on January 18, 1978, but the team survived even that catastrophe to enter the NHL. Their later trials and tribulations might seem minor compared to being left homeless, but the national economic downturn in the late 1980s hit Connecticut particularly hard and threatened the Whalers' existence once again. Baldwin had moved on to Minnesota and Pittsburgh, the club changing hands twice before Richard Gordon assumed total control.

In 1992-93, with the club struggling both on the ice and at the gate, the Whalers were the subject of rumors that they would be relocated, but Gordon pledged to keep the team in Hartford while negotiations with the state and city on a new Civic Center lease carried on into the summer. For long-time fans of the team, it was no more than another chapter in a story which had seen the club make the most out of situations where others might well have thrown in the towel.

Not Easy in Boston

The Whalers faced a major challenge right from day one. Baldwin, John Coburn, Godfrey Wood, and Bill Barnes had been awarded the franchise in November, 1971; they elected to challenge the Boston Bruins for hockey attention in a city where interest in the sport was high. They named the veteran Boston University coach Jack Kelley as the team's first coach and general manager and set about the business of trying to win hockey games and fans.

As might be imagined, the Whalers didn't get prime dates at the venerable Boston Garden, where they found themselves in a line behind both the Bruins and the NBA's Boston Celtics. Still, the on-ice product did just fine, winning the first WHA title by defeating Winnipeg in the championship playoffs. Tom Webster led the attack with 53 goals while Terry Caffrey won WHA Rookie of the Year honors with a 100-point season.

But the WHA and the Whalers didn't exactly win major attention in Boston. By April of 1974 they had relocated to Springfield, Massachusetts, on their way to their eventual home in Hartford. The move made sense; Hartford was building the new showpiece Civic Center as part of a major city renovation project. Rather than battle for fans in Boston, the Whalers would be the first major league team in Hartford.

Before they moved, however, the Whalers played the 1973-74 year in Boston and fielded a somewhat unique team. The 43-31-4 club finished first in the Eastern Division but bowed to Chicago at the start of the playoffs. What made them unusual, however, was the roster: it contained five players who would one day coach in the NHL. There was Larry Pleau, the first player to sign a Whaler contract, who would ultimately have more than one stay behind the Hartford bench; Don Blackburn, who coached the first NHL team to represent Hartford; Rick Ley, a two-year boss of the Whalers; Teddy Green, who wound up leading the Edmonton Oilers; and Tom Webster, who had the head responsibilities in cities as far apart as New York and Los Angeles.

The move down the Massachusetts Turnpike to Springfield came on April 6, 1974, when the Whalers played their first game as a Hartford entity. They didn't actually debut in the 10,507-seat Civic Center until January 18,1977, however, filling the building for an overtime victory against the San Diego Mariners. That team was coached by loquacious Harry Neale, who spent two years with the club before moving to the Vancouver Canucks.

The 1976-77 year was also notable for the performance of Mike Rogers, who would be one of the team's first stars in its new home. He had moved to the Whalers after a season-and-a-half in Edmonton. His speed and shooting quickly endeared him to Connecticut fans while his statistics confirmed that he was, indeed, a special talent. His first full season produced 25 goals, 57 assists, and 82 points, but the numbers got even better when the club moved to the NHL. Partnered with Blaine Stoughton and Pat Boutette, he put together a pair of 100-plus point seasons.

Neale's first team went 35-40-6, finishing fourth in the WHA East and bowing to Quebec in the first round of the playoffs. His second team was not only better, some would say it was remarkable because of the presence of Gordie Howe and his sons.

The Legend Continues

When Gordie Howe decided to return to professional hockey with the Houston Aeros in 1973-74, critics of the new World Hockey Association took it for evidence that the league could not be compared with the NHL. After all, Howe had

TEAM INFORMATION AT A GLANCE

Founding date: 1971 (as New England Whalers
of WHA); 1979 (NHL)

Home ice: Hartford Civic Center Coliseum
242 Trumbull St., 8th floor
Hartford, CT 06103
Phone (203) 728-3366
FAX: (203) 522-7707

Seating capacity: 15,635

Team colors: Green, blue, and white
Team nickname: Whalers
Logo: Letter "W" with a whale's tail on top of it.

Franchise record	Won	Lost	Tie
(1972-93)	703	795	181

turned 45 on March 31, 1973, and had already completed a hockey career with the Detroit Red Wings.

He had spent 25 years with Detroit, playing his first NHL game in 1946-47 and, for the time being, his last in 1971. Along with Maurice Richard, Gordie Howe was the dominant player in the NHL in its post-World War II heyday. He was always mentioned in the hot stove league arguments whenever anyone asked: "Who is the best ever to play the game?"

What the critics of his return to professional hockey didn't understand was that Howe was not only a remarkable athlete, he was also a remarkable man. Determined to play with his sons, Mark and Marty, and equally determined not to have his great reputation diminished by some type of "cameo" appearance, he whipped himself back into shape, defied time, and proved that he could still make pinpoint passes and take body checks.

He twice went over the 100-point level in Houston before the Whalers lured the family to Hartford on May 23, 1977. By then Hartford had to bid against NHL teams now aware that Gordie was not exactly over the hill.

Howe brought more than his sons to the Whalers; he brought his willingness to promote the sport in an area where—although there were plenty of New York Rangers or Boston Bruins fans—many spectators were new to the game. After his playing days finally ended (following the Whalers' first season in the NHL when Howe was 52 but still fit enough to play in all 80 games) he worked as the club's unofficial public relations chief, always ready to spend time with fans of any age.

Howe also showed his generous appreciation for the sport which had been so much of his life, virtually "adopting" Wayne Gretzky in the 1980s when "The Great One" chased down and eventually surpassed records that once were thought unapproachable. Howe was on hand when Gretzky broke them, often the first to shake the hand of a player who earned comparison with all of the sport's best.

The Roof Falls In

Howe's first year in Hartford showed that he could still play very well. He led the team in scoring (34-62-96), and accompanied a couple of other hockey legends, Dave Keon and John McKenzie, when the team had to pack its goods and move up the road to Springfield once again, following the 4:30 a.m. Civic Center roof collapse.

Fortunately no one was killed in the January 18, 1978, disaster; just hours before there had been a college basketball doubleheader in the building, as the snow, which changed to rain in the middle of the night, fell heavily outside. An incredulous public awoke to the news the next morning. The curious braved the aftermath of the storm to drive past the site in the heart of downtown, and the local papers carried aerial photos of the twisted wreckage.

It might also have wrecked the Whalers as a franchise, to say nothing of the then-ongoing talks between the WHA and the NHL for an accommodation that would finally end the lengthy war between the professional leagues. Credit Baldwin and the rest of the Whalers' administration, the city, and the fans for keeping hockey alive through that dark period.

Only 300 fans canceled their season tickets when it was announced that the team would finish the season in Springfield, about 40 minutes up Interstate 91 from the Connecticut capital. In fact, the Whalers' fans turned the next two years and 19 days into "The I-91 Club," which had grown to 4,200 members by the time the Civic Center welcomed the Whalers back to Hartford.

The city and the hockey club also decided to make something out of the disaster which had struck. While the original Civic Center housed nearly 11,000 fans, the decision was made to not only put a new roof on the edifice, but to make it bigger. That meant that Hartford could be in line for a spot in the NHL if the talks between the leagues ever amounted to something solid. They did, in June, 1979. Hartford was still the "Springfield Whalers" until February 6, 1980, but they were now the NHL Whalers.

They were also Don Blackburn's Whalers, Gordie Howe's and Dave Keon's, too. The veterans gave a special spice to the first NHL season, but it was Rogers, with 44 goals and 105 points, fifth best in the NHL, and Stoughton, whose 56 goals tied him for first in the league that season, who put the gas in the tank. The biggest point-scoring Howe was not Gordie, but Mark, developing into a top defenseman who could also skate as a wing when required. He collected 24 goals and 56 assists to finish with 80 points.

Gordie's last year saw him make a "farewell" tour of his old NHL haunts as well as take his game to the many new cities that had come into the league after he "retired" for the first time. He finished with 15 goals and 26 assists, labeling his game "poetry in slow motion" in those final years. He left with a smile on his face and with even his sharpest critics having to admit that, at more than 50 years-old, he wasn't out of place on the ice.

As it turned out, that first Hartford year in the NHL had been more than a bit misleading. The collection of aging players and a few talented youngsters had managed to make the playoffs with a 27-34-19 mark, but it would be six full seasons and three changes of administration before the fans could cheer for a winning team in their rebuilt Civic Center.

Blackburn didn't last the 1980-81 season, but was replaced after 60 games by Pleau, who took over in March. Pleau had been with the organization since its start, serving as a player and broadcaster, then as assistant coach. In April of 1981 he assumed the additional duties of general manager, replacing Kelley as director of hockey operations.

To put it mildly, Pleau had no honeymoon. The club struggled on the ice in 1981-82, finishing with just 21 wins and 60 points. The next season, Pleau appointed Larry Kish, who had been a successful minor league mentor, to the bench job, but that proved no solution. Pleau, himself, came back to the coach's job after 49 games, eventually surrendering the position to his assistant, John Cunniff, for the final 13 games of the year. That spring he would be replaced by Francis, called in from St. Louis to rebuild a club that had gone from success in the WHA to a 19-54-7 NHL season.

No one ever questioned Pleau's desire to see Hartford produce a winning team, but there were plenty of queries about his lack of front office-experience, especially when some trades went wrong during his dual tenure in office. Rogers, for instance, was sent to the New York Rangers on October 2, 1981, for Chris Kotsopoulos, Gerry McDonald, and Doug Sulliman. Rogers had been the club's leading scorer the past two seasons.

Then, on August 12, 1982, Hartford sent Mark Howe to Philadelphia in a blockbuster trade. The big name in return was the Flyers' feisty forward, Ken Linseman, but he never stopped in Connecticut. Instead, he was sent on to Edmonton for Risto Siltanen, who inherited the task of replacing the popular Howe. Howe had not only escaped from the lengthy shadow of his father to become a great player in his own right, he had also become a figure of great courage in Hartford after he was involved in a bizarre accident that changed the way hockey nets are anchored in the NHL.

Howe slid into the old-style cage and became impaled on the triangular piece which used to be part of the system that secured the then-stationary goal to the ice. It took him almost a full season to come back to his full strength after the accident, which alerted the hockey world to the dangers of a non-movable net. Since then, goal cages have been secured by magnetized pins which allow them to come free when players make hard contact.

It didn't help Pleau's administration when Howe turned into an NHL all-star defenseman in Philadelphia in 1983. There was another deal that rebounded, too, although this one could hardly be blamed on the new general manager. Aware that the Whalers needed to acquire goaltending help, Pleau signed Greg Millen on June 15, 1981, as a

free agent from Pittsburgh. Millen turned out to be a stalwart in some of the Whalers' dark days, but the cost under the old NHL system—there really was no actual free agency—was high. Hartford was forced to yield the rugged Boutette and a promising youngster, Kevin McClelland as "compensation" for Millen's signature.

The combination of questionable trades and just plain bad luck was mitigated somewhat by the 1981 entry draft. Hartford was widely rumored to be seeking the Massachusetts schoolboy star Bobby Carpenter, but Washington took him with the third selection. Pleau then named the Ontario Hockey Association's Ron Francis, who was from Sault Sainte Marie, as the fourth overall pick, and Hartford had its first bona fide rookie star.

Although Francis didn't come up to the Whalers until completing his junior requirements with Sault Sainte Marie, his 59 games in Hartford that first season earned him some consideration for Rookie of the Year in the league. Although not blessed with great speed, Francis had the know-how of a much older forward, a soft touch which made his passes especially crisp, and a leadership ability that was apparent even before the age of 20. His first year was a 25-goal, 43-assist effort that netted 68 points, third among Hartford scorers.

Francis would go on to represent Hartford in the mid-season NHL All-Star game each of the next four seasons, while firmly establishing himself as the team's most popular player. When he was traded by Ed Johnston on March 4, 1991, Hartford fans were both enraged by the deal and happy for their local hero.

Francis' reward was a key role on two Pittsburgh Stanley Cup winners after many thankless seasons in Connecticut. The fans and media made it clear that they celebrated his success with the Penguins even as they questioned still another unusual front-office move.

On March 15, 1983, the Hartford Whalers held a somber news conference. Baldwin, who had been criticized for being too involved in hockey matters, announced that he would concentrate on the business end of the operation. Donald G.

Conrad, an executive vice president of Aetna, had been a background figure while Baldwin, as the corporate ownership's Managing General Partner, did the talking. Conrad admitted to Jerry Trecker of the *Hartford Courant,* "We had a game plan, but we've gone off the track. There is nothing more depressing than leaving the Coliseum with a bad taste after a game. I want our fans to go expecting that the team will win."

What wasn't answered that March day was what would happen to Pleau, who had disappeared from the Hartford scene, reportedly dispatched to Western Canada on a scouting mission. Cunniff took the club to the end of the 1982-83 season. There also was no word on who would be the new hockey boss, a "czar" as Baldwin and Conrad labeled the position.

They found out on May 2, 1983, when Emile Francis flew in from St. Louis to assume the mantle. Baldwin stated in the *Hartford Courant,* that "Experience is something this organization has lacked," but refused to label the change "an indictment of the present administration." The man on the street might have thought otherwise.

Pleau remained with the organization as assistant general manager under Francis, and Jack Evans was brought in as head coach. Although the Whalers would be criticized again for picking Sylvain Turgeon in the spring entry draft (they overlooked Pat LaFontaine, Steve Yzerman, and Tom Barrasso) with the second selection, Francis delivered exactly what the front office wanted. He produced Hartford's first NHL winner.

Francis was no miracle worker, but he and the veteran Evans, a no-nonsense teacher, slowly reconstructed a team which had sunk to the bottom of the NHL. Evans' first team improved by 21 points and the second won 30 games, the most in the franchise's six NHL seasons. Ron Francis was developing into one of the most reliable centers in the league, and Millen proved a workhorse in goal, while Emile Francis slowly, but surely, built the team in his typical image.

"The Cat," who had done similar reclamation projects in New York and St. Louis, believed in defensive solidity. He dealt for players who could

AP/Wide World Photos

Mike Liut (in goal)

specialize in things like winning face offs or defending on special teams. He liked loyalty and hard work and he was not afraid to trade a young prospect for a proven veteran.

Most of all, he had a special fondness for goalie Mike Liut, a big netminder who had backstopped Francis' best team in St. Louis. When he had the chance to get him, he moved, although this was another trade which riled some of the Hartford media and fans.

Liut was obtained along with Jorgen Pettersson on February 22, 1985. The price was Millen and another very popular Whaler, ex-U.S. Olympian Mark Johnson. Francis listened to the initial critics, relied on Liut's past performance, and eventually had the last laugh.

The Best Two Years

The next two seasons were the best Hartford hockey has enjoyed. Evans' club won 40 games in 1985-86 with Liut showing both fiery leadership and expertise in goal. He finished with a 3.62

goals-against average in 57 games, then had an outstanding playoff series as the Whalers swept first-place Quebec and extended Montreal to a seven-game Adams Division final. The Canadiens needed overtime to escape that trial, with Claude Lemieux scoring the goal that ended Hartford's best post-season performance 5:55 into sudden-death play.

The Whalers had gotten 79 points and 45 goals from Turgeon that season, Francis had come back from an ankle injury to make his usual key contribution, and there was a strong second season from Kevin Dineen, who had joined the club three years after being a third-round draft choice. Dineen played first at the University of Denver, then with the 1984 Canadian Olympic Team before turning pro.

In fact, the atmosphere was so upbeat in Hartford that the team even got a parade. Francis and his staff were given contract extensions, and The Cat was named NHL Executive of the Year by both the *Sporting News* and the *Hockey News.*

An Adams Division title came in 1986-87, but the season ended with a first-round playoff upset at the hands of Quebec. Still, Evans and Francis had made good on the pledge to make Hartford into a winning team.

Almost as quickly as success had arrived, it began to disappear. Although Evans had posted a 105-91-18 record in his last two-and-a-half years as coach, he was suddenly replaced late in the 1987-88 season after he told the *Hartford Courant*'s Jeff Jacobs that he was contemplating retirement. Apparently, The Cat didn't want to read about such news in the paper.

Pleau was recalled from Binghamton where he had been successful in the American Hockey League, but something had been lost. Relations between the team and the media grew strained; Francis actually lambasted the press at a post-season news conference after Hartford was swept by Montreal in the 1989 playoffs.

Pleau's club had been 37-38-5 in the regular season, with Dineen collecting 89 points and Ron Francis and Ray Ferraro making big contributions, but Liut was no longer at the top of his game and

there was a sense of change once again.

The Whalers had been sold to Conrad and a local developer, Richard Gordon, back in September, 1988. When Gordon eventually took full control, the Emile Francis era ended.

Enter Johnston, Exit Ronnie

The new owner turned to Ed Johnston—a former goalie who had made his administrative name in Pittsburgh—and ex-Whaler Rick Ley as the club's new leadership team in 1989-90. As general manager, Johnston got credit for restructuring the team's scouting system and improving the draft picks, but he also found himself the man in the middle in the second year of his tenure when he traded Francis and Ulf Samuelsson, considered by many fans the heart of the club, to Pittsburgh for John Cullen and Zarley Zalapski. The trade followed a winter of discontent that had seen Francis subject to some criticism from within the organization; that also rubbed the Hartford public the wrong way.

Ley had a winning season in 1989-90, and the Whalers carried Boston to a seventh game in the first round of the Adams Division playoffs. The series was remembered in Hartford for the fourth game, when the Whalers let a big lead, and a possible series upset, slip away. The next year was a 31-38-11 campaign ending in another first-round loss to the Bruins. Ley was replaced by Jimmy Roberts for 1991-92, but the club's slide continued.

With both Gordon and Johnston coming under media criticism, the year ended with still another change of administration. Johnston got the ax this time, replaced by Brian Burke from the Vancouver organization.

Burke brought in Paul Holmgren as his first head coach and adopted a youth policy that saw the Whalers stick with their kids through a 1992-93 season that produced just 58 points, fourth worst in the NHL. The only three clubs behind them were the expansion clubs in Tampa Bay and Ottawa and the two-year old San Jose Sharks.

Making matters worse was Gordon's public revelation that the club was losing more money than he could afford. Connecticut governor Lowell Weicker stepped in to insist that the state would not let the Whalers go, and negotiations between the state, city, and team dragged on through the season.

The crowds which once nearly filled the Civic Center dwindled, especially the important tenants of expensive sky boxes which had been seen as a major source of Whalers' revenue. Instead, the luxury boxes had become part of the problem for a club trying to survive a shaky economic climate.

SOURCES

BOOKS

Fischler, Stan and Shirley Fischler, *The Hockey Encyclopedia,* New York: MacMillan, 1983.
Romain, Joseph and Dan Diamond, *The Pictorial History of Hockey,* New York: Gallery Books, 1987.

PERIODICALS

Trecker, Jerry, *The Hartford Courant,* March 16, 1983, pp. A-1, A-12.
Trecker, Jerry, and Bruce Berlet, *The Hartford Courant,* May 3, 1983, p. A-10.

—*Jerry Trecker* for Book Builders, Inc.

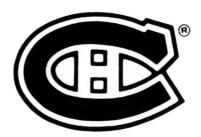

MONTREAL CANADIENS

Le Club de Hockey Canadien are not just another hockey team. They are synonymous with the sport itself, a dynasty encompassing generations of championships, much like the New York Yankees in baseball or the Boston Celtics in basketball (though the passion the Canadiens inspire among their fans, because of hockey's status as Canada's national game, is perhaps even greater than that of Yankee or Celtic fans). For Montrealers, the Habs—short for *Les Habitants,* meaning "the locals"—are a source of pride, contributing both glory and riot to the city's history.

It was in Montreal that the rules of hockey were first standardized by McGill University students in 1875, and it was in that same city, ten years later, that the first factory-made hockey sticks were manufactured. By 1909, Montreal had an estimated 100-plus hockey teams including four professional clubs—the Wanderers, the Shamrocks, the Nationals, and the All-Montreal team. However, in a city that was approximately 70 percent

French-speaking, there was not yet a French-dominated hockey team which could capture that ethnic loyalty. The idea for such a team originated after a November 25, 1909, meeting of the newly formed Canadian Hockey Association (CHA).

The Eastern Canada Hockey Association (ECHA) had thrown one of its teams, the Montreal Wanderers, out of the league. The general manager of the Wanderers, James Gardner, was fuming in a Windsor Hotel hallway over the ECHA's action when he chanced to meet J. Ambrose O'Brien, a wealthy young railroad contractor who owned hockey teams in the mining towns of Cobalt and Haileybury. Gardner and O'Brien discussed forming a new league, and in a meeting held in the same hotel on December 4th, the NHA was formally created.

This new league featured teams from Cobalt, Haileybury, and Renfrew, as well as Gardner's Montreal Wanderers. Gardner further suggested to O'Brien that a French Montreal team, to counterbalance the English-speaking Wanderers, would be a popular attraction. The team would be called the Canadiens, and Jack Laviolette, a local bar owner and former Montreal Shamrock, would be responsible for building the team's roster.

The NHA quickly entered into a bidding war with the CHA for Canada's best hockey players—a struggle which earned the NHA a good deal of criticism but ensured its supremacy. Even before the league's first game, the salary war made headlines, with the CHA's Montreal Nationals filing for an injunction to stop their star, Didier Pitre, from playing for the Canadiens. The Pitre dispute blew over, but the Canadiens' unprecedented payroll—totalling $5,000—had the hockey world buzzing.

The controversy over salaries lured 3,000 fans to Montreal's Jubilee Rink on January 5, 1910, to watch the first game in NHA history, a 7-6 overtime victory over the Cobalt Silver Kings. In those days, seven-man squads played two 32-minute periods; Laviolette was playing point, with Pitre at cover-point, Edouard "Newsy" Lalonde at rover, and future Canadiens co-owner Joe Cattarinich at goal. Montreal center Ed Décarie was the first player ever to gain possession of an NHA puck, and Lalonde, the team's first superstar, scored league's first goal. When regulation time ended with the score 6-6, the officials decided on the spot to hold an overtime period, and the fans and players, who had already begun to leave, were called back.

Hall-of-Famer Lalonde was the league's scoring champ that first year. Playing for several teams over a long career, he would retire with 441 goals in 365 pro games and would go on to coach the Canadiens from 1932-35. Early in his career, Lalonde was known particularly for his bitter rivalry with Quebec Bulldog Joe Hall who, during one game, nearly severed Lalonde's windpipe with his hockey stick. When Hall later joined the Canadiens, however, the two became roommates and friends.

The Canadiens won just two more games in that 12-game season, finishing in last place, but the NHA was off to a promising start. The rival CHA

disbanded barely a week after the Jubilee Park opener. The next season saw a major rule change: the addition of a third 20-minute period. The Canadiens had changed, as well, for wrestling promoter George Kennedy, owner of the Club Athlétique Canadien, had purchased the franchise for $7,500.

The 1910-11 season also marked the rise of a new star in 23-year-old goalkeeper Georges Vézina out of Chicoutimi, Quebec. A quiet family man who eventually fathered 22 children, Vézina's coolness in the crease helped the Canadiens rise to second place. In his first season he gave up an average of 3.9 goals per game, a statistic which decreased to a career 3.49.

Like many early hockey stars, Vézina's career would end tragically; he contracted tuberculosis, and was forced to withdraw from a game against Pittsburgh on November 28, 1925, when he lost consciousness after the first period. Vézina died March 27, 1926, and pro hockey's annual trophy for best goalkeeper is named after him.

"The Flying Frenchmen," as the team came to be called by the press, finished second to Ottawa in 1911. The next few years witnessed rapid change in the hockey world. Rule changes made it a six-man game, new penalties were added, and it was determined that the referee should drop the puck at each face-off.

A new league, the Pacific Coast Hockey Association, was born, competing with the NHA for young players—in fact, Newsy Lalonde defected to the PCHA in 1912 to become it's first scoring champ, returning to the Canadiens the next season. The Habs finished in the cellar without Newsy; however, in 1913-14 they tied the Toronto Blueshirts for first.

Another dismal year followed in 1914-15, as Lalonde refused to play during a contract dispute; he approved of his contract for the following season, though, and came back to lead the league in scoring with 31 goals in 24 games. He also led the team to its first Stanley Cup finals and championship. The finals were played in Montreal's Westmount Arena against Portland, the first time a non-Canadian team had competed for the cup.

TEAM INFORMATION AT A GLANCE

Founding Date: December 4, 1909;
November 22, 1917 (NHL)

Home ice: Montreal Forum
2313 St. Catherine St. West
Montreal, Quebec, Canada H3H 1N2
Phone: (514) 932-2582
FAX: (514) 932-8736

Capacity: 16,197 (17,909, including standing room)

Team colors: Red, white, and blue.
Team Nickname: Canadiens, 1910 present; Habs (les habitants), informal.
Logo: Monogram consisting of red capital "C" with smaller, white capital "H" inside it.

Franchise record:	Won	Lost	Tie
(1917-93)	2,480	1,473	723

Stanley Cup wins (23): 1923-1924, 1929-30, 1930-31, 1943-44, 1945-46, 1952-53, 1955-56, 1956-57, 1957-58, 1958-59, 1959-60, 1964-65, 1965-66, 1967-68, 1968-69, 1970-71, 1972-73, 1975-76, 1976-77, 1977-78, 1978-79, 1985-86, 1992-93

NHL records for most Stanley Cups, most final series appearances (31), most years in playoffs (67), most consecutive Stanley Cups (5), most consecutive years in playoffs (22)

League/Division first-place finishes (34): 1918*, 1919*, 1928, 1929, 1931, 1932, 1937, 1944, 1945, 1946, 1947, 1956, 1958, 1959, 1960, 1961, 1962, 1964, 1966, 1968, 1969, 1973, 1975, 1976, 1977, 1978, 1979, 1980, 1981, 1982, 1985, 1988, 1989, 1992

*first half of divided season
League/Division last-place finishes (3): 1926, 1936, 1940

Both teams were at less than 100-percent strength for the opener, with the favored Portlanders tired from five days of train travel and the Canadiens' Lalonde (flu) and Laviolette (broken nose) hampered. The series alternated between Eastern six-man and Western seven-man rules. Game three of that series (which was tied at one game apiece) was marred by the ejection of Lalonde and Portland's Ernie "Moose" Johnson, inciting Montreal fans to riot.

That game was a 6-5 Canadiens victory, but game four went to Portland by an identical score. In a 2-1 thriller, the Canadiens won the Cup, and the perennial cry of Montrealers, "Les Canadiens sont là"—"The Canadiens are there"—had borne fruit for the first time. Each winning player took home $238; the losers, $208.

World War I was under way, and a single unit of the Canadian Army, the 228th Battalion, included so many top hockey players that it was granted an NHA franchise as the Northern Fusiliers—and went on to beat every NHA club except the Canadiens.

The Army team's mid-season departure for overseas caused a shakeup in the league's composition and schedule. The Canadiens and Ottawa, who had finished first in the first and second halves of the season respectively, met for a two-game series which the Canadiens won. They then went on to lose to the Seattle Metropolitans in the finals—the first time an American team had won the Stanley Cup.

The NHL

The year 1917 marked the birth of the National Hockey League (NHL), and the Windsor Hotel was again the scene of the November 22nd founder's meeting. Montreal had two teams in the new league, but the Wanderers were in financial trouble from the start, and when the Westmount Arena burned down on January 2, 1918, only the Habs were left. Though the league was down to just three teams, the Canadiens were by no means out of trouble; the arrival of Joe Malone, however, played a large part in saving the team.

Malone, a nonviolent player known for his precision play, had been a Quebec favorite until that city's team bowed out of the new league. He scored five goals in the first NHL game ever (a 7-4 Canadiens victory over Ottawa), and went on to become the league's first scoring champ with 44 goals in 20 games—a record which remains the all-time highest goals-per-game average.

Pitre and Lalonde joined Malone among the league's top scorers. Goaltender Vézina held opponents to four goals per game—a low number in those high-scoring times, despite the fact that goalies were now allowed to dive for the puck. The Canadiens finished first in the first half of the season but last in the second half, ultimately losing a two-game playoff to the Toronto Arenas (precursors to the Maple Leafs), who marched on to the Stanley Cup.

The NHL added the blue line in the 1918-19

Hockey Hall of Fame and Museum

Joe Malone

season, a shaky 18-game campaign in which the Canadiens finished first in the first half and second in the second. Lalonde was now player-manager and won the scoring title with 21 goals. Though Montreal defeated Ottawa in the playoffs, sending the Habs to Seattle for the Stanley Cup series, a flu epidemic wreaked havoc with the team, incapacitating five Canadiens.

The final game of that series was never played—the only time in NHL that the Stanley Cup has gone without a victor. Bad Joe Hall, "the meanest" of all hockey players according to Lalonde (who was himself a rival for the title), was hit worst by the plague; he died in a Seattle hospital on April 5, 1919, at the age of 38.

The early 1920s were also not kind to the Canadiens. They finished out of the playoffs in 1919-20, having lost Malone to Quebec (he led the league in scoring, with Lalonde second). Lalonde recaptured the scoring title the following year, but the Canadiens were still not playoff material. Early in the 1922-22 season, disgruntled owner Kennedy sold the team to Joe Cattarinich, Louis Létourneau, and Léo Dandurand for $11,500.

A key personnel change was made when hard-nosed defenseman Sprague Cleghorn and Billy Couture were obtained from the Hamilton Tigers in the NHL's first big multi-player trade. Sprague joined his younger brother Odie to form a powerful scoring and intimidation duo—on one occasion, Sprague put three Ottawa players out of action for two games with injuries. Referee Lou Marsh called the Cleghorns "a disgrace to the noble game of hockey." The brothers went on to finish as the eighth and ninth best scorers in the league.

Lalonde, however, had become a weak spot; after returning from a four-game holdout, he was booed by the Montreal crowd, and was traded to the Saskatoon Sheiks at season's end. From the Shieks, the Canadiens got an all-time favorite, 140-pound Aurèle Joliat. The little guy scored two goals in his first game for Montreal, a 7-2 loss to Toronto. He went on to earn a place among the league's top ten scorers with 22 points, behind teammates Billy Boucher's 27 and Odie Cleghorn's 26. The Canadiens came in second to Ottawa in the regular season, losing to Ottawa in a playoff series that saw owner Dandurand unilaterally suspending Sprague Cleghorn and Billy Couture for vicious play.

Sprague Cleghorn's play continued to trouble the league the following season, when he was the

Hockey Hall of Fame and Museum

Howie Morenz

subject of a special owners' meeting and, though being absolved at first, later received a one-game suspension. Cleghorn was a leading candidate for the first Hart Trophy nevertheless, and Vézina led all goalies with a stingy 2.0 goals-against average. The Canadiens' real find in 1924, however, was a speedy, fearless, 5'9", 165-pound center from Stratford, Ontario, named Howie Morenz.

As a rookie, Morenz was eighth in the league in scoring and played an important role in the playoff series versus Ottawa. Montreal took that series—despite having finished second to Ottawa in the regular season—then defeated Pacific Coast Hockey Association (PCHA) champions Vancouver and Western Canada Hockey League (WCHL) champs Calgary for their second Stanley Cup. In the four-game sweep of Calgary, Morenz led the team with four goals and an assist. The Morenz-Joliat-Boucher line, which scored 12 of the team's 14 goals in the series, weighed an average of 140 pounds, with Morenz the giant of the three.

Local Competition

The mid-1920s were years of NHL expansion. The Montreal Maroons provided new competition for the Canadiens, while teams in Boston, New York, and Pittsburgh increased the popularity of hockey in the United States. The league schedule was expanded to 30 games to accommodate the growing league. The Canadiens began 1924-25 in the Mount Royal Arena but moved to the new Forum in downtown Montreal on November 29, 1924—a game in which a crowd of over 8,000 watched the home team swamp the Toronto St. Pats 7-1.

The Canadiens would split their home games between the two arenas until 1926, when they switched to the Forum permanently. In 1924-25, Canadiens Joliat, Morenz, and Boucher were the NHL's third, fourth, and fifth most productive scorers. The team finished third that season, and would have been unable to participate in the playoffs had the first-place team from Hamilton not gone on strike. Montreal defeated Toronto in the playoffs and went to the Stanley Cup, losing the finals to Victoria of the WCHL 3-1.

The most tragic event of 1925-26 was the death of another star Canadien. During the home opener against Pittsburgh, George Vézina, who had not missed a game in fifteen years, collapsed, hemorrhaging from tuberculosis; he died four months later. Vézina's collapse marked the start of a dreary year for the Canadiens.

The following season the team climbed to second place, with Howie Morenz leading the Canadian Division in scoring and Vézina's diminutive successor in goal, the 5'6" George Hainsworth, winning the first-ever Vézina Trophy as the league's outstanding goaltender. The Canadiens' 35-year-old newcomer Herb Gardiner took the Hart Trophy as most valuable player. A defenseman from Winnipeg who had spent his youth as a surveyor and army officer before joining Calgary of the WCHL, Gardiner was to spend only two seasons as an NHL player, scoring a total of 10 goals and 9 assists—a performance which earned him a place in hockey's Hall of Fame.

Hockey Hall of Fame and Museum

Emile Bouchard

Hainsworth repeated his Vézina Trophy-winning performance in 1927-28, with scoring champ Morenz taking the Hart Trophy and the Canadiens sitting at the top of their division. However, the rival Maroons upset them in postseason play, robbing them of the honor of playing for the Stanley Cup.

Future Hall-of-Famer Hainsworth reached his personal pinnacle the following season, winning his third Vézina Trophy after recording 22 shutouts and allowing only 43 goals in 44 games. Oddly enough, a different goalie, Roy Worters of the New York Americans, won the Hart Trophy, though the Canadiens had handily surpassed the Americans.

Back-To-Back Championships

The beginning of the Great Depression did not stop hockey's growth, with the NHL expanding to a 44-game schedule for 1929-30. Early in the season Morenz broke the nose of Maroons goalie Clint Benedict, prompting the first-ever use of a mask by an NHL goaltender. The Canadiens came in second to the Maroons for the divisional title that year, with Morenz scoring a career-high 50 points.

Ironically, the Maroons' better record meant that they faced the imposing Boston Bruins in the playoffs—and lost—while the Canadiens drove past the Chicago Black Hawks, winning the second playoff game 3-2 in triple overtime. In the opening game of the semifinals, it took 68 minutes of overtime for the Canadiens to subdue the Rangers before reserve goaltender Gus Rivers got the 2-1 victory.

The Canadiens met the Bruins for the Cup—a matchup of the speedy little Morenz against the bruising Eddie Shore in which Morenz ultimately persevered. As Shore said later, "I could never get even with him to give him a good check." The Canadiens won the Cup, 3-0 and 4-3, with Morenz scoring the winning goal.

Johnny "Black Cat" Gagnon joined Morenz and Joliat as the starting line for 1930-31; he was to spend most of his career with the Canadiens, later finishing with the Rangers. Morenz took his second regular-season scoring title with 28 goals and 23 assists, leading the team to a first place finish.

The playoffs against the Bruins were closely contested, and in the closing two minutes of overtime in the tie-breaking fifth game, Montreal defenseman Marty Burke scored the winning goal for Montreal, sending the Canadiens to the Cup finals versus Chicago. It, too, was a tight series, and Morenz, playing injured, had not yet scored a goal.

The Canadiens won the opener 2-1 in Chicago, but two days later the Black Hawks came back by the same score. As the series moved to

Hockey Hall of Fame and Museum

Clint Benedict

Montreal, the Black Hawks won game three, 3-2, before the Canadiens took game four by a 4-2 margin. So far the Montreal goals had been by Georges Mantha, Alfred "Pit" Lépine, Nicholas Wasnie, and Gagnon; Morenz, nine games into the playoffs, had still not scored a goal. Finally, with four and a half minutes to go in the third period of game five, Morenz guided the puck the length of the ice and, weaving through the Chicago defense, scored the winning goal of the finals, earning the Habs back-to-back Stanley Cup championships.

If Montreal fans had known that the Canadiens would not appear in the Stanley Cup finals again until 1944, the Depression might have seemed even bleaker for their city. The special draft that distributed the talent of the defunct Ottawa Senators and Pittsburgh Pirates contributed no new talent to the aging Montreal squad. Though the Canadiens took first place in the Canadian Division, they lost the opening playoff round of 1931-32 to the Rangers.

The following year, Newsy Lalonde returned to Montreal, this time as the team's coach. Desperate for a winning combination, Lalonde replaced Gagnon on the starting front line with Lépine—a move which neither allowed them to overtake Toronto for the divisional title nor overcome New York in the playoffs.

The 1933-34 season finished with the Habs at the same plateau of mediocrity; Joliat, the only Canadien among the league's top ten scorers, celebrated his 500th NHL game on February 8, 1934. The following year was noteworthy for its personnel changes: the Canadiens sent Morenz to Chicago in a multi-player trade, where he scored only eight goals; Gagnon was sold to Boston before being quickly bought back; and owner Dandurand installed himself as head coach.

Unfortunately, the changes did not prevent another playoff defeat at the hands of the Rangers in 1934-35. Out went coach Dandurand and in came player-coach Sylvio Mantha. Though the Montreal native and future Hall-of-Famer had played 13 seasons as a Canadiens defenseman, his coaching record was less than illustrious: Mantha guided his club to a cellar finish in 1935-36 before finishing his playing career in Boston.

In 1935, Dandurand and partners sold the Canadiens to the Canadian Arena Company, backed by Senator Donat Raymond, for $165,000. The franchise would remain under this ownership until 1957, when the Molson brewing family would buy it for a million dollars.

The 1935-36 season was notable for the arrival of former Maroon Hector "Toe" Blake, who would go on to play outstanding hockey for the Canadiens over the next 12 years and coach them during their heyday of the late 1950s. As yet, however, he was not a major factor. For the past two seasons, the Canadiens' only All-Star representative had been Welsh goalie Wilfie Cude. A highly capable goaltender who allowed only 1.57 goals

Hockey Hall of Fame and Museum

Sylvio Mantha

per game in 1933-34 (but who did not play enough minutes to qualify for the Vézina Trophy), Cude would be a much-needed bright spot throughout the otherwise dismal 1930s. He was often plagued by the emotional pressures of his position, however—and according to legend, he once threw a steak at his wife when she asked him about a goal the opponent had scored—and retired suddenly in 1941.

The Canadiens' plight in the mid-1930s was such that the league, recognizing the importance of the franchise to its existence, adopted a special measure giving the team first crack at all French-Canadian players for three seasons. This early example of affirmative action served the team well, and the influx of new, young talent helped the Canadiens to climb from last to first in their division in 1936-37.

Howie Morenz returned to Montreal to be reunited with linemates Joliat and Gagnon. The reunion was marred by tragedy, though: on January 28th Morenz broke his leg in a collision with Eddie Siebert of the Black Hawks and was carried off the ice on a stretcher. The fracture led to an embolism, and Morenz died in St. Luke's Hospital on March 8th. Morenz's number 7 sweater was retired the following season before 8,000 fans. Adding to the Canadiens' troubles, Joliat's bad legs prevented him from matching his earlier skating prowess. The team sank back into the bottom of the standings. The Habs' only bright spot—and a dubious one at that—was that the rival Montreal Maroons folded at the end of 1937-38.

Joliat retired the following season, after 16 years with the Canadiens. Coach Cecil Hart was replaced in mid-season by Jules Dugal. Toe Blake, coming into his own, won the Hart Trophy and was the NHL scoring leader with 47 points.

The team, however, did not fare well, finishing in sixth place in the reorganized seven-team, single-division league. The Canadiens fell to last place the following year, and Blake, though an All-Star for the second straight time, dropped all the way down to a disappointing ninth place on the scoring list.

Hockey Hall of Fame and Museum

Toe Blake (center)

Coach Irvin Takes Charge

The glimmerings of a turnaround appeared in 1940-41, when Dick Irvin, formerly of Toronto, took over the Canadiens' head coaching post. As a scout for Montreal, Irvin had discovered future superstar Maurice Richard, as well as Ottawa junior Johnny Quilty, whom Irvin correctly predicted would win the Calder Trophy as rookie of the year. Irvin's prediction of a fourth-place finish for the Habs, however, did not come true—they moved up but a single notch to sixth. However, the fans sensed good things to come, and a crowd of 12,000 attended the team's home opener.

Canada had been fighting in World War II since 1939, and in 1941 came Pearl Harbor. Though the NHL did not postpone any games, it lost a good many players and a team, the Brooklyn (formerly New York) Americans, to the war effort. The Canadiens again finished sixth, with Blake again the team standout.

Because of wartime pressure on train schedules, the NHL eliminated overtime in 1942, while expanding its schedule to 50 games and solidifying its membership at six teams. In retrospect that year would be remembered as the rookie season of Maurice "Rocket" Richard, though he contributed just five goals before breaking an ankle on December 27, 1942. The Canadiens' hotshots that year, finishing eighth, ninth, and tenth in scoring, were Blake, linemate Elmer Lach, and 5'7" Herbert "Buddy" O'Connor.

A Rocket Lands in Montreal

In a season in which many teams' rosters were depleted by the war, the 1943-44 Canadiens had relatively good luck, losing only Quilty and Kenny Reardon to military service. The institution of the red center line helped to speed up the game, but the Canadiens' turnaround that year had less to do with rule changes or opponents' weakness than with the new strength brought by a recovered Richard and a new star goalie, Bill Durnan—both of whom were medically exempt from military service.

Hockey Hall of Fame and Museum

Maurice "Rocket" Richard

Richard led the famous "Punch Line" that also included Lach and Blake, the three stars joining for a total of 82 goals. The team's 234 goal tally was an NHL record. Setup man Lach specialized in assists, scoring 42 of those to his 24 goals. Durnan was the league's leading goalie with a 2.18 goals-against average, and was first-team All-Star goalie for the first of four consecutive years. Durnan would go on to win the Vézina Trophy in six out of the next seven seasons.

It was the beginning of the Canadiens' first dynasty. In the regular season the Habs were 38-5-7, beating the second-place Red Wings by 25 points. The Canadiens lost the first playoff game 3-1 to the underestimated Maple Leafs, but rocketed back in game two as Richard scored all five Montreal goals in a 5-1 victory, with Blake assisting all five times. The remainder of the Toronto series was a cakewalk, including an 11-0 rout in the fifth game. The finals opened in Montreal against the Black Hawks, who were solid defensively but had only one dangerous scoring line. Coach Irvin used a strategy of wearing out Chicago's Bentley-Mosienko-Smith line with his Punch Line, then bringing in reserves such as O'Connor, Phil Watson, "Murph" Chamberlain, and Ray Getliffe to reinforce the starters.

It worked for the first three games, with Richard scoring a hat trick in game two. In game four, the Black Hawks were ahead 4-1 in the third period when the Montreal fans began jeering at their team, yelling, "Fake! Fake! Fake!" Their pride aroused, Rocket (2 goals) and Blake (the tying goal) brought their team back into overtime, which was decided by Blake's goal at 9:12. For the first time, a team had won eight straight postseason games.

Richard Scores 50

Without question, the Canadiens were an awesome team in the regular season of 1944-45. The Habs finished 38-8-4, 13 points ahead of second-place Detroit. Richard, in his greatest season, became the first NHL player ever to score 50 goals, and the only one ever to do so in a 50-game season. The Punch Line supplied the league's top three scorers, with Lach (80 points, including a then-record 54 assists) first, Richard (73) second, and Blake (67) third.

These three, plus goalie Durnan and defenseman Butch Bouchard, composed five sixths of the All-Star first team. It was the first of three consecutive first-team All-Star years for the 6'2", 210-pound Bouchard, a future Canadiens captain. Lach won the Hart Trophy and Durnan, of course, the Vézina.

But a funny thing happened to the Canadiens on the way to the championship—they were ousted by the third-place Maple Leafs in a six-

game playoff series. Bob Davidson's coverage of Richard shut the Rocket down in the first two games, which Toronto won 1-0 and 3-2. Game three went to the Canadiens, but game four to the Leafs, 4-3. Rallying angrily, the Canadiens took game five, 10-3, a record for total goals in a play-off game; the Leafs, however, came back to take the series clincher, 3-2.

The first postwar season, 1945-46, was a relative off-year for Richard, as he scored only 27 goals; his performance was good enough to send him to the All-Star game, though, along with teammates Bouchard and Durnan. Toe Blake became the first Canadien to win the Lady Byng Cup for sportsmanship, serving only a single two-minute penalty all season while helping his team to another first-place finish.

It was in the postseason, however, that the Canadiens really shone. They swept the Black Hawks in four games, then took three straight against the Bruins—the first two in overtime. The Bruins rebounded for a 3-2 overtime victory in game four, but game five was a 6-3 Canadiens breeze, and the Cup stayed in Montreal.

The Selke Initiative

A new general manager, Frank Selke, took over before the 1946-47 season. Selke, a hockey visionary and former Maple Leafs executive, took the initiative in building a farm system for the Canadiens, a system which would eventually unearth such players as Jacques Plante, Henri Richard, and Doug Harvey.

The 1947 Stanley Cup finals were a classic, the first of several confrontations between the Canadiens and the upstart Maple Leafs. The two clubs had finished first and second in the regular season, and Montreal had again dominated the individual awards, with Richard winning the Hart Trophy and coming in second in scoring.

Future Hall-of-Fame defenseman Ken Reardon was also a first-team All-Star. Although Lach missed the playoffs with a fractured skull, the Habs beat the Bruins 4-1 in the first round. When the

Canadiens won the first game of the finals, 6-0, the outcome seemed certain. In game two, however, Richard (who had been closely covered by Bill Ezinicki) wrenched a knee; Richard, in retaliation, cracked Ezinicki's skull open and slashed another Leaf's eye shut. The Leafs went on to win the game 4-0, and new NHL president Clarence Campbell, a former referee, suspended Richard for the third meeting.

The Leafs won that one as well, 4-2, and though Richard returned for game four, he was held scoreless by the Leafs defense. With three and a half minutes to go and the game tied at one goal apiece, Toronto's Syl Apps went behind the net, stopped, reversed, and sneaked the puck past Durnan for the winning score. Richard scored two goals in game five for a 3-1 Montreal victory, forcing a sixth meeting.

Though the Leafs peppered the Canadiens' goal with shots, the score remained locked at 1-1 until the third period, when a harmless-looking shot by Toronto's Ted "Teeder" Kennedy slipped in, giving the dynastic young Maple Leafs the first in a string of Stanley Cups. The Canadiens, on the other hand, would not appear in a Stanley Cup finals until the same two teams met in 1951.

The fabled Punch Line broke up the next season when Toe Blake was slammed into the boards by the Ranger's Bill Juzda and broke his ankle. Buddy O'Connor, who had been traded to New York, won both the Hart and Lady Byng trophies—an unprecedented feat—and finished second only to Lach in scoring.

The Habs did not make the playoffs that year, but returned to postseason action in 1948-49, largely because of Durnan's ten regular-season shutouts. In the opening round, though, they fell over for the Red Wings' famous Production Line of Ted Lindsay, Sid Abel, and Gordie Howe. A standout during the season was Montreal defenseman Billy Reay, the future great Black Hawks coach, who scored 22 goals and 23 assists.

In 1949-50 the Habs moved up to second place, behind Detroit. Richard emerged from his doldrums with 65-points for the 70-game season. This was the height Richard's great rivalry with Detroit legend Gordie Howe, and for the past two seasons Richard had edged Howe for the All-Star right wing slot. In one memorable game, Howe knocked Richard down, and when Howe's linemate Sid Abel taunted Richard, the Rocket broke the kibitzer's nose. The season was also memorable for the stunning retirement of Durnan in the middle of the playoff series against New York. The sensitive goalie had been booed by Montreal fans throughout the season, and was prone to insomnia and nausea. At last he simply asked to be replaced, saying, "Nothing was worth that kind of agony." The Rangers beat the Habs 4-1.

New Faces in 1950

The 1950-51 Canadiens were revamped to the tune of ten rookies. They brought up 5'7" Quebecois Gerry McNeil to replace Durnan in the nets, and gave tryouts to two junior players who would prove to be superstars: Bernard "Boom Boom" Geoffrion and Jean Béliveau. Béliveau was a diamond in the rough: his outstanding performance in the Quebec amateur had prompted the Canadiens to purchase the entire league, just to acquire the rights to Béliveau.

In Béliveau's two games in the majors he scored a goal and an assist, but the Canadiens felt that the teenager needed further seasoning, and returned him to the Quebec Junior Citadels. Geoffrion, who turned all of 20 in February of 1951, made a more durable impression at first, playing 18 games for the Canadiens and logging eight goals and six assists.

It was Maurice Richard, however, who still led the club, and his 42 goals and 24 assists powered them to a third-place finish and, ultimately, the Stanley Cup finals. (Richard also manhandled a referee, Hugh McLean, in lobby of New York's Piccadilly Hotel, receiving a $500 fine from the league president.) The Canadiens surprised the Red Wings in a six-game playoff series, winning the first two on overtime goals by Richard.

Then came the Maple Leafs in the finals—a series which is still remembered for its closeness,

Hockey Hall of Fame and Museum

Jean Béliveau

as all five games were decided in overtime. Toronto's Sid Smith, the team comedian, won the first game with a backhanded shot. Richard's overtime goal won the second game when he decked veteran Toronto goalie Turk Broda out of the crease for a 3-2 victory. Broda was benched for the remainder of the series in favor of Al Rollins.

Games three and four went to Toronto, and the series stood at three games to one. In game five the Canadiens were ahead 2-1 in the final minute. Toronto coach Lou Primeau gambled, pulling his goalie and putting six skaters on the ice. Primeau's gamble worked: Tod Sloan tied the score with 37

seconds left in the game. At only 2:53 of the overtime period, Toronto's Howie Meeker flipped the puck out from behind the Canadiens net toward teammate Bill Barilko, who slapped a short, hard shot over goalie McNeil's shoulder to extend Toronto's dynasty.

The Canadiens got another chance at the Cup in 1951-52. It was Geoffrion's first full year, and he won the Calder Trophy as the league's outstanding rookie. Another newcomer, left winger Dickie Moore, scored 18 goals in 33 games to inaugurate a brilliant career. Though Richard was not among the league's top ten scorers, Lach was third with 65 points and Geoffrion sixth with 54.

The Habs took second place, a full 22 points behind the league-leading Red Wings, and proceeded to an exciting postseason. The semifinals against Boston lasted a grueling seven games. In the second period of the final matchup, Bruin Leo Labine overturned Richard, gashing the Rocket's head.

The great star, who spent the most of the second period in a clinic, was woozy for the remainder of the game and did not remember his third-period heroics. He must have enjoyed being told how, with blood seeping through his head bandage, he wove around four Bruin defenders and shot the puck into the goal, receiving a four-minute ovation from his home-town fans. "A few times when I got the puck I didn't know whether I was skating toward our goal or their goal," Richard said afterward. But Bruin coach Lynn Patrick said, "A truck couldn't have stopped Richard on that play."

The first game of the finals against Detroit took an unprecedented—and illegal—61 minutes, because a faulty siren had failed to sound at the end of play, allowing the players to continue for an extra minute. Fortunately, no goals were scored during the extra time. Unfortunately for the Habs, they lost 3-1. In game two, Elmer Lach scored the only Montreal goal in a 2-1 loss, and things went downhill from there; the Wings handed the Canadiens two 3-0 shutouts to take the Stanley Cup.

The young Canadiens added still more talent the following year. Goalie Jacques Plante was brought up from Buffalo for three games when

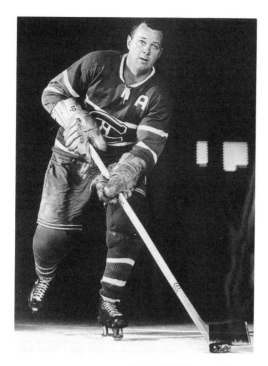

Hockey Hall of Fame and Museum

Doug Harvey

McNeil was injured, and the front office liked what it saw. Béliveau returned for another trial—three games this time, beginning December 18th. He scored five goals in the three games, including a hat trick in his Forum debut. The Habs ended the regular season in a familiar position—second to the Red Wings by 15 points.

Richard had set a new NHL record with 325 career goals on November 8th—the same night Lach scored his 20th career goal. Doug Harvey was a first-team All-Star, and Bert Olmstead, the 6'2" left winger from Saskatchewan, had one of several fine seasons with 45 points. McNeil recorded ten shutouts in goal but was edged out for the Vézina trophy by Detroit netminder Terry Sawchuck.

More proof that goalies are a funny breed came in game six of the semifinals against Chicago. McNeil, feeling the strain, asked to be replaced in the net by rookie Plante for the good of the team. The willing Plante allowed just one goal over the next two games, and the Canadiens advanced to the finals against the Boston Bruins. The Canadiens took game one by a score of 4-2, as injured Bruins' star Milt Schmidt did not play.

Boston won the second game, but their star goalie, Sugar Jim Henry, sprained an ankle, and his replacement, Gordon "Red" Henry (no relation), was a substitute in name only. The third game was a 3-0 Canadiens shutout as McNeil returned to the nets, and in game four the Canadiens took advantage of Red Henry for seven goals—three of which came off Richard's stick—for a 7-3 win.

Out went Red Henry, in came the injured Sugar Jim for game five. Both McNeil and Sugar Jim were outstanding, and at the end of regulation play the game remained scoreless. Then, at 1:22 of the overtime, the 35-year-old Lach took a shot which bounded off Henry's stick. Richard recovered the puck and sent it backward to Lach, who wound up and zipped it into the net. Montreal coach Dick Irvin, who for some Machiavellian reason had predicted a Boston sweep, said, "They sure made a liar out of me."

The Béliveau Era

Jean Béliveau arrived for good in 1953-54, scoring 34 points in 44 games as center for a line whose wings were Geoffrion and Moore. Three Canadiens were among the league's top five scorers: Richard with 67 points (a distant second to Gordie Howe's 81), Geoffrion with 54 and Olmstead with 52. Veteran center Ken Mosdell scored 46 points and made the All-Star first team.

Once again the Canadiens finished the season second to the Red Wings, but this time the gap was only seven points. The Canadiens swept the Bruins in the semifinals—luckily for them, because the finals against the Red Wings were brutal. The first game, in Detroit, was a 3-1 home victory, with Geoffrion scoring the Habs' only goal. The visiting Canadiens evened the series in the next game, with all their scoring—a goal by

Moore and two by Richard—coming in the first period. But the Red Wings took the next two games at the Forum by scores of 5-2 and 2-0. Coach Irvin mulled over his choice of goalies. Plante was playing well and McNeil was rusty, but perhaps the team would respond better for the veteran than for the youngster. McNeil was in for game five in Detroit, and shut out his opponents in a 1-0 overtime win, with Mosdell scoring the sole point.

Game six, after a scoreless opening period, saw Montreal take the lead and hold it for a 4-1 win. In game seven, played in Detroit, Montreal scored first—and in every game of the series so far the first team to score had won. The Wings tied it early in the second period, and both goalies held firm, forcing overtime. Then, four and a half minutes into sudden death, Red Wing Glenn Skov passed across the ice to Tony Leswick, who took a 30-foot shot from the face-off circle.

The puck went over the shoulder of Montreal defenseman Doug Harvey, who swatted at it with his glove, over his own goalie's shoulder and into the net. Bouchard, who saw the action from the Montreal bench, later remembered thinking, "There is no danger there," and being stunned, like everyone else on both teams, when the puck dropped in. The team did not blame Harvey, but they refused, on coach Irvin's orders, to shake hands with the Red Wings afterward.

1954-55 was a wild season, highlighted by the "Richard Riot" of March 17. A few days earlier, Richard had been cut by a high stick in a game against Boston, and had retaliated with his own stick. The president of the league, Clarence Campbell, had warned Richard in the past about illegal use of his stick; determined to teach the Rocket a lesson, Campbell suspended him for the remainder of the season. Fans in Montreal were incensed, for Richard—at that time the leader in the NHL scoring race, a race he had as yet never won—was viewed as the Canadiens' best chance at dethroning the Red Wings.

Campbell's office was flooded with letters from Montreal fans, many threatening Campbell's life; the president would not be intimidated,

though, and he attended the next Canadiens home game versus the Wings to prove it. As the tide of the game turned in Detroit's favor, the Forum crowd began throwing objects at Campbell. Deciding that the situation was out of control, Campbell declared the game over—a Red Wing victory, by forfeit. Enraged, the Montreal crowd stormed into the streets, looting and smashing windows.

Without Richard, the Canadiens surrendered the final game of the season to Detroit, finishing in second place behind the Wings by just two points. Doug Harvey won the Norris Trophy—his first of seven over the next eight seasons—and Geoffrion won the Art Ross Trophy as top NHL scorer with 75 points, surpassing the Rocket by one point; though he approached it several more

Hockey Hall of Fame and Museum

Bert Olmstead

times, Richard would never attain the league scoring title.

Olmstead had a career season with ten goals and 48 assists. In the semifinals, despite the postriot suspension of Richard, the Canadiens defeated the Bruins in five games. But the Red Wings had a 13-game winning streak going, an NHL record that spanned the regular and postseason. They extended it to 15 by beating the Canadiens in the first two Stanley Cup games, both in Detroit.

Back in Montreal, the Canadiens snapped the Red Wings' streak with two victories in which they were outshot by the losers. The teams proceeded to trade home-ice victories, and the team with the home advantage in the seventh game—the Red Wings—took the cup. The Red Wings, a young team, looked like a solid dynasty, but in fact it would be their last moment of glory before the Canadiens took over the league.

The Dynasty Begins with a Toe

Some of the Canadiens' younger players reached maturity in 1955-56, while promising rookies Henri "Pocket Rocket" Richard, Jean-Guy Talbot, and Claude Provost joined up and veterans like Richard, Bouchard, Mosdell, and Olmstead were still productive. Most important, Toe Blake—who had learned the coaching art in Houston, Buffalo, and Valleyfield—had been persuaded by Selke to return to the Canadiens as head coach.

This new combination of players and coach lifted the Canadiens to their highest level yet. Finishing the regular season at 45-15-10, they were 24 points ahead of the second-place Red Wings. Hart Trophy winner Béliveau led the league's scorers with 47 goals and 41 assists, and Rocket Richard and Olmstead were third and fourth with 71 and 70 points. Béliveau, Harvey, Richard, and Plante were All-Stars, and the latter won the Vézina Trophy with a 1.86 goals-against average; Blake was chosen Coach of the Year in his rookie season.

The Canadiens brushed aside the Rangers in

Hockey Hall of Fame and Museum

Dickie Moore

the first round of postseason play, then marched on to face the Red Wings in the finals. This matchup of rivals was not the challenge it had been in past years. In game one, down 4-2 in the third period, the Habs scored four goals in five and a half minutes to overwhelm the Wings, 6-4, and game two continued the shellacking with a 5-1 Canadiens victory.

The third game, in Detroit, went to the home team, but then the Canadiens overcame their Olympia Stadium jinx and took game four with a 3-0 shutout. The climactic game five was a 3-1 win for the Canadiens on enemy ice, in which Béliveau tied Richard's old record of 12 postseason goals, and Bouchard, playing his final game, skated around the rink with the Stanley Cup.

Perhaps a slight letdown led to the Canadiens' finishing second in 1956-57, six points behind Detroit despite the Habs' fearsome collection of shooters. This was the season that the Canadiens' devastating power play, with Geoffrion and Harvey on defense and Béliveau, Rocket, and Moore or Olmstead up front, convinced the league to allow a penalized player to return to the ice after the opposition scored.

Montreal had four of the league's top ten scorers, with Béliveau's 84 points leading the team. Rookie Phil Goyette scored 7 points in 14 games at the start of a stellar 16-year career. Detroit, lead by Gordie Howe and Ted Lindsay, was also a powerhouse; fortunately for Montreal, the Bruins upset the Wings in the first round of the playoffs. In the opening game of the finals, Rocket Richard scored four goals—three of them in the second period—on the way to a 5-1 rout.

The second game was a 1-0 shutout on a Béliveau back-hander past the kneeling, outfoxed Boston goalie. Game three was a relatively routine 4-2 Montreal victory in which the Habs were leading 3-0 after the first period, but in game four, the Bruins capitalized on their home-ice advantage. Back at the Forum for game five, though, the Canadiens were on fire, leading 3-0 after two periods and winning the cup with a penalty-filled 5-1 victory.

The bloody rivalry of the Canadiens and Bruins was to continue the next season. The Canadiens finished with 250 goals, the most any NHL team had ever amassed. Dickie Moore, playing much of the season in a wrist cast, led the league in scoring with 84 points, and Henri Richard was second with 80. Rocket Richard scored his 500th career point on October 19, the first such milestone in the history of the NHL; a month later, however, his Achilles' tendon was almost completely severed in a collision with Marc Reaume of the Maple Leafs.

In February, another crucial injury hurt the team as Geoffrion collided with teammate Andre Pronovost during practice and ruptured a bowel; he was rushed to the hospital for major abdominal surgery and received the last rites of the church. Nevertheless, the Canadiens finished the season with 96 points, 19 ahead of the second-place Rangers, and were represented in the All-Star game by Henri Richard, Moore, Harvey, Plante, and Jean Béliveau.

Topping it off, Rocket Richard and Geoffrion were back—though hurting—for the postseason, helping the Canadiens sweep the Red Wings in the semifinals. In the finals, the Habs faced the underdog Bruins, taking game one by a score of 2-1. Game one of that series was brutal: Boston's Leo Labine broke Provost's nose and several teeth with a stick. ("We can't play unless we're hitting," the Boston general manager admitted. "Take Leo Labine. He's useless unless he's in there hitting someone.")

However, in game four, with the Canadiens ahead two games to one, Bruins' coach Milt Schmidt recommended to his players that they adopt a less physical style of play: if they weren't penalized, he pointed out, the Canadiens couldn't put on the power play.

The Bruins' strategy paid off, and they won the game 3-1 to tie the series. Rocket Richard won game five in overtime on his 18th career playoff goal, and in game six in Boston, Geoffrion put the puck in the net twice during a hectic 5-3 scoring contest. The Canadiens had their third straight Cup.

Dickie Moore took his second consecutive scoring title in 1958-59 with a then-record 96 points. Béliveau was second with 91, but would miss the finals after being body-checked in the semifinals by Glen Skov. It was another easy first-place finish for the Habs, 18 points ahead of Boston, with four first-team All-Stars in Moore, Plante, Béliveau, and defenseman Tom Johnson (who narrowly edged out teammate Harvey). Rookie Ralph Backstrom won the Calder Trophy. In short, just as their older stars were fading (Rocket Richard missed 28 games with a broken ankle), the Canadiens were consolidating their younger talent.

After taking care of Chicago in the semifinals, the Canadiens won the first two finals games

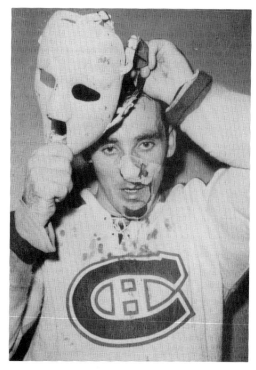

Hockey Hall of Fame and Museum

Jacques Plante

workouts) but as with Columbus' voyage to America, it was Plante's example that people remembered and copied. A new era in hockey safety had begun.

The Canadiens of 1959-60 finished in first place with 92 points, to the Leafs' 79. Three forwards—Geoffrion, Henri Richard, and Béliveau—scored 30 goals or more, and Plante was the stingiest goalie in the league. Many people have opined that this Canadiens squad was the greatest ever. The team's success, while lacking a single outstanding scorer to match, say, Chicago's Bobby Hull, testified to its tremendous depth and balance.

No team had ever won five straight Stanley Cups, but the Canadiens were heavily favored, and rightly so. They swept the Black Hawks in the semifinals and then swept the Leafs in the finals. It was the second and last time a team had won the Cup in eight straight games, for after that the postseason was expanded to three series. The highlight of the finals was Rocket Richard's 82nd career playoff goal in game three—the concluding goal of his career.

against the Maple Leafs by scores of 5-3 and 3-1, then traveled to Toronto for a 3-2 overtime loss. Game four was scoreless after two periods, but the Habs broke the home-team spell with third-period goals by rookie left wing Alvin "Ab" McDonald, Backstrom, and Geoffrion.

In game five, the Canadiens cruised to a 3-0 lead in the first period, going on to win it 5-3. Rocket Richard refused to take a shift as the game came to a close, so as not to detract from his younger teammates' glory.

On November 1, 1959, Andy Bathgate of the Rangers took a dangerous shot at the Canadiens' goal, giving Jacques Plante a gash that required seven stitches. When Plante returned to the game, he was wearing a mask. It was not the first time a goalie had ever sported a mask in a game (Plante himself, who had fractured both cheekbones in practice, had worn one for years during Canadiens

All Things Must End

The end of a career, the end of a decade, and the end of a dynasty coincided. For the next four years, the Canadiens would bow out in the semifinals, though in three of those years they finished first in the regular season. In 1960-61 Jacques Plante was no longer the Vézina Trophy winner, relinquishing that honor to Johnny Bowers of Toronto.

Geoffrion and Béliveau were the league's top two scorers, with Moore and Henri Richard also having excellent years, and Harvey continued his hold on the Norris Trophy. But the lowly Black Hawks defeated them in a six-game playoff, including a triple-overtime win in game three and shutouts in games five and six. If Toe Blake, in punching the referee at the end of game three, was trying to make a point about the officiating, it was apparently not well taken.

Captain Doug Harvey left the Canadiens the following year to be player-coach of the Rangers. In return the Habs got veteran enforcer Lou Fontinato and named Béliveau captain. Jacques Plante received the Hart Trophy as well as the Vézina in another first-place year, while Montreal native Bobby Rousseau won the Calder at the beginning of a long career at right wing.

However, the Canadiens again succumbed to the Black Hawks—led by Bobby Hull and Stan Mikita—in the playoffs. The 1962-63 season was even more frustrating as the team fell to third place behind Toronto and Chicago, and lost the semifinals to Toronto.

The Habs recaptured first place in 1963-64, with Béliveau garnering the Hart Trophy, goalie Charlie Hodge the Vézina, and Jacques Laperriere the Calder. This time it took the full seven games for the Maple Leafs to put down the Canadiens. The 3-1 loss in game seven marked Boom-Boom Geoffrion's last game for Montreal.

After this string of relatively grim years, Frank Selke retired as general manager, giving the helm over to Sam Pollock. In 1964-65 Provost and Backstrom were the Habs' leading scorers with 64 and 55 points respectively. Provost and Laperriere were All-Star first-teamers.

The Canadiens finished second to the Red Wings by four points, then fought their way past Toronto in a rough semifinals. For the finals they faced the mighty Black Hawks without star defenseman Laperriere, whose ankle was broken. Montreal's strategy was for Pete Provost to stick to Bobby Hull like glue.

Easier said than done, but Provost did it, and the Canadiens won game one, 3-2, on a goal by Yvan Cournoyer, the 5'7" right wing from Drummondville, Quebec—another rookie who would bring honor to the Montreal lineup for years to come. The second game was a shutout, 2-0, by plump Montreal goalie Lorne "Gump" Worsley.

Game three, in Chicago, was a 3-1 win for the Hawks. Worsley was injured for game four and Charlie Hodge let five Chicago shots through—including Hull's only two goals of the series—for a 5-1 loss.

But back at the Forum Hodge shut out the Hawks 6-0 in game five. Game six was a Black Hawk victory, apparently because it was played on home ice, and game 7, for perhaps the same reason, clinched Montreal's 12th Stanley Cup.

Béliveau, who had scored the final game's first goal at :14 of the first period, received the first Conn Smythe Trophy for most valuable player of the playoffs, though many considered Provost to be equally deserving of the honor. The Canadiens finished in first place in 1965-66, led by Rousseau's 78 points (third best in the NHL) and Béliveau's 77. Laperriere won the Norris Cup and an All-Star berth. The playoffs against Toronto were violent, marred by 26 penalties in game two and a record 35 penalties (154 minutes) in game three. The Leafs might as well have put down their dukes, for the Canadiens swept the series.

Hockey Hall of Fame and Museum

Henri Richard

The finals against the Red Wings opened in Montreal, and the Wings won the first two games there, 3-2 and 5-2, in large part due to the brilliant saves of 5'8" goalie Roger Crozier. The third game was played in Detroit's Olympia Stadium, where the Canadiens' luck had been lousy—only two wins in as many seasons. In desperation, Toe Blake called up Leon Rochefort from the minors and put him on a line with Henri Richard and Dave Balon, allowing Balon to score the tying goal and Béliveau the winner for a 4-2 triumph.

Game four was a 2-1 Canadiens victory, with Crozier (sprained knee) out of the nets. In game five the Canadiens outskated Howe's aging Red Wings to a 5-1 victory. Game six, played on an 88 degree May day in Detroit, was tied 2-2 in overtime, and Richard "scored" the winning goal when the puck knocked against his leg and into the net.

In 1966-67—the 50th year of the NHL—the Canadiens advanced to the finals despite a rocky regular season in which they finished second to the Black Hawks and in which Béliveau missed 13 games after being accidentally hit in the eye with a stick. In the playoffs, the Canadiens swept the Rangers—among them ex-Canadiens Phil Goyette and an as-yet-unretired Boom-Boom Geoffrion—and then confronted the Maple Leafs, whose roster included seven players 36 years old or older.

Hockey Hall of Fame and Museum

Yvan Cournoyer

The Canadiens' goalie, in contrast, was Rogatien Vachon, a 5'7" 22-year-old from Palmarolle, Quebec, whom opposing coach Punch Imlach derided as a "Junior B" player. Coach Blake bragged in turn about his new tough guys, John Ferguson, Terry Harper, and Ted Harris. The first game went to the Canadiens, 6-2. In game two, Ferguson reinforced his reputation by breaking Maple Leaf goalie Johnny Bower's nose—an incident which did not keep Bowers from recording a 3-0 shutout.

In the marathon game three, Bowers made 60 saves, including 20 in the 28-minute-long overtime, and the Leafs won 3-2. But the 42-year-old Bower pulled a muscle before game four, and it did what a broken nose had not: put him out of action. Terry Sawchuck, a mere youth at 38, replaced him for the remainder of the series. The erratic veteran goalie allowed six goals in game four for a Canadiens win, but only two more goals for the duration of the series, and the Canadiens were out of it in six games.

Coping With Expansion

The NHL doubled its size for 1967-68, an experiment which proved successful. Though the Canadiens lost forward Dave Balon to the Minnesota North Stars in the expansion draft, it did not stop the team from advancing to the Stanley Cup. A highlight of the season was Béliveau's 400th career goal, scored against the Pittsburgh Penguins during the first game between an established team and an expansion team.

Montreal finished the season in first place in the East without having any of the league's top ten scorers on its roster. Its goalies, Worsley and Vachon, shared the Vézina Trophy, and Worsley was the All-Star at that position. Montreal swept Boston in the playoff openers and then ousted Chicago for the division title. The Cup finals were against the St. Louis Blues, whose season record against the Canadiens was 0-3-1. Surprisingly, Blues' goalie Glenn Hall took the Habs into overtime in games one and three, and games two and four were also tight, with scores of 1-0 and 3-2. At the end of four games, however, Montreal had swept the Blues.

The 1967-68 finals marked the last NHL game played in the old Forum, and the day after the series, Toe Blake announced his retirement, giving the reins to Claude Ruel. "I've had enough" Blake said. "The pressure is too much." Another postseason highlight: Jacques Provost received the first Bill Masterson Trophy, given to the hockey player exemplifying perseverance, sportsmanship, and dedication.

The Forum was remodeled for the following season; Béliveau scored the first goal in it and Cournoyer the second, during a 2-1 victory over the Red Wings. The season featured a neck-and-neck for first place between Montreal and Boston, with Montreal triumphing by three points. In a season dominated by high scorers, Cournoyer's 87 points and Béliveau's 82 led the team but not nearly the league. These two forwards, plus defenseman Ted Harris, represented Montreal on the second All-Star team.

Montreal swept New York in the playoffs, then defeated the strong Boston team in six games, three of which were decided in overtime. They then faced the mini-dynasty of the St. Louis Blues for the Stanley Cup. It was something of a grudge match, especially because of the presence on the Blues of ex-Canadien Jacques Plante, whom some Montreal players felt had disparaged them to the press.

Most of the hockey world took the Western Division lightly—including the Habs, who swept the finals, 3-1, 3-1, 4-0, 2-1, for their fourth Cup in five years, their 16th altogether. After this impressive postseason play, the Canadiens' collapse of 1969-70 was quite unexpected. They fell to fifth place in their conference; Laperriere, on the second team, was the only All-Star; and Ruel resigned in December, 1970, to be succeeded by Al MacNeil.

In a time of transition, Béliveau scored his 500th goal on February 11, 1971—he would finish the season with 507. His 700th assist came nine days later. A night in his honor followed on March

24, as did the announcement of his retirement that June. On a more positive note, future star Ken Dryden played his first game in goal and won it, 5-1, against Pittsburgh. The upgraded Montreal team also included the Mahovlich brothers, Frank and Pete.

Montreal finished third in the East for 1970-71, and Dryden's sensational goaltending led them to an upset over the hot-shooting Bruins in the playoffs. The Bruins had outscored Dryden 8-2 through the first game-and-a-half when he suddenly seemed to turn an emotional corner, and the Canadiens rallied to win game two 7-5. In the seventh game of the series, Dryden's saves frustrated Phil Esposito so much that the great Bruin smashed his stick against the boards.

The second round, against Minnesota, was a relative breather, though the North Stars won two of six. The Canadiens faced the Black Hawks for the Cup. As Provost had done in 1965, little Rejean Roule covered Bobby Hull, holding him to just three goals—two of which came on power plays. The Hawks were up by two games when coach McNeil experimented with reshuffled lines, angering Henri Richard into outspoken criticism before the press.

It could have been disastrous, but it seemed to strengthen the Canadiens' resolve not to look bad. In the seventh game, the home team Hawks were leading 2-0 at 14:18 of the second period when goalie Tony Esposito let an easy Jacques Lemaire shot sail into the net. That shifted the

Hockey Hall of Fame and Museum

Ken Dryden (in goal)

momentum, and two Richard goals won the game and the Cup. Dryden was awarded the Smythe Trophy as playoff MVP.

Dryden won the Calder Trophy the following year, having been ineligible during his heroic playoff season. It was Guy Lafleur's first year with the Canadiens, and in 73 games he notched 29 goals and 35 assists. It was also Scotty Bowman's rookie year as head coach. Montreal came in third in the East in 1971-72, losing the opening round of the playoffs to the Rangers.

Defense and Depth

Never down for long, the Habs took first place in the East in 1972-73. On January 8, 6'4", 225-pound defenseman Larry Robinson played his first game for the team, adding to an already astonishingly deep squad featuring All-Stars Dryden (who also garnered the Vézina), defenseman Guy Lapointe, and Frank Mahovlich. In the playoffs, the expansion Buffalo Sabres gave the Habs a surprising six-game run for their money before bowing out. In the semifinal round, the Philadelphia Flyers took the first game, but the Canadiens won the next four.

Despite the presence of two outstanding goaltenders, the first game was a shootout that went 8-3 to the Canadiens. They took the second game as well, but the third, on Chicago's mushy ice, was a 7-4 hometown victory. Though game four was a seminar in goaltending, with Dryden recording a 4-0 shutout, game five was a defensive disaster for both teams as the Hawks won 8-7. In game six in Chicago, "Roadrunner" Cournoyer's speed overcame the slow Chicago ice; his two goals in the third cemented a 6-4 victory, a Smythe Trophy, a record 11th Stanley Cup ring for Henri Richard, and the 18th cup for the team.

Something was missing from the Canadiens in 1973-74: Ken Dryden, who sat out the season as a law clerk after the Canadiens refused his demand for $100,000. Without the Vézina Trophy-winning goaltender, the Canadiens proceeded to give up more goals than any team in Montreal history. They finished second in the East, 14 points behind Boston, and fell to the Rangers in a six-game playoff.

Dryden returned for 1974-75 with a multi-year, million-dollar contract in his glove. It was in that same year that Lafleur bloomed, becoming the third Canadien in history to score 50 or more goals in a season—a landmark he would pass six straight seasons. Lafleur finished fourth in the league with 117 points, with Frank Mahovlich just one point behind him.

Their offense, combined with the defense of Lapointe and Serge Savard (who that year scored a career-high 20 goals and 40 assists), helped the Habs reach the top in the newly formed Norris Division of the Prince of Wales Conference. In the quarterfinals they defeated Smythe Division leader Vancouver in five games.

In the semifinals they confronted the pesky Buffalo Sabres—a team that the Canadiens, despite their high-powered offense, had been unable to defeat all season. The Sabres took the first two games handily, but the Habs came back 7-0 and 8-2 in the next two. Game five was a 5-4 Sabres victory, and game six an easy 4-3 win for the Sabres.

The Flowering

The Lafleur dynasty was about to begin, however, with four straight Stanley Cups from 1975-76 to 1978-79, and four straight first-place divisional finishes, with record-breaking point totals of 127, 132, 129, and 115 in those 80-game seasons. Lafleur led the league in scoring in the first three of those years, and in 1976-77 Steve Shutt became the first Montreal player ever to score 60 goals in a season.

The Canadiens' quick, graceful, non-aggressive style—only 12.2 penalty minutes per game in 1975-76—was the opposite of that favored by their playoff opponents, the Philadelphia Flyers, whose grinding style had earned them the nickname "the Broad Street Bullies." The Habs swept the Flyers in the finals for the Stanley Cup—much to the delight of fans who preferred clean hockey to Philadelphia's bruising tactics—concluding a postseason in which they went 12-1, losing only to the New York Islanders.

In 1976-77 the Canadiens again dominated the All-Star selections, with Lafleur, Robinson, Shutt, and Dryden on the first team and Lapointe on the second. The Habs finished the season at 60-8-12—a record number of wins, and an amazing 49 points ahead of the second-place Los Angeles Kings. The Canadiens were awesome in front of the Forum crowd, losing just one home game all season. Lafleur won the Hart, Ross, and Smythe trophies and Robinson the Norris as the Canadiens glided to another Stanley Cup, losing their only two postseason games to the up-and-coming Islanders before sweeping the Bruins in the finals.

The Isles were a serious threat to dethrone the Habs in 1977-78 but they lost an upset playoff series to the helpful Maple Leafs. The Canadiens

Hockey Hall of Fame and Museum

Guy Lafleur

then eliminated the Leafs for their pains and again bounced the Bruins for the Stanley Cup. This time Boston salvaged its pride by winning two games out of six, but the Canadiens' defensemen, backed up by Vézina winners Dryden and Michel Laroque, held the Bruins to just 12 goals over the entire series.

Montreal's opponents in the 1978-79 Stanley Cup finals were the Rangers, who had upset their crosstown rivals the Islanders for the honor. The Rangers took the first game of the series but were summarily dismissed in the next four. Bob Gainey, a 6'2", 200-pound left wing from Peterborough, Ontario who would spend his entire 16-year career with the Canadiens, won the Smythe Trophy. But the dynastic Canadiens would soon be decimated: Dryden, Cournoyer, and Lemaire all retired after that season, as did coach Bowman.

The Ordinary Eighties

The Canadiens' record during the 1980s would have made most sports teams proud, but in contrast to their previous achievements the decade was a letdown. Between 1979-80 and 1989-90, the Habs won one Stanley Cup, lost one in the finals, and won their division six times, with three second-place finishes. Clearly they were a quality team, but the league itself had changed since the days of the original six.

Hockey talent was spread from Edmonton to the Sun Belt—with Wayne Gretzky showing up in both places. The early 1980s were the years of Mike Bossy and the Islanders' "Drive for Five"; in the later 1980s it was Gretzky establishing a new dynasty in the far north.

There were internal problems in the Canadiens franchise, as well. The front office did a coaching flip-flop in 1979-80, using Boom-Boom Geoffrion briefly at the helm before Claude Ruel returned. The two men had very distinct styles—Geoffrion flamboyant and attack oriented, Ruel conservative, a believer in caution on the ice—and the players' loyalties were torn between them.

Lafleur, the Blond Demon, began to show signs of personal pressure, becoming a lover of nightlife (in sharp contrast to his formerly puritanical image) and habitually making controversial remarks to reporters. However, his 50 goals and 75 assists, third in the league, still propelled the Canadiens to the divisional lead, and Robinson again earned the Norris Trophy. The momentum did not last through the playoffs, though, as the Canadiens bowed out of the playoffs in the quarterfinal round.

In 1980-81 Lafleur played only 51 games, owing to a series of minor injuries, illnesses, and a headline-making, alcohol-related auto accident. The Canadiens still took first place, but fell out of the playoffs even earlier, this time in the preliminary round. Only Robinson, a second-teamer, represented Montreal in the All-Star game.

A trio of Montreal goalies—Richard Sevigny, Denis Herron, and Michel Larocque—shared the Vézina Trophy. After the season, Ruel moved out of the coaching slot into player training. Discipline-oriented Bob Berry, a Montreal native who had successfully coached the Los Angeles Kings, became the new Canadiens' coach.

In 1981-82 a divisional reshuffling took place, with the Canadiens moving into the Adams division. Though their chief divisional rivals were now the Bruins rather than the Kings, the frustrating pattern of solid regular-season finishes followed by early playoff elimination continued.

Despite Berry's motivational efforts, player disunity remained a problem, as did the decline of key veterans. Berry instituted a balanced four-line rotation which was well thought out but which alienated Lafleur, whose starring role was greatly diminished. Brian Engblom, a 6'2", 190-pound defenseman out of Winnipeg, was the only Canadiens All-Star, making the second team. Bob Gainey was named captain, serving in that capacity until his retirement in 1988-89.

A team "first" was achieved in 1982-83 as Mats Naslund, a left winger from Sweden, became the first regular Canadien from Europe. In eight seasons for Montreal the 5'7", 160-pound Swede would score 243 goals and 369 assists before returning to Europe to wind up his career. But the

Canadiens sank to second place, behind Boston, and lost the divisional semifinal. The following season saw a further plummeting, into fourth place with a 35-40-5 record. A changing of the guard was in process, as veterans Lafleur and Shutt reached milestones—Lafleur with his 500th goal and Shutt his 400th on the same day, December 20, 1983, in a 6-0 swamp against New Jersey.

In mid-season, retired veteran Canadiens center Jacques Lemaire returned to the team, this time behind the bench. A superb theoretician who had been Lafleur's chief playmaker during his career, Lemaire had coached in Switzerland, where he had become expert in the new, system-oriented, video-driven style of hockey.

Lemaire's coaching led the Canadiens as far as the conference championship. They defeated their provincial rivals, the Quebec Nordiques, in a series that was marred by ideological and anti-Semitic displays on the part of separatist Nordiques' fans.

The Canadiens then faced the Islanders, who had captured four straight Stanley Cups. The Canadiens won the first two games of the series, largely without the help of Lafleur, who had to plead with Lemaire for playing time in the remaining games. The defensive-minded Islanders shut down the Canadiens for four straight, eliminating them in six games.

Hockey Hall of Fame and Museum

Jacques Lemaire

Another Cup

Lafleur's career with the Canadiens would end the following season. He scored his 518th and final goal as a Canadien on October 25, 1984; on November 26th he announced his retirement. Lafleur would be inducted in the Hall of Fame in September, 1988, and, to the astonishment of the hockey world, would return to active duty as player and coach for the Nordiques.

Despite the mid-season loss of Lafleur, the 1984-85 Canadiens were again on top of the Adams division, but lost the division final. In a postseason front-office move, Lemaire was moved upstairs as director of hockey personnel, assisting

Managing Director Serge Savard. The new head coach for 1985-86 was former assistant coach Jean Perron. The Canadiens finished second to Quebec in the Adams division, Naslund leading the team in scoring with 43 goals and 67 assists. In the divisional playoffs, Hartford eliminated Quebec and Montreal conquered Boston to set up an exciting divisional final, in which 6'1" right wing Claude Lemieux scored the winning goal for Montreal in overtime of the seventh game.

It took only five games for the Canadiens to defeat the Rangers, setting up the first all-Canadian Stanley Cup finals since 1967 between Montreal and the Calgary Flames. The Flames won game one in Calgary. Game two went into overtime, with Canadien center Brian Skrudland, an Alberta native from Peace River, scoring the winning goal against his province's team. At nine seconds, it was the fastest overtime goal in playoff history. The Habs swept the remaining three games, led by the unbelievable goaltending of rookie sensation Patrick Roy. At the age of 20 he became the youngest Smythe Trophy winner ever, logging a 1.92 goals-against average over 20 playoff games.

The 1986-87 Canadiens finished one point behind the Hartford Whalers in the regular season. They advanced as far as the Wales Conference finals against the Flyers, who eliminated them in a six-game series. The conference finals featured a pre-game locker-room-clearing brawl before game one, which began when Lemieux took a shot at the Flyers' goal to end his warmup, evoking the wrath of Flyer Ed Hospodar.

In 1987-88, Naslund won the Lady Byng Trophy and veteran center Guy Carbonneau won the Frank Selke Trophy for best defensive forward. The Montreal goaltending combination of Patrick Roy and Brian Hayward took its second of three consecutive William Jennings Awards for allowing the fewest goals in the regular season. But despite coming in first in the division by nine points, the Habs lost the Adams division final to the Bruins.

Roy ascended to the Vézina Trophy in 1988-89, the first of two consecutive years he would win that award. A formidable goalie on anybody's ice, he was an astounding 25-0-3 at the Forum. Defenseman Chris Chelios, a Chicago native, had a career year, garnering 58 assists and 73 total points, the Norris Trophy, and a first-team All-Star berth. Carbonneau took his second straight Selke Trophy. With that kind of defense and unselfish play—and the leadership of rookie coach Pat Burns, a former police officer—the Canadiens easily took first place in the Adams division, their 115-point total only two behind league-leading Calgary.

They eliminated the Flyers in six games for the conference title, then faced the Flames for the Stanley Cup—the second such meeting in four years, and the Canadiens' 31st Cup finals. The series was tied after two games, when Ryan Walter's goal in the second overtime gave the Canadiens a 2-1 lead. But the Calgary defense outplayed Montreal as the Canadiens could score only six goals in the next three games. Game six marked the first time in Canadiens history that a team other than the Canadiens had won the Stanley Cup in the Forum.

The Canadiens of the early 1990s were a team in flux. Lacking a dominating scorer of the Wayne Gretzky, Mario Lemieux, or Brett Hull variety, they relied on defense and on the increasingly solid goaltending of Patrick Roy to keep them close in games. Roy won the Vézina in 1989-90 and 1991-92, while Carbonneau repeated for the Selke in 1991-92. Carbonneau shared the captaincy with Chelios in 1989, until Chelios was traded to Chicago for center Denis Savard—an offensive specialist who would eventually lead the team in assists.

Veteran Claude Lemieux was traded to the New Jersey Devils for left wing Sylvain Turgeon; the New Jersey connection continued as right wing Stéphane Richer, who had led the Canadiens in goals in 1989-90 and 1990-91, was exchanged for center Kirk Muller as part of a four-player deal. Muller proceeded to lead Canadiens scorers in 1991-92 with 36 goals and 41 assists. Center Russ Courtnall, who led the team in assists and points in 1990-91, was traded to the Minnesota North Stars for left wing Brian Bellows. In 1992 the Canadiens also picked up, on waivers, veteran enforcer Chris Nilan, who vaulted to the team lead in penalty minutes.

The Canadiens finished third in their division in 1989-90, second in 1990-91, and climbed back to first in 1991-92. The 1992 playoffs against Hartford were a tradeoff of home team victories, with Montreal's four home games topping Hartford's three. The division final against Boston was anticlimactic: a sweep by the Bruins, with the fourth game a 2-0 shutout. At season's end, coach Burns stepped down.

The new Montreal coach was Jacques Demers, a Montreal native who as the coach of the

Red Wings had won two consecutive Jack Adams awards as the coach who had contributed most to his team's success.

Though off-season trades had brought Vincent Damphousse and Brian Bellows to Montreal, the team Demers inherited was (with the exception of Patrick Roy) without a franchise player; like the Geoffrion-Richard-Béliveau Canadiens of 1959-60, the 1992-93 team was deep in talent at nearly every position. An emotional coach who was fiercely loyal to his players, Demers took a team with a reputation of cliquishness and infighting and gelled them into an imposing hockey club.

The Canadiens finished the 84-game 1992-93 season with an impressive 102 points, sixth best in the NHL—but only third best in the grueling Adams division, behind Boston and Quebec. Damphousse led the team in scoring with 97 points, with Muller and Bellows not far behind. Muller represented the Canadiens at the All-Star game, along with perennial All-Star netminder Roy.

The first and second rounds of the playoffs, in which Montreal eliminated the Quebec Nordiques and the Buffalo Sabres, were merely a warm-up, and the Prince of Wales conference finals against the Islanders, though challenging, could not compare to the drama to come.

The Stanley Cup finals pitted the Canadiens against their old rivals, Wayne Gretzky's Los Angeles Kings. This was a rivalry in more ways than one, for the Kings' rookie coach was Barry Melrose, who had coached the Red Wings farm team while Demers had coached the Red Wings, and many suspected that Melrose was eager to defeat Demers' team. The Canadiens dropped the first game of the series on their own ice, and with less than two minutes remaining in game two were trailing by a score of 2-1, with the lone Canadien goal scored by defenseman Eric Desjardins.

Demers, knowing that only one team in NHL history had ever come back from back-to-back home losses to win the Stanley Cup, was prepared to gamble. Acting on a hunch, he asked that the referee examine the curve of Los Angeles defenseman Marty McSorley's stick. If the stick was

Patrick Roy

found to be illegal, McSorley would serve a two-minute penalty; if the stick was legal, however, Montreal would be assessed two minutes for delay of game.

Much to the surprise of McSorley, Melrose, and the Forum crowd, the stick was found to be curved beyond the legal limit, and the Canadiens were given a power play. This did not necessarily reassure Demers, for his team had not scored a single power-play goal in the last 32 attempts; hedging his bets, Demers pulled Patrick Roy out of the goal in favor of an extra attacker. Once again, Demers' gamble paid off: with a little over a minute left in regular play, Desjardins put the puck past Kings goalie Kelly Hrudey, sending the game into overtime. It then took Desjardins just 51 seconds of overtime to score again and become the first defenseman ever to score a hat trick in the Stanley Cup finals.

With the series tied at one game each, the Canadiens made the long trip to Los Angeles, where the confident Kings expected to win handily. The Habs, though, were prepared to put up a fight, sending both games into overtime—and winning both on goals by defenseman John Le-Clair. Montreal had set yet another playoff record: nine straight overtime wins. The Canadiens took their three-games-to-two edge back to Montreal, sealing up the series—and their 23rd Stanley Cup—with a decisive 4-1 victory.

As with their last championship, Patrick Roy was named the playoffs' most valuable player. The celebrations were marred, however, as thousands of exuberant Canadiens fans streamed out into the streets of Montreal, causing a riot that left 168 people injured and led to 115 arrests.

With a solid base of talent, the tireless goaltending of Patrick Roy, the leadership of Jacques Demers, and the near-fanatical loyalty of their fans, the Canadiens—the most successful team in NHL history—may well be on their way to yet another dynasty.

SOURCES

BOOKS

Beddoes, Richard, et. al, *Hockey!,* Macmillan, 1969.

Club de Hockey Canadien 1992-93 Yearbook, Club de Hockey Canadien media relations department, 1992.

Devaney, Joe, and Burt Goldblatt, *The Stanley Cup: A Complete Pictorial History,* Rand McNally & Co., 1975.

Germain, Georges-Hebert, *Overtime: The Legend of Guy Lafleur,* Viking, 1990.

Hollander, Zander, *The Complete Encyclopedia of Hockey,* fourth edition, Visible Ink Press, 1993.

Hood, Hugh, *Strength Down Centre: The Jean Béliveau Story,* Prentice-Hall, 1970.

Kariher, Harry C., *Who's Who in Hockey,* Arlington House, 1973.

McFarlane, Brian, *60 Years of Hockey,* Pagurian Press, 1976.

Mouton, Claude, *The Montreal Canadiens,* Key Porter Books, 1987.

National Hockey League Official Guide and Record Book, 1992-93, Triumph Books 1992.

O'Brien, Andy, with Plante, Jacques, *The Jacques Plante Story,* McGraw-Hill, 1972.

O'Brien, Andy, *Les Canadiens,* McGraw-Hill, 1971.

Ronberg, Gary, *The Ice Men,* Crown, 1973.

Ronberg, Gary, *The Illustrated Hockey Encyclopedia,* Balsam Press, 1984.

PERIODICALS

Life, November 23, 1959.

Maclean's, May 15, 1978; November 6, 1978; May 26, 1986.

Newsweek, November 16, 1959.

New Yorker, March 19, 1979.

Sports Illustrated, June 5, 1978; October 23, 1978; December 25, 1978; May 28, 1979; October 8, 1979; May 26, 1986; June 2, 1986; October 13, 1986.

Time, November 23, 1959; April 4, 1978; June 4, 1979.

—*Richard Cohen* for Book Builders, Inc.

OTTAWA SENATORS

The Ottawa Senators team that toiled in the NHL in 1992-93 was a far cry from their namesakes who won six Stanley Cups between 1908-1927 before being disbanded. The first-year Senators posted a horrible 10-70-4 record with only one road win. To bottom out, the Senators endured a humiliating charge that they purposely lost their final game of the year to ensure they would have the first selection in the 1993 amateur draft. A league-sponsored investigation ensued, and the Senators were cleared of charges.

Ottawa finished with the second highest goals-against total for the season, last in power play goals, and next to last in penalty killing proficiency. The team's 202 goals were the fewest by an NHL team since the 1978-79 season. Obviously, the Senators have a long way to go. They plan to improve gradually by emphasizing youth.

The team's chairman, Bruce Firestone, jokes that only his team and the Montreal Canadiens achieved their vision for the 1992-93 season:

Montreal won the Stanley Cup, and Ottawa avoided being the worst team of all time.

The Senators posted the NHL's worst record in 1992-93 with a veteran team. General Manager Mel Bridgman was fired immediately after the season and replaced by Randy Sexton, who began a youth movement. Veterans Brad Marsh and team captain Laurie Boschman, both of whom played with great desire to compensate for depleted skills, were released, along with several other older players. Among a number of swaps of older for younger players, two off-season trades with New Jersey bring the Senators a more youthful look: goalie Peter Sidorkiewicz (age 30) was traded for goalie Craig Billington (27), and, in an exchange of finesse for toughness, Mike Peluso (27) was dealt for Troy Millette (23). Dennis Vial (24) was signed to add more toughness to the defense.

Two highly touted young centers figure most prominently in Ottawa's future. Alexandre Daigle

Founding date: December 16, 1991

Home ice:
Ottawa Civic Centre
1015 Bank Street
Ottawa, Ontario, Canada K1S 3W7
Phone: (613) 564-7275

Seating Capacity: 10,565

Team colors: Gold, red, and black
Team nickname: Senators
Logo: Roman legionnaire caricature within a black circle,
bordered by the franchise name on the one side
and the tips of black wings on the other side.

Franchise record	Won	Lost	Tie
(1992-1993)	10	70	4

(18), pegged as one of the next NHL greats, was the first player selected in the 1993 amateur draft, and Alexei Yashin (19), the Senator's first pick in 1992 (second overall), fulfilled his obligation to Moscow's Dynamo and joined the Senators with great expectations. Daigle had a monstrous 1992-93 season for Victoriaville of the Quebec Major Junior Hockey League, notching 45 goals and 92 assists in 53 games. Also monstrous is Daigle's contract--$12.5 million over five years. Yashin is a great puckhandler and skater. Forwards Dave Archibald (24; 9 goals in 44 games) and Jody Hull (24; 13 goals in 69 games) and defenseman Dmitri Filimonov (20) round out the Senator's emphasis on youth.

Veteran forwards Mark Lamb, Sylvain Turgeon (who led the Senators with 25 goals), and Bob Kudelski, who scored 21 goals in 48 games after being acquired from Los Angeles, all had fine seasons in the Senator's inaugural year and provide coach Rick Bowness with on-ice leadership.

Norm Maciver was the Senator's best player in the team's first season, leading the club with 63 points (17 goals, 46 assists). MacIver was the only NHL defenseman to lead his team in scoring, and he earned a spot on Team Canada's roster for the World Championship Tournament. Brad Shaw and Darren Rumble also played respectable defense.

Harry Neale, an analyst for *Hockey Night in Canada* and a former coach, observed that "in Ottawa, hockey and politics are the same. Hope is always for the future, never for the present." In Daigle, a charismatic presence on and off the ice, and Yashin, considered a mature player at 19, coach Bowness, General Manager Randy Sexton, and Director of Player Personnel John Ferguson have players to count on. Playing in a small venue in one of the NHL's smallest communities, the Senators will not be able to count on novelty and civic pride to sustain the franchise for long. The team entered its second year younger and more hopeful for the future.

PITTSBURGH PENGUINS

As is the case with teams in many other major league professional sports, championships in the National Hockey League often seem to come in cycles. From the 1940s through the NHL's last "pre-expansion" season of 1966-67, for instance, Stanley Cup supremacy was maintained over blocks of years by just three clubs—the Montreal Canadiens, Toronto Maple Leafs, and Detroit Red Wings. In the league's early post-expansion years from 1968 to 1973, the Canadiens and Boston Bruins became the circuit's dominant teams, succeeded in the mid-1970s by the first of the new clubs to achieve excellence, the Philadelphia Flyers. Over the second half of the 1970s Montreal again emerged, followed from 1980 to 1983 by the New York Islanders and then by the Edmonton Oilers, who ruled the NHL for most of the rest of the 1980s.

As the final decade of the twentieth century began, however, a brand new force emerged to dominate the NHL—the Pittsburgh Penguins. The one-time steel capital of America's old industrial "rust belt" heartland had often enjoyed success in the traditional blue-collar sports of major league baseball and NFL football. But prior to 1990 the city's two NHL teams had more often been pretenders rather than contenders, although minor-league pro hockey had been played at championship levels in Pittsburgh from time to time in the 1950s and 1960s.

Early Pro Hockey History

Nineteen years after the reorganization of the National Hockey Association into the National Hockey League in 1917, another new professional hockey circuit destined for long term success was formed out of the ashes of a disbanding confederation as four member cities of the then-ten-year-old Canadian-American League and four more from the international League joined forces in

---

1936 to create the international-American Hockey League. Among the eight communities making up that new circuit—which within a few years was to be renamed the American Hockey League—were Pittsburgh and its longtime cross-state economic, political, and sports rival, Philadelphia.

Ironically, only a few years earlier these oft-competing Pennsylvania entities had been partners of sorts in an odd, essentially unsuccessful, preliminary fling with the NHL. In 1925 the NHL had made its first appearance in Pennsylvania in the form of the Pittsburgh Pirates, but that club pulled up stakes after just five seasons—capped by a disastrous 1929-30 "Depression year" campaign in which the Pirates won just five games (5-36-3)—to move to the opposite end of the Keystone State, where the franchise attempted to begin life anew in 1930 as the Philadelphia Quakers. As bad as the Pirates had been in Pittsburgh, however, the 1930-31 Quakers proved even worse, winning just four times (4-36-4) before folding for good after skating in the City of Brotherly Love for just one desultory season.

Over the AHL's first 31 seasons, from 1936 to 1967, charter member Philadelphia was represented in the league for just nine years—first by the original Ramblers, from 1936 to 1942, and then by the postwar Rockets, between 1946 and 1949. Pittsburgh, on the other hand, was only without AHL hockey for five seasons during that period. In 1956 the original AHL Pittsburgh Hornets suspended operations after 20 consecutive seasons when their ancient arena, Duquesne Gardens, a converted one-time streetcar barn located in the Oakland section of the city, was demolished to make way for an apartment complex.

Pro hockey, however, would not be gone for long. With the renovation of Pittsburgh's downtown district and the dedication on September 17, 1961, of the city's modern new Civic Auditorium, located less than a mile from the confluence of the Allegheny and Monongahela Rivers, the AHL Hornets returned phoenix-like to the ice in 1961-62. Although the club was a dreadful 10-58-2 in its first season back, just a half dozen years later the Hornets both captured the AHL's 1966-67

regular season championship and then swept the Rochester Americans in the Calder Cup finals to bring the Steel City a third AHL play-off title to go along with the two Calder Cups won by the original Hornets in 1952 and 1955.

By the mid-1960s the sports fans of western Pennsylvania had established a strong tradition among themselves of supporting minor pro hockey over the better part of three decades, and with the rebirth of the Hornets in 1961 the AHL was again as comfortable and familiar a feature of the Pittsburgh sports scene as the National League Pirates or NFL Steelers. Therefore when it was announced in 1965 that the NHL would double in size from six to 12 teams with the 1967-68 season, Pittsburgh's strong hockey tradition quickly pegged the city as a leading prospect to become home to one of those half dozen new National Hockey League expansion teams.

Steel City Wins NHL Expansion Franchise

A dozen groups from around North America assembled in New York City on February 8, 1966, to make formal presentations to the NHL Board of Governors seeking to purchase one of the six new franchises being created. As expected, among them was a group from Pittsburgh led by Pennsylvania state senator Jack E. MacGregor and Peter H. Block, a local businessman and MacGregor's law school classmate. The following day the board announced that, as had been the case with the formation of the AHL 30 years earlier in 1936, both of Pennsylvania's two major cities—Pittsburgh and Philadelphia—were in. The other four new NHL clubs would go to St. Louis, Missouri, and the Minnesota "twin cities" of Minneapolis-St. Paul, in the Midwest, and to the Pacific coast population hubs of Oakland and Los Angeles, in California.

As with both Pittsburgh and Philadelphia, the NHL had also once before briefly experimented with putting a team in St. Louis when the original Ottawa Senators (1917-34) moved there in 1934

TEAM INFORMATION AT A GLANCE

Founding date: June 5, 1967

Home ice: Civic Arena
Pittsburgh, PA 15219
Phone: (412) 642-1800
FAX: (412) 281-0382

Seating capacity: 16,164

Team colors: Black, gold, and white
Team nickname: Penguins or Pens
Logo: Skating penguin with a hockey stick

Franchise record	Won	Lost	Tie
(1967-93)	754	954	284

Stanley Cups: 1991, 1992
League last-place finishes (2): 1982-83, 1983-84

and became the St. Louis Eagles. However, as had been the case with the Pirates-cum-Quakers before them, the Eagles folded in 1935 after suffering through a single disastrous (11-31-6) dead-last-place NHL campaign.

While Minnesota and the two California venues had each previously supported minor league clubs, the 1967-68 season would be the first experience with NHL hockey for each. Philadelphia, Minnesota, and Los Angeles also would have to build new arenas for their NHL clubs while Pittsburgh, St. Louis, and Oakland had existing buildings available (or in Oakland's case, already under construction and open by 1966) that met the league's minimum requirement of 12,500 seats.

Pittsburgh's NHL home would be the same Civic Arena (as the Civic Auditorium had since been renamed) that had housed the AHL Hornets since 1961. At the time, the Arena just barely met the NHL's minimum capacity requirements, with

12,508 seats for hockey; new levels and super-boxes were later added in stages between 1972 and 1991, which eventually brought the total for hockey up to 16,284.

With Civic Arena the NHL had also added a most unusual and unique playing venue—the world's only major indoor sports arena equipped with a retractable roof. Civic Arena's 415-foot diameter, 170,000-square-foot, 2,950-ton stainless steel dome consists of eight huge pie-shaped "leaves," six of which can be "folded" back in just two and a half minutes under the other two. This singular design feature therefore makes it possible, if desired, to actually play NHL hockey in Pittsburgh "under the stars."

As the dome is entirely supported by a single massive 260-foot arching cantilevered arm, the arena is also completely free of internal architectural supports that could block spectator sight lines and therefore has no "obstructed view" seating.

When its roof is open, Civic Arena most closely represents a magnificent outdoor band shell and as such has been used for summer concerts and outdoor tennis matches, among other events. When closed, however, the building resembles a huge Eskimo dwelling, which quickly led to the arena being dubbed with its much more familiar, albeit unofficial, nickname—"The Igloo." Not surprisingly, then, when it came to choosing a name for the new NHL team that would play on the Igloo's frozen floor, it became clear to the people of Pittsburgh that only one moniker would really do—"The Penguins."

Building the Original Penguins

As its first general manager (GM), Penguins president Jack MacGregor hired a highly respected veteran minor-league hockey executive, John T. "Jack" Riley, who was then serving as president of the American Hockey League. A one-time player in the AHL with both Hershey, Pennsylvania, and Baltimore, Maryland, during the 1940s, the Toronto-born Riley had moved into coaching and management at only 26. In addition to his extensive behind-the-bench experience, Riley had also served as a GM in both the Eastern Hockey League (Washington, D. C., and Johnstown, Pennsylvania) and the AHL (New York's Rochester Americans) before assuming the AHL's top job in 1965.

To coach the Pens Riley hired 36-year-old George "Red" Sullivan, who had previously coached in the NHL with the New York Rangers from December, 1962, to December, 1965. Between 1951 and 1961 Sullivan was a center in the NHL for nine seasons, collecting 346 points in 557 games with Boston, Chicago, and New York. While the Pens' new coach had fashioned quite a creditable NHL career, his most outstanding season as a player came in 1953-54 with the AHL Hershey Bears. In that single AHL campaign, the 5'10", 160-pound Peterborough, Ontario, native scored 30 goals and assisted on 89 in just 69 games. Sullivan's 119 points not only led the AHL

in scoring in 1953-54, but also established an AHL single-season points record that would stand for 30 years.

As did the other five new NHL expansion clubs, the Penguins stocked their first roster largely by way of the NHL expansion draft held in Montreal on June 6, 1967. However, by the time Riley had finished picking the two goalies and 18 skaters he was permitted to claim from among the players the "original six" clubs had made available, the new Penguins could have just as easily been mistaken for a New York Rangers alumni squad; no fewer than nine of the 20 Pittsburgh picks—Earl Ingerfield, Al MacNeil, Noel Price, Ken Schinkel, Art Stratton, Val Fonteyne, Billy Dea, Mel Pearson, and then-Ranger all-time leading scorer Andy Bathgate—had skated on Broadway at one time or another in their careers.

Riley was not finished, however, for as soon as the draft was completed he added three more ex-Blueshirts when he traded Larry Jeffrey, a left wing he had just drafted from Toronto, to New York for Paul Andrea, Dunc McCallum, and George Konik to bring Pittsburgh's total of Ranger alumni assembled that day to an even dozen.

Among the Penguins' other original roster players were 31-year-old left wing Alvin Brian "Ab" McDonald, a nine-year veteran of the NHL taken from the Detroit Red Wings. McDonald, who had played for the Hornets for most of their Calder Cup season the year before, became the Pens' first captain but only remained with the team for one season before being traded to St. Louis in June, 1968. Thirty-five-year-old defenseman Leo Boivin—who stood just 5'7" but had been one of the most feared body checkers in the NHL for 15 years—also came over from Detroit.

A number of players with long careers already spent in the minor leagues but little or no NHL experience were also acquired by Riley and made the Pens' original club. Among those was 29-year-old Hershey Bears winger Gene Ubriaco, who played with Pittsburgh for its first two seasons and would eventually return over 20 years later to coach the Penguins. Keith McCreary, a 27-year-old veteran minor-league winger who arrived with just nine games of NHL experience with Montreal, would play for the Pens for almost five seasons before being lost to the Atlanta Flames in the 1972 expansion draft.

While the Penguins had taken 23-year-old former Hornet Joe Daley from the Detroit organization and 29-year-old Roy Edwards from Chicago as the two goalkeepers they claimed in the expansion draft, neither of them actually played a game for the Pens in the club's first season. Daley spent 1967-68 on loan to the AHL Baltimore Clippers but eventually played in 38 games for Pittsburgh in the 1968-69 and 69-70 seasons. He was eventually lost in the 1970 expansion draft to the Buffalo Sabres, who joined the NHL in 1970-71 with the Vancouver Canucks.

Edwards, on the other hand, had already left the Pittsburgh organization when the Pens played their first game as he had been traded to Detroit during training camp for Hank Bassen, a colorful 35-year-old veteran netminder with 132 games of NHL experience with Chicago and Detroit in addition to many solid years in the AHL and WHL.

A member of the AHL Hornets for much of the previous five seasons, Bassen had been the hero of that club's play-off run the previous April, appearing in all nine of their post-season games and compiling a league-leading play-off GAA of 1.67 as he helped the Hornets bring the Calder Cup title back to Pittsburgh in 1967.

With many Pittsburgh hockey fans still not at all happy about their beloved champion Hornets being replaced by the as yet unproven Penguins, it was hoped that acquiring the already well known and immensely popular Bassen would help assuage their anger—and also hopefully help at the gate. However, with the surprise emergence of another old AHL war horse, Leslie John "Les" Binkley, as the Pens' first "number one" netminder, Bassen would end up appearing in only 25 games for the Pens before retiring at the end of that inaugural season.

Ironically, Binkley had been acquired by the Pens nine months before the 1967 expansion draft when his contract was purchased from the AHL Cleveland Barons in September, 1966, and he was then loaned to the WHL San Diego Gulls for the 1966-67 season. Binkley, who had celebrated his 33rd birthday on the day of the expansion draft but was still considered a "rookie" in the NHL, appeared in 54 games for the Penguins during their debut campaign and compiled a highly respectable record of 20-24-10, with a 2.88 GAA and six shutouts.

Before leaving Pittsburgh five years later to sign with the Ottawa Nationals of the new World Hockey Association, Binkley collected a total of 58 wins and 11 shutouts in 196 games, with an NHL career GAA of 3.11. (After retiring as a player in 1976 at the age of 42, Binkley became a scout with the New York Rangers for a year and then joined the Winnipeg Jets in a similar capacity for another dozen seasons. In 1989, however, Binkley returned to the Penguins organization after an absence of 17 years to scout for the club that had given him his chance to finally play goal in the NHL almost a quarter of a century earlier.)

Although Binkley was already a veteran of over a dozen seasons of pro hockey when he finally broke into the NHL with the 1967-68 Penguins, at 33 he was still only a year-older than the average player on the team. In fact, with an average age of 32, the first-year Penguins were the oldest of the dozen clubs in the NHL in 1967-68. Nonetheless, 35-year-old Andy Bathgate not only proved to be Pittsburgh's leading scorer, with 59 points on 20 goals and 39 assists, but he also had the highest point total of any player in the new West Division in which the six expansion teams played and was among the league's top-twenty scorers.

NHL Hockey Returns to the Ice in Pittsburgh

The Penguins made their NHL debut at Civic Arena on October 11, 1967, by hosting the most distinguished and successful team in the history of pro hockey, the Montreal Canadiens. Although Bathgate scored the first goal in franchise history that night, the Penguins also suffered their first loss as the Habs edged them 2-1. Two nights later, however, the Pens would collect their first win by beating the St. Louis Blues on the road 3-1. Bathgate scored the club's first ever hat trick in a 3-3 tie with Minnesota on October 18, and three days later Pittsburgh witnessed the team's first home victory—and first ever over one of the NHL's "original six"—as they downed the Chicago Blackhawks at the Igloo 4-2.

Although the Pens had a veteran-laced lineup, their relatively poor record on home ice (15-12-10) kept them from ever rising above fourth place in the West Division for most of 1967-68. As season's end approached, however, it still looked as if Pittsburgh's hockey fans would be treated to NHL post-season action for the first time since the old Pirates had lost to the eventual 1928 Stanley Cup champion New York Rangers in the first round of the play-offs exactly 40 years earlier.

However, as would eventually happen to the Penguins in 13 of the club's first 23 NHL seasons, between 1967-68 and 1989-90, by the time the 1968 Stanley Cup tournament began in the first week of April, the Penguins found themselves on the outside looking in.

The first sign of disaster came when Bathgate's longtime linemate Earl Ingerfield fractured his kneecap in early February and the Pens' scoring leader went without a goal for the next nine games. Defensive winger Ken Schinkel, who had been the Pens' representative in the All-Star Game in Toronto that year, went down next, on January 28, when the veteran's ankle was cracked as he blocked a Bobby Orr slapshot during the course of a 1-0 Binkley-authored shutout in Boston. Then Binkley himself was shelved when he broke a finger against Oakland on March 2nd and was unable to play again until the season's final week.

While the Penguins struggled on with their injury-depleted lineup, the St. Louis Blues and Minnesota North Stars picked up the pace and soon passed them. Although Pittsburgh won its last four games of the year to match both St. Louis and Minnesota with 27 wins apiece, the other two clubs each had more ties and fewer losses than the Pens. With Philadelphia and Los Angeles already holding down first and second place, that left the 27-34-13 Penguins as the "odd-team out," in fifth place, with 67 points and ahead of only the far-distant (47 points) last-place Oakland Seals.

Penguin Losses On and Off the Ice

The Penguins would not only prove starcrossed on the ice over much of their early history, but off the ice as well. Frequently, the club found itself in deep financial straits necessitating an almost constant search for new investors. On March 22, 1968, Donald H. Parsons, a Detroit-based banker and lawyer, and eight other Michigan businessmen became the first such "angels" as the Parsons group bought a controlling interest (80 percent) in the club from the original 20-man syndicate that had acquired the franchise in 1966. Over the next decade the club's ownership structure would undergo three more such financially driven changes.

Turmoil similarly abounded on the ice during the Pens' early years. With team captain Ab McDonald's trade to St. Louis prior to the 1968-69 season for former Philadelphia Flyer captain—and another future Pittsburgh coach—Lou Angotti, the Pens curiously failed to appoint another player to wear the "C" until 1973. Despite leading the club in scoring in 1967-68, Andy Bathgate also disappeared from Pittsburgh's second-year roster when he was loaned to the WHL Vancouver Canucks in October, 1968. He did not return again to the Pens lineup until 1970, when the WHL Canucks folded so that Vancouver could ice an NHL expansion team in 1970-71.

Although GM Jack Riley made a number of trades during the 1968-69 season, the deal that proved to have greatest long-term impact on the future of the Penguins came with little fanfare during the off-season in May, 1968, with the acquisition of 22-year-old left wing Jean Pronovost and defenseman John Arbour from the Boston Bruins for cash and a first-round draft pick in 1969. Although Arbour only appeared in 17 games for Pittsburgh before eventually being sold to the

WHL Canucks, Pronovost would become a mainstay in Pittsburgh for a decade. Over that period the smooth-skating Shawinigan Falls, Quebec, native collected 603 points on 316 goals and 287 assists while appearing in a team-record 753 games. As the Penguins entered their 27th NHL season (1993-94), only the great Mario Lemieux had scored more goals—and Lemieux and Rick Kehoe had collected more total points—in a Pittsburgh uniform than Jean Pronovost.

Among the few highlights of the Penguins' otherwise disappointing second NHL season was the club's first-ever win at the Montreal Forum. On January 2, 1969, the Penguins defeated the Canadiens, 5-2, despite having lost nine of their previous ten games—and then dropped 11 of their next 13. Keith McCreary's 25 goals made him the Pens' only twenty-plus goal scorer that year, and with 52 points (18-34) Ken Schinkel was the club's leading scorer and again represented his team in the All-Star game at Montreal.

With the retirement of Hank Bassen after the 1967-68 campaign, Joe Daley had joined Les Binkley in goal in 1968-69. Each, however, only managed ten wins apiece for the second-year club, which dropped 16 points under the previous season's total on a record of 20-45-11 (51 points) to miss the play-offs again with a fifth-place finish, seven points behind fourth-place Los Angeles.

The season even proved to be a tough one for the club mascot; the Pens' management went to considerable expense to acquire a real penguin and spent two months teaching it to skate. Just before the bird was finally to make its public on-ice debut, however, it contracted pneumonia and died.

At season's end, Red Sullivan became Pittsburgh's first former coach as he moved over to the team's scouting staff. But when the Penguins took to the ice for their third NHL campaign in October, 1969, the players still called their new coach "Red" as Leonard "Red" Kelly took over the club after coaching the Los Angeles Kings through their first two NHL seasons. During his twenty-year playing career, Kelly had won four Stanley Cups as a defenseman with Detroit—and four

more playing center for Toronto—before retiring in 1967. Just prior to coaching his first game in Pittsburgh Kelly's playing was honored with his induction into the Hockey Hall of Fame.

In keeping with his tradition of bringing in experienced players, Jack Riley claimed 37-year-old left winger Dean Prentice, already a veteran of 17 seasons in the NHL, from the Detroit Red Wings in the intra-league Draft in June, 1969, and also grabbed the hard-nosed 26-year-old Glen Sather—who later managed and coached the Edmonton Oilers to a bevy of Stanley Cups in the 1980s—from the Boston Bruins in the same lottery.

From the WHL Canucks Riley added some muscle to his club's lineup when he acquired 28-year-old veteran minor-league center Bryan Hextall, Jr., the rough-and-tumble son of the last New York Ranger to score a Stanley Cup-winning goal (1940) and the father of future Vezina Trophy-winning goalie Ron Hextall.

From Toronto the Penguins got 24-year-old goalie Al Smith, who went on to be the club's busiest netminder over his two seasons in Pittsburgh, during which he appeared in 91 games with a 24-42-17 record (3.07 GAA) and four shutouts. Riley also added center Ron Schock, a Penguin mainstay for eight seasons, from St. Louis at the expense of Lou Angotti and Pittsburgh's first-round pick in the 1971 amateur draft.

Despite Pittsburgh's continued dependence on veterans, in 1969 the club began to seriously look at building a future with youth. Although the Penguins had no first-round pick in the 1969 amateur draft, having traded it to Boston a year earlier for Jean Pronovost, the club came up with what appeared to be its first future young star that June when it drafted 19-year-old center Michel Briere in the third round (26th overall) from Shawinigan of the Quebec League. The personable 5'10", 160-pound pivot became an instant fan favorite in his 1969-70 rookie season, collecting 44 points on a dozen goals and 32 assists to finish third in team scoring behind veterans Dean Prentice and Ken Schinkel.

As would be the case with fellow French-

Canadian Penguin forwards Pierre Larouche and Mario Lemieux, who would follow him to Pittsburgh in the 1970s and 1980s, Michel Briere quickly melted the hearts of the Steel City's sports fans.

But the love affair would end tragically after less than a year when Briere was seriously injured in an automobile accident in northern Quebec on May 15, 1970. The accident occurred just a few weeks after Briere had helped lead the Penguins through their first-ever trip to the play-offs, in which he scored five goals (including the series winner over Oakland in overtime) and assisted on three in ten games against the Seals and Blues. Briere never recovered from his injuries and died 11 months later on April 13, 1971. The Penguins subsequently retired his jersey number, "21," making it the first to be so honored by an expansion club. As of the 1993-94 season, Michel Briere's "21" remained the only number ever to have been retired by the Pittsburgh Penguins.

Although Pittsburgh finished its third season with a record of 26-38-12 and three fewer points (67) than they had scored their first year—when they missed the play-offs—it was enough to give the Pens second place in the West Division in 1969-70 and earn them a spot in the Stanley Cup race for the first time in their history. Kelly's club performed flawlessly in its first-ever post-season series as the Pens swept past the Oakland Seals in four straight games, but in the semi-finals the West Division champion St. Louis Blues ended Pittsburgh's first quest for the Stanley Cup in 42 years by eliminating the Penguins four games to two.

Although Pittsburgh was still 20 years away from making a serious challenge for the Cup, the club's improvement in 1969-70 and strong play-off performance, which had brought them within two games of the Stanley Cup finals, was recognized; Red Kelly was named by the *Hockey News* as its "Coach of the Year." Penguin defenseman Bob Woytowich and the ageless Prentice were also named to the 1969-70 West Division All-Star Team.

With the 1970-71 season Jack Riley became the Penguins' executive director and coach Red Kelly added the GM's duties to his portfolio. In June the club used its first-round pick (7th overall) to select winger Greg Polls from the WCHL Estevan Bruins, and in January, 1971, Kelly sent Glen Sather to the Rangers for defenseman Sheldon Kannegieser and 23-year-old center Syl Apps. By the time Apps left Pittsburgh eight years later he had notched an even 500 points as a Penguin on 151 goals and 349 assists. As of the 1993-94 season, Apps still held fourth place on Pittsburgh's all-time scoring list behind only Mario Lemieux, Rick Kehoe, and Jean Pronovost.

With the addition of Bobby Hull and the powerhouse Chicago Blackhawks to the West Division in 1970-71, along with the strong Blues and improved Flyers, North Stars, and Kings, the Penguins dropped from second- to sixth-place and out of the play-off picture again despite finishing with just two fewer points (62) than the year before on a record of 21-37-20.

While the Penguins had played pretty well at home, where they lost just 12 of 39 games, their road show in 1970-71 was more like a horror show as they won just three times (3-25-11) while being outscored 148 to 95.

"Revolving Door" Ownership Continues

As had been the case almost since the beginning, the Penguins' off-ice financial woes continued to make as many headlines as their on-ice exploits. Just three weeks after the end of the 1970-71 season, the Penguins got their third set of owners in just over four years as the club was acquired by a four-man Pittsburgh-based group of which 38-year-old utility executive Thayer R. "Tad" Potter was the general partner. Potter, a marketing director with Peoples Natural Gas Company whose only previous connection with the team was as a season ticket salesman, took over as chief executive officer of the hockey club.

Meanwhile on the ice, Syl Apps led the club in scoring in 1971-72 with 15 goals and 44 assists to tie Andy Bathgate's then-club-single-season record of 59 points. And for the first time in team history, the Pens not only had a 30-goal scorer, they had two; Jean Pronovost and sophomore Greg Polls both notched an even 30 goals on the season while the NHL's perennial badman Bryan "Bugsy" Watson became the first Penguin to ever exceed 200 penalty minutes in a season with 212.

Goalie Jimmy Rutherford, who had been acquired from Detroit in the intra-league draft in June, carried the major load in the nets, compiling a 17-15-5 record while Les Binkley and Roy Edwards split the rest of the work. Also joining the Penguins that season was 22-year-old Toronto-born defenseman Dave Burrows, claimed in the intra-league draft from the Chicago Blackhawks.

The steady 6'1", 190-pound blueliner would go on to be the Penguins' unquestioned leader on defense for seven seasons until he was traded to Toronto in 1978 for Randy Carlyle and George Ferguson. (He returned in November, 1980, for one more season in Pittsburgh.) In all, Burrows appeared in 573 games as a Penguin, second only to Ron Stackhouse's 621-game total among Pittsburgh blueliners.

Despite receiving a new five-year contract as GM/coach after the ownership change, Red Kelly relinquished the GM's post to Jack Riley on January 29, 1972. Meanwhile Kelly continued to perform his duties behind the Pittsburgh bench for a third full season, which the Penguins finished with 66 points on a record of 26-38-12. It literally took the Penguins until the final seconds of the season, however, to make the play-offs.

First Greg Polls scored with less than a minute to go in their last road game at Philadelphia on April 1st to give the Pens a 4-4 tie and a 3-2-1 edge in the season series over the Flyers. After defeating St. Louis at home the next night 6-2, the Penguins then had to await the outcome of the Flyers' final game of the season at Buffalo. A Philadelphia win or tie would have eliminated Pittsburgh, but incredibly, the Sabres' Gerry Meehan scored with four seconds left in that final game to edge Philadelphia 3-2. Unfortunately for the Penguins, however, their prize for making the play-offs was a series with the Chicago Blackhawks,

who dispatched them easily in four straight games.

Kelly's fourth season behind the Pittsburgh bench, 1972-73, proved to be his last. After a fairly strong start (15-12-2), the club faltered badly over a stretch of a dozen games beginning on December 17, which resulted in a 2-7-3 record. On January 12, 1973, original Penguin Ken Schinkel retired as a player and was named to replace Kelly the next day, becoming the Penguins' fourth coach.

Although the Penguins didn't do any better under Schinkel over the rest of the season (15-18-3), they still improved by 11 points in 1972-73 to 73, with a 32-37-9 record. But with the league's expansion that year to sixteen teams ballooning the West Division to eight clubs, with the addition of the new Atlanta Flames, half of those would now miss the play-offs at season's end. For the fourth time in their first six seasons, the Pens missed the cut as they finished in fifth place in the West, just three points behind St. Louis.

On the positive side, Syl Apps became the first Penguin to average over a point per game as he collected 85 points in 77 contests on 29 goals and 56 assists to lead the team in scoring for the second year in a row. Right wing Al McDonough, who had been acquired in January, 1972, from Los Angeles for Bob Woytowich, collected three hat tricks in the team's first 21 games and finished the year second only to Apps in scoring, with 76 points on a team-leading 35 goals and 41 assists. Mc-Donough's third hat trick was part of an NHL record-setting outburst against the St. Louis Blues at the Igloo on November 22nd, with one of his three markers coming during a flurry of five goals scored by the Pens in a stretch of just 2:07.

Lowell MacDonald, the 32-year-old left winger on Apps' line, finished one point behind McDonough with 34 goals and 41 assists. What made that so remarkable was that MacDonald had missed all but ten games over the previous two seasons while rehabilitating from four separate knee operations. In addition to his offensive output, MacDonald also finished the season at plus-41 for the fourth-best plus-minus in the NHL that year. MacDonald's remarkable comeback earned him the NHL's Bill Masterton Trophy for "dedication to hockey," making him the first Penguin player to win a major-league award.

Comings and Goings—Both Upstairs and Down

While the Philadelphia Flyers were streaking to their first of two consecutive Stanley Cup titles on the western end of Pennsylvania in 1973-74, their western neighbors in Pittsburgh were missing the play-offs for a fifth time in seven seasons. Just a little less than 13 months after taking over the bench from Red Kelly, Ken Schinkel found himself out on February 6, 1974, with the Penguins having won just 14 of its 50 games (14-31-5). He was replaced by Marc Boileau, who had coached the Pens' IHL affiliate the Fort Wayne Komets to both the regular season and Turner Cup play-off titles in 1972-73. (Schinkel remained with the team in a scouting capacity and returned to the Penguins' bench two years later, replacing Boileau in January, 1976.)

On January 13, just 24 days before Boileau replaced Schinkle, GM Jack Riley was himself replaced by Penguins director of player personnel and assistant GM Jack Button. Although he had never played the game and began his career in pro hockey as a publicity man, Button had built a well-deserved reputation as an astute judge of talent who had brought the team such fine players as Al McDonough, Syl Apps, and Dave Burrows, to mention a few.

Four days after taking the job, Button made his first trade, bringing in 24-year-old defenseman Ron Stackhouse from the Detroit Red Wings for Jim Rutherford and Jack Lynch. With the 6'3", 210-pound puck-moving Stackhouse to go along with Dave Burrows, a premiere stay-at-home rearguard, Button had provided the Penguins with a dynamic defensive duo that would eventually serve the team for a combined total of 1,194 games of quality Blueline play.

Jean Pronovost also took over the right wing slot on the Pens' top line with Apps and Mac-Donald during the season, and the trio became know as the "Century Line" as they combined for 107 goals. (McDonough had been traded to Atlanta on January 4th for Chuck Arnason and Bob Paradise.) With 24 goals and 61 assists, Apps compiled his second consecutive 85-point season and finished seventh overall in scoring in the league.

After the "Century Line," however, the Pens' scoring punch fell off considerably and the team was only able to win 28 times (28-41-9) to finish in sixth place in the West Division with 65 points, nine fewer than the second-year, fifth-place Flames.

When GM Jack Button went to Montreal in June for the league's 1974 annual meetings and amateur draft, he knew that even though the Pens had finished sixth in the West Division, he would pick no higher than eighth in the draft as five other teams in the league had finished with worse records than Pittsburgh, and two new franchises—Kansas City and Washington—would get the first two picks.

Button also had to worry about the Montreal Canadiens, who owned the fifth and seventh overall selections, which they had acquired from Vancouver and St. Louis in trades and might well use to claim a certain flashy young French-Canadian player that Button hoped would still be around when Pittsburgh's turn came.

As it turned out, Montreal went for huge Flin Flon Bomber right wing Cam Connor and feisty Kitchener Ranger center Doug Risebrough with their two top picks. Fortunately for Pittsburgh, none of the other high-drafting clubs—Washington, Kansas City, California, the New York Islanders, and Minnesota—looked toward the Quebec League either, which left Button the player he wanted all along, flashy, high-scoring eighteen-year-old French-Canadian center Pierre Larouche of the Sorel Blackhawks. After collecting 31 goals as a teenaged rookie in 1974-75, Larouche would become Pittsburgh's first-ever 50-goal and 100-point scorer in 1975-76.

A few months after drafting Larouche, Button made a second outstanding personnel move when he obtained 23-year-old right wing Rick

Kehoe from Toronto for Blaine Stoughton and Pittsburgh's first-round pick in 1977. Kehoe would play 11 seasons as a Pen, collecting 636 points on 312 goals and 324 assists in 722 games before retiring in 1985 to join the club's coaching staff. Only Mario Lemieux exceeds Kehoe among all-time Penguin point getters.

1974-77: Finally on the Upswing

With the NHL expanding to 18 teams in 1974-75, the East and West Divisions were finally abandoned in favor of two conferences split into four smaller divisions. The Penguins joined the new Norris Division along with Montreal, Los Angeles, Detroit, and Washington to play in the Prince of Wales Conference. This new arrangement seemed to suit the Penguins well; for the first time the club finished a season with a winning record—37-28-15. (No subsequent Penguin squad would reach the 1974-75 team's total of 89 points until 17 years later, by which time the Pens were already two-time defending Stanley Cup champions, with 56 wins and 119 points in 1992-93, finally breaking their old mark by an incredible 30 points.)

With the addition of Larouche and Kehoe, the acquisition of former 50-goal scorer Vic Hadfield from the Rangers for defenseman Nick Beverley, and captain Ron Schock emerging with a career year (23-63), Pittsburgh suddenly became a scoring machine in 1974-75. Only the Canadiens, Sabres, and Bruins managed more goals that season than the Penguins' total of 326. Nine Pens scored 20 or more goals, with Larouche and Hadfield notching 31 each and Jean Pronovost leading the team with 43. (Larouche and Pronovost would both exceed 50 the following year.)

In goal, 25-year-old Gary Inness (who had been signed as a free agent in June, 1973) emerged as the Pens' last line of defense, appearing in 57 games, with a record of 24-18-10 and a 3.09 GAA. Michel Plasse, Bob Johnson, and Denis Herron combined for a 13-10-5 mark in the team's other 27 decisions. Although the Penguins' 89 points were only good enough for third place in the high-powered Norris Division, behind Montreal's 113 and Los Angeles's 105, the Penguins had the sixth-best overall record among the NHL's 18 clubs in 1974-75 and were therefore back in the play-offs—albeit for just the third time in eight years. This time, however, it looked as if the club might actually have a chance to win two or three series.

After sweeping St. Louis in the best-of-three preliminary round in two straight games, the Penguins met the New York Islanders—a club that had joined the league three years earlier and was in the play-offs for the first time—in the best-of-seven quarterfinals. The high-scoring Penguins were expected to take the series with relative ease. If successful, the Pens would get to face their powerful cross-state rivals, the Stanley Cup champion Flyers, in the semifinals.

Pittsburgh's snipers scored 14 times in the first three contests to give the Penguins a commanding three-games-to-none lead over the Isles and ignite Stanley Cup fever in the Steel City for the first time; it was beginning to appear as if the hometown heroes might reach the NHL's "Final Four" without losing a game.

The Islanders—and more specifically, New York goalie Chico Resch—had different ideas, however. After the Isles surrendered an average of 4.66 goals over the first three games, Resch cut the Pens down to a goal-a-game over the next four while Islander shooters foiled Inness a dozen times. Incredibly, in just four days the Pens' seemingly insurmountable three-game lead quickly gave way to a series tied at three games apiece before Resch administered the coup de grace on April 26, 1975, with a 1-0 shutout at the Igloo to finally dash Pittsburgh's 1975 Stanley Cup hopes.

1975: Rescued Again

Six weeks after the Penguins' crushing play-off loss, it began to look as if Pittsburgh would lose their team altogether as the financially troubled club was forced to declare bankruptcy on June 13,

1975. On July 11th, however, the Penguins were rescued once again when Albert Savill, Wren Blair, and Otto Frenzel purchased the team and became the fourth group to own the club in just eight years. Savill, the British-born owner of a Columbus, Ohio, mortgage company who took over as chairman and CEO of the Penguins, had experience in hockey as owner of the IHL Columbus Owls. Blair, a longtime junior hockey executive, former GM/coach of the Minnesota North Stars, and owner of the IHL Saginaw Gears, became the Pens' president and general manager. Frenzel, the chairman of an indianapolis bank, took on the duties of the club's secretary-treasurer.

The Pens appeared to celebrate their latest rescue from oblivion by winning their first four games of the 1975-76 season, during which they outscored their opposition 27-12. As usual, however, the club could not sustain success and, after suffering through a dreadful 5-14-3 stretch in December and January, Blair removed Marc Boileau as coach on January 17, 1976, and returned Ken Schinkel for his second stint behind the Pittsburgh bench. This time the medicine seemed to work as the club went 20-10-7 over the final 37 games of the season under Schinkel and exploded for 339 goals, of which Larouche and Pronovost combined to contribute 105.

With 111 points (53-58), Larouche finished his sophomore year fifth overall in NHL scoring behind only Guy Lafleur, Bob Clarke, Gil Perreault, and Bill Barber. Pronovost (52-52-104) and Apps (32-67-99) also joined "Lucky Pierre" in the league's top ten at eighth and tenth overall, and Lowell MacDonald and Vic Hadfield each also contributed 30-goal seasons. In goal, Michel Plasse led the way with a 24-19-10 (3.45) mark and two shutouts.

With another third-place finish (33-35-12; 82) in the Norris Division behind Montreal and Los Angeles, the Penguins met the Toronto Maple Leafs in the always-scary best-of-three preliminary round of the 1976 Stanley Cup play-offs. With a hot Wayne Thomas in goal, however, the Leafs shut down Pittsburgh's big offense and allowed them just three goals over the three games

while scoring ten on Denis Herron to upset the Penguins and take the series two games to one.

Pittsburgh's 1976-77 season was almost a carbon copy of 1975-76 as far as its record (34-33-11), points (81), and finish (7th overall, 3rd in the Norris), but its playing style was dramatically different. After scoring 339 goals the previous year for an average of 4.23 per game, the Penguins managed just 240 (3 per game) with essentially the same lineup and top forwards. The offensive numbers of Larouche (29-34-63), Pronovost (33-31-64), and Apps (18-43-61) all tumbled as the club's top three scorers dropped from a combined total of 314 points in 1975-76 to just 188 in 1976-77.

The club's scoring drop of almost a goal and a quarter per game, however, was the result of much greater concentration on the defensive aspects of the game, at which Schinkel had himself been so skilled as a player. Consequently, the number of goals allowed also dropped dramatically from 303 to 252, with goalies Dunc Wilson (18-19-8; 5 shutouts) and Denis Herron (15-11-5; 1 shutout) fashioning identical 2.94 goals-against averages.

In exchange for an October draft pick, the Penguins defense also benefited from the August acquisitions of Montreal's permiere shot-blocking blueliner Don Awrey and Los Angeles' fine-checking winger Mike Corrigan.

Unfortunately, however, none of this changed 1976-77's bottom-line results in either the regular season or play-offs. The Penguins not only drew the Toronto Maple Leafs again in the preliminary round of the 1977 Stanley Cup play-offs, but also lost to them again by the same two-games-to-one margin. Although Pittsburgh had managed the minor prize of having the "home ice advantage" for the series this time, both of their losses to the Leafs came at the Igloo.

The "Baz" Bastien Era Begins

Midway through that 1976-77 season, the Penguins underwent another major change in office leadership as 56-year-old Aldege "Baz" Bastien took over as GM from Wren Blair on December 3, 1976. Of all the people to ever manage or coach the Penguins, Baz Bastien had by far the longest association with pro hockey in Pittsburgh.

A one-time All-Star goalie with the original AHL Hornets in the late 1940s, Bastien's playing career was cut short at age 29 when he lost an eye during a scrimmage on the first day of the Hornets' 1949-50 training camp in Welland, Ontario. Bastien remained with the Hornets after his injury, however, and spent most of the next 20 years as an executive and/or coach with the Hornets or Hershey Bears, whom he joined as business manager in 1956 when the original Hornets club folded. Bastien returned to Pittsburgh as GM of the "new" Hornets when the club returned to the AHL in 1961, and in 1966-67 he coached the team to the city's final Calder Cup title.

Bastien wasted little time after the 1976-77 season ended to begin making major changes. First he replaced Ken Schinkel behind the bench with 48-year-old Johnny Wilson. A one-time NHL "Iron Man" when he appeared in 580 consecutive games with Detroit and Chicago between 1952 and 1960, Wilson turned to coaching when he retired as a player in 1962.

In addition to guiding the NCAA Princeton University Tigers, AHL Springfield Indians and AHL Tidewater Red Wings, Wilson had also already coached three other NHL clubs—Detroit, Los Angeles, and Colorado—before being hired by Bastien to coach the Penguins on June 13, 1977.

Once the 1977-78 season got underway, Bastien kept his telephone busy making frequent deals both big and small. In late September he traded team captain Ron Schock to Buffalo for the colorful Brian "Spinner" Spencer, and on October 1st sent Don Awrey's rights to Washington for Bob Paradise. Long-time scoring star Syl Apps went next, along with Hartland Nonahan, to the Los Angeles Kings on November 2nd for Gene Carr, NHL all-time penalty-minute king Dave Schultz, and a fourth-round draft pick in 1978.

Bastien saved his biggest trade for last, however, as he dealt Pierre Larouche and NHL rights to winger Peter Marsh (then playing in the WHA)

to Montreal for veteran center Pete Mahovlich and promising 21-year-old right wing Peter Lee, who had been the Habs' first-round pick in the 1976 Draft. Less than two years earlier, Larouche had been the toast of Pittsburgh as a 19-year-old 53-goal scorer with a then-team-record 111 points. Under the more defensive-minded systems of Ken Schinkel and Johnny Wilson, however, Larouche had become ineffective, only producing six goals and 11 points in 20 games for Pittsburgh in 1977-78 when he was sent packing to Montreal. (With the "Flying Frenchmen" Larouche became a 50-goal scorer again by 1979-80.)

The short term-result of this turmoil was that the Penguins dropped 13 points to 68 on a record of 25-37-18 in 1977-78, largely because the number of goals they allowed ballooned from 252 to 321. By finishing fifth in the Norris Division and 12th overall in the league, the Pens were also out of the play-offs again after qualifying the three previous years. Bastien was looking to the future, however, and believed that the long-term results of his many moves would eventually prove his course a wise one.

Off the ice, the club's financial woes continued until Youngstown, Ohio, shopping mall magnate and real estate developer Edward J. DeBartolo, Sr., purchased one-third of the franchise and agreed to take over the financial obligations of the club. DeBartolo first became involved in sports in 1960 when he purchased Thistledown Race Track in Cleveland and later added Balmoral in Chicago and Louisiana Downs in Shreveport.

The DeBartolo family's first venture into team sports, however, did not come until 1977, with the purchase of the NFL San Francisco 49ers by Edward J. DeBartolo, Jr. On April 5, 1978, four days prior to the Penguins' last game of the 1977-78 season, DeBartolo assumed complete control of the club and installed Vincent J. Bartimo, the GM of Louisiana Downs, as president and chairman.

The management of the club's day-to-day business and policy matters was taken over by 36-year-old Pittsburgh attorney J. Paul Martha, who was named vice president and general counsel. A native Pittsburgher, Martha had first made his name in sports in the football-crazed Steel City as an All American at the University of Pittsburgh in the early 1960s. As the number-one draft pick of the NFL Steelers in 1964, Martha had been a top defensive back with that club for five years before finishing his active playing career with the Denver Broncos in 1970. While still playing with the Steelers, Martha had also attended Duquesne University Law School, from which he graduated in 1969. After his retirement from football, he returned to Pittsburgh and joined the law firm of Reed, Smith, Shaw & McClay.

As the Penguins' fiscal house was being restructured, Bastien continued to make deals as if there were no tomorrow. At the 1978 NHL meetings in Montreal, he obtained promising 22-year-old defenseman Randy Carlyle and six-year NHL veteran center George Ferguson from Toronto for 29-year-old Dave Burrows.

Then, late on the evening of June 14th, Bastien sent the Pens' first-round pick in the next morning's amateur draft to Philadelphia for three members of the Flyers' 1974 and 1975 Stanley Cup teams—center Orest Kindrachuk, defenseman Tom Bladon, and winger Ross Lonsberry.

Jean Pronovost became the next to go when, after a decade in Pittsburgh, he was shipped to the Atlanta Flames in September. The three-way deal with Boston brought the Pens the Bruins' top defensive center, Gregg Sheppard. Dale Tallon, a 28-year-old veteran defenseman, came next from Chicago just before the season opened in October for a second-round draft pick in 1980, and then a week into the season Bastien traded yet another first-round pick (1981) to Montreal on October 18th for promising 22-year-old left wing Rod Schutt, a former AHL Rookie of the Year with Nova Scotia in 1976-77.

With all these changes the team not unexpectedly started the 1978-79 season slowly, with just one win in their first 11 games (1-8-2), and by the end of November was solidly in last place at 5-14-3. But Bastien got the last laugh as his moves finally started to pay off in December, and over the final two-thirds of the season, Wilson's restruc-

tured club compiled an outstanding 31-17-10 record to finish the year in second place in the Norris with 85 points (36-31-13), which earned Bastien Executive of the Year honors.

Twenty-two-year-old center Greg Malone, a 1976 Penguin second-round draft pick, led the team in scoring with 35 goals and 65 points, while rookie goalie Greg Millen (14-11-1; 3.37; 2 shutouts), a 1977 sixth rounder, emerged as an instant fan favorite in net behind veteran Denis Herron (22-19-2; 3.37).

Among the more unusual highlights of the 1978-79 campaign was a home-and-home divisional series with the vaunted Montreal Canadiens on February 21 and 22. The Pens opened the two-game set at home with an impressive 3-1 victory authored by Denis Herron over future Hall of Famer Ken Dryden and the then-three-time-defending Stanley Cup champions for just the Penguins' ninth career victory over Montreal against 50 losses and nine ties. The next night in Montreal, however, the Habs made them pay dearly as the late Bunny Larocque shut out Pittsburgh while the aroused Canadiens shooters pumped a dozen goals past Herron and Millen. That 12-0 drubbing still remains the largest margin by which the Penguins have ever lost a game.

In the play-offs, George Ferguson propelled Pittsburgh past favored Buffalo in the best-of-three preliminary round by first scoring in the third period to tie the third-and-final game of the set and then beating Bob Sauve in the first minute of overtime to defeat the Sabres 4-3. Ferguson's game-and-series winner was also the Penguins' first overtime goal in almost a decade.

The powerhouse Boston Bruins quickly ended the Pens' play-off hopes in the quarterfinals, however, as Bruin goalie Gerry Cheevers held them to just seven goals in four games while Boston's snipers scored 16 times to sweep the best-of-seven series.

The 1979-80 hockey season was dominated by two riveting and virtually unprecedented stories—the Philadelphia Flyers' 35-game unbeaten streak from October to January and the miraculous Gold Medal-winning performance of the U.S.

Hockey Team at the politically charged Winter Olympic Games at Lake Placid in February.

While neither had any direct effect on the overall outcome of the Penguins' season, during which the club dropped a dozen points from 85 to 73 and fell from five games over to seven games under .500 with a 30-37-13 record, the Pens were nonetheless touched by each of these remarkable events.

On December 20, 1979, the Pens visited Philadelphia with a chance to end the Flyers' streak at 27 games and thereby prevent their cross-state rivals from tying Montreal's then-NHL record of 28 games without a loss. The greatly overmatched Pens—who had only managed one win and one tie at the Spectrum in the previous decade—were clearly inspired by the challenge.

As the tense game approached the final buzzer, Pittsburgh was grittily holding on to a 1-0 lead behind the equally inspired goaltending of young Greg Millen, who held his ground as if it were the seventh game of the Stanley Cup finals. Thanks to a controversial penalty called on Penguin blueliner Bob Stewart, however, the Flyers managed to barely escape with their streak intact when Philadelphia defenseman Behn Wilson scored a power-play goal in the game's dying moments for a 1-1 tie—the Pens' sixth deadlock in their last seven games.

Although they failed to end the Flyers' streak, the Penguins had come closer than had many stronger clubs, and their inspirational performance that night drove them on to win five of their next seven games, Pittsburgh's best such stretch of the season. The Flyers, meanwhile, sailed on to eventually better Montreal's record by seven games.

With the end of the Olympics in February, many of the Gold Medal-winning American players turned pro and joined NHL teams. Olympic center Mark Johnson, the Penguins' fourth-round pick in 1977 from the University of Wisconsin, made his NHL debut with Pittsburgh on March 2nd in a 0-0 tie with the New York Islanders.

While Johnson was traded away to the Minnesota North Stars just two years later, his surname eventually graced the Stanley Cup when the Pens finally won it for the first time in 1991 under the guidance of Mark's father, Bob Johnson, who had also been his son's college hockey coach at the University of Wisconsin from 1976 to 1979.

The Penguins made a major change in their physical appearance during the 1979-80 season when they abandoned their longstanding quiescent light blue, dark blue, and white team colors in favor of the far more aggressive black and gold. While the Pens had changed the basic design of their uniforms a number of times over their first dozen seasons, taking the far more drastic step of altering a club's colors is a rare move in sports.

However, with the black-and-gold-clad baseball Pirates as reigning 1979 World Series champions and the similarly tinctured Steelers having won their fourth Super Bowl title in six years just ten days earlier, the Penguins appeared in their sympathetically hued new livery for the first time on January 30, 1980, when they hosted the St. Louis Blues at the Igloo.

(As did the Pirates, the Pens used two differently colored sets of home jerseys—one with white as the basic color, another with gold. This confusing practice was eventually abandoned, however, in favor of using only basic white home jerseys.)

While the Penguins had fallen to 13th place overall in the NHL by season's end, the addition of four refugee clubs from the recently disbanded World Hockey Association to the NHL in 1979-80 increased the total number of teams qualifying for the play-offs from 12 to 16, giving the Pens a berth.

As they had been a year earlier, however, the Pens were again eliminated by the Boston Bruins, with whom they now shared their colors. After their recent Olympic hero, Mark Johnson, scored twice to help upset the powerhouse B's 4-2 in the first game of the best-of-five preliminary round at Boston Garden, the Bruins dominated the Penguins the rest of the way to take the series in five games while out-scoring Pittsburgh over the final four contests 19 to 10.

Eddie Johnston Arrives

After three years behind the Penguins' bench, Johnny Wilson departed to be replaced in 1980-81 by Eddie Johnston, a former outstanding NHL goalkeeper who had retired in 1978 after 16 seasons and 592 games with Boston, Toronto, St. Louis, and Chicago. The last netminder to have played every minute of every game for his club in an NHL season (4,200 minutes in 70 games with Boston in 1963-64), the 45-year-old Johnston had played on two Stanley Cup winners in Boston (1970 and 1972) and had led the EHL Johnstown (Pennsylvania) Jets to a senior amateur title just 40 miles east of Pittsburgh in 1960.

When he joined the Penguins, however, Johnston had just two seasons of coaching experience—one year with the AHL Moncton (New Brunswick) Hawks and another behind the bench of the NHL Chicago Blackhawks, whom he had guided to a first-place finish in the Smythe Division in 1979-80.

While the Penguins finished the 1980-81 season with an identical record to that of the previous year (30-37-13), the club's style was curiously much more wide open, despite coaching by a former goalie, as their goals scored—and allowed—increased dramatically. Rick Kehoe, who had led the team in scoring the year before with 30 goals and 60 points, became the first Penguin to score 55 goals in a season and boosted his team-leading point total to 88 points.

For the first time, however, the club's number-two scorer was a defenseman as Randy Carlyle blossomed from 36 points (8-28) in 1979-80 to 83 on 16 goals and a team-leading 67 assists. Both players were honored at season's end with league trophies as Kehoe collected the Lady Byng for gentlemanly play (six penalty minutes) and Carlyle was named to the NHL First All-Star Team and won the James Norris Trophy as the league's top defenseman.

In the 1981 play-offs the Penguins were again destined to suffer disappointment after almost upsetting a much stronger opponent. As the 15th overall finisher in 1980-81, the Pens met the St. Louis Blues in the best-of-five preliminary round. The Blues had compiled 105 points—33 more than the Pens—and had been second only to the defending Stanley Cup champion Islanders in the regular season. The Pens managed a split in Johnston's old St. Louis Arena stomping grounds, however, and then split again at the Igloo to force the series back to the Gateway City for a fifth and final game.

Although St. Louis had entered post-season play as a favorite to reach the Stanley Cup finals, the underdog Pens forced the ultimate decision as to whether or not the Blues would even survive the opening round into overtime as the fifth game stood tied 3-3 after 60 minutes of regulation play. If the Pens were able to score one more goal, it would be the biggest victory in the club's history. Pittsburgh's Millen did his part to give the team that chance, stopping everything that came his way in the first overtime period, but so too did St. Louis goalie Mike Liut.

Pittsburgh's fairy tale play-off—and season—came to an abrupt end 5:16 into the second overtime period when light-scoring Blues winger Mike Crombeen finally beat Millen. It would be the last goal Millen would allow as a Penguin; just six weeks later he left the club to sign with the Hartford Whalers as a free agent.

1981-82: A New Division—But Play-off Deja Vu

With realignment of the NHL in 1981-82, the Pens moved from the Norris Division to the Patrick, joining the Flyers, Rangers, Islanders, and Capitals. In addition to Pittsburgh now having to face each of these teams eight times during the regular season instead of four, beginning with the 1982 play-offs, all matchups in the first two rounds would be among divisional rivals.

With the then-two-time champion Islanders and the usually contending Flyers and Rangers all now in the Penguins' small universe of possible early play-off opponents, this new arrangement was not good news for GM Bastien as he continued to try building a club good enough to finally play a game in May.

Bastien's first task, however, was to replace the departed Greg Millen, which he did in July by signing 27-year-old free agent goalie Michel Dion, a five-year ex-WHA veteran who had split the previous season between Quebec and Winnipeg. Dion not only ended up carrying the bulk of the load for Pittsburgh in 1981-82 by appearing in 62 games (25-24-12; 3.79), he also started for the Wales Conference in the mid-season All-Star Game and finished third in voting by the league's GMs for the 1982 Vezina Trophy, awarded annually to the NHL's top goalie.

Rick Kehoe led the team in scoring for the third consecutive season (33-52-85), followed again by All-Star defenseman Randy Carlyle (11-64-75), who quarterbacked the Pens' power-play to a league-leading 99 goals. Pat Boutette, a 29-year-old veteran center who had come over from the Whalers as part of the compensation for Hartford's signing of Greg Millen, was close behind at 23-51-74.

Pittsburgh's top goal scorer in 1981-82, however, was 20-year-old rookie center Mike Bullard—the Pens' top pick (ninth overall) in the 1980 draft—who collected 37 on just 145 shots to lead the NHL in shooting percentage at 25.5. In the fistic department, defenseman Paul Baxter—who was the all-time penalty minute leader in the WHA when that league folded in 1979—led both the Pens and the NHL in penalty minutes with a still-team-standing record 409.

While Pittsburgh finished 12th overall in the league, with 75 points on a record of 31-36-13, the Penguins were forced to immediately confront the NHL's best team during the regular season, the Islanders, who had finished 43 points ahead of Pittsburgh over the 80-game schedule with 118. As they had against St. Louis the previous spring, however, the Pens not only gave their powerful new Patrick Division rivals a scare, they came within 141 seconds of pulling off the biggest play-off upset in years.

After being decisively outplayed in the first two games in New York, where they were blown out by the Islanders 8-1 and 7-2, Dion and the Penguins stunned the champions in Pittsburgh with suddenly stellar goaltending and tight play-off-type checking. Rick Kehoe won game three when he scored 4:14 into overtime to beat the Isles 2-1 and also scored the winner in game four, which the Pens took with relative ease 5-2 to even the best-of-five series at two games each. As had been the case the previous two play-off years, the underdog Pens had again forced a much stronger opponent to a fifth and final game in the opening round.

The tense rubber game of the series was played in New York on April 13, 1982. As he had in the previous two contests, Dion continued to stand tall in the Pittsburgh net while the Pens managed to take advantage of the few chances the Isles gave them to fashion the slim 3-2 lead they held as the clock ticked down to the final three minutes of regulation time. Just under two and a half minutes from upset heaven, though, a Pittsburgh clearing pass eluded the stick of Penguin defenseman Randy Carlyle and was picked off by Islander winger John Tonelli, who beat Dion to tie the game at 3-3 with just 2:21 left in regulation time.

For the second consecutive year the Pens were involved in a fifth and deciding play-off game that had gone into overtime. It almost ended happily for them when rookie Mike Bullard got a fabulous scoring chance early in overtime—only to be thwarted by Islander goalie Billy Smith.

A short time later Tonelli ended the suspense by beating Dion at 6:10 to give New York the game 4-3 and the series three games to two. While the Islanders would go on to win their third consecutive Cup a few weeks later, the came-so-close-again Pens had begun a long journey in the other direction as they would not make a another play-off appearance for seven years.

1982-83: The "Dark" Years Begin

The 1982-83 campaign would be the first of six consecutive lost seasons of NHL hockey in

Pittsburgh. All semblance of defense disappeared as the Pens allowed a team record 394 goals while scoring just 257 on their way to a 30-point drop from 75 to 45 and a dead-last-place record of 18-53-9. The season's low point came with an 18-game winless streak (0-17-1) from January 2nd to February 10th, which featured 11 consecutive losses. Then, on March 15, 1983, tragedy struck when Baz Bastien was killed in an automobile accident while returning home from a team dinner.

Coach Eddie Johnston took over the vacant GM's chair on May 27, 1983, and on July 20th named former (1968-69) Penguin center Lou Angotti to replace him behind the bench. The then-45-year-old Toronto native had spent the previous two seasons coaching Pittsburgh's AHL farm clubs in Erie, Pennsylvania, and Baltimore. Angotti had also coached briefly (6-20-6) in the NHL with St. Louis in 1974.

While the 1983 draft was a strong one, with such future NHL stars as Pat LaFontaine, Steve Yzerman, Tom Barrasso, John MacLean, and Cam Neely all available, none would be there when Eddie Johnston got to make his first pick as Bastien had exchanged first round picks with Minnesota the previous October in a deal that also had sent George Ferguson to the North Stars and brought the Pens Ron Meighan and Anders Hakansson.

The last-place Penguins, therefore, had to sit quietly while all the top talent was plucked from the slate before finally getting to pick 15th overall. Johnston used his devalued first rounder to take Peterborough Petes left wing Bob Errey, who, although he played serviceably for Pittsburgh for a decade, only once scored over 40 points in a season as a Penguin. Meanwhile, Meighan and Hakansson managed to contribute a total of just 29 points in their combined Penguin careers.

Although Johnston was denied the opportunity to get one of the several sure Hall of Famers available in the 1983 draft, as it turned out, he was able to convert part of Bastien's mistake into a huge long-term benefit before the start of the next season. On September 9, 1983, Johnston pre-

sciently traded Hakansson to the Los Angeles Kings for the rights to Kevin Stevens, then an 18-year-old Massachusetts-born left wing who was just about to start his rookie season at Boston College. A sixth-round pick (112th overall) of the Kings the previous June, Los Angeles GM George Maguire apparently had second thoughts about the judgment of his scouts as he let the 6'3", 220-pound Stevens go to Pittsburgh just three months later for a player who eventually provided the Kings with just 31 goals in two and a half seasons.

Stevens, meanwhile, became a college All-Star by the end of his four-year career at BC and then played for the United States in the 1988 Olympics before finally turning pro with the Pens in March, 1988. He more than proved to be worth the five-year wait as by 1991-92 Stevens had become a 50-goal scorer and finished that year second only to teammate Mario Lemieux in NHL scoring, with 123 points (54-69).

June 9, 1984: Drafting a Savior

Despite a 51-goal season by Mike Bullard, 1983-84 saw the Penguins dress an incredible total of 48 different players on their way to finishing with the worst-ever record in club history—16-58-6 for 38 points—and costing Lou Angotti his job.

That dismal campaign proved a blessing in disguise, however, as it provided the Penguins with the one and only "key" that would ever be available to unlock the treasure chest containing the biggest draft prize in NHL history. While the 1984 NHL entry draft was not as deep as 1983's, there was no doubt that one player in it would prove to be more valuable than all the rest put together.

As did the Los Angeles Kings, the Penguins had a sorry history of trading away their first-round draft picks, having done so in seven of the previous 14 draft years. Fortunately for Eddie Johnston, however, that was not the case in 1984, when he had a shot at the draft's top pick if the Pens finished the campaign with the worst record in the

NHL. As the 1983-84 season wound down to its final six weeks, only the Penguins and New Jersey Devils remained "in the running" for that first overall pick in the June entry draft, with no other teams even close to being as bad as these two Patrick Division patsies.

With a 3-17-1 finish capped by six consecutive losses, the Pens "beat out" the Devils for that first overall pick by three points 38 to 41; so on June 9, 1984, Johnston wasted no time in claiming his prize—18-year-old French-Canadian wunderkind Mario Lemieux.

In his just-completed final season of junior hockey with Laval in the Quebec league, the 6'4", 210-pound Montreal-born center had amassed an incredible 282 points (133-149) while fashioning a 61-game scoring streak. Ten days later—and after a certain degree of posturing on both sides—Lemieux inked his first Penguins contract, on June 19, 1984.

In addition to Pittsburgh's own pick, Johnston had also stockpiled two others in the first round through trades made the previous few months. With Winnipeg's ninth overall pick (acquired on May 5th for Randy Carlyle), the Pens selected defenseman Doug Bodger from the WHL Kamloops Blazers. Right wing Roger Belanger was taken 16th overall with Philadelphia's first-round pick, which Pittsburgh got as part of a four-player, three-draft-pick deal made on October 23rd that had sent Rich Sutter to the Flyers to join his twin brother, Ron.

To replace Angotti, Johnston had hired former Los Angeles King and Montreal Canadien mentor Bob Berry on June 4, 1984 as the eighth man to coach the Penguins. With Lemieux in the lineup, Berry's club made a modest fifteen-point improvement in 1984-85, finishing with 53 on a record of 24-51-5.

Although the team still missed the play-offs—and would continue to do so for yet another four years—the addition of Mario Lemieux had made the Penguins an instant attraction wherever they played. Lemieux was Pittsburgh's starting center on the 1984-85 season's opening night in Boston and before he left the ice had scored his first NHL goal on his first-ever shot as a pro.

By season's end the big rookie had collected a total of 43 goals and, with 57 assists, became just the third first-year player in NHL history (after Peter Stastny and Dale Hawerchuk) to score 100 or more points. To no one's surprise, Lemieux also went home that summer with the first of many NHL awards to come his way over the years as he became the first Penguin player to win the Calder Memorial Trophy as NHL Rookie of the Year. Lemieux also represented the Penguins in the 1985 All-Star Game in Calgary and, with two goals and an assist, led the Wales Conference to a 6-4 win and was named the game's MVP.

The Penguins improved another 24 points in 1985-86 to 76 (34-38-8) but missed the play-offs again when they stumbled down the stretch (3-12-1) to finish just two points behind the fourth-place New York Rangers. Still, Lemieux only continued to get better as he finished the season second only to Edmonton's veteran "Great One," Wayne Gretzky, in league scoring, with 141 points (48-93), while fashioning a 28-game scoring streak. Lemieux also collected his second major award as he was named the winner of the Lester B. Pearson Award, presented by the Players' Association to the outstanding player in the NHL. Another highly touted young Penguin did not do as well, however, as 18-year-old center Craig Simpson, the Pens' top pick (2nd overall) in 1985, had a disappointing rookie season with just 28 points (17-11) in 76 games.

With seven consecutive victories—including three in overtime—to begin the 1986-87 season, it looked as if the Penguins might finally be back in the play-offs by April, 1987, for the first time since 1982. But with just four wins (4-15-4) during a six-week stretch between mid-December and late January and an 0-5-1 run in March, the club again finished in fifth place, with 72 points on a 30-38-12 record, four points behind the Rangers.

Nonetheless, Lemieux broke the 50-goal plateau for the first time with 54, despite missing 17 games, and produced his third consecutive 100-point season with 103. The Penguins' fifth consecutive non-play-off year, however, finally cost

Bob Berry and assistant coach Jimmy Roberts their jobs at season's end.

In June Eddie Johnston tapped 43-year-old Pierre Creamer to replace Berry behind the bench for the Penguins 21st NHL season, 1987-88. Creamer, who had previously coached both Montreal and Verdun in the Quebec junior league, came to the Pens after three successful seasons in the AHL as coach of Montreal's top farm club, the Sherbrooke Canadiens, whom he had guided to a 102-point season in 1986-87. Johnston's biggest move came on November 24th, however, when he sent Craig Simpson, center Dave Hannan, and defensemen Moe Mantha and Chris Joseph, whom the Pens had drafted 5th overall the previous June

to the Edmonton Oilers for Dave Hunter, Wayne Van Dorp, and the key player in the deal—All-Star defenseman Paul Coffey.

As expected, Lemieux had another outstanding season, with 168 points on 70 goals and 98 assists, ending Wayne Gretzky's seven-year stranglehold on the Art Ross Trophy—and eight-year grip on the Hart Trophy (MVP)—bringing both pieces of silverware to Pittsburgh for the first time. In addition, Lemieux was again named the All-Star Game MVP, with six points (3-3), including the game-winning goal in overtime. With 319 goals as a team, the high-scoring Pens led the Patrick Division—but also gave up the most, surrendering 316.

AP/Wide World Photos

Mario Lemieux (66)

In 1987-88, for the first time in nine seasons, the Penguins finished over .500, with a 36-35-9 record for 81 points; but all five other teams in the division also posted winning records, and the season ended with the Patrick's six clubs in a virtual dead heat. The Islanders took first place with a modest 88 points, but just four points separated the other five in the final standings to make the race for the last three available play-off berths truly a game of musical chairs.

Washington and Philadelphia ended up tied with 85 points each on identical 38-33-9 records to take second and third. Three points back, New Jersey and the Rangers also tied, at 82, in the race for the final berth, but the Devils got the nod for their first time ever by winning in overtime at Chicago on the final night of the season.

Thus, despite the Penguins finishing their year with an impressive 11-5-0 run, a six-game losing streak in late February proved too much to overcome, and they finished in sixth place, trailing the division champion Islanders by just seven points—and the fourth-place Devils by just one.

With no play-offs in Pittsburgh for the sixth consecutive spring, the DeBartolos decided that the time had come to make some changes in senior management. On April 14, 1988, Hall of Fame goalie Tony Esposito was named vice president and replaced Eddie Johnston as GM, although Johnston was retained in the organization as assistant GM.

Prior to joining the Pens, the 45-year-old Esposito had been working for the NHL Players Association since his retirement in 1984. Coach Pierre Creamer was released on June 14th after just one season and two weeks later was replaced by 50-year-old Gene Ubriaco, who 21 seasons earlier, in 1967-68, had been a member of the Penguins first team.

Ubriaco, who, like Esposito, was a native of Sault Ste. Marie, Ontario, already knew most of the Penguin players well, having coached many of them with the AHL Baltimore Skipjacks over the previous five years. As Pittsburgh's top farm club from 1983 to 1987, Ubriaco had led the Skipjacks to a 102-point season in 1983-84 and to a

berth in the Calder Cup finals in 1984-85 without being offered the Penguins when changes were made behind the bench in 1984 and 1987. Just prior to the 1987-88 season, however, the Pens moved their minor-league affiliation from the AHL Skipjacks to the IHL Muskegon (Michigan) Lumberjacks, which forced Baltimore to operate as an independent club for that season.

Without a source of players under NHL contract, Ubriaco's club not unexpectedly finished dead last in the AHL, with just 35 points (13-58-9). It was after that dismal season that the timing finally proved right for Ubriaco to get his long-awaited chance at coaching in the NHL.

The first two major trades made by ex-goalie Esposito were for help between the pipes. On September 1st he picked up 25-year-old Wendell Young from Philadelphia for a draft pick. While Young had not yet been a first-string NHL goalkeeper, the previous May he had made pro hockey history by leading the AHL Hershey Bears to a 12-0, three-series sweep through the Calder Cup playoffs while playing every minute of all dozen wins.

On November 12th, however, Esposito made a much more important long-term goaltending move as he obtained former Vezina and Jennings Trophy winner Tom Barrasso from the Buffalo Sabres for defenseman Doug Bodger and 18-year-old left wing Darrin Shannon, who had been Pittsburgh's top pick (4th overall) in the draft the previous June.

1988-89: Finally Back in the Play-offs

The Penguins' 1988-89 season was all Mario Lemieux as he won his second consecutive scoring title with 85 goals and 114 assists for a stratospheric 199 points. Two other Penguins also joined him in the three-digit range as sophomore right wing Rob Brown collected 115 (49-66) and Paul Coffey added 113 (30-83) as he quarterbacked the Pittsburgh power play to an NHL record 119 goals. On New Years' Eve, Lemieux also provided the fans with a most unusual virtuoso performance as he became the only player in NHL history to score one of each of the five possible types of goals—even strength, power play, shorthanded, penalty shot, and empty net—all on the same night during an 8-6 home-ice victory over New Jersey.

Although the Pens only improved by a half dozen points to 87 on a record of 40-33-7, that proved good enough to move them from last to second place in the Patrick Division, just five points behind the first-place Washington Capitals.

More importantly, however, it also ended Pittsburgh's embarrassing seven-year play-off drought. For the first time since April 13, 1982, the Pens took to the ice for a post season contest, on April 5, 1989, as they faced the New York Rangers in the best-of-seven division semifinals. And for the first time since Pittsburgh's first-ever play-off series against Oakland in 1970, the Penguins swept a set in straight games, four games to none, while outscoring the Broadway Blueshirts 19-10.

With the Pens' victory over the Rangers and the Flyers' upset elimination of the first-place Caps, for the first time ever Pennsylvania sports fans were to be treated to a pro hockey play-off matchup between the teams representing the Keystone State's two major cities, longtime rivals Philadelphia and Pittsburgh. The series turned out to be quite a memorable one as the two clubs split the two opening pairs of games at the Igloo and the Spectrum to set up an unforgettable fifth game played back in Pittsburgh on April 25th.

By the time that wild contest ended, the two clubs had come within one goal of tying the NHL record for total goals in a play-off game (18), and Mario Lemieux personally tied two league marks for a single Cup game with five goals and eight points as he led the Pens to a no-holds-barred 10-7 victory.

While the Flyers tied the series at three apiece with a 6-4 win in the sixth game in Philadelphia to force the Penguins to a seventh game for the first time since their ill-fated collapse against the Islanders in 1975, Pittsburgh appeared to get a big break in the deciding contest when star Flyer goalie Ron Hextall was unable to play. Instead, the

Flyers had to use Ken Wregget, who had only made three appearances in the Flyer nets since having been traded to Philadelphia from Toronto in early March. Unfortunately for the again star-crossed Penguins, however, Wregget—whom the Flyers would trade to Pittsburgh three years later—played like an All-Star as he held the Pens' offensive machine to just one goal while the Flyers thwarted Tom Barrasso for four to prevent the Penguins from having ever won a second-round series.

As is often the case prior to a team making its transition to greatness, the preceding season is often marked by considerable turmoil and unexpected disappointment. The 1989-90 season proved just such a year for the Penguins as by mid-November they were wallowing in a 5-10-2 record and seemed directionless. First goalie Tom Barrasso broke his wrist in the season's fourth game, on October 14, and was lost for the next 23.

Then, two months after his return, his young daughter was diagnosed with leukemia and he took a leave of absence until late March so he could be with her while she underwent special medical treatment in Los Angeles. By season's end, Barrasso had only been able to appear in 24 games (7-12-3; 4.68) while Wendell Young carried the bulk of the load with 43 appearances (16-20-3; 4.17), backed up by Frank Pietrangelo (8-6-2; 4.33) in 21 games.

As the Penguins entered the season's stretch run, a serious back injury to Mario Lemieux kept him on the sidelines for all but the last of the club's final 22 games—though he still managed to lead the team in scoring with 123 points (45-78) and finish fourth overall in the league. His ongoing back problems forced him out after the first period of a 4-3 Penguins overtime win against the Rangers in New York on February 14.

Lemieux was seeking to extend his then-46-game scoring streak (45-78-103), the second-longest in NHL history. Although he returned for the final game of the season and collected a goal and an assist in a 3-2 overtime home-ice loss to Buffalo, that defeat left the 32-40-8 Pens with 72 points, one fewer than the fourth-place Islanders, and out of the play-offs again.

The 1989-90 season did have some very bright spots, however, as two young forwards whom Tony Esposito had brought into the organization in June, 1988, emerged as key offensive forces on the team. Center John Cullen, a 24-year-old graduate of Boston University, had been inked as a free agent after compiling a remarkable 157-point (48-109) rookie season with the IHL Flint (Michigan) Spirits in 1987-88, which had made him that league's scoring champion, Rookie of the Year, and MVP.

After a gratifying 49-point (12-37) rookie NHL season in 1988-89, Cullen almost doubled that to 92 points (32-60) in 1989-90 while playing on a line with two rookie wingers, ex-Olympian Kevin Stevens (29-41) and Esposito's other key 1988 acquisition, 22-year-old right wing Mark Recchi (30-67), who was quickly proving to have been a steal as Pittsburgh's fourth-round pick in the 1988 entry draft.

The "Patrickification" of the Patrick Division Penguins

In addition to their fortunes on the ice, the Penguins also made plenty of news off the ice in 1989-90. The slowdown in the economy and reverses in real estate and the retail and shopping mall businesses led the DeBartolo family to start looking for a buyer for the Penguins even though attendance figures and team support had swelled markedly in the years since the arrival of Lemieux.

Aside from that distraction, frequent front office intrigues seemed to seriously affect relationships among the owners, Esposito, Ubriaco, and many of the players. All this finally came to a head on December 5th when GM Esposito and coach Ubriaco were dismissed and replaced by one man—Craig Patrick, the grandson of the man after whom the Penguins' own home Patrick Division was named.

The then-44-year-old Patrick came to his new position both with outstanding bloodlines and sterling credentials. The grandson of Hall of Famer

and NHL patriarch Lester Patrick, the son of Lynn Patrick, and the nephew of Muzz Patrick—all of whom had played for, coached, and/or managed the New York Rangers between 1926 and 1964, Craig Patrick had also both managed and coached the Rangers during his own six seasons on Broadway from 1980 to 1986.

A graduate of the University of Denver, Craig Patrick played all or part of eight seasons in the NHL with California, St. Louis, Kansas City, and Washington between 1971 and 1979 before beginning his coaching and management career as both assistant GM and assistant coach of the 1980 Gold Medal-winning U.S. Olympic hockey team. After leaving the Rangers, Patrick had gone back to his alma mater to serve as the University of Denver's director of athletics prior to returning to the NHL to take over the Penguins.

While Craig Patrick did not really want to return to the NHL as a coach, he stepped behind the Penguins' bench for the remainder of the season so that he could evaluate firsthand exactly what he had and thereby determine what changes he would need to make. While the team played fairly well under Patrick over the next few months, it still struggled far too often on the road. It also appeared that the Pens had come to depend far too much on Lemieux to win as the club managed only five victories (5-12-4) in the 21 games he missed despite having eight other players on the squad who scored between 20 and 33 goals in 1989-90.

While missing the play-offs on the final day of the season was clearly a disappointment, in a way it proved another blessing in disguise as the Pens' poor stretch run gave Craig Patrick the fifth overall selection to work with in what most NHL scouts figured would be one of the strongest drafts in years.

As expected, Owen Nolan, Petr Nedved, Keith Primeau, and Mike Ricci—the unanimously acknowledged top-four available prospects—were the first four players taken in the 1989 entry draft, held at B.C. Place in Vancouver on June 16, and were therefore not available when Patrick's turn came to announce Pittsburgh's choice. While many expected the Penguin GM to pick another of the rugged North American-born junior players still left in the deep field, to their surprise he instead claimed a fancy-skating 18-year-old Czechoslovakian right wing named Jaromir Jagr.

Regardless of how the "big four" taken ahead of Patrick's unexpected choice eventually performed, none could match the immediate impact on their teams that Jagr had in helping to make the Pens a champion within the following 12 months.

Acquiring Jagr was far from the only important personnel move Craig Patrick made in the week surrounding those 1990 NHL meetings, however; on June 12th, Patrick hired Hall of Fame coach and former Buffalo GM Scotty Bowman as director of player development and former University of Wisconsin and Calgary Flame mentor Bob Johnson as head coach. Just prior to the draft he also dealt his second-round pick to Calgary for veteran winger Joey Mullen, who—although in his mid-30s—quickly became one of the Penguins' most effective leaders and productive scorers. Then, in July, Patrick signed 34-year-old former Hart Trophy-winning center Bryan Trottier, a veteran of four Stanley Cups with the Islanders and a man who truly knew what it took to be a champion.

While Patrick continued to rebuild the Pens over the summer, the club's prospects for 1990-91 were dealt what might have been a fatal blow when Mario Lemieux's back problems finally forced him to undergo surgery on July 11 to repair a herniated disc. The time required for his recovery and rehabilitation forced the Penguins captain to miss the first 50 games of the campaign and often left him playing in considerable discomfort when he returned. While Lemieux's long absence could well have been an excuse for the Penguins to "tread water" for the season, the unfailingly positive and enthusiastic Bob Johnson quickly made it clear that that was not about to happen.

As a coach, the 59-year-old Johnson had been noted as a master teacher—and superb motivator—since he first stepped behind a bench at Warroad High School in his native Minnesota in 1956. While he had been a hockey coach and/or

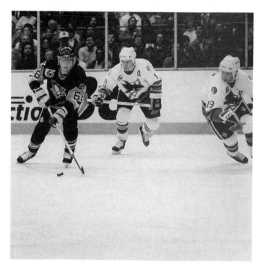

Jaromir Jagr (68)

administrator for almost 35 years when he came to Pittsburgh, by far his greatest success and acclaim had come during his 15 seasons (1966- 82) coaching the University of Wisconsin Badgers, with whom he won three NCAA championships.

In 1982 "Badger Bob" left the college ranks to take over the NHL Calgary Flames for five years and led them to the Stanley Cup finals for the first time in 1986. He left Calgary in 1987 to become executive director of USA Hockey, the supervisory organization for all amateur hockey in the United States.

After a modest 10-7-2 start through mid-November, the Pens struggled over the next dozen games at 2-9-1, ending with a 4-1 loss at Chicago on December 11, which dropped them into fifth place for almost a month. On December 11th and 13th, however, Patrick made two key deals that started the club on a 16-5-0 run and moved them to within striking distance of the first-place Rangers.

On the 11th, Patrick acquired defensemen Larry Murphy and Peter Taglianetti from the Minnesota North Stars for journeymen blueliners Jim Johnson and Chris Dahlquist, and on the 13th he plucked veteran Czech center Jiri Hrdina from Calgary for bellicose blueliner Jim Kyte.

An excellent puck-moving blueliner, Murphy complimented Paul Coffey and provided another good point shot on the power play. Taglianetti brought both toughness and solid defense. The 32-year-old veteran Hrdina was acquired to help his teen-aged countryman Jagr adjust to playing hockey in North America. Just over a week later on December 21st Patrick made a third deal, sending talented but erratic right wing Rob Brown to Hartford for former U.S. Olympian Scott Young.

Although Mario Lemieux finally returned to the lineup in late January, the club stalled again in February (4-8-2) before Patrick made his biggest move—right at the trading deadline. On March 4th the Penguin GM sent his club's then-leading scorer, John Cullen, defenseman and 1986 first-round draft pick (4th overall) Zarley Zalapski, and minor-league center Jeff Parker to the Hartford Whalers in exchange for Whaler captain and all-time leading scorer Ron Francis, "in-your-face" Swedish defenseman Ulf Samuelsson, and stay-at-home blueliner Grant Jennings. While at the time the deal was quite controversial and unpopular with Pens fans, within three months it would prove crucial to the club's successful run for the Cup.

The trade's immediate result was a strong 9-3-1 finishing run, which by March 17th had pushed the Pens into first place in the Patrick Division, past the New York Rangers, who had held that top spot for 141 consecutive days. When the regular season ended two weeks later, the Pens were still there and, with 88 points on a 41-33-6 record, claimed their first-ever regular season divisional title. With 133 points (40-73), right wing Mark Recchi led the club in scoring and finished fourth overall in the league, behind only the Kings' Wayne Gretzky and St. Louis linemates Brett Hull and Adam Oates.

The best-of-seven opening round of the playoffs brought the Penguins face to face with the club they had "beaten out" in the competition for the rights to Mario Lemieux seven years earlier, the fourth-place New Jersey Devils. But as had been the case during the seven-game regular season series between the two Patrick Division rivals (won by Pittsburgh four games to three), New Jersey proved to be no pushover. The Devils won the opening game at the Igloo 3-1, then took the Pens into overtime before Jaromir Jagr scored at 8:52 of the first extra period to even the series. After splitting the next two games in New Jersey, the Devils forced the Penguins to the wall by upsetting them again in game five in Pittsburgh 4-2.

With first-string goalie Tom Barrasso having already lost three times in five games while giving up 17 goals, Johnson decided to make a change for the do or die sixth game and went with backup Frank Pietrangelo despite the fact that he had never played a single minute of Stanley Cup action. Johnson's hunch paid off as the 25-year-old former University of Minnesota netminder not only beat the Devils, 4-3, to even the series, but then shut them out 4-0 in game seven to move Pittsburgh on to the Patrick Division finals against the Washington Capitals.

As in the first round, the Pens again lost the opening game at home, 4-2, before evening the series with a 7-6 overtime win. With Pietrangelo having surrendered ten goals in the first two games, however, Johnson returned Barrasso to the nets; he responded by holding Washington to a single goal in each of the next three games as the Pens beat the Caps four games to one to advance to a third-round series for the first time in their history.

Their competition this time, however, was the far tougher Adams Division champion Boston Bruins, a club that had finished the season with a dozen more points than Pittsburgh (100 to 88). The Bruins also held huge career regular season (64-20-16) and play-off (7-2) advantages over the Penguins, and at Boston Garden the Pens had only won a total of seven games (7-42-6) in 24 years.

But the Penguins didn't seem to mind; for the first time since joining the NHL in 1967, they finally got to play a game in May when they opened the Wales Conference Finals in Boston on May 1, 1991. As they had in their two previous series, the club lost its opening game, 6-3, and went to overtime in the second. This time, however, Pittsburgh lost game two as Boston center Vladimir Ruzicka celebrated May Day by scoring 8:14 into OT to beat the Pens 5-4 and take a two-games-to-none lead in the series. Unfortunately for Boston, though, that would prove to be their last hurrah as Barrasso and Lemieux took over and led the Penguins to four consecutive victories during which the Bruins were outscored 20-7. In six games against Boston, Lemieux had 15 points (6-9) while Stevens (6-4) and Recchi (2-8) had ten each.

While the Penguins might well have been considered underdogs in 1991 in their quest to reach their first Stanley Cup finals after missing the play-offs in seven of the previous eight years, their opponents in the championship series—the Minnesota North Stars—were even greater longshots. After finishing the season with just 68 points on a record of 27-39-14, however, the North Stars had suddenly became play-off supermen.

In the first two rounds the Stars upset both of the NHL's top-two overall finishers in 1990-91—the Chicago Blackhawks and St. Louis Blues—and then knocked off the defending Stanley Cup champion Edmonton Oilers in the Campbell Conference Finals.

For the fourth consecutive series, the Penguins lost the opening game, as the North Stars edged them at the Igloo 5-4 for their 13th postseason victory of the year against just five losses. Pittsburgh then came back to win three of the next four games, although they outscored the North Stars by only four goals (20-16) through five games as they took to the ice for game six at the Met Center in Minnesota on May 25th.

A North Star win would send the series back to Pittsburgh for a seventh and final game, but it quickly became clear that the 1991 play-offs would end that night as Pittsburgh scored eight unanswered goals while Tom Barrasso allowed none to earn his first career play-off shutout, 8-0. With 44 points (16-28) in 23 games, Mario Lemieux finished as both the leading scorer in the 1991 play-offs and winner of the Conn Smythe Trophy as the Stanley Cup MVP.

Triumph and Tragedy

For the first time since the AHL Hornets had won the Calder Cup in 1967, Pittsburgh celebrated a pro hockey championship in 1991. While the players had obviously done the work on the ice and proved themselves a tremendously talented team, it is unlikely that the Penguins would have won the Cup in 1991 without the inspiration and guidance of their coach, Bob Johnson. No man who has ever stood behind a bench exuded more enthusiasm for the game than "Badger Bob," who lived by one motto—"It's a great day for hockey!" That was always the gospel by which Johnson coached—and his teams played.

The off season for both the Penguins and their coach would be short and busy. For Craig Patrick and the club's front office the summer was not without its distractions as negotiations to sell the team were under way in earnest. Bob Johnson would also have little time off to enjoy his first pro championship as he immediately began preparation to assemble and coach the United States team that was to participate in the Canada Cup tournament to be played in September.

After a brief but intense training camp in Pittsburgh, Johnson took his Canada Cup team out for a grueling schedule of exhibition games, which ended in western Canada in late August. On August 29th, a few hours after returning to Pittsburgh, where Team USA's opening game of the tournament would be played, Johnson collapsed at dinner with his wife and was rushed to the hospital, where he underwent emergency surgery for what proved to be multiple brain tumors.

Left unable to speak or walk, Johnson returned to his home in Colorado Springs to recover. Although it was hoped he would eventually be able to once again coach the Penguins, Bob Johnson died at his home on November 26, 1991, almost six months to the day after having guided the Penguins to their first Stanley Cup title. (In honor of their coach, each member of the team wore a patch on their shoulder with the word "Badger" on it for the rest of the season, and Johnson's motto, "It's a great day for hockey," was painted on the Civic Center ice.)

On October 1st, Craig Patrick had named Penguins director of player development and recruitment Scotty Bowman interim head coach in the hope that Johnson might eventually be able to come back. The winningest coach by far in NHL history in both regular season and play-off competition, Bowman was nonetheless the antithesis in coaching style to Johnson. Whereas Bob Johnson was at times almost boyishly enthusiastic and always positive no matter what, Bowman was a far more stern taskmaster and a consummate tactician whose previous teams in St. Louis, Montreal, and Buffalo had always been known for their highly disciplined and often suffocatingly defensive style of play.

On November 19, 1991, the NHL approved the transfer of ownership of the Penguins from the DeBartolo Corporation to a group consisting of Howard Baldwin, Morris Belzberg, and Thomas Ruta, with Baldwin becoming the team's new president and governor. After brief front office experience with the Philadelphia Flyers, Baldwin had been founder and managing general partner of the WHA New England Whalers in 1972. He later served as president of that league from 1977 to 1979, when the circuit folded and the Whalers and three other ex-WHA clubs joined the NHL.

Baldwin continued as managing general partner of the NHL Hartford Whalers until the club was sold in 1988 and in 1990 was briefly involved in the purchase of the Minnesota North Stars, which kept that club from moving to California, but sold his interest in the Stars to Norman Green prior to the start of the 1990-91 season.

Meanwhile on the ice, the contrast between the coaching styles of Scotty Bowman and the late Bob Johnson was proving a shock to many of the younger, more offensive-minded Penguin players, and by February some members of the team were almost in open revolt. While this friction may have been only partly to blame, the Penguins' performance began dropping from a strong 22-13-4 record on New Years' Eve to just .500 (27-27-8), with an ugly 8-4 home loss to lowly Hartford on

Hockey Hall of Fame and Museum

Scott Bowman

February 27th. By then it had also become clear that if the Pens did not quickly right themselves, they might well go from being 1991 Stanley Cup champions to missing the 1992 play-offs altogether.

For the second year in a row, however, GM Craig Patrick brought a struggling Penguin club out of its lethargy with another big late-season trade. On February 19th, Patrick dealt perennial all-star defenseman Paul Coffey to Los Angeles for defensemen Jeff Chychrun and Brian Benning and the Kings' top pick in the 1992 entry draft. Patrick then sent Benning, the L.A. draft pick, and high-scoring 23-year-old right wing Mark Recchi to the Philadelphia Flyers for goalie Ken Wregget, 6'6" Swedish defenseman Kjell Samuelsson, and the Flyers' captain, right wing Rick Tocchet.

Within ten days of the trade, the Pens started to right themselves, beginning with a 5-2 win at Buffalo on February 29th, and finished out the season with a strong 12-5-1 run to take third place on a 39-32-9 record for 87 points.

Still, whether or not the Penguins would get to defend their Stanley Cup title became an open question with three games to go in the season; on April 1st the NHL Players Association went on strike, causing the first work stoppage in the league's 75-year history. For ten days it looked as if there would be no 1992 Stanley Cup play-offs, but on April 10th the strike was resolved, and the final week of the schedule was completed on April 16th. Despite missing 16 games due to continuing back problems, Mario Lemieux reclaimed the scoring title from Wayne Gretzky with 131 points (44-87) in just 64 games, and on March 22nd he recorded his 1,000th career NHL point in only his 513th game.

1992: Princes Again—Stanley Cup II

As it had been against New Jersey the previous spring, the opening round of the 1992 play-offs, against the Washington Capitals, proved to be the year's most difficult for the Pens. After losing both games in Washington to open the series, Pittsburgh won the first game played at the Igloo—only to be blown out in the second 7-2 and fall behind three games to one. But the Pens were by now at their best when their backs were against the wall, and they swept the final three games to take the set in seven games. Lemieux outdid even himself in the set with an incredible 17 points (7-10) despite missing the first game with a shoulder injury.

In the Patrick Division finals the Pens met the regular season champion New York Rangers—and surprisingly, for the first time since 1989, won the opening game of a series. While the Rangers came back to take the second contest, the Penguins lost far more than the game when Mario Lemieux suffered a broken left hand after being slashed by Ranger center Adam Graves. But the Penguins stayed in the hunt as the two clubs split the next two games in Pittsburgh, with both contests being decided in overtime, before Pittsburgh unex-

pectedly took another lead in games with a gutsy 3-2 victory at Madison Square Garden in game five. By then, Lemieux was able to return to the lineup for game six, at the Igloo, which the Penguins won with relative ease 5-1 to upset the Rangers four games to two and again deny the Broadway Blues a chance to return the Stanley Cup to the Big Apple for the first time since 1940.

After struggling through the first two rounds, the Penguins were finally on a roll and would not drop another game in their final two series as they swept the Boston Bruins in the Wales Conference Finals and the Chicago Blackhawks in the Stanley Cup Finals, outscoring those two powerful opponents by a cumulative 34 to 17.

Despite having missed six of Pittsburgh's 21 playoff games, Lemieux won his second consecutive Conn Smythe Trophy. With 34 points (16-18) in just 15 games, the Penguin captain again captured the play-off scoring crown, followed by three of his teammates—Kevin Stevens (13-15-28), Ron Francis (8-19-27), and Jaromir Jagr (11-13-24).

1992-93: Dynasty at Last?

While the Pittsburgh Penguins finished the 1992 playoffs as two-time defending Stanley Cup champions, they did not take on the mantle of a dynastic club until the 1992-93 season. Not only did the Penguins lead the Patrick Division from virtually the opening day of the campaign, the club also dominated the overall league standings, finishing with a team record mark of 56-21-7 for 119 points—30 points more than they had collected in any previous year. What made this feat all the more remarkable, however, is that the Penguins accomplished it with their star player, Mario Lemieux, sidelined for a total of four games with heel and back problems—and another 20 games over six weeks while undergoing treatment for Hodgkin's Disease.

After three consecutive injury-plagued (although still productive) years, Lemieux absolutely dominated the NHL over the 1992-93 season's first half, breaking the 100-point plateau in just 38 games, with his 37th goal and 64th assist of the year coming against the Toronto Maple Leafs on New Years' Eve.

Less than two weeks later, however, the shocking announcement was made that Lemieux had been diagnosed with early-stage nodular lymphocytic-type Hodgkin's Disease, a serious but fortunately highly treatable form of cancer. The 28-year-old Penguin star immediately began six weeks of radiation treatments while his understandably shaken teammates—and the hockey world—wondered if would ever be able to play again.

Lemieux's course of radiation treatments ended on the morning of March 2nd and remarkably, that very same night the Penguin captain made his emotional return to the lineup, collecting a goal and an assist in a 5-4 loss in Philadel-

phia. Three nights later, he was shutout in a 3-1 loss to the Rangers but then went on a scoring binge that saw him amass 29 goals and assist on 25 more in the season's final 18 games.

Included in that stretch was a pair of consecutive four-goal games against Washington and Philadelphia, respectively, on March 18th and 20th, and a five-goal outburst against the Rangers at Madison Square Garden on April 9th. The Pens had compiled a respectable 10-8-2 record while Lemieux was under treatment for cancer, and though the club lost during the captain's first two games back, the Pens then went on a remarkable 17-game winning streak before ending the season with a 6-6 tie in New Jersey, the same team they would face in the first round of the play-offs.

With 56 points in the 20 games after his return, Mario Lemieux accomplished perhaps the single most remarkable feat of the 1992-93 NHL

NHL President John A. Ziegler presents the 1991-92 Penguins with the Stanley Cup

season by either a player or team—winning the league scoring title despite having missed over a quarter of his team's games.

With 69 goals and 91 assists, Lemieux's 160 points beat out second-place finisher Pat Fontaine of Buffalo by a full dozen points and ensured the Penguin captain his fourth Art Ross Trophy. That performance also earned Lemieux his second Hart Trophy as the season's MVP, his third Lester B. Pearson Award as the NHL players' choice of the league's top performer, and the NHL's Bill Masterton Memorial Trophy for "perseverance, sportsmanship and dedication to hockey."

The Penguins first play-off opponent, the New Jersey Devils, had earned that dubious honor by finishing fourth in the Patrick Division on a "tie breaker" behind the New York Islanders, with whom they were otherwise even in points (87) and overall record (40-37-7). While the third-place Islanders were facing and upsetting the second-place Washington Capitals, the Devils proved no match for the streaking Penguins.

After 6-3 and 7-0 Pittsburgh victories at the Igloo and a 4-3 win at New Jersey, the Pens had extended their overall unbeaten streak to 20-0-1—and their play-off winning streak over two years to 13—before the Devils finally broke both skeins when they beat the Penguins in game four 4-1.

With a 5-3 victory in game five, however, Pittsburgh moved on to the Patrick Division Finals against the Islanders, clearly still "prohibitive" favorites to repeat as Stanley Cup champions for the third consecutive time. If ever a team looked as if it were going to be a dynasty, it was the Pittsburgh Penguins as they opened their series with the Islanders on Sunday, May 2nd.

Not only had the Islanders finished 32 points behind the Pens, they would also have to face them with the additional handicap of being without their top scorer, Pierre Turgeon, who had been blindsided by the Caps' Dale Hunter while celebrating a goal late in the third period of the Isles' series-clinching game against Washington.

Although Hunter's vicious crosscheck earned the aggressive Cap veteran a long suspension to start the 1993-94 season, it also separated Turgeon's shoulder, making him unavailable for at least the first five or six games of the Penguin series. Unlike the super-talented Pens, however, the Isles did not have anything like the supporting cast that Pittsburgh had when Lemieux was on the shelf in January and February.

What the Islanders did have, however, was legendary coach Al Arbour, who had molded his young club over the season into a sum far greater than its parts while Penguin coach Scotty Bowman—admittedly also one of the most successful bench bosses in NHL history—had guided his team with a far more "distant" hand.

Many believed that this difference in styles would eventually prove a major factor in the series, assuming that when push came to shove, the far more talented Penguins appeared to play with less team cohesion and spirit than the younger, more emotional, and ultimately hungrier Islanders. Thus, even without their best player, the Islanders believed they could beat the Penguins and did just that in the opening game of the series to capture "home ice" in a surprising 3-2 New York road win.

While the Pens rebounded with a convincing 3-0 Tom Barrasso shutout in game two and then regained their home-ice advantage in game three with a 3-1 victory, the Isles tied the series with a second win in game four, 6-5, to reduce the set to a far more uncertain best-of-three series. With a three-point night (2-1) Lemieux led the Penguins to a decisive 6-3 victory in the fifth game, however, and it appeared that the defending champs were finally coming out of their "slump" as they returned to long Island expecting to clinch the Patrick Division play-off title.

For the third consecutive game the high-scoring Penguins scored at least five goals, but the surprisingly resilient Islanders stunned Tom Barrasso and the Penguins with seven for a clutch 7-5 victory to tie the series at three games each and force Pittsburgh's back to the wall in a winner-take-all seventh game.

While the Penguins were still favored to win the series—and the Cup—they could not have been encouraged by looking at what had happened to the other seven teams that had finished first or second in their divisions in 1992-93, all of which had already been knocked out of the play-offs.

None of those teams, however, could boast the combination of four 100-or-more-point scorers (Mario Lemieux, Kevin Stevens, Rick Tocchet, and Ron Francis), the league's top plus-one defenseman (Larry Murphy at +45 and 85 points), and the league's winningest goalie (Tom Barrasso with 43), which bolstered the Penguins as they stepped on the Igloo's ice on the sweltering evening of Friday, May 14th. But as Islander goalie Glenn Healy said after New York's upset win in game one, "We don't have to be better than the Penguins, we just have to play better than them."

As if an omen of things to come, the Penguins almost immediately lost one of their top guns as 55-goal scorer Kevin Stevens was carried off the ice midway through the first period when he was stunned by a collision with Islander blueliner Rich Pilon and fell face first to the ice, fracturing his nose and cheek. Pittsburgh nonetheless dominated the game territorially, outshooting the Islanders 26-11 over the first two periods.

But the superb goaltending of Glenn Healy canceled that advantage, holding Pittsburgh to one second-period goal by Ulf Samuelsson, which was soon countered by one by Islander winger Steve Thomas.

Although the Penguins continued to pepper Healy, the Islanders finally took the lead during the first ten minutes of the third period with the first goal of the play-offs by little-used winger David Volek and the fourth by Benoit Hogue to give New York a 3-1 lead, which they held until the final four minutes of regulation time, when Ron Francis scored at 16:13 to bring Pittsburgh back to within one.

As the Penguins' season appeared to tick down to its final minute, Bowman pulled goalie Tom Barrasso for an extra attacker and miraculously, Ron Francis, then Rick Tocchet, deflected a point shot by Barry Murphy past Healy to tie the match at 3-3 with exactly one minute left in regulation to force the series-deciding game into overtime.

Eleven years earlier, the Islanders' John Tonelli had scored a similar late goal to keep the then-upstart Penguins from prematurely ending New York's Stanley Cup defense, which forced an early series-deciding game to overtime, where the champion Isles eventually prevailed. This time, however, the Isles would come out on top as underdogs as David Volek stunned the Penguin faithful with a blast from the top of the right circle that beat Barrasso cleanly, thereby subjecting the Penguins to one of the most remarkable upsets in Stanley Cup history.

In June, Penguin coach Scotty Bowman resigned his post to accept the position of coach of the Detroit Red Wings. He was replaced behind the Pittsburgh bench by former Penguin coach and GM Eddie Johnston, the man who had drafted Mario Lemieux almost a decade earlier and had later served as GM of the Hartford Whalers. In late August, GM Craig Patrick added another Stanley Cup-winning veteran to his lineup when he traded rookie center Shawn McEachern to the Los Angeles Kings for hard-nosed defenseman/winger Marty McSorley.

Though in 1993 the Penguins had failed to win their third consecutive Cup title and would thus not establish themselves as a "dynasty," Mario Lemieux and company remained in residence in the Steel City as the club entered the mid-1990s. As such, the unexpected break in the NHL's championship "cycle" looked as if it might well be just a temporary one.

—Bruce C. Cooper

QUEBEC NORDIQUES

The Quebec Nordiques didn't join the National Hockey League until 1979-80, when the NHL and the rebel World Hockey Association (WHA) came to a merger agreement, but any review of the Nordiques' life must start with those heady days when they challenged the Montreal Canadiens for support in "La Belle Province."

Quebec City is the provincial head of Quebec's government and the French-speaking center of life and culture in French-Canada, but the "grand ville" had always played second fiddle to the renowned Montreal Habitants when it came to ice hockey. The best local talent—most notable among them, Guy Lafleur—went from area rinks down the road to Montreal where the Forum waited.

Thanks to territorial rules that prevailed in the pre-expansion days of the NHL, the Montreal Canadiens snapped up the bevy of youngsters annually produced in the hockey-mad region along the St. Lawrence River. Quebec had to be

content with Canadian Junior Hockey, their Remparts the team where Lafleur carved out his earliest fame.

When the WHA became more than just an idea, six area businessmen put together a consortium to pursue a team for Quebec. On February 11, 1972, the group headed by Jean-Marc Bruneau purchased the San Francisco franchise of the WHA. Soon after, Marius Fortier got the support of influential Quebec citizens, including Premier Jean Lesage, so the team launch of May 5 included $2 million in capital, $1 million raised through personal endorsements. Suddenly, Montreal had company in Quebec.

The Nordiques made news before they ever played a game, signing two famed Montreal Canadiens. One, Jean Claude Tremblay, a 13-year veteran of the "bleu, blanc et rouge" team, stayed with Quebec for seven seasons, but the other, coach Maurice Richard, lasted just two games in his new home. Later Quebec would be coached by ex-Habs Jacques Plante and Jean Guy Gendron, but the real battles between the two franchises had nothing to do with personnel.

The serious Quebec Provincial issue in those days of WHA-NHL warfare revolved not around player deals but around the brewery rivalry between Molson, so long associated with the Canadiens, and O'Keefe, which took a major share of ownership in the Nordiques in 1976. The competition obviously involved advertising, but more than that, television.

The Canadiens had long enjoyed a monopoly on weekly French-language *Hockey Night in Canada* broadcasts, a Canadian TV habit. Montreal and Molson were not interested in sharing the wealth with another team, to say nothing of another league. Even after the NHL accepted Quebec and the three other WHA survivors, Montreal remained the Saturday night tenant on CBC television. O'Keefe and the Nordiques had to cut their own television deals on another network, a situation unchanged into the early 1990s.

A Style Is Born

On the ice, the Quebec Nordiques wasted little time in establishing themselves in their home market. By playing an attacking style of hockey, the type favored in the region as evidenced by the wide-open Quebec Major Junior Hockey League, the Nordiques not only entertained fans, they also quickly created some individual stars whose scoring feats were to define the WHA years. All told, there were seven WHA seasons and plenty of heroes to keep the crowds coming to the Quebec Coliseum. If Coach Richard lasted only two games, replacement Maurice Filion was there for the long haul, and some of the team's first stars shone right on into the NHL days.

It took three seasons before Quebec reached the WHA playoffs, but, from the start, Tremblay proved that he had plenty left after a lengthy NHL career with Montreal. In 1972-73 he led the team in scoring from his defense position (14-75-89) and led the WHA in assists. He topped that output in 1975-76 with 12-77-89. In addition to Tremblay, the Nordiques had great stars in Serge Bernier, Real Cloutier, Rejean Houle, and Marc Tardif, plus goaltender Richard Brodeur, a Quebec fixture until reclaimed by the New York Islanders when NHL clubs were allowed to take players they had drafted during the battle with the rival league. Bernier, Cloutier, Houle, and Tardif were all special players worth a second look.

While the hockey purists might well argue that NHL expansion and the very existence of the WHA served to dilute the overall quality of professional hockey, the opposite can be asserted when you look at the talent that found room to flourish with the creation of new teams.

Players who might never have cracked the elite six-team NHL that prevailed until the 1967-68 expansion suddenly had a stage on which to perform. Many took it with aplomb. Serge Bernier, for instance, had broken in with expansion in 1968-69 and collected 77 points in the 1970-71 season with the Philadelphia Flyers. When the Nordiques were born, the Padoue, Quebec, native elected to take his chance in the new league.

At 6' 1" and 190 pounds, Bernier played eight years as a center in a Nordique uniform and demonstrated his range of skills. Twice he topped the 100-point level and in five seasons produced 30 or more goals. He had a standout 1976-77 WHA playoff campaign when he rolled up 36 points in just 17 games, scoring 14 goals and adding 22 assists. He was 32 years old when the Nordiques finally gained their NHL spot, by then past his prime.

Real "Buddy" Cloutier went directly from Quebec junior hockey to WHA stardom. He was just 18 when the Nordiques signed him, playing 63 games in the 1974-75 season for 26-27-53 figures. In those days, players like Cloutier, a native of St. Emile, Quebec, were still thought too young for the rigors of the professional game, but Cloutier's rapid development suggested otherwise. At 19, the 5' 10" 185-pound right wing was a 60-goal scorer in the WHA during the first of four consecutive seasons that saw him get 50 or more. He finished 1975-76 with 114 points in 80 games, a sug-

TEAM INFORMATION AT A GLANCE

Founding date: May 5, 1972 (World Hockey Association)
March 30, 1979 (National Hockey League)

Home ice: Colisee de Quebec
2205, ave du Colisee
Quebec, Quebec, Canada G1L 4W7
Phone: (418) 529-8441
FAX: (418) 529-1052

Seating capactiy: 15,399

Team colors: Blue, white, and red.
Team nickname: Nordiques
Logo: Stylized red and blue letter "N" next to hockey stick and puck.

Franchise record	Won	Lost	Tie
(1979-1993)	433	544	147

League last-place finishes: 1989, 1990, 1991.

---

gestion of what lay ahead. Cloutier's subsequent seasons read this way: 66-75-141, 56-73-129, 75-54-129. And lest one suppose that these figures owed much to the WHA's lack of defensive talent, Cloutier, when the Nordiques finally joined the NHL, got 42 goals and added 47 assists in just 67 games. He was hampered by injury in 1980-81, but rebounded the following year to get 97 points with 30 goals, 67 assists. Clearly, Cloutier knew where the net was.

At Home With Both

Rejean Houle was a player who spent parts of his career with both of the Quebec franchises. He broke into the NHL as a 20-year-old in 1969 with Canadiens and spent four seasons in the Forum before signing with the Nordiques. From 1973 to 1976 he played the WHA game with devastating effect, getting 40 goals in 1974-75 and following that up with a 51-goal season. He then went back to Canadiens and was a consistent, if not as spectacular, performer.

Marc Tardif, on the other hand, started in Montreal, then chose the WHA and never looked back. Born in Granby, Quebec, in 1949, the left winger made his NHL debut in Montreal, playing 18 games in the 1969-70 season. He stayed three more years, scoring 31 goals in 1971-72 and adding 25 the next year before accepting a WHA offer to head west with the new Los Angeles franchise. After a 40-goal debut season there, he wound up in Quebec midway through the 1974-75 season.

Even critics of WHA hockey had no trouble spotting Tardif as a truly gifted goal scorer. He struck for 71 in his first full season as a Nordique

---

(1975-76) and followed with 49 and 65 the next two years. He led the WHA in goals, assists, and points that first year and did the same again in 1977-78. When the NHL-WHA merger came the goals didn't stop. He scored 41 in his first full NHL season and topped the 30 mark in two of the next three years although no longer a youngster.

The Nordiques put together six straight winning WHA seasons after finishing the first year seven games under .500. The new team was exciting and high-scoring, one of the truly successful franchises in the expansion league. Having established a winning habit, they carried it into their early NHL years, a fact which made the difficult second half of the 1980s, when Quebec sunk to the bottom of the league, that much harder to take.

The Nordiques won the WHA Canadian Division in 1974-75 but lost the WHA play-off title to the Houston Aeros, a team featuring Gordie Howe and his sons, Mark and Marty, playing on the same line. A year later Tardif, Cloutier, Houle, and Bernier all topped the 100-point mark, and Tremblay finished with 89 as the Nordiques fired away on all burners.

But it was in 1976-77 when they finally won everything, finishing first in the WHA East, then beating New England, Indianapolis, and Winnipeg, to capture the Avco Trophy, emblematic of WHA supremacy. Maybe the lords of the NHL didn't take notice, but the populace of Quebec City did.

When the merger came after the 1978-79 season, the Nordiques were well-endowed. They kept Bernier, Cloutier and Tardif, although Richard Brodeur was taken by the Islanders. Even better, they named Michel Goulet their first NHL draft pick, a choice that would last for many seasons.

Two Results in Season One

The first NHL campaign was not a winner on the ice, but the Nordiques certainly made a tremendous gain outside the boards. While the team struggled in with a 25-44-11 season, Goulet making his debut with 54 points and Cloutier leading the team at 42-47-89, the management team of Michel Aubut and Gilles Leger was achieving a coup of its own.

The Quebec pair had gone to Eastern Europe in a cloak-and-dagger mission to obtain the signatures of two of Czechoslovakia's finest players, Anton and Peter Stastny. The brothers agreed to come west at a time when relations between the North American pros and the East European Socialist states were far from friendly. The agreement meant that the two great international players would have to forgo appearing for their native country in future world and Olympic competition—not an easy decision in that day—and eventually led to the third, and eldest brother, Marian, joining them in Quebec.

Not even the most optimistic Nordique fan—and, most likely, not Aubut and Leger, either—could have predicted the impact that the Stastny brothers would have on hockey in the NHL. Peter was a big, strong player with wonderful balance, a powerful shot, and the kind of temperament most NHL coaches would die for.

He never seemed to tire (although he admitted that going from the much shorter European seasons to the 80-game NHL grind was the hardest adjustment he'd had to make) and instantly earned the respect of all opponents with his competitive spirit. He was 24 when he came West, already an experienced international who had proven his abilities in those hotly contested Soviet-Czech games that spiced World Hockey tournaments.

He was especially adept at scoring power play goals and equally irritating with his ability to play both strong offense and defense. His first season was a 39-70-109 work of art, a Calder Trophy-winning year that helped to destroy any ideas that Europeans couldn't become a major force in the NHL.

Anton, the youngest Stastny brother at age 21 when he made his NHL debut, was a smoother artist, but every bit as much of a problem for defenses. He began his NHL stay with a 39-46-85 announcement and helped transform the Nordiques in a single season. A left wing, he was a definite prospect, but not yet a recognized star like his two older brothers.

The third Stastny, Marian, an acknowledged Czech superstar, arrived the next season in 35-54-89 fashion to complete the threesome. The real veteran at age 28, he was a right winger, so his arrival completed a Stastny line. Quebec had not only played its cards with the daring grab of the Bratislava trio, it had come up trumps.

When Peter Stastny finished his Nordique career, his 10 seasons in Quebec left him the franchise's all-time leading scorer. He scored

AP/Wide World Photos

Goalie Daniel Bouchard

1,048 points in 737 games (a 1.42 point-per-goal average) to finish more than 100 points ahead of Goulet. His 668 assists were nearly 200 more than his nearest challenger. Anton ranked third in scoring after nine seasons, collecting 252 goals and 384 assists in 650 games, while Marian played four seasons, scored 98 goals, and finished with 241 points. He was ninth overall on the Nordiques' scoring list after the 1991-92 season, right behind Tardif's 244 NHL points.

Enter the Little Tiger

Quebec might not have emerged as NHL power so quickly had the Nordiques not been fortunate enough to discover a coach whose personality and fiery competitive temperament complemented the players and the region so well. Born June 12, 1946, Michel Bergeron was just 34 when he replaced Maurice Filion behind the bench in the 1980-81 season to begin a seven-season stay in Quebec. The Nordiques never missed the play-offs during that tenure, one which saw Bergeron alternately inspire and cajole his players while winning the respect of fans and the media throughout the league.

Nicknamed "Le Petit Tigre," Bergeron was a master of public relations in both English and French, just as he was a master tactician on the ice. He seemed to revel in the heat of the Quebec City-Montreal confrontations and convinced his players that his style and approach to the game would win. He began his coaching career in Montreal midget hockey, then moved to Quebec Major Junior Hockey League's Three Rivers Draveurs, where he took the team to a pair of Memorial Cup finals in 1978 and 1979. The next step was into the NHL, working with the Nordiques as an associate coach with Filion. He took complete charge behind the bench on October 20, 1980, just seven games into the season.

The Bergeron era had begun with a fourth-place finish in the Adams Division and a first-round loss to the Philadelphia Flyers in the Stanley Cup play-offs, but there was much better to come.

Michel Goulet

In 1981-82, Quebec was fourth again in the division, but their 33-31-16 record represented the first NHL winning season for the franchise.

Peter Stastny showed what a tremendous player he was, with 46 goals and 93 assists carrying him the 139-point level. Cloutier went 37-60-97, and Marian Stastny, still full of vigor after a full European-based career, came up with 35 goals and 54 assists in his debut NHL year. In the nets, Dan Bouchard won 27 games and posted a 3.86 goals-against average.

Even the most die-hard Nordique fan might not remember much about those statistics, good as they are. But there probably isn't anyone who pays even passing attention to hockey in the Province of Quebec who has forgotten what happened in the first round of the 1981-82 Stanley Cup play-offs. After five dramatic games, Quebec eliminated regular season Adams Division champion

Montreal in the fabled Forum. The new boys on the block, who had struggled for recognition in their WHA days and endured second-class status as an expansion team, had won their NHL spurs by defeating their mighty neighbors.

That year Dale Hunter became an instant hero for Nordique fans with a goal 22 seconds into overtime of the fifth game to win the Battle of Quebec. The Nordiques went on to knock out Boston in another series that went the limit, again capturing the decisive game on enemy ice, but they couldn't match the powerful New York Islanders and fell in four straight games in the conference finals.

Goulet Steps Forward

Michel Goulet had been the hidden prize on the day that the Nordiques gained their official NHL place. He was already well known in Quebec, having starred in the city with the Quebec Junior Hockey League, but he turned pro in the final year of the WHA. The Nordiques claimed him 20th overall in their first entry draft.

A natural left winger with a hard left-sided shot, Goulet was a native of Peribonka, Quebec, and only 18 when he played his first pro game in the WHA. It was no surprise, then, that it took a while for him to put everything together in the National Hockey League. Once he did, he was a consistent big gun, rolling up six straight 90-points-plus seasons, four times topping the 100-point level. He was a first-team all-star in 1984, 1986, and 1987, and won second-team recognition in 1983 and 1988. He played in five mid-season all-star games between 1983 and 1988.

In 1982-83 Goulet finished behind only Peter Stastny in team scoring, his 57 goals the best on the club in a 34-34-12 season. After another fourth-place Adams Division finish the Nordiques were victims of a bit of revenge, with Boston knocking them out of the playoffs in the first round. The other big news came after the season when the Nordiques dealt Cloutier to Buffalo for Andre Savard, Tony McKegney, and Jean Francois Sauve.

Goulet won his first team scoring title in 1983-84 with another big year. He scored 56 goals and added 65 assists to nip Peter Stastny 121-119 on the club leader board. Bergeron used four goaltenders that season with Bouchard still doing the bulk of the work, but there was a 23-game stint by Clint Malarchuk, a netminder who would one day be Quebec's main starter. For the second straight year the play-offs brought a first-round loss. This time it was Montreal's payback turn, and they won a 4-2 battle.

Bergeron's team was still to peak. In 1984-85 the Nordiques went 41-30-9 and finished second in the Adams Division. Peter Stastny finished 32-68-100, and Goulet was right on the mark in goal scoring once again, totaling 55 this time. Mario Gosselin, Richard Sevigny, and Bouchard shared the goaltending work, all of them below the 3.50 goals-against mark.

The play-offs brought reward this time. First Buffalo fell, 3-2, then the Nordiques gained their second post-season success at the expense of the Canadiens in another nail-biting confrontation. The Nordiques won three overtime games in the seven-game showdown, once more eliminating their arch rival in the Forum.

Mark Kumpel's goal at 12:23 of the first extra period won the first game in the Forum, 2-1, but Montreal went to Quebec City on level terms after winning the second, 6-4. Game three was a shoot-out; Dale Hunter again wore the overtime hero's hat with a goal at 18:36 that gave the Nordiques a 7-6 victory. But Montreal evened the score again with a 3-1 victory.

Now the series took on a life of its own. The final three games all went to the visiting team, making a mockery of the NHL's much-vaunted "home ice" advantage in the play-offs. The Nordiques easily won game five, 5-1, but had to keep the champagne on ice when they were beaten in their own building, 5-2, three nights later. The finale, on May 2, 1984, was decided—quite fittingly—by a Peter Stastny goal 2:22 into still another overtime. But the emotion invested in such a series left the Nordiques spent: they fell to Philadelphia in the conference final in six games.

An Adams Division title came in the 1985-86 season, the first championship Quebec had won in the NHL. No prizes for guessing who led the way—by now it was Peter Stastny, Goulet, Anton Stastny, and Dale Hunter who drew most of the attention from friends and foe alike. Peter had 41 goals, Goulet netted 53.

What happened next was totally unexpected in two cities: the Hartford Whalers, longtime rivals dating back to WHA days, rose up and stunned the Adams champs in three straight Stanley Cup games. What had looked so much like Quebec's year to challenge for play-off honors ended before it began. In Hartford, the victory signalled the arrival of the Whalers' best NHL team.

The Downward Spiral

For five consecutive years Bergeron had put winning teams on the ice in Quebec. The team was balanced, attractive to watch, and had a fiery approach to the game that appealed to the partisan fans in the old city. There was no warning that the 1985-86 year was to be the high-water mark, and no immediate indication that it would be the last winning year in Quebec for years to come.

The decline can be partly explained by the fact that key players were aging, but there were still major contributions from Goulet and Peter and Anton Stastny well into the period of decline. The fact that Bergeron was lured away to coach the New York Rangers after the 1986-87 season was also significant, but Quebec's fall from contender status to Adams Division also-ran owed more to the fact that the whole division tightened its defensive web around the once free-skating Nordiques.

Even Montreal, nicknamed "the Flying Frenchmen" in their heyday, had become a more grinding type of hockey club, a necessary style in a division containing proud Boston, an Emile Francis-rebuilt Hartford franchise, and a Buffalo team that also had learned the value of solid checking. The wide-open game of the past was found increasingly found wanting. Quebec had some bad

luck, too. Just when coach Ron Lapointe was getting the necessary experience to rebuild the club, he was forced out of action on December 15, 1988, and later underwent surgery for a tumorous kidney. That ended his NHL coaching career.

The Nordiques first turned to Jean Perron, then persuaded Bergeron to return for another turn in 1989-90, but that ended in disaster. The old Bergeron touch wasn't there and even the return of an aging Guy Lafleur to the city where he had become a junior hockey idol couldn't prevent a dreadful 12-61-7 season. On May 4, 1990, Pierre Page was named general manager and the process of retooling the Nordiques for the last decade of the century was undertaken once again.

Good Draft Choices

While the records were poor and success fleeting—there was a play-off victory over Hartford in 1987 but no other Stanley Cup action for five years—there were some signs that life would be better when Quebec's succession of draft choices began to mature. In 1987 they traded Dale Hunter and Clint Malarchuk to Washington in a deal that included the Capitals' number-one pick. That turned out to be Joe Sakic, one of the youngsters who would become the foundation of the Quebec revival in the new decade.

In 1988 the Nordiques chose defenseman Curtis Leschyshyn and forward Daniel Dore with their two first-round picks, while 1989 saw them take the Swedish youngster Mats Sundin. Because these were 18-year-old kids there was no immediate return on the selections, but it was to Quebec's credit that they made no attempt to force-feed their prospects. In that same 1988-89 year when the club won only 27 games, they had two Canadian Junior Hockey award-winners in Bryan Fogarty and goalie Stephane Fiset.

The collection continued in 1989-90 when the "reward" for that 31-point season was number-one pick Owen Nolan, while another long season in 1990-91 again left the Nordiques with the first choice. They named Eric Lindros, the most talked-about Canadian junior prospect in ages, even though it was widely reported that Lindros did not wish to play in Quebec. Page resisted the temptation to trade the young man for immediate help, waiting an entire year while Lindros stayed in the juniors. Eventually, on June 30, 1992, Quebec got six players and two draft choices from the Philadelphia Flyers as Lindros moved on without ever playing a game for the Nordiques.

That huge deal, plus the signing of Russian star Valeri Kamensky in 1991 and the maturation of all the younger players who had been picked during the Nordiques' "Dark Ages" created a new team in 1992-93. Quebec was back on the winning side of the ledger again, fighting for the Adams title right to the final week of the season. A first-round play-off loss to Montreal, the eventual Stanley Cup winners, didn't sit well with the Nordiques' faithful, but the fact that Page had led the team back into a proud NHL position was probably reward enough for supporters who had never deserted their hockey team.

SOURCES

BOOKS

Diamond, Dan, *The Official National Hockey League 75th Anniversary Commemorative Book,* NHL Publications, 1991.

Fischler, Stan and Shirley, *The Hockey Encyclopedia,* MacMillan, 1983.

Romain, Joseph, and Dan Diamond, *The Pictorial History of Hockey,* Gallery Books, 1987.

Additional information obtained from such sources as *NHL Official Guide & Record Book,* various editions of *Sporting News Hockey Guide & Register,* and other media guides & yearbook information, including key dates in history from *Quebec Nordiques.*

—*Jerry Trecker* for Book Builders, Inc.

PACIFIC DIVISION

© Disney

ANAHEIM MIGHTY DUCKS

There has never been an expansion team in professional sports quite like the Anaheim Mighty Ducks. Even before a Duck played a puck, the franchise ruffled feathers in the sports world. (Even one of the team's players, Stu Grimson, had problems with the club's name, preferring to think of himself as a "muscular water fowl.") Those who take their sports seriously believe the Mighty Ducks are making a mockery of hockey, while those who prefer fun with their games find the Ducks a mighty source of entertainment and amusement, even before they take the ice.

The team's nickname is taken directly from a movie—*The Mighty Ducks*—about a misfit kid hockey team coached by a yuppie lawyer as part of his community service sentence for drunk driving. After much slapstick fun on and off the ice, both the team and the coach earn respect by the end of the movie. The movie was produced by Disney studios, and the Mighty Ducks of the NHL are owned by Michael Eisner, Chairman of Dis-

ney. Legend has it that Eisner liked the movie so much he bought his way into the NHL for $50 million.

The Ducks, then, enjoy the mighty financial backing and the shrewd marketing and merchandising skills of the Disney empire. But even with this backing and potential, will they be taken seriously? Is this hockey, or hokey?

Take the team's logo, for instance—a cartoonish goalie mask exaggerated to accommodate a duck's bill. It may not be a stately or aggressive-looking logo, but as sale's attest, it has found favor with the public. The team will play in a state-of-the-art venue that cost $103 million and boasts plenty of glass and marble. The Anaheim Arena has been renamed The Pond, and management plans to treat fans with numerous contests and mascots, including a whole new slew of Disney characters.

The hockey game will only be part of the event. For instance, in the team's first press conference Eisner, NHL Commissioner Gary Bettman, and Bruce McNall, Chairman of the NHL Board of Governors brandished duck calls and quacked out the team's theme song. Goofy, yes, but Disney has proven that goofy sells. While the NHL lags far behind other professional sports leagues in marketing savvy, the Mighty Ducks have already made an immediate impact: season ticket sales reached 11,500—a phenomenal figure—by mid-July, the logo is a hot item on sportswear, and the franchise is certainly drawing plenty of media attention.

On the ice the Mighty Ducks can only hope to be as offensive, or fun. Making the best of a weak talent pool drained by two previous expansions in the 1990s alone, General Manager Jack Ferreira drafted a team experienced on defense and in goal. Ferreira has an impressive resume. He most recently assisted in launching the San Jose Sharks franchise for the 1991-92 season. Assistant General Manager Pierre Gauthier helped transform the Quebec Nordiques into one of hockey's brightest young teams.

The team is coached by well-respected Ron Wilson. According to Mark Whicker of the *Orange County Register*, Wilson "was famous as a Vancouver assistant (coach) for using video to amuse and motivate."

"We'll use the (*Mighty Ducks*) movie at first," said Wilson. "That has some highlights. We don't have any highlights of our own yet."

Wilson comes from a strong hockey background. Both his father, Larry, and uncle, Johnny, played and coached for the Detroit Red Wings.

Ducks on Ice

The Mighty Ducks defense will be anchored by their goalies. Guy Hebert, their first pick in the expansion draft, backed up Curtis Joseph in St. Louis. Vying with Hebert will be Ron Tugnutt, a perennial prospect who has yet to blossom. The defense can best be described as "mature," with Alexei Kastonov (33, drafted from New Jersey), Bill Houlder (26, Buffalo), Randy Ladoceur (33,

Hartford), and Bobby Dollas (28, Detroit).

Forwards taken in the draft by the Mighty Ducks totalled only 73 goals for their respective NHL teams the previous season. Best of the flock is Terry Yake (24, Hartford), the only forward to tally as many as 20 goals during the 1992-93 campaign.

Anatoli Semenov (31, Vancouver), who will battle Yake for the first line center position, was a 20-goal scorer for the Edmonton Oilers in 1991-92 but slipped in only a dozen for the Tampa Bay Lightning the next year. The remaining forwards are in their mid-20s without notable NHL achievements. With their first selection in 1993's amateur draft, the Mighty Ducks chose Paul Kariya, an 18-year-old Canadian of Japanese descent. Kariya is touted as an excellent playmaker and is already viewed by some hockey analysts as the Ducks' best forward.

A prolific scorer for the University of Maine in 1992-93, Kariya was the first freshman to win the Hobey Baker Award as top collegiate player. Kariya is expected to practice with the Canadian National Team and to play for them in the 1994 Winter Olympics before joining the Mighty Ducks late in their first season. The Mighty Ducks hope to earn some respect while Kariya undergoes his apprenticeship. The large volume of season ticket sales and the curiosity of the public have already indicated a strong degree of interest in this fun-generating franchise.

While the Mighty Ducks are an immediate sensation at the gate and in the stores, they will be hard pressed to win as many as 15 of 84 games on the ice, and any more than that would be a Disney fantasy come true. Meanwhile, *Mighty Ducks II* is already being filmed and is expected to be released by the end of the season—the NHL season that is. By then, coach Wilson will have his own team highlight films to amuse and, hopefully, to motivate.

SOURCES

Inside Hockey: Yearbook '94, September, 1993.
Sports Illustrated, October 11, 1993.

TEAM INFORMATION AT A GLANCE

Founding date: December 9, 1992

Home ice: The Pond at Anaheim
2695 E. Katella Blvd.
Anaheim, CA 92806
Phone: (714) 704-2700

Seating Capacity: 17,500

Team colors: Black, teal, gray, and white
Team Nickname: The Mighty Ducks
Logo: Goalie mask exaggerated to accommodate a duck bill, set over diagnally crossed hockey sticks in a black circle within a wedge-shaped, teal-colored backdrop.

AP/Wide World Photos

NHL Commissioner Gary Bettman attends the introductory press conference conducted by Mighty Ducks owner Michael Eisner (at podium)

CALGARY FLAMES

When Calgary won the 1989 Stanley Cup, there were undoubtedly some fans in Atlanta who shared in the moment. If the Georgia city no longer had an NHL team, at least the Flames had spent a fair part of their history in the Southern United States, testimony to an era when the expansion of the National Hockey League was part of the war for turf, prestige, and players with the rival World Hockey Association.

The Flames spent eight full seasons in Atlanta before relocating to western Canada, but they are firm fixtures on the Canadian prairies now. Arch rivals with Edmonton, Calgary now plays in the beautiful Olympic Saddledome and has built a hockey heritage of its own in the space of just over a decade.

After a checkered history beset with playoff miseries and the misfortune to be just down the road from one of the sport's greatest dynasties, Calgary got it just right in 1989 when they won the Stanley Cup. But the road to the top was not easy.

The Atlanta Flames were created for the 1972-73 season, well ahead of the NHL's announced expansion schedule and the subject of more than one question about the league's concern with the WHA. Although the official line was to ignore the fledgling rivals, the presence of another major professional hockey league was a real concern for the NHL. The 1970s were wide-open as sports boomed across North America; even the powerful National Football League had been forced to make peace with an upstart American Football League just years before. There was every reason for the NHL to take the threat of the WHA seriously, even if they didn't acknowledge their concern.

In *A Thinking Man's Guide to Pro Hockey,* Gerald Eskenazi suggests that the folks who decided to put franchises in Atlanta and on Long Island were reacting to the existence of their rivals. The WHA had announced its presence in the summer of 1971, not long after the NHL had decided against expansion until at least 1974-75. The league had even passed a resolution requiring a unanimous vote before more teams could join pro hockey's elite. Suddenly, however, things were different and that vote forgotten.

"In an about face, a week after the WHA had announced it was in business and was going to have a New York franchise, the NHL suddenly granted franchises to New York [the Islanders] and Atlanta," Eskenazi writes, "and was going to expand in 1972—two years earlier than it had planned to do. In addition, it said it was going to expand again in 1974 and planned to have 24 teams in North America by the decade's end. Cynical observers saw the league's move to Long Island and further expansion plans as a ploy to rid itself of the WHA.... And by moving to Atlanta, the NHL would also get the inside track on the new Atlanta Coliseum [the Omni] which the WHA had hoped to invade. The NHL for the first time was in the Deep South."

A Grand Experiment

Whatever the motivation, the NHL's grand attempt to take hockey into the American South ultimately was terminated when the Flames moved to Calgary, but there are people who insist that Atlanta was considerably better hockey territory than the naysayers allowed. Certainly the team was no expansion punching bag, needing just two seasons to better the .500 mark and never experiencing a losing season again. What Atlanta's Flames did not do, however, was win post-season games. They made the Stanley Cup playoffs six times in eight years, and sometimes started a series as favorites, but never captured one. In the final analysis, that playoff jinx may have been the reason they never quite penetrated deeply enough into the Atlanta sports fans' consciousness.

Bernie "Boom-Boom" Geoffrion, one of the great Montreal Canadiens, was Atlanta's first NHL coach. He wasn't all that deep in talent in the first season but had two goaltenders of quality, Phil Myre—once the Canadiens' heir apparent—and

Daniel Bouchard. Myre finished with a 3.03 goals against average in 44 games, Bouchard was a 3.09 in 34, and the Flames were a creditable 25-38-15 in their first year. Compare that to the Islanders' 12-60-6 or California's 16-46-16 in the same season, and it is easy to see that Atlanta was far better than might have been expected.

In their second year, buoyed by the addition of Calder Trophy winner Tom Lysiak, Geoffrion's troops finished fourth in the Western Division and almost had a winning year. They were 30-34-14, well-behind the Western Division champion Philadelphia Flyers, who swept them out of the Stanley Cup playoffs in four straight games en route to the championship.

Bouchard finished fourth among goalies that season with a 2.77 GAA and five shutouts, while Lysiak began what would be a solid career in Flames' colors by leading the team in scoring with 19 goals, 45 assists, and 64 points. He had been the number two pick in the 1973 draft of junior hockey talent, chosen from Medicine Hat. It was an outstanding pick for the Flames; trouble was the number one that season was a player named Denis Potvin. He went to the New York Islanders, eventually having a hand in four straight Stanley Cup triumphs for the Flames' expansion partners.

A Winning Year, but No Playoffs

Additional expansion in 1974-75 meant that the Flames were relocated into the newly-created Patrick Division, alongside Philadelphia, the New York Rangers, and the New York Islanders, as the NHL grew to 18 teams. That proved to be a mixed blessing.

Geoffrion didn't survive the season behind the bench, leaving with a 22-20-10 winning record. Fred Creighton took over and kept the Flames on the winning side of the ledger for the first time in their history, but the 34-31-15 record wasn't enough to land them a playoff spot. They were last in the Patrick division with 83 points, a finish better than seven other NHL teams; but the

TEAM INFORMATION AT A GLANCE

Founding date: 1972

Home ice: Olympic Saddledome
P.O. Box 1540, Sta. M
Calgary, Alberta, Canada T2P 3B9
Phone: (403) 261-0475
FAX: (403) 261-0470

Seating capacity: 20,123

Team colors: White, red, and gold.
Team nickname: Flames
Logo: Letter "C" with flames on back side.

Franchise record	Won	Lost	Tie
(1972-93)	793	632	255

Stanley Cup Victories (1): 1988-89
First-place divisional finishes (3): 1987-88, 1988-89, 1989-90

new playoff system denied them a Stanley Cup shot while others went forward.

Lysiak proved that there was no sophomore jinx by again leading the club in scoring. He had support from a rookie, Eric Vail, whose first season of 39 goals (tops on the team) was part of a 60-point campaign that won him the Calder Trophy as the NHL's top rookie. Vail registered his 39 goals on just 177 shots, and his shooting percentage of 22.0 was topped only by Jim Pappin of the Chicago Black Hawks.

Bouchard and Myre were stingy again, too, both allowing fewer than 3.00 goals per game. Bouchard finished fifth in the NHL—behind such greats as Bernie Parent, Rogie Vachon, Ken Dryden, and Tony Esposito—with a 2.78 GAA, a mark equalled by a New York Islander who would gain his own share of NHL fame, Billy Smith. Myre's five shutouts placed him fourth behind Parent (12), Vachon, and Esposito.

All But the Cream

The next five seasons in Atlanta would have been gladly accepted by many teams in the NHL. The team never had a losing year, developed some additional stars, and made a sagacious trade or two. But playoff success eluded Atlanta every season.

Lysiak again set the pace in 1975-76, as the Flames went 35-33-12 and finished a solid third in the Patrick, 15 points ahead of the Rangers. Vail's production fell off sharply from his rookie year, but Curt Bennett, who had been acquired from the Rangers back in 1972, stepped forward with his best campaign in an Atlanta uniform. Bouchard and Myre were still a formidable goaltending tandem. The only thing missing was a little luck in the playoffs. This time the Flames lost to Los Angeles in two straight games at the start of the spring showdown.

Atlanta repeated the scenario a year later, a

.500 season, enough to get them home eight points clear of the Rangers; Lysiak still the consistent number one scorer; and Vail back to his first-year form. Flame rookie named Willi Plett, who would develop into one of the sport's most noted workers, won the Calder Trophy off a 56-point season. But Atlanta again fell to Los Angeles in the playoffs, this time two games to one.

Is There a Good Rut to Be In?

Atlanta had certain parts of the NHL formula down absolutely pat by the 1977-78 season, but the problem was that third place Patrick Division finishes and first round Stanley Cup losses weren't boosting season ticket sales to knockout numbers in the Omni. This was a pretty good hockey club, but it wasn't a great one and the numbers made that fact clear.

The 1977-78 team went 34-27-19, quite respectable, but the 87 points were 24 shy of the Islanders, who had, after all, accompanied Atlanta somewhat hastily into the NHL fold. While the Long Islanders now seemed poised to challenge for the very top in the game, the Flames were sputtering along well enough, but without the look of a club that was about to make the breakthrough to the top.

Lysiak and Vail again led the scorers, Guy Chouinard began to make good on his expected promise with a strong showing in just his second full season in the league, and Bouchard's 2.75 goals-against mark was excellent. But the Flames were again kayoed at the first tier of Stanley Cup action, falling 2-0 to Detroit this time.

A year later might have marked the turnaround for the Flames in Georgia, but it was not to be. The team's best record (41-31-8) was good for 90 points, but just fourth place in the Patrick Division. Five other NHL teams had more than 90 points that season.

Bob MacMillan, acquired in a December, 1977 trade that sent Myre and Bennett to St. Louis, emerged as a star with a career season. MacMillan scored 37 goals, picked up 71 assists, and finished with 108 points, a performance which earned him the Lady Byng Trophy for excellence on the ice combined with gentlemanly play. He had been assessed only 14 minutes in penalties during 79 games.

Chouinard, a 50-goal marksman, was right behind his teammate with 107 points that year, and Bouchard led the NHL in wins with 32. But none of that was enough to boost the Flames among the elite. They lost 2-0 to Toronto in the first round of the playoffs.

If that's hard to understand, consider what kind of season this was: Chouinard's 50 goals would have made headlines two decades before. In 1978-79 he was no better than fourth in goal scoring behind the Islanders' Mike Bossy (69), the Kings' Marcel Dionne (59) and the evergreen Guy LaFleur in Montreal, who bagged 52. MacMillan's 71 assists were 16 fewer than league-leader Bryan Trottier of the Isles and his 108 points left him 26 short of the same Islander in the race for the Art Ross Trophy.

The standards were rising every season. Yes, they were helped by the inevitable expansion-based inflation, but the game was opening up, too, as players like Wayne Gretzky and his Edmonton Oiler teammates made their NHL debut. The Atlanta, then Calgary, franchise would know all about that in the years to come, of course.

A Final Season

Maybe the last Atlanta season in Georgia was snake-bit from the start. Al MacNeil had taken over as coach and the club had acquired Garry Unger—a player who had the longest consecutive games streak among NHL players from St. Louis in the off-season. Late in the year, following the "Miracle of Lake Placid," where the USA won a completely unexpected Olympic Gold Medal, American goalkeeper Jim Craig played a game in the Flames' goal. None of the talismans worked.

Although Atlanta finished 16 points clear of Washington in the Patrick Division and had another winning season, the playoff story remained unchanged. Only the post-season executioner was different, the New York Rangers this time performing the 3 games to 1 ritual.

Unger had seen his string of consecutive games interrupted on December 21, 1979, after 914 games, and Craig never translated his Olympic stardom into NHL greatness. The bright spot in the last campaign in Atlanta was Kent Nilsson, a refugee from the World Hockey Association whom the Flames had reclaimed from Winnipeg. Nilsson finished with 93 points to outdistance the rest of his mates.

Atlanta fans never saw him again, however. By the 1980-81 season, the Flames, still bearing their bright red jerseys and the same nickname, had become the seventh NHL franchise to locate in Canada.

It was a move that many cynics had long expected, "proving" that hockey wouldn't fly in the American Sun Belt, but it wasn't a change that brought instant new fortune to the team. They moved into small Calgary Stampede Corral and awaited better things. It took almost a decade for all of it to happen.

Not a Bad New Home

When Calgary exchanged the Omni (15,141 seats) for the Stampede Corral (7,242) what they lost in capacity they may have made up in home-ice advantage. In 146 games in the compact, cozy arena, the Flames lost only 28 regular season and four playoff games. Included in their sojourn was a January 2, 1983, victory over a Soviet National Team that was otherwise making light work of the National Hockey League's best.

It was not until October 15, 1983, that the Calgary Olympic Saddledome—a facility which ranks among the finest in the world—opened for business. Now Calgary plays before regular capacity crowds of 20,130, but that was just a dream when Nelson Skalbania purchased the Atlanta franchise on May 21, 1980, and announced that the team would be relocated in Alberta.

In terms of timing, Skalbania's move to Calgary couldn't have been better. The city had not been one of the four old World Hockey Association venues admitted to the NHL two years before, but there was no doubting its sporting interest. Long a Canadian Football League bastion, Calgary's fans had been credited with "creating" the mania which now annually surrounds the Grey Cup, Canada's football finale. They were overdue NHL attention, and the fact that another Alberta team was located just up the pike in Edmonton merely added to the logic of the switch.

Finally, a Playoff Win

The first year in Calgary could have been an extension of the years in Atlanta. The Flames finished third once again in the Patrick Division, but Nilsson exploded into all-star form. He set a Flames' record with 131 points, accumulated on 49 goals and a record haul of 82 assists, but didn't win any awards in the end of-season-voting. There were a couple of other centers ahead of him: Edmonton's Wayne Gretzky and the Islanders' Bryan Trottier.

Nilsson finished nearly 50 points ahead of the next Flame, Chouinard (31-52-83), while Plett was third on the scoring list despite accumulating 239 penalty minutes, fifth highest in the NHL (but still more than 100 behind Vancouver's Dave "Tiger" Williams).

This was also the season when there was a change in resident goaltenders for the Flames. Bouchard, having carried the load through most of the team's first decade, was traded to Quebec for Jamie Hislop in a January, 1981 move that established Pat Riggin and Rejean Lemelin in the nets. Lemelin, in particular, would play a key role over the next several years, although Riggin was the harder worker in 1980-81, appearing in 42 games to the 26-year-old Lemelin's 29. Lemelin, however, had the better GAA, 3.24 to Riggin's 3.83.

The playoffs proved to be a vastly different story from the frustration which had accompanied the team in Atlanta. Chicago was quickly swept aside in the best-of-five first round. Calgary won 4-3 and 6-2 at home, then completed their business with a 5-4 victory in Chicago Stadium. The quarterfinal was full of drama, with Calgary winning twice on Philadelphia ice as they eliminated the Flyers—who had been Stanley Cup finalists the year before—in a seven-game thriller.

But the story ended there. Minnesota came into the Stampede Corral and won the first game of the semifinal, then proved unbeatable at home. That single slip in game one meant the Flames could never get an edge in the series, and as they fell 4-2. Minnesota then was beaten in five games by the Islanders, the second of four straight New York Stanley Cups.

Trouble Up the Road

Who knows how much hockey history Calgary might have created for Alberta in that first decade if they had not had the misfortune of being the second-best team in the province? The Flames developed a succession of All-Stars during the tenure of coaches Al MacNeil, Bob Johnson, and Terry Crisp, and became one of the premier clubs in the National Hockey League, but they always were measured against their rival from Edmonton. The Oilers were on course to succeed the Islanders as the great NHL team of the 1980s and Gretzky was setting unbelievable records. Although Calgary held its own in the famous "Battles of Alberta," there was no doubting that the Oilers cast exceptionally long shadows.

The high point for Flames' fans came in the 1985-86 season when they eliminated the arch rival Oilers in the Smythe Division finals. That prevented Edmonton from winning a possible five straight Cups and remains one of the most dramatic series in recent playoff history. But the season ended, ultimately, in disappointment, when Calgary fell to Montreal in the Stanley Cup Finals in just five games. At other times, as in the 1981-82 season, there was the kind of post-season disappointment that die-hard Flames' fans had come to know too well. That team finished 12th overall

and was swept in the first round of playoffs by Vancouver. This despite the fact that Lanny MacDonald, a future All-Star and team mainstay, had been acquired from Colorado. Nilsson played only 41 games so had no chance to emulate his great previous season, and MacNeil was replaced as coach when it was all over.

Badger Bob Goes North

The appointment of Bob Johnson as head coach in 1982-83 was not without controversy. Johnson had made the University of Wisconsin Badgers one of the great American collegiate hockey powers, and was so well known for his loyalty and affection at the institution that he proudly carried the nickname, "Badger Bob."

But Johnson was a "college coach" and that was not the usual recommendation for work in the NHL. Indeed, there was more than a bit of tension between the traditionalists who populated the NHL and the growing number of collegians who were starting to be a force in the game. The acceptance of the U.S. college system as a source of players had long been fact, especially in the era after the WHA took shape, but the conventional wisdom suggested that "rah rah" college methods wouldn't work over the 80-game NHL schedule, nor with hardened pros.

Johnson changed all that. An enthusiastic ambassador for hockey, he would spend endless hours talking about his favorite game with anyone who would listen. "Badger Bob" stepped off the Wisconsin campus into the NHL and served five years behind the Calgary bench. Of course there was a transition period, and not all of the seasons were exceptional, but Johnson slowly sold the team on his approach and was the mastermind behind that big win over Edmonton in 1985-86.

The Flames' First All-Star

In Johnson's first season, 1982-83, Calgary finished 32-34-14 and eliminated Vancouver in the first round of the playoffs, before running into

PROFILE	Lanny McDonald

Lanny McDonald came to Calgary in 1981-82 after building a career in Toronto and Colorado. By the time the Flames won the 1989 Stanley Cup, McDonald had become the symbol of the club, a 16-year veteran of the NHL seeking to cap his playing days with the ultimate prize.

McDonald scored one of the goals in the Cup-clinching victory, an historic occasion when Calgary became the first visiting team to end a Stanley Cup Final series in the Montreal Forum. The last time a Montreal team lost the Cup in Montreal was in 1928, but then it was the Montreal Maroons, not the Canadiens, who were beaten on home ice. But McDonald kidded that he had been around even for that 1928 occasion. "I was only a rookie then . . . I didn't play in the game," he told reporters in the euphoria of the Calgary victory. It was a remark typical of a player known for his sense of humor, his remarkably luxurious mustache, and his tenacious skills that accounted for 500 career goals and 1006 NHL points before he retired.

One intrepid reporter, in fact, got the cutting edge of McDonald's humor when he tried to get the Calgary player to talk about life with that gigantic mustache. "How do you eat ice cream," he asked. "With a spoon," McDonald replied.

Hockey Hall of Fame and Museum

the Edmonton buzzsaw and bowing out in five games. It was notable for McDonald's team record 66 goals and second-team all-star selection. He was the first member of the Flames to attain recognition among the elite 12 players, chosen by a vote of hockey writers across the league at the end of the season.

In goal, Calgary had acquired Buffalo's Don Edwards in a draft weekend deal, so Johnson split the work evenly between the newcomer and Lemelin, a tactic that would last the better part of three full seasons. The 19-year old Mike Vernon, a Calgary native, played two games that year. It would be his turn in 1989, when he would lead the

Flames to a Stanley Cup.

While McDonald was the veteran around whom much would revolve in the next six years, the ensuing seasons saw the introduction of a number of important players who would eventually help Calgary to the very top of the league.

Hakan Loob and Al MacInnis both put in their first full-time seasons in 1983-84, as the Flames showed marginal improvement to 34-32-14. They took Edmonton all the way to a seven-game Stanley Cup series, before falling in the decisive game at Northlands Coliseum. Both Loob, 30-25-55 in his debut year, and MacInnis, 11-34-45, were recognized as rookie all stars.

A year later, big Joel Otto's name appeared on the Calgary team sheet for the first time, while the Flames obtained one of those players equally known for talent and intangible leadership, John Tonelli, in the 1985-86 campaign. That was also the year they added Joey Mullen from the St. Louis Blues, a move that would pay off at the highest level in the Stanley-Cup-winning season, when Mullen was a first-team all star.

A Flirtation With the Cup

Johnson twice guided Calgary to 95-point seasons, first in 1984-85, when the team finished sixth overall, and again in 1986-87, when they compiled an identical 46-31-3 record. Paradoxically, both of those Calgary teams were beaten in the first round of the Smythe Division playoffs by Winnipeg.

In between those campaigns, in 1985-86, the Flames finished 40-31-9 during the regular season. That year saw the memorable victory over Edmonton in the Smythe Division finals and a seven-game triumph over St. Louis that won the conference playoff before the championship season ended with a 4-1 series loss to Montreal in the Stanley Cup Finals.

The 1985-86 team had been retooled by the mid-season addition of Mullen, who played 29 regular-season games with the Flames after being picked up, and Tonelli, who arrived for just nine games at the end of the year but was available for crucial playoff duty. For Edmonton coach Glen Sather, they were the vital additions who helped turn things upside down in the playoffs.

"I've always worried about Calgary. And when they made the trades for Mullen and Tonelli it really finished off their team," Sather told Jim Matheson, a veteran Edmonton sports writer who summarized the NHL season in *The Sporting News Hockey Guide and Register.*

But the Oilers—winners of two straight Stanley Cups and possessing Gretzky at his prime, Paul Coffey, Jari Kurri, and a host of other stars— were still heavy favorites to repeat as champions.

They had finished a whopping 30 points ahead of Calgary in the regular season, compiling a 56-17-7 record that spread-eagled the NHL. Gretzky had a remarkable 52-163-215 season that made him the Art Ross Trophy winner by 74 points. The runner-up was a young Mario Lemieux of Pittsburgh, but he could barely see "The Great One" in the distance.

So how did Calgary do it? Edmonton fans will always remember that Steve Smith, a rookie defenseman, inadvertently shot the puck off his own goalie, Grant Fuhr, to "score" the decisive seventh-game goal for Calgary in a series dubbed "The Uncivil War" by the media who watched it unfold. Gretzky, however, told Matheson that it was not a case of a mistake costing Edmonton the playoff.

"Calgary won fair and square," Gretzky said. "We had an unfortunate goal in the last game, but we shouldn't have been in the position of having to play a seventh game anyway," Matheson writes. The Edmonton sports writer then went on to explain why the Flames were able to produce one of the game's big upsets.

"The Oilers lost three games at home to the Flames, allowed Calgary to score the first goal and dictate the style of play in six of the seven games and scored just six goals in the four losses," he states in *The Sporting News Guide and Register* for the 1986-87 season.

Johnson's tactics also had plenty to do with the outcome. Coffey told Matheson, "Every time I carried the puck and got to center five guys were on me. I felt like I was in Boston Garden." Kurri had no explanation for his dry-spell. "I have no excuses," he said, "When you score 68 goals in the regular season and only two in the entire playoffs you have to expect criticism. I was fighting the puck."

Rookies in the Final

The Calgary victory wasn't the only strange result in that 1985-86 post season. Philadelphia, Washington, and Quebec had been the next four

Joe Nieuwendyk

The Canadiens had a strong playoff, troubled only by the surprising Whalers who took them to a seventh game. A rookie goalie, Patrick Roy, averaged 1.92 goals-against in the playoffs, and first year coach Jean Perron seemed to push all the right buttons. Calgary contributed to a bit of Stanley Cup history when they also used a rookie (Vernon) in net during the finals, marking the first time since 1945 that rookies had lined up in hockey's most important series. But the Flames won only the first game.

The series was marred by a brawl that followed the fourth game. NHL President John Ziegler assessed a record $42,000 in fines after the bench-clearing mess, which was ignited by Montreal's Claude Lemieux and Calgary's Jim Peplinski. Perron agreed with Ziegler's statement that "There was absolutely no excuse for what happened," when he said, "This was crazy."

But Matheson also reports that Peplinski took a somewhat lighter view of the wild finish: "He (Lemieux) grabbed my hand and pushed it into his mouth," the big Calgary forward said. "I didn't know I'd have to worry about cannibalism."

League Champs, But No Cup

Edmonton regained its supremacy with consecutive Stanley Cup wins the next two seasons, although the 1987-88 Flames actually won the regular season title in the Smythe Division and finished first overall in the NHL to claim the President's Trophy. That was Terry Crisp's first year behind the Calgary bench. The highly-successful junior coach succeeded Johnson when "Badger Bob" took a position in United States Hockey administration.

Crisp's first team had a first-team all star in Loob, and a pair of second-team all stars on defense, Brad McCrimmon and Gary Suter. It had two plus 100-point scorers, Loob and Mike Bullard, and a full season from Calder Trophy winner Joe Nieuwendyk who came out of Cornell University and had immediate success in the NHL. Nieuwendyk scored 51 goals, one more than

finishers behind Edmonton in the overall points race, but none survived the divisional round. The Flyers, who had played in the previous Stanley Cup Final, were knocked out by the New York Rangers. Washington also fell to the Rangers, while also Quebec was stunned by the Hartford Whalers. By the time the semifinals took shape, the Montreal Canadiens were facing the Rangers, while Calgary was paired against still another outsider, St. Louis.

AP/Wide World Photos

Terry Crisp

Loob, and finished with 92 points, while Suter, the defenseman, accumulated 91 points, largely on the strength of 70 assists.

There was also Tim Hunter (337 penalty minutes) to add a bit of muscle tone to the Calgary game, and Vernon, who was still enjoying top-flight status in goal.

That's why the playoffs ultimately proved so disappointing. After a first round 4-1 series win over Los Angeles, the Flames were snuffed in four straight games by Edmonton. The Oilers may not have been first in the regular season, but they weren't yet ready to concede their Stanley Cup, especially not to Calgary.

Joey Mullen, a kid who had grown up playing hockey not on the wide open Canadian prairies but in New York City, picked 1988-89 to have his career year. He was one of nine NHL players to exceed the 100 point level that season, and his total of 110 broke Jimmy Carson's record for an American-born player. He won the Lady Byng Trophy and was voted first-team all-star right wing.

In the off-season the Flames pulled some daylight robbery in a trade with St. Louis, nabbing Doug Gilmour in a multi-player trade which cost them Bullard but little else. Gilmour would prove to be one of the key ingredients in a team that dominated the NHL. He finished with 85 points, tied with Loob as the second leading scorer on the team.

Calgary also had a full-season from the Czech Jiri Hrdina and picked this season to introduce little Theoren Fleury to the rest of the National Hockey League. Chosen 166th overall (Calgary's ninth choice) in the 1987 entry draft, the 5' 6", 160-lb. center-wing proved to have that talent which irritates even the best of players: a combination of speed, shooting touch, and a feistiness that saw him become a fan favorite even as he got under the skin of opponents.

Loob, Nieuwendyk, MacInnis, and Vernon were still very much there, while the Flames also provided additional depth in goal with a full season from Rick Wamsley. MacInnis, a second-team all star on defense, led all of the Flames in playoff scoring and won the Conn Smythe Trophy as the outstanding player in the Stanley Cup Finals. Vernon led the post-season goalies with 16 wins en route to a second-team all star berth. Nieuwendyk's second straight 50-goal season equalled the Islanders' great Mike Bossy, the only other player to achieve the feat in his first two years in the NHL.

It all added up to gaudy statistics: 54 wins, 17 losses, 9 ties, and 117 points in the regular campaign, the President's Trophy as the best team in the NHL, and top seed in the Stanley Cup play-offs.

This time there was no disappointment in post-season, though the Calgary survived a real first-round scare against Vancouver. They needed seven games to get by the Canucks, but were not taken to the limit again. Los Angeles fell 4-0, Chicago lasted just five games, and the Flames got revenge against Montreal in the Finals, winning the Stanley Cup in six games. They clinched the

Cup in the Montreal Forum, thus marking the first time in NHL history that a visiting team had won the trophy in the Forum.

That first round series against the Canucks, however, came very close to ending everything for Calgary. Vernon was heroic in goal, particularly in the seventh game when he stoned Canucks' shooters on several great chances. That performance allowed Joel Otto to win it for the Flames in overtime and let Crisp tell the world, "Vernon gave us a stay of execution," according to Jim Matheson in *The Sporting News Guide and Register, 1989-90.*

Fleury emerged from the finals as something of a folk-hero, his darting style of play attracting the attention of fans across the land. His second-period goal won the first game 3-2, and his post-game comment, "This one was for my mum. Mother's Day," endeared him to the listeners.

Matheson described the combination of Fleury's speed and MacInnis's immense talent this way when he wrapped up the series for *The Sporting News Guide and Register, 1989-90*: "While Fleury was buzzing, MacInnis was stinging."

Matheson also noted the series' coaches on the particular attributes of the series' two stars. The Flames' Crisp was quoted as saying, "He [Fleury] is like an Indian rubber ball. You throw him against a wall and he keeps bouncing back. He's a little guy who plays like a big man. He's a pest." Of MacInnis, who scored twice in the opening game win, Montreal's Pat Burns admitted, "On his first goal (a 40-footer), they could have put a piece of plexiglas in front of the goal and it wouldn't have made a difference. Patrick [Roy] wasn't going to stop it."

MacInnis tormented Roy and the Canadiens throughout the finals, running his consecutive game scoring streak to 17 games. Teammate Rick Wamsley, who had the task of facing him in practices, sympathized with the opposing netminders who had to deal with his big shot in the *Sporting News Guide.* "He's got the type of shot where you have no idea where it's going to go," he said. "There's no anticipation so you start spreading out and hope it hits you."

AP/Wide World Photos

Al MacInnis

In the end, when the Cup was safely on the shelf in Calgary, Crisp commented that the trophy might well have been won the year before, when the Oilers shot the Flames out of the playoffs in four games. He allowed that it had been "a very long summer."

No Immediate Encore

As good as that Calgary team was, there was no Stanley Cup encore. MacInnis was now established as a first-team NHL all star defensemen and the Flames added—not without some debate—another Calder Trophy winner in 1989-90 and repeated as Smythe Division champions. They were then unceremoniously bumped out of the playoffs by an old rival, Greztky, who now lined up in the black-and-silver of the Los Angeles Kings.

The Rookie of the Year that season was no kid, but a 31-year old Soviet named Sergei Makarov. He had played most of his career with the team many regarded as the best club squad in the world, CSKA Moscow, the Soviet Army team. With the Soviet Union slowly coming apart at the seams, the exodus of hockey talent to the NHL began, and Makarov, chosen way back in 1983 when Calgary gambled on his availability, finally reached the NHL. Although some writers grumbled about the fact that he was not a true rookie, they voted according to the rules and named him the league's best first year player for his 86-point season.

The Flames—under new coach Doug Riesebrough—and the Kings battled for the regular season Smythe title in 1990-91, with Los Angeles finishing in front by the narrow margin of 102-100 points. Calgary then collapsed to fifth place in 1991-92. Risebrough moved into the general manager's chair, and veteran Canadian Olympic coach Dave King was installed as head coach for the 1992-93 season, as the Flames hoped to build again toward the heights of the previous decade.

Although the Flames finished second in their division with 97 points, it was 3rd-place Los Angeles who emerged to represent the Smythe Division in the Campbell Conference finals of the playoffs.

SOURCES

BOOKS

Eskenazi, Gerald, *A Thinking Man's Guide to Pro Hockey,* E.P. Dutton, 1972.
Fishler, Stan and Shirley Fishler, *The Hockey Encyclopedia,* MacMillan, 1983.
Matheson, Jim, *The Sporting News Hockey Guide & Register,* 1986-87 and 1989-90 editions.

OTHER

Various *NHL Official Guide & Record Book*, Sporting News *Guide and Register* for basic statistical data.
Various Calgary Flames media guides & yearbook information.

—Jerry Trecker for Book Builders, Inc.

EDMONTON OILERS

There are sites and arenas that define the sports they house. Center Court at Wimbledon, Yankee Stadium, the Rose Bowl, Churchill Downs: all bring the best in tennis, baseball, football or horse racing immediately to mind. In the 1980s, there was no better place for an ice hockey devotee than Northlands Coliseum. Perched high over the ice in the circular press facility which gives an unparalleled view of the action, all the patterns, the speed, the thinking which combined to make the Edmonton Oilers the team of the decade become apparent.

Wayne Gretzky in all his splendor—accompanied by the likes of Glenn Anderson, Paul Coffey, Grant Fuhr, Jarri Kurri, Kevin Lowe, and Mark Messier—redefined the game for a new age.

The Montreal Forum and Toronto's Maple Leaf Gardens still conjure up the image of high-class hockey for most Canadian and U.S. fans, but Northlands was the place where hockey's revolution took place. The Oilers not only played the game at a higher pace with the accent on full-throttle attack, they combined their speed and passing wizardry with a defensive philosophy which their opponents in Stanley Cup playoffs found suffocating. Coach Glen Sather had the perfect blend of imagination and tenacity, and his Oilers will remain indelibly etched on the memories of those who saw them at their best.

Incredibly, Northlands was also the home of one of the sport's most dramatic moves, when, in the summer of 1988, the Oilers sent Wayne Gretzky, the game's greatest player, to the Los Angeles Kings in a megadeal that rocked the sports world. Two years later the Oilers proved they could still be the best in the game, winning a Stanley Cup without "The Great One."

That made it five Cups in ten years, a host of individual and team records, and a firm place in NHL hockey history for a team that had begun life in the lightly regarded rival World Hockey Association.

It Started in the WHA

The Alberta Oilers began life as one of the founding franchises in the WHA in 1972, and immediately struggled not only for recognition but for their very existence. Playing in the old Edmonton Gardens, the first team missed the playoffs altogether, and the second, now called the Edmonton Oilers, was eliminated in the first round of the post-season while attracting an average of just 4,429 fans.

The opening of Northlands on November 10, 1974, with a crowd of 15,326 in attendance, marked the first steps toward major league status for a team which still faced growing pains. Bill Hunter and Dr. Charles Allard, who had been the club's guiding forces since opening day, stepped aside at the end of the 1975-76 season, as Vancouver businessman Nelson Skalbania acquired a share of the club along with entrepreneur Peter Pocklington. That was to be a turning point in Oilers' history.

Pocklington acquired Skalbania's interest in the team on March 2, 1977, becoming the only Edmonton shareholder. Fully in charge, the man who would earn the affectionate nickname "Peter Puck" began to reshape the Oilers.

The first major move came with the appointment of a player, Glen Sather, as head coach. "Slats" had been a hard-working left winger with six NHL teams before moving to the WHA and the Oilers in 1976-77. What he lacked in pure talent, he made up for with his ability to read the game and his work rate. He also learned from every team and coach he played for; when he took over at Edmonton he was only 34 but hockey-wise well beyond his years.

Sather was given the additional job of Director of Hockey Operations at the start of the 1977-78 season, a fortuitous appointment. It granted Sather a free rein to create his kind of club and placed a young, innovative coach in position to assemble some of the finest young talent in the game.

Pocklington made three other moves in 1978-79 that ultimately cemented the Oilers place in

Peter Pocklington

history. First, he tapped Barry Fraser as chief scout, one of those positions that hockey insiders regard as the engine room of any franchise. Over the next several years, Fraser would prove uncanny at spotting young talent to fit the team Sather was building.

Second, as the Indianapolis Racers were disbanding in the closing days of the struggling WHA, Pocklington plucked three players from the club then owned by his old partner, Skalbania. As the Oilers' official club history states, "two ... Peter Driscoll and Eddie Mio will become trivia answers in the future, but the third was a spidery thin 17-year old by the name of Wayne Gretzky."

Finally, Pocklington executed his master stroke, signing Gretzky to a 21-year personal services contract that would make the 18-year old one of the game's wealthiest players and ensure he

TEAM INFORMATION AT A GLANCE

Founding date: 1971 (WHA);
June 22, 1979 (NHL)

Home ice: Northlands Coliseum
Edmonton, Alberta, Canada T5B 4M9
Phone: (403) 474-8561
FAX: (403) 471-2171

Seating capacity: 17,053

Team colors: White, blue, and orange
Team nickname: Edmonton Oilers
Logo: A drop of oil

Franchise record	Won	Lost	Tie
(1980-1993)	364	199	81

Stanley Cup Wins (5): 1983-84, 1984-85, 1986-87, 1987-88, 1989-90

---

would remain with the Oilers if merger with the NHL ever came.

The Summer of 1979

The announcement that Edmonton—and the other survivors of the WHA's long struggle with the older circuit—had long waited for was made in May, 1979. The Oilers, along with the Hartford Whalers, Quebec Nordiques, and Winnipeg Jets, joined the National Hockey League and the World Hockey Association disappeared.

It did not take long for the Sather-Fraser team to make an impact in the new league. On August 9, 1979, the Oilers, although selecting 21st overall in the NHL draft, plucked Kevin Lowe, Mark Messier (48th), and Glenn Anderson (69th) in their first dip into the youth talent pool. In retrospect it seems inconceivable that players of such talent as Messier and Anderson could be available in the third and fourth rounds of a draft, but that was testimony to Fraser's talent for seeing something in players that other scouts and organizations overlooked. He soon would become legendary among the game's insiders for that special sense.

One reason why Fraser's picks slipped past other observers was that he and Sather were looking for something that the rest of the NHL still didn't have as its number one priority: speed. A year later the Oilers would grab Paul Coffey and Jari Kurri, then add goaltender Andy Moog in the same draft. How many teams have gotten six potential all stars in two drafts?

A year later the drafting magic touch produced goaltender Grant Fuhr, taken eighth overall and first by the Oilers at a time when conventional wisdom often said that first-round picks weren't to be spent on netminders. That same draft netted Steve Smith, on the team's fifth choice and

111th overall. Who said that gems are never found low in the amateur draft? Edmonton was proving that all it took was an exhaustive evaluation of the available players and a clear sense of what to draft for.

The groundwork for one of hockey's great teams had been laid by these drafts; Gretzky was now surrounded by some of the quickest talent in the game. Sather let them play, often in the face of the critics who decried the wide-open, "outscore 'em" type of hockey that the Oilers seemed to advocate. What the critics missed was the fact that the defense was simply young and aggressive, not faulty. As men like Coffey and Lowe developed into back-line stars and support came in the form of players like Randy Gregg and Charlie Huddy, the Oilers turned into a high-scoring attacking team with a defense that could match the best in the sport. And Fuhr, it turned out, was an absolute magician in goal, his glove hand remarkable, his reflexes uncanny, and his competitive temperament seemingly near perfect.

It would not be long before the rest of the hockey world was making an annual pilgrimage to Edmonton to see the Stanley Cup presentation.

Gretzky, Immediately Gretzky

No player had come into the National Hockey League facing greater expectations than Gretzky, who had acquired the nickname, "The Great One," while still a youth. He came into the league with a potentially suffocating burden of expectations, but all of the publicity and anticipation served only to inspire this special player.

Jay Greenberg, the respected hockey writer who covered the great Philadelphia Flyers' teams, reminds us what Gretzky had already "achieved" before he ever skated in an NHL game. Writing in *NHL: The World of Professional Hockey,* Greenberg said, "A limited number of times a century a brain outraces a hormone and the world marvels. In the rarest of cases the child prodigy is given the equal gift of an early maturity to handle his genius. And Wayne Gretzky handles it. He handles it so well that he's almost too good to be true.

"He was skating before he was 3, joined a team of 11-year olds when he was 6, was interviewed for the first time when he was 8; he shared a head table with Gordie Howe at 10, scored 378 goals in 85 games when he was 11, was called the next Bobby Orr at 12, and left home to play junior hockey when he was 13. He had an agent at 14, graduated to Junior A and was profiled in *Sports Illustrated* at 16, signed his first professional contract when he was 17 and became a millionaire on his eighteenth birthday."

This all occurred before Gretzky ever played a game in the NHL. There were cynics who wondered if the rough, tough world of the best professional hockey wouldn't bring him down a peg or two. Sather, however, was supremely confident.

"You get one like him every ten years. There is a Howe and a [Bobby] Hull and an [Bobby] Orr and there is Gretzky. He adjusts to all situations well because he is very mature. Don't let the age fool you," the Oilers coach said.

Greenberg related that Gretzky, himself, set a first-year goal of finishing third in NHL scoring, an achievement that would equal his previous WHA season. He did better than that, finishing even with the Kings' Marcel Dionne with 137 points, but having to settle for second place in the Art Ross Trophy race because Dionne had two more (53) goals. Gretzky didn't finish second again for seven years, finally surpassed by the first player to be compared to "The Great One," Mario Lemieux.

What Made Him Great?

Any discussion of Edmonton and the fabulous decade of the 1980s must begin with the qualities which separated Gretzky from the rest of his contemporaries. He was by no means the fastest skater, surely not the strongest; he didn't have the hardest shot and certainly would not win many physical battles, but Wayne Gretzky was yards ahead of everyone else in technique and intellect.

Like the greatest performers in the arts, he always made the difficult look easy, and he always seemed to have more time than anyone else on the ice. He created space for himself, because he was always thinking ahead of the opposition. He scored countless goals for the simplest of reasons; he always went to where the puck would be, while others chased after where it had just been.

Gretzky perfected two aspects of the game that others in the NHL too often neglected. He operated like a magician from behind the net, holding the puck almost casually before flicking a precision pass onto the stick of a cutting teammate. He was so good at seeing the whole ice surface, so adept at avoiding checks and maintaining possession, that he became the most deadly man in the sport from a position almost no one but the great Russian stars of the 1970s thought was important enough to maintain.

His long, cranelike, swooping reach made him one of the most effective penalty killers in the history of the game. Indeed, getting a man-advantage against the Oilers was often a disadvantage, so good was Gretzky at poking the puck away from a slower opponent, then sending the short-handed attack off in the opposite direction.

But Gretzky was not just the best at several aspects of his game, he was actually better than the sum of the parts. He made all around him better because he attracted opponents' attention to himself, then was completely unselfish as a passer. He also was so polite and self-effacing, yet also so supremely self-confident, that his career was never marred by superstar tantrums or jealousies.

Jay Teitel, writing a Gretzky profile for *The Official NHL 75th Anniversary Commemorative Book*, captures the man this way: "It wasn't just numbers; it was the images, too. Slowly, and with a relentlessness to match our reluctance, the pictures of our adult hockey years were becoming Gretzky pictures. Gretzky gliding folded-over to the open faceoff circle, his stick on his thighs, his pale eyes up and to one side, his gaze positively eerie and foreheadless under his helmet, his sweater, as always, hitched up (by now he was actually using Velcro to make sure it stayed that

Wayne Gretzky

way). Gretzky veering inside the blue line with that precipitous slant, coming across the slot with the puck, waiting, waiting, till not just the opposing goalie but the entire opposing team, you got the feeling, had committed itself (half of them falling down in a mysterious surrender), then pushing a totally ordinary ice-bound shot into the center of the net. Gretzky setting up behind the net in his 'office,' head paradoxically down as he looked for the cutting defenseman, distinguishing between teammates and opponents by the color of their hockey pants, so he wouldn't have to waste time looking all the way up (he once complained to a fellow Oiler that he had trouble playing against the Islanders because their pants were the same blue as the Oilers'). Gretzky churning up the wing outside a defenseman, then putting on the brakes in that patented move to let the play catch up; Gretzky faking the huge wind-up on the slapshot,

---

cocking once, cocking twice; Gretzky kneeing the air and punching it like a ramshackle adolescent after a goal; Gretzky hounding an opposing defenseman while killing a penalty, chipping and hacking and taking a ride because he could do that with the best of them too. Gretzky being Gretzky."

The Numbers Also Speak

As Teitel says, Gretzky, the player, was even more impressive than the numbers he put up in Edmonton. But those statistics not only tell the story of one great player's career, they also chronicle the rise of his team to NHL superpower status.

From the first NHL season through the great trade of August 9, 1988, Gretzky surpassed himself so many times that it became almost impossible to keep up with the accomplishments. He led the league in scoring eight straight years; scored 92 goals in the 1981-82 campaign; collected the fastest 50 goals in the history of the sport in the subsequent campaign, achieving the feat in the first three months of the season; registered 163 assists in 1985-86, a year when he totalled 215 points; scored 50 or more goals eight times, 70 or more four times, and 87 once in addition to that 92-goal year; twice scored more than 40 points in the Stanley Cup playoffs, five times collected 30 or more. And that doesn't take into account the awards he won and the individual game feats which fill page after page in team media guides.

Blessed with perhaps the greatest player in hockey history, Edmonton rode the wave with him. More than that, Sather and assistant John Muckler created a team which played off the star. They complemented him with skaters who could react to the unexpected, and with others who provided the necessary muscle to protect their greatest asset. And Sather had the courage to let the game Gretzky orchestrated become the game of the Edmonton Oilers, this at a time when many still did not believe that you could win a Stanley Cup without a commitment to grinding, wear-them-down hockey. As it turned out, the Oilers could

Paul Coffey

play that game, too, if necessary, but they preferred to operate at full throttle, like kids on a pond with the wind at their back.

Getting Started in the NHL

Edmonton's first NHL season produced a 28-39-13 overall record and a fourth-place Smythe Division finish, better than many cynics had expected because the four ex-WHA teams had been given little chance to make an impact in the "tougher" climate of the NHL. The Oilers posted one more win than Hartford, another WHA survivor, to make the playoffs. Both Winnipeg and Quebec finished last in their respective debut seasons.

Gretzky, Messier, and Lowe were part of that debut as was a big left winger named Dave Semenko. A 6'3", 200 pound wing, Semenko—a carryover from the WHA Edmonton Oilers—was a player known more for his physical style of play than any goal-scoring records. But Semenko was considerably more than a fighter; he could skate well enough to keep up with his speedy teammates, and he picked his spots when it came to asserting himself.

In addition he was one of the most popular figures in the community, his soft-spoken style and huge off-ice smile a marked contrast to the dark-haired enforcer he portrayed on the ice. Ultimately, he would be known as Gretzky's protector, a player who made certain that no one took liberties with "The Great One."

Having made the playoffs in their first year, Edmonton didn't last long, but they left a calling card. The Philadelphia Flyers took them out in three straight games, but needed overtime goals from Bobby Clarke in game one and Ken Linseman in game three to subdue a pesky opponent.

Year two produced a similar record, the 29-35-16, 74-point finish just five points better than the previous season. Kurri came on board that year to collect 75 points, Gretzky gave a hint of what was to come when he tallied 164 points, and Glenn Anderson made his first season a 53-point learning experience. Gretzky finished the year with a five-point game against Winnipeg and became the youngest player in NHL history to win the Art Ross Trophy. He was 20 years, 2 months old that April. Finally, defenseman Risto Siltanen, another of the slick-skating speedsters whom the Oilers were busy collecting, finished with 53 points to establish an Edmonton record for a back liner.

The Oilers woke everybody up in the NHL when the Stanley Cup playoffs started. They chose the opening series against the fabled Montreal Canadiens to make their first great statement, winning twice in the Forum, then completing the sweep at home. Andy Moog, the rookie who had played only three games in the regular season, won all three games in the Oilers' nets. Gretzky had proved a key to the first round victory, but even his magic presence wasn't enough against the defending champion New York Islanders in the next test. The Isles won, 4-2, on the way to their second of four straight Cups.

Building Toward the Cup

Edmonton's first winning season came in 1981-82, a remarkable 48-17-15 year that gave hockey its first real look at what Sather and Fraser were putting together out in Alberta. This was the first season for Coffey, who burst into the NHL with an 89-point "announcement" that he was present. Messier continued to mature, lifting his point tally to 88, while Kurri finished the season with 86. But the fact was plain: Edmonton had found a defenseman who could complement Gretzky and finish second in team scoring. That was scary to the opposition.

Gretzky scored his 92 goals that season and added 120 assists to put together an unbelievable 212-point tally that had old hands shaking their heads; these were numbers that no one could have imagined a decade before. Along the way he broke Guy Lafleur's record for consecutive game scoring, then shattered another fabled record, Maurice Richard's 50 goals in 50 games. Richard had done it in 1944, just getting to the imagined barrier; Gretzky ripped five goals past Philadelphia on December 30, 1981, to reach the 50-goal plateau in just 39 games. He did it so quickly that the anticipated media countdown never even had time to get organized.

There was also a 12-game goal-scoring streak by Dave Lumley, one short of the 13 established by Los Angeles' Charlie Simmer, and Grant Fuhr played 23 consecutive games without a loss between October and January. The Edmonton goal-scoring machine seemed unstoppable. On March 28, 1982, Messier and Lumley had the Oilers ahead of the Kings, 2-0, in just 24 seconds, a record for the fastest goal-scoring start to any NHL game. Edmonton finished that year with 417 goals (a record they would ultimately surpass in 1983-84), eight players who registered 20 or more goals, and every reason to think the club would make an impact in the playoffs.

AP/Wide World Photos

Mark Messier

The precocious Oilers still had a lesson to learn, however: fourth-place Los Angeles, who finished 48 points behind the Smythe Division champs, stunned them in the best-of-five first-round series. The Kings won three games to two, including a game in which they trailed 5-0 and rallied to win, 6-5, in overtime.

The First Cup Final

Edmonton made no such mistakes in the next Stanley Cup playoffs, marching all the way to the finals against the Islanders, before their inexperience at the very highest level finally caught up with them.

The 1982-83 season was another remarkable offensive show. The 47-21-12 record was powered by four players with more than 100 points, Gretzky (196), Messier (104), Kurri (104), and Anderson (104). Coffey added 96. It was a scoring rate that earned comparison with the 1970-71 Boston Bruins, previously the bellwether of NHL teams. That Boston club had Phil Esposito, Bobby Orr, John Bucyk, and Ken Hodge all score over 100 points and was considered by many the incomparable attacking team. But times were changing with the advent of this Edmonton bunch, and they were setting new standards.

There were a couple of additional moves that played a role in the continuing growth of a hockey juggernaut: John Muckler had moved alongside Sather on the bench as co-coach, offering a quiet approach to contrast with his fiery boss; and the Oilers acquired Ken Linseman, a forward with a feisty reputation but a studious, thorough approach to the game, who would add both fiber and toughness to the wide-open Edmonton style.

Another addition may have passed with less notice, but it is hard to underestimate the value of Randy Gregg to the Edmonton Stanley Cup pursuit. A big, red-headed back liner, Gregg was a university man who combined hockey with medical studies. He played with an upright precision, teaming on a defense that now included reliable Charlie Huddy, veteran Lee Fogolin, the ever improving Lowe, and the spectacular Coffey.

It was no surprise when the Oilers again dominated the Smythe Division nor were their individual accomplishments unexpected. It was only the scope of the achievement which had onlookers still taking the occasional second look. Gretzky started the year at full throttle, scored in his first 30 games, and had 76 points by December 7, just two months into the season. After 50 games he had 61 goals, a mark he would equal two years later. Four players, Gretzky, Anderson, Messier, and Kurri topped the 40-goal mark to set an NHL single-season record. Lowe's seven-point game against Pittsburgh in February, 1983, set a record for Oiler defensemen. And Edmonton's 22 road victories was a franchise mark.

In retrospect it was not truly surprising that Edmonton did not win the 1982-83 Stanley Cup. They had all the pieces in place but had not been thoroughly tested in the post-season grinder. The team had never before played even three series after the regular season, and they came into the spring of 1983 with such momentum that it may actually have worked against them.

The first three rounds in the Campbell Conference playoffs simply didn't extend the Oilers. They swept Winnipeg, 3-0, outscored Calgary by 35-13 in a five-game victory, then battered Chicago in four straight to advance to the finals. They won games by 8-4, 8-2, and 6-3, in addition to one close one, 3-2, against the Black Hawks.

The media who descended on Edmonton that May were divided as they assessed the final round; some thought that this Oiler team was so strong that nothing could deter it. Others looked at the veteran Islanders, still possessing Billy Smith in goal, Denis Potvin on defense, and a collection of forwards that included some of the best forecheckers in the game, and voted for New York.

The opening game in Northlands Coliseum turned out to be pivotal. Just before game time it was learned that Mike Bossy, the top Islander scorer, would not play because of an injury. Any edge that might have given Edmonton evaporated when Smith played incomparably in goal; the Islanders won, 2-0, to reassert their command of hockey. Edmonton had played 198 consecutive games without being shutout (Smith had done it then, too) and this loss put them behind for the first time. Veterans that they were, the Islanders went for the jugular and swept the next three.

When it was over, Sather told the assembled media, "I feel tremendous pride in this team. I hope we'll be around for a long while, but I hope we don't see the Islanders again. I'm sure what we've learned from this series can't be measured right now. It takes steps to win, to learn how to be champions."

And Gretzky admitted, "My job is to put the puck in the net and I didn't do that, but one thing about this organization is that we don't hang our heads. We'll learn and correct our mistakes and

be a better hockey team because of this. The Islanders are a great team."

Birth of a Dynasty

Sather didn't exactly get his wish—Edmonton saw the Islanders again in the next final—but he and Gretzky were absolutely right. The lessons were absorbed and the Oilers did return a better team in 1983-84. Indeed, they e-merged as the best team for the rest of the decade, a team so wonderfully conceived and balanced that they became a joy to behold, perhaps even for the rivals they swept aside with an inevitability that might otherwise have grown monotonous.

At the start of the season there may have been more than one cynic who recalled the apparently rash prediction of Oilers owner Peter Pocklington, who had issued a challenge to the NHL traditionalists when Edmonton entered the league. Although he subsequently has admitted he didn't know how hard it would be to accomplish, Pocklington had vowed that the Oilers would win a Stanley Cup within five years of their acceptance into the league.

They did, after defeating those Islanders in five games, earning the respect of the outgoing champions even as they inherited their mantle. "I don't feel badly about turning the Cup over to them," Islanders captain Denis Potvin said at the end of New York's reign. "They're truly a worthy champion. This is one great, great team passing the Cup along to a team that is great."

The Oilers' 1983-84 team was astonishingly good. They finished 57-18-5, scored an NHL record 446 goals, and had a .744 winning percentage. Their individual feats were every bit as remarkable: Gretzky scored 87 goals, added 118 assists, and won the Art Ross Trophy with 205 points; Coffey stepped into the history books with a 40-86-126 season that stamped him as one of the finest attacking back liners ever to play; Kurri scored 52 goals and wound up with 113 points; and Messier went 37-64-101 as the Oilers again had four 100-point producers; Anderson just missed making it five, finishing 54-45-99.

There had, truly, never been a hockey attack like this one from Northlands. And, while it might still have been fashionable to say that Edmonton just outscored people, the two goaltenders could not be overlooked. Moog played 38 games and compiled 3.86 goals-against-average while Fuhr had a 3.91 mark in 45 appearances. What those statistics don't show is that both netminders were big-game goalies, excellent under pressure.

There were plenty of additional memories from 1983-84. Gretzky established a club record with an 8-point game as the Oilers battered New Jersey, 13-4, in a November game that produced a rare outburst from the Oilers' star. Perhaps because the assault came against an old friend, Ron Low, "The Great One" lashed out at the Devils, who had begun the season with a 2-18 record: "It's not funny, it's disappointing. These guys better get their act together ... [they're] ruining hockey. They putting a Mickey Mouse Operation on the ice."

Pat Calabria, writing the season review in *The Sporting News Hockey Guide and Register 1984-85,* continues the story, noting that Gretzky's words stung the Jersey organization and fans to such an extent that he sent a telegram of apology to Devils' chairman John McMullen. When the Oilers later played in Byrne Arena, fans turned out in Mickey Mouse ears to razz the Oilers' star.

If that intemperate slip proved Gretzky human, most of the rest of the team's season added to the evidence that he was more likely the spark of a superhuman team. In December, the Oilers established a club record for the longest undefeated spell on home ice, 12 games.

In January, Fuhr set a record for shutout goaltending, going 95 minutes, 57 seconds without yielding a goal. He blanked Calgary in the final 26:46 on December 26, 1983, Boston on December 30, and Minnesota for 9:11 on January 4, 1984. Gretzky went 17 consecutive games with at least one assist, another NHL record. Gretzky set possibly his most unapproachable record, going 51 consecutive games with at least one point, a feat comparable to Joe DiMaggio's great 56-game hitting streak in baseball.

Glen Sather

During the span, which ran from October 5, 1983, through January 27, 1984, Gretzky scored 61 goals and collected 92 assists. Ironically, the streak ended against the Los Angeles Kings, for whom Gretzky would eventually play. In February, Pat Hughes, not one of the Oilers most often listed among the team's top players, scored five goals against the Calgary Flames, while Gretzky picked up his 10th hat trick of the season, to tie his own NHL record, in a game against Pittsburgh.

At the end, the Oilers had established team records for goals, goals per game (5.58), and shorthanded goals (36); Fuhr set an NHL record for goaltenders with 14 assists and finished ahead of 62 NHL regulars in the race for the Art Ross Trophy; and Anderson's 54 goals beat his own record for Edmonton right wingers by six.

Then came the playoffs and Edmonton's coronation as the best in hockey. There was a tough Smythe Division final, a seven-game war with Calgary, to spice the story, but most of the post-season was exactly like the regular year. Winnipeg, Minnesota, and the Islanders tried, but couldn't offer a real challenge. The Jets and North Stars didn't win a game against the Oilers, while the Islanders won just one in the final series.

Pat Calabria explains that the Oilers understood the magnitude of their task in 1984, especially in the aftermath of their Campbell Conference victory over the North Stars. He quotes both Gretzky and Coffey to show the motivation that carried Edmonton into the finals.

"All of a sudden, after the game, the clincher against the North Stars, the whole room went hush. Our attitude was 'we haven't won anything yet.' We sat down in the room and about all we could tell ourselves was, 'OK, we've done well up to now ... but all we've done is get to the place we're supposed to be.' We had to think all summer and throughout the season of getting to the Stanley Cup finals. We waited a long time to get back to the finals with the series tied, 0-0," Gretzky said.

And Coffey, the marvelous defenseman, was even more direct: "You don't play to win the Campbell Conference championship. It's the Cup that counts. Forty years from now nobody will worry about who won the Campbell Conference."

The final series may well have turned in the first game, played at Nassau Coliseum. The Islanders, no longer the indomitable force they had been, were still champions and chasing a piece of Cup history themselves, a fifth-straight title. They still had Smith in goal and an excellent team.

Fuhr picked that May 10, 1984 game to quiet any and all critics about Edmonton's defensive shortcomings. He turned aside 34 Islander shots with an array of outstanding saves. Kevin McClelland, acquired from Pittsburgh in mid-season, got the only goal, and Edmonton took a 1-0 win. They lost the next game on the Island, 6-1, but with the series shifting to Northlands for the next three games the sense of change was obvious.

In fact, Edmonton thoroughly dominated the remaining games winning 7-2, 7-2, and 5-2, to leave no doubt that the torch had been passed. Mark Messier won the Conn Smythe Trophy, and it was party time in Canada's great Northwest.

More to Come

There will always be some who suggest that Edmonton should have won five consecutive Cups in this era, but four in five years will have to do. Upset by the Calgary Flames in a wonderfully dramatic 1986 series, they missed their chance at that little bit of history, but almost everything else went exactly right following the first Cup triumph.

Philadelphia was beaten in a five-game final series in 1985, then extended the Oilers to seven games in 1987, while Boston was swept in 1988. There seemed to be nothing even the strongest teams could do against the machine that just purred on.

Even injury to Messier, limiting him to just 55 games in 1984-85, hardly made a dent. Mike Krushelnyski became the latest addition to the Oiler attack. Joining the usual Gretzky (208 pts.), Kurri (135), Coffey (121) trio, big Mike weighed in with 88 points to help make up for Messier's absence. Moog (3.30) and Fuhr (3.87) were again solid in goal.

The season included an NHL-record unbeaten run of 15 games at the start of the campaign, eight Oilers on the mid-season All Star team, and an NHL-record season by Kurri, who became only the third player—and the first right wing—ever to get 70 goals in a season. He finished with 71.

In the playoffs, Gretzky set still another NHL record with 47 points—on 17 goals and a record 30 assists—and picked up the Conn Smythe Trophy. Meanwhile Coffey set a new standard for playoff defensemen (12-25-37), and Kurri's 19 goals tied the playoff mark set by the Flyers' Reg Leach back in 1975-76.

Coffey won the Norris Trophy as the NHL's top defenseman, and Kurri picked up the Lady Byng, while Gretzky won the Hart Trophy for the sixth consecutive season.

A Rare Setback

The machine was oiled and ready in 1985-86, but Calgary got in the way in the Smythe Division finals, the only dent in the Edmonton armor during the glory era. Gretzky, by now, was finding that matching his own feats was no easy task, but he managed it, nonetheless. Collecting at least one point in 77 of the 80 games he played, Gretzky set a record with 163 assists, eclipsing in assists alone the 152 points (goals plus assists) that represented the highest scoring total by any other NHL player that year. And don't think he was the recipient of cheap assists, either.

Edmonton sportswriter Jim Matheson, writing in *The Sporting News Hockey Guide and Register, 1986-87* quoted Chicago co-coach Roger Neilson on the subject: "Wayne should get a point and a half for some of the assists he gets, the way he sets up his teammates."

Coffey was impressive that year, too, getting at least one point in 28 consecutive games from his defenseman's position and breaking Orr's record for back liners with 48 goals. "It's an honor to be mentioned in the same sentence with Orr," said Coffey. Watt commented, "The record wasn't tainted in any sense. He went end-to-end, split the defense, went one-on-one with the goalie [Wendell Young] and put it away. It was a classic, typical Bobby Orr goal." Coffey finished the year one point shy of Orr's record 139-point haul for a defenseman.

The post-season soured some of the memories, though, and may have inspired the Oilers to the next two Cups. They lost in seven games to Calgary in a series where they never struck top form, allowing the Flames to dictate the pattern of action far too often.

The irony was made worse by the fact that the decisive goal in the seventh game was actually shot into the Edmonton net by Oiler defenseman Steve Smith, whose clearing pass struck Fuhr and rebounded into the wrong cage. To Smith's credit, the young defenseman accepted the misery of the moment and went on to build an outstanding career.

Two More Stanley Cups

That loss might have been a setback for some teams, but look at what an Oilers' official club history, produced for the 1986-87 media guide, had to say: "With the lesson of defeat clearly etched in their minds, the Edmonton Oilers entered the 1986-87 season with a new-found commitment. There was very good reason for optimism.

Consider that they have Glen Sather at the helm. He is not only considered to be the top General Manager in the league, but also possesses the best winning percentage in the league as a coach. He has surrounded himself with two of the most able coaches in hockey in John Muckler and Ted Green and the team has talent far beyond the expectations of every other NHL team.

"Wayne Gretzky is in a league by himself.... Paul Coffey has been named the NHL's outstanding defenseman two years running. Jari Kurri is the top goal scoring European ever to play in the league. Mark Messier and Glenn Anderson continue to amaze everyone with their high speed talent. Grant Fuhr and Andy Moog are considered the best goaltending tandem in the world. And the supporting cast is second to none. Although there are never any guarantees of success in professional sport, the Edmonton Oilers have all the ingredients to make it."

In some other NHL team literature you'd take such hyperbole with a grain of salt. In the case of Edmonton, even the publicists had a hard time exaggerating the truth.

The 1986-87 season saw several Oiler players reach career milestones. Messier—by now acknowledged to be every bit as valuable as Gretzky because of his combination of speed, muscle, dedication, and desire to win—played his 500th Edmonton game on October 21, 1986; Kurri collected his 700th career point and his 350th career goal; and Anderson reached the 300 career goal level in March at Toronto. In addition, seven Oilers played for Team NHL against the Soviet Union at Rendez-Vous 87 in Quebec.

The playoffs included a record-setting 13-3 rout of Los Angeles (Gretzky had six assists to tie a playoff mark), a sweep of the Winnipeg Jets, and then a thrilling final series victory over a tough Flyers' team. Philadelphia won games five and six to put some fear into the Oilers before Edmonton won the finale, 3-1. Kurri got the game-winner at 14:59 of the second period and also had an overtime decider in the second contest.

The fourth Cup was won in 1987-88 in a manner that may never be equalled. The Oilers needed five games to sweep the Boston Bruins 4-0, because a power failure in ancient Boston Garden stopped the fourth game when the teams were tied, 3-3, and the Oilers were looking to finish off their post-season business. They went back to Edmonton two days later and did it.

"This year was the most fun I've ever had playing hockey.... from our Canada Cup win over the Russians, with the great team and great players we had, to the Oilers being underdogs to Calgary in the playoffs ... to winning it all again," Gretzky said at the end of the year.

It wasn't exactly a typical Gretzky year. He lost the Hart Trophy and the Art Ross Trophy to the league's new wunderkind, Pittsburgh's Mario Lemieux, and the summer would bring that unbelievable trade, but for the Oilers the end result was just the same. Calgary was creeping up on them, winning the regular season Smythe Division crown, and there were signs of mortality about the Edmonton club. But they were hardly ready to

AP/Wide World Photos

Bill Ranford

concede the highest rung on the ladder.

Gretzky, by the way, wasn't exactly reduced to average status. An injury sidelined him for 16 games—the first time he had missed a significant amount of regular season action—but he still led the NHL in assists with 109 and added 40 goals. Messier gathered 111 points and Kurri picked up 96, but Coffey was gone, having been traded to Pittsburgh in November in a seven-player exchange that rocked hockey.

Coffey had been in disagreement over terms, but the decision to move him still caught the sport by surprise. Later it would be seen as evidence that the club was not afraid to trade established stars for young prospects rather than commit to long-term contracts at high salaries.

In the playoffs the Oilers rediscovered their old magic. In fact, they were almost perfect. Winnipeg won only once in the first round and Calgary was swept aside in the Smythe finals, with Gretzky winning the second game in the Olympic Saddledome on an overtime goal and the Oilers then closing the door at home. Detroit managed to win once in Joe Louis Arena, but Kurri's goal in the 12th minute of overtime decided game four and the Oilers needed only one more win to reach the finals.

The final was hard-fought but ultimately one-sided. The Bruins lost 2-1 and 4-2 in Edmonton, then fell 6-3 in the third game in their old home building. When the lights went out in game four, the only question was whether Edmonton would need to return home to nail down the Cup. The NHL decided not to chance an after-midnight restart, fearing for the crowd's ability to safely exit should the power fail again, so the Cup presentation did, in fact, take place at Northlands on May 26.

You could have searched all of Alberta that evening and not found anyone who would have predicted the next major event in Oiler history. Edmonton fans were talking about the next Stanley Cup conquest, but behind the scenes, moves were taking place that would shock Canada and the hockey establishment.

Gretzky Goes West

On August 9, 1988, the Oilers acquired Jimmy Carson and Martin Gelinas, plus first round draft picks in 1989, 1991, and 1993, as well as a reported $15 million in cash from the Los Angeles Kings. In return they sent Mike Krushelnyski, Marty McSorley ... and Wayne Gretzky to the West Coast. Reporters across North America scurried to double check the news coming across the wires. Gretzky had been traded. It was hard to think of a comparable blockbuster trade in sporting history.

There were immediate rumors that Pocklington made the deal because he needed the cash, but Gretzky, himself, deflected some of the pressure by saying that he wanted to move on. He had married a Hollywood starlet and was not averse to changing homes. He also acknowledged a mission to promote hockey in the United States. Canadian listeners found all that hard to swallow—some even ranted against the transfer of a "national treasure" to the Americans—but life went on in Edmonton. In fact, it went on better than anyone might have expected.

The Oilers initially slumped to third in the Smythe Division in 1988-89, but they would rebound to second a year later and win a fifth Stanley Cup, their first without "The Great One" to orchestrate the charge.

The 1988-89 team was not devoid of stars. Kurri put up another strong season, finishing 44-58-102, and Carson did his best to "replace" an icon, finishing with 49 goals and 51 assists. Messier, although bothered by nagging injuries, contributed 94 points and the redoubtable Esa Tikkanen, a player who had emerged as one of the league's toughest forwards, was still very much in the forefront. But there was a certain irony in the playoffs when the Gretzky-led Kings defeated the Oilers in the first round. Wayne, himself, allowed that he had mixed feelings when the seven-game series went his way. Calgary, Edmonton's Alberta rivals, went on to grab the Cup and bragging rights in the annual western-Canadian war.

Their 1989-90 Stanley Cup victory, therefore, was all the sweeter for an Oiler team that had something to prove. Finishing second in the Smythe Division during the regular season, the Oilers were inspired by Mark Messiers' career year (45 goals, 84 assists, and 129 points). Petr Klima, a sometimes unpredictable Czech, had been acquired from Detroit in mid-season and there was a surprising hero in goal, Bill Ranford, who was picked up from Boston. The latter pair would turn out to be stars in the final.

Before that, the Oilers had to negotiate a seven-game first round battle against Winnipeg and a second-round rematch against the Kings. This time it was no contest against their former star, as Edmonton swept Los Angeles in four games. The Campbell Conference title came in six games against Chicago, so it was on to the final against Boston once again. The Bruins had gotten by Hartford, Montreal, and Washington—the latter two series in impressive fashion—so when the series began in Massachusetts, it was expected that this might be the year that one of the NHL's original six teams could exact revenge.

The opening game turned out to be a gem, lasting well into the wee hours of the morning before Klima, only a sometimes-used forward, scored the winner—after 55 minutes and 13 seconds of overtime—to give Edmonton a 3-2 triumph. Although Boston showed character to win game three in Northlands Coliseum, that first game result set the tempo for a five-game Oiler victory. They paraded the Cup in Boston on May 24, and few denied that they had overcome any questions about their corporate wisdom. They had made the "Trade of the Century" but were still able to claim hockey's most sought-after trophy.

The Oilers lost Jari Kurri before the 1990-91 season when he signed a two-year contract with the Milan Devils of Italy. In August, Fuhr admitted that for seven years he had battled with drug abuse. The league promptly suspended him (but reinstated him in less than a year. Hampered by injuries, the team's performance declined as they finished at 37-37-6 and lost in the Campbell Conference Finals to Minnesota in five games. Ted

Green replaced John Muckler behind the bench after the season.

In 1991-92, Edmonton finished the season at 36-34-10. The Oilers traded Mark Messier to the Rangers and Grant Fuhr to the Maple Leafs. A *Detroit News* contributor remarked, "Sather's house of mirrors is crumbling. His salary budget might prevent him from ever again icing a Stanley Cup contender." Things only got worse in 1992-93, as Green saw his team miss the playoffs for the first time in 14 years and post a club-record 50 losses. Owner Peter Pocklington shouldered much of the blame for not coming up with the cash to sign and keep star players. During the year, Edmonton dealt veterans Murphy, Tikkanen, and Lowe.

Controversy swirled in Edmonton, because many fans believe Pocklington was going to move the team to Hamilton, Ontario. He negotiated a new lease with the operators of the Northlands Coliseum, and for the 1993-94 season, the Oilers remained in Edmonton. As part of the new Pacific Division which has two expansion teams, Edmonton's chances for a playoff berth improved considerably.

Yet the self-imposed draining of talent continued as Edmonton traded their only 30-goal scorer, Petr Klima, to Tampa Bay for future considerations before the 1993-94 season. A *Hockey Illustrated* reporter noted, "Just five years ago they won their fifth Stanley Cup in seven years, but it's been a virtual fire sale ever since the selling off of Gretzky." A *Detroit Free Press* writer summed up, "Ted Green has the hardest job in the NHL, trying to win with a minor league club because the ownership won't pay major league wages."

Sources

BOOKS

Diamond, Dan, *The NHL's Official 75th Anniversary Commemorative Book*, NHL Publications, 1991.

Fischler, Stan and Shirley Fischler, *The Hockey Encyclopedia,* MacMillan. 1983.

Matheson, Jim, "Season Review," *The Sporting News Hockey Guide and Register, 1986-87,* St. Louis, 1987.

Teitel, Jay, "Gretzky—Doubt Dispelled," *NHL: The World of Professional Hockey,* Rutledge Press, 1982.

PERIODICALS

Detroit Free Press, October 5, 1993.

Detroit News, October 6, 1992.

"The History of the Edmonton Oilers," 1986-87 Edmonton Oiler media guide.

Calabria, Pat, "Season Review," *The Sporting News Hockey Guide and Register, 1984-85.*

Trecker, Jerry, 1983 Stanley Cup coverage columns and stories, *The Hartford Courant.*

—*Jerry Trecker* for Book Builders, Inc.

LOS ANGELES KINGS

On February 8, 1966, 12 groups from around North America made formal presentations to the National Hockey League's (NHL) Board of Governors in New York City for one of the six new franchises up for grabs. Five of these groups sought to place a team in Los Angeles. Prior to the meetings, the group most observers believed to have the best chance of getting the nod for southern California was headed by Dan Reeves, the owner of both the National Football League's (NFL) Los Angeles Rams and Western Hockey League's (WHL) Los Angeles Blades.

When Reeves had purchased the WHL's Victoria, British Columbia, franchise in 1961 and moved it to Los Angeles, he did so with an informal understanding that he would receive "encouragement" from the NHL (with which the WHL had a formal working agreement until 1964) if and when the major league circuit elected to expand. Reeves thus believed—apparently with some justification—that he would have the inside track for

an NHL franchise in Los Angeles. In addition, Reeves' Blades held the hockey lease to the publicly owned Los Angeles Memorial Sports Arena in Exposition Park. The Sports Arena—which could seat almost 14,000 for hockey—was also the only indoor arena in southern California at the time that could meet the NHL's requirement for a minimum of 12,500 seats.

The other four groups to make bids to the NHL for a Los Angeles-based franchise were the owners of the Metromedia broadcasting chain; American Football League (AFL) Buffalo Bills owner Ralph Wilson; Tony Owens, a television producer and husband of actress Donna Reed; and media and sports mogul Jack Kent Cooke, the owner of the National Basketball Association's (NBA) Los Angeles Lakers and part owner of the NFL's Washington Redskins.

Cooke surprised the four other applicants when he sweetened his proposal by offering to build a new, privately financed arena to accommodate at least 16,000 fans. "You have to be impressed with anyone who offers to build a new building," reasoned Montreal Canadiens' Governor David Molson.

Cooke, a 53-year-old Canadian expatriate who had become a U.S. citizen by a special Act of Congress in 1961, pointed out two obvious major advantages of such a new facility over the existing Sports Arena in his presentation to the league.

The first was the far greater revenue potential of a franchise located in a building with approximately 2,000 additional seats. The other was the control over the availability of playing dates Cooke would have in a building that he owned. This was an especially important consideration in Los Angeles where the Sports Arena was controlled by the highly political—and notoriously difficult to deal with—Los Angeles Coliseum Commission.

"The Coliseum Commission is supposed to be an administrative body," Cooke explained to the Los Angeles Times, "but instead the commissioners use it as a power base for themselves personally. I made two applications—one for a long term lease for the Lakers, and a second for the right to sign a lease for hockey if I were awarded an NHL franchise. The commissioners rejected both applications and only offered me a two year lease for the Lakers. When I replied that such a ruling was completely unacceptable, Ernest Debs (an LA County Supervisor and influential member of the Coliseum Commission) replied—and these were his exact words—'Take it or leave it.'"

"I looked at him for a moment," recalled Cooke, "and said, 'Well then I've just decided that I am going to build my own arena!'" Thus, in what he would later describe as "a spur-of-the-indignant-moment decision," Cooke made a commitment to build, less than two years, the largest and most lavish indoor arena in southern California—The Forum.

The day following the bid presentations, the NHL's Governors announced that Jack Kent Cooke was awarded the franchise for Los Angeles. Cooke was ecstatic: "I'm an American now, but I feel like I've just been elected King of England. I feel like I'm one echelon above the President of the United States."

Among Cooke's first tasks was to name his new club. While most of the other new teams sought suggestions from the public, Cooke was so confident in his own judgement and marketing ability that he elected to handle the naming himself. He decided upon the name "Kings" because it alluded to British royalty, and he felt the letter "K" had a "strong" sound.

For team colors, Cooke kept to regal hues, selecting gold and royal purple (which he immediately dubbed "Forum Blue").

Like many other professional sports teams owners, Cooke was first and foremost a salesman. Born and raised in Hamilton, Ontario, Cooke grew up in a relatively well-to-do household. When the stock market crashed in 1929, however, the 18-year-old Cooke quit high school to sell encyclopedias and work as a stock exchange runner. Cooke eventually became associated with Roy Herbert Thomson who, as Lord Thomson of Fleet, built what many considered to be the greatest newspaper empire in the world.

Cooke eventually became a multi-millionaire through his holdings in newspapers, radio and television. Cooke's passion, though, was sports, and he entered the business end of athletics when he purchased the minor league baseball Toronto Maple Leafs of the Triple-A International League. The team flourished under Cooke's stewardship, and he was named minor league executive of the year in 1953.

Along with such other baseball executives as Branch Rickey, Cooke later attempted to start a third major league—the Continental League. After the effort failed, Cooke decided to move to the United States. He soon purchased a 25 percent interest in the Washington Redskins. In 1965 Cooke expanded his sports holdings by purchasing the Los Angeles Lakers for more than $5 million and, the following year, added his new NHL franchise for an entry fee of $2 million.

TEAM INFORMATION AT A GLANCE

Founding date: 1967

Home ice: Great Western Forum
3900 W. Manchester Blvd.
Inglewood, CA 90306
Phone: (310) 419-3160

Seating capacity: 16,005

Team colors: White, black, and gray.
Team nickname: Kings.

Franchise record	Won	Lost	Tie
(1967-93)	818	944	300

Division First Place Finishes (1): 1990-91

Building the Kings

Cooke's first important task after being awarded his NHL franchise was to make his promised new arena a reality. Time was crucial as the six new teams were scheduled to take to the ice in just 21 months. After considering five potential sites, Cooke purchased a 29-acre tract of land in Inglewood that had been part of a golf course.

Situated across the street from the popular Hollywood Park Racetrack and just a ten-minute drive from Los Angeles International Airport, the location for the new arena was perfect. Less than five months after being awarded his NHL franchise, Cooke's design for the arena was complete, the site purchased, and the financing arranged; on July 1, 1966, Cooke broke ground for his "fabulous" Forum.

With his new arena under way, Cooke's next task was to bring in a hockey staff to prepare for the expansion draft in June of 1967. The first man Cooke selected to help him build his club was Larry Regan, a 36-year-old native of North Bay, Ontario. A one-time NHL rookie of the year with Boston, Regan had played with the Bruins and Toronto Maple Leafs from 1956 to 1961.

He then joined the American Hockey League's (AHL) Pittsburgh Hornets for a season as player-coach before spending three years managing and coaching in Innsbruck, Austria. Regan then returned to North American and had been playing with the AHL Baltimore Clippers when Cooke hired him. Regan would spend the 1966-67 season scouting the NHL and minor leagues for players to select in the expansion draft.

For general manager, Cooke tried unsuccessfully to convince Clarence "Hap" Day, the 65-year-old Hall of Famer who had played, coached, and managed with the Toronto Maple Leafs, to come to Los Angeles. Cooke later offered a job to Scotty Bowman without result.

Cooke had still not yet given Regan any title other than "scout," but when they headed to Montreal for the 1967 NHL Meetings, Regan made all of the club's picks. Following the expansion draft, during which the Kings and the other five new teams each selected two goalies and 18 skaters, Cooke officially named Regan general manager.

The first two players taken by each new club in the draft were the goalkeepers. As did most other teams, Regan went immediately for experience between the pipes, selecting 18-year NHL veteran Terry Sawchuk from Toronto (where he had just helped the Leafs win a Stanley Cup). Wayne Rutledge, a 25-year-old New York Ranger prospect from the CPHL Omaha Knights, was picked as Sawchuk's backup. Regan later second-guessed himself about selecting 37-year-old Sawchuk, who would only spend one season with the Kings. "I should have gone for youth and taken Bernie Parent from Boston," he admitted.

Sawchuk was the only established player that Regan picked that day. He later explained that he wanted a fast, young team that he could keep together and allow to develop as a unit. In keeping with that philosophy of building from within, the Kings were the only expansion team that did not make a single trade during their opening season.

Cooke's announced that he had purchased Eddie Shore's famous AHL club, the Springfield Indians. This provided Los Angeles with an additional source of talent (they acquired the rights of the players owned by the Indians), and gave them complete control of the primary minor league club on which their young players would be developed. Among the players acquired with Springfield who made an immediate impact on the Kings were defensemen Bill White, Dale Rolfe, and Dave Amadio. Center Brian Kilrea, another Springfield acquisition, would score the first goal in club history.

The Kings hired a coach in an unusual way—they drafted one. With their 18th pick in the expansion draft, the Kings selected 20-year NHL veteran center Leonard "Red" Kelly from the Stanley Cup champion Toronto Maple Leafs. This unexpected move enraged Toronto owner Stafford Smythe who had figured that, at age 39, the extremely popular Kelly was too old to interest any

of the new teams and could therefore safely be left unprotected in favor of a younger player. Smythe immediately tried to put Kelly back on the Leafs' protected list, but the Kings were adamant. After some negotiation, Toronto agreed to trade Kelly to the Kings for 22-year-old defenseman Ken Block whom the Kings had taken in the previous round. Kelly, a player on eight Stanley Cup winners with Detroit and Toronto, formally announced his retirement as a player and was immediately named the Kings' first coach.

First Season Opens

Four months after the draft, the Kings and the five other expansion teams opened their debut NHL seasons. The Kings were the only club not yet ensconced in its permanent home arena; The Forum was not scheduled to open until December 30th. When the Kings' hosted the Philadelphia Flyers for their first game, the teams played 20 miles southeast of Los Angeles, in Long Beach. That night, October 14, 1967, the Kings officially took to the ice for the first time at the Long Beach Arena before a crowd of 7,035.

If the Kings' first period of hockey were any indication of things to come, the club probably would have ceased operations after just those 20 minutes. The first bad omen had occurred a day earlier—on Friday the 13th—when goalie Terry Sawchuk hurt his elbow in practice. This injury prevented the veteran of almost 1,000 NHL regular season and playoff games from taking to the ice in the opener. Rookie Coach Kelly was thus forced to start rookie goalie Wayne Rutledge.

Rutledge was understandably nervous. So too, apparently, was his defense. Just 52 seconds into the game, Flyer winger Bill Sutherland dumped the puck into the Kings' end only to have Los Angeles defenseman Bob Wall deflect it past a startled Rutledge for the first goal scored against the Kings. Although the Flyers were only credited with three shots on goal in the opening period, they scored twice. That first period proved to be an aberration, however, as the Kings scored four goals to win 4-2.

The next night the King hosted the Minnesota North Stars and won 5-3. Then the club tied road games in Oakland and St. Louis. For their fifth game, the Kings met one of the NHL's "original six," beating the Blackhawks at Chicago Stadium 5-3. Los Angeles finally tasted defeat for the first time with a 4-2 loss in Toronto on October 24th. Nonetheless, after six games, the youthful Kings were riding high in the NHL's new West Division with an excellent 3-1-2 record. NHL hockey had officially arrived in southern California.

The Forum Opens

After splitting their first 17 home dates between the Long Beach Arena and the Los Angeles Memorial Sports Arena, the Kings finally moved into their permanent home on December 30, 1967. The visitors were again the Philadelphia Flyers. However the crowd of 14,366—even though it was smaller than the new arena's 16,005 capacity for hockey—was still more than twice the size of the one that had witnessed the Kings beat the Flyers in that first game played at Long Beach in October.

Cooke had endured a great deal of skeptical criticism in the two years since he had announced plans to build his own arena. With The Forum's completion and Hollywood-style grand opening, Cooke had again proved what a motivated individual entrepreneur can accomplish.

The Kings' new home included a swanky members-only restaurant, The Forum Club, located just a few steps from the ice. Seventy percent of the arena's orange and gold theater-style seats were located between the goal lines, none was more that 170 feet from the ice, and all featured an unobstructed view.

"It's quite outstanding," Lord Thompson of Fleet told the *Los Angeles Times*. "The Forum is the most beautiful arena I've ever seen, and it takes someone with Jack Kent Cooke's guts to do something like this himself. He's quite a salesman, you

know, and I'll bet this will be a good investment for him. And despite what you might hear, this is his. He built it with his money." While Cooke's Forum garnered rave reviews, unfortunately he and the crowd were left disappointed by the Kings performance as the Flyers shut them out 2-0 in the nationally televised game.

Despite going into their first NHL campaign with the youngest team of the six expansion clubs, the Kings' 200 goals were the most scored by any of the six new teams, and they compiled the best record of any of the Western Division clubs (10-12-2) against the NHL's "original six." In goal, rookie Wayne Rutledge was the team's top netminder with a 2.87 goals-against average and 21-15-5 record, while veteran Terry Sawchuk was 10-17-5. Center Ed Joyal was the Kings' leading scorer with 57 points, and rookie winger Bill "Cowboy" Flett led the team with 26 goals.

The Kings ended their inaugural campaign with a record of 31-33-10. Had it not been for a controversial disallowed goal in their final game of the season, which left them with a 2-2 tie against the last place Oakland Seals, the Kings would have finished in first place in their division in 1967-68. (Instead the Kings would have to wait 23 seasons before finally winning a regular season divisional crown.)

Having qualified for the playoffs that year, the Kings' first taste of Stanley Cup action came against the Minnesota North Stars. After leading three games to two, the Kings lost the next two games. The seventh game of the series would prove to be the final appearance in the King nets for Sawchuk. He was traded to Detroit for Jimmy Peters two days before the 1968-69 season.

Drafts and Trades

After their strong inaugural season, the Kings quickly became an NHL doormat. Only two years after narrowly losing the Western Division title, Los Angeles collapsed and finished with just 38 points and 14 wins—48 points behind that year's divisional champion, the St. Louis Blues. These

1969-70 Kings stood alone in last place, 20 points behind Oakland and Philadelphia who both recorded a meager 58 points.

One reason for the Kings' many subpar seasons was the practice of trading high draft picks. According to play-by-play broadcaster Jiggs McDonald, the voice of the Kings for five seasons, Cooke learned this procedure from football coach George Allen. McDonald recalled, "I joined them for lunch one afternoon during the Kings' first season and listened to Allen, then coach of the Los Angeles Rams, convince Mr. Cooke to relinquish draft choices for players who could help his team then. Allen told him that 'It's far better to have a known quantity now than an unknown quantity later.'"

While Allen's approach may have worked in football, it turned out to be a disaster for the Kings. Nonetheless the trading of first-round draft picks was standard procedure during Cooke's reign. Among the players Los Angeles acquired in exchange for its various first-round picks were Gerry Desjardines, Skip Krake, Eddie Shack, Randy Rota, Bob Murdoch, Terry Harper, Gene Carr, Glen Goldup, Ron Grahame, Jerry Korab, Rick Chartraw, and Bob Janecyk.

Most of these men were journeymen or players past their prime. The players acquired with Los Angeles' traded picks, however, were some of the game's most productive performers, including Reggie Leach, Steve Shutt, Andre Savard, Mario Tremblay, Pierre Mondou, Ron Duguay, Ray Bourque, Phil Housley, Tom Barrasso, Claude Lemieux, and Ed Olczyk.

Another trade that hurt the Kings, but helped the Philadelphia Flyers win a pair of Stanley Cups, came on January 28, 1972 when the two clubs carried out an eight-player deal. The Kings sent center Ed Joyal, right wing Bill Flett (the team's top two scorers in 1967-68 and 1968-69), left wing Ross Lonsberry (the leader in 1969-70), and defenseman Jean Potvin to Philadelphia for forwards Bill Lesuk, Jimmy Johnson, Serge Bernier, and defenseman Larry Brown. While Bernier had one strong season for the Kings, none of the four helped make the team a winner.

AP/Wide World Photos

Marcel Dionne (16)

Not all of the Kings' trades were bad, however. On September 3, 1970, the club acquired veteran left wing Bob Pulford from Toronto for Garry Monahan and Brian Murphy. After two seasons as the Kings' captain, Pulford retired as a player in 1972 to become the team's coach.

In Pulford's five seasons behind the Los Angeles bench, the Kings compiled a 178-150-68 record, including a mark of 42-17-21 in 1974-75 for a team record 105 points. Another future captain and coach, winger Mike Murphy, came in a trade from the New York Rangers on November 30, 1973.

Rogie Vachon and Marcel Dionne—two of the greatest "impact" players in the history of the Kings prior to Wayne Gretzky's arrival in 1988—also arrived in Los Angeles via trade. Vachon, the Kings' all-time goaltending leader in games (389), wins (171), shutouts (32), and goals-against average (2.86), was acquired from the Montreal Canadiens on November 4, 1971, for Denis DeJordy, Dale Hoganson, Noel Price, and Doug Robinson.

Dionne, Los Angeles' first Hall of Famer and the club's all-time scoring leader, also came relatively cheaply—although Cooke's deal nearly prompted Coach Bob Pulford to quit. On June 23, 1975, the Kings sent the Detroit Red Wings hardnosed winger Dan Maloney—the player Pulford considered the heart and soul of his club—along with 35-year-old defenseman Terry Harper and a second-round draft pick in exchange for Dionne's rights. When Dionne ended his career in 1989, he was third on the NHL's all-time scoring list with 1,771 points, 1,307 of which had come with Los Angeles between 1975 and 1987.

Although the Kings seldom had a high draft pick to work with, the club's scouting staff uncovered numerous late-round picks who achieved All-Star status in the NHL. The best of these sleepers was right wing Dave Taylor, a 15th round pick (210th overall) in 1975. After graduating from Clarkson College in 1977, Taylor joined the Kings, becoming just the second player to score 1,000 points in a Los Angeles uniform. Midway through the 1991-92 season, the 36-year-old right wing achieved the distinction of being the only player to appear in 1,000 games with the team.

Center Butch Goring, the Kings' fifth and final pick (51st overall) in 1969, spent almost 11 seasons in Los Angeles, collecting 659 points for fourth place on the club's all-time scoring list. Goalie Billy Smith, the all-time leader in Stanley Cup wins, was another fifth round Kings' pick (59th overall in 1970), but he was lost to the New York Islanders in the 1972 expansion draft. Mario Lessard, the Kings' top goalie for four seasons, was the 156th player selected in the 1974 Draft.

In 1980 the Kings' scouting staff came up with another scoring ace in center Bernie Nicholls who was selected 73rd overall. He collected 758 points on in just 605 games as a King before being traded to the New York Rangers on January 20, 1990, for Tomas Sandstrom and Tony Gran-

ato. Left wing Luc Robitaille, the Kings' most prolific scorer during the late 1980s and early 1990s—after Wayne Gretzky—was taken 171st overall in the ninth round of the 1984 draft.

The Forum's Revolving Door

In contrast to the club's first season, 1968-69 saw the Kings begin to fall apart both on the ice and in the front office. By season's end, Regan and Kelly refused to speak to each other, and Kelly resigned as coach after the team finished in fourth place. He was replaced by Hal Laycoe, an NHL defenseman for 11 seasons during the 1940s and 1950s, who had been coaching the WHL Portland Buckaroos. Laycoe lasted just 24 games, however, and was fired after an 8-1 home loss to St. Louis on December 13, 1969, with a record of just 5-18-1. (Three of Laycoe's five wins were against the equally hapless Oakland Seals.)

General Manager Regan then promoted Springfield Indians' coach Johnny Wilson, another veteran ex-NHL player, to take over for Laycoe. Regan hired Doug Harvey, his friend and former Baltimore Clippers' teammate, to assist Wilson. By then, however, the Kings were in free fall and won just nine of their remaining 52 under Wilson and Harvey who were both dismissed at the end of the season.

Regan subsequently named himself the team's fourth coach in just four seasons and led them to an improved 25-40-13 record in 1970-71. By early in the 1971-72 campaign, however, it was clear that the players were no longer responding to Regan either. Following a mark of 2-7-1, Regan replaced himself with Fred Glover.

Although the 5' 9" Glover had only played briefly in the NHL in the early 1950s, he was a legend in the AHL where he was that league's number two all-time leading scorer. The Kings players seemed unimpressed with their new coach's credentials, finishing the 1971-72 season in last place for the second time in three years.

Cooke's revolving door for coaches compelled *Los Angeles Times* columnist John Hall to state, "There sits The Forum, on the corner of Manchester and Prairie. On one side is the Inglewood Park Mortuary, on the other side, Hollywood Park. It's a toss up as to which of the three has laid to rest the most good men!"

The Kings' woes resulted in both dismal records and sparse crowds. Even during some of their better years, Kings' audiences seldom reached 10,000—and on many nights were far closer to 7,000. About the only time the place filled up was when one of the popular East Coast teams—Philadelphia, New York, or Boston—came to town. On those nights, many in the stands cheered for the visiting team.

Another reason for low attendance was that Los Angeles' hockey fans, used to paying for minor-league admission for the Blades, balked at NHL ticket prices. Yet one of the reasons that owner Cooke had envisioned success for a Los Angeles NHL franchise was that some 550,000 of his transplanted countrymen lived in the area. The Kings' failure to develop a loyal fan base prompt-ed the frustrated Cooke to complain that "the half million Canadians in southern California must have moved here because they hated hockey!"

The Pulford Years

After four seasons of turmoil behind the bench, the Kings finally found stability in the coaching department in May of 1972, when 36-year-old center Bob Pulford retired to become the club's skipper. As a player, Pulford was a highly disciplined and stoic practitioner of his sport. His demeanor remained unchanged after he assumed coaching duties, but his club's collective personality was much different.

"It was a terrible situation," Pulford told Lyle Spencer of *The National* many years later. "The attitude in Los Angeles was probably the worst I'd ever been associated with. There was no pride. The character of the players was terrible. The whole atmosphere just wasn't conducive to playing hockey."

To convert the motley and disorganized Kings into winners, Pulford knew the club had to develop self discipline, internal leadership, and the willingness to sacrifice. Pulford made it clear that he would get rid of players who gave less than a full effort.

In 1971-72, the Kings had allowed the most goals in the league, 305, 99 more than they scored. With Pulford's emphasis on team defense and discipline, however, that differential shrank to just 13 in 1972-73. Although the Kings again missed the playoffs by finishing sixth in the eight-team West Division, they had improved by 24 points over the previous year to notch a record of 31-36-11.

The club's most important addition in 1972-73 was the late season acquisition of 22-year-old winger Dan Maloney from the Chicago Blackhawks. Mal-oney was exactly the kind of player Pulford wanted to provide on-ice leadership for his club.

The building process continued over the next summer as defenseman Bob Murdoch was acquired from the Canadiens. In September veteran winger Bob Nevin, Pulford's teammate in Toronto in the early 1960s, came over from Minnesota. On November 30, the Rangers sent winger Mike Murphy and defensemen Tommy Williams and Sheldon Kannegeiser to Los Angeles in exchange for blueliner Gilles Marotte and left wing Real Lemieux.

The first major change in the Kings' front office occurred on December 17 when General Manager Larry Regan resigned and was replaced by Jake Milford. Milford was a longtime minor league general manager and scout in the New York Ranger organization whom Cooke had hired the previous summer to run the Kings' WHL Portland Buckaroos farm club.

In 1973-74 the Kings reached .500 for the first time in their history with a 33-33-12 record, scoring two more goals than they allowed. More important, however, was that their third-place finish in the West Division earned them a playoff spot for the first time since 1969. Although the Kings lost their first-round series to the Blackhawks, the games were close—two losses were 1-0 shutouts, and the Kings only allowed ten Chicago goals in five games.

Pulford's Kings appeared to be on the verge of becoming a force in the NHL. The Kings opened the 1974-75 season at the Spectrum against the Stanley Cup champion Philadelphia Flyers. The Kings' backup netminder, Gary Edwards, faced the high scoring Flyers and All-Star goalie Bernie Parent.

By the end of the first period, however, it was the Kings who had taken charge and were leading 2-0. The game ended as a 5-3 Los Angeles victory, with Edwards brilliant in goal by stopping 34 of 37 Flyer shots. The Kings then went to Montreal where—with Edwards again in goal—they tied the Canadiens, and continued undefeated until their seventh contest of the season. Loss number two came only in mid-November. After 26 games, the Kings had a stellar record of 15-2-9.

By season's end, the Kings had compiled a record of 42-17-21 good for 105 points and second place in the newly formed Norris Division. In just three seasons, Pulford had converted the Kings from the worst team in the NHL to one of the best—and, with the exception of goalie Rogie Vachon, did so without a single "star" player.

The Kings' 1974-75 leader in both goals (31) and points (72), for example, was 37-year-old journeyman Bob Nevin (who had averaged just 45 points a season in his 16-year career). The Kings' secret was not high scorers, but balanced scoring. No fewer that seven Los Angeles players collected between 24 and 31 goals that season.

The most important factor behind the Kings' glorious season, however, was team defense and goaltending. The Kings' goal-keeping tandem of Vachon and Edwards allowed only 185 goals. In 54 games, Vachon fashioned a 27-14-13 record with a career best goals-against average of 2.24 and finished a close second to Flyer center Bob Clarke in voting for league MVP honors. Even more impressive was the record of Vachon's backup, Edwards, who posted a spectacular 15-3-8 mark.

For the first time in the history of Los Ange-les, the city was excited about its hockey team, and the Kings were the talk of the town as they confidently prepared to open the 1975 Stanley Cup playoffs with a best-of-three preliminary round series against Pulford's old club, the Toronto Maple Leafs. While the Kings had finished the 1974-75 season 25 games over .500, the Leafs were a mediocre 31-33-16. Moreover, in the five regular season meetings between the two clubs, the Kings had manhandled Toronto, 4-0-1, and out-scored them 24-7.

The Leafs gave the Kings a scare in the series opener when they forced the game into overtime. Mike Murphy scored to give the Kings a 3-2 victory. The series resumed two nights later in Toronto, and again the underdog Leafs fought the Kings to a 2-2 draw after 60 minutes. This time, however, it was Toronto's Blaine Stoughton who scored in overtime to tie the series and send it back to Los Angeles for the series deciding game.

The Leafs chartered a flight to Los Angeles immediately after the game, but, incredibly, the Kings waited until the next morning to fly back, arriving just a few hours before game time. That night the Kings' glorious season came to a premature end as the Leafs upset them 2-1 in a fight-filled contest.

Pulford was so distraught over the loss that he was unable to meet with the media after the game. "That was the most devastating thing that ever happened to me in hockey," Pulford said many years later. "After having such a great year, with such a great team—it was a bitter, bitter disappointment. I don't think that I've ever really gotten completely over it."

The stunning playoff loss would not be the last blow Pulford would suffer before the opening of the next season. On June 23rd, the Kings acquired Marcel Dionne and Bart Crashley from the Detroit Red Wings. Although Pulford had pursued Dionne for some time, owner Cooke got involved in the deal and gave away the one player Pulford considered absolutely "untouchable" on his team—Dan Maloney.

Cooke's trading of Maloney and his subsequent squashing of another deal Pulford had arranged to get Dave Keon from Toronto was more meddling than the coach could take. Pulford announced he could no longer work for Cooke under those circumstances and quit. However Cooke refused to release Pulford from his contract which had two more years to run. The players also pleaded with Pulford to stay because they knew he had made the team a winner.

In the years Dionne played for the Kings, he led the club in points eight times while becoming one of the game's all-time greatest players and premier scorers. However the Kings never really recovered from the loss of Maloney's leadership and dropped 20 points in 1975-76 to a record of 38-33-9.

The outstanding defensive style that Pulford had instilled in the club also disappeared, and the club gave up 265 goals—80 more than they allowed in 1974-75. Yet the Kings again finished second in the Norris Division in 1975-76. Unlike the previous spring, however, the 1976 playoffs would bring Pulford and his team some solace.

After eliminating the Atlanta Flames with two excellent defensive games, the Kings faced the powerful Boston Bruins in the best-of-seven quarterfinals. While the Bruins won the first game at Boston Garden relatively easily, the Kings came back to even the series in game two. After a 6-4 Los Angeles victory at The Forum in game three, the Bruins won the next two contests to force the Kings to the brink of elimination in game six at The Forum. "I'll never forget that sixth game," Pulford recalled. "It was the most memorable of all my years in Los Angeles. I can still hear and feel the ovation the crowd gave us when we stepped on the ice that night—and the game that followed more than lived up to it."

The Kings trailed the Bruins 3-1 in the third period, but Pulford's club would not give up. Left wing Mike Corrigan scored at 10:50 to bring the Kings within a goal of Boston. Then with just 2:12 left Corrigan scored again—after being tripped by Boston goalie Gerry Cheevers—to tie the game at 3-3 and send it into overtime.

"Both clubs had great chances in the overtime and the action was end-to-end," Kings' play-by-play broadcaster Bob Miller explained. "Then at 18:28 Butch Goring beat Cheevers from 30 feet out with his second overtime game winner of the series. After mobbing Butch along the boards, the players hoisted him to the shoulders of Mike Corrigan and Dave Hutchinson and carried him off the ice. I've never seen anything like that in a hockey game before or since."

With that thrilling 4-3 come-from-behind victory, the series went back to Boston for a seventh and final game. The Bruins won 3-0 behind Gerry Cheevers' third shutout of the series, but the Kings' inspirational performance did much to help them regain their lost pride. The 1976-77 season a virtual carbon copy of the previous year, with the Kings again finishing second in the Norris Division, beating Atlanta in the first round, and falling to the Bruins in six games in the playoffs.

The tenures of Bob Pulford and Jake Milford in Los Angeles both came to an end with the 1977 playoffs as each resigned to run another NHL club. (In July Pulford was named general manager/coach of the Chicago Blackhawks while Milford became general manage general manager of the Vancouver Canucks.) In Pulford's five years behind the Kings' bench, the acerbic coach amassed a record of 178-150-68. "I'll always remember my five years in Los Angeles with extreme pride—pride in the team, the players, and the fans," Pulford told Lyle Spencer of *The National*. "While we didn't accomplish the ultimate goal, we came a long way."

Arrivals and Departures

Pulford's replacement for the 1977-78 season was 45-year-old Ron Stewart, a right wing with 21 years' NHL experience who had coached the Kings' AHL Springfield club to a Calder Cup title in 1975 and then guided the Portland Buckaroos to the WHL Patrick Cup finals. Meanwhile 56-year-old George Maguire, a longtime scout and minor league general manager, took over as general manager.

Stewart lasted only one season as coach, but another new arrival in 1977-78, Dave Taylor, would eventually have the longest tenure of any player or coach in club history. After graduating from Clarkson College in 1977, the right wing made the Kings after only a brief minor-league stint in Ft. Worth. He would remain as one of the club's most consistent contributors for 15 years.

The Kings fell to third place in the Norris Division in 1977-78 with 77 points and were quickly knocked out of the playoffs by Toronto. The club made several player changes, however. All-star goalie Rogie Vachon left the Kings after the season to sign with Detroit as a free agent. In mid-season, an injury to right wing Hartland Monahan opened up a spot for Taylor on Dionne's line. With the promotion of minor-league left wing Charlie Simmer from Springfield the following season, the elements of the most productive offensive unit in the team's first quarter-century—the "Triple Crown Line"—were joined.

Signed by the Kings' as a free agent in 1977, Simmer was called up to Los Angeles as the club began a grueling eight-game road trip in early January of 1979. Rookie Kings' coach Bob Berry, who had skated with Simmer the year before while a player/coach of the Indians, placed him with Dionne and Taylor for the first time in Detroit on January 13, 1979. The trio clicked immediately, accounting for six goals in a 7-3 Los Angeles victory that night. Except when injured, they would remain together as a unit almost continuously for more than five years.

Simmer collected 21 goals and 48 points over the rest of the 1978-79 season while Taylor's second year output jumped from 43 to 91. Dionne finished the season with 59 goals and 71 assists for a career-high 130 points, just four fewer than Bryan Trottier's league-leading 134. Meanwhile, Vachon's spot in goal was assumed by 24-year-old Mario Lessard who finished his rookie NHL season with a 22-15-10 record and 3.10 goals-against average.

In 1978-79, the Kings returned to .500 with a 34-34-12 record, but they were again eliminated from the playoffs in two games, this time by the eventual Stanley Cup finalist New York Rangers. After being downed convincingly 7-1 in the series opener in New York, the Kings' season ended with a 2-1 overtime loss in Los Angeles in game two of the best-of-three preliminary series—a contest best remembered for a spectacular 25-minute bench-clearing brawl at the end of the first period.

After almost 15 years, Jack Kent Cooke left the Los Angeles sports and entertainment scene when he sold his California Sports, Inc. empire (comprising the NHL Kings, NBA Lakers, and The Forum) in the summer of 1979 to local entrepreneur Dr. Jerry Buss for $67.5 million. The 46-year-old Buss, who had moved to Los Angeles from his native Wyoming in the mid-1950s, had built his fortune through his real estate investment business with large holdings in California, Nevada and Arizona.

"Triple Crown Line" Flourishes

In 1979-80, their first full season together, the "Triple Crown Line" combined for 146 goals and 328 points. Simmer collecting a team-leading 56 goals despite missing 16 games with a knee injury. Taylor notched 37 goals while also being sidelined for 19 contests with knee problems. Dionne won the Art Ross Trophy as the NHL's top scorer for the only time in his career with 137 points—beating out 19-year-old Wayne Gretzky of the Ed-monton Oilers on the final day of the season. While Dionne and Gretzky actually had the same number of points, Dionne was declared the champion because he had two more goals than Gretzky (who won the scoring title for the next seven years).

Simmer, Dionne and Taylor had their best year as a unit in 1980-81 as they combined for 161 goals and 352 points. All three broke the 100-point plateau to become the league's top scoring line that year. The remarkable offensive output of the "Triple Crown Line" and the outstanding goaltending of Mario Lessard (35-18-11 record; 3.25 goals-against average) returned the Kings' to the league's elite with 99 points on a record of 43-

24-13—an improvement of 25 points over the previous season.

While the Kings appeared ready to make a strong playoff run that April, disaster struck with 15 games to go in the regular season schedule when Simmer suffered a terrible break to his right leg which would sideline him until the following November. Without their high scoring left winger, the Kings were no match for the New York Rangers, and they fell easily, three games to one, in the best of five preliminary series. New York outscored Los Angeles 23-12.

Hard Times Again—Then a Miracle

The 1981-82 Los Angeles club tumbled 36 points to a ten-year low of 63 points on a record of 24-41-15. Curiously the 1981-82 Kings' lineup was not very different from the one that had been so effective the previous year. Defensively, however, the team allowed nearly one more goal per game while their scoring output dropped by 23 goals.

The coaching situation also became unstable; Bob Berry resigned as Kings' coach on May 22, 1981, after a contract dispute and was almost immediately named head coach of the Montreal Canadiens. Berry's departure ended a nine-year stretch over which just three men—Bob Pulford, Ron Stewart and Berry—had guided the Kings. Over the next 36 months, however, six other men would serve as coach of the club.

The first of these was 48-year-old Parker MacDonald, Berry's assistant coach the previous year. A veteran of a dozen seasons as a player in the NHL, MacDonald became the ninth coach of the Kings. MacDonald had replaced Jackie Gordon behind the bench of the Minnesota North Stars 17 games into the 1973-74 season and coached them for the remainder of that campaign. MacDonald then spent the next six seasons as general manager/coach of the AHL New Haven Nighthawks where he enjoyed considerable success, twice reaching the Calder Cup finals.

After three seasons under the highly disci-

plined Berry, the Kings had trouble adjusting to MacDonald's easy-going approach, and he was relieved after just 42 games with a record of 13-24-5. MacDonald was replaced on January 11, 1982, by 52-year-old Don "Fred" Perry who came to his new post after 30 successful seasons playing and coaching in the minor leagues, but no NHL experience. Perry spent most of his playing career in the rough-and-tumble Eastern Hockey League where there were few—if any—tougher than the 6'2", 210 pounder.

Shortly after joining the Kings, however, Perry found himself the center of controversy when he was suspended by the league after winger Paul Mulvey—the recently acquired "policeman"—complained that he was demoted to the AHL because he had refused Perry's orders to leave the bench to aid his outnumbered teammates during a brawl. Assistant coach Brad Selwood took over behind the Kings' bench during Perry's six-game absence.

Although the Kings' record over the rest of the season was 11-17-10, and the team finished in fourth place in the Smythe Division, the 1982 playoffs would see the Kings produce a true "miracle on ice." On April 10, 1982, the club pulled off one of the most remarkable come-from-behind victories by a decided underdog. In the "Miracle on Manchester," the Kings overcame a 5-0 third period deficit to beat the heavily favored Edmonton Oilers 6-5 in overtime to take a two-games-to-one lead in their first-round series.

Although the Oilers came back with a 3-2 win in the next game to tie the series and send it back to Edmonton, the Kings took the fifth and final game with relative ease, 7-4, despite being outshot 43-31. With that, the Kings had unexpectedly won their first playoff series since 1977—and just their fourth in 15 years in the NHL.

Two nights later, Los Angeles opened their next series in Vancouver and lost 3-2. The two teams split the next two games, but the Canucks prevailed in games four and five to take the best-of-seven set, four games to one. Just 11 days after performing their "Miracle on Manchester," the Kings' season was over. Nonetheless, the team had left Los Angeles with one of the most memorable nights in the history of professional sports.

Although the Kings improved by three points in 1982-83, their chance at another miracle was impossible as they finished in fifth place in the Smythe Division and missed the playoffs for the first time since 1973. Mario Lessard, who two years earlier was a second team All-Star, won just three of 19 games. The bulk of the goaltending load was carried by Gary Laskowski, a undrafted college goalie who had made the team as a walk-on in training camp.

The 1983-84 campaign started off even worse for the Kings; Perry was replaced behind the bench on January 25 after posting a record of 14-27-9. Rogie Vachon, who had rejoined the club first as a goaltending consultant and then assistant coach after finishing his playing career with the Boston Bruins in 1982, took over for two games while owner Buss decided how to restructure his floundering club.

Five days later, Buss completely reorganized the Kings' management. He named Vachon the club's new general manager, replacing the increasingly ineffective George Maguire. Buss got veteran NHL coach Roger Neilson to take over behind the bench. Recently retired King winger and former team captain Mike Murphy was also added to the staff as an assistant coach. By season's end, however, the Kings still had their worst record in a dozen years at 23-44-13.

The Pat Quinn Era

When Neilson joined the Kings he had expected a management position to be added to his portfolio after the season. When that never materialized, he left. Vachon considered his choices carefully; the distractions in Los Angeles had often resulted in a lack of on-ice discipline and intensity among King players, and this was especially true when they were not guided by a "firm" hand.

Vachon needed a man who could get his team to focus first and foremost on playing winning hockey. He more than found him in 41-year-old John Brian Patrick (Pat) Quinn.

A veteran of nine NHL seasons (1968-77) as one of the toughest defensemen in the game, the imposing 6'3" 225 pound Quinn had already achieved success behind the bench during his tenure as coach of the Philadelphia Flyers from 1979 to 1982. Under Quinn in 1979-80, the Flyers had also achieved one of the most remarkable feats in the history of pro sports; the club went 35 games without a single loss (25-0-10).

Although Quinn compiled 141-73-48 record in Philadelphia, he was relieved with eight games remaining in the 1981-82 season when his club faltered down the stretch. Vachon, who had played against Quinn during his NHL career, knew that his new coach always treated his players fairly and had commanded great respect from his Flyer teams. Under Quinn, the character of the Kings changed dramatically as the club regained direction and played with purpose.

With his coach in place, Vachon began to restructure the Kings. None of the nine goalies who had played for the Kings over the previous four seasons appeared in another game for the team. Instead the 1984-85 Kings went with a pair of NHL rookies in goal—Chicago-born Bob Janecyk whom Vachon acquired from the Chicago Blackhawks on June 9, 1984, and 1980 draft pick Darren Eliot, who had spent the previous year with the Canadian Olympic team.

Vachon then traded 30-year-old Charlie Simmer—the Kings' number-two scorer the previous season—to the Boston Bruins for a first-round draft pick. Later in the season, Vachon added two veterans, Steve Shutt and Dave "Tiger" Williams, to the team at very little cost. Guy Lefleur's longtime linemate in Montreal, the speedy Shutt came over from the Habs in November for a tenth-round draft pick, but retired after the season. Williams—the NHL's all-time leader in penalty minutes by a huge margin—was acquired from the Detroit Red Wings in March for cash and remained as the Kings' very effective "policeman" until 1987.

The Kings showed a marked revival in Quinn's first season, 1984-85, jumping 23 points

When Pat Quinn was originally hired to coach the Kings in 1984, he was told that general manager Rogie Vachon might take a different position in the organization within two years or so, and if that happened, Quinn would be considered for the general manager post. It was agreed that if the club were not able to offer Quinn a suitable management position after he completed his second year, he would be free to explore other options during the final year of his contract. To facilitate this arrangement, it was also agreed that Quinn's contract with the Kings would not be registered with the league office so that any discussions he might later have with another club would not constitute tampering.

When no management position was offered to Quinn by the Kings after his second year, he began to plan for what he would do after his contract expired. Because Quinn had just completed his law degree, he was considering entering law practice in Philadelphia. On December 8, 1986, however, the owners of the Vancouver Canucks contacted his long-time legal advisor and personal representative in Atlanta to inquire if Quinn would be interested in joining the Canucks as president and general manager after he had completed his coaching responsibilities with the Kings at the end of the 1986-87 season.

When the Canucks had entered the NHL in 1970, one of the players the club had taken in the expansion draft was Quinn, a 27-year-old defenseman with the Toronto Maple Leafs. While he remained in Vancouver as a player for just two seasons before being lost to the Atlanta Flames in the 1972 expansion draft, Quinn's commanding presence on the ice and later behind the bench had long been admired there. In 16 NHL seasons, however, the Canucks had never yet reached championship level (they were usually much below that). By the 1986-87 campaign the club was on its seventh general manager.

Quinn met Frank and Arthur Griffiths, the Canucks' owners, in Los Angeles on December 18 to discuss their proposal and signed the contract in Vancouver five days later. After returning to Los Angeles, Quinn advised Vachon that he would be retiring from coaching after the season to accept the front-office position with the Canucks.

Upon receiving this news, the Kings offered Quinn a very large raise to stay on as coach, but he turned it down. Although he had not requested it, the Canucks paid Quinn as signing bonus to seal the agreement. One week later, however, word of Quinn's agreement with the Canucks was leaked to the press; with this public disclosure, the Kings' removed Quinn from behind the bench on January 9, 1987. Assistant coach Mike Murphy was named as his replacement for the remaining 38 games of the season.

Although Quinn had kept the Kings fully apprised of every step of the process and his actions conformed to his agreements with the club, the Kings nonetheless filed a grievance with the NHL against the Canucks for tampering. Quinn was immediately "expelled" by NHL President John Ziegler pending a league conducted investigation. The Canucks were eventually assessed a heavy fine (later rescinded by the Court) and Quinn was prohibited from assuming any duties with the Canucks until the date of expiration of the Kings' contract or from coaching in the NHL for three years.

Quinn officially became president and general manager of the Canucks on May 1, 1987, and on January 31, 1991, took over from Bob McCammon as head coach. In 1991-92, Quinn's first full season behind the Vancouver bench, he led the Canucks to the best season in their history with 96 points on a 42-26-12 record and a first-place finish in the Smythe Division.

to 82 on a record of 34-32-14. Bernie Nicholls became a 100-point scorer for the first time with 46 goals and 54 assists. For the first time since 1982, the Kings returned to the playoffs but had to face the defending Stanley Cup champion Edmonton Oilers in the best-of-five first-round series. Their playoff series was closely matched, but the Oilers prevailed in three straight games, although two of the contests were decided in overtime.

In 1985-86, Quinn's second season, the Kings suffered both offensive and defensive collapses, dropping 29 points from the previous season's total with a dismal record of 23-49-8. Only the Detroit Red Wings had a worse mark that year. During the season, General manager Rogie Va-chon made seven trades involving 22 players or draft picks as he tried to help his underperforming club.

Bruce McNall Arrives

The Kings recovered in 1986-87 to finish fourth and make the playoffs, but the season in Los Angeles was marked by one significant arrival and two unexpected departures. While maintaining his ownership of the Lakers and The Forum, Jerry Buss began to divest himself of his NHL team when he sold a significant minority interest in the Kings to Bruce McNall, a 37-year-old local entrepreneur (who would eventually become the sole owner of the team in March of 1988). Over the next five years, the activist McNall would become one of the most influential owners in the league, and in 1992 he was elected Chairman of the NHL Board of Governors.

Departing the Los Angeles scene were coach Pat Quinn and the Kings' all-time scoring leader, Marcel Dionne, who both unexpectedly left the

AP/Wide World Photos

Luc Robitaille

club during the second half of the season. Quinn's exit came on January 9 when he was "expelled" by league President John Ziegler because he had signed an agreement in December of 1986 to become president and general manager of the Vancouver Canucks when his coaching contract with the Kings expired at the end of the 1986-87 season.

After much controversy and a league investigation—but no hearing—conducted by NHL General Counsel Gil Stein, Quinn's expulsion was rescinded effective at the end of the season when he would then be permitted to join the Canucks. Quinn was prohibited, however, from coaching in the NHL for three years. In the meantime, assistant coach Mike Murphy had taken over for Quinn behind the Kings' bench on January 10. Murphy collected his first coaching victory three nights later as the Kings defeated the Canucks 4-0.

Marcel Dionne's departure came on March 10 when he was dealt to the New York Rangers at the NHL trading deadline. In return the Kings got Tom Laidlaw, a solid blueliner in his seventh NHL season, and 23-year-old center Bobby Carpenter, the Massachusetts-born former high school wunderkind who the Washington Capitals had picked third overall in the 1981 entry draft. (The talented but sometimes temperamental Carpenter had been traded to the Rangers by the Caps just ten weeks earlier after finally wearing his welcome in Washington.)

Dionne, who was completing his 12th season in Los Angeles, had one year left on his contract but had been seeking an extension. However with 25-year-old Bernie Nicholls joined that year by 18-year-old center Jimmy Carson and 21-year-old winger Luc Robitaille to give the Kings three young high scoring forwards, Vachon was reluctant to make a commitment beyond 1988 to 36-year-old Dionne. When Ranger General Manager Phil Esposito expressed interest in Dionne and willingness to extend his contract, Vachon made the deal. "It was a combination of a few things," Dionne told the Associated Press after the trade. "I talked to the general manager to renegotiate

and I could see that I was struggling a lot in the last couple of months. I didn't think I was going to get anyplace (in the negotiations) so that's why the trade happened. I'm still surprised that it all happened, but sometimes you have to stand up for what you believe and I think it's time for me to go." For most Kings' fans, however, Dionne's departure was completely unexpected.

For the third consecutive year, Los Angeles faced the Edmonton Oilers to start the playoffs. After winning the opening game 5-2 against the defending Stanley Cup champions, the Kings dropped four straight while being outscored 32-20 in the series.

McNall, a Los Angeles native who turned his childhood hobby of collecting ancient coins into a highly successful business while a doctoral candidate in Roman history at UCLA, became president of the Kings in September of 1987. In March of 1988, he took over the club completely when he bought out Busses' majority interest in the franchise to become the Kings' sole owner. While hockey was McNall's first venture into team sports, he had already experienced considerable success as the owner of a thoroughbred racing stable and a motion picture production company.

The Kings struggled badly over the first two months of the 1987-88 season, and Mike Murphy was let go after 27 games with a 7-16-4 record. General Manager Vachon filled in for one game, a 10-3 loss in Washington, before AHL New Haven Nighthawk coach Robbie Ftorek was promoted to take over the Kings. Ftorek, an acerbic 36-year-old native of Needham, Massachusetts who had his greatest success as a player as a high scoring center in the WHA from 1974 to 1979, led the Kings to a 23-25-4 record over the final 52 games of the season and into the playoffs. For the third consecutive time, the opening round proved to the Kings' last, as the first-place Calgary Flames polished them off in five games.

When the Kings left the ice after their final playoff game on April 12, they could not have fathomed that by the following fall the club would be the center of international attention. The Kings would sport a completely different look as the familiar gold and "Forum Blue" they had worn for 22 would be replaced by silver and black uniforms and a new team logo. And taking the first face-off before the Kings' first opening night sellout crowd would be the most famous player in hockey, Wayne Gretzky.

Gretzky Takes L.A.

On May 26, 1988, Edmonton Oiler captain Wayne Gretzky carried the Stanley Cup around the ice at Northlands Coliseum after helping his club sweep the Boston Bruins in the finals. It was the fourth time since 1984 that the 27-year-old Gretzky had been given this happy task. As had been the case in each of the Oilers' other three championship seasons, their captain had also been the league's leading playoff scorer.

There were stories about this remarkable feat in the various Los Angeles newspapers, but none of them received particular prominence or garnered much interest. As usual, hockey had already been over in southern California for more than a month, and all eyes turned to baseball's Dodgers. The local media was much more interested in another story out of Edmonton, Gretzky's July 16 wedding—mostly because his new bride, Janet Jones, was an Los Angeles-based film star.

August is generally a uneventful month for hockey in Los Angeles, but Tuesday, August 9, 1988, was different. The afternoon *Los Angeles Herald Examiner* carried a six-column banner across the top of page one that said: "Kings trade puts Gretzky on Los Angeles Ice." Page one of the sports section carried a similar banner: "Another Magic Man in Inglewood".

Just five months after taking full control of

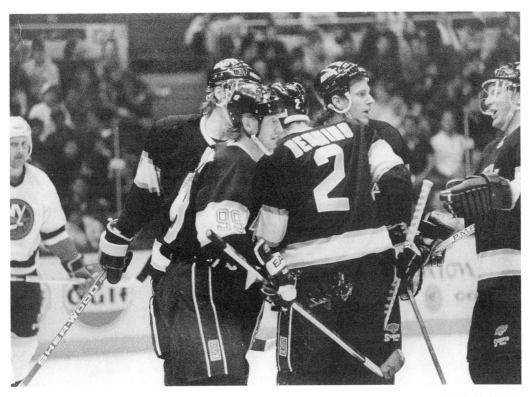

AP/Wide World Photos

Wayne Gretzky

the Kings, McNall had made the biggest deal in his life—and in the history of the National Hockey League—as he brought one of the most famous athletes in the world to Los Angeles. In exchange for Jimmy Carson, Martin Gelinas, three future first-round draft picks, and $15 million in cash, the Oilers had traded Wayne Gretzky, Marty Mc-Sorley, and Mike Krushelnyski to the Kings. After 22 seasons as a virtual sports nonentity in Los Angeles, the Kings were suddenly "Hollywood."

"It's hard to leave a place you've been happy for ten years, Gretzky told the *Herald Examiner* by telephone from McNall's private jet before a press conference. "I'm really excited about coming to Los Angeles. Hopefully I can turn around what has been a losing franchise into a winner and create a lot of excitement."

McNall had paid about $20 million for the Kings' franchise. With the cash paid to Edmonton and the contract given to his new star player, Wayne Gretzky had cost McNall much more than that. "I'm a fan," McNall said, "and I want to see hockey become a major-league sport in Los Angeles. This is the way to do it. Ask fifty people to name a Kings' star player and one or two might know. Ask fifty people in Los Angeles who Wayne Gretzky is and all of them will know."

It did not take long for McNall and the Kings to begin to get a return on his investment. Everywhere in trend-conscious Los Angeles people were wearing silver and black Kings' hats, shirts, and jackets. Broadcast rights fees skyrocketed, as did advertising revenues. The Kings were finally a hot ticket in Los Angeles, and soon each time they played, every Forum seat was filled.

Wayne Gretzky played his first regular season game as a King on October 6, 1988, as the Detroit Red Wings visited The Forum. At 12:54 of the first period, number 99 scored the first Kings' goal of the season, and by game's end had added three assists in the 8-2 Los Angeles romp. Two nights later the Kings beat Calgary 6-5 in overtime, and then posted the same result against the New York Islanders the next night. The Boston Bruins fell next to the Kings, before Gretzky and company finally tasted defeat for the first time

at the hands of the Philadelphia Flyers in the Kings fifth game.

Gretzky collected a team record 168 points on 54 goals and 114 assists in 1988-89, while frequent linemate Bernie Nicholls had a career season with 70 goals and 80 assists for 150 points. By season's end, the Kings had fashioned a 42-31-7 record and finished in second place in the Smythe Division with 91 points—seven more than the third place Oilers. As fate would have it, that meant Gretzky and the Kings would face the defending Stanley Cup champions in the opening round of the playoffs in what would prove to be a highly emotional series requiring a full seven games to decide.

While the Kings' had Gretzky, the Oilers' still had most of the rest of the players who had won four of the last five Cups. Edmonton employed that playoff experience to take three of the first four games. By the time the series was over, however, the Kings had upset the champions four games to three.

Had the Calgary Flames not survived their opening round series against the Vancouver Canucks—in which the underdogs' gritty shooters twice hit the post in overtime of the seventh game before falling to the Flames—the Kings may well have gone all the way to the finals in 1988. After their close shave with Vancouver, though, the Flames regained their composure and swept past the Kings in four straight. (Calgary eventually went on to win the Cup by beating the Montreal Canadiens in the finals.)

Despite compiling a record of 65-56-11 since taking over the Kings' bench, Coach Robbie Ftorek's dour approach had worn thin by the end of the 1988-89 campaign and he was let go. His replacement was 40-year-old Tommy Webster, a one-time WHA scoring star and veteran minor league and junior coach who had led teams in the AHL (Adirondack), CHL (Tulsa), and OHL (Windsor) to playoff championships in his ten-year bench career.

Webster had also briefly coached the NHL's New York Rangers in 1986-87 before an inner ear problem, which was later corrected by surgery, forced him to quit because he was unable to fly.

The Kings also got a new captain—and their home arena a new name—with the start of the 1989-90 season. After three years as Kings' captain, Dave Taylor surrendered the "C" to Gretzky (who had served the same role with the Oilers from 1983 to 1988).

Meanwhile, The Forum's name officially changed to The Great Western Forum, and the base red-orange hue of the arena's exterior disappeared in favor of a deep blue to match the color scheme of the building's new corporate sponsor, the Great Western Bank.

To the new captain's distress, however, the Kings again repeated their pattern of regressing after a strong season by finishing the 1989-90 campaign in fourth place in the Smythe Division with 75 points and a record of 34-39-7. The season was not without its dramatic highlights. On October 16, the Kings faced the Oilers at North-lands Coliseum in Edmonton, with Gretzky entering the game one point shy of Gordie Howe's league record 1,850 career points.

Gretzky quickly tied Howe's mark with an assist just 4:32 into the game but failed to collect another point through the rest of the first two periods. Also early in the second period Gretzky was hit hard by Oiler defenseman Jeff Beukeboom and began suffering dizzy spells in the dressing room during the second intermission. Although coach Tom Webster was reluctant to allow him to play the game's final period, Gretzky insisted.

Gretzky was still without a second point on the night as the game reached its final minute of regulation time, with the Oilers holding a 4-3 lead. With Kings' goalie Mario Gosselin pulled for an extra attacker, Gretzky beat Edmonton netminder Bill Ranford at 19:03 of the third period with a backhand shot to tie the game and break Howe's record.

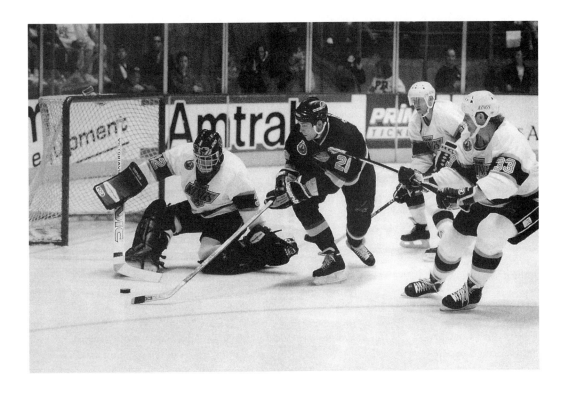

Kelly Hrudey (in goal)

After an emotional ten-minute ceremony to recognize Gretzky's achievement, the final :53 of regulation time were played and the teams began a five-minute sudden death overtime period. Gretzky struck again with another backhand shot to win the game for the Kings in overtime, 5-4, and earn himself his 1,852nd point.

On the trade front in 1989-90, Vachon made one of the boldest deals in team history at mid-season as he sought to give the Kings some much needed grit and toughness up front. On January 20, 1990, he dealt the club's number three all-time leading scorer (758 points), Bernie Nicholls, to the New York Rangers for high scoring—and no-toriously feisty—Swedish right wing Tomas Sandstrom, and 26-year-old left wing Tony Granato, a 1988 U.S. Olympian. The trade was announced at a news conference in Pittsburgh just prior to the 1990 All-Star Game in which Nicholls was scheduled to represent the Kings.

With the Kings fourth-place finish in the Smythe Division, they met the defending Stanley Cup champions—the powerful Calgary Flames—in the opening round of the playoffs for the sec-ond year in a row. After splitting the first two games in Calgary, the Kings won game three in Los Angeles in overtime, and then stunned the Flames with a 12-4 thrashing to take a three-games-to-one lead in the series.

With a 5-1 home ice win for Calgary in game five, the Flames seemed to regain their compo-sure as the two clubs returned to The Great West-ern Forum for game six. That contest proved one of the most dramatic ever played in Stanley Cup history, and made a case for the use of instant replay by NHL offices.

With just 1:43 to play in regulation and the Flames holding a precarious 3-2 lead, Kings' defenseman Steve Duchesne beat Calgary goalie Mike Vernon to tie the game at 3-3. To make matters worse for the dispirited Flames, Gary Roberts took a penalty for interference at 19:01 and 14 seconds later referee Denis Morel gave Joe Nieuwendyk two minutes for charging, leaving Calgary two men short. The Flames survived this severe disadvantage through regulation and into overtime as the two teams played cautious hockey with each looking for the perfect shot to end the game.

At 17:37 the Flames seemed to get that per-fect shot when Doug Gilmour slipped the puck un-derneath Kings' goalie Kelly Hrudey's pad and just over the line. Although television replays sub-sequently showed that the puck had clearly crossed the line, referee Morel disallowed it. Despite Calgary's vehement protest, play was resumed and the first overtime period concluded with the score still tied at 3-3.

The controversial game—and the Flames' Stanley Cup reign—finally ended early in the sec-ond overtime period when Kings' winger Mike Krushelnyski blindly flipped the rebound of a shot by Duchesne at the Calgary net and scored for a 4-3 Los Angeles series-clinching victory.

For the second consecutive year, the Kings had eliminated the defending Cup champions in the first round. However the controversy over the Flames' disallowed goal eventually led to the in-stitution of a video replay judge at every NHL game beginning in the 1991-92 season. Mean-while the Kings went on to meet their traditional playoff rivals, the Edmonton Oilers, only to be outscored 24-10 in a four-game Oiler sweep.

The 1990-91 season, Gretzky's third in Los Angeles, finally saw the Kings emulate their leader's high standards as the club surpassed the 100-point plateau for just the second time in their history on a record of 46-24-10. The club's 46 wins broke the club's single-season mark of 43 set in 1980-81. Most important, for the first time in the Kings' 24 NHL seasons, they had finished in first place in their division.

With 163 points on 41 goals and 122 assists, Gretzky won his ninth Art Ross Trophy as the NHL's leading scorer—beating out Brett Hull of St. Louis by 32 points. Kelly Hrudey became the first regular (over twenty games) Kings' net-minder to finish a season with a goals-against average under 3.00 as he compiled a 26-13-6 record and had a career-best 2.90 average with three shutouts. Backup goalie Daniel Berthiaume, who had been acquired from Minnesota just before the start of training camp, was also a strong 20-11-4 with a 3.31 goals-against average.

For the first time since their disastrous first-round collapse to Toronto in three games in 1974, the Kings entered the playoffs as favorites to get out of their division. If successful, the Kings would face the Norris Division victor in the Campbell Conference finals (which had been won by the Smythe Division representative for nine consecutive years). As a Smythe team had also won six of the previous seven Stanley Cup titles, the odds of the Gretzky-led Kings bringing the Cup in Los Angeles in 1991 seemed quite realistic.

The Kings opened the 1991 playoffs against the Vancouver Canucks who had finished a distant 37 points behind them. Vancouver won the opening game in Los Angeles and looked as if they might take the second game as well, but the Kings staved off such a disaster with a 3-2 overtime victory. Vancouver then took another lead in the se-

ries with a 2-1 overtime win in game three before the Kings finally woke up and swept the next three, outscoring Vancouver 17-6, to move on to the division finals for the third year in a row.

As had happened to the Kings so many times in the past, however, the second round would again prove their limit. Although the Kings had finished the regular season 25 points ahead of the defending Stanley Cup champion Edmonton Oilers, that club again proved that it knew how to win in the playoffs. After the Kings won the opening game of the series 4-3 in overtime, the Oilers took four of the next five games. For the 24th year in a row there would not only be no Stanley Cup in Los Angeles. (Instead the big prize in 1991 went for the first time to Mario Lemieux's Pittsburgh Penguins.)

In an effort to surround Gretzky with some of the same key offensive talent that he worked with so successfully during his four Stanley Cup

AP/Wide World Photos

Barry Melrose

years in Edmonton, Vachon made a pair deals before and during the 1991-92 season to bring the Kings two of the most prolific scorers in the history of the game. On May 30, 1991, he acquired the rights to ex-Oiler right wing Jari Kurri, the number two all-time leading Stanley Cup goal scorer behind Gretzky, by way of a three-way trade with Edmonton and Philadelphia, giving up Steve Duchesne, Steve Kasper, and a fourth-round draft pick. (The Finnish-born Kurri had spent the 1990-91 season playing in Milan, Italy.)

Vachon's second deal came on February 19, 1992, in a three-way trade with Pittsburgh and Philadelphia that brought the Kings the NHL's all-time leading scorer among defensemen, Paul Coffey, from the Penguins where the former Oiler blueliner had just collected his fifth career Stanley Cup ring.

Despite the presence of these two former Oiler greats at Gretzky's side, however, the Kings dropped back to second place in 1991-92 behind the suddenly powerful Vancouver Canucks. For the seventh time in their last eight trips to the playoffs, the Kings again faced the Oilers. For the fifth time they came up short as Edmonton won the opening round series with relative ease, four games to two, to close out the Kings' first 25 years in the National Hockey League.

Following the 1991-92 season, Tom Webster was relieved after three years as head coach—during which the Kings had a record of 115-94-31. Although Webster's winning percentage of .544 was better than any coach in Kings' history, his recurring inner ear problems had forced Webster to miss a number of games behind the bench.

In addition, Webster had displeased his employers and the fans when he was suspended on several occasions by the league for incidents relating to the abuse of officials his hurling of a stick at referee Kerry Fraser during a Forum game in November of 1991. Rumors also circulated that Gretzky was still miffed about being benched by Webster and had influenced the firing.

Vachon also changed jobs in the off-season as he was named assistant to Kings' owner and Chairman Bruce McNall. He was replaced as general manager on June 25, 1992, by 45-year-old Nick Beverley, an 11-year veteran NHL defenseman who had worked in the Kings' organization since his retirement as a player in 1980. Prior to becoming the Kings' fifth general manager, Beverley had served the club as a minor-league head coach, NHL assistant coach, pro and amateur scout, player personnel director, and Kings' assistant general manager.

To replace Webster the Kings named 36-year-old Barry Melrose, a former WHA and NHL defenseman, as the club's 17th coach. Although Melrose only began his coaching career in 1987, he had already won playoff titles in junior hockey with the 1987-88 Memorial Cup champion Medicine Hat Tigers of the WHL, and in the pros the previous year as coach of the AHL Calder Cup champion Adirondack Red Wings. (Melrose, the second consecutive Kings coach with experience in the Red Wings's system, had been pegged to eventually replace Bryan Murray as Detroit coach, but team officials could not match Los Angeles' offer.)

The Kings' 26th NHL season proved to be one of unexpected highs and lows almost from the opening day of training camp. The team's first setback came just a few days into training camp when Wayne Gretzky made what he expected to be just a brief return to Los Angeles for the birth of his third child on September 14. Although the 31-year-old superstar had felt fine in the first few days of workouts, almost immediately after returning to Los Angeles, he began experiencing debilitating pains in his upper body and was soon hospitalized for tests.

After more than a week of uncertainty the answer finally came back—the Kings' captain had developed a highly unusual disc problem in his upper back which was inoperable and could only be treated by extended rest. Sudden there was a real possibility that the greatest player in the history of the game—who had only missed 39 games in 14 seasons— might never appear in another game.

Funny thing happened when the season got under way; instead of folding without Gretzky, the

Kings became a virtual juggernaut. By their 31st game on December 12, the club was atop the Smythe Division and at 20-8-3 carried the third best overall record in the league, behind only Pittsburgh and Montreal.

Veteran Kelly Hrudey and rookie Rob Stauber were providing the club with exceptional goaltending while Robitaille, Granato, Sandstrom, and an apparently rejuvenated Jari Kurri were scoring with abandon. The almost three months of rest did wonders for Gretzky as his pain subsided and he began to skate again, and by late December was practicing with the team with a hoped for return by mid-January. The Kings, however, suddenly became cold over their next 31 games, falling from first place to fifth with a 7-20-4 run despite Gretzky's return on January 6.

In an effort to shake up the slumping club, General Manager Nick Beverley traded away the second highest profile player on the team, Paul Coffey, to the Detroit Red Wings along with young journeymen forwards Jim Hiller and Syl-vain Couturier on January 29. In return the Kings got hard-nosed right wing Marc Potvin and former University of Wisconsin center Gary Shuchuck—both of whom had played on Melrose's Calder Cup team in Adirondack—and reacquired former Kings' 50-goal scorer Jimmy Carson who had been one of the key players in the Wayne Gretzky deal with Edmonton in 1988. (In March another former King veteran also returned as defenseman Mark Hardy was acquired from the New York Rangers for center John McIntyre.)

The Kings' low point of the 1992-93 season came on February 13, with a dreadful 10-3 home loss to the Washington Capitals that dropped them below .500 for the first time that season. Two nights later, however, the club rebounded with a 3-0 Kelly Hrudey shutout over the first place Vancouver Canucks which finally seemed to break their slump. The Kings went 15-10-3 over the season's final two months.

With a record of 39-35-10 at season's end, the Kings edged out the Winnipeg Jets by one point for third place in the Smythe Division. (Their old playoff nemesis, the Edmonton Oilers finished fifth and would miss the postseason for the first time in their history.)

The Kings met the second-place Calgary Flames in the first round of the playoffs, downing them four games to two. The Kings next took on their old coach, Pat Quinn and his powerful Vancouver Canucks, who had won the Smythe Division with 101 points and had manhandled Los Angeles during the regular season.

After splitting the first four games of the series, the clubs returned to the Pacific Coliseum on May 11 for game five. After almost four hours of furious hockey, Shuchuck scored at 6:31 of the second overtime to give the underdog Kings a 4-3 victory and a chance to advance beyond the second round in the playoffs for the first time with a victory in one of their next two games. As it turned out, the Kings needed just one of those chances to earn a 5-4 victory two nights later.

The Kings' opponent in the Campbell Conference Finals was the Toronto Maple Leafs. Under new coach Pat Burns and his assistant, former Kings' captain and head coach Mike Murphy, the Maple Leafs were a team that believed in itself and had finished the year with a club record 99 points.

With Doug Gilmour, Wendel Clark, Dave Andreychuk, and Glenn Anderson leading the way up front and super rookie Felix Potvin staring in goal, the Leafs first upset the powerful Detroit Red Wings in the Norris Division semifinals and then took another seven games to dispatch the plucky St. Louis Blues in an equally tense division final to earn the right to meet the upstart Kings.

The Kings split the first four games with Toronto with each club winning once on the opposition's ice. The fifth game was tied after 60 minutes. This time, however, it was the home team that potted the crucial overtime goal to take the series lead as Gretzky's old Edmonton teammate Glenn Anderson scored at 19:20 of overtime to beat the Kings, 3-2.

Then in Los Angeles two nights later, Toronto captain Wendel Clark tied the game at 4-4 with a clutch goal at 18:39 of regulation time with leaf goalie Felix Potvin pulled for an extra attacker. It took just 1:41 of overtime for the suspense to be ended, however, as Wayne Gretzky collected the 105th playoff goal of his NHL career to send the series back to Toronto for a seventh and deciding game. Gretzky exploded for three goals—his eighth career playoff hat trick—as the Kings edged Toronto 5-4 to earn their first berth in the Stanley Cup Finals. Their opponent was the 23-time champions, the Montreal Canadiens.

The Kings opened the finals with a 4-1 victory over the unbelieving Habs. It looked as if the Kings would go home with a commanding two-games-to-none series edge as they held a 2-1 lead in game two with less than two minutes to play. With just 1:45 left in regulation, however, the Montreal bench challenged the curve on King winger Marty McSorley's stick.

Upon measurement, it was found to be illegal by referee Kerry Fraser. It then took Montreal defenseman Eric Dejardins just 32 seconds to score on the power play to tie the game at 2-2. Then just 51 seconds into overtime, Dejardins—who had scored but five goals in 60 previous Stanley Cup games—completed his first hat trick to give the Habs a thrilling 3-2 comeback victory.

Montreal's goal on the "illegal stick" power play seemed to defeat the Kings; they never recovered. The Habs won both games in Los Angeles—again in overtime—with both game-winning goals being scored by utility winger John LeClair. The Canadiens then dominated on their home ice, holding the Kings to just 19 shots on Conn Smythe Trophy-winning goalie Patrick Roy.

After the game a disappointed Gretzky stunned the hockey world when he indicated that he might retire. The "Great One" finally announced that he would return to the Kings for the 1993-94 season. A few days later, however, his longtime teammate with both the Oilers and Kings, Marty McSorley, was traded back to the Pittsburgh Penguins. While Gretzky and the Kings fell just short of bringing the Stanley Cup to Los Angeles, top-flight hockey had finally arrived in town.

—*Bruce C. Cooper*

SAN JOSE SHARKS

Hockey found its way to San Jose by following a circular path not unlike a mode of attack favored by sharks. The story begins in the north part of San Francisco Bay, winds through Cleveland and Minneapolis, and circles back to the southern-most portion of San Francisco Bay. Near there lies the city of San Jose with its population of 782,248 according to the 1990 census, making it the 11th largest city in the United States. The market, then, is certainly large, but is there enough interest in San Jose and the Bay area to sustain a hockey franchise? Early results from this second try are resoundingly positive.

During the late 1980s, the city of San Jose went fishing for a major sports franchise. Among various incentives, the city promised to build a stadium to lure a professional baseball team (specifically, the San Francisco Giants) or an arena to house a basketball or hockey team. At about the same time the Minnesota North Stars hockey franchise was in financial trouble. North Stars' own-

ers George and Gordon Gund threatened to move the team unless attendance improved and unless substantial improvements were made to the team's home arena and its lease on the building. The NHL, however, had recently nullified attempts by the St. Louis Blues franchise to relocate to Saskatchewan for fear of losing a major market and were not about to be without a franchise in the hockey hotbed of Minnesota. (That was then, of course; the Minnesota North Stars eventually became the Dallas Stars in 1993.)

The Gunds sold the North Stars in 1990 for $38 million. Then, for $50 million they purchased a new NHL franchise to be located in San Jose and to begin play in the 1991-92 season. As part of the deal, the Gunds were allowed to take with them significant players from the North Stars' farm system--a controversial agreement that immediately depleted a team that surprisingly reached the Stanley Cup finals in 1991 before losing to the Pittsburgh Penguins.

The arrival of the San Jose Sharks franchise in the Bay area completes a circle. George Gund, based in San Francisco, became involved in hockey early in the 1970s as a minority owner of the California Golden Seals, located in Oakland. The franchise had struggled since entering the league for the 1968-69 season, when the NHL expanded from six to twelve teams.

George Gund and his brother, Gordon, eventually became majority owners, moved the franchise to Cleveland in 1976, and renamed the team the Barons. The Gund family is based in Cleveland, where they built a banking, brewing, and coffee empire worth over a billion dollars. After two lackluster seasons, the Cleveland Barons merged with the Minnesota North Stars, another hapless franchise, with the Gunds as owners. Later, of course, the Gunds sold the North Stars and completed the circle by bringing hockey back to the Bay area.

Observers wondered if the Gunds would have better luck with Californian hockey the second time around. After all, with their bright green and gold jerseys, cute logo, and white skates, the California Golden Seals immediately established an identity and were fairly strong on the ice for an

Bob Gaudreau (center) is presented the Leonard M. Fowle Award by Fowle (right)

TEAM INFORMATION AT A GLANCE

Founding date: May 9, 1990

Home ice: Cow Palace, 1991-93; San Jose Arena, 1993—

Address: 525 W. Santa Clara Street
San Jose, CA 95133
Phone: (408) 287-7070

Capacity: Cow Palace, 11,000; San Jose Arena, 18,000

Team colors: Pacific teal, gray, black, white
Team Nickname: Sharks
Logo: Shark biting a hockey stick in half

Franchise Record	Won	Lost	Tie
(1991-1993)	28	129	7

expansion team. However curious they looked and played, though, they failed to stir significant interest.

The Sharks started much stronger, inspiring a feeding frenzy for tickets and merchandise. The team sold 7,500 season tickets for their first two seasons at San Francisco's Cow Palace (capacity 11,000), their home until construction of a new arena in San Jose was complete. The team's logo, which features a shark gnashing a hockey stick, became a phenomenally hot-selling item on sportswear before the Sharks ever played a game.

The Sharks posted a 17-58-5 record during their first season, respectable for an expansion team. Pat Falloon, the team's first selection (second overall) in the 1991 amateur draft, made an immediate impact by scoring 25 goals. Though plagued by injuries, veterans Kelly Kisio (11 goals in 48 games) and David Bruce (22 goals in 60 games) made important contributions. Among the players formerly with the North Stars' organization, Rob Zettler was a steadying influence on defense.

More important, young prospects that moved from Minnesota's to San Jose's farm system gained experience with the Shark's top minor league affiliate, the Kansas City Blades, providing hope for the future—great hopes, considering the Blades won the International Hockey League (IHL) championship. Former Minnesota players fed to the Sharks include forwards Rob Gaudreau (23 years old in 1993) and Ed Courtenay (25), defensemen Tom Pederson (25) and Doug Zmolek (22), and goalie Arturs Irbe (26).

Hope was all the Sharks were left with following their disastrous 1992-93 season—the worst second season by any team in NHL history. The Sharks lost an NHL record 71 games, sported the league's worst home record (8-33-1), and endured a 17-game losing streak during the Christmas holiday season. The Sharks scored the second fewest goals in the league (208) and allowed the most (414). Pat Falloon missed half the season with injuries and scored only 14 goals.

Still, there were bright spots. Kisio, who had made a career of playing on third and fourth lines,

AP/Wide World Photos

Kevin Constantine

scored 26 goals, assisted on 52 others, and made the All-Star team. Linemate Johan Garpenlov tallied 22 goals, and Rob Gaudreau scored 23. Defenseman Sandis Ozolinsh was one of the brightest rookies in the league until suffering a knee injury that limited him to 41 games.

The Sharks' miserable on-ice performance was complemented by turmoil among their three-headed management team. Coach George Kingston was fired following the season. General Managers Dean Lombardi and Chuck Grillo took on more defined roles: Lombardi oversees day-to-day operations and Grillo is in charge of scouting and drafting.

Kevin Constantine, who coached the Kansas City Blades to the IHL championship in 1991-92 and into the playoffs in 1992-93, became the

Sharks' new coach before the 1993-94 season. At 34, Constantine is the youngest head coach in the history of the NHL. The Sharks should rise from the murky depths in 1993-94 since the NHL has added two more expansion teams—the Florida Panthers and the Anaheim Mighty Ducks; the Ducks should finish behind the Sharks in the Pacific Division.

The team made several trades and drafted or signed as free agents a host of European players. Jimmy Waite (24, acquired from Chicago), will battle Irbe for goaltending duties; Jeff Norton (27, New York Islanders), a rushing defenseman, will add offense to the defensive corps, while Gaeten Duchesne (31, Dallas), a defensive specialist, will add defense to the offense.

The Sharks also acquired Sergei Makarov (35) and signed free agent Igor Larionov (33), who spent three years with Vancouver before playing on a Swiss team in 1992-93. Makarov and Larionov, along with now-retired Vladimir Krutov, formed the famed K-L-M line for USSR teams that dominated international hockey during the 1980s.

In the 1993 amateur draft, the Sharks traded their first pick (second overall) to Hartford for the Whalers' first pick (sixth overall), Makarov, and two lower picks. The Sharks then selected Russian Viktor Kozlov (18, 6-5, 200 pounds), potentially forming a new K-L-M line. Indeed, Kozlov idolized the original alphabet-run threesome while growing up; Makarov was his favorite player.

The Sharks have invested heavily in European talent, drafting 20 non-North American players, including 13 of their top 15 picks, from 1991 to 93. Their East European contingent includes Czechs Jan Calhoun (31), Jaroslav Otevrel (25), and Michael Sykora (20); Latvians Ozolinsh and Irbe; and Russians Alex Cherbayez (20), Mikhail Kravets (30), and Andrei Nazarov (19, 6-4, 230 pounds)—the second of two first round selections (10th overall) in the 1992 amateur draft—to go along with K, L, and M. These comrades and young talents such as Falloon, Gaudrea, Zmolek, and Mark Rathje (19, 6-5, 200 pounds), the team's first pick in the 1992 amateur draft (3rd overall) form a group of players whose success is as difficult to predict as they are to interview.

With strong season ticket sales, enhanced attendance at the team's brand new, 18,000 seat San Jose Arena, a more focused management group, and a commitment by the team and community to support one another through growing pains and language barriers, the Sharks have potential for moving up in the standings.

VANCOUVER CANUCKS

When the National Hockey League finally reached British Columbia in 1970-1971, elated Western Canadian fans could hardly have know what they were in for. The debut of the Vancouver Canucks franchise finally established the NHL on the Canadian West Coast, creating a coast-to-coast presence in Canada, where hockey had long been a television staple. The opening of the franchise, however, also ushered in 20 years of sometimes frustrating hockey as the club struggled to shake off a post-season jinx that lasted 11 seasons before the 1981-82 year turned unexpectedly golden.

Vancouver reached the Stanley Cup final in that wonderful spring as the Pacific Coliseum rocked to full houses of white-towel waving fans, but the New York Islanders, in the midst of their domination of the sport, swept four straight games to put the would-be Cinderellas to bed early.

That remarkable April and May didn't signal a string of success for the Canucks, however. It would be another 10 years before Vancouver sur-

vived a first round playoff series, but the arrival of two great youngsters, Trevor Linden and Pavel Bure, redirected the franchise's fortunes in recent seasons. Two Smythe Division championships, if not another run to the Stanley Cup finals, have served as the reward for a patient rebuilding process.

Hockey Goes West

On May 22, 1970, the National Hockey League awarded a franchise to the Vancouver Canucks. That was three years after the NHL had created its first expansion division, one that included two California teams, but not a British Columbia franchise. That decision rankled Western Canadians who had long supported the popular Canadian Broadcasting Corporation's Hockey Night in Canada telecasts, so the eventual award of the franchise to the country's third-largest city came as no surprise. The fact that 12,000 season tickets were sold for the inaugural season was not only proof of British Columbia's interest in hockey but the basis of a support which would stick with the team in the early years.

Getting a team was no guarantee of success, however, a fact that Canucks' fans would soon discover. They would endure four difficult seasons without seeing playoff hockey, watching a team that proved unable to collect 60 points in a season. The early years saw two 24-win seasons (1970-71 and 1973-74), but the losses hit 50 in the second campaign and were never lower than 43. Life was hard in a league where the established teams had a long head start. Moreover, the available talent pool had thinned noticeably because of emerging competition from the newly-created World Hockey Association.

Still, the first four seasons had some pleasant memories. The opening year, for instance, proved to be a bit misleading to the home crowds, because the Canucks started that 1970-71 season 10-3-2 in the Pacific Coliseum, a pace they could not sustain. Frustration was more often the byword: on February 25, 1971, the Canucks gave up three goals to the Boston Bruins in an NHL record 20 seconds; after 85 games without being blanked, Vancouver was shut out in successive games on Oct. 20-22, 1971; and when the Canucks finally recorded a shutout of their own, goalie Dunc Wilson stopping 34 Toronto Maple Leaf shots, Vancouver still didn't win the game. The Leafs' Bernie Parent returned the shutout favor, making 20 saves in the 0-0 game, still the only scoreless tie in Canucks' history.

Kurtenbach and Quinn From Day One

Gary Doak, from Boston, was a "name" selected by Vancouver in the NHL expansion draft, having played with the Bruins' Stanley Cup winners, while veteran Orland Kurtenbach, Pat Quinn, and Rosaire Paiement were also selected back on June 10, 1970. While Doak did not achieve laurels with his new club, Kurtenbach was the team's first captain, played the first four seasons, and collected the fans' first three Most Valuable Player Awards. He eventually took a turn at coaching.

Quinn, another original Canuck, would later return to build the team into a Smythe Division power at the start of the 1990s, while Paiement would become the first Canuck to score four goals in a game, achieving the feat against Buffalo on February 9, 1971.

Seven days later, Paiement enjoyed a five-point game in a 5-4 victory over the defending Stanley Cup champion Boston Bruins, a night that saw both Paiement and Andre Boud-rias become the Canucks' first 20-goal scorers.

In the NHL entry draft of amateur players, the Canucks picked second behind the other new club, Buffalo. The Sabres chose Gilbert Perreault while Vancouver selected Dale Tallon. Both went on to fine NHL careers, although one can only wonder what might have been had the coin flip favored the Canucks.

1982 Wasn't The First Final

The Vancouver Canucks have only appeared in one Stanley Cup final, their 1982 match against the New York Islanders. The city, however, had played host to the finals in 1923, although not many fans of the modern club remembered that the old Vancouver Maroons, Ottawa Senators, and Edmonton Eskimos had played for the coveted Cup in British Columbia.

All of the games were played in Vancouver, as Ottawa won the Stanley Cup with a team that included the fabled King Clancy. The host Maroons were beaten three games to one by Ottawa, who then took the Cup by winning two further games from the Edmonton Eskimos. Before that, the Vancouver Millionaires of 1914-15 had won the Stanley Cup by sweeping Ottawa in a three-game series played in British Columbia.

TEAM INFORMATION AT A GLANCE

Founding date: May 22, 1970

Home ice: Pacific Coliseum
100 North Renfrew St.
Vancouver, British Columbia, Canada V5K 3N7
Phone: (604) 254-5141
FAX: (604) 251-5123

Capacity: 16,123

Team colors: White, black, red, and gold
Team nickname: Canucks
Logo: Representation of a hockey skate with word "Canucks" making up blade.

Franchise record	Won	Lost	Tie
(1970-93)	654	910	272

Perreault, of course, was an offensive dynamo during his Sabres career, while Tallon, an NHL All-Star in his first season, was a quality defenseman ultimately traded to Chicago for goaltender Gary Smith and Jerry Korab three years later. Doak, too, was part of a trade, moving from Vancouver to the New York Rangers in a November 16, 1971, deal.

The early seasons also were notable for a turnover of coaches as the Canucks scrambled to find a winning formula. Hal Laycoe was behind the bench in the first two seasons, followed by Vic Stasiuk, who took charge in 1972-73. Bill McCreary and Phil Maloney were on duty in 1973-74 before Maloney finally established himself with the club's first winning season in 1974-75.

It's Hard to Catch Up

Getting started, especially for a team on the opposite coast from most of the rest of the league, was not easy. Gerald Eskenazi, in *A Thinking Man's Guide to Pro Hockey* recalls that first season when the Canucks "had to travel more than 65,000 miles—compared to 25,000 for the eastern teams. The Canucks would have stretches of seven games in 11 days. Their closest competitors, the California Golden Seals, were more than a thousand miles away in Oakland."

Eskenazi sympathizes with Laycoe, a former NHL player in the pre-expansion days, who was forced to create not only a team, but "whip them into a unit that could live out of suitcases and exist in hotels."

Not surprisingly, it didn't work, although the Canucks did not finish last in the Eastern Division. They were placed there along with newcomers Buffalo in defiance of geography as the NHL took steps to reorganize its divisions, and the presence of a weak Detroit Red Wings team enabled the 24-46-8 team to finish sixth out of seven, a point ahead of the Wings. The successful debut of

Tallon on defense, coupled with the fact that the attack had some balance, if not superstars, were positive signs.

But Laycoe put the situation in perspective in *A Thinking Man's Guide to Hockey*, relating an incident wherein Eskenazi recalled a game when the Canucks were outshot 52-16 and the coach admitted, "Isn't it a hell of a note on expansion when you have to compliment your players on a beating like that?"

There was a "Philosophy"

None of the rigors of the first year were unexpected by hockey veterans. Canucks general manager Normand "Bud" Poile, in fact, took many of the tribulations in stride. He had previously led another expansion team, the Philadelphia Flyers, so had some idea what he was getting into, although as Eskenazi reports, his philosophy was a combination of tongue-in-cheek humor and a reliance on veterans.

"A guy's got be crazy to start an expansion team twice. You need a good wife and it helps to be nuts," he said. But he also had a plan that relied on players like Kurtenbach, a well-traveled, but well-respected, centerman. "I needed a nucleus," Poile said. "I looked at the other clubs in expansion that had made a lot of changes and didn't improve themselves."

Kurtenbach eventually did just what Poile expected, providing solid leadership, but he was injured midway through the first season at a time when the Canucks were still holding their own. Without him, the club tumbled. Kurtenbach eventually played 52 games in the initial season and performed at a point-a-game pace (21 goals and 32 assists) that emphasized the impact of his absence.

The club's second season was not an improvement, although Kurtenbach and Boudrias shared the team scoring lead and Wilson arrived as a solid goaltender. There simply weren't enough pieces in place to compete in a league where Boston still had Bobby Orr, the Canadiens could turn

to a parade of talent, and Chicago had the Hull brothers, Stan Mikita, and goaltender Tony Esposito. Vancouver struggled home at 20-50-8, finishing last in the Eastern Division.

Vic Stasiuk took the coaching reins in 1972-73 but had no magic wand. Jocelyn Guevremont, a highly-touted defenseman who had been selected as a member of Team Canada in the famous first hockey showdown against the Soviet Union, and Tallon were still present on the backline, but both players saw their point totals drop from the year before.

Right wing Bobby Schmautz led the team in goals (38) and points (71) but only four players managed 20 or more goals. Wilson saw his goals-against average inflate to 3.94, and his back-ups all conceded goals at better than a 4.50 rate. The team finished 22-47-9, ahead only of the latest expansion entry, the New York Islanders.

McCreary and Maloney shared the reins in 1973-74 when the Canucks again finished ahead of only the Islanders. Gary Smith had arrived to play goal, however, as a result of a trade to Chicago in which Vancouver surrendered Tallon, and right winger Dennis Ververgaert made his Vancouver debut with a 57-point season. Despite finishing 24-43-11, the organization pointed to these performances as positive signs.

Suddenly, Success

Perhaps because of the long time building, Vancouver's Smythe Division championship was all that much sweeter. Maloney, the fourth head coach in the club's five-year history, guided the team to a 38-32-10 season and into the playoffs for the first time ever. In fact, the team's 86 points would prove to be the most a Vancouver team would amass until the 1991-92 campaign.

That year was marked by a number of notable achievements. Andre Boudrias became the club's first career 100-goal scorer when he nailed the game winner in a November triumph against the New York Rangers; netminder Smith became the first Canuck ever voted to the NHL All Star team and played half of the game in the Montreal Forum backing up starter Bernie Parent; and Ken Lockett set a club record that still stands when he registered back-to-back shutouts.

Smith played the lion's share of the games in goal, compiling a 32-24-9 overall record and a 3.09 goals-against average as the Canucks edged St. Louis by two points in the race for the Smythe Division championship. Chicago, in third place, was just two points behind St. Louis, a measure of the battle Maloney's team had to win.

Boudrias led the team in scoring, as he dished out 62 assists as part of a strong season. The assists, coupled with his 16 goals, gave Boudrias 10 more points than Don Lever, whose 38 goals topped the Vancouver scorers.

A major reason why Vancouver had just enough firepower to secure the division title was the addition of John Gould, a right wing who had been acquired from Buffalo in December 1973. Although Gould's 9-year NHL career saw him score 131 goals, his next two seasons in the Canucks' colors were by far his best. In 1974-75 he potted 34 goals, his personal career high, following up with 32 the next campaign. His 65 points placed him third on the first Vancouver team to finish above the .500 mark.

There was another factor in the Vancouver triumph that deserves mention: the Canucks power play functioned at the 20.8 per cent level, second best in the Smythe Division, while their penalty killers were the best in the five-team circuit.

Montreal Proves No Reward

The euphoria of a Smythe Division title didn't last long, however. After a first round Stanley Cup bye, the Canucks found themselves matched against Montreal in the fabled Forum in a best-of-seven series. Despite Garry Monahan's winning goal in the second contest in Montreal, a 2-1 Vancouver victory, the Canucks ultimately could not contain the Canadiens' great Guy Lafleur. He collected three game-winning goals in the series, including one at 17:06 of overtime of the fifth

game as Montreal clinched a 4-1 series win to end the glorious Vancouver season.

There was certainly no disgrace in the loss. Lafleur had become a 50-goal scorer for the Canadiens in that season, achieving a then-rare milestone, and the veteran hockey fans in Vancouver knew all about the legendary Montreal franchise. After all, they had been reared on televised hockey, which featured Montreal and Toronto long before the NHL ever thought of growing beyond its six-team base.

Goaltender Smith collected the official club MVP and was also the fans' most valuable selection that season. Bob Dailey, a 6-foot, 5-inch, 220 pound defenseman, collected the Babe Pratt Award, the fans' recognition of their top backliner. Dailey's 48 points (12 goals and 36 assists) were the most he would collect in four seasons at Vancouver, although he contributed 15 goals in the ensuing season.

Dailey was partnered by three players who had been acquired in significant trades. On October 14, 1974, Vancouver had acquired Gerry Meehan and Mike Robitaille from Buffalo in a trade that sent Guevremont and Bryan McSheffery to the Sabres. Then, a month later, the Canucks added Ab DeMarco in a trade with Pittsburgh. Robitaille went on to lead the defensemen in the important plus-minus category.

There's an Encore, of Sorts

Vancouver wasn't able to build on that 1974-75 campaign, although Maloney led the club to a second-place Smythe Division finish a year later, when the team finished 33-32-15 to record consecutive winning seasons, a feat which would not be equalled again until the 1990s. This time the Canucks fell a point short of Chicago in another race to the wire. They built a nine-point cushion over third place St. Louis, however, and had every reason to think that a corner had been turned.

Smith again had a good season in goal, his 3.50 goals-against average belied by his 20-24-6 overall record. Lockett played more than he had the year before, finishing 7-8-7 with a 3.47 goals-against record. The team goal-scoring was balanced, with five players collecting 20 or more. Right winger Ververgaert led the way with 71 points, including 37 goals, and was selected to represent the Canucks in the NHL All-Star Game. There he set a record with a pair of goals just 10 seconds apart in the game played in Philadelphia's Spectrum.

Gould had a second successive strong season with his 32 goals in 70 games while Lever (25 goals and 40 assists for 65 points) and center Chris Oddleifson (16-46-62) both chipped in with important contributions. Oddleifson also scored two short-handed goals in a 5-5 tie against Toronto, becoming the first Canuck to achieve that feat. There was immediate playoff disappointment, however, when the Canucks were bounced right out of the playoffs in two straight games by the New York Islanders.

Disappointment, Then All-Star Hosts

In each of the next two seasons, the team failed to qualify for the playoffs, but there were a couple of major compensations.

On January 25, 1977, the National Hockey League All-Star Game was played in the Pacific Coliseum with popular Canuck Harold Snepsts representing the home team. And, in one of those sometimes overlooked trades that pop up around the time of the NHL draft, the Canucks acquired the rights to Thomas Gradin in a deal with the Chicago Blackhawks. Gradin would ultimately prove to be one of the foundation stones of a resurgent Vancouver club, assuming the organization's career scoring lead by January 4, 1984, when he passed the team's first major star, Lever, with 408 points in a Canucks' uniform.

The acquisition of Gradin was by no means a straightforward decision. The NHL lagged behind the rival WHA in the introduction of foreign players, as several hockey critics were outspoken in their view that players from Scandinavia, used

to the wider rinks and less physical European style of play, would not be able to stand up to the 80-game pounding (and playoffs) that awaited each NHL player. Born in Solleftea, Sweden, Gradin was one of several imports who would prove the critics dead wrong.

Gradin made his NHL debut at the age of 22 in the 1978-79 season and scored 20 goals, a figure he would surpass in each of the next four seasons. In the 1981-82 campaign he logged 37 goals and 49 assists in 76 games. Gradin missed only nine games in his first five years at Vancouver, proof positive that the foreign-trained players could tolerate NHL-style hockey very well.

In 1976-77 the Canucks were fourth in the Smythe Division, but so close was the race that they were just two points out of second place. While St. Louis secured first place with 73 points in a division where none of the five teams posted winning records, Minnesota finished on 64, Chicago and the Canucks on 63. Chicago won one more game than Vancouver to finish in third and get the last available playoff spot.

There was a noticeable drop in offense as no Canuck reached the 30-goal level and a trade of goaltenders, a straight swap with Minnesota that sent Cesare Maniago to Vancouver in exchange for Smith, didn't work magic. Maniago, 17-21-9 with a 3.36 goals-against average, still had a better season than did Smith in Minnesota (10-17-8, 3.99).

In an effort to shake things up, other fixtures of the club just three years before were traded. Gould was sent to Atlanta in December and Dailey was moved to Philadelphia in January. Robitaille played in only 40 games in his last season.

On the plus side, Snepsts, who would go on to become of the leading figures in the 1981-82 team and a tremendously popular player, had made his debut in 1975-76 in steady, if unspectacular fashion by leading the defensemen in plus-minus. He repeated as plus-minus defensive leader in 1976-77 as he established himself as a regular who could be counted upon.

The following year was once again not a banner season for Vancouver. Chicago won the

Smythe Division by a whopping 24 points over second-place Colorado. The Canucks were third, two back, but the team's overall figures were unimpressive. Winning just 20 games, the team allowed 320 goals, a figure exceeded by only four other teams. It was clearly time for a change of direction.

Harry Neale Takes Over

The next three seasons were alike in one sense: Vancouver never posted a winning record and lost in the first round of the playoffs each year. But there was a significant change in the makeup of the team. Harry Neale took over as coach in 1978-79 to work with general manager Jake Milford. Together the pair retooled the franchise to such an extent that the 1982 Stanley Cup finals appearance was the result.

There were some significant trades, especially the February 8, 1980, deal when the popular Lever was dealt to Atlanta as Vancouver acquired Darcy Rota and Ivan Boldirev. Rota, a left winger, collected an even 100 goals in the next three-plus seasons at Vancouver and added some muscle as well. The 5-foot, 11-inch, 180-lb. left winger topped the 100-minute mark in penalties twice. Boldirev was a well-traveled native of Zranjanin, Yugoslavia, who played with Boston, California, Chicago, and the Flames before moving to Vancouver.

Another left-sided shooter, Boldirev was a six-foot centerman who usually flirted with the 70-point mark every season. He always seemed to produce goals, and his presence immediately helped in that department. He scored 16 times in 27 games after the February trade and went on to add 59 more in the next two seasons.

Then, just 10 days later, the Canucks traded Rick Vaive to Toronto for the irrepressible David (Tiger) Williams, a player whose physical presence was legendary around the league. Vaive had joined the Canucks after the NHL-WHA merger, his rights acquired from Birmingham, where he had picked up 26 goals and 59 points as a 19-year

old prospect. He had collected 13 goals in 17 games for the Canucks in his debut season when Milford swung the deal for Williams, then a 25-year old noted more for penalty minutes than goals. In fact, Williams racked up 338 minutes in the sin bin in 1976-77 with Toronto, adding 298 more two years later, both NHL-leading totals. It was a tradition he continued in Vancouver, where he served 343 minutes in his first full season and 341 in the Stanley Cup final year, but there was another facet to Tiger's game that opponents ignored to their peril. He could score goals, getting eight in just 23 games in his 1980 debut in Vancouver, followed up with 35 the next season and 17 in the 1981-82 campaign. His competitiveness was unquestioned around the circuit.

On Oct. 6, 1980, Milford swung the deal that filled the last piece of the puzzle for the eventual finalists, acquiring goaltender Richard Brodeur in a exchange of draft picks with the New York Islanders. Then 28, Brodeur was already a veteran professional netminder, but he had spent the first seven of his seasons with Quebec in the World Hockey Association. On a team that often featured a wide-open attack, Brodeur was a steady, often spectacular goalie.

After his first season of 24 games, when he conceded goals at a 4.75 per game rate, he grew considerably more stingy. In his last full WHA season he had gone 25-12-2 with a 3.11 goals-against average when plucked by the New York Islanders as a consequence of the NHL merger agreement, which allowed the veteran league's teams to reclaim their rights to WHA players.

Brodeur, however, whose rights were owned by the Islanders, was going to a team that was putting together a Stanley Cup juggernaut. He played just twice for the Islanders, who already owned the imposing goaltending duo of Glenn (Chico) Resch and future Hall of Famer Billy Smith. There was no way past that blockade to a starting job, so Brodeur was rested and ready when snapped up by Vancouver.

In his first season with Vancouver Brodeur played 52 games and recorded a 3.51 goals-against average. The next year, the season when Vancouver nearly grabbed the golden slipper, he was 3.35 in the same number of starts. His playoff figures were even better as he posted an 11-6-0 record and 2.70 goals-against average against some of the best snipers in the sport.

Stan Smyl, Mr. Canuck

Captain for eight seasons (1982-1990), a gritty, hard-working winger who could both score goals and play the defensive, physical game that coaches love, Stan Smyl came to epitomize the heart and competitiveness of the Canucks. When he retired on July 3, 1991, to become an assistant coach, he held the club records for games played (896), goals (262), assists (411) and points (673). His No. 12 jersey was retired the following November, making him the first Canuck so-honored by the club.

Statistics don't tell everything about Smyl's 13-season career in Vancouver, however. His leadership was as important as his stats, a fact reflected in some additional honors: he was honored as team MVP three times, the same number of times that the fans voted him their similar honor. And, while he twice led the club in scoring (1979-80, 1982-83) his checking and his passing were as equally as important to the club.

It Still Takes Time

Patience was required as the rebuilding took place, however. The seasons in Neale's first three seasons behind the bench were noteworthy for regular season improvement, but the playoff jinx persisted; the Canucks had still never won a post-season series by the end of 1980-81.

Lever, however, had set a club record of 437 consecutive games before—ironically—breaking his cheekbone in the game that established the mark, and Stan Smyl, en route to establishing himself as Mr. Canuck, had a remarkable 1979-80 campaign, a season in which he led the team in goals, assists, points and penalty minutes in the same campaign.

In 1978-79, Vancouver finished second behind Chicago in the Smythe Division, still the weakest of the NHL's four circuits. The Blackhawks won the title despite finishing below .500 and the Canucks' record of 25-42-13 was only marginally better than the year before. Ron Sedlbauer, who would be traded to Chicago in the next season, led the attack with 40 goals, but it was the appearance of players like the rookie Gradin, Smyl, and a better overall balance that was encouraging.

In the playoffs, Neale's team threatened to create a real shock when they upset Philadelphia 3-2 in the opening game at the Spectrum. The Canucks couldn't close the door at home, though, losing 6-4. The final game was a 7-2 Philadelphia rout.

The improved regular season performance continued in 1979-80 as the Canucks went 27-37-16. Glen Hanlon was the bulwark in goal that season, playing 46 of the games and limiting opponents to 3.47 goals against, while Gradin's 75-point season was another step up for the Swede. Smyl, leading the team in plus-minus and in scoring, was the club's MVP, while Hanlon collected the Molson Cup, awarded on the basis of three-star selections after each game.

Chicago and St. Louis also improved their performances, however, so the Canucks actually slipped back to third in the Smythe Division and wound up matched against Buffalo in the first round of the Stanley Cup. Although the Canucks won at home after losing the first two games of the best-of-five series, the Sabres closed them out in the fourth game at the Pacific Coliseum.

In the 1980-81 regular season Vancouver finished 28-32-20, but St. Louis zoomed away from the whole of the NHL that season to finish twenty-nine points ahead of Chicago in the Smythe; the Canucks' 76 points left them 31 points behind of the Blues. It was little reward for the rebuilding that was clearly taking the team closer to a contending position.

In Brodeur's first season in the nets the team produced eight 20-goal scorers, with Williams the unexpected leader with 35 goals. Gradin slumped back to 21 goals, but added 48 assists to finish as Vancouver's overall scoring leader.

Better, But Not Title Stuff

There was no reason to suspect in March 1982 what life would be like in Vancouver in the following May. Neale had the team headed toward a 30-33-17 finish that would be good enough for second place in the Smythe Division, but the team's performance was hardly head-turning stuff. Both Williams and defenseman Kevin McCarthy had been voted to the All-Star team the year before while Snepsts and Smyl continued to establish records for both proficiency and longevity.

Ivan Hlinka, a Czech rookie, was a major addition to the team, his 60-point (23 goals and 37 assists) performance a record for a first year player that would later be tied by the Russian Pavel Bure. The rest of the cast was well-known. There was good goal-scoring balance, led by Gradin's 37, but players like Smyl (34 goals), Boldirev (33) and winger Cam Fraser (28) upped their ante. In goal, Bordeur went 20-18-12 (3.35 goals against) and Hanlon, sharing the duty, was 8-14-5 (3.95) until traded late in the season to St. Louis.

Snepsts was voted best defenseman by the fans, Doug Halward, another backliner, claimed the Unsung Hero award, and Gradin picked up the most exciting player trophy. Brodeur was the choice as MVP by both club and fans.

Still, those efforts didn't add up to a Smythe Division championship or anything really that close. When the books were closed on the regular

---

The Uniforms: Wild and Controversial

It is impossible to think of the Vancouver Canucks without thinking of the black-red-and-orange jerseys that attracted comment, both positive and negative, across the NHL in the 1980s. Featuring a somewhat abstract V on the front, the uniforms were starkly different from what the rest of the clubs wore. Traditionalists, somewhat like the early critics of change in baseball attire, scoffed when the sweaters first appeared; later they came to be collector's items among fans who found them delightfully different.

season, there was Edmonton atop the Smythe with 111 points, everybody's choice to sail through the playoffs. Vancouver finished second, 34 points behind with a 30-33-17 record, just two points ahead of Calgary. The Los Angeles Kings, despite winning only 24 games and finishing fourth, were in the playoffs thanks to the NHL's practice of sending four teams from each division into the Stanley Cup fray.

Not many people in Vancouver would have bet the farm that their team would play in the Stanley Cup finals that year. Yet it happened; explaining why is a bit harder.

Worth the Wait

Perhaps it all changed on March 20, 1982, in Quebec City, one of those games that sometimes spice an NHL season. After an altercation that eventually involved the crowd, both Neale and Halward were handed suspensions by the league. Neale was banned for 10 games, Halward for seven, and Roger Neilson took over behind the bench for the suspended mentor. Things were never quite the same in Vancouver the rest of the year.

Neilson, a studious type whose passion for the finer points of hockey extended to an unending study of the game, earned the nickname Captain Video for the hours he spent dissecting his team's and the opposition's techniques. If he wasn't the most demonstrative behind the bench—in fact his style stood in stark contrast to the ebullient Neale—he managed to get his points across to a team that was looking for a pattern that could translate the undoubted regular season improvement into postseason success.

It happened just that way. Neilson's concentration on defense fitted the style of a team that had hard-working forwards, including Smyl, Williams, and Rota, who weren't afraid to check. The Canucks also had big, strong defensemen who were adept at the "stay at home" game that Neilson advocated.

And behind all of it stood Richard Brodeur, about to have one of those playoff series that every opponent dreads. Brodeur emerged in the playoffs as a "hot" goalie, the kind who wins Stanley Cups. Followers of the game eventually called him "King Richard."

Williams scored a goal 14:20 into overtime to give the Canucks their first overtime win in Stanley Cup history, a 2-1 decision at home, as Vancouver swept Calgary 3-0 in the first round, with Brodeur showing the form that would carry right through the four rounds. He compiled a 1.55 goals-against average in the first-round series, beaten only five times while facing 108 shots.

Next came a 4-1 series win over the Los Angeles Kings, who had stunned the favored Oilers in the first round, a series marked by wild scoring games that included a 10-8 Los Angeles decision on Edmonton ice. Vancouver's defensive style put the clamps on the Kings, but the first four games were all nail-biting, one-goal-margin affairs. Vancouver won three of them, one in overtime, then finished the Kings off in the Pacific Coliseum by a 5-2 score. The team that had never won a playoff series was now in the Campbell Conference finals.

Surely their luck would run out against a Chicago team that had been riding a similar postseason wave, but the experts didn't read the momentum correctly. The Chicago Stadium was a raucous place when the series opened April 27, but the game that might have held the key to a grinding series turned out to be tight, tense and long. When Jim Nill—acquired in the trade that sent Hanlon to St. Louis—scored after 28:58 of overtime the Canucks had a vital 2-1 victory and the inside track in a series that defied the odds.

Chicago came back to win the second game, a match that contained an incident that sparked Vancouver's fans. Neilson, Williams, and Gerry Minor were ejected from that game when they waved white towels at the referee after a penalty call that led to a Blackhawks' goal by Denis Savard. When the series went west, those towels became a symbol of Vancouver's defiance.

Vancouver won twice in Pacific Coliseum, where the fans were suddenly loud, perhaps inspired by the antics they had seen displayed on television in the venerable old Chicago Stadium. Traditionally staid and hockey-wise, the Vancouver public was now completely sold on Neilson's miracle crew. The final game in Chicago was a 6-2 Vancouver romp. Two days after the heavily-favored New York Islanders had swept Quebec, the Islanders, reigning as lords of all hockey, learned that their opponent in the final would be a most unexpected crew.

By now the Pacific Coliseum had become a sea of white, with fans waving "victory" towels to exhort their heroes, but the final series opened on Long Island. Vancouver needed one more miracle, at least a win on enemy ice, to have a chance to take the story to its conclusion. The fact that their own home building had been long-ago booked for a Western show, meaning that there would be three days between games in British Columbia when the series finally reached the Pacific Coast, was testimony to the past history of a team that simply wasn't expected to be playing in May.

For almost 80 minutes the Canucks' dream lived on against the potent Islanders, who were on the way to their third of four consecutive Stanley Cups. In the first period, Gradin scored after just 1:29, then again at 17:40. In between the Islanders had gotten two of their own, so when Denis Potvin scored with nine seconds left in the first period the knowing wags in the press box at the Nassau Coliseum acknowledged that it was just a matter of time. They weren't convinced that Neilson had transformed the Canucks from pretenders to contenders, but the experts were almost fooled.

Smyl and Boldirev wiped out a Potvin second period goal so it was 4-4 after 40 minutes, then Nill put Vancouver ahead just 3:06 into the third and final period. For the next 12 minutes Islander fans agonized. Chances came and were wasted until Mike Bossy converted passes from John Tonelli and Bryan Trottier to tie the game at 15:14. The contest went into overtime.

The Unkindest Cut of All

That overtime not only sealed the season for Vancouver, it probably anointed the Islanders. As they so often did, the defending champions found a way to win. With the game apparently headed for a second extra period a wayward clearing pass from the tired Snepsts, a giant all night long, allowed Bossy to snap a winning shot past Brodeur with just two seconds remaining in the first over-

Canucks Captains

Orland Kurtenbach, 1970-71 to 1973-74
1974-75, no captain named
Andre Boudrias, 1975-76
Chris Oddleifson, 1976-77
Don Lever, 1977-78
Don Lever, Kevin McCarthy, 1978-79
Kevin McCarthy, 1979-80 to 1981-82
Stan Smyl, 1982-83 to 1989-90
Dan Quinn, Doug Lidster and Trevor Linden, 1990-91
Trevor Linden, 1991--

time period. That goal deflated the bubble; with Billy Smith starring in goal and the Islanders' balance all-too-evident against the gritty Canucks' all-out effort, New York swept the next three games.

Vancouver put up a brave fight in game two, losing 6-4, but their effort was spent. When the series went west, Smith recorded a shutout in game three as New York won, 3-0. Smith was almost as good in the final, winning 3-1, the only Canuck goal coming off the stick of Smyl late in the first period.

No one had expected the Canucks to be in the final so the post-series rhetoric was as expected. The winners praised the losers for their effort; Vancouver fans acknowledged the Islanders' superiority. Beneath it all, however, was the undercurrent; Vancouver had tasted success in hockey and wanted more.

Stars Shine, No More Miracles

Neilson stayed on as coach for 1982-83, Neale stepping up to the general manager's office with Milford's retirement. The momentum from the previous season, however, was lost. Despite club record-setting seasons from Smyl and Rota, who established marks for right and left-wings respectively, the 1982-83 team finished third in the Smythe Division and lost once more in the opening round of the playoffs. The magic couldn't be bottled and stored. Smyl's 88 points set a then-club record for scoring, although it would be surpassed a year later by Patrik Sundstrom.

An overall record of 30-35-15 was disappointing in the wake of an appearance in the finals, but that was only part of the problem. Edmonton, fueled now by the routinely terrific Wayne Gretzky, simply blew apart the division, finishing with 106 points, 36 more than the third-place Canucks. Gretzky scored 196 points and three other Oilers topped 100 that season. Such exploits made it hard to get too excited about the marks of Smyl and Rota, mere mortals in an era when the superstars were writing the script.

Such comparisons were unfair, however. Rota led the NHL in shooting percentage, his 42 goals coming on just 103 shots. Smyl was at the top of his game as well, while Gradin's 86-point (32 goals, 54 assists) season would do honor to anyone. Brodeur turned in a 21-26-8 season that saw him yield 3.79 goals per game.

The obvious problem was seen on the plus-minus stats sheet, however, where all but Rota finished in negative numbers. Somewhere between the epiphany of spring and the reality of the next fall, Captain Video's lessons had been lost. The defensively tight Canucks of the Stanley Cup playoffs gave up 309 in the following campaign. The oddity was that the figure was still best in the run-and-gun Smythe. The problem was that the Canucks' offensive output of 303 was last in the circuit, 121 behind the number posted by those flying Oilers.

When the playoffs began there was no repeat of the previous season. Calgary needed 12:27 of overtime to win the first game of their best-of-five series but triumphed, 4-3. They lost only once, at the Pacific Coliseum, before wrapping up a 3-1 series success over the Canucks with an overtime victory in game four.

The Neilson Era Ends

That 1983-84 team not only had Sundstrom's 91-point campaign but also a 45-goal outburst from Tony Tanti, who became the fastest player in Canuck history to score 20 goals, needing just 21 games to achieve the mark at the season's start. Gradin scored his 400th point during the 1983-84 season, and Sundstrom set a club record with a seven-point game against Pittsburgh. There was no greater reward, however, than another third place finish with a 32-39-9 overall record and first-round playoff elimination, capping a year that promised more than it ultimately delivered.

By the end of that season Neale had replaced Neilson behind the bench. Neale didn't complete the 1984-85 campaign, though, as the Canucks slumped to 25-46-9 and a last-place finish in the Smythe. Bill Laforge finished the year with Tom Watt named to take over in 1985-86.

The season was notable for Gradin's 500th NHL point, acquired on March 8, 1985, in a 4-3 victory over the Los Angeles Kings, while Smyl passed Lever as the all-time career goal-scoring leader when he got his 187th goal on February 27 in an 11-5 loss at Detroit.

The Canucks were weak on defense all season; they yielded an NHL-high 401 goals-against and finished a staggering 50 points behind the champion Edmonton Oilers.

Watt's initial season included a loss in the playoff first round and may have been equally notable for a trade made after it was over. On June 6, 1986, the Canucks sent Cam Neely, who had been their 1983 first round draft choice, to Boston for Barry Pedersen. On paper it looked like a trade of established stars from one coast to the other. Unfortunately for Vancouver, Neely's contributions in Boston eventually made it look like the Bruins had gotten the better of the exchange.

In the 23-44-13 campaign of 1985-86, Vancouver finished fourth in the division and was quickly eliminated by Edmonton when the playoffs started. The Canucks radically improved the defense over the course of the regular season, cutting down the goals-against to 333. The squad nevertheless wound up with exactly the same number of points as the season before. Smyl reached the 200-goal milestone in November and Brodeur achieved his 100th career win, the first Vancouver goalie to hit that level.

Quinn Comes, But Not Easily

The next year was to be one which saw the Canucks embroiled in an ongoing dispute with the NHL over their hiring of Pat Quinn, who agreed to become president and general manager of Vancouver while coach of the Los Angeles Kings. NHL President John Ziegler suspended Quinn and fined both teams, but the move eventually took place to Vancouver's great benefit. Watt served as coach for all of the 1986-87 season, but the Canucks' improvement to 66 points (29-43-8) wasn't enough to get them into the playoffs. They finished at the bottom of the Smythe Division.

The season included a notable feat by Petri Skriko, who scored three hat tricks in the space of eight days, registering 12 goals and 2 assists between November 17 and November 23, the hottest spell by any Canuck in history. The outburst came in just five games.

With Quinn as GM and his former Philadelphia Flyers' cohort Bob McCammon as head coach in 1987-88, Vancouver began to rebuild. The selection of Trevor Linden as the overall No. 2 draft choice in 1988 was a master stroke, soon to be followed by an even better pick. In the 1989 entry draft, the Canucks gambled on Russian Pavel Bure, the 113th choice overall, because it was quite uncertain whether the great young defenseman would be allowed to leave the old Soviet Union to play in the NHL. He did, of course, and the rest is history.

AP/Wide World Photos

Pavel Bure

McCammon's first season actually produced a poorer record than Watt's previous year (25-46-9) but the Canucks returned to playoff action in 1988-89 for the first time in three seasons when they finished fourth in the Smythe Division with a 33-39-8 record. What was even better was the defense, which allowed only 253 goals, second best in the Smythe and third-best in the NHL.

In the playoffs, Vancouver pushed division champion Calgary into a seven-game showdown before being eliminated in a dramatic final game. Linden set a club mark with four points in one game and the sixth game in Vancouver—the first time the Canucks had ever played a sixth game in post-season—was marked by a three-goal burst in 2:18 en route to a 6-3 victory.

The Russian Connection

Vancouver General Manager Pat Quinn flew to Moscow on July 1, 1989, to sign Igor Larionov, then a star member of the all-conquering Soviet Union national team. Larionov and USSR teammate Vladimir Krutov didn't turn the NHL on its ear when they made their Vancouver debuts in the 1989-90 season, but Quinn's aggressive move into a then-tricky marketplace was an early sign that NHL clubs were going to explore the slowly-opening Soviet hockey program. The arrival of Pavel Bure on October 31, 1991, may be seen as an even more important signing, the acquisition of a superstar, but it was the trailblazing signings of Larionov and Krutov that paved the way for Bure's NHL career.

In June, three Canucks were finalists for major NHL trophies, another first in Vancouver history. Linden was runner-up to the Rangers' Brian Leetch for the Calder Trophy, McCammon finished behind Montreal's Pat Burns for the Jack Adams Trophy, and Kirk McLean, the goaltender who had been acquired in a major trade with New Jersey in September, 1987, was third in voting for the Vezina Trophy.

Linden racked up 59 points, including 30 goals, in his first NHL season, while McLean finished 20-17-3 with a 3.08 goals-against average. Both would continue to star as the club improved in the next four seasons. Linden hit the 75-point level in 1991-92 while McLean put in an NHL-leading 63 starts in 1989-90.

Although Vancouver missed the playoffs in 1989-90, finishing 25-41-14, they were on the way back. Quinn replaced McCammon as head coach in 1990-91, Smyl retired to complete a fine career, and the Canucks edged out Winnipeg for the final Smythe playoff spot after a 28-43-9 season. The Canucks twice led their Stanley Cup first round series against Smythe champion Los Angeles, 1-0 and 2-1, but the Kings rebounded to win the final three games, including two in the Pacific Coliseum to close the campaign for Vancouver.

The Linden and Bure Era Begins

Pavel Bure arrived in 1991-92 to win the Calder Trophy as the NHL rookie of the year. He was the first Vancouver player to capture a major league award, but his 60-point (34 goals, 26 assists) season was just a taste of the future. Vancouver finished first in his rookie year and repeated again in 1992-93 when the Bure account included 60 goals and widespread recognition that he was one of the top players in the game.

Before the great young Russian's signature was on a Vancouver contract, Linden had signed a multi-year deal that made him the highest-paid player in Canuck history. When Bure signed 10 days later and made his NHL debut against Winnipeg in early November the Canucks were on their way toward a Smythe Division title and a 96-point season. That was the best-ever performance by a Vancouver team, as were the 42 wins, although both would be immediately surpassed a year later.

The playoffs saw Vancouver post only its second-ever first round series win, a hard-fought seven game battle against Winnipeg. But the Canucks were upset victims in the second round, as their old rivals from Edmonton snatched a 4-3 overtime victory in the opening game and rode that momentum to an eventual six-game success.

Along with Bure's Calder Trophy, Quinn picked up the Jack Adams Trophy, thus becoming the first NHL coach to be named coach of the year with two different teams. He was also tapped by *The Sporting News* as coach of the year, while McLean's second-team All-Star berth marked another first in franchise history.

Linden, Cliff Ronning, Igor Larionov, and Bure topped the team's offense while McLean, playing 65 games, finished 38-17-9 with a gaudy 2.74 goals-against average. Bure's immediate contributions were all the more remarkable since he joined the team after the start of the season and did not have the benefit of easing his way into the NHL style of play. Bure's talent was unquestioned; his fast adaptation to the NHL game simply marked him as an extra-special catch.

The 1992-93 season was even better, although there was another disappointment at playoff time. With Bure becoming the first Vancouver player to top the 100-point level (he finished with 110), the Canucks set team records for wins (46) and points (101) while winning the Smythe Division for a second straight year.

They eliminated Winnipeg in a six-game first round series, but fell to the surprising Kings in the divisional final, a heartbreaking double overtime loss in game five at Vancouver the turning point in a dramatic series.

SOURCES

BOOKS

Diamond, Dan, ed., *The Official NHL 75th Anniversary Commemorative Book,* NHL Publications, 1991.

Eskenazi, Gerald, *A Thinking Man's Guide to Pro Hockey,* E.P. Dutton & Co., 1972.

Fishler, Stan, and Shirley Fishler, *The Hockey Encyclopedia.* MacMillan, 1983.

The NHL Official Guide & Record Book. 1971-1993.

The Sporting News Hockey Guide. Sporting News, 1980-1993.

—*Jerry Trecker* for Book Builders, Inc.

THE STANLEY CUP

The Stanley Cup, the symbol of professional hockey supremacy in North America, is known simply as the "world's oldest trophy continuously competed for by professional athletes." What has grown to become the magnificent three-and-a-half foot gleaming trophy presented annually to the playoff champions of the National Hockey League (NHL) began life just over a century ago as a modest 7-1/2 by 11-1/2 inch silver rose bowl that cost just ten guineas (about $60) to purchase. Since being donated in 1892 by Lord Stanley of Preston Frederick Arthur (the 16th Earl of Derby and sixth Governor General of Canada from 1888 to 1893), the Stanley Cup has become virtually priceless.

North America's three major league professional team sports—basketball, football, and baseball—have a newly manufactured trophy meant to be kept permanently by each year's winning team. The Stanley Cup is unique in that Lord Stanley dictated that his Cup was to remain in perpetual competition and never become "the property of any one team, even if won more than once." In a century of competition between 1893 and 1993, a total of 126 separate Cup title challenges or playoff championships were contested for it, including 35 prior to 1910 which involved one or more amateur clubs.

It is doubtful that any sports trophy has had a more egalitarian history or been competed for in a greater variety of venues than the Stanley Cup. Cup championship games have occurred in such diverse locations as Quebec City, Los Angeles, Winnipeg, Pittsburgh, Kenora (Ontario), Seattle, Bloomington (Minnesota), Detroit, Vancouver, Ottawa, Montreal, Toronto, Edmonton, Victoria, and Halifax among others.

Since first being offered up for competition as an amateur challenge trophy "to be held for year to year by the champion hockey team in the Dominion (of Canada)," the Stanley Cup has had perhaps the most colorful—and convoluted—history of any piece of sports silverware in the world.

Today the Stanley Cup is competed for exclusively by the highly skilled—and highly paid—professional NHL players who come from all over the world to play the fast and dynamic game. The hockey played when the Cup was born a century ago, however, was a far different one.

The Dominion Hockey Challenge Cup

"I have for some time been thinking that it would be a good thing if there were a challenge cup which should be held for year to year by the champion hockey team in the Dominion," the Governor General noted in a flowery message delivered on his behalf at a March 18, 1892, dinner of the Ottawa Athletic Association. "There does not appear to be any such outward sign of a championship at present and considering the general interest which matches now elicit, and the importance of having the game played fairly and under rules generally recognized, I am willing to give a cup which shall be held for year to year by the winning team."

In the four years after Lord Stanley of Preston and his large family arrived in Ottawa from England when he was appointed Governor General of Canada in 1888, all seven of his sons had become enthusiastic and reasonably skilled hockey players. At the constant behest of two of them, Arthur and Algy, and of his aide-de-camp, Philip D. Ross, Lord Stanley agreed to help encourage the sport and its play by "people who matter" by donating a challenge trophy. Thus in early 1892 he dispatched Captain Colvill, another of his aides, to find and purchase a suitable piece of silver to serve as such an award.

When Colvill returned to Government House in Ottawa he brought with him a fluted silver bowl, which would soon be engraved with the new trophy's name—"Dominion Hockey Challenge Cup"—on one side, and "From Stanley of Preston" surrounding the Stanley family crest (a swan with wings extended under a coronet) on the other. Although Lord Stanley's original trophy was physically dwarfed by the tall, highly ornate Amateur Hockey Association of Canada's six-year-old "Senior Championship Trophy," the new Cup was unique in that it could be challenged for by any hockey club in the Dominion.

Lord Stanley's new Challenge Cup was to be administered by a self-perpetuating board of two trustees who would have "absolute authority in all situations or disputes over the winner of the Cup." The original trustees Stanley appointed were Philip Ross and Ottawa's Sheriff, John Sweetland.

According to Lord Stanley's original "terms of presentation" as published in the *Montreal Gazette* on February 23, 1894, the trustees were "to suggest (the) conditions to govern competition. In case of any doubt as to the title of any club to claim the position of champions, the Cup shall be held or awarded by the trustees as they might think right, their decision being absolute."

Another condition that Lord Stanley placed on his trophy was that "each winning team have its club name and year engraved on a sliver ring fitted to the Cup." By 1991 that had led to the filling up of every part of the bowl, both inside and out, and nine variously sized rings. This caused the trophy to grow over the years to a height of some three-and-a-half feet.

In addition, since 1928 the names of each champion's players, coaches, trainers, managers, and owners have been engraved (including those of the only three women whose names appear on the trophy—Detroit Red Wings' president Marguerite Norris, Calgary Flames' co-owner Sonia Scurfield, and Pittsburgh Penguins' president Marie-Denise DeBartolo York).

The Cup also includes the names of three teams not credited as Cup winners—the 1914-15 Ottawa Senators, 1915-16 Portland Rosebuds and the 1917-18 Vancouver Millionaires. While all three of these teams defeated the defending Cup champions in their own league's playoffs—and then quickly had their names engraved on the Cup—each was subsequently defeated in the NHA-PCHA playoffs and therefore never officially qualified as a Cup champion.

Lord Stanley's deed of gift also specified that

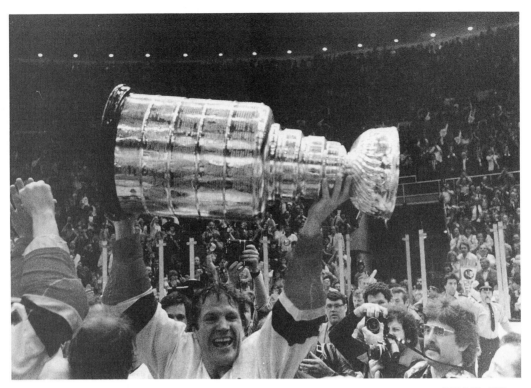

AP/Wide World Photos

The Stanley Cup

each winning club must agree "to return the Cup in good order when required by the trustees in order that it may be handed over to any other team which may win it."

This last condition would try the patience of the Cup's trustees over the next century. While the Cup has always been returned (although not always willingly), its condition was often not nearly as good as it had been when awarded. In fact, no trophy has ever been more "used"—or abused—than the Stanley Cup. It is for that very reason that the Cup presented today is not the original silver bowl which was first awarded to the Montreal Amateur Athletic Association in May of 1893.

After 75 years of "hard use" Lord Stanley's original Cup had become so fragile and brittle with age that it was retired in 1969 and placed on permanent display in the Hockey Hall of Fame in Toronto. Some of the tribulation the Cup had endured include being battered by its overly enthusiastic winners, clumsily repaired in an Edmonton auto body shop, occasionally stolen, used as a flower vase, left overnight in Ottawa's frigid Rideau Canal, forgotten by the side of a road in Montreal, and almost pitched into a lake by a disgruntled Kenora team executive.

Since 1969, however, its place atop the NHL's playoff championship trophy's massive barrel-shaped base has been occupied by a painstakingly fashioned re-creation faithful in every detail (including scratched initials and cracks) to the original. In addition, it was made using the same 19th century silversmithing techniques with which the real Cup was crafted.

Lord Stanley gave Canada's young national sport the Cup which would soon became universally know by the name of its donor, but he never attended a championship hockey game and did not witness its first presentation. With a 7-1-0 record in the five-team AHA's 20-game season, the veteran Montreal club beat out the Ottawa Generals.

By then, however, Lord Stanley and his seven hockey-playing sons had returned to England after the death of the Lord's elder brother and his consequent accession to his late father's Earlship. Under the terms of Lord Stanley's gift, any Canadian hockey team that the Cup trustees considered a legitimate contender could then challenge the AHA champion for it. None did in 1893, and Montreal was the first ever Stanley Cup champion.

Over the Stanley Cup's first century, Montreal would be its home far more often than any other city. Over that period six different clubs representing Montreal—AAA, Victorias, Shamrocks, Wanderers, Canadiens, and Maroons—would win the Stanley Cup a total of 41 times. Of all those winners, however, the Cup's centennial champion—the Montreal Canadiens—have been by far the most prolific, capturing a record 24 Cup titles between 1916 and 1993.

The Cup's First Decade

Over its first decade, the winning of the Stanley Cup would be dominated by teams from Montreal. Formed in 1884, the Montreal Amateur Athletic Association (AAA) was hockey's first "dynasty," having won the AHA title for seven consecutive years when they became the first Stanley Cup champions in 1893. The AAA repeated as Stanley Cup champions the next year but for the first time it took a playoff to determine the winner as four of the AHA's five teams were tied at 5-3-0 at season's end.

With two of the four contenders from Montreal, it was decided that all playoff games would be contested there. Quebec immediately withdrew to protest the ruling. The Ottawa Capitals agreed to the Montreal venue in exchange for a guaranteed berth in the championship game. That was

contested between the AAA and the Victorias on March 17, 1894, and was won by Montreal 3-2. Montreal AAA then retained the Cup by downing Ross's Capitals 3-1 behind a pair of goals by Billy Barlow. Ross, the only man involved in the creation the new trophy to ever see it competed for, would never be a part of a Cup winner.

The first official challenge for the Stanley Cup was made in 1895 by Queen's University of Kingston, Ontario. This resulted in one of the most unusual playoff games in the history of any sport. When the AHA season ended on March 8, the defending champion AM's archrival, the Montreal Victorias, had won the league's 1895 season title. The Vics assumed that as the AHA's new champions they would defend the Cup against the challenge from Queen's University.

However, Cup trustees Ross and Sweetland ruled that since the MA held the cup when the challenge had been accepted, they—and not the Victorias—would defend the challenge. The trustees declared that the Victorias would become the new Stanley Cup champs only if the AAA beat the challenging club from Queen's University. If the University club won, however, the Cup would go to Kingston. Fortunately for the Vics, the AAA beat the Kingston schoolboys easily to save the Cup for their cross-town rivals.

The first successful Stanley Cup challenge came the next year when the powerhouse Winnipeg Victorias of the Manitoba Hockey League ventured east at mid-season and shut out their Montreal namesakes 2-0 to take the Cup west for the first time. Eleven months later, however, the Montreal Vics traveled to Winnipeg and overcame on early 3-0 deficit with the first hat trick in Stanley Cup history (by Montreal's Ernie McLea) for a 6-5 victory over the Winnipegers to return the Stanley Cup to eastern Canada.

As repeating AHA champs, the Montreal Victorias kept the Cup in both 1897 and 1898 without being challenged, after which the circuit folded and was replaced by the Canadian Amateur Hockey League.

In February of 1899, the Vics survived another mid-season challenge from their Winnipeg counterparts. Montreal opened the two-game, to-tal-goals series by defeating Winnipeg 2-1 in Montreal. With just three minutes left in the second game with the home team holding onto a 3-2 lead, Montreal defenseman Bob McDougall viciously slashed Winnipeg rover Tony Gingras across the back of the leg—for which referee J.A. Findlay assessed him a two-minute penalty. Incensed by what he considered grossly insufficient punishment, Winnipeg captain Dan Bain pulled his team off the ice and refused to continue the game.

Insulted that his integrity had been questioned, referee Findlay left the rink and headed home only to be pursued on a dogsled by the two teams' managers who finally persuaded the unhappy official to return. After nearly an hour's delay, the referee and the hometown Montreal Victorias were back on the ice. Winnipeg's Bain refused to bring his team back, and therefore the game and the Cup were forfeited to Montreal.

Less than two weeks later, however, the Victorias lost their four-year hold on the Stanley Cup when the Montreal Shamrocks upset them 1-0 before a crowd of 8,000 to break the two clubs' deadlock for first place in the CAHL on the final day of the season.

Two weeks later the Shamrocks turned back Queen's University 6-2 in a one-game challenge, defeated Winnipeg in another mid-season challenge in February of 1900, and downed the Halifax Crescents 10-2 and 11-0 in March.

In January of 1901, the Winnipeg Victorias finally got the Cup back—after five years of assiduous effort—by defeating the Shamrocks in two straight games and withstanding a challenge from the OHA champion Toronto Wellingtons a year later. In March of 1902, however, the Cup ended its second brief western hiatus when its original champs, the Montreal AAA, took it back from Winnipeg in a challenge series. The Cup would not leave Quebec or Ontario again for a dozen years.

In February of 1903, the Winnipeg Victorias played for the Stanley Cup for an eighth and final time, but the AAA defeated them in Montreal in four games. At season's end, however, the AAA surrendered the Cup for the final time as the Montreal Victorias and the former Ottawa Generals—now called the "Silver Seven"—tied for the CAHL title with identical records and faced off in a two-game, total-goals playoff for the Cup which the Silver Seven won.

The "Silver Seven's" Reign

Perhaps no appellation in hockey carries more mystique than that of the "Ottawa Silver Seven," despite the fact that they appeared in Stanley Cup play under that name for only three years. Nonetheless their pride, skill, toughness, and many feats were so great that decades later they were voted as Canada's most outstanding hockey team of the first half of the 20th century.

In the 36 months between March 1903 and 1906, the Silver Seven won or defended the Stanley Cup 11 times, surviving challenges from the Rat Portage Thistles, Winnipeg Rowing Club, Toronto Marlies, Montreal Wanderers, Brandon Wheat Kings, Dawson City Nuggets, Queen's University, and Smiths Falls. They finally lost the Cup in an intra-league playoff to the Montreal Wanderers. The Silver Seven's 1903 playoff defeat of the Victorias had also brought the Stanley Cup back to Canada's capital city for the first time since former Governor General Lord Stanley had donated it a decade earlier.

The "Silver Seven" adopted its name from silver nuggets that club manager Bob Shillington had presented to each of the team's seven players in recognition of their winning season. (At this time hockey was still played with seven men on a side, in two 32 minute periods without substitutions.)

Among the stars of the Silver Seven's Cup teams were Hall-of-Fame right wing and team captain Alf Smith, a scorer and tough guy, and defenseman Harvey Pulford, another Hall of Famer, who not only played on the Silver Seven's Stanley Cup teams, but also played on four championship football teams with the Ottawa Rough

Riders, four national lacrosse titlists with the Ottawa Capitals, and was the heavyweight boxing champion of Eastern Canada from 1896 to 1898.

With the likes of Smith and Pulford, there was no tougher team in hockey than the Silver Seven as the Winnipeg Rowing Club found out after losing a 1904 series to Ottawa and leaving town aboard what the newspapers dubbed the "hospital train." With the "flying" Gilmour brothers (Billy, Dave and Suddy), Harry "The Rat" Westwick, and the talented yet diminutive center/rover "One-Eyed" Frank McGee, no team in hockey could score like the Silver Seven either. In goal, the Silver Seven featured yet another Hall of Famer in John "Bouse" Hutton. As did Pulford, all-around athlete Hutton also played on Canadian championship football (Rough Riders) and lacrosse (Capitals) teams.

While the Silver Seven appeared in a total of 11 playoff series in the three years they held and defended the Stanley Cup, two of those sets are particularly memorable in the fabled history of Stanley Cup play. The first involved the most improbable—and one sided—challenge series in Cup history while the other featured the greatest one game almost comeback in a century of Cup competition.

After being forced to defend the Cup four times in January, February, and March of 1904, the Silver Seven were not challenged again until early in the 1904-05 season. The colorful chairman of the Dawson (Yukon) Athletic Club, Colonel Joe Boyle, offered to bring his team the Nuggets, to take on the best that organized hockey had to offer.

With their surprising challenge accepted, Boyle's rag-tag group of players managed one practice in Whitehorse before leaving on December 19th by dogsled in 20 degree below zero weather to begin their 4,000-plus mile journey to Ottawa. After a journey of 22 days the Klondikers finally reached the Canadian capital on January 12 and were forced to face off against the Silver Seven at Dey's Rink the next day. (Ottawa had refused Dawson City's request to postpone the series for a week, citing conflicts with their league schedule.) While the Nuggets managed to score two goals against the Ottawas, Dawson City's inexperienced 17-year-old goalie Albert Forrest—the youngest player in Stanley Cup history—surrendered nine. Nonetheless Boyle was pleased with his club's performance and wired them that "The beating is no disgrace. We still have a chance to win the Cup."

Boyle was apparently happier with the Nuggets loss than the Silver Seven were with their win, however. The Ottawas were especially annoyed by the smug Klondikers who had ridiculed Frank McGee after the first game because he had scored only once and had "not lived up to their expectations." In the second game, the Silver Seven crushed Dawson City 23-2 with 23-year-old McGee scoring 14 goals, a still-standing mark.

While Boyle's club completed a fairly respectable barnstorming trip around Eastern Canada (which was made in order to earn the money to pay for their long trip home), their dismal showing in the Stanley Cup challenge against Ottawa caused the trustees to change the rules of future challenges. All subsequent challengers would be required to play each other until a single club was left.

The Silver Seven's other memorable Stanley Cup series also proved to be the last one in which they would ever play under that name. After breezing through challenges in late February and early March of 1906, the Silver Seven finished their first season in the Eastern Canada Amateur Hockey Association (ECAHA) tied with the Montreal Wanderers with a 9-1-0 record.

This led to a two-game, total-goals series to decide both the ECAHA title and the possession of the Stanley Cup. In the first game in Montreal, the inspired Wanderers embarrassed the seemingly dynastic Silver Seven and Ottawa goalie Billy Hague 9-1 behind four goals by Ernie Russell. In the second game three days later, the Silver Seven would have to outscore the talented Wanderers—who featured goalkeeper Doc Manard, center Pud Glass, and the great Lester Patrick in their lineup—by nine goals to retain the Cup.

To help improve their slim odds, the Silver Seven quickly acquired the services of the day's greatest goalie, "Peerless" Percy LeSueur (he had played against Ottawa just over a week earlier for Smiths Falls in their unsuccessful Cup challenge). After falling behind 1-0, the Silver Seven exploded and scored nine unanswered goals (including five by Harry Smith) to tie the total-goals set at 10-10 with a little over nine minutes to go in the final game.

Although the Silver Seven kept pressing, it was the great Lester Patrick who beat LeSueur for the series go-ahead goal and then added an insurance marker less than two minutes later to give Montreal a 12-10 overall victory. After an interminable delay and much name calling, Ottawa finally produced the Cup and surrendered the much tarnished and abused bowl to the new champions, the Montreal Wanderers.

Hockey—and the Stanley Cup— Turn Pro

Except for two months in early 1907 when the Cup would be held by the Kenora Thistles, the Wanderers held onto it until 1909 when it was again returned to Ottawa in the hands of new ECHA champion Senators. In the three years since it had left, however, ice hockey—and competition for the Stanley Cup—had seen a radical change.

Up until that time hockey in Canada had always been regarded strictly an amateur sport. That did not mean that many of the better players were not paid, but they got their money quietly and under the table. In 1906, however, the ECAHA realized that to remain competitive it would have to permit some professionals to play openly on amateur teams.

Prior to the 1906-07 season, therefore, the ECAHA allowed teams to pay players as long as they disclosed their professionalism. Although teams such as Montreal AAA and the Victorias remained amateur, others such as the champion Wanderers soon became fully professional. Over the transition period when both amateurs and pros

played together this mixture led to endless protests to the trustees.

In 1908 the first team representing an exclusively professional league, the Toronto Trolley Leaguers of the Ontario Professional Hockey League, challenged for the Stanley Cup and met the Wanderers in a one-game, sudden-death match played in Montreal. Although the game was tied four times and Hall of Famer Edouard "Newsy" Lalonde scored twice for Toronto in his first Stanley Cup game, Ernie Johnson and Bruce Stuart scored late goals for the Wanderers to retain the Cup.

The last two amateur clubs in the old ECAHA—the Montreal AAA and the Victorias—dropped out of the circuit in 1909. The league then removed the word "Amateur" from its title. Thus when the ECHA Ottawa Senators won the new league's title, they became the first Stanley Cup champion representing an entirely professional league.

The following year the National Hockey Association (NHA) was formed with the Colbalt Silver Kings, Haileybury, Renfrew Creamery Kings, Montreal Wanderers, Ottawa Senators, Montreal Shamrocks, and the Montreal Canadiens.

With the emergence of true professional hockey, the sport exploded over the next decade. New pro leagues joined the ranks, including the Eastern Professional Hockey League, the Patrick brothers' Pacific Coast Hockey Association (PCHA), the short-lived Western Canada Hockey League (WCHL), and the National Hockey League (which was formed in 1917 out of the ashes of the NHA). Over this turbulent period, many teams and leagues came and went as pro hockey sought to establish itself as a major league sport.

Over this same period the Cup's trustees also made major changes in Stanley Cup competition. In 1912 they ruled that no challenges would be played until after the regular season was completed and that games played among eastern clubs would use the NHA's new six-man system instead of the seven-man hockey played by the PCHA.

In 1914 the first of 13 consecutive annual confrontations between the championship teams from the east and west was played when the PCHA Victoria Cougars traveled to Toronto to take on the NHA champion Toronto Blueshirts. Although the best-of-five series was never officially sanctioned by the Cup's trustees, it was played nonetheless. The owners were more than happy for the extra gates it provided, and Toronto won the set in three straight games.

The following year the trustees finally approved a formal agreement between the NHA and PCHA that the two league's respective champions would meet each year to determine the Stanley Cup champion. With that, all further outside challenges for the Cup ceased.

The Stanley Cup headed west of Ontario in March of 1915, when Frank Patrick's Vancouver Millionaires swept the NHA champion Ottawa Senators. Although the Montreal Canadiens brought the trophy back east in 1916, the Habs were thoroughly embarrassed in 1917 by the PCHA Seattle Metropolitans. After winning the opening game of the series 8-4, the Canadiens were blistered 21-3 in the next three games as the Metropolitans brought the Stanley Cup "south of the border" to the United States for the first time.

The Habs 9-1 loss in the final game of the series also proved to be the last game ever played by a team representing the National Hockey Association. Eight months later, on November 22, 1917, the NHA was dissolved in a meeting room in the Windsor Hotel in Montreal and was reborn as the National Hockey League (NHL).

NHL Gained Stanley Cup

While the Stanley Cup would continue to be competed for between the pro hockey champions from the east and west until 1926, it would only be won by a non-NHL club one more time after 1917. Lester Patrick's former PCHA Victoria Cougars, which were then a part of the of the shortlived WCHL, defeated the Canadiens for the Cup in 1925 in another championship fraught with controversy. And as with many of the controversies in the history of Cup play, this one took place not on the ice but off of it.

The Hamilton Tigers finished first in 1924-25, edging the Toronto St. Patricks by a single point in the newly expanded NHL. With the expansion of the league that year, however, the owners also lengthened the season from 24 to 30 games and added a third team to the playoffs—which meant that the regular season champs would have to wait for the completion of a new semifinal round before facing off for the league championship series.

While the owners of the other league clubs had increased their players' salaries and bonuses to reflect the addition of three weeks and six games to the NHL schedule, no such provision had been made by the Tigers' owners for their players. Thus when the regular season ended on March 9, the Hamilton players announced that they would not play the winner of the semifinal between Toronto and Montreal for the NHL title and a Stanley Cup berth unless each of the team's ten players were paid an additional $200.

Incensed, NHL president Frank Calder immediately suspended the entire team, fined each man $200, and announced that the winner of the Toronto/Montreal series would represent the NHL against the WCHL for the Stanley Cup. Thus it was the Canadiens and not the regular season champion Tigers who traveled to British Columbia to meet the Cougars for the Stanley Cup.

As the WCHL champs again in 1925-26, the Cougars defended their Stanley Cup title against the NHL Montreal Maroons in the first series played in the newly constructed Montreal Forum. With a trio of shutouts by Hall-of-Fame goalie Clint Benedict, however, the second-year Maroons swept the Cougars to become the sixth Montreal-based club to win the Stanley Cup. This was also the last Stanley Cup game ever played involving a non-NHL club.

Within a few weeks after the series ended, the financially strapped WCHL folded and sold its players to the NHL. Most of the players found jobs with the bevy of new U.S.-based teams that were entering the expanding circuit. Thus by 1926-27, the nine-year-old NHL was the only surviving major professional hockey league, and by default it gained exclusive control of the Stanley Cup.

In 1947 a confidential agreement between the league and the Stanley Cup trustees was executed that allowed the NHL to determine all the conditions of competition for the Cup. One of those conditions was that it could only be competed for by "major league" clubs of which, of course, the NHL was to be the sole arbiter.

The only non-NHL club to offer a formal challenge to the NHL champion for the Cup after 1947 was the AHL powerhouse Cleveland Barons, a club which had applied for an NHL franchise in 1952. The NHL Board turned down the Barons' application on the specious grounds that the club did not have "sufficient financial resources." Before the 1952-53 season, Barons' owner James Hendy issued a formal challenge to the NHL to play for the Cup following the 1953 NHL playoffs if the Barons won the AHL Calder Cup that year—which they did.

The NHL claimed that no matter how good the Barons or any other non-NHL club might be (and during the days of the six-team NHL many so-called "minor league" clubs were very good indeed), the AHL was not a "major league" and therefore the Barons did not qualify to issue a challenge for the Stanley Cup.

The Modern Stanley Cup

With the NHL's assuming exclusive control of hockey's greatest trophy in the 1926-27 season, the modern Stanley Cup era had arrived. During much of the almost seven decades since the NHL took formal charge of the Stanley Cup, it has been held by one "dynasty" club or another. That was not the case, however, during the turbulent 20 years between 1926 and 1946, during which Canada and the United States both experienced the Great Depression and World War II. During that era, eight different teams—the Ottawa Senators, New York Rangers, Boston Bruins, Montreal

Canadiens, Toronto Maple Leafs, Chicago Black Hawks, Montreal Maroons, and Detroit Red Wings—all won the Cup at least once. All six of the clubs that would comprise the NHL between 1942 and 1967 also won a title in the seven play-off years of 1938 to 1944.

In the years since World War II, however, the trend reverted to the dynastic traditions of the Cup's early history, with the Canadiens, Red Wings, Maple Leafs, Islanders, Oilers, and Penguins all dominating Cup play at one time or another. The Canadiens won five consecutive titles from 1956 to 1960, four out of five from 1965 to 1969, and four more in a row from 1976 to 1979.

In 1974 the Philadelphia Flyers became the first of the post-1967 expansion clubs to win the Cup, which they repeated in 1975 before losing the 1976 finals to the Canadiens. From 1980 to 1983, the New York Islanders captured four consecutive titles. The WHA refugee Edmonton Oilers won five Cup championships in the seven years between 1984 and 1990.

Stanley Cup playoff formats have also gone through many alterations since the NHL's formation. In 1917-18—when the NHL finished its first season with just three clubs—the league played a 20-game regular season schedule split into two halves. The winners of each half played a two game, total-goals series for the right to meet the PCHA champion in a best-of-five Stanley Cup final. Since then, the Stanley Cup format has been altered 23 times as the league has grown, although many of the changes have been relatively minor ones.

The Stanley Cup trophy has also changed to make more room for the literally thousands of names that have been added to it over the years. When the NHL took it over in 1926, the trophy was still less than a foot high with the original Cup still dominating the modest base upon which it was mounted. An additional ring was added in 1928, as its base began to take on the appearance of a small wedding cake.

By 1932 that base had been replaced with a narrower but taller cigar shaped one which brought its height up to just under two feet. With the continued addition of new rings, by 1947 the overall trophy—which had by then acquired the slightly uncomplimentary moniker of the "elephant's leg"—had reached an ungainly height of well over four feet. It was finally remodeled in 1948, and again in 1958, into the contemporary three-and-a-half foot tall, two-tiered barrel-shaped trophy.

With the filling in of the last open space on the bottom of five large rings of the "barrel" portion of the trophy in 1991, the top ring of those five containing the Cup winners from 1928 to 1940 was removed and retired to the Hockey Hall of Fame in 1992. A new blank ring was added at the bottom upon which the names of the winners from 1992 to 2004 will be engraved.

In the history of the Stanley Cup no player has broken more records than Wayne Gretzky. By 1993, he owned all the most important NHL playoff scoring records (most career goals, assists, and points) and also held the record for the total number of official individual Stanley Cup records simultaneously held or shared by any one player—13. In 180 Stanley Cup games through the 1993 playoffs, Gretzky had scored 110 goals and assisted on 236 for 346 points. Among the "Great One's" other all-time playoff marks are most career game-winning goals (21), most points in a playoff year (47), most Stanley Cup hat tricks (8), and most points in a Stanley Cup Final series (13).

When it comes to superlatives in the shear numbers of games, playoff years, and Cups won, however, it helps to have played for the Canadiens. In total playoff appearances nobody surpasses defenseman Larry Robinson who skated in the vast majority of his 227 career Cup games—the equivalent of almost three full regular seasons of extra hockey—between 1973 and 1992 with the Canadiens. (He also holds the additional mark of never having missed the playoffs in 20 NHL seasons.)

No player has had his name engraved on the Stanley Cup more often than another Canadien great, Henri "Pocket Rocket" Richard, who played on 11 Cup winners between 1956 and 1973. Coach "Toe" Blake, who led the Habs to eight titles from behind the bench between 1956 and 1968, leads the way for coaches. (He also won three Cups as a Canadiens' player.)

With the growth of the NHL from three teams and a 20-game schedule in 1917-18 to 26 teams and an 84-game slate in 1993-94, the length of the playoffs has also grown exponentially. No Stanley Cup game had ever been played as late as April prior to 1920, nor had it ever taken more than ten days from start to finish to determine a winner. By the Cup's centenary, however, the four best-of-seven rounds of playoffs took almost two months to complete and the entire 1993 final series between Los Angeles and Montreal was played in the month of June.

With the 1994 National Hockey League playoffs, the Stanley Cup, the "world's oldest trophy continuously competed for by professional athletes," begins its second century as the ultimate symbol of professional hockey supremacy in North America. When Governor General Stanley first donated it as the "Dominion Hockey Challenge Cup" in 1892, the English aristocrat did so more as a favor to his amateur hockey playing sons and to snobbishly encourage participation in the game by "people who matter." The Cup—and the game—have both changed radically since his little silver bowl was first presented to the Montreal AAA in May of 1893. Winning the Stanley Cup is now recognized as one of the world's premier sports achievements.

—Bruce C. Cooper

PROFESSIONAL

SPORTS TEAM

HISTORIES

INDEX

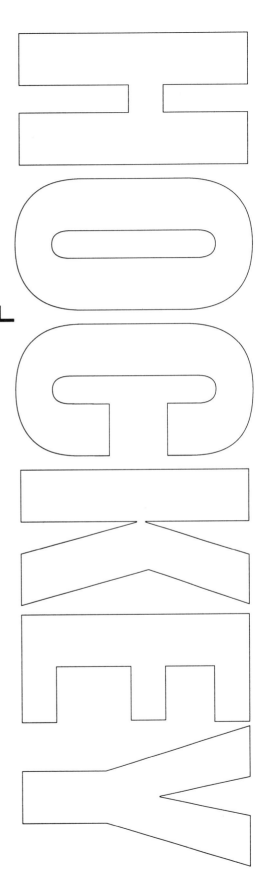

Index

Belanger, Roger 339
Belfour, Ed 153, 154
Béliveau, Jean 300, 301, 302, 304, 306, 307, 308, 309
Bellows, Brian 165, 166, 169, 315, 316
Belzberg, Morris 168, 347
Benedict, Clint 9, 67, 68, 222, 295
Bennett, Curt 371, 372
Benning, Brian 20, 347
Bentley, Doug 140, 141, 142
Bentley, Max 133, 140, 142, 223, 224, 225
Berenson, Red 193, 194, 197, 198, 200, 202, 204
Bergen, John J. 74
Bergeron, J.C. 119
Bergeron, Michel 81, 82, 83, 358, 359, 360
Bergevin, Marc 119
Bernier, Serge 100, 354, 356, 401
Berry, Bob 313, 339, 340, 407
Berthiaume, Daniel 416
Bertuzzi, Larry 113
Berube, Craig 128
Bettman, Gary 15, 16, 124, 365, 367
Beverley, Nick 331, 418
Billington, Craig 319
Binkley, Les 325, 327, 329
Bishop, Jim 183
Blackburn, Don 284
Bladon, Tom 99, 105, 334
Blair, Wren 112, 156, 260, 331, 332
Blake, Toe 9, 142, 255, 296, 297, 298, 299, 300, 304, 308, 309, 452
Block, Ken 400
Block, Peter H. 322
Bodger, Doug 276, 339, 341
Bodnar, Ausut 222
Bodnar, Gus 142
Boe, Roy 41, 42, 50
Boesch, Garth 222
Boileau, Marc 330
Boivin, Leo 202, 324
Boldirev, Ivan 433, 437
Boll, Frank 216

Bordeleau, Christian 200, 236
Boschman, Laurie 319
Bossy, Mike 48, 50, 51, 53, 54, 55, 57, 107
Bouchard, Butch 299, 304
Bouchard, Daniel 357, 358, 370, 371, 373
Bouchard, Emile 294
Boucher, Billy 293
Boucher, Frank 9, 65, 66, 67, 68, 70, 72, 73, 223
Boudrias, Andre 156, 430, 431
Bourne, Bob 57
Bourque, Ray 33, 249, 266
Boutette, Pat 282, 285
Bower, Johnny 147, 226, 227, 228, 231
Bowman, Scotty 106, 191, 194, 195, 199, 273, 274, 276, 277, 311, 313, 344, 346, 347, 350, 351
Bowness, Rick 243, 320
Boyle, Joe 448
Bradley, Brian 118
Brewer, Carl 183, 227, 231
Brian, Alvin 324
Bridgman, Mel 25, 30, 106
Briere, Michel 327, 328
Brimsek, Frankie 250, 255, 256
Brind'Amour, Rod 209
Broda, Turk 218, 219, 220, 222, 224, 301
Brodeur, Richard 354, 356, 434, 435, 436
Bromley, Gary 272
Brooks, Herb 40, 79, 80, 168
Brophy, John 233
Broseker, Gord 34
Broten, Aaron 31
Broten, Neal 164, 165, 166, 167, 168, 169
Brown, Doug 33
Brown, Larry 100, 401
Brown, Rob 341
Brown, Walter 250
Bruce, David 423
Bruneau, Jean-Marc 353

H

L

M

Mitchell, Irving Felt   74
Modano, Mike   168, 169
Mogilny, Alexander   278, 279
Mohns, Doug   150, 160
Monahan, Garry   401, 431
Monahan, Hartland   122
Moog, Andy   266, 383, 387, 391, 392
Moore, Dickie   140, 143, 302, 304
Moran, Lois   66
Morel, Denis   415
Morenz, Howie   9, 136, 293, 294, 295, 296, 297
Morrison, Jim   179
Mortson, Gus   222, 225
Mosdell, Ken   302, 304
Mosienko, Bill   140, 141
Mowers, Johnny   176
Muckler, John   279, 280, 386, 388, 395
Muldoon, Pete   149
Mullen, Joey   193, 344, 376, 378
Muller, Kirk   29, 31, 316
Mulvey, Paul   408
Murdoch, Bob   244, 401, 404
Murdoch, Murray   65
Murphy, Brian   401
Murphy, Gord   20
Murphy, Larry   344
Murphy, Mike   404, 405, 408, 411, 419
Murphy, Ron   11, 74, 147
Murray, Bryan   32, 124, 126, 127, 188, 191
Murray, Terry   127
Myers, Bob   53
Myre, Phil   52, 106, 370, 371, 372

N

Nanne, Lou   53, 160, 161, 167
Naslund, Mats   313
Nazarov, Andrei   424
Neale, Harry   186, 282, 433, 434, 435, 436, 438

Nedved, Petr   343
Neely, Cam   266, 267, 438
Neighbor, Frank   7
Neilson, Roger   84, 86, 232, 274, 408, 436, 437, 438
Nesterenko, Eric   146, 147, 150
Nevin, Bob   227, 228, 404
Newell, Dave   34, 106
Nicholls, Bernie   85, 402, 411, 413
Niedermayer, Rob   20
Nieuwendyk, Joe   377
Nilan, Chris   315
Nill, Jim   437
Nilsson, Kent   239, 240, 373, 374
Nilsson, Ulf   78, 237, 238, 239, 240
Noble, Reg   6, 212
Nolan, Owen   343, 360
Nolet, Simon   24, 96
Nonahan, Hartland   333
Norris, Bruce   171, 183, 184
Norris, Jack   261
Norris, James D.   133, 171, 174, 179, 269
Norris, James, Jr.   74, 142
Norris, Marguerite   179, 444
Norton, Jeff   424
Numminen, Teppo   243
Nykoluk, Mike   102, 232
Nystrom, Bob   44, 50, 51, 53, 107

O

Oates, Adam   193, 202, 208, 209, 267
Oatman, Eddie   4
O'Brien, J. Ambrose   289
O'Connor, Buddy   222, 298, 299, 300
Oddleifson, Chris   432
Olausson, Frederik   244
Oliver, Harry   252
Oliver, Murray   160, 161, 259
Olmstead, Bert   228, 302, 303, 304
O'Neill, Brian   15, 34
O'Ree, Willie   259

T

Tabaracci, Rick   128
Taglianetti, Peter   344
Takko, Kari   167
Talbot, Jean-Guy   77, 200, 304
Tallon, Dale   334, 428, 430
Tambellini, Steve   26, 53
Tanti, Tony   438
Tardif, Marc   354, 355, 356
Taylor, Billy   219, 259
Taylor, Dave   402, 406, 407, 414
Taylor, Fred   3
Terreri, Chris   39
Tessier, Orval   152
Thomas, Bill   68
Thompson, Cecil   253
Thompson, Cliff   12, 259
Thompson, Edwin G.   22
Thompson, Errol   233
Thompson, H. Percy   7
Thompson, Paul   137, 139, 140, 175
Thoms, Bill   216, 218
Thomson, Jimmy   222
Tichy, Milan   20
Tinordi, Mark   169
Tocchet, Rick   60, 112, 350, 351
Tonelli, John   51, 55, 56, 337, 376
Torrey, Bill   19, 41, 42, 43, 44, 46, 49,
   50, 51, 53, 55, 56, 57, 59
Trecker, Jerry   286
Tremblay, J.C.   353
Trottier, Bryan   46, 47, 49, 51, 53, 54,
   55, 57, 58
Tucker, John   119, 275
Tugnutt, Ron   366
Turgeon, Pierre   57, 59, 60, 128, 277,
   278, 279, 350
Turgeon, Sylvain   286, 287, 315, 320
Turner, Dean   78

U

Ubriaco, Gene   324, 341, 343

Ulanov, Igor   244, 246
Unger, Garry   200, 201, 372

V

Vachon, Rogie   150, 308, 309, 402,
   404, 406, 408, 409, 411, 417
Vadnais, Carol   51, 77, 103, 263, 264
Vail, Eric   372
Vaive, Rick   233, 433
van Boxmeer, John   273
Van Dorp, Wayne   340
Van Impe, Ed   104
Vanbiesbrouck, John   20, 79, 80, 85
Vasko, Elmer   143
Veitch, Darren   122, 123
Verbeek, Pat   31, 33
Vernon, Mike   375
Ververgaert, Dennis   430, 432
Vézina, Georges   290, 292, 293, 294
Vial, Dennis   319
Villemure, Gilles   76
Volek, David   60

W

Waite, Jimmy   424
Wakely, Ernie   198, 199
Walker, Jack   172
Wall, Bob   400
Walsh, Stephen   58
Walter, William Ryan   122, 123, 125
Walton, Mike   99
Wamsley, Rick   378, 379
Wares, Eddie   176
Wasnie, Nicholas   295
Watson, Bryan   329
Watson, Harry   222
Watson, Jimmy   99, 106
Watson, Joe   96
Watson, Phil   69, 71, 74, 299
Watt, Tom   241, 242, 438
Webster, Tom   81, 282, 414, 417
Weiland, Cooney   138, 175